Survival
of the City

Survival
of the City

LIVING AND THRIVING
IN AN AGE OF ISOLATION

Edward Glaeser
and
David Cutler

PENGUIN PRESS   *New York*   2021

PENGUIN PRESS

An imprint of Penguin Random House LLC

penguinrandomhouse.com

LIBRARY OF CONGRESS CATALOGING-IN-PUBLICATION DATA

Names: Glaeser, Edward L. (Edward Ludwig), 1967– author. | Cutler, David M., author.
Title: Survival of the city : living and thriving in an age of isolation /
Edward Glaeser and David Cutler.
Description: First edition | New York : Penguin Press, 2021. |
Includes bibliographical references and index.
Identifiers: LCCN 2021008290 (print) | LCCN 2021008291 (ebook) |
ISBN 9780593297681 (hardcover) | ISBN 9780593297698 (ebook)
Subjects: LCSH: City and town life—United States. | Urban health—United States. |
Epidemics—History. | COVID-19 Pandemic, 2020– —Social aspects—United States. |
COVID-19 Pandemic, 2020– —Economic aspects—United States. |
Urban economics. | Urban policy—United States.
Classification: LCC HT123 .G563 2021 (print) |
LCC HT123 (ebook) | DDC 307.760973—dc23
LC record available at https://lccn.loc.gov/2021008290
LC ebook record available at https://lccn.loc.gov/2021008291

Printed in the United States of America
1st Printing

Set in Adobe Caslon Pro
Designed by Cassandra Garruzzo

FOR OUR DAUGHTERS,

Kate Cutler, Allie Cutler, and Eliza Glaeser,
in the hope that the cities of their
futures will be full of more hope than fear,
more kindness than anger, and
more wisdom than folly.

CONTENTS

Survival
of the City

Chapter 1

THE CITY BESIEGED

Cities can die. Earthquake and invasion doomed Knossos, the mighty Cretan city that housed the mythic minotaur. Cities often decline. Cleveland, Pittsburgh, and Liverpool are all far smaller today than they were in the 1930s. Urban triumph is never guaranteed.

The decline of a city is a terrible thing to watch. It might begin with a factory closing. Some of the factory's workers then cut back on spending at local stores; other workers, those with the most education and opportunities, leave the city altogether. The tax base declines, and the city both raises its taxes and cuts its spending on police, schools, and parks. Crime increases. New businesses stay away. More people leave. Economic trouble begets social trouble, which begets more economic trouble.

For the past half century, urban decline has mostly come from deindustrialization, the exodus of factory jobs from erstwhile municipal powerhouses like Detroit and Glasgow. That crisis occurred because urban density no longer offered much of an advantage to massive, self-contained, highly automated manufacturing plants. But uncontrolled pandemic is an even more existential threat to the urban world, because the human proximity that enables contagion is the defining characteristic of the city.

If cities are the absence of physical space between people, then the social distancing that began in March 2020 is the rapid-fire deurbanization of our world. Data from cellular phones, provided by SafeGraph, shows that the number of trips Americans took for recreation and shopping dropped by 40 percent between March 14 and March 24 of 2020.

A pandemic that travels by air poses a threat not only to urban health but also to the urban service economy that provides jobs for most modern city dwellers. For workers without an advanced degree, the ability to serve coffee with a smile provided an economic safe haven after the factories mechanized and left once wealthy metropolises. Those jobs seemed safe because no matter how much we globalize, fresh lattes will never be exported from China to Soho.

When that barista's smile becomes a source of peril rather than pleasure, those jobs can vanish in a heartbeat. Before the 2020 pandemic, 32 million Americans, or twenty percent of the employed labor force, worked in retail trade, leisure, and hospitality. One fifth of America's leisure and hospitality jobs vanished between November 2019 and November 2020. Between the third quarter of 2019 and the third quarter of 2020, UK employment in accommodation and food services declined by more than 14 percent, and 22 percent of those who still have jobs in the sector are on some kind of furlough. If all of the world's face-to-face service jobs permanently disappear, the results will be catastrophic, both for cities and for the global economy.

The irony of our pre-2020 complacency toward pandemic risk is that the triumph of the city owes much to victories over prior plagues. The semi-urban inhabitants of the first human settlements were less healthy than their hunter-gatherer ancestors, partially because communicable disease deaths were more common in denser areas. Cities long depended on net migration from the countryside to replace their dead. But by 1940, vaccination, sewers, and antibiotics allowed life expectancy in urban areas to catch up to rural life expectancy. By 2020, urbanites lived longer than people in rural areas, and that mortality gap was growing—at least before the reappearance of mass contagion.

Unfortunately, COVID-19 is unlikely to be a one-time event, unless governments take pandemic preparedness far more seriously. As global mobility has grown, actual or potential pandemics have become more common. Between 1900 and 1980, only a few outbreaks threatened all of the United States: the influenza pandemic of 1918–19, the Asian flu (1957–58), and the Hong Kong flu (1968). The first of these was terrible, but our memory of it dimmed over time. Since the 1980s, the country has experienced HIV/AIDS (1980s–present), the H1N1 flu (2009), the Zika virus (2015–16), and now SARS-CoV-2 (2020), which we will hereafter refer to as COVID-19, the disease it causes. COVID-19 is itself the third in a series of coronaviruses to jump from bats to humans, following SARS in 2002 and MERS in 2012. Then there are the near misses, like Ebola (2013–16, 2018–20) and the Marburg virus (1998–2000, 2004–05). If pandemic becomes permanent, then a good share of workers may decide never to go back to their downtown offices.

Contagious disease is the most obvious threat to urban life in 2020, but it is not the only one. A Pandora's box of urban woes has emerged including overly expensive housing, violent conflict over gentrification, persistently low levels of upward mobility, and outrage over brutal and racially targeted policing and long prison sentences for minor drug crimes. These seemingly disparate problems all stem from a common root: our cities protect insiders and leave outsiders to suffer.

Gentrifiers move into ethnic neighborhoods because regulations have made it too difficult to build more affordable housing in other areas. The regulations that limit new construction protect the high housing values and views enjoyed by incumbents, but exclude the young and the poor who also want an urban future. Reductions in urban crime enable the well-heeled to safely enjoy a midnight stroll, but police stop and frisk lower-income minorities who try to do the same thing. If a policeman gets too rough, then his union stands up for him, but there is no equivalent organization protecting disadvantaged youth. Suburban and private schools enable prosperous parents to ignore the enduring dysfunction of many big-city school districts.

Before 2020, our cities flourished as enclaves for the wealthy, but they were failing in their great mission of turning poor children into prosperous adults. Our cities, and our countries, must be opened again for outsiders. Business and land use regulations must be reduced and rewritten. Schools must be strengthened. Policing must both prevent crime and respect every citizen. Pandemics must cease so that urban entrepreneurs can again create opportunity, even in the poorest neighborhoods.

Remaking a system built for insiders into a machine for empowering outsiders will take years if not decades. Unfortunately, the threats to urban life capture our attention fleetingly then slip out of consciousness as our minds flit to other concerns. The Occupy movement of 2011 sought to expose the inequities of the Great Recession. The killing of George Floyd led millions to feel anger and shame over the long and sustained mistreatment of African American men and women by the police. Like contagious disease, persistent poverty and racial injustice must be addressed if cities are to thrive once more. Yet fighting any of these problems requires sustained collective effort, not a short burst of outrage. To protect our cities, we must manage not just months of protest, but years of learning, implementing, and executing.

After nearly a year of social distancing, Zooming to work, and police protests, cities look even more vulnerable than they did at the onset of the COVID-19 pandemic. Almost 70 percent of American workers with advanced degrees switched to remote work in May of 2020, and 48 percent remained remote in November. Many wondered why they hadn't been dialing it in before the pandemic. In chapter 7 of this book, we will argue that even if face-to-face work returns, as we believe that it will, companies and workers have become less anchored to particular places. Better-educated

Zoomers may reconsider their commitment to cities that offer expensive housing, painful commutes, and political rancor. Unfortunately, technology has not created an exit option for the less educated: only 5 percent of people who had not finished high school were working remotely during May 2020.

The Demons of Density

Physical illness plays an outsized role in this book, but this is not a book about disease. This is a book about the problems that can come with urban scale and proximity, and the fight to tame the city's downsides. Plagues spread from city to city across the lattice of global trade and travel, and then from person to person within the crowded confines of urban space. They are the most terrible demons of density. But traffic congestion, crime, and high housing costs are also common companions to city life. These ills have festered and made cities less livable.

Gulfs of inequality have been a part of urban life for thousands of years. Plato wrote in *The Republic* that "any city, however small, is in fact divided into two, one the city of the poor, the other of the rich; these are at war with one another." The fight against the downsides of density requires a truce in that war. Such a truce should be possible, because city building is not a zero-sum game. In most cities, both poor and rich would benefit from more home building, from better schools, from more humane policing, and from widely available health care that provides a stronger defense against future pandemics.

The impact of catastrophe is always mediated by preexisting social strength or weakness. The Black Death struck Constantinople in 541 CE during a period of instability. It led first to political chaos and then to centuries of rural poverty. In contrast, the plagues that slaughtered nineteenth-century urbanites, like cholera and yellow fever, did not stop the growth of New York, Paris, and London, partially because those cities came together and strong leadership made them resilient. Collectively, they invested in mighty infrastructure projects, like New York's Croton Aqueduct and the Parisian sewers, that made those cities safer. In our own time, New York shrugged off the terrible terrorist attacks of September 11, 2001, because the city worked together and rebuilt itself.

But the New York of 2021 is far more fractured than the New York of 2001. The pragmatic consensus that emerged after the city's near bankruptcy in the 1970s has come undone. In 2011, demonstrators seized Zuccotti Park, practically in the shadow of the memorials to 9/11. The Occupy movement and the police response to it divided the city that had seemed so united. New York was hardly alone: the Occupy movement took over public squares from Boston to Berlin.

In the years since, divisions have widened, creating more urban vulnerability. Two months after the COVID lockdowns had begun, a policeman killed an African American man in broad daylight in Minneapolis, by pressing his knee against the man's neck for over eight minutes. Anger about the terrible racial disparities in police violence, perhaps reinforced by angst from months of lockdown, led streets to explode as they had not since the late 1960s. In some areas, city leaders, either out of fear or sympathy with the protesters, allowed whole districts to become lawless, leading to such new neighborhood names as Seattle's "Capitol Hill Autonomous Zone." Urbanites across the world took stock of their cities' responses to racial disparities and found them lacking.

Any effective response to those inequities will require financial resources, and those have already been strained by the pandemic. Local finances are as precarious as they have been since the 1970s. Less employment and fewer shoppers mean lower local tax revenues. Schools face added difficulties providing classes safely. Transit systems receive far fewer fares, and little sure prospect of a quick comeback. Unlike the federal government, cities cannot print money or borrow trillions.

At the same time, people are in a progressive mood, as they were in the 1960s, and they want more for those who start with less. Those who have been left out want change. We understand and sympathize with that impulse: our urban inequities are terrible. Yet when cities try to play Robin Hood, as they did in the 1960s, businesses and the rich pick up and leave. Protesters want to defund the police, but wealthier urbanites will decamp for safer suburbs if crime rates start to rise, and the poor and vulnerable will suffer most.

If people decide that cities are too unsafe, either because of disease or crime or declining public services, we will move to a world not of cities, but of enclaves. The rich will live in their own luxurious retreats, keeping their exposure to the poor to a bare minimum. Middle-income people will form their own havens of stolid respectability, and the poor will inhabit what remains. Whatever mixing can be done remotely will. With less connection between rich and poor, economic opportunity will diminish. As the urban tax base declines, disadvantaged areas will have even fewer public services: schools will educate less well; police forces will be smaller, which may lead to more brutality and more crime. As violence increases, crime will particularly terrorize poor, minority neighborhoods as it has in the past.

A world in which enclaves replace cities is a world impoverished. Even for the rich, spatial isolation rarely provides long-term safety. The patricians who fled Rome's swelter for the comforts of Capri in the late years of the empire were still killed by plagues and doomed by the fall of the capital city. In our own time, one of the first hot spots of COVID-19 was New Rochelle, New York, a suburb half an hour outside Manhattan. In December 2020, some of the highest COVID-19 areas of the country included the wealthy enclaves of Beverly Hills, Palos Verdes Estates, and Hancock Park, all in or near Los Angeles.

There is a way to bring cities back stronger, but it is not simple. The path starts by recognizing that cities can only fund services that help the poor if they can also attract the jobs that pay taxes. Consequently, the answer is not to just tax and spend more. The spending must be smarter and strengthen the entire city. Taxpayers must believe that the government will use their money wisely and treat them with respect. This must happen at all levels— international, national, and local. We must also recognize that we do not have all the answers. We must have the humility to learn before we can transform.

Fortunately, for all the currents that buffet them, cities are stubbornly durable things. By and large, the greatest cities in the world in 1700 are still among the greatest cities in the world today: Beijing, London, Tokyo, and Istanbul. Cities have structural advantages that are nearly impossible to rep- licate. A fabulous panoply of people and firms creates plentiful opportunities for employment, especially in service sector jobs, that are just not present in lower-density parts of the world. Cities have museums and parks, architec- ture and restaurants.

The most important lesson from months of lockdown and protest is surely that human contact—real, in-person contact—is precious. Whenever the lockdowns were eased, people rushed back out to connect with other people, health consequences be damned. After watching a white policeman kill a prostrate African American man, people came together to air their anger, even at the risk of their own health. The most important gift of the city is that it enables us to be close to one another, to learn and befriend, to connect and collectively rejoice. Humanity will not walk away from that gift, especially if our cities can be better protected from the demons that haunt them.

Who Are We and Why Did We Write This Book?

We are two Harvard economists who have been friends and worked together for about thirty years. We are both suburban parents who generally live lives that are quite exciting to ourselves, but that most people would find fairly dull. We are certainly not cool urban hipsters or cultural warriors, but we do love cities and worry about their future. We started this book in May of 2020, because we felt an urgent need to bring the tools of economics to the debates that were raging about urban life and death during the pandemic.

COVID-19 does not kill everyone who develops it. Indeed, the vast bulk of people live. However, many of those who survive suffer long-term impairments—respiratory disease, cardiac disease, and other complications. We fear the same will be true about cities. Urban life as a whole will outlast COVID, but not every city will. And some that survive might be permanently impaired. We wrote this book because we hope that better policy can limit the damage that COVID does to cities, and to the people who live in them.

While we have written many papers together over the years, on topics as varied as racial segregation, obesity, smoking, and opioids, we come from two different subfields: health economics and urban economics. The core specialty of one of us (Cutler) is the functioning of the health system and the public role in that system. The core specialty of the other (Glaeser) is the economic life of the city and public policies that surround our urban world. We believe that both specialties are vitally needed to make sense of policy making at this juncture.

We also differ in our political past. One of us (Cutler) served in the Clinton White House and on the Obama presidential campaign and has been engaged with Democratic health policy for decades. The other (Glaeser) has been a traditional East Coast Republican, who idolized Alexander Hamilton long before Lin-Manuel Miranda made him a pop icon, and generally worked with city governments of any party from the outside. We have both compromised at some points about policies discussed in this book, and we think that is a good thing. Americans, and the world in general, should remember that policy progress almost invariably involves compromise and that no single person has all the answers.

Compromise is not mediocrity. It is not even moderation. There were compromises between British and American leaders as they launched the greatest amphibious assault of all time on June 6, 1944. Indeed, we are radical in our desire to strengthen the world's cities. We are just not radical on a conventional left-right spectrum.

We see three elements that must be woven together to protect urban life. First, there must be a shared strength that serves the city, which means more accountable and capable governments and the balancing power of civil society. Second, cities must enable the freedom to flourish. Third, governments, entrepreneurs, and all of us must have the humility to learn.

Shared Strength That Serves

An old aphorism notes that "there are no atheists in foxholes." So too we might add that "there are no libertarians in cities." Some public management is needed to mediate the problems that come from cramming millions together into a dense landmass. The pro- and anti-government divide that split rural and urban America during the 2020 election partially reflects the fact that urbanites need government more than the residents of lower-density America.

Governments of the world should be willing to spend enormous amounts to ensure that pandemics are as uncommon as possible. One of us (Cutler) estimated that COVID-19 would cost the US economy $16 trillion by the time it was done. With costs that large, it is worth spending hundreds of billions of dollars to avoid future pandemics. The trick is to ensure that money is spent effectively.

What creates effective, accountable government, what we call "the shared strength that serves"? Effective public and private action requires clear objectives and leadership that is both empowered and held responsible for success and failure. We must measure the things that we care about, like the respect that police show for the community. Leadership must have sufficient human and material resources to achieve that success.

Contrast the disastrous response to COVID-19 by many governments throughout the world with that of the companies like Pfizer and Moderna that developed vaccines at warp speed. The global quest for a vaccine gave those companies a clear objective. Their chief executive officers could be rewarded with the glory and financial rewards of victory or the embarrassment and career consequences of failure. Those companies could hire or fire scientists or expand or repurpose labs in a heartbeat, without seeking the approval of Congress or the city council.

Political leaders can be transformational. The vital nineteenth-century health improvements came from monumental public shared efforts, like the building of sewers and aqueducts. Empowered leaders, like former mayors and crusading doctors, spearheaded those communal victories. Wealthy taxpayers supported robust spending, which went toward a clear public mission. By contrast, America's national health programs were generally designed to insure the elderly and the poor against medical expenses, not to enhance health most efficiently. America adopted a legislation-heavy solution for health care with Medicare and Medicaid, with little executive public health capacity. That structure explains why the US spends by far the most on medical care of any country in the world, and was among the worst in preventing deaths from

COVID-19 during 2020: the mission of America's public health insurance programs was never modified to protect public health or prevent contagion.

While city governments expanded in the nineteenth century, national governments grew most in the twentieth century. In some places, like England, national public capacity replaced local public capacity. The National Health Service was a huge organization run nationally. In the US, the federal government became a great regulator, taxer, and spender, but not a big employer. Even today, almost two thirds of all public employees in the United States work in local government; only 13 percent work in the federal government—the bulk of those in the post office and military. But a small executive branch doesn't mean limited government, as illustrated by the vast spending of America's social insurance programs.

Clear objectives have typically made urban governments less ideological. They are more often dominated by centrist mayoral executives than by more partisan legislative city councils. A Republican, former New York City mayor Fiorello LaGuardia, famously opined that "there is no Republican or Democratic way to clean the streets." The same nonpartisan pragmatism also ruled the nation when the country's work consisted primarily of fighting the Axis powers. Arthur Vandenberg, the isolationist turned internationalist Republican senator declared that "politics stops at the water's edge."

In contrast, ideology will always dominate politics if government acts primarily to shuffle money from one set of citizens to another, as often happens at the national level. Fans of that redistribution will argue for bigger government. Opponents will argue for lower taxes, and so it has been for American politics since 1980. Your two authors have often been on opposite sides of that debate. But we share the view that going forward the executive functions of our national government must become more effective, partially to protect our cities. The menaces of the twenty-first century require more national strength, just as defeating cholera required local strength in the nineteenth century. Only national governments can muster the resources to preemptively research and prepare for the next pandemic, and to deal with it when it arrives.

Because disease affects the less healthy first, our mutual interdependence requires policies that strengthen society's weakest links, those who are most likely to spread disease. This requires better health care for the poor and better policies toward health-related behaviors, including obesity and opioid addiction.

To get a more effective national government, we must first collectively agree on shared objectives—like preventing pandemic and extending life spans. We must then judge our national leaders on their ability to achieve those objectives, just as we already fire our mayors when they take too long to clear the streets of snow in winter.

The fight against global pandemic requires not only more national competence, but also a multinational entity that monitors the globe for new outbreaks and speedily closes the travel routes that spread death. Across the world, a plague that begins in an Indian pit latrine or a Chinese open-air market can infect billions. Even the best-run countries were flattened by COVID-19. To be effective, a multinational anti-pandemic agency must look more like NATO than the United Nations. After World War II, NATO was given a clear mission—preventing an attack on its members by the Soviet Union—and a budget commensurate with it. NATO was spectacularly successful. In the same way, a revitalized international health organization must monitor the emergence of any new infectious disease and set rules about disease risk, reporting, and travel.

To reduce the risk of global pandemic, the rich world should be willing to contribute more to ensure better sanitation in the world's poorest cities. The price of that aid could be the enforcement of bans on excessive mixing of humans, bats, pigs, and other animals involved in spreading viral disease, along with limits on excessive use of antibiotics that might seed the next superbug. At the extreme, the country-members of NATO-for-health can ostracize those nations that permit particularly unsafe practices. Either the threat of trade and travel sanctions will nudge countries into enforcing hygienic regulations, or the imposition of those sanctions should stop the spread of disease from those countries.

State and local governments must also become stronger, and that strength must serve rather than oppress. In the wake of the killing of George Floyd, the calls to "defund the police" have become loud. Yet a poorer police department will provide neither more safety nor more respect for the community. The answer is not defunding but defining the mission of the police to include both crime reduction and upholding civil rights. A young woman of color has a right to walk safely home from school that is just as precious as the right of a young man to be free from police harassment. The girl will not be safe if the police are defunded, but the boy will not be safe unless the police are reformed.

In the 1990s, America tilted one way. We adopted draconian punishment rules like "Three Strikes and You're Out" because of terrible crimes committed by people who should never have been on the streets. But those policies punished "not wisely but too well." The mass incarceration of young men shows not only a lack of humanity but also stupidity. A smarter society should be able to target its punishments toward those who truly endanger the community.

As we embark on a quest to reform criminal justice, we must heed the advice of Robert Heinlein and Milton Friedman: "there ain't no such thing as a free lunch." If we want better policing, we will have to pay more, not less, for it. But in exchange, we can demand accountability.

Public accountability also requires shared strength of a different form: nongovernmental alliances that can balance and enhance public power. As Alexis de Tocqueville observed almost two centuries ago, "among democratic nations all citizens are independent and weak," and "therefore they all sink into a state of impotence, if they do not learn to help each other voluntarily." Luckily for the United States, "Americans of all ages, conditions and all dispositions constantly unite together." Tocqueville's sunny assessment of America's civil society assuredly overstated the case even in 1830. In 2021, the US feels more like a nation of dividers than uniters, and societies everywhere are increasingly polarized, but Tocqueville's line that people "can achieve almost nothing by themselves" remains true.

The ability to enable cooperation is among the greatest of urban assets. Shared strength in the twenty-first century will require more collaborative, private effort, especially if we are to ensure that public strength does not turn into public tyranny. The whole point of a government that is capable enough to prevent pandemics is to empower individuals to forge their own destinies. Cities require both effective government and empowered individual freedom, which does not sit comfortably within the ideological boxes of today's partisan politics.

The Freedom to Flourish

There is an ancient German phrase, "stadtluft macht frei": "city air makes you free." That phrase expressed a medieval legal reality: no noble could reimpose bondage on a serf who had been living in a city for a year and a day. The phrase also expresses the more essential truth that cities are places of possibility, with a cornucopia of social delights and a phalanx of prospective employers. In the twentieth century, city air meant freedom to the traveler coming to New York from the czar's Russia or the Jim Crow South. Along with its woes, Pandora's box also held hope.

Today, younger urbanites see less to be hopeful about. They are angry about the inequities of urban life and a perceived lack of opportunity. There are haves and have-nots, and the haves seem to get it all. Cities will always be unequal places, but that inequality is only tolerable when cities are seen as engines of growth. Poorer people must see the gain from urban life. They must feel the possibility of finding a brighter future. When that future fades, the desperate turn to demagogic calls for the bluntest forms of redistribution.

There are smart and effective ways of promoting upward mobility, including better pre-K programs, tax subsidies for the working poor, and better vocational training. We should do all of these and more. But canceling commercial rents for prosperous businesses makes little sense, and neither does canceling student debt for the children of the wealthy.

In a sense, the enthusiasm that many have for redistribution from the rich represents an awareness that our cities have become a rigged game that favors insiders over outsiders. Over decades we have accumulated rules and institutions that favor the old over the young, homeowners over renters, insiders over outsiders. Thus, people who bought houses a long time ago are guaranteed nice views and pretty parks, but people new to the area cannot afford to buy a house or even rent because prices are too high. Many schools are dominated by teachers' unions, and some police departments are run by their worst officers. It is not that individuals are bad—though of course some are—but that the system is not working. Too many cities have coasted on the prosperity of the privileged rather than on empowering the upward mobility of the less fortunate. That empowerment needs better education and fewer barriers to entrepreneurship, especially among the poor.

Gentrification is often seen as a problem, but it is really a symptom of other urban woes. Urban residents of all stripes are victims of policies that artificially constrain the growth of city space. Los Angeles is the site of many gentrification battles, which is particularly sad since that sprawling city once practically stood for Latino opportunity in America. Los Angeles is not particularly dense, and it could easily handle abundant extra building, especially if the new structures were high-rises that occupied little land. But Los Angeles sharply restricts the amount of new construction through local zoning rules, as does most of coastal California and many of the more expensive places on the planet. Since there is so little new space, there is more conflict over the old space. If the city allowed more growth, then there would be room for all and rents would be lower.

Our cities must do more to empower outsiders to start businesses, to build homes, and to learn new skills. To do that, there must be fewer regulations that serve little purpose other than protecting the current homeowners from nuisance or current businesses from competition. The right answer to today's unlevel playing field is not to create an equally inefficient system that favors a different set of insiders, but rather to open our cities up to everyone.

Many businesses shut their doors during 2020, which is why speedier permitting is more necessary than ever. In cities with sky-high rents pre-COVID-19, landlords can and will reduce rents to lure people and businesses back. Lower rents are likely to attract younger, scrappier firms that had been priced out of our most expensive cities. Some richer people will decide that life outside the city fits their needs better. Our metropolitan areas will become a bit more affordable and a bit grittier, and that's all right. They will also become younger, and those younger urbanites need a government that says yes more often to their dreams.

For years, urban retail space had been converting from stores that sold goods to places that sell experiences. Bookstores were becoming cafes. That process was derailed by the pandemic, and ground-level vacancies remain visible in once-fashionable shopping streets. But that real estate is too valuable to remain empty. Once the pandemic ends, creative urban entrepreneurs will convince landlords that lower rents are better than no rents.

While demand for commercial real estate is likely to decline in dense downtowns, demand for urban residences seems likely to remain robust. People will still want housing, and many hunger for the excitement of an urban neighborhood. If demand for residences is more robust than demand for office space, then the long-standing process of converting business space into homes will speed up. All of this requires change, and change requires freedom.

The Humility to Learn

Better urban education is the most important public tool that exists for transforming poor children into middle-class adults. Yet just spending more on schools is unlikely to generate flourishing in the inner city. Many urban school districts already spend far more per pupil than suburban schools, and their outcomes are still poor. We do not oppose spending more on schooling. We most emphatically favor more investment in our collective human capital. But that investment will be far more effective if we first focus on understanding what works.

Some of the urban problems that we will discuss in this book, like the high cost of urban housing, have clear solutions, like allowing more housing to be built. Other problems, like the poor performance of many urban schools, do not. The third major theme of this book is that our cities must become learning machines. We must recognize where we are ignorant and try to fill in the gaps of our knowledge.

The stellar performance of New Zealand during the pandemic reflects both its location as an isolated island and the commitment to learning made by prime minister Jacinda Ardern and director-general of health Ashley Bloomfield. The two key steps in New Zealand's safety were the initial strict lockdown, which was hardly unusual, and basing the decision to reopen on widespread testing of the asymptomatic, which was unique and extraordinarily successful.

Where American states like Florida and Texas reopened without knowing the prevalence of the disease in the population, New Zealand reopened only when population-level testing allowed them to know that the disease had truly vanished. The American error was not the reopening decision itself, but the failure to base the reopening decision on a serious measure of the disease. Good science does not mean knowing all the answers. It means having the humility to recognize the limits of one's knowledge and then embracing the tools needed to learn more. After all, if a scientist isn't wrong sometimes, then that scholar is not producing very imaginative hypotheses.

The early history of COVID-19 illustrates the folly of viewing scientists as infallible. The scientific leader of the public fight against the pandemic told Americans on March 8, 2020, that "there's no reason to be walking around with a mask." A spokesman for the World Health Organization, an entity that mixes science and politics, offered the view that "although travel restrictions may intuitively seem like the right thing to do, this is not something that WHO usually recommends." These opinions were not baseless, but they proved to be wrong. Much as we wish it were otherwise, the two of us have made our share of mistaken claims and prognostications.

Individual scientists don't know everything off the bat, which is why we have scientific inquiry. We have experiments and randomized controlled trials, not just for vaccines but also to evaluate the impact of putting body cameras on police. These are the tools of effective government in the twenty-first century. We live on a complex planet and our cities are complicated organisms. We must embrace a constant need to learn.

The Plan of the Book

This book is divided into ten chapters, eight of which lie between the introduction and the conclusion and carry the book's main arc. The first four chapters deal primarily with the mental and physical health of cities. The last four chapters address the economic and social challenges that were laid bare by the pandemic. All chapters include both our diagnosis of the problem and suggestions for policy remedies.

Pandemic spreads across cities, within cities, and within individuals themselves. Chapter 2 deals with the spread of contagion from metropolis to metropolis. For millennia, cities have hosted the ports and harbors that welcome boats carrying ideas, goods, and bacteria. The golden age of Athens was dimmed by the plague that entered that city from its Port of Piraeus. The hopes of reestablishing Roman order throughout the Mediterranean world were dashed when *Yersinia pestis*, the bacteria behind medieval Europe's Black Death, appeared in Constantinople in 541 CE.

This chapter covers the early history of pandemics and the efforts to fight those pandemics through quarantines. The medieval quarantines provide the earliest models for the restrictions on international travel that we use today, like the ban that many countries imposed on travelers from China in January 2020. In the US, that measure was ineffective, since people went from China to Europe and from there to the US. Chapter 2 ends by proposing our model of a NATO for health to do better next time.

The third chapter addresses the spread of disease within cities and focuses on the great plagues of the nineteenth century, especially cholera. Those diseases strengthened the sense of connection between rich and poor and ensured that sewers and aqueducts reached not only the elegant townhouses of New York's Washington Square but also the tenements of the not-too-distant Bowery. Those investments were expensive, but the payoff has been enormous. The whole world has a strong interest in ensuring that the cities of developing nations become safer: more sanitary, better protected from antibiotic-resistant superbugs, and the like. Rich countries should be willing to invest in those cities in exchange for safer conditions going forward.

Ultimately, the outcome of a pandemic depends on the fight between the individual and the disease. COVID-19 was particularly likely to kill the elderly and the obese. Other diseases disproportionately kill those who smoke, use illegal drugs, or engage in unsafe sexual practices. The fourth chapter discusses the behaviors that determine the health of a city and its vulnerability to pandemic.

Urbanization and industrialization bear much responsibility for the mass-prepared foods and sedentary lifestyles that directly explain high obesity rates. Even still, the residents of better-educated cities are much healthier than rural Americans. The opioid epidemic, for example, largely began in low-density locations because physical pain was more prevalent in those places. In recent years, opioid deaths have urbanized, partially because cities are more hospitable to illegal drug markets. In this chapter, we discuss targeted interventions against unhealthy products, such as harsher penalties for deceitful marketing, and the link between healthy behavior and schooling. That link helps justify a renewed emphasis on educational opportunity.

The fifth chapter focuses on the health system itself. How can the US spend so much on health care and not have the ability to contain infectious disease? The roots of our medical dysfunction lie in a system that is focused on private health rather than public health, and on care for the sick rather than promoting health. That system, in turn, reflects America's national predilection for a minimalist government that dispenses dollars but does not create executive capability. Health insurers of all stripes have spent trillions on chronic disease but have neglected contagious disease. Our health system needs to anticipate future pandemics and prepare plans to beat them.

In the sixth chapter, we pivot to the shorter-term economic consequences of the pandemic. Past plagues killed people but did little or no damage to the economy. The Black Death actually left the survivors richer, since the wealth of subsistence agriculturalists rises when there is more land per farmer. The 1918–19 influenza was a short, sharp shock, but the economy quickly recovered. Industrial products are still typically safe to ship, even when the industrial workers are themselves unwell.

By contrast, the modern urban service economy is much more vulnerable to an airborne pandemic. Masks help, but the risk of infection still takes away a lot of the fun of going out for a cup of tea. Even if people are allowed to go out to bars, cafes, and restaurants, many will not if pandemic is in the air. There is no obvious fix for this problem. We can provide short-term payments to the unemployed to reduce economic hardship, but we cannot save every small business ruined by the pandemic. The utterly crucial nature of these face-to-face service jobs for employing ordinary people makes it all the more vital that we make sure that pandemic never happens again. We must also ensure that entrepreneurship becomes easier post-pandemic. To generate more of the freedom that is needed to flourish, business regulations should be subjected to cost-benefit analysis and cities across the world should experiment with pro-entrepreneurship institutions like one-stop permitting.

In the seventh chapter, we turn to the longer-term consequences of the pandemic, especially the move to remote working. For forty years, futurists like Alvin Toffler have argued that electronic interactions would make face-to-face meetings unnecessary and that would lead to massive out-migration from cities. For forty years, they were wrong. Then, suddenly, they were right. Has Zoom replaced the conference room?

The evidence suggests disruption but not a hinge of history. Simple tasks, like working in a call center, can be done well remotely, but there is evidence that remote workers learn less than their in-person counterparts. Recent research suggests that the workers who sign up for remote jobs are less committed and productive than workers who want to be live. New hiring for remote jobs, including architects, aerospace engineers, and environmental scientists, had not recovered by the end of 2020, while new hiring for non-remote jobs, like painters, messengers, and stock clerks, had largely come back. For many jobs, even highly intellectual jobs, working face-to-face increases productivity. Unplanned interactions in the hallways and in common spaces are often the key to progress. Just as importantly, remote working is rarely as joyful as being in the same room.

Ultimately, cities will remain strong because they are places that allow us to exercise our deeply human love of personal connection. Yet even if creative firms remain committed to face-to-face interaction and cities, they are not committed to any particular city. Relocating from New York or San Francisco to Miami or Austin has never been easier. The increased mobility of firms means that cities will have to compete more fiercely to attract the global talent that powers local economies. That competition, in turn, limits the ability to raise local taxes to help the urban poor.

Chapter 8 then turns to the social strength of cities. A new wave of internecine conflict has weakened cities and made pandemic response more difficult. Public transit systems were unwilling to enforce rules about mask wearing, partially because they were terrified of producing viral videos, like the one taken in Philadelphia showing white cops dragging an African American man from a bus by force. We focus on gentrification battles in Los Angeles, which illustrate the larger sense of struggle over urban space. Gentrification is a long-standing but not particularly difficult problem to solve. If cities don't have enough space, create more. In a place with abundant demand, more space requires only the elimination of the land-use regulations that prevent the construction of taller, denser buildings.

But there are sources of urban strife other than constraints on urban space. Many of these are battles between insiders and outsiders. In chapter 9 we turn to two conflicts that do not have the same simple legislative solution as the gentrification wars: policing and schools. The Black Lives Matter protests in the summer of 2020 were motivated by police brutality, but this requires executive reform, not a simple legal fix like defunding the police. We need police protection, but we also need respect for all. The solution lies in a robust reform program that embraces two policy goals: safety and accountability for civil rights. That dual mandate requires us to measure both crime and community satisfaction with police service. We must then hold city leaders and the police accountable for both outcomes. As we ask more of the police, we are likely to spend more, not less.

The path forward for urban schooling is less clear. Police departments have proven quite malleable over time. Policing styles and crime rates have often changed swiftly; schools have not. One possibility is to allow outsiders to compete to provide vocational training—after hours, on weekends, and over the summer. Since vocational skills can be measured, it will be easy to pay for performance. To ensure that those courses lead to employment, cities need to make business permitting easier, which is particularly necessary given the vast number of businesses that will need to be reborn following COVID-19.

We end the book with a chapter summarizing our policy conclusions and our fundamental optimism. Cities have been engendering miracles of collaborative creativity since Socrates and Plato bickered on an Athenian street corner. The age of urban miracles need not be over. Indeed, it must not be. But we will have to work intelligently and pragmatically to make sure that cities are more open to outsiders and less vulnerable to the demons, like contagious disease and terrible inequities, that can often accompany density.

Chapter 2

WILL GLOBALIZATION LEAD TO PERMANENT PANDEMIC?

T he first well-chronicled urban plague occurred in Athens in 430 BCE. According to Thucydides, the epidemic began "in Ethiopia in upper Egypt and spread from there into Egypt itself and Libya and much of the territory of the King of Persia," before reaching Athens by sea. At the time, Athens was the undisputed trading capital of the Mediterranean, one of the world's largest cities and the most cosmopolitan polis in Europe. Pericles had proudly proclaimed that "our city is open to the world," and so it was.

Athens was at war with Sparta. The whole region sought safety from enemy hoplites behind the city's walls, but those barriers provided no protection from illness that entered by sea. The plague raged for the next four years. As many as one quarter of Athenians died, making the case fatality rate perhaps twenty-five times that of COVID-19. Without the plague, Athens might have won the Peloponnesian War. As it was, the city-state surrendered in 404 BCE.

As long as people have lived in cities, they have battled infectious disease.

The first farming and livestock settlers seem to have died more often than earlier hunter-gatherers. Living near animals brought humans into contact with diseases ranging from sleeping sickness to tetanus to tuberculosis.

Yet despite the danger, people have been coming to cities for millennia. During wars, cities are often safer than rural areas; many of those who died in Athens were farmers who had fled before the Peloponnesian soldiers. Traders come to cities that serve as centers of commerce and knowledge. Those merchants provide jobs and opportunity, but global trade and travel also provide pathways for pathogens.

This chapter highlights the fundamental vulnerability of cities to contagious diseases that enter through their harbors and airports and then tear through crowded streets. The same physical proximity that enabled Socrates to talk to Plato also enabled the flow of the Athenian plague. But this chapter also emphasizes that this urban weakness can be fought, as long as the fight is carried on collectively. In the modern world, this collective action must be global.

The oldest means of preventing the spread of pandemic is quarantine—isolating those who are sick, or those who are well if the sick are too numerous. The Athenians did not try to quarantine, but the Venetians, the French, and countless others did. Quarantine only works if potentially infected people are prevented from entering the city completely; any crack in the wall can let in the plague.

Quarantining is easier than the social distancing that became the norm in 2020. Locking the disease into a well-defined locale is far less onerous than keeping away from individuals one by one. But the history of quarantines also shows numerous instances of failure, because officials didn't want to inconvenience merchants or because the disease leaked through the barrier, perhaps carried by an errant mosquito or rat. Only effective governments have been able to enforce effective quarantines.

The quarantine model provides a plausible path toward protecting our urban world, but it requires vastly better monitoring of new outbreaks and the ability to shut down global travel at a moment's notice. The World Health Organization is far too weak to play this role in its current formulation. Instead, we need an empowered organization beholden (at least initially) to a much smaller number of nations. We need a NATO, not a UN. We discuss how to create such a system at the end of this chapter. We begin with the age-old urban bargain, where the city provides its choicest gifts— the interactions that bring us joy and make us rich and creative—in exchange for the risk of death by contagion.

The Mediterranean Lattice, and the Plague That Killed Pericles

Herodotus, sometimes known as the father of history, arrived in Athens around 448 BCE. Born in Halicarnassus, a Greek colony in Asia, he journeyed widely through the connected world of the Eastern Mediterranean. His histories are rich with folklore, probably gained from travels to Tyre and Babylon, Egypt and the Black Sea. Finally, he came to Athens and started making history profitable, by writing fulsome tributes to the city-state and its victories over Persia. Plutarch, who was not a fan, said that Herodotus "flattered the Athenians for a great sum of money he received of them." And so the craft of historical writing was born.

Herodotus's wanderings illustrate both the first glimmerings of globalization and the magnetic pull that Athens exerted on far-flung talent. Pericles's own paramour, the beautiful and wise courtesan Aspasia, was born in Asia. Anaxagoras, like Herodotus, came from Anatolia, bringing a whole school of philosophy in his head. He inspired the young Socrates. The mathematician Theodorus relocated to Athens from North Africa. Protagoras, a

Thracian immigrant to Athens, was preeminent among the professional teachers of philosophy known as Sophists, at least according to Plato.

In the fifth century BCE, Athens was the cultural center of the Mediterranean world. Like all large cities, Athens had the size and wealth to support highly specialized occupations, like teaching philosophy and writing unctuous local histories. Talent came and went, enabling former Athenians to seed the growth of Greek culture from Spain to India.

Herodotus answered Pericles's call for colonization and went to the Athenian outpost of Thurii in southern Italy. Protagoras would write Thurii's laws. The great tragedian Aeschylus left Athens to die in Sicily. Aristotle, who lived a century later, was Athens's most famous intellectual export. After coming to the city to study at Plato's Academy, he returned north to tutor Alexander the Great. His intellectual influence extended the reach of Athens deep into the Indus Valley and then returned via the domes of Baghdad to shape the meandering course of Western thought.

We remember best the ideas that leaped across Athens's Mediterranean network, but the network's primary purpose was commercial, not intellectual. Before the age of Roman roads, large trading cities could exist only on waterways. Boats provided the only plausible means of long-distance transportation. Like most large cities, Athens relied on imported food. Demosthenes reported that Crimea alone sent 4.8 million liters of grain to the city during the fourth century BCE. In return, Athens exported olive oil, luxuriously painted vases, and silver coins extracted as tribute.

As Athenian power waxed in the middle fifth century, the city tried to transform its network into an empire. The Delian League started as a loose anti-Persian confederation, with "allies who were originally independent states and reached their decision in general congress." Athens's power and influence over the league increased, and Sparta, the dominant land power in Greece, pushed back. In 432, the Spartans demanded that the Athenians cede control over their client states. Pericles responded that it would be "slavish to give in to them," and the war was on.

Pericles's strategy seemed foolproof. He sheltered his people behind the city walls ("which are just as strong as anything they could build") and sent the unbeatable Athenian navy out to raid and pillage at will ("we have nothing to fear from their navy"). The Spartans came and tore through the Athenian hinterland, but Pericles correctly foresaw that they couldn't break through the city's defenses. He was also right that the fleet "could harass the coastal states of the Peloponnesus with relative impunity."

But viruses and bacteria can enter a city that is barred to armed hoplites. Athens teemed with refugees from the Spartan onslaught, and it was open to the sea through its port of Piraeus. Plague entered Athens and started its slaughter. Thucydides, an Athenian general, was there, caught the disease, and survived to write about it. Pericles was not so lucky. He died, as did his legitimate sons.

No one knows whether the disease was bubonic plague, typhus, smallpox, measles, or something else entirely. Symptoms included high fever, diarrhea, head and body aches, and pustular rash. Virtually all of Athens caught the plague. The refugees were "particularly affected," because "there were no houses for them, and, living as they did during the hot season in badly ventilated huts, they died like flies." So said Thucydides. Just as in the case of COVID-19, the disease spread disproportionately to health-care workers, who were "dying like sheep through having caught the disease as a result of nursing others." Their efforts made little difference, for the plague "carried away all alike, even those who were treated and dieted with the greatest care." Unlike COVID-19, "those with naturally strong constitutions were no better off than the weak to resist the disease."

Some of Thucydides's most famous lines describe how plague destroyed the urban order: "men, not knowing what would happen next to them, became indifferent to every rule of religion or law." Consequently, "Athens owed to the plague the beginnings of a state of unprecedented lawlessness."

The plague killed Athenians by the tens of thousands, but it did little damage to Sparta's less dense farmland. The mysterious illness "never affected the Peloponnese at all, or not seriously; its full force was felt at Athens, and, after Athens, in the most densely populated of the other towns." Every plague finds it easier to spread when people are packed more tightly, which is why contagious disease disproportionately threatens cities, at least initially. Our modern world is so connected that a disease that enters America through New York City and Seattle can still do its worst damage in the Dakotas.

To be sure, neither plague nor military defeat ended Athens's cultural creativity. Plato was born in the city just as the plague was winding down, and lived for another eighty years. His conversations with the older Socrates provide one of the best examples of how face-to-face interactions can change the course of history. Yet Athens never again reached the soaring heights that it had under Pericles. As the great historian of illness William McNeill put it: "The disease inflicted a blow upon Athenian society from which it never entirely recovered."

Urban Plagues before Athens

Thucydides's writing provides us with a remarkable picture of the Athenian plague, but contagious diseases haunted human settlements long before 430 BCE. The scholarly investigators who try to understand historical health through ancient skeletons and other evidence think that the transition from hunting and gathering to settled agriculture led to a substantial rise in infectious illness.

The earliest hominids were not disease-free. Some organisms, like lice, pinworms, and salmonella, seem to have been with us since before we were human. Diseases like sleeping sickness and trichinosis may have traveled from animals to people even when we hunted in small packs without domesticated animals.

The agricultural revolution that led to sedentary settlements about twelve thousand years ago created higher human density levels and more opportunities for infection from domesticated livestock. Close proximity to pigs has long had its hazards. A distinguished anthropologist of early disease, George Armelagos, emphasizes that the "products of domesticated animals such as milk, hair and skin . . . could transmit anthrax, Q fever, brucellosis, and tuberculosis."

The coming of the city meant that even more humans and animals would be packed together, in close proximity to each other and to each other's waste. Records of pre-Athenian plagues are limited, but the Book of Exodus suggests that something terrible happened in urban Egypt over three thousand years ago. Some biblical scholars date the events in that book to the twelfth century BCE, which means that those ten Egyptian plagues occurred at the same time as the general collapse of Bronze Age civilization. The events of the *Iliad*, in which a plague strikes the Greek army besieging Troy, may have also occurred in the same time period. Sanskrit sources have been claimed to mention a contemporaneous plague in Babylon.

These shreds of evidence lead some to suspect that the collapse of the Bronze Age civilization itself occurred because of an early pandemic that spread through the connected cities of the Eastern Mediterranean. If disease played a significant role in that catastrophic event, then we have our first example of urban contagion wreaking havoc with humanity. An even deadlier second example occurred almost exactly one millennium after the Plague of Athens.

The Coming of the Black Death

For five hundred years after the plague that killed Pericles, the Mediterranean seems to have generally been pandemic-free. Large, land based, and endowed with an anti-trade ethos that banned senators from commerce, the Roman Republic spent centuries subjugating its near neighbors. Massive grain shipments increasingly came to the capital, but these were tribute from the conquered territories of Spain and Egypt rather than the result of a complex web of trading journeys.

From our vantage point, it is impossible to parcel out credit for those relatively healthy centuries between 400 BCE and 100 CE. Roman aqueducts, limited contact with outsiders, and blind luck surely all played a role. Whatever the cause, the absence of plague made it possible for the Roman Republic to stretch its borders; Marius, Pompey, and Julius Caesar took Roman armies across the Mediterranean world and turned a republic into an empire.

Rome was a military powerhouse, but the city was also a center of art and knowledge. The architecture of the Pantheon, the poetry of Virgil, the oratory of Cicero, and Pliny's natural history provide examples of human creativity at its best. Perhaps the genius of Rome is less original than that of classical Athens. Nonetheless, the city on the Tiber produced a steady flow of brilliance that shows the full capacity of human minds connected to each other by a dense city. Urban proximity linked Virgil to his fellow poets Horace and Propertius and to their arch-patron Maecenas, Augustus's cultural impresario.

As the Roman Empire extended and Rome's trading network stretched deep into Asia, pandemic returned to Europe. In 166 CE, "the Han histories record that Roman subjects reached Chinese territory." While "this new encounter ought to have marked the beginning of a new international commerce not only in merchandise, but also in ideas and information," it was "instead the harbinger of something much more ominous."

The Antonine Plague that came out of Asia may have killed between 10 and 14 percent of the Roman population between 165 and 180 CE. It could have been measles or smallpox, and the Chinese empire seems to have been afflicted by a pandemic at roughly the same time. A second pandemic came to Rome in 250 CE. That outbreak may have helped convert Rome to Christianity, because "one advantage that Christians had over their pagan contemporaries was that care of the sick, even in times of pestilence, was for them a required religious duty," and "the teachings of their faith made life meaningful even amid sudden and surprising death."

The Antonine Plague struck during the epoch of the "Five Good Emperors," when Rome seems to have been particularly well governed. Consequently, the plague killed, but it did not destabilize society. The second plague struck during more uncertain times and added to the political chaos of the third century, which was only ended by the long, successful, and brutal reigns of Diocletian and Constantine. Diocletian began the process of splitting the empire, and Constantine built the eastern capital of Constantinople. That city, also known as Byzantium, would serve as the urban core of a Roman empire for a millennium after the fall of Rome itself.

In his Foundation trilogy, Isaac Asimov wrote about how the wisdom of a collapsing Galactic Empire was preserved in a distant planet packed with scholars and merchants. In the fifth century, Constantinople seemed ready to play that role for Rome. While Visigoths and Vandals sacked the mother city, Constantinople built the high, thick walls that would protect its people until Mehmed II came with his cannons a millennium later. The walls were "built just in time," for while Attila the Hun was eager to subdue both halves of the Roman Empire, "the Huns had not the patience, the skill nor the discipline required for protracted siege warfare."

The learning of the classical world was preserved in Constantinople's Pandidakterion, which was something like a university packed with dozens of chaired professors spouting Greek and Latin. Even as "the vacant throne of Italy was abandoned to lawless barbarians," as Gibbon put it, the Eastern emperors promulgated new legal codes. Just like Asimov's Foundation, Constantinople kept its wisdom safe, waiting for the right moment to burst out and reclaim the West. The Dark Ages could end after a few decades rather than many centuries.

The moment for imperial renewal seemed to have arrived in 533 CE. The first generation of barbarian conquerors, such as the Vandal chief Genseric who sacked Rome in 455, had died and been replaced by squabbling descendants.

Justinian sent forth his warlord Belisarius to defeat the Vandals and re-establish Roman control over part of the Italian peninsula. Belisarius brought back to Constantinople the former riches of the Western Roman Empire such as "gold and carriages in which it is customary for a king's consort to ride," and the "treasures of the Jews, which Titus, the son of Vespasian, together with certain others, had brought to Rome after the capture of Jerusalem." But Belisarius got no chance to rest on his laurels.

There was infighting in Italy, again between royal cousins, and Justinian again sent Belisarius into action. The Byzantine general's battle with the Goths lasted for another three years. He captured the Gothic capital of Ravenna in 540 CE and returned to Constantinople, but his triumph turned into catastrophe. The contemporary observer Procopius writes that "during these times there was a pestilence, by which the whole human race came near to being annihilated." Procopius wrote in Attic Greek (the dialect of Athens), like Thucydides, and he was deeply influenced by the Athenian. Like Thucydides, Procopius claims that the disease came out of Africa: "it started from the Aegyptians who dwell in Pelusium" and "from there it spread over the whole world." The modern scientific literature suggests instead that the plague originated in central Asia.

Unlike the earlier Plague of Athens, our medical knowledge of Justinian's plague is reasonably good, primarily because of DNA found in early medieval cemeteries. Justinian's plague appears to be the first well-recorded appearance of that archenemy of humanity: the *Yersinia pestis* bacterium, aka the Black Death. That serial slaughterer seems to have evolved from less virulent bacterial ancestors that infected Eurasians during the Bronze Age. The standard view is that *Yersinia pestis* emerged out of central Asia and traveled along the Silk Road to Europe.

The first wave of *Yersinia pestis* was to haunt Europe, as well as parts of Asia and Africa, for at least the next century. *Y. pestis* is a bacterium spread largely by fleas. A flea bites a human, and regurgitated blood enters the body. Once inside a human, the bacteria enter the lymphatic system and settle in the lymph nodes. There, they colonize and reproduce, spreading throughout the body. Swollen lymph nodes are termed *buboes*, hence the name "bubonic plague." Symptoms appear within a week—fever, chills, weakness, and internal bleeding. Skin and other tissues may turn black and die (hence the name Black Death). Roughly half of the people who caught bubonic plague died before the advent of modern medicine, though in some settings the mortality rate may have been much higher.

Yersinia pestis DNA have been found in the teeth of a twenty year-old Swedish farmwoman who died five thousand years ago. That evidence led a team of scientists to conclude that *Yersinia pestis* was present in the Bronze Age "mega-settlements of Eastern Europe," where "living conditions in these sites were unprecedented compared to previous human populations" because of high population densities and proximity to animals. Prehistoric agricultural density may have enabled an even earlier wave of plague, which then "contributed to the Neolithic decline," and "paved the way for the later steppe migrations into Europe."

If the forensic examiners of the ancient world are right, then the deadly dance between density and disease goes back over five thousand years. Technological progress, like the plow, leads to population growth, urbanization, and trade. Bacteria come along for the ride, leaping from animal to human.

If the pandemic is sufficiently severe, civilization collapses and there is a return to lower-density living. Perhaps this is what happened to those agrarian "mega-settlements" of the Ukraine and Romania over five millennia ago, but we have far better records of the damage done to Justinian's city in 541 C.E.

Procopius's narrative of the plague is harrowing: "death came in some cases immediately, in others after many days, and with some the body broke out with black pustules about as large as a lentil and these did not survive even one day." With some, "a vomiting of blood ensued without visible cause and straightaway brought death." As "the disease in Byzantium ran a course of four months," "the tale of dead reached five thousand each day, and again it even came to ten thousand and still more than that."

Procopius echoes Thucydides by writing that "confusion and disorder everywhere became complete," but the public response in Constantinople was better than it had been in Athens. One of Justinian's agents kept "giving out the emperor's money" and "burying the bodies that were not cared for." While Thucydides described a city bent on having one last fling, Procopius writes that "those who in times past used to take delight in devoting themselves to pursuits both shameful and base, shook off the unrighteousness of their daily lives and practiced the duties of religion with diligence." Fear of damnation works wonders among people who were "supposing that they would die immediately."

In the spring of 2020, the streets of New York City were eerily empty. The same was true a millennium and a half ago in Constantinople, as the Byzantines seem also to have practiced social distancing. Procopius writes that "it seemed no easy thing to see any man in the streets of Byzantium, but all who had the good fortune to be in health were sitting in their houses, either attending the sick or mourning the dead." Unfortunately, isolation from other humans does not ensure protection from the bite of a flea.

The plague did not completely end Justinian's attempts to reconquer Italy.

He sent Belisarius back in 544 CE, but with a trifling force of four thousand, a quarter of the number that he had taken to North Africa a decade earlier. The general battled on. Constantinople would maintain its presence in Ravenna for another two centuries, but this was no new Pax Romana. The representatives of Byzantium in Italy became just another set of local belligerents dusting it up with the Lombards and the Franks and contributing to the general chaos of early medieval Europe.

The plague came and went for another two centuries. Estimates are that this first wave of the Black Death killed as many as fifty million people. It fatally weakened both the Roman and Persian Empires, which opened the way for the Arab conquests of Asia and North Africa during the seventh and eighth centuries. Waves of disease and warfare tore apart the urban world of the Roman Empire and led to centuries of largely rural poverty in Europe.

This interpretation of the end of the classical world provides an apocalyptic vision of pandemic. A thriving urban civilization is first weakened by disease and then divided politically. External marauders take down the weaker half and replace it with even weaker kingdoms. The stronger half remains and prepares to reestablish control, but plague prevents reconquest and further enervates the remaining outpost of civilization. People retreat to isolated farms, where they are preyed upon by roaming bandits, who eventually settle down and dignify their thieving by calling themselves nobles.

Shades of Social Distancing

Today, the Black Death is generally treatable. Antibiotics cure most cases. But Alexander Fleming only discovered penicillin in 1928. In the Middle Ages, social distancing was the only possible response. The same was true for COVID-19 during most of 2020.

Isolating the sick from the healthy is a reasonable response to a contagious pandemic, but different types of social distancing come with different costs and efficacy. The oldest form of social distancing is simply to remove the sick from the community. Leviticus 13:46 may be humanity's oldest public health warning: "all the days wherein the plague shall be in him he shall be defiled; he is unclean: he shall dwell alone; without the camp shall his habitation be." The Indian Lepers Act of 1898 empowered "any police officer" to "arrest without a warrant any person who appears to him to be a pauper leper." After some bureaucratic procedures with a magistrate and the inspector of lepers, the officer was to send the "pauper leper" to "a leper asylum, where such leper shall be detained until discharge by order of the Board or the District Magistrate." The act was only fully repealed in 2016.

Few modern societies are willing to condemn a sick person to the wandering life of a medieval leper. Further, individual exile may not be effective. In New York City a century ago, "Typhoid Mary" Mallon was forcibly quarantined because disease and death came along with her cooking. She was eventually released from her first quarantine "on her pledge to give up her vocation of cook" and "not handle the food of others," but "she violated every detail of her pledge" and "cooked in hotels, restaurants and sanatoria." In the case of bubonic plague, exiling the sick does little good as long as the fleas and rats remain. For diseases with human-to-human spread, exiling the visibly sick will not protect the healthy if the disease can be spread before the person is symptomatic, as in the case of COVID-19.

A second form of social distancing is for each family to self-isolate, like the Byzantines who were "sitting in their houses" in Procopius's narrative. That strategy carries the large costs that millions experienced during their own personal COVID-19 lockdowns. The downsides of family isolation are more extreme for the poor, who live in homes too small for comfort and who must work in proximity to others to survive. Only 13 percent of Americans with a high school degree or less were able to work remotely during May of 2020.

In rich countries, prosperity and technology made it possible to self-isolate and still receive food and other necessities. There was no Amazon Prime in sixth-century Constantinople. A long hibernation is impossible unless one has a store of calories, but for most of history, city dwellers had no such stores.

For most of the premodern plagues, family isolation would be both costly and useless. Distance from people does not guarantee distance from fleas and rats; yellow fever can be spread by mosquitoes to otherwise isolated households. Cholera oozes through the water system to strike families sheltering at home. As we will discuss later, the whole theory of contagious disease was questioned during the nineteenth century, partially because social distancing did so little to protect against yellow fever and cholera.

The third and fourth social distancing techniques are more effective, less personally costly, and involve the isolation of the place rather than the person. The third, more common strategy is to establish a quarantine barrier around one's community in the hope of stopping disease from entering. The fourth strategy is to establish a barrier around the source of the plague to stop the disease from getting out. At the end of this chapter, we will discuss the feasibility of imposing such a cordon sanitaire around the source of any future pandemic.

Thinking in terms of place and community is unnatural to people who have been taught they are autonomous human beings. We expect social policies and products that are catered toward our own idiosyncratic needs, not targeted toward the larger community. But with contagion, the community becomes crucial. Any disease that enters into a neighborhood can infect anyone, which means that good policy making must be much more communally focused. We shall revisit this theme often.

The Invention of Quarantine:
Dubrovnik and Venice

In the aftermath of Justinian's plague, trade collapsed. Cities shrank to small towns. The population of Rome, perhaps 1,000,000 at the time of the Caesars, fell to 30,000 a millennium later. As humanity retreated into the autarky of isolated rural communities, pandemics abated. To be sure, the life of a medieval serf was far from healthy. Nutrition was terrible. Hygiene was worse. There are plenty of infectious diseases that do not turn into pandemics, and the peasantry of medieval Europe knew many of them.

Gradually, trade reemerged both in the Mediterranean and among northern cities, like Bruges and Lübeck. Ties between European towns deepened and extended through Constantinople to the Silk Road. By the thirteenth century, Europe had access to a trade network that could move luxury fabrics and spices over vast distances. Cities like Venice and Dalmatia's Dubrovnik were key nodes on that lattice. But a network that can move bales of wool can also move the rats and fleas that carry *Yersinia pestis*.

Dubrovnik's picturesque red rooftops and sturdy city walls became famous to millions of *Game of Thrones* viewers as a stand-in for the city of King's Landing. But Dubrovnik has greater historical import than as a fictional victim of dragon fire. It successfully linked the East and West for over half a millennium. Dubrovnik's origins lie in the invasions that overran much of the Byzantine Empire in the wake of Justinian's plague. Refugees from an older Roman city fled before early Slavic invaders and established a refuge protected by mountains and waterways. As Europe recovered in the centuries after 750, Dubrovnik—or Ragusa, as it was known then—grew as a port. The city remained under the loose control of Byzantium until 1205, and it served as a conduit between the ancient empire and the growing cities of Italy.

Ragusa's independence was ended by the freebooting Venetians during the Fourth Crusade. In a sense, Venice was Ragusa on steroids. It was the greatest connector between East and West. It was the greatest trading power in the Eastern Mediterranean. In 1204, Venetians partnered with crusaders to sack Constantinople and conquer the remnants of the Roman Empire. The Venetians and their cross-bearing allies took down the largest city in Christendom and seized Byzantine treasures, such as the four bronze horses they brought back to grace the facade of San Marco.

Ragusa, along with the rest of the Dalmatian coast, was also acquired as war booty. For 153 years, the Ragusans had to pay tribute to their Venetian overlords, much as the cities of the Delian League once paid tribute to Athens. Yet Ragusa, like Venice, was one of the best-governed cities in the world. Ragusa's strong institutions enabled it to become the first Western city to organize a coherent public health response to the plague.

The Black Death reemerged in Asia during the early fourteenth century, after a five-hundred-year hiatus. *Yersinia pestis* then tore through the cities of China and blazed its way along the Silk Road to Constantinople and then Ragusa. The fleas that carried the disease could travel on rats or directly on the traded fabrics, like wool, that were such a large part of medieval commerce. Perhaps one fourth of Europe's population died in the first years of this second Black Death pandemic. In 1348 alone, Ragusa lost somewhere between 10 and 50 percent of its population. Plague came again to the port in 1357, 1361, and 1371.

But Ragusans learned how to protect themselves. In May 1363, when "news about the epidemic in Apulia and Marche regions of Italy" arrived, Ragusa's leaders decided to "forbid travelers from those regions to enter the city," and "likewise, Ragusans were not allowed to travel to those regions." Region-specific travel bans can work when one knows where the disease is located, though by the time the US banned travel from China on January 31, 2020, COVID-19 had already spread far and wide.

Fourteen years after their travel ban, the Ragusans went further and adopted the first quarantine regulations, "Veniens de locis pestiferis non intret Ragusium vel Districtum," or "travelers from places of plague shall not enter Ragusa or its environs." The rule established two places of quarantine—the rocky islet of St. Mark and the town of Cavtat. Ragusans were forbidden from visiting these areas, even to bring food, and that prohibition was enforced by a sizable fine.

Quarantines are now so ingrained that it is easy to miss the brilliance (and blind luck) of this initial innovation. The Ragusans figured out that the plague could be brought by both the sick and the apparently healthy. They guessed that a lengthy isolation period would enable the plague to run its course. As it turns out, two weeks would have been fine since the plague's incubation period is typically less than seven days. They understood enough to keep the plague victims far away from their major population centers. They imposed a penalty structure that was effective and easy to enforce. England wouldn't have its first quarantine regulation until 1663.

Surrounding visitors with a watery moat provided a model for quarantine that was imitated for centuries. Ships from diseased ports had to shelter on the island of Ratonneau before entering Marseilles. America's own Ellis Island was used to quarantine immigrants until 1954. The fictional Vito Corleone spends a lonely forty days on the island after immigration officials diagnose him with smallpox in *The Godfather Part II.*

Quarantine provided a middle way between complete openness and shutting down trade routes entirely. Before 1377, Ragusa had turned travelers away, but that meant an end to all commerce. Quarantine permitted some trade, while still reducing the flow of disease.

Inbound ships and their trading partners will always want to speed things up. The collective interest lies in isolation—the individual advantage comes from connection. This divide between individual and collective interests remains key today. During the COVID-19 crisis, many countries and even US states asked travelers to self-quarantine upon arrival. But self-quarantine is hard to enforce, and it is a good bet that many flouted the rules.

The Ragusans didn't just establish Europe's first quarantine. They created a shared strength to protect the city: elected public health officials were empowered with broad authority to enforce these and other rules. In 1390, the city appointed officiales contra venientes de locis pestiferis (officials against travelers from places of plague). After 1397, these health officers were elected annually and, after 1426, they served without pay. Ragusa, like Venice, was an aristocratic republic, and its leadership positions, including the plague fighters, were almost exclusively patricians. Venice followed Ragusa's lead in 1486, and "by the middle of the sixteenth century all the major cities of Northern Italy had permanent Magistracies of public health."

Ragusa would eventually up the isolation time to forty days for travelers arriving on land; *quaranta*, which means "forty" in Italian, provides the root of the word *quarantine*. The choice of forty days may have owed more to biblical authority than strictly scientific knowledge. After all, Jesus wandered for forty days in the wilderness. Moses spent forty days in the clouds of Mount Sinai. Noah traveled forty days on his ark. And the Israelites wandered in the desert for forty years. Those models of social isolation seemed to place quarantine on solid spiritual ground.

The Venetians called their isolating island Lazzaretto, after Lazarus. During its long history, it held both travelers and sick Venetians. The Venetians embraced social distancing in the fifteenth century, not only quarantining travelers but also sending their own sick to their "lazaretto." Sometimes, "entire districts within cities were quarantined." Just as in 2020, physical mobility was limited by fiat, and "women and children" were "confined to their homes" or "forbidden from leaving their parish." It is hard to know whether these onerous and highly discriminatory restrictions actually saved lives.

Venice is also associated with the social distancing of doctors through the use of protective equipment. The beaked nose of the plague doctor's mask is a highlight of the Carnival of Venice today, although credit for the mask's invention is typically given to Charles de Lorme. De Lorme was an early seventeenth-century French court physician who appears to have been smart enough to figure out that wearing some personal protective equipment helped a medical professional's chance of surviving a pandemic.

Venice targeted their system of quarantine with the help of "an information network of daily reports of Venetian consuls in Mediterranean areas" and "detailed interrogation of sailors who arrived in Venetian ports." If there was a plague outbreak anywhere, the Venetian authorities wanted to know and to immediately impose quarantine on ships that had been exposed to that plague. Any successful twenty-first century cordon sanitaire will require an even more sophisticated early warning system.

A recurrent theme of this book is that slowing the spread of disease requires both medical knowledge and effective government. Enforcing quarantine is difficult because private interests don't align with social interests. A merchant in fifteenth-century Ragusa wanted to bring his goods into the city as quickly as possible, rather than sit for a month on a rocky island. The sick of seventeenth-century Venice would rather stay in their homes than be shipped off to a plague hospital. Plenty of Americans chose to party in August at South Dakota's Sturgis Motorcycle Rally rather than shelter in place. Quarantine was as successful as it was only because the governments of both Venice and Ragusa were among the most competent of their day. In fact, in many ways they look better than the US or UK government did at the outbreak of COVID-19. When governments are less capable, quarantine and social distancing are harder to enforce.

Why Did Europe Survive
the Black Death?

The Black Death slaughtered millions of Europeans, but it didn't end the European resurgence. In a terrible way, it made surviving Europeans richer, by increasing the amount of land per person, which we will discuss in chapter 6. The great difference between the first round of *Yersinia pestis* and the second lies in the political events that followed each outbreak, which reinforces the point that the impact of disasters is determined by the strength of civil society.

The first round of the Black Death came on the heels of the destabilizing invasions that brought down Western Roman Europe. Justinian might have been able to reestablish order, but his prospects always teetered on a knife-edge. Moreover, the empire's ultra-urban, highly centralized model of imperial rule was particularly vulnerable to a pandemic that brought chaos to the capital.

The second round of *Yersinia pestis* arrived when Europe was decentralized, defense oriented, and in a stable, long-run political equilibrium. Dynasties were well established. The feudal order had been in place for centuries. The second Black Death was not rocking an already unsteady boat.

Between 550 and 1450, the Europeans spent an inordinate amount of time fighting one another. They developed military technologies, like the castle, and borrowed others, like gunpowder, which probably came from China along the Silk Road. When Suleiman the Magnificent's Ottoman army arrived at Vienna in 1529, he faced walls and a highly organized defensive force of Spanish musketeers and German pikemen.

The continent was geared for defense, and the smaller population that survived the plague could still garrison Europe's castles. Europe's borders changed little between 1300 and 1400, even as millions died. That stability meant that Europe's economy could continue to grow, despite the horrors of the plague. The comparison of the two rounds of Black Death leads us to wonder whether the world in 2021 will look more like the instability of 540 or the stability of 1350.

In most of history prior to 1492, we think of Europeans being afflicted with disease imported from elsewhere. Thucydides credits the Athenian plague to Ethiopia. *Yersinia pestis* likely came from central Asia, though some suggest an ancient European origin. That perspective reflects the biased focus of European historians on events in Europe. If sixth-century Europeans spread plague to central Africa through some long-forgotten trade route, Europeans never wrote about it.

But thanks to a Franciscan missionary, we have a written record of how the Spanish unleashed a terrible pandemic upon the Aztecs: "when the smallpox began to attack the Indians it became so great a pestilence among them throughout the land that in most provinces more than half the population died." While New Spain (or Mexico) was "extremely full of people," smallpox "had never been seen" before the Spanish arrival. The population had no immunity, and some of their generally healthy habits, like bathing communally, may have helped spread the disease.

In 1633, the Pilgrim William Bradford noted the losses inflicted by smallpox on the Native Americans of Massachusetts: "they fell down so generally of this disease as they were in the end not able to help one another, not to make a fire, nor to fetch a little water to drink, nor any to bury the dead." Some estimate that up to 90 percent of the native population died of diseases that came from Europe, making it easier for a small number of early colonists to establish themselves in North America. The colonists were exposing largely nonurban North Americans to diseases that had spread for centuries around Europe's cities.

When Quarantine Failed:
Yellow Fever in Philadelphia

Europeans turned to quarantine again and again in the eighteenth and nineteenth centuries when new pandemics traveled along with clipper ships in that previous age of globalization. Just as our modern travel restrictions did little to keep COVID-19 out of America or the UK, those earlier quarantines kept out neither yellow fever nor cholera. The story of yellow fever in Philadelphia cautions us against too much reliance on travel bans, and reminds us that other investments, like the city's public water system, can help populations survive when a disease makes it through the cordon sanitaire.

As sailing ships connected continents, more diseases wandered the globe. The Europeans who crossed the Atlantic brought American diseases back to Europe. Syphilis seems to have been a prime example. Since Africa became part of the triangular trading routes, African diseases, like yellow fever, got thrown into the mix. Yellow fever is an arbovirus, transmitted by infected mosquitoes, not by airborne droplets. Both the virus and the *Aedes aegypti* mosquitoes that carry it are thought to originate in Africa, where the disease still kills tens of thousands of people annually, despite the existence of a functional vaccine since 1937.

Slave ships traveled the terrible Middle Passage from Africa to the Americas for centuries carrying water barrels along with their human cargo. A wooden barrel is a perfectly pleasant environment for an *Aedes aegypti* mosquito to inhabit. So these death-dealing insects crossed the Atlantic in style, often killing their shipmates as they went. Yellow fever became endemic in the American tropics and would regularly travel northward to American cities from 1691 to 1761. Then, for thirty years, the terrible disease stayed away not only from the US, but also largely from the Caribbean.

The historian Billy Smith's *Ship of Death* tells a remarkable tale about how yellow fever came again to kill urban Americans. Eighteenth-century London coffeehouses were great intellectual connectors: Old Slaughter's Coffee House on St. Martin's Lane provided both coffee and information for Dr. Samuel Johnson, Thomas Gainsborough, John Dryden, and even that early intercontinental traveler, Benjamin Franklin. Old Slaughter's also hosted a remarkable meeting of early abolitionists, who dreamed up a utopian scheme that went horribly awry, both for the schemers and for thousands of Americans living far away.

The plan was to form a colony for freed slaves on the African island of Bolama, now part of Guinea-Bissau. The English would buy the island and hire local Africans to help with the planting. The result would be a profitable plantation, operated entirely without coercion. It must have seemed like a brilliant scheme on a damp London afternoon warmed only by Old Slaughter's coffee and abolitionist dreams.

The group took three ships to Africa and landed on Bolama. The locals initially attacked, killing seven men and kidnapping eight women and children, but the idealistic colonists persevered and eventually purchased the land. The women and children were mostly returned too. Unfortunately, the mosquitoes proved deadlier than the Africans, and the graveyard started to fill. The settlement shrank as yellow fever continue to kill, and their ship—the *Hankey*—traveled across the Atlantic, bringing fever first to the Caribbean and then to Philadelphia.

The yellow fever epidemics that raged between 1793 and 1805 became the first major health crisis of the new American republic. They also marked the beginning of the great intellectual battle over the nature of illness that would split the world's best medical thinkers for a century.

There were two theories of epidemic. The miasma theory emphasized that disease came from bad air (literally, miasma), which itself was a result of poor environmental conditions, including fetid water and a polluted atmosphere. The miasma theorists called for aqueducts and the eradication of filth. The contagion theory emphasized the risks of proximity to other humans and stressed the use of quarantine. With hindsight, the contagionists were right about the science, but the policy recommendations of the miasma school were often perfectly sound. Filth doesn't cause bubonic plague, but if getting rid of the filth also gets rid of the rats, then filth-reducing policies will certainly help.

The celebrated Dr. Benjamin Rush—signer of the Declaration of Independence, surgeon general of the Continental Army, professor at the University of Pennsylvania, and "the father of American psychiatry"—was the most prominent early American adherent of the miasma theory. As a young man, Rush had treated yellow fever patients, and he knew the symptoms when they began to appear in Philadelphia in 1793. He sent his family to safety outside the city. Twenty thousand other Philadelphians also fled to the countryside to escape the disease. Rush stayed to fight the illness, but despite his ministrations, yellow fever would kill one tenth of the city's population.

Rush was as brilliant a doctor as eighteenth-century America possessed, but his errors during the yellow fever epidemic were as glaring as his successes. Rush convinced himself that African Americans were not susceptible to yellow fever: "in no one instance have the black people been infected with the malignant fever which now prevails in our city." Consequently, Rush emphasized "the safety and propriety of employing black people to nurse and attend persons infected with this fever." The African American community of Philadelphia responded magnificently, throwing themselves into the maws of the epidemic for the common good. Unfortunately, Rush was completely wrong and large numbers of the heroic caretakers died.

Rush's medical cure for yellow fever involved copious bloodletting combined with high doses of mercury. When the first bloodletting did not work, he let even more blood flow. He was wrong, but his observations on contagion were an interesting mixture of insight and error. Rush had no use for contagion theory. In 1804, he wrote that "the separation of the sick from the healthy has been repeatedly tried to no purpose to check the progress of our yellow fever," and that "it originates frequently in half a dozen places in our city remote from each other and at the same time." Consequently, "stories with respect to the contagious nature of yellow fever" are "not only erroneous but highly ridiculous." Rather, yellow fever "can spread only in an atmosphere contaminated by exhalations from putrid animal and vegetable matters." For that reason, he held that quarantines were not only "unnecessary and nugatory," they were downright evil.

Rush wasn't being unscientific. He was drawing from his copious observations of the spread of yellow fever in Philadelphia, and it didn't look like contagion to him. Of course, it wasn't spread by strictly human contact at all.

Rush's foil in the yellow fever debate was none other than the first secretary of the treasury, Alexander Hamilton. Drawing on his Caribbean roots, Hamilton argued for "bark and wine cure"—use of quinine bark and diluted Madeira wine. Quinine would have been fine had Philadelphia suffered an outbreak of malaria; it was no use against yellow fever. Madeira also had no medical value, but at least it might have lifted spirits.

Quarantines fail either because they are porous or because they are imposed too late, like the travel bans that came into operation long after the US was filled with travelers exposed to COVID-19. Philadelphia's quarantines and lazaretto may have failed for both reasons. Mosquitoes can travel over water for hundreds of meters, so the distances needed for a yellow fever quarantine need to be much larger than for a plague quarantine. We can't know if infected mosquitoes traveled from quarantined ships to the mainland in 1793, but it is possible.

More importantly, by the time the city was ready to impose a quarantine in 1793, the mosquitoes were already well entrenched citywide. The city moved too late and the mosquitoes had found plenty of human hosts. A mosquito-borne epidemic will temporarily end when frost grounds the insects, but that doesn't mean the disease is done. Come spring, the sickness often reappears, even if ships are put under quarantine. Both yellow fever and Zika virus can be transmitted from infected *Aedes aegypti* to their progeny, and the larvae hatch in the spring. Philadelphia would end up being afflicted for years. In a sense, Rush was right that the land itself had become a source of illness.

The true understanding of yellow fever would have to wait for Walter Reed in 1901. Reed was the chairman of the United States Army Yellow Fever Commission, formed to investigate the disease after the terrible toll it took during and after the Spanish-American War. Reed himself was testing a hypothesis that he credited to the Cuban doctor Carlos Finlay, who suggested in 1881 the idea that mosquitoes carried the infection.

While Benjamin Rush had yellow fever wrong, his broader policy impact was vast. Indeed, Philadelphia was a pioneer in American water systems precisely because Benjamin Rush misunderstood the causes of yellow fever. Better sanitation meant eliminating pools of standing water that made it easier for mosquitoes to breed. The miasma school's emphasis on urban cleanliness is almost always sensible advice, even if cleanliness is not a surefire protection against contagion.

Quarantines continued to be common, despite the prominent enthusiasts for miasma, partially because there really wasn't much else to do. In the American South, yellow fever outbreaks became seasonal events. In places with mild winters, the infected mosquitoes themselves, and not just their children, can survive until the spring. During yellow fever outbreaks, far-flung communities would impose "shotgun quarantines" that blocked all movement into their jurisdiction and disrupted commerce throughout the South. The costs of this uncoordinated local imposition of quarantine led Southerners, who had just fought a civil war against the federal government, to demand more federal control over quarantine policy.

Philadelphia demonstrates the practical limits of quarantines and barriers to mobility. When a disease appears, the quarantine walls have to go up immediately, and they need to be strict. A half measure that comes even fifteen days too late can be near useless. The fear is that maybe the modern world will never be able to rely on barriers to mobility for protections against the plagues of the future.

Philadelphia does offer some hope amid the pessimism. Because of a combination of scientific error (the miasma theory) and common sense (clean water is good), the city invested in a public water system that enabled it to become more resilient against future pandemics. In a world where we can never be sure that we will keep the next pandemic locked up, we need health systems and human bodies that are as fortified as possible against future infections.

Constraining the Spread of Disease with a Cordon Sanitaire in the Sixteenth and Twenty-First Centuries

Quarantines keep out disease and isolate healthy communities. With those uncoordinated shotgun quarantines, a maze of local barriers cut off perfectly safe travel from one healthy community to another. The far less costly form of quarantine is to lock the disease in, rather than locking it out. But that requires both a strong early warning system and the ability to erect a hard wall locking people into a sick city.

When the plague appeared in the Maltese city of Birgu in 1523, guards were sent to prevent anyone from leaving the town. The disease seems to have been kept within the city's walls. Three hundred years later, the

Maltese tried to repeat that trick by barricading their larger cities in response to a plague outbreak late in the Napoleonic era. That time they moved too slowly to stop the spread of the disease.

The village of Eyam in England's Derbyshire provides the most heroic example of voluntary sequestration. Plague came to the village tailor from London in flea-infested clothing sent during the Great Plague of 1665. As the deaths started, two clerics—one a Cambridge-educated Anglican and the other a more popular Puritan—took the courageous step of urging the villagers to barricade themselves in from the outside world. They made arrangements with the nearby Earl of Devonshire to deliver food, in exchange for "payment in pools of vinegar or streams to prevent it carrying the contagion." The Anglican priest's wife perished in the plague. According to some accounts, "259 of a population of 330 died," but the larger population outside the village was spared.

Self-isolation during an outbreak of plague requires the kind of self-sacrifice that comes naturally only to those who have listened to a surfeit of Puritanical preaching. In most cases, however, locking in a district requires force, because the townspeople are desperately trying to flee. Roads and bridges leading out of Philadelphia were blocked during the yellow fever epidemic of 1793 by non-Philadelphians trying to contain the spread of the disease. Yet twenty thousand Philadelphians still escaped.

Whereas a quarantine is the imposition of a waiting period for entry into an area, a cordon sanitaire is a barrier that blocks the flow of potentially diseased individuals out of an epidemic zone. The most natural place for a cordon sanitaire is a national border. Empress Maria Theresa blocked the border with the Ottoman Empire in 1770 to stop the spread of plague. The term *cordon sanitaire* was first used in 1821 when the Duc de Richelieu blocked the border between France and Spain along the Pyrenees to prevent yellow fever from coming north out of Barcelona. Countries could also have easily enforced bans on international travel during the COVID-19 crisis, which would have at least prevented the spread of new virus variants across the globe.

Involuntary restrictions on movement within countries are more difficult. China managed to stop the flow of people out of Wuhan in 2020 and effectively contained the spread of the virus within the country, but the Chinese government is far more authoritarian than its Western counterparts. Similarly, Marshal Tito stopped the spread of smallpox in Yugoslavia with enforced vaccination and containment. Tito was not constrained by democratic due process.

A NATO for Global Health

Can we imagine an early warning system that will stop the spread of pandemic in the twenty-first century? The big challenge is that early shutdown requires both the instant advertisement that a terrible disease has arrived, and the immense display of public might required to impose a cordon sanitaire around an entire city or region. Open societies are good at spreading information, but bad at limiting the freedom to move. Dictatorial societies are good at restricting mobility, but bad at advertising their failings. Yet if containment is going to work, we need to combine the virtues of both systems and avoid their downsides. Here are four ideas that might help.

First, create an international norm that requires and rewards information sharing about new illnesses. Medical standards are one way to do this. If the norm is that every hospital has some connection to the international community, and if members of that community require a commitment to information sharing, then perhaps the tendency to cover up new diseases can be countered.

Second, the information-sharing protocol should be endorsed by international organizations and agreed to by treaty. Every hospital should have at least one officer who is trained to report any new contagious disease into a global monitoring system. That system can then be watched by scientists worldwide. In the United States, for example, states have laws requiring that their governments be notified about some infectious diseases; those states, in turn, relay the data to the Centers for Disease Control and Prevention. Thus, information about any new infectious disease is spread to the relevant authorities. The same could be true internationally.

Third, countries need to be ready to shut down international travel swiftly, and to focus not only on direct sources of contagion, but also on indirect sources. Shutting down travel to and from China early in the COVID-19 pandemic would have been reasonable. But waiting until the end of January was ineffective because the virus had already left the country. An effective system would screen international travelers from affected regions immediately after a new outbreak is reported in the global monitoring system. The system would actively monitor, and sometimes exclude, countries that allow high-risk practices. The error should be on the side of less, rather than more, interaction with pandemic-prone areas.

Fourth, countries need to put in place systems for sequestration of an impacted region that still respect basic human rights and dignities. A legal structure needs to be designed ex ante, with safeguards, that can be imposed quickly once there is an outbreak. That sequestration makes sense only if the pandemic is caught early enough, but at the very least, countries can have their approach in hand before a plague emerges.

To implement these policies, the world is going to need a new form of global health alliance. The international body most responsible for monitoring the spread of epidemics, the World Health Organization (WHO), is unfortunately not up to the task. The WHO was formed in 1948 as a part of the

United Nations. By and large, the WHO is staffed by health professionals.
Over the years, it has done enormous good. It led the fight to eradicate smallpox and has pushed vaccinations for children. It is currently pushing to improve access to quality health care throughout the world.

But the WHO is poorly equipped to deal with disease outbreaks. On
January 14, 2020, for example, the WHO tweeted that "preliminary investigations conducted by the Chinese authorities have found no clear evidence
of human-to-human transmission of the novel #coronavirus (2019-nCoV)
identified in #Wuhan, #China." This echoed official Chinese information,
virtually word for word. But by then it was known by scientists in Wuhan
and elsewhere to be false. Indeed, there was already a case of human-to-
human transmission in Thailand. Delay in recognizing the truth in early
January was critical because it allowed vast numbers of people to travel to
and from Wuhan for the Chinese New Year. Had a cordon sanitaire been
imposed earlier, or even had appropriate doubt been cast on Chinese claims,
the disease might have been better contained. It is hard to miss the twin
facts that Chinese statements about COVID-19 were taken too seriously
and that China is a major funder of the WHO.

The WHO was also late to sound the alarm about Ebola in 2014. It was
clear in the spring of that year that there was an Ebola outbreak in West
Africa. The WHO did not take public action until six months later. In this
case, the WHO was trying to buffer an economic shock to a poorer part of
the world.

Several factors inhibit the WHO's ability to stop pandemics. Fighting
illnesses needs to be a technical issue, not a political one. Scientists need to
judge the virulence of new diseases, calculate their likely spread, and convey
relevant knowledge. The WHO sees itself as being partly a technical agency
but also a political body, where major world health issues are discussed and
debated. Politics and science rarely mix well. Thus, when a large donor like
China does not want to be identified as the source of an outbreak, the WHO

plays it down, and when West African countries are afraid of losing trade revenue if they are seen as centers of disease, declaring an Ebola epidemic is delayed.

By contrast, technical agencies, like America's Centers for Disease Control and Prevention and the National Institutes of Health, Germany's Robert Koch Institute, which has a public health mandate, and the UK's National Institute for Health Research are all acknowledged to be scientifically grounded and run. Their decisions are made by technical experts who follow rigorous criteria and thus come with a scientific imprimatur. Their funding is not predicated on specific decisions they make—though obviously if they fail to do their job, stakeholders will push to cut their funding. As a result, they have the trust that other political agencies do not.

The WHO also lacks the power to investigate. In January of 2021, China blocked WHO inspectors from entering the country to better understand the origins of the COVID-19 pandemic. The organization must rely on country-provided information and accept any restrictions on access that countries may impose.

Membership in the WHO is open to every member of the United Nations (UN) that accepts the WHO constitution, and consequently, the WHO has the same unwieldy structure as the United Nations General Assembly. Like the UN, the WHO has little real power. The scale of pandemic threat facing the world requires a more muscular global partnership that looks more like NATO than the UN.

NATO is perhaps the most successful example of a technically oriented alliance of great powers. NATO's purpose is "to guarantee the freedom and security of its members through political and military means." The shared mission is then translated into strategic concepts: collective defense, crisis management, and cooperative security. The NATO secretary general is often a politician, but military leaders are highly placed.

In addition to its split mission and limited scope for action, the World

Health Organization is woefully underfunded, and is continually scrambling for cash. The WHO budget is roughly $2.5 billion per year, which must cover pandemics and every other health condition in the world. A single big hospital in the United States will have a budget that is bigger. As a result, money spent on pandemic preparedness quite literally gets taken from immunization campaigns. NATO's annual budget is roughly the same size as the WHO's, even with a much smaller mission (a war fought by NATO would generally use people and material from member countries). Even the Centers for Disease Control and Prevention, which is also woefully underfunded, has a budget that is three times greater than the WHO's. The Food and Drug Administration's budget is twice as large.

Finally, the World Health Organization has a decision-making process that is not designed for rapid action. The governing board of the WHO has thirty-four members, drawn from six areas of the globe. Major operational decisions are made by the World Health Assembly, which represents all member states. Consensus bodies often work off a "lowest common denominator"; the UN system is a prime example.

Interestingly, NATO also works by consensus; all decisions, even in committees, are unanimous. This may not be the best model for a revamped world health agency. The difference is that NATO's primary decision—what to do if a country is attacked—has been settled in advance. The NATO charter declares that an attack on one is an attack on all. Thus, there is no ambiguity among possible aggressors about how NATO would view any military strike.

A better international pandemic organization must start with a small number of client states, so that its objectives and governance are kept clear. It must be focused on a single goal: preventing the international spread of contagion. It must be scientific; all practices contributing to pandemics must be called out. It must have the ability to investigate without restraint. There must be consequences for countries that fail to limit risks. And it must be sufficiently resourced. After World War II, the West invented such a structure, and it defended Europe from the Soviet Union for forty years. The threat of global pandemic is similarly dire and requires no less a commitment.

Even with such a structure, pandemics can still occur. The risk will never be zero. In this chapter, we have focused on the first source of urban vulnerability. Cities are nodes on a global network, and they provide the ports of entry for any new disease. Since that vulnerability involves cross-national connectivity, it cannot be fixed by cities themselves: a parliament of mayors does not have the power to negotiate treaties governing the movement of people across countries. A multinational organization—NATO for health—provides one path toward making cities safer against infection from abroad.

We next turn to the second source of vulnerability: the easy spread of contagion across densely crowded cities and slums. City governments themselves reduced that source of contagion in the West during the nineteenth century. In poor world megacities, that vulnerability remains. Since diseases that evolve in an Indian slum or a Chinese wet market can spread throughout the world, wealthy nations must help those poor cities to take care of their own today.

Chapter 3

CAN INDIAN SEWERS MAKE INDIANA HEALTHIER?

I n the spring of 2020, the world was both isolated and unified. Families huddled alone—if they could—and avoided everyone else. But the entire world faced the same pandemic. Mothers in Kalamazoo and Kampala both worried about whether they could risk taking their sick children to see the doctor. Silicon Valley software engineers and Saigon street vendors were both putting on masks. Make no mistake, the pandemic was far deadlier and more economically harmful for the poor. We will return to that theme many times. Yet ultimately, no one was spared from the plague's reach. Everyone—rich and poor alike—faced fear, dislocation, and discomfort.

Natural disasters—even great tsunamis—have a limited geographic scope. Most wars are restricted to a small number of combatant countries. Even World War II left South America and sub-Saharan Africa virtually untouched. But a pandemic like COVID-19 threatens every person on the planet. The danger of disease spreading around the globe reminds us that we are all connected. If in nothing else, then at least in our ability to make each other ill.

If the emergence of a disease in the poorest places on earth can endanger the richest places on earth, then wealthy countries have a purely selfish reason to make investments that reduce illness in developing nations. Spending Western aid dollars to improve the sewers in sub-Saharan Africa and India isn't just humanitarian; it is in the West's self-interest. The COVID-19 pandemic is costing trillions. Spending billions to reduce disease prevalence in developing world cities today can reduce the risk of a future, possibly costlier, pandemic.

The previous chapter asked whether we can cut the ties between countries and communities when a new plague emerges. We may be able to do a better job of limiting global travel than we did in the early days of 2020, but we can never eliminate the risk that a new virus will appear and slip into the world before anyone notices. If a single country, like America or the UK, tries to eliminate travel to some riskier countries permanently, then the disease could still pass through any apparently low-risk country that kept its borders open. America can't really isolate itself unless it completely walls itself off, which would mean far fewer jobs in vacation destinations like Florida and California and no more travel abroad for Americans. Even goods would struggle to get across the border.

Poor world cities in the twenty-first century suffer from many of the same contagious diseases that afflicted Western cities in the nineteenth century, including cholera and typhus fever, but the number of people who die from these illnesses is far fewer today. Our medical responses have improved, thanks to antibiotics and oral rehydration therapy. Yet an approach to public health that allows diseases to emerge and trusts in antibiotics to reduce their harm risks producing antibiotic-resistant superbugs that can decimate whole populations.

In this chapter, we focus on nineteenth-century illnesses, especially cholera, and the battle for urban health. The collective creation of aqueducts and sewers is arguably the most important achievement of government before the twentieth century. Building that infrastructure required institutions that were strong enough to manage major engineering problems and to secure massive levels of financing. As private interests often run counter to social interests, the city's health also required sanitary regulations enforced by public agents. Those agents needed to earn enough trust that the community would tolerate the punishment of people who didn't follow the rules.

The wealthy world would also benefit from hygienic regulations in the poor world today, such as rules that separate humans from bats and monkeys. But how can richer nations induce Brazil to limit agricultural incursions into bat-infested areas of the rain forest or Asian countries to shut down wet markets? If high-income countries were to increase their public health aid for poorer places, that aid could be contingent on enforcing rules that reduce viral spread. The price of noncompliance could be exclusion from travel networks.

In nineteenth-century cities, the spread of contagious disease taught rich American urbanites that they needed to care about their poorer neighbors. In the twenty-first century, we are connected not only to people within our polis but to the entire world. Thus, the nature of our intervention will need to grow. If we want to stay healthy, we need to make sure that everyone around the world stays healthy as well. This involves caring about sewers in India and open-air markets in China. It also involves fretting about frenchfry consumption in Los Angeles, but that is a story for the next chapter.

The Coming of Cholera

At the start of the nineteenth century, effective government meant cannons not aqueducts. Over the next one hundred years, the public sector increasingly took on responsibility for limiting plagues, which is something of a turning point in the history of government. Before 1815, monarchs were praised largely for acquiring land and protecting their own subjects from conquest. Gradually, governments started providing something positive for their people. The first Napoleon is still remembered primarily for his brilliant battles and final catastrophic collapse, but the military misadventures of his nephew, Napoleon III, are eclipsed by that later emperor's work modernizing the streets and sewers of Paris after 1853.

Francis Rawdon-Hastings, whom we shall refer to as Rawdon, epitomized public service in the pre-1815 era of largely militarized government. His great-grandfather had participated in an earlier English government's conquest of Ireland and Rawdon grew up in County Down. Rawdon followed his ancestors into public service by buying an army commission. He led the third and final British assault during the Battle of Bunker Hill, and may have personally executed Joseph Warren, giving American freedom its first martyr. But Rawdon is famous more for his adventures in India than in the American colonies.

Rawdon went to India in 1813 and was soon at war, first with the Nepalese and then with the mighty champions of Hindu India: the Marathas. Rawdon assembled 110,000 men, and by early November 1817, he was making stately progress across the mountainous region of Bundelkhand. On November 13, 1817, Rawdon reported that "the dreadful epidemic disorder which has been causing such ravages in Calcutta, and the southern provinces, has broken out in camp." He knew it to be "a species of cholera morbus," that was so deadly that "if immediate relief be not at hand, the person to a certainty dies within from three to five hours."

To understand the backstory behind this outbreak, we must move from Rawdon's journal to a report written by a far more junior member of the British colonial administration, whose more benevolent role suggests the path from a state that kills by the sword to a state that protects with the sewer. The relative importance of generals and doctors in the 1820s is well illustrated by the fact that Rawdon is splendidly buried in a beautiful Maltese garden while Dr. James Jameson's remains reside in a swampy, overgrown graveyard in Kolkata. His memorial pillar reads "to the memory of James Jameson, Esq., Surgeon, Secretary to the Medical Board, who died 20th January 1823, aged 35, universally respected for his talents and acquirements, as well as esteemed for every social virtue." Jameson died young, possibly of cholera, and left behind a twenty-three-year-old Irish wife.

Jameson is known today primarily because of his *Report on the Epidemick Cholera Morbus* written in 1820. The young doctor sent out 238 questionnaires to medical professionals throughout India to ask about their experience with the disease. Just like any serious social scientist, Jameson bemoaned the low response rate to the survey. In fact, he received serious answers from 42 percent of his correspondents, which is not bad given the spread of the pandemic and the condition of Indian roads in 1819.

Jameson believed that before 1817, cholera had been "endemical in Bengal" but limited to "certain parts of the year," "restricted to particular places," "not very commonly fatal," and "its attacks were chiefly limited to the lower classes of inhabitants; whose constitutions had been debilitated by poor, ungenerous diet, and by hard labor in the sun." Something like cholera clearly had existed around the Ganges delta for ages. Portuguese traders reported a cholera outbreak as far away as their Indian outpost of Goa in 1543. But the mildness of Jameson's description suggests that, perhaps, this earlier form of Bengalese cholera may not have been quite the same terrible *Vibrio cholerae* that devastated India after 1817.

Jameson's words capture the horror of this new outbreak: "on the 28th of that month [August] it was reported to Government, that the disease has suddenly appeared epidemically in Jessore, a populous town situated in the delta of the Ganges; that was attacking all classes indiscriminately; and was cutting off from twenty to thirty persons daily; and that inhabitants, astonished and terrified at the unaccountable and very desperate nature of its attacks, were flying in crowds from the place, as the only means of escaping impending death." Jameson noted "the marked disposition of the disease to follow the course of rivers," which could mean either that the disease was in the water, or that it was carried by waterborne travelers.

Cholera swept through dense, but largely rural, India like the Grim Reaper. Jameson writes that "after the middle of September, the disease, now strictly epidemical extended itself in every direction; within the short space of a few weeks stretching from the most easterly parts of Poorneea, Dinagepore, and Sylhet, to the extreme borders of Balasore and Cuttack; and reaching from the mouths of the Ganges nearly as high as its junction with the Jumna." In one month, the disease seems to have traveled over five hundred miles, which is remarkable in a world of oxcarts and slow river craft.

Like most observers of plagues throughout history, Jameson was mystified by its movements: "it at once raged simultaneously in various and remote quarters, without displaying a predilection for any one tract or district more than for another; or anything like regularity of succession in the chain of its operation." The lands east of the Ganges were largely left untouched, but Dhaka and Patna were ravaged. The disease may have mutated as it traveled, sometimes becoming less harmful and sometimes becoming deadlier. Jameson notes that "a new stream of the pestilential virus, now apparently propagated by regular succession," emerged from Allahabad (now Prayagraj).

This new variant of the disease "did no great mischief, until . . . it reached the Centre Division of the Grand Army, then encamped, under the personal command of the Marquess of Hastings," which was Francis Rawdon's formal title. Among Rawdon's men, "the disease put forth its strength, and assumed its most deadly and appalling form." The combination of disease and warfare reappears, over and over again, throughout human history.

Both Rawdon and Jameson describe how the disease spread from poor Indians to well-fed Europeans, which is the reverse of the movement of COVID-19 from well-paid biotech researchers and Italian vacationers to poorer waiters and janitors. Jameson writes that "after creeping about, however, in its wonted insidious manner, for several days among the lower classes of the Camp followers; it, as it were in an instant, gained fresh vigor, and at once burst forth with irresistible violence," and that "the old and the young, the European and the Native, fighting men and Camp followers alike, were subject to its visits; and all equally sunk in a few hours under its power grasp." By the end, cholera "outstripped the most fatal diseases, hitherto known, in the destructive rapidity of its progress."

Some of Rawdon's soldiers correctly blamed the water supply: "there is an opinion that the water of the tanks, the only water which we have at this place, may be unwholesome and add to the disease." Rawdon was skeptical—"I do not think there is anything in the supposition"—but nevertheless, he began carrying one thousand sick men toward the waters of the Pahuj River. On the next day, he reports that "the march was terrible" and that "above five hundred have died since sunset yesterday evening," including ten of his own servants.

On November 16, the disease began to abate. Rawdon explained the slowing pace of death, because after infecting first those who "were predisposed to receive the infection," the disease then "made its impression more weakly, and thence more tardily, on persons whose bodily temperament was not so ready to admit it." Like COVID-19, cholera targets those with preexisting conditions. Rawdon writes that "debility from previous illness, or from low living, seems to have invited the attack."

Finally, on November 19, the army reached a "broad and clear stream," which "was sufficient to cause universal exultation among the troops and camp-followers." They were right to have hope. On the next day, there was "thus far a favourable change that few new cases, in proportion to former days, have been sent to the hospital, and the quality of the attacks appears not so virulent." From that point onward, there was "a diminution in the activity of the pestilence." Rawdon survived that terrible week to triumph over the Marathas. His success led to another 130 years of English control over India, much of which would be an unmitigated public health disaster for the subcontinent. In Western cities, civic leadership would pass from warlords to doctors but the old exploitative state lived on in the colonies.

Cholera would occur and reoccur during the nineteenth century and kill perhaps 35 million Indians. Millions more would die during the third bubonic plague epidemic that began in the 1890s. The influenza pandemic of 1918–19 killed over twelve million in the parts of India directly controlled by the British, and many more in the princely states. Both bubonic plague and influenza were brought into India from elsewhere, probably on British ships, but India also exported diseases, like cholera, that slaughtered Americans and Europeans. When the world is connected, diseases that fester anywhere can spread everywhere.

The globalization of the nineteenth century, like the globalization of the twenty-first century, created health challenges for the entire world, as diseases moved from the Ganges to London and Chicago. Yet in Western Europe and the United States, the pestilence was offset by massive investments in hygiene and medicinal breakthroughs. While the more isolated places in the poor world may have remained safe from contagion, India was connected enough to catch new diseases, but the British Raj was not interested in massive investment projects to protect the natives.

The British elites living in Delhi's suburban Civil Lines during the nineteenth century received clean water and sewers. During the twentieth century, the British could move into New Delhi, a segregated, modernized, Europeanized capital. But in old Delhi, where the poorer Indians lived, "until 1928 excrement and refuse were dumped within the city, in the ditch, and in pits close to town." What Delhi needed then and what the cities of the developing world need now are the game-changing investments in clean water and sewers that were built, largely as a response to cholera, in the wealthy world. Sporadic, almost feeble, expenditures on new water tanks, or open sewers, could not protect nineteenth-century Delhi and cannot protect twenty-first-century poor world megacities from the scourge of contagious disease. If we are not careful, they cannot protect people in rich countries either.

Cholera Travels West

Six great waves of cholera afflicted the world between 1817 and 1923. In 1817, after its apparent mutation, the bacterium spread to Indonesia and the Near East. That first epidemic came to an end in 1824, possibly because of an unusually cold winter.

The second pandemic began in 1826, again emerging from the Ganges delta, traveling over land, across the mountains of Afghanistan, and reaching Russia by 1829. The czar's quarantines and cordons sanitaire were too late and too unevenly implemented to stop the disease from killing one hundred thousand of his subjects. Preexisting political distrust meant that conspiracy theorists whispered that the disease had been spread by doctors and the government. Russia's plague-ridden cities erupted first into protests and then riots, like American cities in 2020. The Poles of Warsaw had never accepted the legitimacy of their Russian overlords and the city rebelled in November 1830.

Like Rawdon, the Romanov czars were traditionalists, lords by right of conquest who had neither the desire nor the ability to produce clean water. They were, however, happy to unleash their armies on their own citizens. The blaze of artillery fire ended Russia's cholera riots and the Warsaw rebellion, but the disease continued marching west, carried by the czar's army.

In 1831, the British imposed quarantine on Russian ships, but the czar's troops had already spread cholera throughout the Baltic region, just as Chinese tourists had spread COVID-19 through Northern Italy by the time the

US imposed its travel ban on China. By October 8, 1831, the disease had come to Hamburg. Two weeks later, it entered England through Sunderland, a port with a particularly lax quarantine.

For three hundred years, the British had built roads and canals that crisscrossed their island. For three hundred years, English mariners had explored new continents and conquered distant lands in the name of king, country, and commerce. Yet England had no public health infrastructure to protect itself against the intercontinental flow of deadly bacteria. Governments had over four hundred years of experience with quarantine by 1831, but in Sunderland "no efficient measures of precaution were adopted, and the intercource [sic] of vessels from foreign ports with the River Wear, was apparently as unrestricted as at any former period of perfect security." Britain paid a fearsome price for its carelessness. More than 20,000 Britons died from cholera in 1831 and 1832. London lost over 5,000. Glasgow lost over 3,000.

On the fifteenth of March, cholera first appeared in the French port of Calais, presumably carried by English smugglers who eluded the French quarantine. By the twenty-fourth, the disease struck Paris. A contemporary source reports that more than 38,000 caught cholera in France in April of 1832 alone, and more than 16,000 died. The same source credits cholera with a total of 94,666 kills in France in 1832, which means that the death rate was more than three times higher than France's death rate from COVID-19 in 2020. One out of every fifty Parisians perished, and in two central districts, the death rate was over 5 percent.

The German poet Heinrich Heine was an eyewitness to the horror. As in Rawdon's army, "the cholera evidently first attacked the poorer classes." Just like wealthier Manhattanites in 2020, "the rich fled away and, well packed with doctors and drugs, took refuge in healthier climes." The Paris of Honoré de Balzac, Alexandre Dumas, and George Sand shone with artistic brilliance, but also seethed "with bitter discontent that money had become a protection also against death." Pandemics do more harm when they strike cities already at war with themselves. The Parisians, who had overthrown one monarch in 1830, would take to the barricades again in the summer that followed the cholera spring, in the failed uprising that is so vividly portrayed in Victor Hugo's *Les Miserables*.

New York City Responds to Cholera

Cholera reached the New World in the spring of 1832. Quarantine might have protected North America from the disease, but again, weak governments failed to enforce the rules. Canada's quarantine station "merely separated those who were obviously ill from those who appeared sound," and "the latter were permitted to continue immediately." US quarantines were no more effective.

Our colleague Charles Rosenberg, the eminent historian of disease, writes that by the summer of 1832, outside New York City "the roads, in all directions, were lined with well-filled stagecoaches, livery coaches, private vehicles and equestrians, all panic-struck, fleeing the city, as we may suppose the inhabitants of Pompeii fled when the red lava showered down upon their houses." As in 2020, only "the poor, having no choice, remained," and because they were "living in crowded, filthy rooms they were perfect victims for cholera." The 1832 cholera outbreak killed over 3,500 New Yorkers, which is slightly more than 1.5 percent of the city's population of 220,000. This death rate may have been below that of Paris during the same year, but it is five times New York City's death rate from COVID-19 in 2020.

While we may wonder what the COVID-19 pandemic will do to the wealthy world's cities, we should never think that pandemic will stop the growth of population in the poor world's megacities. America's nineteenth-century cities were far deadlier than cities in low-income countries are today, and people still came by the million. The world's poor will still come to

Nairobi and Mumbai, even if contagious diseases disproportionately slaughter those city's slum dwellers, who certainly caught COVID-19 far more often than their richer neighbors.

The movement to tame the demons of density in nineteenth-century New York City took decades and the collective efforts of wealthier urbanites who understood the need to strengthen the entire city. John Jacob Astor bequeathed an enormous gift to the reading public that would eventually evolve into the New York Public Library. Theodore Roosevelt Sr., the president's father, was a cofounder of the American Museum of Natural History, the Metropolitan Museum of Art, and the Children's Aid Society. Peter Cooper tried to make the city more equitable through education.

Stephen Allen is less well-known than these luminaries but he was as important to creating New York's shared strength. Allen served as the first elected mayor of New York City from 1821 to 1824, and "spearheaded one of the greatest public health initiatives nineteenth-century America had ever seen—the rebuilding of the New York City water supply." As the leader of the commission that built the Croton Aqueduct, he helped move governments from taking lives to saving lives.

Allen's father was a "superior and expert" carpenter who died of yellow fever while working for the British army in Florida when Allen was only two. Allen's mother "consented to permit" him to apprentice to a sailmaker, and in fairly short order, Allen became one of the most successful sailmakers in a city that was rapidly becoming one of the greatest ports in the world. His first wife died when he was thirty-five in 1802, and he "was left with a family of seven children to educate and rear." He apparently enjoyed parenting so much that he married again and sired another nine children.

When Tocqueville wrote that Americans "constantly unite together," he could have been describing Allen. At one point in his memoirs, Allen lists fifteen major organizations in which he held office, from the "American Bible Society" to the "New York Hospital and Lunatic Asylum" to the

"American Prison Discipline Society." The most important of Allen's associations was with the Tammany Society, of which he served both as treasurer and as president, or more properly grand sachem.

For 150 years, Tammany Hall's political machine dispensed patronage, welcomed immigrants onto the voting rolls, and, occasionally, robbed the city blind. When Boss Tweed ruled Tammany Hall and New York City, every contract was an opportunity for illicit gain. Tweed Courthouse still stands as a temple to corruption because builders who had been paid vastly more than their costs would promptly kick most of the cash back to Tammany. Yet Stephen Allen, champion of clean water, was a steadfast Tammany man, who called the organization "partly political and partly charitable" and said its objects were "to inculcate the principles of liberty and the rights of man" and "to assist unfortunate members."

Tammany Hall was a political machine even then, although it wasn't yet Tweed's corrupt piggy bank, but Allen floated above Tammany's muck untouched by its scandals. Even in the cholera year of 1832, Allen ardently lobbied for the creation of a Tammany Bank, promising that "any assistance I can give for advancing the interests of Old Tammany will be cheerfully afforded." Yet New York politician Thurlow Weed, a Tammany hater if ever one existed, described Allen as a man with "a clear head and a sound heart" who "brought industry, intelligence and integrity with him" when he was elected to the New York State Assembly.

Allen's terms as mayor overlapped with the yellow fever outbreaks of 1821 and 1822, and after the deadly summer of 1822, Allen embraced a public health agenda of "bringing in of good and wholesome water" because it was "connected with the health and prosperity of the city" and that goal ought "never to be lost sight of until its accomplishment was consummated." As mayor, Allen started by surveying "the route from the best source of supply to the city," but was ousted from office before he could do anything more. Manhattan's water remained largely unfit to drink for more than another decade. While Philadelphia had begun its public waterworks program in 1799 and improved it fifteen years later, New York had largely trusted its water provision to the Manhattan Company, a private company with neither a clear mission nor sufficient resources to solve the city's water needs.

Aaron Burr founded the Manhattan Company with help from Alexander Hamilton, and they made sure that the water company could also operate a bank. As the profits from banking were greater than the profits from clean water, the company focused on lending rather than piping. Its descendant corporation remains with us today: the Bank of the Manhattan Company merged into the Chase Manhattan Bank which merged into JPMorgan Chase.

While the Manhattan Company was busy banking, Allen continued pushing for clean water. In 1831, the Common Council of New York City sent a draft bill up to Albany requesting permission to build an aqueduct to the Bronx River. The state legislature declined to act. In 1832, cholera struck New York City and the case for better hygiene became even stronger.

The aqueduct's advocates marshaled their political forces. One of the sons of the Erie Canal–building governor DeWitt Clinton wrote an engineering report extolling the virtues of an aqueduct carrying water from Croton. Young Clinton suggested the costs would be minimal and the benefits extraordinary, which provided an early model for the wildly optimistic projections about infrastructure projects that have been common ever since. They elected a former alderman and health board official, Myndert Van Schaick, to the state senate to champion clean water.

In 1833, the governor of New York appointed Stephen Allen to be one of the new water commissioners. He was then elected the commission's chairman and the great work of his life began. The aqueduct succeeded because the commission had a clear objective that was agreed to by all. It had a competent leader with a lifetime of political connections and know-how, who had the ability to hire and fire. An empowered, impatient boss is usually the first necessity to produce something great.

Allen actually fired the project's first engineer, a distinguished West Point professor, for moving too slowly. He admired the man as a "ripe scholar" and a "good mathematician," but he came to believe that he did "not possess that practical knowledge," which Allen "deemed necessary to carry on a work of so much importance to the City." It is hard to imagine a political appointee who would second-guess his chief engineer today, but Allen grimly went through every detail of the plan. He wanted action and a new engineer, and he got both.

In 1837, construction of the aqueduct began. It would take five years for the clean waters to flow into the city, and Allen was gone before it was done. He was removed as commissioner for political reasons in 1840, but Van Schaick remained and kept watch over the project until 1860. Their aqueduct was a dazzling achievement that required both public spending on a grand scale and an independent leader of competence and reputation. Croton cost nine million dollars, which represents four cents out of every dollar earned in New York City for six solid years.

Other cities and towns followed the models of Philadelphia and New York. One of us (Cutler) coauthored a paper fifteen years ago that estimated the impact on mortality of clean water across the nineteenth-century United States by using the relatively random timing of the introduction of new technologies, like water filtration, in different cities as a natural experiment. The paper concluded that "clean water was responsible for nearly half of the total mortality reduction in major cities, three-quarters of the infant-mortality reduction, and nearly two-thirds of the child mortality reduction." The ratio of benefits to costs was 23 to 1, which makes clean water among the single best investments that any government has ever made. Once in a while, infrastructure really is revolutionary, and governments can do enormous good.

Sewer systems were equally transformative. One might think that piped water becomes less critical when a city builds sewers that remove the waste that pollutes local wells. Research by our colleagues Marcella Alsan and Claudia Goldin finds that the opposite is true. Sewers are more valuable when there is clean water, and clean water is more valuable when there are good sewers. Health requires shutting down all of the ways in which bacteria can travel into your body, not just one half of the paths of waterborne illness.

In the US, sewers, like water systems, were largely local investments that expanded public strength of city governments. In the UK, sewers were championed by national leaders and debated in Parliament. When the Thames became a sort of fetid swamp, the queen herself had to abort her pleasure cruises, and the halls of Parliament, which abut the river, became malodorous. The Great Stink of London occurred in 1858 during "one of the hottest summers on record, with the Thames emitting a sickening smell as a result of the sewage of over two million inhabitants being discharged into the river."

London's sanitary master builder, Joseph Bazalgette, was already ensconced as chief engineer to the city's Metropolitan Board of Works during that hot, smelly summer. Bazalgette became chief engineer for the city's sewer commission in 1852, two years before Dr. John Snow unlocked the secret of cholera in Soho. By 1858, Bazalgette had a plan, but not the money, to fix London's waste problem.

The Great Stink brought London's filth right under the noses of the great and good. Benjamin Disraeli, chancellor of the exchequer, politician of genius, orator of renown, took up the cause of the Thames and the sewer. On July 3, 1858, he told Parliament:

> That noble river, so long the pride and joy of Englishmen, which has hith-
> erto been associated with the noblest feats of our commerce and the most
> beautiful passages of our poetry, has really become a Stygian pool, reeking

with ineffable and intolerable horrors. The public health is at stake; almost all living things that existed in the waters of the Thames have disappeared or been destroyed; a very natural fear has arisen that living beings upon its banks may share the same fate; there is a pervading apprehension of pestilence in this great city; and I am sure I am only taking a step that will have been anticipated when I ask for leave to introduce a Bill which will attempt—and I trust the attempt will be successful—to terminate a state of affairs so unsatisfactory and fraught with so much danger to the public health.

Disraeli's plan was for the costs to be eventually covered by property taxes paid by the residents of London. In wealthy cities, infrastructure should be funded by its users. But since lenders weren't going to trust the Board of Works with millions, the national government would guarantee the loan. Disraeli was sure that the cost would not be less than 3 million pounds, or about 360 million pounds today.

With those funds, Bazalgette "constructed the system of intercepting sewers that protected London's water supply from its sewage and spared the capital further epidemics of waterborne diseases." His sewers are still used today, and one can reasonably argue that funding London's sewers may be the greatest achievement of Disraeli's career as a statesman. The British national commitment to urban sanitation has no counterpart in US history, and that legacy remains today. The speedier UK rollout of vaccines in early 2021 partially reflects a national health capability that could design and execute a plan without working through fifty different state governments.

Making America's cities safe required a revolution both in government and in public finance. The cost of the Croton Aqueduct and London's sewers were high but not unusual for clean water. At the turn of the twentieth century, America's cities and towns were spending as much on sewerage and clean water as the federal government was spending on everything except for the post office and the army. This spending was possible only because municipal bond markets had grown and cities had access to a river of external investment that did not exist in 1858, when Disraeli needed to backstop Bazalgette's borrowing. That growth, in turn, reflected both the increasingly global nature of finance and the ability of local US governments to convince bond buyers that they would be repaid. The lifesaving strength of local governments depended on strong and collective leadership, good engineering, and fiscal prudence.

In some cases, cities directly owned their municipal waterworks. Milwaukee was famous for its successful "sewer socialism." In other cases, water was produced by quasi-independent public entities, like the Croton Aqueduct Commission. These independent organizations skip the rules of public bureaucracy and some of the worst aspects of municipal corruption, but they work only with someone prominent and capable like Stephen Allen at the helm. When poorly governed countries (and US states) establish "independent" parastatal enterprises that are staffed with semi-competent cronies, then they serve only to provide an excuse for the elected officials to blame someone else.

Private water companies can also work, but they need to be regulated. A private provider will cut costs, but they will also cut corners if services aren't watched by citizens or government. The work of the economic historian Werner Troesken shows that private water companies systemically underserved their African American consumers. Providing clean water to the poor is not a naturally lucrative task, which is why the Manhattan Company spent more time banking than building water pipes.

It may seem obvious that when the public sector is weak, the private sector should step in, but that conclusion is often wrong. Consider a public regulator that is setting the fees that a private water company can charge its customers. If the public sector is strong, then the system may work. If the public sector is modestly weak, then the private company will skimp on quality and convince the government to let it raise its rates. If the public sector is utterly inept, then it will end up subsidizing the private company with massive tax dollars and the taps will still be dry.

There is no absolute rule about public or private provision of water or any public service. Deng Xiaoping wisely adhered to the adage that "it doesn't matter if a cat is black or white as long as it catches mice," meaning that competence, not ideology, should determine the nature of production. When it comes to water systems in the developing world or anywhere else, neither public nor private is inherently better. The right answer is a ruthless pragmatism that chooses the appropriate institution based on local conditions. In some cases, cost efficiency is particularly important, and private companies have the edge. In other cases, the critical task is to provide water to the neediest, and a public entity is more likely to serve that end.

Incentives and Infrastructure: Dr. Stephen Smith and the Board of Health

In sub-Saharan Africa today, well-meaning donors build water mains but expect ordinary householders to pay for the final connections. These installations can cost over $1,000, which is a lot of money in a country like Zambia, where per capita output is less than $2,000 per year. Consequently, poorer households don't connect to the system. This is the last-mile problem. People are even less willing to pay for sewers than for water, because most of the costs of dumping waste are borne by one's neighbors. A healthy city requires policies that ensure that people will pay for services that protect everyone else.

For twenty-five years after the Croton Aqueduct was built, New York

City also faced a last-mile problem, and its citizens continued to die from cholera. The second cholera epidemic continued to kill for many years. A third cholera wave emerged, again from India, around 1846, and spread throughout the world. While the second epidemic struck Great Britain relatively lightly, the third killed 10,000 in London alone during the years 1853 and 1854.

Dr. John Snow was working with the poor in Soho during that outbreak when he solved cholera's mystery. He noticed that the cases were all clustered around a particular water pump. He noted that the brewery workers who didn't drink the water weren't getting sick. He removed the handle of the water pump, and the neighborhood's cholera outbreak ended. This simple experiment led to the conclusion that cholera came through the water, and his success essentially sparked the field of epidemiology. Of course, Snow didn't actually see the cholera bacterium, and it would take another fifty years before the germ theory of disease became universally accepted. Nonetheless, after 1854 a growing number of physicians believed in the link between water and cholera.

On the other side of the Atlantic, more than 5,000 New Yorkers died from cholera in 1849, well after the Croton Aqueduct was completed, including Glaeser's great-great-great-grandfather (Dr. James Ashley). Connecting to the Croton system was expensive and most New Yorkers were poor. There were slightly more than 2,300 free hydrants scattered throughout Manhattan, but water is heavy to carry. Immigrant households stuck with their shallow wells and their pit latrines and they continued to catch cholera. Death rates were higher in the 1850s than they had been in the 1830s before the aqueduct was built. Density levels had risen markedly and clean water didn't reach into the city's most desperate neighborhoods.

The nineteenth century produced an abundance of medical heroes who still fill our imaginations. Dr. Louis Pasteur's eyes gleam from his pince-nez as he provides us with pathogen-free milk. Robert Koch, his German archrival, stares back, reminding us that it was he who identified the bacterial source of cholera. Florence Nightingale carries her lamp to the bedsides of soldiers suffering from typhus. Excluded by Nightingale from her regular staff, perhaps because of her color, Mary Seacole waits outside offering tea and comfort.

Dr. Stephen Smith is a lesser-known member of this pantheon, whose importance stems mainly from his work bringing the public sector into the service of health. He helped New York's local government evolve into a more effective and benevolent entity, by building the institution that would make the aqueduct and the sewer system far more effective. He was also the founder of the American Public Health Association, but that came after his work in New York.

Smith came from a "small farm in the highlands" of New York and worked at New York City's Bellevue Hospital as a doctor and teacher from 1854 to 1891. Like John Snow, Smith looked for spatial patterns that would enable him to grasp the links between illness and the urban environment. About his work in the 1850s, he later wrote that "upon examination of the records of admission of patients, I discovered that from one tenement house upwards of one hundred cases had been received." When he visited the house he found a "fever nest," where "the doors and windows were broken, the cellar was filled with sewage, every room was occupied by families of Irish immigrants who had but little furniture and slept on straw scattered on the floor." He went to the police and urged them to shut down the tenement. They refused.

In New York at the time, government agents couldn't help. No law gave the police the right to shut down a tenement, and anyway, the cops had other things to do, like taking bribes. To clean out the tenement, Smith went to William Cullen Bryant, the poet and editor of the *New York Evening Post*. With Bryant's support, he visited the tenement owner and threatened both a lawsuit and exposure in the paper. The landlord probably could have won in court, but ridicule in the *Post* was a different matter. The tenement closed.

Smith couldn't just clean up the city going building by building. He needed new laws and better enforcement of the existing ones. He needed public support, and to get that he coordinated a wide alliance of powerful men like Bryant and Peter Cooper. They came together and formed the Citizens' Association of New York that sponsored Smith's landmark 1865 report on New York City hygiene, which included the work of twenty-nine different physicians.

That report depicts a city of sanitary horrors. The doctors tested one of the wells that still supplied water to the poor and found that it "contained not less than forty-eight grains of solid matter in the gallon, half of this being putrid organic substance." The doctors noted that "the neighbors using it are greatly troubled with diarrhoeal disease" and archly observed that "it would be surprising indeed if they were not." Perhaps more powerful were the sketches of individuals, such as the child "emaciated to a skeleton, and with that ghastly and unearthly look which marasmus impresses on its victims," who "has reared its feeble frame on a rickety chair against the window sill, and is striving to get a glimpse at the smiling heavens whose light is so seldom permitted to gladden its longing eyes."

At this time, the massively corrupt Tammany boss William M. Tweed was firmly in control of New York City, and his interest in sanitary reform was minimal. Smith and his allies instead went to the state legislature, which was the standard track for city reformers looking to bypass Tammany. In 1866, the state passed a Metropolitan Health Bill, and the next year, it passed the Tenement House Act. That law required one indoor toilet for every twenty residents and a window for every room. The toilet requirement was helpful, but slumlords found it easy to get around the window rule. The law never said that the window had to face out into a street or courtyard or offer "a glimpse at the smiling heavens." If the law wanted a window for every room, builders would give every dark interior room a window onto another dark interior room.

The Metropolitan Health Bill created the Metropolitan Board of Health, which could handle enforcement without any help from Tweed and his corrupt cops. The board of health was run primarily by doctors. Smith himself was its first leader. It had its own inspectors, picked by the doctors, not the city police who had previously ignored Smith. Tenement owners who didn't pay for connections to the water system faced fines. Local wells were driven out of business. The system was far from perfect, but death rates started to decline. Cities need incentives as well as infrastructure.

New York's board of health provides something of a model for developing world cities today. To solve their own last-mile problem, they will either need to find public funding to subsidize vast numbers of water connections or follow New York's lead and start fining landowners that don't connect to the water mains. The corruption of local police forces should make us wary about any new legal requirements that provide police with another excuse to extort the poor. But if the fines are small and imposed intelligently, then perhaps more urbanites can be induced to switch to clean water.

Smith was less successful on the national stage. In early 1879, Congress authorized a National Board of Health that would supervise quarantines at major ports and make up for the weakness of local health boards in states like Louisiana, which was blamed for allowing yellow fever to rage up the Mississippi in 1878. For four years, the National Board of Health did good work, but it was never truly empowered and its funding was not renewed in 1883.

Smith knew that the board was too weak to last and pushed for a more robust and durable national commitment to public health. As one later scholar wrote, "Stephen Smith, of all the national sanitarians, saw the importance of a National Public Health Service." He knew that "congress would lose interest in the National Board of Health, but would continue to support a service agency that had fulltime career officers and was incorporated as an integral part of national government machinery." We will take up the story of Smith's dream in chapter 5.

The secretary of the National Board of Health was Colonel George Waring, who would spearhead the next phase of New York City's fight against filth. Like Benjamin Rush, Waring believed that miasma generated disease, the false belief that motivated many of the most important nineteenth-century achievements in public health. Waring drained the swamps of New York's Central Park, designed Memphis's sewer system, and took over the sanitation department of New York City in 1895.

By that year, Waring had both a national reputation and enormous expertise. He had a single-minded mission to clean the city's streets. He "accepted the commissionership" with the mayor's "positive assurance" that he "should not be interfered with in the matter of appointments and dismissals, and that I should have my own way generally."

Before Waring's appointment, "the practice of standing unharnessed trucks and wagons in the public streets was well-nigh universal," which "made complete street cleaning practically impossible." Mobs rioted when Waring set his street cleaners to seize the trucks, but the empowered sanitation chief persisted and "within less than six months from the inauguration of Mayor Strong, these vehicles had all been removed."

Like Smith, Waring helped make local government the guardian of the city's health, and to do that, both Smith and Waring had to punish people. Waring went after the trucks left in the road. Smith fined landowners who didn't connect to the water system. Despite the mobs, New York City ultimately accepted these punishments because the city trusted Smith and Waring, and because the city understood the widespread need for street cleaning and sanitation. The population did not, however, accept that they couldn't go to a beer hall on Sunday. Mayor William Lafayette Strong's reform movement paid a fearsome political price when his police commissioner, Theodore Roosevelt, tried to shutter the saloons on the Sabbath. Later in this book, we will discuss how the city becomes more vulnerable when citizens no longer trust that penalties will be administered only to protect the common good.

To create a shared strength that serves, there must be leaders who have the power to accomplish goals and the ability to put the larger interests of the city ahead of local complaints. They must also be able to impose penalties that deter behavior that harms the whole. But that power cannot be absolute. Waring could fight back against the local mobs, but he was also completely accountable to Mayor Strong. As Waring himself wrote, "His power to dismiss me is unlimited, and he could get rid of me any day if I did not suit him; but so long as I should remain, I was to be the real head of my department."

Back to the Front

In the late nineteenth and early twentieth centuries, America's city governments became stronger and more oriented toward serving their citizens, but the national government became drawn into foreign adventures. When Teddy Roosevelt moved from Mayor Strong's city administration to the Department of the Navy, he helped push a reluctant President McKinley into war with Spain. America's victories during that "splendid little war" led Waring to Havana, where he was commissioned by McKinley to improve the sanitation. Waring died in Cuba of yellow fever, another victim of the diseases that so often accompany the military adventures of nation-states.

A far more catastrophic health event followed Europe's descent into the madness of war in August of 1914. Just as plague traveled along with Rawdon-Hasting's Indian army, World War I brought a truly global pandemic. The war spread disease so widely because it moved so many people across the planet.

Before 1800, pandemics were often carried across space by animals rather than humans: witness the mosquitoes that brought yellow fever to North America or the fleas and rats that brought the Black Death to Europe. Since 1910, human beings have become the primary vector of intercontinental disease, bringing influenza, AIDS, and COVID-19 in boats and planes across oceans. Humans now move more quickly, and transportation has become more sanitary. It is hard to imagine a Boeing 787 packed with either rats or mosquito-infested barrels of standing water, but a fourteenth-century cog traveling from Calais to the Thames estuary could easily have had both.

Dr. Jameson's narrative suggested that cholera changed shortly before the terrible 1817 outbreak. The influenza pandemic of 1918–19 may have begun with the transmission of a flu virus from animals to humans in a military camp in Étaples, France, around 1916, but there are also suspicions that the so-called Spanish flu actually started in Kansas. What seems relatively clear is that the Spanish flu did not originate in Spain. The flu is associated with Spain only because the Spanish were more forthcoming about the extent of the problem. Crowded, unsanitary conditions on military bases then enabled the disease to spread.

The influenza pandemic of 1918–19 is the closest historic parallel for the COVID-19 pandemic of 2020. Both diseases traveled easily through the air from human to human. For both diseases, massive investments in water systems and sewerage provided no safety. Neither disease brought forth a quick cure. In both cases, vaccines provided some hope, but that hope proved illusory in 1919. One difference between the Spanish flu and COVID-19 is that COVID-19 particularly kills the elderly, while the influenza had the unusual feature of slaughtering the young and healthy, perhaps because of an extreme immune system response or perhaps because of a lack of exposure to similar diseases.

The influenza pandemic was vastly deadlier than COVID-19, killing perhaps 50 million people out of a global population of 2 billion. In 2020, the global population is about four times larger, but COVID-19 deaths have been over 90 percent fewer. The difference seems most extreme in India, which lost perhaps 15 million to the 1918–19 influenza and 150,000 people to COVID-19 in 2020, but COVID-19 has not yet run its course.

The 1918–19 pandemic yields a few clear lessons. Disease follows in the footprints of war. Super-spreader events are important. Large public gatherings, such as Philadelphia's Liberty Loan Drive parade, seem to have infected thousands. Masks are likely to have been helpful, but, then as now, some individuals objected to them vociferously.

In the 1918–19 pandemic, many cities tried to enforce lockdown rules, similar to those embraced during 2020. But the data linking those rules with influenza mortality is surprisingly unclear. Our economics department colleague Robert Barro has meticulously linked these "non-pharmaceutical interventions," or NPIs, with subsequent mortality. He finds that "although an increase in NPIs flattened the curve in the sense of reducing the ratio of peak to average death rates, the estimated effect on overall deaths is small and statistically insignificant." Translating from statistics, the interventions seem to have delayed, but not eliminated, deaths from the pandemic. But does that mean that lockdowns aren't effective or that the typically one-month-long lockdowns of 1919 were just too short?

Perhaps the most important lesson of 1918–19 is that airborne pandemics have the potential to produce "the most deadly single event in recorded history." The COVID-19 pandemic has so far killed vastly fewer people, but it too reminds us that we do not have the tools to stop this kind of pandemic once it starts. That means we must limit the primary channel of new pandemic creation: the transmission of viruses and bacteria from animals to humans.

Humans, Bats, and the Threat of Pandemic in the Developing World Today

The path to global pandemic has three steps: a disease starts, it spreads locally, and then it spreads globally. The previous chapter discussed stopping the third step of the pandemic's path—cutting the flow of people across countries and continents after a pandemic first appears. A complementary approach is to prevent the human incursion of the disease in the first place, and its local spread. These actions involve separating humans from animals and improving the health climate in an area, through health-related infrastructure such as clean water.

Most pandemics are zoonotic, meaning that the disease starts with a leap from animals to humans. As best can be told, mammals seem to have given us COVID-19 (bats), Ebola (bats), AIDS (chimpanzees), Lyme disease (deer and mice), and the Black Death (rodents, transmitted with the help of fleas). Mosquitoes are the source for yellow fever, malaria, and dengue. Birds are thought to be the most common source of influenza. The origins of measles and smallpox are lost to history, but it is possible that they also have nonhuman roots.

Most pandemic diseases circulate for some time around their initial human hosts before they are carried elsewhere. But as the frequency of travel increases, the time between first infection and global spread has shrunk. Smallpox was circulating around Eurasia probably fifteen hundred years before it was carried to North America. AIDS emerged in the Congo by 1930, but it didn't come to the US for another half century. COVID-19 had only a few months in isolation in Wuhan before it came to Europe.

The zoonotic origins of most recent pandemics suggest the need to reduce the physical proximity between humans and animals, particularly wild animals and bats. Domesticated animals are generally less of a threat because their movement is limited and their health is usually monitored.

Most of the wealthy world is pretty good at segregating humans and feral creatures, although the sprawl of Americans out of cities into lower-density living has reduced our species' isolation. The Northeast of the US spends its summers in fear of bites from ticks that transfer Lyme disease from deer and mice to humans. Eastern equine encephalitis is a mosquito-borne threat that has emerged in the swampier areas of New England. Wild birds provide its current reservoir. But we have not seen a major pandemic move from animal to human in the wealthy world since the H1N1 influenza virus appeared at the end of World War I.

Mosquitoes have long been one of humanity's most deadly nemeses. Public health efforts created more space between us and the deadly carriers of malaria and yellow fever long before we actually understood those illnesses. The ancient Romans built the Cloaca Maxima to drain fetid water away from living areas. Dr. Benjamin Rush wanted to clear standing water away from the docks of Philadelphia in the 1790s. Waring drained Central Park. Mussolini assembled an army of one hundred twenty-four thousand Italians to fill in the Pontine Marshes near Rome. Mao exerted similar efforts against malarial marshes and mosquitoes, which were considerably more successful than his locust- and famine-inducing campaign against the sparrow. Antimalarial efforts may be expensive, but at least humans don't actively subvert public efforts to "drain the swamp." Few people really want mosquitoes nearby.

Urbanites were generally less happy about getting rid of their horses, pigs, and sheep, which were once as much a part of city life as traffic congestion. Horses provided transportation. Dairies and piggeries were ubiquitous. The poor kept free-ranging sheep and goats for food and sustenance. For many urban health advocates, the fight to control animals was as important as the fight for clean water. Catherine Brinkley and Domenic Vitiello, two scholars of urban planning at the University of Pennsylvania, write that "boards of health were created first and foremost to regulate animal agriculture, and most of their work across the nineteenth century involved policing animals."

Philadelphia passed a law in 1705 that tried to restrict the roaming of stray cattle and hogs, but a century later, the pigs were still freely eating their way through the streets of the City of Brotherly Love. The pigs' supporters claimed that free-ranging hogs cleaned up the city. Whatever the merits of the argument, Philadelphia lacked the public policing capacity to control large numbers of stray animals. In the 1860s, city reformers "issued ordinances to prevent driving of animals in certain streets at certain times of day," but small urban dairies and piggeries remained. New York City had twenty-three thousand dairy cows as late as 1903.

As transportation costs fell and pasteurization spread, it became easier to ship milk, beef, and other agricultural products from distant areas with cheaper land. Urban horses were pushed out by the car. As demand for urban animals fell, regulators found it easier to impose and enforce sweeping zoning ordinances, starting with New York City's 1916 law that restricted agriculture across vast amounts of urban space. These zoning laws, like building regulations more generally, may have been turned into tools for preventing the construction of low-cost housing, but they were often initially motivated by genuine public health concerns.

In recent years, dedicated urban farmers have rediscovered the joys of a small garden on a rooftop or in a park. These activities are perfectly sanitary and recall the eighteenth-century urban planners who thought that urban agriculture made a city both more beautiful and healthier. Trees do provide oxygen. But an urban vegetable garden is a far cry from the free-ranging goats that can often be seen in developing world neighborhoods, like Mumbai's Dharavi.

Domesticated animals that have lived for millennia around humans pose less risk than proximity to wilder creatures, like apes, bats, and camels. It is speculated that AIDS started with hunters seeking chimpanzee meat in West Africa. Middle East Respiratory Syndrome, or MERS, likely passed to humans through the care of sick camels. The live animals in the wet markets of Wuhan may have provided COVID-19's pathway from bats to humans, possibly through Malayan pangolins.

Bats are particularly large reservoirs of viruses, including SARS, MERS, COVID-19, and Ebola, possibly because of their flying lifestyle. Some researchers hypothesize that bats' "elevated metabolic body temperatures from flight, mimics the fever response" and enables them to safely contain viruses. Others emphasize their consumption of disease-ridden insects.

The risks created by bats made the COVID-19 pandemic somewhat predictable to serious virology researchers. One article published in March 2019 by researchers at the Wuhan Institute of Virology (no less) and the University of the Chinese Academy of Sciences presciently noted that "it is highly likely that future SARS- or MERS-like coronavirus outbreaks will originate from bats, and there is an increased probability that this will occur in China." Increasing the physical distance between humans and bats seems like a good first step, including shutting down open-air markets where the two species co-exist along with other mammals.

One recent study's findings "suggest that global changes in the mode and intensity of land use are creating expanding hazardous interfaces between people, livestock and wildlife reservoirs of zoonotic disease." A 2020 workshop on biodiversity and pandemics concludes that "conservation of protected areas, and measures that reduce unsustainable exploitation of high biodiversity regions will reduce the wildlife-livestock-human contact interface and help prevent the spillover of novel pathogens." The risks of zoonotic disease strengthen the case for living in compact urban spaces that do not encroach on the habitats of the wild.

There have been fledgling attempts to put together lists of unsafe practices, and this should continue. Alongside this, lawyers, economists, epidemiologists, and others must craft rules and institutions that enforce the appropriate separation between humans and animals. The first step is to obtain international agreement on a set of rules. The second step is for local governments to create mechanisms to enforce those rules, like Stephen Smith's board of health. The third step is for international governments to monitor the local governments. This is another job for our proposed NATO for health.

With COVID-19 in mind, come back to the example of coronaviruses in bats. There are certainly areas where proximity between people and bat caves poses too much risk to allow human settlement or agriculture nearby. The local government must be convinced to turn this area into some sort of national park, perhaps allowing tourists but no permanent habitation. If the country is rich, then it has plenty to gain from a global agreement to limit future pandemics and should be willing to set a good example. If the country is poor, then richer countries could provide some form of compensation for the loss of agricultural revenue, perhaps aid for urban sanitation projects. US foreign aid packages, such as Plan Colombia, have long been used to build local support for the War on Drugs. US foreign aid seems to buy countries' votes in the United Nations, so aid should also be able to buy some public hygiene.

America's current foreign aid budget is modest, but still unpopular, which provides little precedent for aggressive quid pro quo spending in the developing world. At the same time, Americans have been willing to provide oceans of cash to foreign allies when fighting either a hot or a cold war. The Marshall Plan was both generous and popular. John F. Kennedy established the United States Agency for International Development (USAID) in 1961 as one of "our political obligations as the single largest counter to the adversaries of freedom." The key to such efforts is self-interest. For our own health, as well as that of the world community, America and other rich nations must now be in the business of fighting pandemics. Aid that limits the spread of diseases is as hardheaded as aid that aims to stop the spread of communism.

Enforcing separation between humans and animals is also tricky. In richer places, laws work well, and rich farmers can generally be scared off by threat of disease or litigation. In poorer places, enforcement is harder, but technology can improve monitoring. For example, using satellites or drones, we can now spot human or agricultural settlement in a wilderness area from the sky. Richer countries, perhaps through some collective agency, could provide satellite monitoring of the protected area. That agency could report those violations to the world community, which can demand local action or impose some external punishment, like travel bans or the loss of aid.

Since an outside agency is providing monitoring, that agency can recommend some form of punishment. If the country is receiving aid, then that aid can be cut, but that threat works only if the agency is credible. The aid must flow if the rules are followed and stop if the rules are broken. If the violations are more extreme, then the increased pandemic risk creates a rationale for limiting international travel to and from that country. There needs to be coordination across nations, so that countries block travel simultaneously. The threat of ostracization from global networks then provides incentives for local and national governments to remove the farmers who have decided to locate near the bats. Moreover, sanctions that prevent the flow of people can reduce the risk of pandemic even if they don't induce better behavior.

Clean Water for Hyderabad and Lusaka

Our colleague Marcella Alsan is both a Harvard University economist and a practicing infectious disease physician. She spends part of her life lecturing in classrooms in Cambridge, Massachusetts, and part working in hospitals, including the Mahatma Gandhi Medical College and Hospital in the Indian city of Hyderabad, along with others in Africa and South America. Through her clinical work abroad, she became involved in a study measuring the presence of antibiotic resistant bacteria in Hyderabad.

Bacteria have a variety of strategies for developing resistance to antibiotic drugs, including pumps that push out the molecules and enzymes that cleave the drugs to mutations in the antibiotic target. Health-care providers facing such illnesses then need to use cocktails of medication and stronger therapeutics. The threat looms that resistant super bacteria will emerge and create the same kind of global risk posed by COVID-19 or other recent viruses.

India still has plenty of waterborne diseases today, but these illnesses, including cholera, are far less likely to be fatal than they were in the past. Oral rehydration therapy works for cholera itself, and antibiotics are readily available for most other things, sometimes as a secondary therapy for cholera. But antibiotics are used too much, in India as in rich countries of the West. As a result, we risk breeding antibiotic-resistant bacteria. One study estimated that there were 519 million antibiotic prescriptions for outpatients in India in 2014, or 412 prescriptions per 1,000 Indians. Generic drugs are abundant and cheap. Hyderabad itself is a pharmaceutical-producing powerhouse, soon to house a showcase "Pharma City."

The combination of abundant waterborne illness and abundant antibiotic production creates the perfect conditions for growing superbugs. Dr. Alsan's work in Hyderabad discovered that more than 3 percent of seemingly healthy people in the city were carrying around antibiotic-resistant bacteria. Dr. Alsan's study is based on pregnant women who came to the hospital for an early checkup, so there is no reason why they should have highly antibiotic-resistant bacteria in their urine. Yet they did.

These women had been living in a city filled with people who are exposed to illness and have access to drugs that had once been seen as miraculous but have come to be used as a substitute for strong public health measures. If we allow this process to continue, we risk the emergence of new international killers that could do far more harm than COVID-19.

The most natural and humane way to reduce the risk of future pandemics is to make cities throughout the world healthier. This requires medical research and clinical work, like that done by Dr. Alsan in Hyderabad, but also the same forms of sanitary infrastructure that made the cities of the developed world livable. Wealthy countries can and should help finance those investments. This financing should be a quid pro quo for adopting other sanitary regulations, like keeping away from bats.

This type of grand bargain requires a sustained commitment, not just some seed funding for water mains. Sub-Saharan Africa faces the same last-mile problem today that New York experienced after the Croton Aqueduct. Rich donor countries build water pipes, but poor residents aren't able to pay the final connection fee. To become healthy, countries and the international community are either going to have to subsidize that last-mile link, or do what Dr. Stephen Smith did in New York City and send out the health inspectors to fine property owners who don't connect to the system.

Maintenance is at least as important as new construction. One of us (Glaeser) studies water in Lusaka, the capital city of Zambia. On the best days, water is available only during daylight hours, but in the poorer parts of the city, the water pipes break regularly. Sometimes water isn't available for days on end.

There are two types of water customers in Lusaka. Some pay by the month. Some pay by the gallon. If the water pipes break, the water company still gets paid by its customers who pay by the month. The customers who pay by the gallon don't have to pay until the water starts flowing again. The company has a financial incentive to get the water flowing to the households who pay by the gallon, so that is where it puts its effort. With the supply of water, maintenance is as important as initial construction. Companies will invest in maintenance only when they face the right financial incentives.

When the water pipes stop working, people turn to other water sources. They send their daughters longer distances for water. These young women then spend less time on schoolwork when the pipes break. The water they carry seems to be less safe, because children suffer from diarrhea more often after the pipes break. Respiratory ailments generally have more to do with cooking fires and air quality than with water, but when the water stops flowing in Lusaka, respiratory illnesses increase, presumably because handwashing declines.

Clean water is the most basic job of urban government. It is tempting to say that the cities of the developing world are ultimately responsible for their own water supply. Yet the multitrillion-dollar cost of the COVID-19 pandemic to the wealthy world means that wealthy nations cannot look the other way. Rather, we all have to contribute to the prevention of future waterborne plagues. Fortunately, we have successful examples. The rich world had the same problems over a century ago and finally solved them. Our challenge today is to replicate that around the globe.

Preventing pandemic disease requires action at the international level, at the city level, and at the individual level. In the next chapter, we turn to the spread of disease within the human body itself. We focus on the behaviors that cities enable, including consumption of unhealthy food and use of illegal substances, which can make our bodies and thus our world more vulnerable to the consequences of contagion.

Chapter 4

CAN OUR BODIES BE
MORE PANDEMIC-PROOF?

When COVID-19 first hit Baltimore in March 2020, physicians at the Johns Hopkins Hospital were in for a surprise. They had expected the patients to be elderly, as they had been in China and Italy. But the Baltimore patients were younger, and they were disproportionately obese.

Everyone was affected by COVID-19, but some were affected more than others. In the US, African Americans were 40 percent more likely than whites to be diagnosed with COVID-19 and nearly three times more likely to die from it. Hispanics were at higher risk as well. In the UK, people of Asian and Caribbean heritage were at higher risk. There are many reasons for these disparities, not all of which are fully understood. For this pandemic, as for many contagious diseases, pre-pandemic illness was a major risk factor in disease exposure and fatality. Over 98 percent of those who died from COVID-19 in Massachusetts in 2020 had preexisting conditions. Close living quarters were also important. Almost 40 percent of US COVID-19 deaths in 2020 occurred in nursing homes.

Health-related choices shape both our vulnerability to pandemic and who lives and dies more generally. Heroin needles helped to spread AIDS during the 1980s, first to users and then to their sexual partners. The opioid epidemic continued to kill during the COVID-19 lockdown, as "more than

40 states have reported increases in opioid-related mortality." Cigarette smoking contributes to the conditions that make COVID-19 more deadly, and might play an even bigger role in the airborne plagues of the future.

Chapter 2 emphasized that cities are vulnerable to pandemics because cities provide the pathways across oceans and continents for bacteria and viruses, as well as for goods and ideas. Chapter 3 described how urban crowding enables disease to spread more readily, especially among the urban poor who live in the slums of low-income megacities or people anywhere who can't afford to shelter in place. In this chapter, we focus on how urban abundance and inequality can enable lifestyles that make our bodies more vulnerable, both to contagious disease and to death more generally. Urban innovations include not only art and philosophy but also the Oreo cookie and the open-air drug market.

Urban abundance plays out differently on Park Avenue, where portions are small and exercise is frequent, than in poor neighborhoods where fried food provides an affordable—if unhealthy—escape into pleasure. Like all else in health, obesity, opioid abuse, and cigarette smoking follow education and income. Twenty-eight percent of college graduates are obese, as opposed to 40 percent of those without a bachelor's degree. Opioid overdose deaths have increased far more among those without a college degree. Smoking rates are nearly three times higher among those with a high school degree or less than among those who have completed college.

The segregated nature of our cities means that different cultures coexist, and while the culture of elite neighborhoods can be positively puritanical, the culture of poorer places can be more accepting of many health-harming behaviors. The abstemiousness of the rich itself isn't entirely free: the suicide rate in self-denying Manhattan is a solid 33 percent higher than in any of the other four boroughs. Yet that does little to reduce the large life-expectancy differences between rich and poor parts of the city, which can be as much as ten years on average.

The magnitude of modern urban inequality poses enormous challenges for cities, partially because wide disparities diminish the sense of a shared destiny. The mortality gap between rich and poor is particularly awful. For generations, children have sung about how on the doomed *Titanic* "the rich refused to associate with the poor" and "so they threw them down below, where they were the first to go." Even the youngest sense the wrong reflected in the fact that only 26 percent of third-class passengers survived the iceberg, compared to 62 percent of first-class voyagers. How different is the modern city from the *Titanic*?

The great challenge in reducing health disparities is that death reflects not just access to medical care, which can be altered by policy, but behaviors such as smoking, obesity, and use of illegal drugs. None but the most dictatorial governments can tell people what snacks they can and cannot consume. Even Mayor Bloomberg of New York, among the most health-oriented mayors in history, didn't try to limit total consumption of sugary soda, but only to restrict soda sizes to less than sixteen ounces. The New York State Court of Appeals didn't even give him that victory.

Health behaviors have been long known to explain much of the difference in mortality across space. Almost fifty years ago, the great health economist Victor Fuchs noted that "in the western United States, there are two contiguous states that enjoy about the same levels of income and medical care, and are alike in many respects," and yet, "the inhabitants of Utah are among the healthiest individuals in the United States, while the inhabitants of Nevada are at the opposite end of the spectrum." Fuchs explains that "differences in life-styles account for differences in death-rates." Alcohol and tobacco have long been ubiquitous in Las Vegas casinos and absent from observant Mormon households.

There is no single policy fix for changing health-related behaviors. The lowest-hanging fruit is to reconsider policies that make things worse, like subsidizing corn production and looking the other way at illegal opioid marketing. Opioids are then paid for by public insurance programs, like Medicaid and Medicare, as well as private insurance and individual households. Nudges that encourage health, especially in public schools, also seem sensible. Sometimes the social costs of unhealthy products, like cigarettes, are high enough to justify taxing those products.

Even so, health behaviors will always create difficulties for society. We'd prefer it if people were attuned to risks and abstained from unhealthy behavior on their own, but people should have the freedom to do their bodies a bit of harm, and they always will. Individual character cannot be dictated by the government. But it can be encouraged in the classroom, the job site, and the breakfast table.

Across the world, schooling is the strongest predictor of health at the individual level; educated people are less likely to smoke, drink heavily, or be obese. Education can give people healthier options. Moreover, investing in schooling can improve health not only because risky behavior declines with one's own education, but also because risky behavior falls with the education of the people around you. The social norms that shape our behaviors also shape our health, which in turn helps explain why some places were so much more vulnerable to illness in general and to COVID-19 in particular. Marshaling these social norms will be key to preparing society for pandemics that may yet come.

The Health of Cities
and the Company You Keep

Which places face death most frequently? To answer that question, one of us (Cutler) worked on a project using massive amounts of data, including Social

Security records, which allowed us to measure mortality rates at every age for people living in each city. Using these mortality rates, we estimated how many years the typical forty-year-old had to live. For example, if half of people die one year and half the next, the average life expectancy would be one year (the average of one half year of life for those dying in the first year and one and a half years of life for those dying in the second year).

The variation in life expectancy across areas is enormous. Among the one hundred most populous cities in the United States, the highest life expectancy at age 40 is 45.4 years, in San Jose, California. The lowest is 41.0 years, in Las Vegas, Nevada. That 4.4-year gap between living to 81 and living to 85.4 is larger than the life-expectancy gains that would come from eliminating all cancer deaths in the US. If we could somehow cure every case of breast cancer, lung cancer, prostate cancer, and the like, life expectancy would increase by only 3 years. The gap between San Jose and Las Vegas is thus equivalent to completely eliminating cancer deaths in high life-expectancy areas—and then some.

High life-expectancy areas include those with large, well-educated populations. San Francisco, Boston, and New York all join San Jose at the top of the list. The bottom of the list includes rust-belt cities like Gary, Indiana, along with cities across the South, such as Birmingham, Alabama, and Oklahoma City. These areas have less-educated populations, in some cases because high-wage factory jobs did not require much formal schooling, and in some cases because of the legacy of the Jim Crow South.

Behaviors, healthy and unhealthy, are shaped by our friends and neighbors. If I don't know any smokers, then it is far less natural for me to light up. Teenagers who are exposed to cigarette or marijuana smoking, e-cigarette vaping, or alcohol use are more likely to try those substances themselves. Peers can influence behavior by changing norms, by introducing new products, or by making social connections to suppliers, such as drug dealers. The stores in one's neighborhood reflect the preferences of those who live nearby. Consequently, a person is likely to buy different products depending on whether they live surrounded by fast-food lovers or vegans.

San Jose, Boston, and New York all have many rich people. Perhaps the reason why people in these areas live a long time is that the ultra-rich can buy things that lead to longer lives—healthier foods, gym memberships, and the like—while the rest of the population cannot. In the study described above, we also had the income tax records matched to the mortality records. Thus, we could look at the difference in life expectancy across cities for people with different levels of income.

Surprisingly, the life expectancy of the rich is pretty similar everywhere. To paraphrase Tolstoy, rich people are all (more or less) alike. The big differences across space appear in the mortality of poor people. A forty-year-old living in the bottom fourth of the income distribution in New York can expect to live another forty-two years. In Gary, Indiana, it is five years less. Among people in the top one quarter of the income distribution, the gap in life expectancy is only two years. This is particularly surprising because sky-high New York City rents mean that, holding income constant, the poor in New York are effectively even more disadvantaged.

The differences across other cities mirror the gap between New York City and Gary. The correlation is not subtle. It jumps off the page. Those cities where people live longer have better-educated populations. They are richer and have more of an upper middle class. The life-expectancy gaps are strongest for the poor.

Equally important is what longevity is not related to. The longevity of the poor is not tied to the share of people who are insured or the amount of medical spending per person. It is not that those are unimportant for health; when sick, access to medical care matters a great deal.

But what matters most at the population level is whether the population becomes sick in the first place, and that is largely determined by behaviors.

The smoking rate among low-income people is 30 percent lower in New York City than in Gary, Indiana. Obesity is also 30 percent lower in New York. Lower rates of tobacco use and obesity mean less heart disease, cancer, musculoskeletal disorders, and a host of other conditions. In every way we can tell, New York is a healthier city than Gary, Indiana.

The finding that some cities are healthier than others is true throughout the world. In the United Kingdom, people in London live on average more than five years longer than people in Glasgow. The British speak of the "Glasgow effect"—as in, why is health so poor in Glasgow?—in much the way that epidemiologists speak of the "French paradox"—how can the French eat like they do and not die like flies? Health insurance is universal in both London and Glasgow, and the social safety net is generally strong, certainly stronger than in the US, but London is richer and better educated.

In France, Paris has the highest life expectancy. In Spain, it is Madrid. In Germany, it is Munich. In Italy, it is Trento, rich and high in the mountains near Austria; the province containing Milan is also near the top. In Canada, the healthiest people and behaviors are found in the areas around Vancouver, Toronto, and Ottawa. Not all of these are national capitals, nor are they all densely populated. But all are rich and well educated.

However, even in generally healthy cities, there are many people who die too young. Take New York City, our earlier poster child for the health of the poor. Life expectancy on the Upper East Side of Manhattan is eighty-six years. Take the one-hour subway ride south and then east to Brownsville in Brooklyn. In those twelve miles, life expectancy falls by about eleven years— almost one year per mile. In the Camden borough of London, life expectancy for women is eighty-seven years of age. Go sixteen miles east, to Barking and Dagenham, and life expectancy is five years lower.

What cause of death is present in Brownsville that is absent from Manhattan's Upper East Side? There isn't one. The causes of death are similar in the two neighborhoods, but each cause of death is more prevalent in

Brownsville. Violent death is more common in Brownsville, but so are heart disease and cancer. Infant mortality rates are also higher in Brownsville. Indeed, Brownsville is more unusual in its level of the "natural causes" of death than in homicide.

Brownsville's excess deaths do not come out of thin air. The smoking rate in Brownsville is twice that of the Upper East Side. Obesity rates in Brownsville are ten times those found in the least-obese parts of Manhattan. Brownsville has among the highest rates of HIV and hepatitis C infections of any area of New York City. All of this adds up and subtracts from life expectancy.

The pre-2020 health patterns within New York City were largely repeated during the COVID-19 pandemic. The poorest quarter of zip codes in the city have four times the number of COVID-19 cases as the richest quarter of zip codes. For many reasons—more essential workers, multigenerational housing, greater use of public transportation—COVID-19 hit Brownsville far harder than the Upper East Side.

Some of that difference reflects the fact that wealthier Manhattanites had the luxury to Zoom their way to work, or to stop working altogether. One of us (Glaeser) together with two coauthors linked COVID-19 cases in New York with mobility records from cell phones and subway turnstiles. During the fatal months of April and May 2020, a 10 percent decline in the number of trips by people living in an area was associated with a 20 percent drop in the number of cases.

There is a back-and-forth dance between the rich and poor parts of New York that engenders employment but can spread illness. There are 127,500 restaurant and food service workers who are employed in Manhattan, yet fewer than 40,000 of those workers live on that island. The barista working at a Starbucks on the Upper East Side lives perhaps in the Bronx. Almost 75,000 of New York City's total food-service population live in Queens and another 65,000 live in Brooklyn. More than 10,000 restaurant and food service workers reside in the middle-income Jackson Heights and North Corona neighborhoods of Queens, where 90 percent of the population is nonwhite, 60 percent of the population is foreign-born, and median household income is $55,000. Another 5,500 live in the Hunts Point area of the Bronx, where median household income is less than $25,000. There is no way for a Manhattanite to avoid people from other boroughs without living like a hermit.

And the rich spread disease to the poor as well. COVID-19 was carried across continents by the rich, who then seeded the disease to lower-income areas. Cross-city travel is far more common among the wealthy than among the poor. As the disease spread, the rich then cloistered themselves, but the poor continued to move around, if they were lucky enough to still have a job. As they moved, they continued to get sick. The rich parts of Manhattan could cut their movement. The poorer residents of Brownsville had to leave their homes to make enough money to pay the rent.

With contagious disease, even living near a city puts one at risk. New Rochelle in Westchester County was the site of the first COVID-19 outbreak in New York. Patient Zero was a lawyer who commuted mostly between New Rochelle and a law firm in midtown Manhattan. It is not known if the lawyer contracted COVID-19 in Manhattan or elsewhere, but whatever the source, even the suburbs are not safe. Like the game Six Degrees of Separation, everyone interacts with everyone else with just a few links.

Urbanization, Exercise, and Obesity

One quarter of adults in New York City are obese, but more than half of those hospitalized for COVID-19 in March 2020 were in that category. Among those aged forty-nine or younger, 60 percent were obese. The biology of obese people makes COVID-19 far more serious: their higher levels of ACE2 allow entry of the virus into cells, they have reduced lung volume as the diaphragm is pushed into the lungs, their blood is more likely to clot, they have fewer and less effective immune cells, and so on. The Centers for Disease Control and Prevention suggests that individuals are at highest risk of severe COVID-19 illness if they have any of a series of risk factors, including cancer, chronic kidney disease, respiratory difficulty, serious heart disease, diabetes, immunocompromised state, and obesity. In addition to its direct effect, obesity is a risk factor for many of these other conditions. Smoking is as well.

Just as high levels of obesity have made COVID-19 deadlier in rich world cities, low levels of obesity may have protected the world's poorest urban places. More than 50 percent of the residents of Mumbai's slums appear to have developed COVID-19 antibodies by July 2020, yet the death rates were quite low in Mumbai, and across India as a whole. One possible reason is that the residents of India's slums are too poor to be overweight.

Living in a city doesn't appear to make one heavier. The obesity rate in Manhattan is 15 percent, as opposed to 26 percent in the rest of New York State. The obesity rate in San Francisco is eight percentage points less than the rate in California as a whole. Even Cook County, home of Chicago, with an obesity rate of 28 percent, has less obesity than the rest of Illinois. Yet the long arc of urbanization and prosperity is responsible for creating the conditions that have led to widespread obesity. As cities have made humanity wealthier, they have also enabled us to eat more and sweat less.

While many factors determine one's weight, a simple framework focuses primarily on calories in and calories out. When people consume more calories than they burn, they store that extra energy on their bodies. In 1800, and even in 1900, Europeans and Americans expended a great deal of calories just doing their work. Farming could be backbreaking, and early industrial labor didn't mean sitting in a padded chair.

Cities played an outsized role in creating the technologies that made work sedentary. In nineteenth-century Chicago, Cyrus McCormick made mechanical reapers that reduced the effort needed to chop down wheat and corn. In Detroit, Ford created an automated assembly line that enabled the parts to move and the workers to stay put. Ford's cars then reduced the need to walk to train stations or to the grocery store. During the twentieth century, machines replaced even more human energy and so people burned fewer calories.

But using less energy won't lead to an obesity epidemic if the consumption of calories falls proportionately. Between the 1920s and the 1960s, calories per capita declined by about 10 percent in the United States, offsetting the rise of the car and the declining amount of physical effort. By the 1960s, we were almost as sedentary as we are now and yet our obesity rate remained around 15 percent through the late 1970s. By 2015 that rate had risen to 40 percent.

The rise in American obesity since the 1960s appears to be almost entirely about eating and drinking more. In one of our earlier papers together, the two of us along with Jesse Shapiro evaluated food consumption trends between the mid-1970s and the mid-1990s. The US government gets a picture of changing eating patterns by asking a random sample of the population to fill out food diaries about what they eat. The diaries are kept for a few days and then analyzed. Of course, people don't tell their diary everything. Caloric intake seems too low in the surveys, especially given the weight of the diarists, but the trends in consumption seem accurate and match trends found in food production.

Between 1970 and 2000, weights rose nearly ten pounds per person, while the total food supply in the US increased from 3,300 calories per day to 4,000 calories per day. Correcting for calories lost due to food waste, calories consumed grew from 2,054 calories per day to 2,560 calories per day. An extra 500 calories per day per person means that we've increased our food consumption by one fifth over thirty years. According to the food diary data, daily caloric intake increased by 268 calories for men and 143 calories for women. This alone can explain the ten-pound weight increase. A rough rule of thumb is that in human populations, an additional 100 calories per day leads to ten extra pounds in steady state.

Why has food consumption increased since 1970? Perhaps in the distant past of nineteenth-century industrial Manchester, urban diets consisted mostly of basic starches and canned meat. Back then, we stayed thin because we were poor. Eating was difficult to afford and not that much fun. Yet by 1970, we were rich enough to afford copious calories and there were plenty of tasty things to eat. One could watch Julia Child on PBS and whip up a perfectly splendid French meal, perhaps finished by a chocolate soufflé.

In 1970, we had money and we had the capacity to make good food, but we didn't have as much temptation right at hand. The best explanation for the rise in caloric consumption and obesity is that the time cost of accessing flavorful food has plummeted, owing largely to the advent of processed foods, which were themselves produced largely by urban innovators. More than three quarters of the calories in purchased foods in the United States comes from moderately or highly processed foods. This includes frozen french fries and desserts, canned foods, breads and cereals, premade meals, candy, and soda. In the 1950s, processed foods were rare. Today, they are ubiquitous.

If food takes less time to prepare, then it is easier to eat between meals. Between the 1970s and the 1990s, men reported 240 calories more per day on "snacks," and women reported 160 more calories. In the surveys, a typical snack in the 1970s was bread and butter; by the 1990s, it was potato chips and a soda. New technologies meant that sugary, salty, tasty food had become cheap and available in vending machines, supermarkets, and corner grocery stores throughout the world.

The data in other countries are less clear. Data from British food diaries suggest that calories consumed have decreased over time, possibly because of underreporting. There is a clear trend of eating less at home and more out, and people probably do a worse job of reckoning their calories consumed eating (and drinking) down at the pub. Unfortunately, there has been less research on this question in the British context than in the American.

Innovation and Obesity

As society urbanized, the process of transporting agricultural output to city tables began. Subsistence farmers were generally responsible for almost every step in their own food production process, from sowing the wheat to baking the bread. Urbanites depend on someone else to grow their food. At the end of the nineteenth century, city dwellers were sent fairly basic products, like flour and frozen sides of beef, which they transformed on their own into edible food. Over the course of the twentieth century, more and more of that transformation was taken out of the household and brought into the factory or the supermarket.

Urban brilliance helped to make the food products both tastier and easier to access. The now Google-owned Chelsea Market occupies an entire Manhattan block, from Fifteenth to Sixteenth Street and from Ninth to Tenth Avenue. Today, the building is full of culinary creativity, but it has an even more important past as the National Biscuit Company's signature bakery. That factory was something of an innovation machine that leveraged the wisdom of both Nabisco's competitors and its workforce.

Nabisco's most famous piece of intellectual borrowing was the idea for a cookie made of two chocolate biscuits attached with a white cream. The first cookie that fits this description was named Hydrox and was manufactured in Kansas City by the Loose-Wiles Biscuit Company. The second and more successful cookie sandwich, bearing the name of Oreo, was produced by

Nabisco in New York City and Chicago. Nabisco had a process allowing any employee to suggest a cookie for test baking. The author E. B. White, who wrote both *Stuart Little* and *Charlotte's Web*, visited the Nabisco factory in 1931 and came away impressed by how the trial runs were just "placed in an open rack by the water cooler" for anyone to sample.

The key to Nabisco's mass-produced cookies, or any mass-prepared food, is safely retaining taste during the long trip from the factory to the customer's mouth. To do this, one must control the atmosphere, prevent spoilage due to microorganisms, protect flavor, preserve moisture, and control temperature. Innovations in food processing and packaging over the past few decades have improved our ability to achieve each of these tasks.

"Controlled atmosphere packaging" and, more recently, "modified atmosphere packaging" allow food manufacturers to shape the gaseous environment in which their foods are stored. In the case of fruits, vegetables, and other foods with living cells, these technologies slow down ripening and prevent spoilage. For packaged goods such as fresh pasta, prepared salads, and cooked chicken, control of the atmosphere inside the package can greatly lengthen food durability.

Preservatives have also added to shelf life. Some preservatives prevent the growth of mold, for example on bakery items, while others prevent the growth of bacteria. Hydrogen peroxide sterilization (approved in 1981) and stretch-wrap films (introduced in 1976) have made it easier to eliminate and seal out harmful microorganisms. Since the 1970s, food irradiation has advanced, although the diffusion of this technology was slow until the Food and Drug Administration allowed more widespread use starting in 1986.

A persistent problem in food processing is that packaging can adversely impact food flavor. The 1980s saw advances in "flavor barrier" technology, which involves materials specially tailored to prevent migration of flavor-related chemicals to and from the food. In addition, the food industry has increasingly made use of chemists as flavor specialists to design tastes to suit consumers' whims. These chemists home in on what makes certain foods desirable and synthesize it in the laboratory. These artificial flavors can then be added to make pre-prepared food more appealing. Who wants regular potato chips when you can have chips with that zest of "sweet Maui onion" or "mesquite barbecue"?

Temperature and moisture pose a challenge for frozen foods. If moisture builds up in the package, ice crystals can form, which separate ingredients and alter the food's texture. Oxidation dehydrates food in the freezer, which is commonly called "freezer burn." Advances in polyethylene plastics and other materials have improved control over the internal moisture of food packages, which means a longer freezer life and better flavor.

New household technologies have improved taste and reduced preparation times. Microwave ovens were developed in the 1940s as an outgrowth of radar technology. They became widely available in the 1970s. As late as 1978, only 8 percent of American households had microwaves. By 1999, 83 percent did. Refrigerators have also improved.

Consider the ordinary loaf of bread. Baked bread, as opposed to dry cookies, becomes moldy after three or four days in a normal, slightly damp room. That is not enough time to bake the bread at a central location, distribute it to homes via grocery stores, and then have people eat a complete loaf. For bread to be mass-produced, it had to last longer.

Preservatives enabled mass marketers of white and wheat bread to break the tyranny of time. The most popular is sorbic acid, which occurs naturally and was first isolated in 1859. In the late 1930s, chemists in Germany and the US discovered that sorbic acid slowed the growth of mold. In 1953, America approved the acid as a food additive, and it became commonplace. Today, sorbic acid is bought and sold in industrial bulk and mixed into bakery products of all kinds, as well as into cheese and wine. The result is a near-ubiquitous supply of baked goods that can last for days or even weeks. Preservatives reduce the need to shop regularly, which in turn reduces the time cost of food.

The magnates of the Industrial Revolution, like Henry Ford, pushed down unit costs by selling on a grand scale to rich and poor alike. Nabisco followed the same model and put Oreos in cupboards and bellies throughout the world. Yet mass-marketed flavorful treats proved to have a particular appeal to their poorer customers, and so the obesity gap—and the mortality gap—between rich and poor grew larger.

Mr. Spud and the Rise of the French Fry

A whole literature has emerged documenting the link between neighborhood poverty and the fulsome availability of fast food. Some studies focus on one single metropolitan area, like Los Angeles, and find results such as "poorer neighborhoods with a higher percentage of African American residents have fewer choices and more fast food restaurants." Other papers take a nationwide perspective and document patterns like "predominantly black urban neighborhoods had a statistically higher proportion of fast-food restaurants among all available restaurants." Even outside the US, researchers find things like a positive correlation between "neighborhood deprivation and the mean number of McDonald's outlets per 1,000 people."

Nonetheless, the speed that is inherent in "fast food" appeals to rich and poor alike. Before COVID-19, 37 percent of all adults aged over twenty and 42 percent of families earning more than 3.5 times the federal poverty level ate fast food daily. The poor actually eat fast food less often than middle-income Americans, but the well educated seem to do a slightly better job of stopping that consumption from increasing their waistlines.

The McDonald's french fry has practically come to symbolize both a quick stick of deliciousness and the unhealthy eating opportunities that abound in inner cities. A large order of fries at McDonald's comes in at 490 calories, about the same as the total calorie growth in food supply between 1970 and 2000.

Baked, boiled, and mashed potatoes have been a large part of the American diet for centuries. But before World War II, those potatoes were generally cooked and eaten at home. French fries were a delicacy, both at home and in restaurants, because of the work involved in peeling, cutting, and frying. One man had a supersized role in changing that.

Jack (J.R.) Simplot, potato entrepreneur extraordinaire, was born in a "sod-roofed log cabin" in Iowa and transformed himself into the King of the French Fry, whose vanity license plate read MR. SPUD. Simplot's family moved to Idaho, and he dropped out of school at age fourteen to farm. According to his *New York Times* obituary, "an early profit on some pigs allowed him to become a potato farmer." He founded the J.R. Simplot Company in 1929 when he was only twenty years old.

Like Nabisco, Simplot was a food innovator, although decidedly not an urbanite. He bought a mechanical potato sorter to reduce labor costs. He first adopted fertilizers to improve yields, and then started mining phosphate himself. By 1940, Simplot became the largest shipper of Idaho potatoes.

During World War II, food needed to be moved even longer distances to feed GIs in Europe and the South Pacific. Simplot adapted by dehydrating his vegetables, starting with onions and then moving on to potatoes. He built the largest dehydrating plant in the world. Hungry soldiers would eat almost anything, and so the poor taste of the dehydrated potatoes wasn't a problem. But dehydration hardly seemed like a promising way to woo pickier postwar consumers.

Simplot's star chemist Ray Dunlap discovered the secret to the mass-produced french fry in 1945: refrigeration. Simplot initially thought that frozen potatoes would turn to mush, but he bought Dunlap a large freezer anyway. A few months later, Dunlap had figured out that precooked (or blanched) french fries would keep their flavor through freezing.

The resulting potato retained its taste and could be cooked in an oven instead of a fryer, which made it easier to buy french fries at a grocery and eat them at home. In the 1960s, Simplot partnered with Ray Kroc and became the largest supplier of the iconic McDonald's fries. Simplot built a dedicated factory for the fast-food giant. By the time he died at the age of ninety-nine, the king of Idaho potatoes was worth $4 billion.

Simplot was not a villain. He was an entrepreneur who figured out how to deliver a product cheaply and efficiently that billions of people have enjoyed eating. Unfortunately, his products—mass-produced french fries—are far less healthy than the home-cooked potatoes that preceded them. More choices may make people happier, but they do not guarantee svelter figures.

The ability to make food centrally and deliver it to people is a technological change that caused both the cash cost and the time cost of processed food to fall relative to fresh food. Large production plants make bread and french fries with less labor than is required at home or in corner bakeries. That reduced cash costs. But even more importantly, the industrial production of food lowers the time cost of accessing food. The time needed to amble to the vending machine is much less than the time needed to bake something yourself. Watching reruns of Julia Child today, one is struck by how many hours the preparation and cooking process took.

The connection between technological change and the growth of obesity can explain the rise in weight patterns around the globe. Obesity has increased everywhere, but particularly in English-speaking countries. The US, the UK, Canada, and Australia are generally less regulated than continental Europe. In particular, they are much less picky about food regulation. For example, the German Reinheitsgebot, or beer purity law, dates from 1516 and permits only hops, barley, water, and yeast in beer. There is no equivalent regulation in the UK or US, which reflects both a common-law tradition that relies more on litigation than on regulation and an earlier move from farm to factory, which put a higher premium in the US and UK on the ability to ship and preserve beer.

England's reputation for terrible food, which lasted well into the 1980s, partially reflected the country's rapid industrialization. Poor nineteenth-century factory workers accepted boiled and canned food that was far worse than the fresher food consumed by otherwise poorer Provençal or Bavarian peasants. In the twentieth century, the French and the Germans used regulations to protect their culinary traditions. Their rule-makers cast a particularly dim eye on preservatives.

Why Does Faster Food Mean More Food?

The simplest explanation for why mass-prepared food increases obesity is that time is a cost like any other, and as time costs fall, food consumption rises. That is true, but when the financial costs of food fell between 1920 and 1970, total caloric consumption did not go up. The real cost of flour, bacon, and eggs declined by 33, 31, and 59 percent respectively between 1918 and 1970 in the US. Yet calories consumed went down.

Making tasty treats easily accessible on demand has an even larger impact on consumption than just making them cheaper, probably because it is harder to say no to temptation that is right in front of one's eyes. Common advice to people quitting smoking or alcohol is to not keep cigarettes or liquor in the house. Why does this strategy work? After all, cigarettes and alcohol are just a short walk or drive for most people. The answer is that even a few minutes of effort may be enough to discourage consumption. Cigarettes that are nearby may be too hard to resist. If smoking involves getting dressed to go out and perhaps half an hour of time, it may not be worth it.

People are extremely sensitive—sometimes excessively so—to instantaneous gratification. It is almost as if there are two selves, one that cares only about immediate pleasure and another that makes rational trade-offs between the present and the future. The first operates when cookies are in the next room; the second when we have time to think.

Unfortunately, entrepreneurs can figure out how to use our impulses to make a sale. Ray Kroc's creation of a fast-food nation was not some random act. He knew that fast would sell because people have trouble saying no to a Big Mac that is right there. People are more obese because entrepreneurs have developed ways to provide more instantaneous deliciousness than in the past. Our waistlines spread because our urban world is an innovation machine, for good and ill.

These technological gains have done plenty of good, by reducing the time spent in preparation, cooking, and cleaning. Americans, on average, spend twenty minutes less per day in these chores than they did in the 1970s. For married women, it is closer to an hour. Moreover, few of us would want to return to menus common during the 1930s. Spaghetti served with ketchup, anyone? At the same time, average weights have increased about ten pounds.

Entrepreneurs of Oblivion

The Lower East Side of Manhattan has plenty of artery-hardening eateries, from the McDonald's on First Avenue and Sixth Street to Katz's legendary delicatessen on Houston Street. But that part of the city has also been a distribution center for a more dangerous form of consumption: illegal drugs. In the 1980s, Tompkins Square Park, which is barely a block from the McDonald's, housed an infamous open-air market. In the pages of the *New York Times*, Mayor Ed Koch bewailed the "stubbornly persistent plague of street dealers in narcotics whose flagrantly open drug dealing has destroyed the community life" of the nearby Alphabet City neighborhood.

Cities enable almost all markets, but urban density has a particular edge when it comes to selling illegal products, like drugs, that are more difficult to transport, advertise, and distribute. Those drugs, especially opioids, then made both the AIDS epidemic and the COVID-19 pandemic deadlier. Heroin needles were and still are a primary mode of AIDS transmission. The terrible strain of social isolation during COVID quarantines appears to have led to even larger numbers of opioid overdoses. From a public health perspective, the 250,000 drug overdose deaths between 2015 and 2018 make the opioid epidemic almost as problematic as the COVID-19 pandemic. The urban propensity for narcotics abuse is another significant source of urban vulnerability.

Opium and its derivatives are old companions of humanity. Around 3400 BCE, the ancient Sumerians referred to the opium poppy as a "joy plant." The ancient Greeks, Egyptians, Persians, and Indians all knew about the pleasures and risks that came from the poppy. During the European Age of Exploration, opium joined tobacco and tea as one of the lucrative drugs that clipper ships carried across the waves. The town of Belmont in suburban Boston is named after the estate of a notable opium dealer. Great Britain fought two wars in the 1800s so that British ships could carry Indian opium into China. Twenty percent of Chinese men may have been opium users at the start of the twentieth century.

Opioids ease pain, induce euphoria, and depress respiration and cardiac activity. Consequently, overdosing is easy even among tolerant users. Heroin is a particularly deadly derivative of the opium poppy. For intravenous heroin users, a lethal dose is only six times larger than a usual dose. Opium's desirability and lethality have led to repeated cycles of addiction and avoidance. Typically, the cycle begins because some entrepreneur figures out a new formulation of opium that allegedly eliminates the risk. Consumers buy the story and start using. Eventually, everyone figures out that the new opioid is just as deadly as the old opioids. That realization doesn't help the addicts, but new addictions decline and opioids fall out of fashion, at least for a while.

In 1676, the London physician Thomas Sydenham combined opium and alcohol to promote a wonder drug called laudanum that reduced pain with allegedly little risk. A quarter century later, Dr. John Jones was bemoaning the drug's terrible effects in *The Mysteries of Opium Reveal'd*. He noted the "inability or listlessness to do any things except it be while the Opium operates," but warned that quitting opium could lead to "intolerable . . . anxieties," and even a "miserable death."

In 1804, the German pharmacist Friedrich Sertürner separated an alkaloid that he named morphine from opium. He hoped, with little evidence, that morphine would be safe. Merck sold the drug commercially, and Sertürner himself became an addict, as did thousands of soldiers during the Civil War. In 1872, the *Annual Report of the State Board of Health of Massachusetts* perpetuated the lie that morphine was "free from the more objectionable properties of opium," but also reported that a state assayer found that "among the most dangerous preparations of morphia are those now prescribed and sold by uneducated or villainous individuals as so-called 'cures' for persons afflicted with the uncontrollable appetite for opium."

By the 1880s, morphine had proved itself a path toward addiction and death. Chemists, like Pierre-Jean Robiquet, had long searched for a safer opioid. Robiquet discovered codeine in Paris in 1832. Sixty years later, Felix Hoffmann was trying to produce codeine when he created a more powerful form of morphine, which Bayer would sell as Heroin. Bayer claimed that "Heroin is completely devoid of the unpleasant and toxic effects of opium derivatives." In 1900, the *Boston Medical and Surgical Journal* (the forerunner of the *New England Journal of Medicine*) contained the note that Heroin "possesses many advantages over morphine as a respiratory sedative," especially an "absence of danger of acquiring the habit." Heroin was marketed as a cough suppressant and to ease childbirth, but it was obviously both deadly and addictive. Bayer did better with Felix Hoffmann's other painkiller: aspirin.

For almost eighty years, experience with heroin soured American doctors on opioids. Heroin had a market, but it was illegal. The police forces of the US and Europe were not strong enough to block the flow of the drug entirely, although individual drug rings could be disrupted. The French Connection that processed Turkish opium in Marseilles and shipped it to the US was broken up in the early 1970s. But Afghanistan and Southeast Asia proved to be equally adept at growing poppies for export to the US market.

Big cities like New York and Miami were the natural entry point for imported drugs. Dense urban markets, like the one in Tompkins Square Park, made it easier to sell and avoid detection. The presence of heroin addicts in the cities of the US and Europe during the 1970s and 1980s then proved to be even deadlier when AIDS appeared.

Transmitting AIDS is much harder than transmitting COVID-19, which is why it never posed the same existential threat to cities. In urban America, the disease's spread was most terrible before it was understood, during an age in which people didn't realize that unsafe sex wasn't safe. Drug users also didn't know that sharing needles helped spread the bloodborne illness.

Unfortunately, sharing needles is a very efficient way to spread HIV. After sharing roughly one hundred needles with someone who is HIV positive, a person has a 50 percent chance of becoming HIV positive themselves. Scott County, Indiana, a patch in the southeastern part of the state, was the center of an HIV outbreak in 2014 because one addict had HIV and needle sharing was common. Roughly 1 percent of the county population developed HIV. The situation became so bad that the conservative Republican governor and later vice president, Mike Pence, approved a needle exchange program.

Consequently, heroin abuse became an accomplice to the AIDS epidemic. The advocates of drug legalization can well argue that if heroin were legal there would have been far less needle sharing. Yet the tragic story of the post-1995 opioid pandemic makes it hard to believe that we can ever tolerate the deaths that might come with widespread opioid use. Deaths from opioids are fewer in countries that have decriminalized narcotics, like Portugal and Switzerland. But even in these places, opioid deaths remain a scourge.

The Coming of OxyContin

In 1995, Purdue Pharma received approval to sell OxyContin, the latest supposedly low-risk opioid. OxyContin's alleged safety came from two features. First, the drug had a time-release "Contin" system that would moderate the size of the dose and consequently the degree of dependence. Second, OxyContin used oxycodone, which had less of a history of abuse in the US. The fondness of prominent Nazis for oxycodone had perhaps reduced its appeal in America. Before telling the OxyContin story, we must note that one of us (Cutler) has been involved as an expert witness on behalf of counties and states in litigation against opioid manufacturers, distributors, and dispensers.

The path of OxyContin began in Brooklyn in 1913 with the birth of Arthur Sackler, who almost epitomizes urban upward mobility. Sackler's parents were immigrants. He worked his way through college and medical school, partially as a copywriter for an ad agency that specialized in medical products. Sackler was a successful doctor, but his real genius was in marketing. Along with his two brothers, Sackler bought Purdue in 1952 and revolutionized drug sales starting in the 1950s with "detailing [visits to doctors' offices to persuade them to prescribe the drug], free samples, free food and drink, flashy journal advertising and mailings."

Marketing was also the magic behind Purdue's opioid machine. To sell OxyContin, one Fall River, Massachusetts, doctor received more than six hundred visits from Purdue after 2008 and a "consulting contract worth up to $48,000 to promote Purdue opioids." That doctor allegedly prescribed 180,000 Purdue opioid pills, worth more than $1.4 million.

Effective marketing often skirts the strictest rules of truthfulness. To woo physicians, Purdue promoted a 1980 letter to the *New England Journal of Medicine* noting that among "11,882 patients who received at least one narcotic preparation, there were only four cases of reasonably well documented addiction in patients who had no history of addiction." The problem was that this was for highly supervised inpatients. Yet Purdue represented it as a general indication of safety. In a 1998 video, a doctor argues that opioids "should be used much more than they are for patients in pain" because "in fact, the rate of addiction among pain patients who are treated by doctors is much less than one percent."

The alleged safety of OxyContin was proved to be a lie in less than five years. Users started crushing time-release tablets to get the full dose of oxycodone at once. As the number of pills increased, so did the number of fatalities. The death rate from drug overdoses in the US rose from below 5 per 100,000 in 1990, despite the crack epidemic, to over 15 per 100,000 in 2015.

This new drug wave was entirely legal. Thus, the urban drug market was somewhat less important—though it did smooth the flow from those with prescriptions to those without. Instead, the first wave of opioid deaths occurred in more depressed parts of rural America. The National Drug Intelligence Center report of 2001 found that "the Pike County, Kentucky, Coroner reported 19 Oxycontin-related deaths during the calendar year 2000." In July 2001, *The New York Times* published "The Alchemy of OxyContin," which reported that "the earliest reported cases of OxyContin abuse were in rural Maine, rust-belt counties in western Pennsylvania and eastern Ohio and the Appalachian areas of Virginia, West Virginia and Kentucky."

Policy makers started to crack down on the legal opioid market. In 2003, the FDA warned Purdue that "your advertisements thus grossly overstate the safety profile of OxyContin," and that "failure to respond to this letter may result in regulatory action, including seizure or injunction, without further notice." That same year, the DEA called for the "rapid reformulation" of OxyContin to "reduce the abuse of the product, particularly by injection." Later that decade, state governments began prescription drug monitoring programs to enable physicians to learn the number of prescriptions that their patients were receiving. States added eighty-one new controlled substance laws between 2006 and 2012. Lawsuits began to target Purdue Pharma, along with other opioid manufacturers.

In August 2010, OxyContin was reformulated to reduce the potential for abuse. Physicians started prescribing opioids less, especially to new patients. Overall shipments of legal opioids fell by 27 percent from 2010 to 2017.

But these reforms could not end the opioid epidemic, because people were addicted and illegal suppliers were ready to replace pharmacies. One third of opioid users switched to other drugs after OxyContin was reformulated. Of those who specified a new drug, 70 percent named heroin. Initially, an almost corporate system developed to supply heroin shipped out of Mexico, where buyers called dealers, who then delivered heroin on demand.

A few years later, a much cheaper factory-produced alternative started being shipped out of East Asia. Fentanyl is fully synthetic and far more potent than heroin. As illegal drugs are less predictable in their strength and purity than legal drugs, they are more likely to lead to accidental overdose. Fentanyl is so concentrated that it can be shipped via US mail and is almost impossible to catch. The tremendous narcotic power in fentanyl made it both an ideal drug to smuggle and a leading cause of overdose deaths.

As opioids shifted from a largely legal market to a largely illegal market, opioid deaths became more urban. Prior to 2005, urban areas experienced a higher drug overdose rate than rural areas. During the decade from 2005 to 2015, that reversed; rural counties that got hooked on opioids, thanks to their doctors' prescriptions, surged past urban counties in their overdose death rates. After 2016, urban areas became deadlier once again. The fentanyl gap between urban and rural America is not as large as the urban-rural gap in crack cocaine once was, but it is still significant.

Opioids also increase America's health inequality, as opioid overdose deaths are three times higher for those with only a high school degree relative to those with a college degree. The less educated work in more physically demanding jobs, and suffer more pain in their backs, joints, and muscles. Even standing on one's feet all day, something required of few Americans with advanced degrees, can create lasting pain, especially if one is carrying around extra pounds. The hope that OxyContin would create an escape from that physical pain made it appear a godsend for the working poor. It proved to be a curse.

Low levels of life satisfaction—despair—can also leave some people looking for outs, and opioids are one such out. Across individuals and countries, more income is associated with more happiness and life satisfaction. The connection between unhappiness and rising mortality, especially among lower-income prime-aged American males, has led economists Anne Case and Angus Deaton to collectively refer to opioid overdoses, suicides, and alcohol-related liver disease as "deaths of despair."

The urban supply of illegal opioids and prevalence of despair made both cities and the poor disproportionately vulnerable to opioid overdoses during the COVID-19 pandemic. The Centers for Disease Control and Prevention has yet to release its numbers for the year 2020, but preliminary reports suggest that the number of overdose deaths will reach a new high. According to one article, "stresses related to the COVID-19 pandemic, such as economic strains, as well as COVID-19—related isolation and other factors hindering treatment and support for people with substance use issues, may have contributed to the current rise in overdose deaths." Addiction to opioids is a source of physical and mental vulnerability that makes pandemic even deadlier.

Illegal drug use affects cities in other ways as well. The crack cocaine epidemic of the 1980s and 1990s led to high murder rates, as rival gangs fought over cocaine territory. High crime rates caused people to flee cities, which resulted in a lower tax base, which led to an increased fiscal burden on remaining residents and a further round of urban flight. The long sentences imposed for drug crimes generally, and particularly for crack cocaine, helped spur the massive increase in incarceration that tore apart urban neighborhoods. We will return to these issues in chapter 9. Fortunately, the opioid overdose epidemic is not as violent as the crack epidemic and has not led to the same burst in mass imprisonment.

Reducing Deceit through Better Incentives

There are many culprits in the opioid epidemic. The federal government not only permitted the prescribing of OxyContin after 1995 but actually subsidized its use through public health insurance programs, including Medicare and Medicaid, that did not restrict utilization. Environmental conditions mattered too. Physical pain, which is disproportionately rural, and low levels of life satisfaction, which are more common in some cities, predict opioid use.

However, it is hard not to put much of the blame for the opioid crisis on

Purdue Pharma itself and the companies that imitated it, for their misleading campaign of deceit and addiction. Along with them are the distributors and dispensers of opioids, who did not fulfill their obligations to guard against improper use. If actions by these firms had been more appropriate, then the opioid epidemic would have been nowhere near as deadly.

Sadly, the prioritization of profits over public health is an old story. Big tobacco, as well, tried to hide the health costs of cigarettes for decades. In response to landmark studies in the early 1950s showing that cigarette smoking was associated with lung cancer, tobacco companies set up a phony Tobacco Institute Research Committee (TIRC) to search for the truth about smoking and health. Alas, several decades of no doubt arduous research by the TIRC failed to solve the issue. Even in the early 2000s, most tobacco company CEOs would not admit under oath in congressional hearings that smoking caused cancer.

The same pattern may have played out with food manufacturers. The industry and its representatives obfuscated the dangers of sugar and obesity for years, pushing instead the idea that fat and cholesterol were the causes of heart disease. Meat producers have used their political clout to water down recommendations to eat less beef and pork. The makers of electronic cigarettes have been accused of hiding information about nicotine content and addictiveness, and illegally marketing to teens.

Most profit-seeking companies will try to overstate the benefits of their products and understate any hidden costs, like the risks of addiction and death. We cannot hope to eliminate greed from the human condition. And we recognize that much good can come from pursuit of a dollar. Adam Smith, the father of economics, famously wrote that "it is not from the benevolence of the butcher, the brewer, or the baker, that we can expect our dinner, but from their regard to their own interest."

Yet, the incentive to mislead is particularly pernicious in the case of addictive goods and goods that harm health. If a firm misleads a consumer into buying a defective television, the TV can be returned and the money taken elsewhere. If a firm misleads a person into using a health-harming product, the health damage may be irreversible. The chance of permanent harm is especially acute when the product is addictive. In that case, lasting damage may result from even fleeting malfeasance. Opioid manufacturers claim that they do not bear responsibility for deaths from heroin and illegal fentanyl since they do not produce those products. But for many users, it was the legal drugs that led people to become addicted and ultimately to transition into illegal drug use.

We have a system of tort law that allows customers to sue for deceit, but the incentives for liability seem too weak to stop companies from selling addictive and deadly products. To date, penalties for opioid malfeasance have been a small fraction of the profits made from that misconduct. The ratio of cigarette penalties to cigarette profits is even lower. With those incentives, firms are rational to hide the truth, hope their deceit is not discovered, and pay a fine if it is.

One possible reform is to increase the damage payments so that they exceed the profits made from the misconduct. At the individual level, the possibility of jail time for corporate leaders might have an even larger impact. If a drug dealer can be sentenced to jail for illegally selling OxyContin on the street, then perhaps a pharmaceutical CEO ought to be jailed for illegally promoting the same drug.

The case for penalizing deceit is particularly strong when not only the user but also those nearby suffer from the drug. Smoking harms nonsmokers who share their air. The World Health Organization estimates that 1 percent of all the deaths in the world from all causes were related to secondhand smoke in 2004. One in four motor vehicle accidents in the US involves an alcohol-impaired driver. And excessive opioid use helps spread HIV.

Why Does Education
Protect against Disease?

In a sense, obesity is far more understandable than being thin. Throughout human history, people have derived pleasure from consuming sweet, salty, and fatty foods. Our bodies have evolved to eat whenever food is available; who knows when it will next be plentiful? The residents of Brownsville may not be able to afford a Park Avenue co-op, but during normal years, they can afford plenty of fare that many (including us) find delicious, including pizza, ice cream, and fast food. Quite reasonably, they choose to consume those affordable luxuries. The weird thing is the Upper East Siders who abstain, either because they want to look sleek or because they actually care about their health. It takes a lot of vanity, education, or self-control to convince oneself to forgo that second chocolate chip cookie.

As educators, we certainly hope that schooling can generate a well of skepticism about product claims. As social scientists, we know that education is associated with longer life expectancies and healthier behavior. We suspect that for many educated people (including ourselves), healthier behavior is driven partially by a desire not to seem weak-willed or foolish, rather than greater knowledge about health or any real moral virtue. After all, how could a health economist ever play down being spotted with a cigarette?

But whatever the cause, smoking, excessive drinking, obesity, illegal drug use, and unsafe sex all decline with years of education. Schooling also increases the odds of wearing a seat belt, having a smoke detector at home, having a radon detector, testing for lead paint, having a mammogram or Pap smear (among women), having a colonoscopy, receiving a flu vaccine, and taking recommended medications.

In some areas, education's impact seems to have little or nothing to do with greater knowledge about risky behavior. There is virtually no one in the population who doesn't know that smoking is harmful, that excess weight is bad for health, and that having a designated nondrinking driver reduces motor vehicle accidents. Rather, education seems to matter for other reasons. Education may increase mental bandwidth to change behavior or increase the income necessary to purchase health-improving goods. Years of schooling means having more experience making sacrifices today for benefits tomorrow and developing more trust in the scientific process. Whatever the reason, cities that wish to improve their health should stress greater education for all their citizens.

Moreover, education has spillover effects; even lower-income people have healthier behaviors when they live in areas with more college graduates. At least part of this is a result of public policy. In New York City, the tax rate on cigarettes is $5.85 per pack, including both state and local taxes. In Indiana, the tax is $1 per pack. Restrictions on smoking indoors, in bars and restaurants, and in other settings are also more common in states where there are more college graduates.

Peer effects are important as well. When some people quit smoking, that has a spillover effect on others. People are more likely to smoke or drink with company than if they are alone. If one's coworkers do not smoke, a new employee is less likely to take it up. If one's peers have already quit, managing withdrawal may be a little easier.

Protection from the Pandemic

During a pandemic, a city, even a country, is only as healthy as its sickest group. A global plague reminds us that addressing health behaviors is as much a matter of civic need as it is of personal compassion.

We can try to stop pandemics from starting at all, by keeping away from sources of novel virus strains and improving the sewers and sanitation in developing world cities. We can work to slow the spread of contagion across cities with smarter quarantine regulations and rapid-fire adoption of social distancing. We can fight pandemics medically with vaccines and cures. But the ultimate battle occurs within the human body itself, where the disease is fought by the immune system. Robust pre-pandemic health makes surviving almost any plague easier.

Behavioral change is possible. Half the people in the United States who ever smoked have quit, despite the fact that nicotine is among the most addictive substances known. Opioid addiction has declined in some areas—especially where treatment has become more available—though sadly, deaths will remain high for many years because of the large stock of addicts and seemingly unstoppable supply of fentanyl. Behaviors are not immutable; they are just difficult to change. A central challenge for cities is to make that happen.

Reducing harmful health behaviors is also important because those behaviors divert funds that could be used for other services. The medical conditions that account for the largest increase in spending over time directly result from adverse health behaviors: heart disease, some cancers, and musculoskeletal pain. To fix this will require addressing the medical system as well. We turn to that next.

Chapter 5

WHY DID SO MUCH HEALTH-CARE SPENDING PRODUCE SO LITTLE HEALTH?

Preventing pandemics is inherently a government responsibility. Communal actions must be taken, people must be quarantined, and responses must be coordinated. The public sector response was vital in fourteenth-century Ragusa and nineteenth-century Philadelphia, and it remains so today. Yet while America has built a public health insurance system that spends over $3 trillion annually on medical care, it never built a system to fully protect and promote the health of the public. Even in recent years, as the need for pandemic preparation became increasingly apparent, powerful insiders in the medical and insurance sectors combined with public dysfunction to make it nearly impossible to reorient the direction of the medical system.

Over 350,000 Americans died from COVID-19 in 2020. Adjusted for the higher US population, this death rate was more than double that of Germany or Canada, even though Germany spends one third less than the US on medical care and Canada spends half as much. The US death rate was thirty-three times higher than the rate in Japan and fifty times higher than the rate in South Korea. Singapore and Taiwan collectively lost fewer than 40 people to COVID-19 in 2020; the city of Lubbock, Texas, with one one-hundredth the population of those two countries, had ten times more deaths. And Asian cities were disadvantaged relative to US cities because they are much closer to China and thus more likely to have received infected visitors before the risk became apparent.

A central theme of this book is that the vulnerability of large, dense, interconnected cities requires an effective, proactive public sector: a shared strength that serves everyone. That strength begins with the right objectives and depends on accountable leaders who are empowered with sufficient resources. America's health-care system shows what happens when there is a decentralized health system that is incredibly well endowed but has misidentified objectives and little, if any, empowered leadership.

Much of the blame for America's poor performance during the pandemic has focused on President Trump and his administration. This is appropriate. The Trump administration broke every rule of crisis management during the COVID-19 outbreak. But that story is also incomplete. Personalizing the problem exonerates the broader health system of responsibility for the failure. In reality, the health system failed as well.

Three aspects of health care suggest that even a better leader would have had difficulty managing COVID-19. First, America's health-care system focuses on private medical care, not public health. It worries about diseases that affect individual people, not the potential for an epidemic that envelops us all. Second, the system focuses on caring for the sick rather than promoting health. It encourages treatment of acute illness rather than prevention and spends vastly more on chronic than communicable diseases. Third, America is tolerant of enormous disparities in health care, as in everything else. While millions of Americans have superb medical insurance and live lifestyles that are as healthy as any German or Swiss, other Americans remain without any medical plan. These chinks in the armor are an invitation for pandemic illness.

This set of problems occurs in other countries as well, though typically to a lesser degree. Medical care systems in all countries are disproportionately focused on the treatment of individual disease over public health. But most countries have a stronger public health system than the US, especially the Asian countries that had so few COVID-19 deaths. All developed countries but the US have universal health insurance, which does something to reduce health inequities.

This chapter will not present a blueprint for fixing health care nor make the case for any specific reform—though we both have views on the topic and one of us (Cutler) has written two books on the subject. This book is not the place for the lengthy discussion that health-care reform needs. We will, however, talk about what governments must do to prevent pandemic illness: codify a stronger mission to protect the health of the nation against contagion and put in place operational ability commensurate with that task.

Health Care Is Sick

The underperformance of American health care during the COVID-19 crisis is symptomatic of longer-standing failures in the system. In a recent international survey of satisfaction with health care, the US ranked fourteenth out of eighteen countries. Far more Americans believe the US health-care system needs to be "completely rebuilt" in comparison with people in other nations, who are more likely to believe their medical system needs only "minor changes." Even the insured population in the US reports more dissatisfaction than the populations elsewhere. The US ranks last in life expectancy and last in infant mortality among the eleven wealthiest countries in the Organisation for Economic Co-operation and Development (OECD).

The one example of true American exceptionalism in health care is spending. The US spends $11,000 per person on medical care. The next-highest-spending country, Switzerland, spends under $8,000. The average among rich countries is closer to $6,000. The UK is under $5,000. Given that low level of spending, the British naturally worry far more about access and less about costs than do people in countries that spend more. All told, the US spends roughly $20,000 more per family on health care than do residents of other countries. A good share of the earnings growth received by the middle class is paying for health care, and not rent, material goods, or education. Legendary investor Warren Buffett has called health care a "tapeworm on the economic system." The worm gets bigger by the year.

This disparate spending might be justifiable if US health care were materially better than elsewhere, but it is not. Chronic diseases such as high blood pressure, high cholesterol, and diabetes are less well controlled in the US. Acute illness is treated more intensively in the US, but outcomes are not better. There is no area of medicine where the US is obviously superior to our closest comparators.

If one wants to understand the dysfunction in health care, the best way to do so is to follow the money. In any system, how the money flows determines how the system behaves. Let us take the case of cardiovascular illness—care for people with heart disease, strokes, or related ailments. If a person has a heart attack, rushes to the hospital, and has a stent inserted, then Medicare pays about $15,000. If the person is insured by a private company, the fee might be twice as much. The procedure itself takes about an hour, with a night or two in the hospital.

Now roll the tape backward and think about what could have prevented the heart attack. Many patients with heart attacks have a history of high blood pressure or high cholesterol. An office visit to monitor these conditions (perhaps half an hour) will generate only a $100 fee for the doctor. And should the doctor notice that the patient has not reordered or filled their

medication prescriptions and decide to call the patient to give them a re-
minder, there is no reimbursement at all. Reminding a patient to use medication is not "doctoring"—though it does save lives. It is unsurprising that
virtually every medical center has advanced cardiac capabilities, but few
doctors spend the resources to ensure that their patients take their medications.

The American system of providing high reimbursements for more intensive care is not the result of a well-reasoned decision; rather, it occurred by
happenstance. Early in the twentieth century, doctors had fees for different
services; naturally, more intensive care was reimbursed more highly than less
intensive care. A price list for a hospital in the 1930s shows a charge between
$4 and $10 per day for a room, depending on the number of people in the
room and the location in the hospital. Operating rooms cost $7.50 for minor
surgery, $17.50 for major surgery, and $20 for emergency evening surgery.
The costs of giving birth were $40 to $70, depending how long the mother
stayed and how many other women were in the room. At the time, a routine
physician visit might cost about $5. It typically took place in the patient's
house.

Those prices were paid out of pocket. The first fledgling health insurance
plan appeared in 1929, when Baylor Hospital (now Baylor University Medical Center) in Texas realized that they would need to care for people during
the Great Depression regardless of their ability to pay. To limit their total
costs, they set up a prepayment plan to finance care. For fifty cents per
month, people were guaranteed up to three weeks in the hospital if they
needed it.

During World War II, employers used health insurance to get around
wage and price controls. The federal government capped cash compensation
but not employee benefits. Employers could attract workers by offering them
extras, like health care. After the war, the tax code was changed to exclude
health insurance from taxation. Since wages and salaries are taxed but health

insurance is not, employees save tax dollars when they get their health care at work.

Private insurers generally paid the prices that physicians and hospitals charged their uninsured patients. Car insurance companies didn't try to fix the price of a Buick. Why should a health insurance company try to fix the price of a surgery? Insurers concentrated on risk pooling—enrolling as many people as possible and using the premiums from the healthy to pay for the care of the sick. But as more people were insured, the prices charged became less meaningful. If the insurance companies were going to pay for everything, then the hospital could get away with higher prices.

Thomas Jefferson's Welfare State

Those higher prices, coupled with the growing recognition that medicine could cure the sick, motivated a massive commitment to health insurance for the elderly and the poor. Through Medicare and Medicaid, the federal government spends enormous amounts of *money* on medical treatment yet has very little *control* over the system. The largest single budgetary agency in the US government is the Centers for Medicare and Medicaid Services (CMS), which runs those two programs. The budget of CMS is nearly $1 trillion annually. This budget is administered by a mere 6,000 people, which means that the average employee is overseeing $167 million of public spending. By contrast, the US military spends less money ($732 billion in 2019) and employs 1.3 million people. The federal commitment in health care is almost entirely to pay the bills, while the funding of the military reflects robust executive power.

This divergence between dollars and control is no accident; the political party that crafted America's safety net was also the party of Thomas Jefferson and states' rights. Throughout the nineteenth century, the champions of big government were Alexander Hamilton's Federalists, the Whigs who adored tariffs and infrastructure, and the Republicans who imposed national control on the rebellious Southern states. Their opponents, including both Thomas Jefferson and Andrew Jackson, favored a quasi-egalitarian libertarianism (at least among whites) and opposed federal power, which they saw as primarily helping rich insiders. Their twentieth-century heir, Woodrow Wilson, titled his 1912 election manifesto *The New Freedom* and railed against "a small number of men who control the government to get favors from the government." He proclaimed that "I don't want a lot of experts to sit down behind closed doors in Washington and play Providence to me."

In that election, there was a genuine vision of a centralized Hamiltonian approach to health care. Teddy Roosevelt's Bull Moose Party platform called for "the union of all the existing agencies of the Federal Government dealing with the public health into a single national health service" that would have "such as additional powers as may be necessary to enable it to perform efficiently such duties in the protection of the public from preventable disease" and support "the promotion of vital statistics and the extension of the registration area of such statistics, and co-operation with the health activities of the various States and cities of the Nation." Roosevelt never got his wish.

Channeling Thomas Jefferson came as easily to Harry Truman as it did Woodrow Wilson, not just with boosterish phrases like "As long as we remain free, the spirit of Thomas Jefferson lives in America," but also with a more serious commitment to a small central government: "I am determined that stringent economy shall govern all peacetime operations of the Government." When Truman called for national health insurance in 1945, he asked that "the Federal Government should provide financial and other assistance for the construction of needed hospitals," but "not construct or operate these hospitals." He wanted "more generous grants to the States than are provided under present laws for public health services," but not an empowered federal public health agency.

Truman wanted everyone to have "ready access to all necessary medical, hospital and related services," through an "expansion of our existing compulsory social insurance system." Yet he strongly rejected "socialized medicine" and promised that "our voluntary hospitals and our city, county and state general hospitals" could "retain their administrative independence" so that doctors would not "work as employees of government." He wanted spending without public management, and that is ultimately what happened to America's health care.

Truman's vision soldiered on. The 1960 Democratic platform ambitiously affirmed "the right to adequate medical care," which would take the form of "medical care benefits for the aged as part of the time-tested Social Security Insurance system." In that election, "there was probably no issue on which Kennedy as a candidate was more solemnly pledged" than health care. Again, this was presented as a Jeffersonian right, not as Hamiltonian public action, and as a "right," this commitment didn't come with strings. The platform disparaged any attempt to limit costs by providing care only to the needy: "we reject any proposal which would require such citizens to submit to the indignity of a means test—a 'pauper's oath.'" A "means test" could have meant more spending for outsiders, but that isn't the way to win elections.

In 1962, Congress took up the King-Anderson Bill, which followed Truman's formula of inserting health care into Social Security. The American Medical Association went into overdrive to fight what it called "the most deadly challenge ever faced by the medical profession." One particularly feisty New Jersey physician, J. Bruce Henriksen, spearheaded a movement of doctors who would "refuse to participate in the care of patients under the provision of the King-Anderson Bill" while they would "continue to care for the medically indigent, young and old, as we have in the past." The Senate killed King-Anderson by a narrow margin in 1962, despite the fact that Kennedy had "swung his present great personal popularity into the campaign for the bill."

After President Kennedy's death, President Lyndon Johnson placed health care high on his priority list. This involved working with "the most powerful man in Washington," Wilbur Mills, the Arkansas Democrat who was chairman of the powerful House Ways and Means Committee. Johnson and Mills were both legislative masterminds, and they were both Southern Democrats. As one political scientist writes about the Southerners who led America's legislatures after World War II: "the concern for states' rights was prominent—yet these Southern leaders would prove willing to subordinate this principle repeatedly in order to advance their substantive policy priority for public assistance."

In March 1964, Johnson nudged Mills on the King-Anderson health bill: "There is not anything that has happened in my six months or that will happen in my whole term in my judgment that will mean more to us as a party or to me or you as individuals than this legislation." He still deferred to Mills's fiscal acumen and legislative might: "if you don't know more about ways and means than I do, then you hadn't been applying yourself and I know you have." Mills listened, particularly after Johnson won a landslide election in 1964. As Mills later told an interviewer, Johnson "had espoused it [Medicare] in his campaign, you know, and here he was elected by a 2 to 1 vote, which was a pretty strong endorsement of it, I thought." Consequently, "I thought the time had come to pass it."

We can never know how much of the limited, purely financial structure of Medicare and Medicaid reflected a limited-government Jeffersonian tradition or the opposition to government controls from entrenched doctor and insurer groups—the American Medical Association and private insurers. Perhaps without these opponents, President Johnson and Wilbur Mills would have embraced the model of the British National Health Service that began operation in 1948, or the Swedish system that followed in 1955, or the Canadian system being enacted about that time. Whatever the cause, the outcome was a health insurance system that did not cover the majority of Americans and that sharply limited the government's room to maneuver.

Wilbur Mills put together a "three-layer cake" of a bill: the King-Anderson plan for hospital cost insurance with his own Kerr-Mills law's medical aid for the poor and a new element that would provide insurance for non-hospital doctor's bills. The bill sailed through the House and the Senate. Johnson signed it into law in Independence, Missouri, in the Harry S. Truman Library. President Truman became the first American enrolled in Medicare.

The Jeffersonian model of a safety net meant that the government was there to pay, not to decide on appropriate health care. Medicare and Medicaid are open-ended entitlements, with a commitment to cover any "medically necessary or appropriate" therapy. These programs built on the existing private system of paying more for intensive, generally curative care. This safety net did not expand the federal government's remit into protecting the nation's health, nor did it empower the federal government to select investments that yielded the biggest health benefits per dollar. The flaws in that design have only become more obvious over time, and yet the political power of well-organized senior citizens alongside America's overall political malaise have made Medicare weak, expensive, and seemingly impossible to touch.

Unsurprisingly, medical spending rose more rapidly under Medicare and Medicaid than projections at the time suggested. Ironically, the high cost of Medicare moved even Wilbur Mills, a famous fiscal conservative, into an alliance with Ted Kennedy to push America toward a single-payer system. But Mills was somewhat too fond of the bottle and an Argentine stripper named Fanne Foxe. The two were caught driving drunk at 2:00 a.m. Foxe tried to flee by jumping into the Tidal Basin, ironically right in front of the

Jefferson Memorial. Mills resigned from the Ways and Means Committee two months later. Single payer never happened.

Why Does America's
Health Care Cost So Much?

In the early 1960s, around the time Medicare and Medicaid were enacted, US medical spending was a bit higher than in other countries, but not much more so. In 1960, the US and Canada both spent about 4 percent of national income on health, slightly above other rich countries. As other nations put in place the controls that come with a universal system, a gap developed. US expenditures rose to the top of the pack. By the 1980s, the US was spending 2 percent more of its GDP on health care than Canada. Today, the US-Canada medical spending gap is over 6 percent of GDP.

Where does the US spend all its health-care money? One out of every four dollars in the US medical system goes to administration, which costs twice as much as cardiovascular disease and three times as much as cancer. In Canada, the share devoted to administration is less than half as large.

Every doctor's office and hospital in the country has a wealth of people whose sole job it is to help with the paperwork. Is the patient covered for those services by that insurer? Enormous energy is spent keeping clinical records. Did the patient have anemia? What about a history of diabetes? Each insurer requires separate information, so forms are filled out on an insurer-specific basis. Before payment is approved, the insurer might request documentation as to whether the doctor tried the cheaper drug before prescribing the expensive one. If the service is approved, payment comes later, and keeping track of the money involves even more administrative time. Insurers employ their own army of bureaucrats, who determine which services are covered every time they are requested and which require prior authorization, which drugs are preferred on the formulary and which are not, and whether the amount the doctor wants to bill is reasonable or too high.

Canada avoids this paperwork by having simpler rules. The amount of revenue that hospitals receive is set in advance. With that money, hospitals are expected to treat everyone who needs aid. No individual bills are filed. Physicians are paid per service, like in the US, but there is less haggling over price and authorization. The government sets the rate paid per service and all physicians are reimbursed that amount—a decidedly non-Jeffersonian level of federal control. If spending needs to be lowered, the government can unilaterally reduce what is paid to physicians. If the use of a particular technology is deemed to be excessive—for example, there are too many MRI scans being performed—the government will not authorize additional scanners to be acquired.

Canada's rules can be heavy-handed, but they come at much lower administrative costs. Our point is not that the Canadian system is inherently better or worse than the American one; our point is simply that the single-payer model is administratively cheaper.

The second way that the US spends more is by paying more for the same service. One famous paper examining international medical spending exclaimed, "It's the Prices, Stupid." Prescription drugs are the most notorious example. A vial of insulin costs ten times more in the US than in Canada. Some Americans die because they choose to limit insulin when they cannot afford it. Pharmaceutical companies charge more in the US than in other countries because they can.

In the United Kingdom, the National Institute for Health and Care Excellence (NICE) sets a limit on what it will pay for each new drug, which is again not very Jeffersonian; pharmaceutical companies must price below that level or they cannot sell. Since most drugs cost very little to produce once they have been developed, companies can make a profit even with a low price per user. In contrast, the US has no central negotiator. If one insurer does not cover a new drug but its competitors do, then the stingy insurer will lose customers to its rival. The same is true for physicians. Canadian doctors can't charge more than the moderate fees allotted by the government and cannot bill patients privately for services covered by Canada's Medicare. In the US, if a provider balks at an insurer's price, it can make it up with patients from other insurers.

The cost of the US system does have benefits. Pharmaceutical companies argue that they need the returns from high prices in the US to finance research and development for new drugs. Paying doctors more encourages top students to apply for medical school. Because highly educated people in the US earn relatively more than highly educated people in other countries, if the US did not pay its doctors enough to match, more top students would switch to other occupations. Everything in economics involves tradeoffs, and this is no exception.

The third difference between the US and Canada lies in the way that medicine is practiced in the two countries. Americans do not see the doctor more than Canadians. In fact, physician visits and hospitalizations per person are lower in the US than in most other rich countries. One reason that pandemics pose greater risk for the US is that there are fewer hospital beds per capita than in other wealthy nations.

But when people do receive care in the US, that care is more intensive. With the same report of back pain, people in the US are more likely to receive an MRI. They are more likely to get an opioid and more likely to get back surgery. Cardiologists in the US are more likely to insert stents in people with mild chest pain. In Canada, diet and exercise are the more common prescription. These patterns just follow the money. US physicians earn more from inserting stents than physicians do in other countries.

All these differences are natural outgrowths of the way medical care is set up. The line from Lyndon Johnson and Wilbur Mills to today is relatively straight.

Insurance and the
Incentive to Innovate

Expanding insurance coverage in the 1950s and 1960s led to more use of medical care. That was part of the goal. The unanticipated side effect was the innovation avalanche that came from the interaction of insurance that promised to pay, scientists that wanted to cure, and companies that wanted to earn. In hindsight it is clear, but in foresight it was not: if insurers stand ready to pay for any beneficial new medical procedure, then entrepreneurs will produce a robust stream of new pills, devices, and procedures.

There is good and bad in such incentivized innovation. Perhaps the most hopeful part of the fight against COVID-19 was the explosion of new vaccine candidates in 2020. Producing a vaccine is often not a moneymaker; the vaccine is given to healthy people, who are generally not willing to pay as much for prevention as sick people are for treatment—though COVID is perhaps an exception. As a result, single-payer countries will sometimes commit to buy vaccines before they even exist, to spur invention. In July 2020, no one was surprised when the United Kingdom "signed deals for 90 million doses of promising coronavirus vaccines that are being developed."

A far more significant precedent was set in the same month, when the US government signed a contract with Pfizer and BioNTech to pay $1.95 billion for 100 million vaccine doses, deliverable in December 2020. In the face of a catastrophic pandemic, the US government essentially adopted the single-payer model by committing to provide free vaccines to ordinary citizens that were bought at a centrally negotiated price. As we write in January

2021, vaccines are being made available in the US and UK, though the pace in the US is much slower than was planned. The faster distribution of vaccines in the UK reflects the centralization of health-care responsibilities that became visible even in 1858, when Disraeli waxed poetic about sewers.

COVID-19 is not the only example of speed in vaccine development. The H1N1 vaccine of 2009 was developed with similar rapidity. The first case of H1N1 was detected in Mexico in March of that year; the first US case was diagnosed on April 15. By April 24, the H1N1 genome had been decoded. Mid-September saw the approval of four vaccines; a fifth was approved in November.

Prepaying for COVID-19 vaccines was an easy decision, because the social and economic value of those vaccines is enormous. The open-ended commitment of Medicare to pay for other forms of innovation has both costs and benefits. Billions gain from the generous incentives baked into the US medical system. Yet those incentives have also helped make American health care amazingly expensive.

Medical technology has changed the treatment of almost every health problem. Return to our example of heart attacks. In the late 1940s, when Harry Truman was pushing for national health insurance, the standard treatment for a heart attack was bed rest—six weeks in a hospital bed, followed by six months in bed at home. The theory was that strain on the heart would lead to additional harm. Coronary angiography was developed in the late 1950s, and this allowed physicians to image the heart muscle and determine how badly it was damaged. Fledgling efforts to bypass the occluded arteries ultimately proved successful in the 1960s. Medicare payment then helped coronary artery bypass surgery to become more common. In the early 1980s, physicians developed balloons to implant in occluded arteries. Inflating the balloon created a path for blood to flow to the heart. Wire mesh stents were then developed to keep the artery open. These surgical techniques cost more, but they also save lives.

The process of technical innovation happened in area after area of medicine. Indeed, the technological revolution of medical care led to the birth of entirely new specialties. In the early twentieth century, doctors were generalists who were expected to treat the sick, operate if appropriate, and attend deliveries. Today, there are forty specialties and eighty-seven subspecialties recognized by the American Board of Internal Medicine, and those specialists cost more. According to the physician recruiting and staffing firm Merritt Hawkins, emergency medicine specialists earn about $350,000 annually, dermatologists earn about $420,000, and orthopedic surgeons earn about $540,000 per year. The average doctor of internal medicine (the typical primary care physician for adults) earns about $250,000.

The value of more intensive care can be enormous. One of us (Cutler) wrote a book arguing that spending more on new therapies developed over time was worth it, because the spending improved health outcomes. The cardiac technologies noted above are a prime example. But technology can also be overused. In Canada, stents are inserted far less often than in the US and yet survival after a heart attack is no less common in Canada.

While innovations that generate new fees come fast and furious, the system has been slow to respond to unreimbursed needs, such as improving access to care. At the start of the COVID-19 epidemic, people were asked to stay home, and physicians were leery about bringing sick people to their offices. Thus, millions of medical care visits were cancelled. There is an obvious alternative to in-person visits: telemedicine. Video visits are straightforward for anyone with broadband service; phone calls are easier still. In response to COVID-19, an entire telemedicine industry was invented overnight. In no time, telemedicine became ubiquitous. Hooray for physicians for making this happen! But why did it take COVID-19 for people to be able to Skype with their doctors? The fact that tele-visits didn't pay was surely part of it.

Because of our open-ended, Jeffersonian commitment to medical care, the United States is unique in the extent of its bias toward expensive treatment. We accept that taxpayers will pay for health care without empowering representatives of those taxpayers to limit costs. Single-payer systems have their flaws, but at least the entity that does the spending decides how much to spend. Private insurance also finds it hard to cut costs. If one insurer cuts what it pays physicians or limits spending overall, then its enrollees suffer because their preferred doctors may refuse to treat them. Medicaid pays lower fees, and consequently one third of physicians do not accept new patients covered by Medicaid at all, and many of the rest accept only some Medicaid patients.

Over time, the unconstrained growth of medical spending became more problematic, particularly when the economy performed poorly, as it did after the two oil price shocks of the 1970s. Employment fell, the economy went into severe recession, and governments and businesses alike needed to cut spending.

The first attempts at cost control were relatively weak. Public and private insurers tried to limit physician charges to the "usual, customary, and reasonable" rates in the area. Over time, insurers set up systems to determine how much "doctoring" was involved in everything that happened to the patient. The more the doctoring, the higher the reimbursement. The federal government introduced such a system for hospitals in the 1980s and physicians in the 1990s. Private insurers generally followed the public approach, though the rate paid per medical service was higher in the private sector.

Such efforts controlled prices, but also created an administrative nightmare. Billions of dollars are spent determining exactly who is eligible for which services and how much will be paid for them. The painful bureaucratic effort lowers what each insurer must pay, but it was not enough.

Rationing Health Care
in the Land of the Free

The United States, like all countries, rations medical care. There, we have said it. We have used the R-word. The next time a politician tells you that the US should not have a single-payer system because it would involve rationing, stop listening and vow never to vote for them. The difference is not in *whether* countries ration medical care but in *how* they do so.

In single-payer countries, rationing is done at the aggregate level. Canadian hospitals live with a fixed aggregate budget and regulations that limit purchases of new equipment and operating room expansions. In the US, we use high prices to discourage care and ration the system's limited capacity. The US has no centralized form of rationing, but it rations health care nevertheless. Insurers try to get patients to use less care by charging them co-payments, which allegedly give patients more "skin in the game." To limit expensive branded drugs, patients can be charged as much as several thousand dollars for a month of pills, even though the cost of actually manufacturing the pills is negligible. An emergency department visit can also cost thousands.

One quarter of privately insured people in the US are in a "high deductible health plan" that makes them responsible for paying for the first few thousand dollars of care. The hope is that people in these plans will cut back on expensive, but unproductive, health care. Unfortunately, numerous studies show that people are bad at deciding which care is valuable and which is not. People certainly cut back when the cost of care is higher, but they cut back on less and more valuable care equally. Higher co-payments mean fewer discretionary imaging procedures (which are often not cost effective), but also fewer prescriptions that maintain low levels of cholesterol (which are extremely cost effective).

Another rationing method is to scrutinize doctors' actions and eliminate care that is deemed inappropriate. "Prior authorization" and "utilization management" are the phrases of art. If a physician recommends elective surgery, ensure first that medication therapy has been tried. What about physical therapy? There is so much that doctors can do, and thus so much that can be questioned. The typical insurer has a few thousand rules for prior authorization of medical services, and another few thousand for pharmaceuticals.

Health policy analysts endlessly debate the advantages and disadvantages of the centralized and decentralized rationing methods. Our point is not to choose among them. But whatever one feels abstractly about centralized and decentralized rationing, the pandemic era changes the calculus. In a pandemic, we never want people who might be infected to wait it out because they cannot afford the emergency room fee, or to not take their antibiotic (if the cause is bacterial) because of cost. In a pandemic world, one wants to lower the amount that individuals pay for care to protect us all.

Leadership and the COVID-19 Disaster

America's public response to COVID-19 was neither strong nor effective. The US was slow to recognize the extent of the problem, and consequently the country's borders were left open for far too long. America was slow to implement widespread testing, and never accepted the need to randomly test the asymptomatic. Even our expensive hospitals proved unprepared for the pandemic, despite the number of near misses that have regularly appeared as canaries in the coal mines.

By early January 2020, many observers saw that a COVID-19 epidemic was a real possibility. Both Taiwan and Singapore shut the flow of people from China. However, the Trump administration had pulled its infectious disease experts from China and dismantled the National Security Council unit focused on global pandemics. Travel to China was shut down on January 31, but travel continued to flow to and from Italy and other highly infected regions throughout the world.

Testing was an even bigger mess. By late January 2020, the World Health Organization had a functional test to detect COVID-19. However, the Centers for Disease Control and Prevention (CDC) decided to develop its own, fancier test. Where most tests, like the WHO's, focus on identifying two parts of the COVID-19 genome, the CDC added a third part to identify a wider family of coronaviruses (including SARS and MERS). This third part was unnecessary to identify COVID-19. The reagents in this third part also became contaminated—samples known to be free of COVID-19 came back positive for the virus. Fixing this took weeks; in the end, the CDC simply chose to ignore this third test.

But the impact of this delay was enormous. During this time, universities and private labs were not allowed to implement their own tests, further setting back knowledge of the disease's spread. An exasperated Anthony Fauci, director of the National Institute of Allergy and Infectious Diseases and a member of the administration's COVID-19 task force, told Congress: "The idea of anybody getting [tested] easily the way that people in other countries are doing it—we're not set up for that. Do I think we should be? Yes. But we're not."

Treating people who contracted COVID-19 was also hampered by poor preparation. Doctors and nurses need adequate supplies of protective equipment, such as masks and gowns, the training to know how to use them appropriately, rigorously enforced infection control measures, and cancellation of nonessential medical services such as elective surgery and routine physician visits. Yet US hospitals keep on hand only the level of personal protective equipment (PPE) and ventilators that they need on an ongoing basis. They assume that if they need more, they can buy it at the appropriate time. But in a pandemic, every institution is trying to buy PPE at once. Unless the market can produce more in total, not everyone can get it. The holdup was particularly great with COVID-19 because many of the PPE producers are in China and were either shut down or supplying the Chinese market.

The federal government neither procured more supplies nor did it reallocate equipment from less needy to more needy areas. The result was a black market for protective equipment: high prices and secret supplies going to the highest bidder. Many had no idea how to obtain the necessary PPE. Frontline caregivers in hard-hit areas wound up with inadequate protection. The same situation played out with ventilators and even the swabs and reagents needed to test people.

President Trump has rightly received much blame for the inchoate American response to the crisis. He was about as far from the calm competence that one would want, and voters punished him with electoral defeat, just as they once punished Herbert Hoover for his less-than-coherent response to the Great Depression. One academic paper concluded that "Trump would likely have won re-election if COVID-19 cases had been 5 percent lower."

But COVID-19 is not the first disaster that the United States has botched. In 2006, the nation watched in shock at the catastrophic failure to respond adequately to Hurricane Katrina. At the time, there was widespread condemnation of President Bush, just as the COVID-19 disaster has led to disparagement of President Trump. Yet the testimony given in 2006 by our colleagues "Dutch" Leonard and Arn Howitt remains relevant today: "Given the pre-existing conditions of preparation in the nation and in the region—infrastructure, capabilities, systems, and people—as of the middle of August 2005, and given what the storm was going to do, it is therefore important to realize that no one could have led the response to this storm in a way that could have produced a high performance . . . or even, perhaps, an adequate performance."

Howitt and Leonard were not trying to exculpate President Bush—and

President Trump's crisis management deserves to be condemned. But it is also important to depersonalize the problem. There is a natural tendency in politics to focus on the person in charge, and to think that if we just got a new leader, then things would be better. Howitt and Leonard were correctly emphasizing that switching the president does nothing—unless that change also comes with systemic investment in crisis management.

Good crisis leadership may seem like a magical charismatic art, like Horatius on the bridge defending ancient Rome or Joan of Arc hoisting the fleur-de-lis. But handling a hurricane requires planning far more than heroism. Often, crisis management requires delegating control to specialized leaders who have expertise and experience in similar crises. President Coolidge empowered Herbert Hoover during the Great Mississippi Flood of 1927 because Hoover had done a stellar job managing food aid to Belgium and elsewhere during and after World War I. Managing crises requires the hard administrative effort to design systems that work together when there is no time to waste on miscommunication. As Howitt and Leonard put it:

> First, agencies develop an array of capabilities in advance: They craft plans, design procedures, procure equipment, train responders and leaders, and practice carrying out operations. Second, they develop methods for rapidly designing response efforts that can adapt to novel events. Third, they organize and coordinate response actions in real time to manage the deployment of resources.

Examples of successful pre-disaster preparation abound. Our hometown of Boston has long rehearsed for mass-casualty events, which requires coordination among police, fire, emergency medical personnel, and hospitals. Consequently, when the marathon bombing occurred in April 2013, several hundred people were injured, but there were only three deaths. No one who made it to a hospital alive died.

A plague rolls out more slowly than a catastrophic flood or major terrorist attack, and that provides leaders with a bit more time to react. Yet a pandemic reaches deep into every household and social function, which places an even greater burden on the public response. The need to plan in advance is particularly crucial when a crisis moves like wildfire.

The Failure to Prepare for Pandemic

America's weak performance during the pandemic reflects our failure to preemptively invest in a robust public health system—the one that Teddy Roosevelt wanted and that could have done better to prevent and treat COVID-19. The state of Massachusetts allocates about $600 million annually for the Department of Public Health. In contrast, the largest private health-care provider in the state, Mass General Brigham, has a budget of nearly $14 billion. Before 2020, Massachusetts had no contact tracers on staff (no other state did either). When the pandemic began, it found them by partnering with an organization that works in Haiti and Lesotho.

While US medical spending gets whatever it needs, the public health infrastructure in the US hangs by a thread; even the smallest disruption can overload it. The budget of the Centers for Disease Control and Prevention is about $22 per person per year. The federal, state, and local public health system as a whole spends about $300 per person per year. This covers everything from monitoring infectious disease outbreaks and contact tracing to ensuring childhood vaccinations to designing obesity reduction programs. The Medicare program by itself spends eight times that amount, and Medicare is but one fifth of the nation's spending on medical services. By another metric, public health is the one area of health care in which Canada significantly outspends the US.

Spending little on public health might be sensible if public health dollars are ineffective, but the opposite is true. The Centers for Disease Control and Prevention is acknowledged as the world leader among public health agencies. Indeed, many of the most important health interventions of the past century have come from public health, including new vaccines, advances in water and food safety, safer cars and roads, and reduced tobacco use. If there is any part of government that seems to have earned additional spending, it would be public health.

The failure to fund public health is part of the larger problem that our private and public insurance programs are set up primarily to cover acute illness costs, not to prevent disease. A person with high cholesterol can be treated with diet, exercise, and medication. If they are not, they will be more likely to suffer a heart attack or stroke, and treating that costs real money. Yet only half the people diagnosed with high cholesterol bring their cholesterol under control. The same is true for people with hypertension. Even fewer successfully control their diabetes. If we did a better job managing cardiovascular risk, we would live longer and spend less overall.

A good health system is like a pyramid. It has a wide base of primary and preventive care, including public health and basic medicine. Above that, but smaller in size, is routine inpatient care, such as care for acute illness and trauma. At the top is subspecialized care for patients in severe need. By contrast, the US resembles an inverted pyramid. We have specialists galore (two thirds of doctors, compared to half in Canada) but a shortage of primary care physicians, like the geriatricians who care for the elderly. Ten thousand baby boomers per day turn sixty-five, yet the United States trains fewer than four hundred geriatricians a year.

A strong public health system is vital during a pandemic. Testing is critical, because if we don't know who has the virus, the only way to prevent spread is to quarantine everyone indefinitely. But mass testing can only be overseen by the government. When someone is confirmed to have the disease, their contacts—including family, friends, and the people who sat next to them on the subway—need to be traced. Everyone who comes into contact with the virus should isolate until they are virus-free, which requires about two weeks for COVID-19. Only the government can enforce isolation. If hospitals become overwhelmed because a large share of the population is sick, then the government needs to supply more capacity or move sick patients to other areas.

The distinction between medicine—care for the individual—and public health—care for the population—is understandable but not desirable. Health insurance systems were set up to work with doctors. Water and sewer systems were overseen by engineers. With differing skill needs and different training, there was no reason for the two branches of health care to merge. But for the vast bulk of modern disease, which spans the two—the need to stop smoking and to treat people with heart disease, for example—the separation is damaging.

Ironically, public health was at one time far larger than medicine. As we have already discussed, nineteenth-century governments spent vast sums on health-related infrastructure, like aqueducts and sewers. Many of the medical giants of the nineteenth century—including Walter Reed and Louis Pasteur—were public employees who spent their lives fighting communicable diseases. But after World War II, perhaps because the US had long avoided a major pandemic, policy focused nearly exclusively on medical insurance. When the costs of medical care rose, public health spending was crowded out, which left the US with limited public capacity to prevent the deadly march of COVID-19.

COVID-19 was a shock, but it was likely that the US would face a pandemic at some point. The world has dodged several close calls over the past two decades. The George W. Bush administration got lucky that the 2005 avian flu was mostly contained to Asia. The Obama administration got lucky three times: the H1N1 pandemic of 2009 was not as deadly as it might have been, the MERS outbreak of 2012 remained largely in Asia, and the Ebola outbreak of 2014–15 was contained in West Africa. Bill Gates of Microsoft fame gave a TED talk in 2014 arguing that the United States was not ready for a pandemic. The talk has been viewed nearly forty million times. Reflecting their experiences, both the Bush and Obama administrations created playbooks to reduce the risk of pandemic. Both administrations also simulated responses to virus outbreaks that were eerily similar to COVID-19. However, neither administration dedicated the resources needed to make pandemic prevention a lasting and well-funded public responsibility. Congress did not do so either.

Other countries heard the drumbeat of near-pandemics and were better prepared for COVID-19. The South Korean government was elected in part because its predecessors were seen to have botched the effort to handle the MERS outbreak. Consequently, Korea acted swiftly when it learned that a woman who was COVID-19 positive attended a church service in the city of Daegu. There were over one thousand people at the service. The possibility of a city- or countrywide COVID-19 outbreak was high. South Korea moved immediately to contain the spread. Everyone who was at the church service, along with their contacts, was found. Many were ordered to self-isolate. And the population of Daegu, whether symptomatic or not, underwent massive testing. Within a month, the potential outbreak was contained.

South Korea was not alone in its achievement. Countries with notable success testing, tracing, and isolating people with COVID-19 include Germany, Australia, New Zealand, Singapore, Taiwan, and Canada. The East Asian countries had gone through pandemic scares in recent memory, particularly SARS, and consequently were more attuned to what was needed. The US and the EU also saw those scares, but ignored them. Their populations paid a fearful price. And no population paid more than the residents of American nursing homes.

The Tragedy of the Nursing Homes

The greatest failure of the US health system during the COVID-19 debacle was the death of tens of thousands in nursing homes. Soldiers' Home is a long-term care facility in Holyoke, Massachusetts, ninety miles west of Boston. The home serves veterans who need nursing care and help with dressing, eating, and other activities of daily life. "Care with Honor and Dignity" is the nursing home's mission. Opened in 1952, Soldiers' Home was capable of handling 248 veterans. The typical count in recent years was around 150.

The first sign of a patient with COVID-19, Veteran 1, came in late February 2020. Staff suspected the veteran had COVID-19 when other causes were ruled out and the patient remained sick. That old soldier had dementia and a history of respiratory illness, but the facility delayed testing until March 17. Isolation rooms had been set aside and a protocol for isolation had been developed, but Veteran 1 continued to live with three roommates. He wandered freely and spent time in the common room—which, contrary to protocol, was left open for veterans and staff.

A positive test result for Veteran 1 came back on March 21. At that point, Veteran 1's three roommates were moved out of his room. Plastic was put up to cover his room's door, but Veteran 1 was still not moved to an isolation unit. Senior leaders thought isolation was unnecessary because people living and working in the unit had already been exposed. The staff who treated Veteran 1 continued to rotate across units in the facility, moving the virus from area to area. Soldiers' Home had personal protective equipment, but it was not reliably used, and staff were not adequately trained in how to use it. Some personnel wore gowns, some wore masks, and some wore neither.

Over the next week, more veterans in the dementia unit became ill. Staff called families to discuss their Medical Orders for Life-Sustaining Treatment (MOLST), the equivalent of Do Not Resuscitate orders. But patients and staff suspected of having COVID-19 were not isolated. On March 27, a decision was made to combine residents from a second dementia unit into the first unit. No one has taken responsibility for that decision, including the (twenty-hour-per-week) medical director. The rationale for the move was apparently that a large number of staff were out sick with COVID-19—or perhaps didn't come to work because they were afraid of contracting the disease—and thus it was impossible to operate two separate dementia units.

The move was "total pandemonium" that turned into "a nightmare." Staff said it "looked like a war zone." The combined dementia unit was not big enough for both sets of patients. Cramped into such close quarters, "one veteran [was] taking his last breaths while the veteran next to him [was] eating his meals without the privacy of curtains." Within a few days, many residents had died of COVID-19 and an enormous number were sick. At that point, the state called in the National Guard, which sent sick patients to hospitals, treated the less severely ill, and tested hordes of residents and staff. From late March through mid-June, there were ninety-four deaths at Soldiers' Home, about three times the expected number. Another seventy-three residents tested positive for COVID-19, as did eighty-three employees.

Retribution was swift. In late June, the superintendent of the nursing facility and the state's director of veterans' services were both fired. The superintendent of Soldiers' Home, who resigned shortly after his firing was overturned by a court, was deemed "not qualified to manage a long-term care facility." He had a distinguished twenty-four-year military career and apparently good political connections, but no experience in health-care management. Both the superintendent and the medical director were later indicted and charged with criminal neglect.

But the fault lies as much in our system for treating those at the fringes of life. Running a nursing home is not as complex as running an acute care hospital, but it is not much less. Yet the pay is vastly different. Hospital CEOs earn about $1 million per year. Nursing home CEOs earn about a third as much. At Soldiers' Home, the superintendent's salary is $122,000 annually, below the pay of an intensive care unit nurse in Boston. Is it any wonder that nursing homes have difficulty attracting top-tier talent?

Across the US, nearly four-tenths of deaths from COVID-19 occurred among people living in nursing homes. In Massachusetts, the share is higher. COVID-19 struck both poorly rated nursing homes and homes with high ratings. Preventive care for the frail is just not a focus of a medical care system oriented toward paying for intensive care for the acutely ill.

We spend a huge amount of time tracking the paperwork moving between hospitals and insurers, but pay little attention to the workers traveling across nursing homes. The economists Keith Chen, Judy Chevalier, and Elisa Long looked at the movement of smartphones between nursing homes during the COVID-19 pandemic and found that more than 5 percent of smartphones that visited one nursing home visited a second nursing home. Even when these homes were supposed to be in lockdown, people traveled from home to home, probably because they were piecing together a living working multiple jobs. That movement provided a pathway for the disease. The study concluded that "49 percent of COVID cases among nursing home residents are attributable to staff movement between facilities." If true, then stopping that movement could have saved tens of thousands of lives, at a cost probably of less than a billion dollars.

Nursing home workers move so often because so many of them work multiple jobs, earning close to the minimum wage. Many nursing homes employ certified nurse assistants and personal care aides, whose salaries start at $15 per hour. In contrast, registered nurses in hospitals earn three times more, and the pay for specialized nurses, such as nurse anesthetists, is even higher. To save on labor costs, many nursing homes employ staff for slightly less than the number of hours necessary to qualify for benefits such as health insurance (how ironic to work in the medical sector during a pandemic and yet not be insured). Consequently, nursing home workers may not get tested when they are exposed to disease and may have to work at several different homes to get paid for enough hours to earn a living.

Poor nursing home workers often live in poor urban neighborhoods. They rely heavily on public transportation, which exposes them to infectious diseases that they may bring to work. It is not known how Veteran 1 in Soldiers' Home contracted COVID-19. However, one nursing home employee in New Jersey, where many patients died of COVID-19, commuted to work in a van "that also made pickups in Newark," which at the time had "the highest reported number of cases and deaths from the virus in Essex County." In cities with high rates of COVID-19 infection, nursing homes were also more likely to experience COVID-19 infection.

Many nursing home patients are covered by Medicaid; they are old and poor. In Massachusetts, Medicaid payments for long-term nursing home care average about $200 per day, which includes the cost of the room and board plus nursing and other staff care. A typical hotel room in Boston costs much more than that (let alone a room in a hospital, which might cost a few thousand dollars per day). Moreover, apart from the unusual event of a criminal investigation, there is practically no accountability for nursing home operators. We designed a health insurance system to protect the elderly from acute hospital bills, but not to care for them when they suffer from long-term frailty.

The Weakest Link

Pandemic disease has an uncanny ability to find the weakest link in the chain and attack there. Having broken the chain at one point, the whole structure may topple. Singapore provides a near-miss example of how this can happen even in states that seem like paragons of public competence.

In early 2020, Singapore was a COVID-19 success story. Despite being close to China, the country was containing COVID-19 well. Border control kept most foreigners out. There were small numbers of cases circulating, but the number was not rising. People washed their hands frequently and stayed home when sick. Anyone with the virus was isolated and their contacts were traced and also isolated; elaborate surveillance and a world-famous public health system helped. For those not infected, daily life went on as usual.

Singapore's government provides a true model of shared strength, with a robust cadre of well-paid and competent bureaucrats. But the city-state's public sector has rarely seen its job as serving the nonvoting migrant workers, who are true outsiders. Singapore relies on low-wage foreign labor to construct its buildings and clean its streets; some two hundred thousand people live in crowded apartments on the outskirts of the city. The immigrants earn more in Singapore than they would at home, but by the standards of Singapore, their pay is low and their housing is worse. As many as fifteen to twenty people crowd into a room. With such a high occupancy rate, social distancing is impossible, and even counting the sick is a challenge. Predictably, that is where an outbreak occurred, in the first half of April. COVID-19 cases skyrocketed.

The government of Singapore, worried about a nationwide catastrophe, imposed a "circuit breaker." Foreign workers were told to stay in their dormitories. Immigrant areas were quarantined. Throughout the city, nonessential businesses were shut, schools were closed, and mask wearing was mandatory. Over the next two months, COVID-19 cases subsided. By June, Singapore started a slow reopening. The crisis was averted, but the living conditions of Singapore's foreign workers pose a permanent risk to that otherwise impressive island of public capability.

With noncommunicable illnesses such as heart disease or cancer, a selfish person can pretty much ignore the suffering of others. When infectious diseases abound, however, one person can put an entire society at risk. In the nineteenth century, wealthy New Yorkers cared about the health of poor

New Yorkers because cholera, or any infectious disease, could spread easily from the poor to the rich. But by 1965, and certainly by 2019, chronic illnesses drew all the attention. Wealthy Americans in 1965 worried about paying for their parents' surgery and cancer treatments. They worried less about global pandemics. Had they done so, there would have been a far stronger emphasis on preventing communicable disease for everyone in the community. With contagious disease, any weak link can cause the entire chain to break.

The US has a patchwork of health insurance systems: private coverage for the working population, Medicare for the elderly, Medicaid for those with low income, and a host of smaller ways of obtaining insurance. Those who fall between the cracks wind up uninsured. That underinsurance is a problem, because it makes it difficult to control pandemic disease. It is a weak link in the chain. If cities want to protect themselves from infectious diseases, they will need a health system without cracks. Singapore has one—sort of— as does most of the rich world. The US does not.

Leading through Learning

America's founders took great pains to limit the authority of the president, yet historically, Americans have deferred to their chief executive officer—or his designated representative—during moments of national crisis. In the United Kingdom, the power of the prime minister is sharply checked by the need to constantly cultivate a parliamentary majority. Yet during great wars, Lincoln, Churchill, and Franklin Roosevelt provided extraordinary leadership that has been admired ever since.

Pandemics share some characteristics with wars. The population, or at least a portion of it, risks losing their lives. People are called upon to make sacrifices for the greater good, and the proper balance between freedom and safety may be unclear. Leaders must make decisions that combine technical expertise and moral judgment. Should we close churches and synagogues? Should we mandate masks?

Both crises have clear objectives—winning the war and minimizing the number of deaths from the disease—and a series of associated lesser goals, such as limiting economic harm, preserving basic freedom, and enhancing public morale. America's leadership during the time of COVID-19 collectively failed along all these dimensions. America's death toll was large, the economic carnage was enormous, and the public came through the pandemic with far less sense of solidarity than either other countries today or the US itself after past crises, like World War II.

By contrast, some countries and regions, including New Zealand and Taiwan, produced superstar leaders during the pandemic. New Zealand experienced only 25 COVID-19 deaths in 2020 and fewer than 2,100 cases of the disease. Containment is easier in isolated islands than in Europe or the US. Nonetheless, the remarkable team of prime minister Jacinda Ardern and director-general of health Ashley Bloomfield deserve much credit for keeping the death in their country far below that in a single Massachusetts nursing home.

Ardern's adult life has been almost entirely political, to the point that she brought her baby with her to the UN General Assembly, making her the first national leader to do so. Bloomfield is a doctor whose life has been wholly focused on public health. Together they form a very effective partnership, where a combination of science and good judgment determines policy, and an effective politician persuades the people to follow.

New Zealand began its response to COVID-19 on February 2, 2020, when it banned travel to and from China and entered what they called Alert Level 1, which began communication campaigns about handwashing and social distancing. This intervention was limited, but it would be another twenty-six days before New Zealand had its first confirmed case. While travel restrictions increased, New Zealand remained reasonably relaxed until March 15, when the country had eight confirmed infections. By that time, the experience in Italy and Spain illustrated how terrible the pandemic could be, and New Zealand knew the extent of the threat. America also had that knowledge, but chose a different and deadlier path.

Between March 16 and March 25, New Zealand ratcheted up its COVID response, closing borders except for returning citizens (who were required to self-isolate), banning large gatherings, and jumping up to Alert Level 3. By March 25, New Zealand had 205 confirmed cases and entered Alert Level 4, which was essentially a complete national lockdown. New Zealand's Parliament decided that a temporary loss of freedom was an acceptable price to pay for life. Ardern was empowered and she issued a stay-at-home order with "few exceptions." Returning New Zealanders lost the option to self-isolate. Their quarantine was managed by the state.

The country did things that scientists were advocating everywhere. Contact tracing had been put into place even in February and was scaled up as the cases began to emerge. Testing was widespread, including testing the asymptomatic, which is the only way to learn the true prevalence of the disease. The number of new cases started to decline after April 10, but the amount of testing increased substantially after that point. Consequently, New Zealand's leaders had the single most important element in decision making around a pandemic: knowledge. By April 28, the prevalence declined to the point where Ardern and Bloomfield could allow the Alert Level back down to 3, permitting a bit more freedom.

During the first week of May, New Zealand started to have days with no new cases. Still, they kept on testing thousands. That testing then enabled them to drop the Alert Level to 2 by the middle of May. Since that point, the number of New Zealand cases has generally been tiny with the sole exception of a modest mid-August outbreak, strangely associated with a cold storage facility. The government responded again to that outbreak with massive levels of testing, and the disease almost entirely vanished.

By the end of the year, a grand total of twenty-five New Zealanders had died from COVID-19, which is a small fraction of the number who died in the Soldiers' Home that we discussed above. Moreover, the overall loss of freedom probably ended up being less in New Zealand than in most of America. The Alert Level 4 lockdown was more extreme, yet it was short. Americans, Europeans, and Britons still struggled with limitations on mobility and recreation for almost another year. One clear lesson is that a temporary, extreme lockdown is vastly more effective than half measures that last far longer.

The final tribute is that Ardern won a thumping reelection in October of 2020. Her Labor Party received a larger share of votes in the parliamentary election than any party since 1949. Ardern wasn't a coldhearted technocrat. She exuded compassion and humanity, famously reassuring children that "we do consider both the Tooth Fairy and the Easter Bunny to be essential workers." Still, she succeeded because she ran an anti-COVID campaign with far more information about the disease than most of her peers.

The power of science is not that scientists are always right. Plenty of scientists made the wrong guesses about COVID-19 in February and March of 2020. The power of science comes from its ability to learn and adjust its recommendations. The most important scientific insight in February 2020 was not about wearing or not wearing masks or about closing borders, but about the vital need to test widely and contact trace. We could only fight the disease if we knew what was happening. New Zealand knew. America did not.

The other superstars of COVID-19 management were in East Asia: South Korea, Taiwan, and, more unevenly, Singapore. These countries have strong, capable governments that value expertise. Most East Asians knew enough to wear masks when there was a risk of an airborne pandemic, which was a lesson that took many months for Americans to learn. Taiwan was attuned to COVID-19 because it had done poorly with SARS. The vice president of Taiwan is an epidemiologist. Singapore also underperformed in the control of SARS; COVID-19 was a chance to demonstrate what they had learned. All these places emphasized the need to measure.

Typically, success meant widespread testing, a strict national lockdown, and closed borders. Essentially, a return to quarantine, but quarantine done right. Lockdowns work when they are combined with enough testing to know that the disease is gone, before reopening occurs. The cardinal error of both the US and much of the EU was the failure to measure, which meant that reopening after a first lockdown was followed by another wave of illness and then more lockdowns.

Some European countries did far better than others. Germany and the Canadian province of British Columbia had extremely successful early responses to COVID-19, although at the time of our writing, cases have started to spike once more in both places. The German Chancellor, Angela Merkel, has a doctorate in chemistry and has provided steady leadership for Germany and Europe for fifteen years. Neither Merkel nor her administration moved quickly in response to the pandemic that was unfolding south of the Alps. Indeed, her health minister, who has no medical or scientific background, regularly downplayed the threat of the virus through April. The German government didn't take serious action until March 22, but then it did several things really well.

Germany has a strong federal structure like the US, meaning that state governments generally have control during a crisis. In the US, no one tried to get a common state response, and the national government actually encouraged Sunbelt states with low numbers of cases to reopen while the pandemic was raging in northern states. On March 22, Merkel brokered a deal where all the German states agreed to certain minimum regulations, like the closure of restaurants and a 1.5-meter minimum distance between nonfamily members in public spaces. Individual states could go beyond these rules if they wanted, and some essentially imposed complete lockdowns.

While the US was floundering to manufacture enough tests that could take a week or more to produce results, Germany had a testing system that delivered a verdict in under three hours by using a German rapid COVID test that was released on March 26. Once again, there was widespread testing of asymptomatic populations, and by late April, Germany began reopening. The company that produced the test, Bosch, is owned by a charitable foundation, and there was nothing that prevented Americans from using the Bosch technology. Americans spurned it out of national pride.

Germany's initial success involved national coordination on a short but effective lockdown and plenty of testing. They didn't get it right initially, but they learned quickly. They also had the advantage of having prepared in advance for just such a pandemic and having a public institution—the Robert Koch Institute—geared toward fighting a pandemic.

The Way Forward

To prepare for future pandemics, the US will need to make sure that our vast ocean of health-care spending does more to deliver health, rather than just pay for sickness. This will mean spending less in total, and getting more for what we spend. A key part of focusing on health outcomes is to direct more spending toward public health in general, and pandemic preparedness in particular. We must also reduce the number of weak links, by making sure everyone gets covered.

The Affordable Care Act (ACA) enacted a series of policies designed to reduce the incentives for excessive care. These policies have worked—to a point—and medical spending growth has slowed. But these changes have not radically transformed the medical system, which remains too costly and poor at prevention. We need more and stronger reforms to limit or at least to target future spending growth. The COVID pandemic created something of a national consensus on the need to provide some care for everyone—insiders and outsiders alike. Even the Trump administration announced that it would pay for COVID-19 testing and treatment for the uninsured—though not for the suspected case of COVID-19 that turns out to be something else. The Affordable Care Act focused on coverage as well. To prevent the next pandemic, we cannot leave so many people outside the health-care system.

Finally, we desperately need serious pandemic preparation. Vaccine capacity must be ready, testing must be common and easy, contact tracers need to be on staff, and isolation needs to be economically feasible. That means a plan, including more investment in capacity now. Only a fool waits until the storm is brewing to repair a leaky roof.

We must reform and invest to reduce the risk of future pandemics, primarily to decrease the number of future deaths. But pandemics also have the capacity to create tremendous economic harm. For very good reasons, it is worth spending many billions to avoid the loss of future trillions.

Chapter 6

DO ROBOTS

SPREAD DISEASE?

T he COVID-19 pandemic was both a health disaster and an economic catastrophe. In February 2020, America was enjoying its 128th straight month of economic expansion. By April, the unemployment rate hit 14.7 percent, its highest level since the Great Depression. American GDP shrank by almost 10 percent during the second quarter of 2020, the largest drop on record. In the UK, GDP during that quarter was 20 percent lower than one year earlier.

Past pandemics didn't make work disappear. The medieval serfs who survived the Black Death were better off economically because the plague produced labor shortages and higher wages. Neither cholera nor yellow fever disrupted nascent nineteenth-century manufacturing industries. The economic chaos of 2020 reflects a global economy that has become dependent on human contact, where person-to-person contagion can put all of our prosperity, and especially the employment of the less educated, at risk.

The urban face-to-face economy is both vital and vulnerable to airborne pandemic and public lockdowns. For centuries, machines have eliminated jobs that demand ordinary physical work. Over the past thirty years, computers have provided a nonhuman "substitute for the routine tasks found in many traditional middle-wage jobs," like taking dictation. In-person service industries provided a safe haven for workers when manufacturing was out-sourced and bookkeeping was automated. Wealthier urbanites were willing to pay extra if their cappuccino was served with good cheer and a compliment.

For most of history, new forms of work have come with new forms of interaction, such as the close collaboration on Henry Ford's assembly line or the face-to-face food service at McDonald's. These interactions, many to many and one to one, have created new scope for contagious outbreaks. This chapter chronicles how job-creating innovations, like the crowded factory, have needed new investments in health, and how new investments in health have enabled new modes of employment to prosper. Looking forward, an economy without widespread joblessness requires new forms of interactive employment to replace the rote jobs that have been automated away, but those jobs will only exist if we eliminate the risk of plague. It is not just our health but our economic future that depends on reducing the risk of pandemic.

Unfortunately, the entrepreneurship that creates opportunity has been declining for decades, partly because governments enact regulations that favor insiders over outsiders. Bans on food trucks protect existing restaurants from competition. State-level licensing for occupations like auctioneers and hairdressers make it harder to enter those occupations or to relocate across states. The best educated entrepreneurs escape the morass of state and local regulations by innovating in cyberspace, but ordinary people whose knowledge is focused on the physical don't have that option. Creating one-stop permitting offices can streamline the start-up process and make it easier for new firms to replace old jobs with new jobs, which is always helpful and particularly vital for recovering from COVID-19.

We need to rethink other barriers as well as regulations on start-ups. The same historic-preservation rule that entitles wealthier urbanites to keep their pretty view forever can prevent a poorer household from starting a grocery store. We turn to the regulation of space in chapter 8. Here, we focus on entrepreneurship and the vulnerability of a face-to-face economy.

When Pandemic Produced Prosperity: The Black Death

Pandemics have always been terrible, but they haven't always led to poverty. In medieval Europe most people were subsistence farmers, and the bubonic plague led to prosperity, not famine. The logic is simple. In an agricultural world, the food available per person is roughly determined by the amount of land per person. As long as the population has the physical capacity to farm more land, fewer people leads to more output per person. The ratio of people to arable land can increase by either boosting the amount of land, perhaps by conquering neighboring areas, or by reducing the number of people. The Black Death wiped away a third of Europe's population. Thus, for every acre that a peasant once farmed, another half acre was made available by the peasant who died. The land-owning nobility took as much as they could, but competition to attract workers meant that some of the new wealth also went to ordinary people.

The impact of the Black Death was profound. British economists Stephen Broadberry, Bruce Campbell, Alexander Klein, Mark Overton, and Bas van Leeuwen described how in England, the economic "status quo was abruptly and dramatically transformed by outbreak of the Black Death which in 1348–49, within the space of 18 months, reduced the population by 46 per cent," and consequently "the economy registered an immediate gain in GDP per head of 30 per cent." As the number of agricultural workers dropped, landowners had to pay more to attract labor. The price paid for a basic farm job like threshing and winnowing seems to have risen by over 35 percent between the early 1340s and the early 1370s.

The nobility tried to fight the laws of supply and demand by dictating lower wages and restricting their workers' mobility. England and France passed ordinances in 1349 trying to cap incomes at pre-plague levels, but France revised its statute in 1351 and allowed wages to rise by one third. The English efforts also seem to have failed, as suggested by the wage data discussed above. Individual barons may have been able to terrify their peasantry into submission, but market forces are hard to overrule. Moreover, "the landowners could not be united" because "those landowners who had suffered most would welcome the freedom of peasant movement," since it enabled them to replace missing workers, "while those who had suffered least would oppose it." Only in Russia were the magnates able to impose a "second serfdom" on their peasants as conquest and emigration increased land-to-labor ratios in the seventeenth century.

The effects of the Black Death go even further. Economists Nico Voigtländer of UCLA and Hans-Joachim Voth of the University of Zurich have written that by increasing employment opportunities for women, "the Black Death set into motion a virtuous circle of higher wages and fertility decline that enabled Europe to maintain unusually high per capita incomes" for centuries.

In a sense, the economy of Europe—as well as society as a whole—had become more resilient to pandemic between 540 and 1350 CE by becoming simpler, poorer, and more fragmented. Chapter 2 discussed the earlier Plague of Justinian, which was disastrous along every dimension. The economy of Constantinople didn't benefit from having fewer people—cities thrive because of their density. The waves of war and conquest that followed the deadly flea created centuries of instability and poverty.

In the fourteenth century, increasing agricultural wealth fed the demand for "luxuries" like cloth that was woven in towns. This, in turn, helped spur the urbanization of the fifteenth century, which then set the stage for the

Renaissance. Italy's cities were devastated by the Black Death itself, but in the aftermath of the plague, urbanization rose from 8.6 percent in 1400 to 14.9 percent in 1500. In the northwestern water-linked region that includes England, the Netherlands, and Belgium, urbanization rose steadily from 3.9 percent in 1300 to 6.3 percent in 1400 to 8.5 percent in 1500. By 1700, almost one in five of those northerners lived in a city. Arguably, *Yersinia pestis* both started and ended the Middle Ages, first by ending Justinian's dream of reimposed Roman order and then by launching centuries of urban creativity.

Pandemics are generally more harmful economically to cities. If a city's population falls, then urban real estate may become more abundant, but extra office space does far less for an accountant's productivity than extra land does for a farmer's harvest. The economic harm of an urban outbreak depends partially on the extent to which commerce spreads disease, which then determines whether the threat of sickness shuts down commerce.

Samuel Pepys and the Infested Wig

At the time of the Black Death, Europe's greatest commercial cities, including Venice, Genoa, and Florence, were in the south, but, as the historian Jonathan Scott writes, "between 1500 and 1800, as Europe established its first global colonies, the Anglo-Dutch North Sea region overtook the Mediterranean as the epicenter of material and cultural capital." The closely tied cities of London and Amsterdam led Republican revolts and sent their mercantile fleets across the globe. As their urban populations increased, their economies grew both more interconnected and more prone to suffer from contagious illness.

The last major appearance of *Yersinia pestis* on English soil occurred in 1665 when London was already a great city with a population of 460,000. The plague led wealthier urbanites to decamp to lower-density locales, but it didn't dissuade those who remained from buying urban services. We know something about life during the plague from the prolific diarist Samuel Pepys, member of Parliament and administrator of the navy. Pepys kept his diary for a decade starting in 1660. On the fourteenth of July, 1665, as plague ravaged the city, Pepys wrote that he went "to the Old Exchange, by water, and there bespoke two fine shirts of my pretty seamstress."

Pepys was clearly happy to see the attractive woman and to acquire the new garments despite the thousands dying around him. He didn't know the cause of the plague, but visiting a tailor probably created little extra risk since the infected fleas could get you in bed as easily as in a shop. He probably would have noticed if the young woman was suffering from the pneumonic version of the disease that enables person-to-person transmission through airborne droplets. In that case, he might have stayed away and reduced the risk of personal contact.

Pepys gamely bought shirts, but other products seemed riskier to him: "it is a wonder what will be the fashion after the plague is done, as to periwiggs, for nobody will dare to buy any haire, for fear of the infection, that it had been cut off of the heads of people dead of the plague." He had bought a wig earlier that he "durst not wear, because the plague was in Westminster when I bought it." Cloth sent from London had infected the village of Eyam, which we earlier presented as a pioneering example of self-quarantine, so Pepys was right to fear flea-carrying fibers.

The switch to cotton during the mechanization of the late eighteenth century reduced the risk that textiles would spread disease, because cotton takes better to high-temperature cleaning. Consequently, fears of infected fabric didn't restrain the global trade in cloth that was central to the early Industrial Revolution and the growth of port cities like New York and Liverpool. Eliminating the risks created by moving food long distances would be even more important for urban growth.

While Pepys kept the wine merchants and oystermen in business, London's economy could handle a collapse in the wig trade. London's economic vulnerability was limited because like all premodern megacities, it was a political capital. As long as the government had access to resources that didn't depend on customs revenues, such as bond financing and taxes on internal commerce, then there would be money in the city, even if quarantines shut down trade with the outside world. Pepys's own income was guaranteed by his place as chief secretary of the admiralty, and he was willing to spend his wealth on local products, which in turn employed workers throughout the city.

Making Manufacturing Safe for Workers: The Peels and Public Regulation

The Industrial Revolution was a true hinge of history, an event that ended perpetual poverty by replacing and enhancing human labor with machines. Before the creative outburst that emerged from Birmingham, Manchester, and other mill towns, incomes had stagnated for two thousand years. After the Industrial Revolution, economic growth became the new normal. Thousands of old jobs were destroyed by devices that spun and wove. But millions of new jobs were created to produce goods and services that no one had even imagined in 1750.

The massing of labor in factories, just like the massing of people in cities, enables the spread of disease. Tuberculosis killed English mill workers in 1820. Crowded poultry plants were COVID-19 hot spots in 2020. To reach its full triumph, the industrial age required improvements in hygiene that kept both workers and customers safe. The combinations of private and public action that reduced the risk of illness from mass production and distribution in the nineteenth and twentieth centuries provide examples of how to lower the risks that cities face today.

During the early Industrial Revolution, mechanical innovations like the flying shuttle, the water frame, and the spinning jenny revolutionized the manufacturing of fabric for clothing, one of humanity's most basic needs. Those innovations meant a switch from labor to capital-intensive production and from weaving at home to working in large factories. The machines were expensive, and they became more efficient as industrial establishments grew larger. Factories are like specialized cities that enable both the sharing of infrastructure and the division of labor.

In Manchester, the town that became England's "Cottonopolis," the early industrializers saw little financial reason to reduce the risk that their workers would get sick. Factory owners still had to pay the same wages for labor whether or not they invested in sanitation. There was a plentiful supply of poor workers who were willing to put up with unhealthy work conditions, especially if they were underage apprentices who had no choice about it. Even adult workers can find it difficult to assess the risk of getting sick, whether in eighteenth-century Manchester or twenty-first-century America. What exactly makes a warehouse safe from typhus or COVID-19?

The Peels of Manchester illustrate the intertwined nature of industrial job creation and public hygiene. The first Robert Peel, who lived from 1723 to 1795, was an innovator of products, such as his "parsley" patterned calicos, and production techniques. He employed his neighbor, James Hargreaves, who invented the spinning jenny. Peel's embrace of labor-saving devices made him a target of Luddite anti-machine violence, but the new technology made him productive and wealthy enough to own twenty-three mills.

His son, also Robert, whom we shall just call Peel, lived from 1750 to 1830 and became even wealthier. He was one of an estimated ten British millionaires in 1799 and employed over fifteen thousand workers, including over one thousand young apprentices. When a "fever" struck one of Peel's mills in 1782, he initially did nothing.

But Manchester had its share of well-intentioned reformers. One local advocate interviewed nearly two hundred people about the epidemic and petitioned Peel to stop the nighttime shifts. Peel indignantly responded that "no man in his senses would have complied." The petitioners then turned to the local magistrates, who were sympathetic and demanded an investigation. They summoned Dr. Thomas Percival, a Mancunian herald of the public health movement, who prefigured both London's John Snow and New York's Stephen Smith.

Cities speed the spread of knowledge, and at Percival's time a "wide river of medical learning which flowed from Padua to Leyden was in full flood when it continued its course to Edinburgh, which city, in turn, had become the leading medical school of the civilized world." Percival followed that flood backward, studying first at the University of Edinburgh and then Leyden. He later became friends with Benjamin Franklin and wrote children's stories that would be read by the young Jane Austen. He supposedly coined the term *medical ethics* and wrote a pioneering pamphlet on the topic, which had an outsized influence on the American Medical Association. He wrote scientific papers identifying former Roman outposts around Manchester and tested the water quality throughout southern England. In 1775, he published a pathbreaking, data-filled essay that concluded that "great towns are in a peculiar degree fatal to children." He also worked to improve public health in prisons, among the most crowded of public buildings.

Percival studied the outbreak at Peel's mill. He was unable to conclude whether the disease had started in the mill or been brought from elsewhere, but he was confident that the mill's dense, unsanitary conditions had "supported, diffused and aggravated" the illness. His report proposed increased cleanliness and better ventilation, and called for work hours to be restricted, especially for children. The magistrates agreed but they had no legal power to interfere, which was what the New York City police claimed in the face of Stephen Smith's call to close a tenement. They did, however, urge widespread dissemination of the report.

Peel's reputation may have suffered, but Peel's factories were Peel's property, and in 1784, he could do what he liked with them. In 1789, contagious disease returned to his mills. Once again, Percival was brought in and once again he recommended sanitary improvements.

Percival's influence in Manchester meant that he didn't just butt heads with Robert Peel. They mixed within the same circles, so they met and they talked. Cities enable the interaction and communication that can sometimes change hearts and minds. In 1802, Peel, by then a member of Parliament, dropped his opposition to mill regulation and introduced the Health and Morals of Apprentices Act of 1802, which he shepherded through Parliament. This act required better ventilation and more sanitary factories. It limited working hours for apprentices and forced mill owners to provide some basic education. The legislation was a small step that proved difficult to enforce, but it was the beginning of the public effort to stop workplaces from breeding disease, especially among the young.

Why did Peel become Parliament's strongest supporter of sanitary regulation? The most benevolent view is that under Percival's benign tutelage, his heart grew softer and he came to care more for his workers. This Grinch-like transformation is possible, but the idea of a kinder, gentler Peel is belied by his ardent defense of the slave trade five years after he led the move to regulate factories. Moreover, Peel could have unilaterally improved conditions in his own mills, and he did not do so.

An alternative view is that Peel didn't like being seen as a villain, but he also didn't want to lose any competitive edge to his rivals. Peel was therefore willing to pay the extra costs of sanitation as long as everyone else had to pay as well. As one of the age's industrial giants, Peel probably found it easier to afford the costs of cleaner mills, which meant that the regulation may have helped him relative to his smaller, scrappier competitors. George Stigler, who won a Nobel Prize for his work on "regulatory capture," argued that powerful incumbents, like Peel, often support regulations to protect them against competition from outsiders. For example, restaurateurs in modern Detroit may ardently advocate for rules that bar food trucks from the city.

Before the rise of the regulatory state, lawsuits provided the primary means of rectifying harms to property or health. As long as laborers can sue their employers for illness or injury then that should induce those employers to make their workplaces safer. But in nineteenth-century America, the legal doctrine of "assumption of risk" meant that workers couldn't sue their employers for injuries despite high death tolls. The US's Federal Employers' Liability Act of 1908 enabled injured railroad workers to file lawsuits for compensation, and that encouraged a shift to safer trains.

Did workplace safety increase people's willingness to do industrial labor? A robust literature finds that in the modern world riskier work pays more— people need to be paid higher wages to take on jobs that come with more physical risk. Historical data is more equivocal. One study finds that "child workers received higher hourly earnings in industries associated with more days lost to illness, but adult workers generally did not." Nonetheless, a poster recruiting young women for the cotton mills of Lowell, America's "City of Spindles," promised both that workers "will be properly cared for in sickness" and that "none but active and healthy girls will be engaged for this work."

While the hungry poor in Dickensian England may have been grateful for an industrial job even if it came with a heightened risk of "fever," society as a whole was increasingly unwilling to accept factories that were death traps. If industry was to survive the scrutiny of the increasingly empowered English middle class, then it needed the safety rules that started with the second Robert Peel. Public pressure similarly demanded workplace safety in 2020. Even when urban service workers and some of their customers were willing to accept the risk of COVID-19, governments still enforced lockdowns to reduce the spread of the pandemic.

The second Robert Peel's son, yet another Robert Peel, became the statesman who fought for urban safety as the "father of modern policing," with

British bobbies named in his honor. He was also the prime minister who split his party by ending the Corn Laws that restricted the flow of grain into England. The safety of shipped food would become central during the later industrial age. To urbanize, cities needed more calories than could be produced locally and these had to be shipped from far-off, less populated lands. But in order to grow to meet this demand, the food industry first needed to convince its customers that food that traveled over long distances would not spread sickness.

The path to safety in shipped textiles foreshadowed the process of making food safer. Historically, England specialized in sheep. For centuries, it exported wool to Europe. The machines of the Industrial Revolution required hardy fibers, and cotton was consequently a better match with Manchester's early mills. The switch to cotton fabric came with a surprise sanitary dividend: unlike wool, cotton keeps its shape after being washed in extremely hot water. Woolen fabric had long been a host for the fleas that carried the Black Death, but sufficiently hot water in a scrub pail eliminates almost any risk from cotton fabric. The basic principle that heat purifies would also be a guiding star for food safety.

Pasteurization and Urbanization

Economic pressure was more important in making manufacturing safe for customers than it was for creating workplace safety. Customers avoid products that seem unsafe, especially when those products are meant to be ingested. Chicago's beef barons worked assiduously to convince a skeptical public that cattle slaughtered in the Midwest could be safely shipped to New York in refrigerated railcars.

The mass production and shipment of food offered the possibility of allowing cities to expand enormously, if only the health risks could be contained. As long as New York City had to produce food nearby, as it still did in 1830, its population was constrained. As the city increasingly came to use all of North America as its breadbasket, butcher, and dairy, the scope for urban expansion increased.

For millennia, cities fed themselves on imported grains, such as the rivers of wheat that came to the Rome of Caesar Augustus or the oceans of rice that fed Tokugawa Tokyo. Grains can be contaminated, but cooking at high temperatures generally kills off living organisms. The ergot fungus, which can turn rye bread deadly, kills not because of contagion but because it contains the ergot alkaloid, which is not removed by cooking. Nineteenth-century Americans would eat ketchup rather than fresh tomatoes, because the poisons that were assumed to exist in the dangerously red-looking vegetable had presumably been destroyed by cooking and vinegar.

The struggle to move meat across the North American continent is one of the great epics of American history. That saga touches artistic works like Howard Hawks's film *Red River*, with its oedipal battle between the cattle drivers played by John Wayne and Montgomery Clift, and Theodore Dreiser's novel *Sister Carrie*, whose protagonist comes to Chicago and lives near the stockyards. The quest to unlock the agricultural wealth of the American hinterland created urban outposts like Kansas City and Cincinnati and spurred the building of canals and railroads.

An ancient and reasonably hygienic technology for transporting meat is to march live animals to an urban butcher, who then slaughters them for local consumption. Daniel Drew, one of the nineteenth-century's most successful wizards of Wall Street, began his career as a drover, driving cattle into New York City. His first watered stock literally involved cows that were given abundant drinking water to boost their weight and sales price. But the challenges involved in moving animals on foot led to an increasing dependence on salting, railroads, and refrigeration to move food longer distances.

The ancient practice of salting preserves food by eliminating liquid that can house bacteria. Pigs transform grains into meat calories more efficiently than cows, and so they have long provided the dominant form of salted meat. Today, Americans eat 50 percent more processed pork than fresh pork, but vastly more fresh beef than salted beef, especially in the form of hamburgers. Salted pork's appeal also owes something to the meat's sweetness. The success of Cincinnati—America's "Porkopolis"—stemmed from slaughtering pigs, which were fed with the agricultural riches of the Ohio River Valley and shipped by water to the markets of the East.

The bovine edge over pigs came from the cow's greater mobility, which is well illustrated by John Wayne's cinematic cattle drives. The basic model was that the beef would travel on the hoof from Texas or Iowa to a western outpost of the rail system, such as Abilene or Chicago. The cattle could then be crowded into railcars and shipped east.

But shipping live cows is expensive. They carry extra nonedible weight and require feeding on the trip. However, if the cows were slaughtered in Chicago and shipped as is, the beef would be rotten by the time it reached New York. The meat could be salted to a point of sanitary safety, but urban customers were willing to pay far more for fresh beef. What to do?

In this case, the solution was cold rather than heat. Gustavus Swift began as a drover and butcher in Eastern Massachusetts. He moved west to get closer to the great herds of cattle. Eventually, he gravitated to Chicago's enormous Union Stock Yards, which were established by an alliance of railroad companies to encourage the movement of meat. Swift's place in meatpacking history was ensured by his development of the refrigerated railcar, which originally just meant blocks of ice placed over dressed beef. The cold prevented the growth of bacteria, although good hygienic practice still required plenty of heating before biting into a steak.

An even greater challenge was enabling urbanites to consume food items that were not generally cooked—like wine and milk products. The sophisticated urban societies of East Asia appear to have invented a version of the process now named for Louis Pasteur centuries before the birth of the famous French scientist.

The Western adoption of pasteurization had its roots in the scientific debate over the spontaneous generation of living organisms, such as bacteria. In one of the great battles of nineteenth-century science, the French chemist Louis Pasteur faced off against the far older and in many ways more distinguished naturalist Félix Pouchet before the French Academy of Sciences. Pasteur showed that when sterilized liquids were placed in sealed swan-necked glass containers, there was no subsequent growth of microorganisms. These organisms appeared only in containers that were exposed to outside dust. This discovery convinced the academy to award him a prize of 2,500 francs, more than $40,000 in today's currency.

Pasteur correctly grasped that wine and milk were spoiled by bacteria. Consequently, the liquids could be preserved and shipped if they could be first sterilized and then sealed. The challenge is to not destroy all of the microbes that give character to a bottle of Lafite Rothschild and allow it to evolve in the damp cellar of your chateau. Pasteurization therefore is limited to a short burst of heat that typically falls short of 100 degrees Celsius. To taste the difference between a light pasteurization shock and ultra-high temperature (UHT) pasteurization, just compare a glass of Parmalat's UHT milk with a glass of standard "fresh" milk. The UHT milk can be stored without refrigeration for months because high heat destroys far more of its microorganisms, but Americans raised on low-temperature pasteurization tend to find the Parmalat's taste too industrial and perhaps too sweet—the high temperatures caramelize some of the milk.

The combination of pasteurization, refrigeration, and better packaging enabled the shipping and storage of food in cities. Milk-borne disease killed many nineteenth-century urban children. Twenty-first-century city kids see nothing but wholesome goodness in the white liquid. Sanitary advances also enabled food production to become industrial. Instead of small farms producing tiny batches of milk and eggs, food came to be produced by great industrial conglomerates, like the French company Lactalis that owns Parmalat.

Lactalis is the largest dairy producer in the world, but it is still small relative to the even more massive companies that specialize in producing prepared food, ready for consumption right out of the container, such as the parent company of Nestlé and Nabisco, Mondelēz. Nabisco's iconic bakery on Chicago's South Side once employed 2,400 people in a 1.8 million square foot behemoth of a building that turned out 192 million pounds of cookies annually. As we discussed in chapter 4, Nabisco's bestsellers, like Oreos and Newtons, were some of the first examples of mass-produced precooked food. Nabisco provided both jobs for industrial bakers and food for urban eaters around the world.

At about the same time that Nabisco was pushing its Uneedas and Oreos, Upton Sinclair published his blockbuster expose *The Jungle,* a fictional account of Chicago's meatpacking industry. Sinclair intended to build sympathy for the labor movement, but as he himself later wrote, "I aimed for the public's heart, and by accident hit it in the stomach." His disgusting depictions of meatpacking built enthusiasm for the Meat Inspection Act and the Pure Food and Drug Act which were both passed in 1906. A whole public apparatus has emerged, in the US and elsewhere, to ensure that food products are properly labeled and adhere to sanitary standards. The Pure Food and Drug Act also gave us the legal apparatus that evolved into the War on Drugs.

How important have these regulations been for eliminating foodborne illness? Long-lived consumer businesses like Nabisco have good reason to build and maintain reputations for product quality. Liability lawsuits can also deter lesser-known companies from selling sufficiently unsafe goods. Yet even in 2008, infant milk formula tainted by melamine led over fifty thousand Chinese to become ill. There were surely some American food producers that would have similarly cut corners over the past century if it were not for the oversight of the FDA.

Improvements in food safety enabled the growth of cities, which in turn allowed further economic expansion. A constant threat of foodborne illness would have limited urban menus to safe, simple products and reduced the appeal of urban density. Why would one want to live in a city that served only hardtack and gruel?

The transportation of food remained safe in 2020, even though meatpacking plants became hot spots for disease transmission. Unlike automobiles or refrigerators, meatpacking remains labor-intensive, not capital-intensive. The idiosyncrasies of chickens and cows make it hard to mechanically process them without destroying them. Consequently, meat packers hire low-wage workers, and they are not separated from each other by vast machines. Today, the average textile mill, the modern equivalent of Peel's plants, has over 1,500 square feet of space per worker. The average food manufacturing plant has under 570 square feet per worker. Proximity between laborers still enables the spread of pandemic, especially when employers do little to protect them. Nonetheless, the innovations that protected consumers from getting sick from their food continued to work as millions hunkered down and turned to Amazon for their groceries.

The Industrial Economy Proves Pandemic-Proof

The influenza pandemic of 1918–19 was far more lethal than COVID-19. In America, about 675,000 people died from that pandemic, which as a fraction of population is the equivalent of over 2 million deaths today. It is estimated that one third of the world's population caught the flu, though no exact number is available. As in the COVID-19 pandemic, cloth masks became ubiquitous, countries shut their borders, and cities experimented with enforced social distancing.

Given the death tolls and the mode of transmission, the influenza pandemic would seem likely to have been just as disruptive to local economies as COVID-19. Yet it was not. François Velde of the Federal Reserve Bank of Chicago has done a remarkable job investigating the economic consequences of the influenza pandemic. He finds that "industrial output fell sharply but rebounded within months," and "retail seemed little affected." There was "no evidence of business failures or stressed financial systems." He concludes by confirming the 1946 verdict of the pioneering classifiers of business cycles Wesley Clair Mitchell and Arthur Burns that the downturn was of "exceptional brevity and moderate amplitude." What explains the difference between 1918–19 and 2020–21?

The influenza recession was so mild because the nature of work was so different in 1918 from what it is today. In 1910, 31 percent of Americans worked on farms and 38 percent were manual laborers. In 2015, farmers made up less than 1 percent of America's workforce, and the share of manual laborers had dropped to 20 percent. In 1910, 44 percent of America's nonagricultural employees were in manufacturing, transportation, and public utilities. That share had fallen to 12.5 percent by 2015. No farm was going to shut down out of fear of influenza. Most of the factories kept humming too, as they did in 2020, when the unemployment rate among manufacturing workers remained at only 9 percent through June.

Some forms of retail trade experienced an influenza dip in 1918, but just as today, other businesses expanded. Velde reports that sales by Woolworth, J.C. Penney, and Kresge dropped by 13 percent in October 1918 relative to August of the same year, but the mail-order businesses of Sears, Roebuck and Montgomery Ward boomed. Both drugstores and department stores sold more during the pandemic.

In 1918, people weren't that rich, relative to today, and they spent a larger share of their earnings on essentials. Spending on basic needs stays steady during a pandemic, even if there is some risk in grocery shopping. Spending on discretionary luxuries that involve human interactions falls far more dramatically with widespread disease. Discretionary high-end activities had become more important in the far wealthier world of 2020.

In 1910, only 14 percent of America's non-farmers worked in service occupations outside the home, while 14.5 percent of workers not on farms were in "domestic service" or "personal service." Those categories, which included vast numbers of live-in maids, have essentially disappeared. To be sure, many wealthy families have nannies or au pairs, but the number of such workers is relatively limited. Prosperous Americans are still paying other people to cook their food and iron their shirts, but these tasks are done by a professional outside the home, not by live-in servants.

The disappearance of widespread domestic service strikes us as a win for human dignity. But the professionalization of the service economy has made it more vulnerable to pandemic. Influenza did not lead many households to fire their live-in maids in 1918. If anything, a wealthier family would become more dependent on her to brave the risks of shopping. The service economy in 2020 is highly specialized and involves large numbers of customers interacting with large numbers of service professionals. That network is efficient and productive, but vastly more socially interactive and consequently more prone to contagion.

The Path from Manufacturing to Services

In the century since the influenza pandemic, the wealthy world has changed dramatically. We now spend much of our incomes on products and experiences that are optional, luxuries rather than necessities. We now work in services rather than manufacturing. Many of these services are delivered face-to-face. An economy with a large share of employment providing luxury services in face-to-face interactions is almost destined to collapse when confronted by an airborne pandemic.

Over the past twenty years, much anxiety has emerged over the future of work in an age of machine learning and robotics. What remains for humans to do in a world in which machines can seemingly do everything? The replacement of human beings by mechanical devices is not some new trend. Robert Peel the elder was doing just that when he earned the wrath of local craftsmen with his spinning jennies.

But Peel's technological innovations didn't lead to joblessness, any more than efficient Boulton and Watt steam engines led to a conservation of coal. The great English economist Stanley Jevons noted 150 years ago that more efficient engines led to more coal consumption, because people figured out more uses for steam engines that used less fuel and were consequently less costly to operate. That Jevons paradox is relevant almost everywhere. Electric cars emit less carbon than conventional cars, but they are also cheaper to drive longer distances. Thus, we should expect additional driving encouraged by electric vehicles to undo some of the energy savings created by more fuel-efficient engines.

The global industrial boom of the nineteenth and early twentieth centuries reflected a vast increase in the use of machines to produce thousands of different and often new products. The first wave of industrialization meant more cloth for everyone, as the mills of Manchester sent their calicos across the globe. The second wave fueled transportation, as railroads crossed the American continent. Trains also enabled the horizontal spread of cities that were increasingly organized around subways and streetcars.

Machines replaced some people, but they also created vast numbers of new jobs. People were richer and so they ate more. They had more clothes and traveled longer distances. Every new machine could have led to a disappearance of work, but the combination of human ingenuity and seemingly unquenchable material desires kept the factory floors full of workers, who were reasonably safe from disease because of the regulatory process begun by the second Robert Peel.

Through the middle of the twentieth century, urban growth was oriented largely around manufacturing plants, like Nabisco's bakeries in Chelsea and Chicago. The Allied victory in World War II required an explosion of manufacturing. Thus, England had a burst of aircraft production in 1940 and 1941 that won the Battle of Britain. American factories produced even more planes in 1943 and 1944.

The massive construction of armaments meant that 16.5 million Americans were in manufacturing in January 1944. That figure represented 45 percent of America's paid private-sector workforce. America's industrial army was 40 percent larger than the combined uniformed army and navy at the height of World War II. Factory employment dropped sharply at the end of the war, as the riveting Rosies, the women who had made so many tanks and planes and guns, returned to their homes, but then it began to grow once more. America's manufacturing labor force reached its maximum in June of 1979, just shy of 20 million workers.

But that would be the high-water mark. Indeed, as a fraction of total nonfarm employment, manufacturing peaked at 39 percent in November 1943 when British planes, built outside of Manchester, were just beginning to bomb Berlin. After the war, manufacturing represented 32 percent of America's nonfarm employment through the summer of 1953, but then that share began to decline. By the time John F. Kennedy spoke in Berlin ten years later, manufacturing's share of nonfarm laborers was down to 27 percent. When Saigon fell to the North Vietnamese in April 1975, fewer than 22 percent of workers were in manufacturing. The share of the workforce in manufacturing fell below 16 percent in 1990, 12 percent in 2001, and held between 8 and 9 percent between 2009 and 2020. The figures are comparable for other wealthy countries: fewer than one in ten Britons work in manufacturing. Manufacturing's share of French employment is below 12 percent.

The decline of industrial employment didn't mean that America stopped making physical goods. They were just made by machines rather than people. A capital-intensive, machine-intensive manufacturing sector could supply all of America with its core material needs, such as clothing, food, and transportation. As a result, American workers started to do other things. They looked for more interesting and varied retail experiences. They generated better vacations and more fun. People moved from manufacturing into jobs that put them into contact with other people.

The total number of Americans providing services rose from 24 million in 1944 to 131 million at the start of 2020. Eighty-six percent of American workers are service providers; the figures for the United Kingdom are comparable. Between 1945 and 2004, the number of Americans working in retail trade as salespeople, cashiers, and stockers rose from 3.5 million to 15.8 million. Over the same period, the number of workers in leisure and hospitality, which includes restaurants and hotels, rose from under 2.2 million to over 12 million.

While retail trade employment stagnated between 2004 and 2020, leisure and hospitality continued to expand. On the eve of COVID-19, that sector employed 16.9 million workers. At the start of 2020, as many Americans worked in restaurants (12.3 million) as in factories (12.8 million).

If we group retail trade, hospitality, and leisure together, perhaps calling it the face-to-face service economy, it grew from under 5 million workers in 1939 to over 32 million workers in 2020. Before COVID-19, it employed one fifth of the American labor force. Whereas Americans without a college degree in 1953 could make good money working on an assembly line, by 2020 the face-to-face service economy was a better bet for someone who didn't want to sit through more algebra.

The health risks inherent in the rise of that face-to-face economy would have been quickly obvious in the unsanitary eighteenth century. But until 2020, we didn't seem to notice that the face-to-face service sector could both spread a pandemic and be crushed by a pandemic.

Two less vulnerable sectors also continue to dominate the American labor market: professional and business services, which had 21.5 million workers before COVID, and education and health services with 24.5 million workers. Professional and business service providers, such as lawyers and architects, often have advanced degrees. This group didn't generally telecommute before COVID-19, but they can do so, and many did after the pandemic struck. When these knowledge-intensive workers stopped going to the office, that further depressed the demand for the restaurants and shops that used to supply them during the day.

Education and health service workers are often directly or indirectly paid by tax dollars. Because children continue to need education and people continue to get sick, even in recessions, those two industries have been traditionally immune from economic downturns. In a departure from the past, however, many health-care workers were paradoxically laid off early in the pandemic. Future state and local budget cuts may also mean more teacher layoffs.

Machines are extremely good at routine tasks, such as producing almost any physical object that does not need to be embedded in its surroundings. Robots are great at welding car parts together. Computers are good at doing routine intellectual tasks, including basic accounting. As yet, humans have retained the edge in three key areas: creativity, person-to-person interactions, and nonroutine or highly embedded physical tasks.

Extreme creativity seems likely to remain a human monopoly for decades if not centuries. How could a machine be da Vinci or Einstein? Some tricky cognitive tasks also befuddle even the brainiest machines. IBM's famed supercomputer Watson was unable to improve on the diagnosing of cancer. But there are lesser creative tasks—such as producing an amusing song list for a birthday party—that should be well within the province of a properly trained machine. The creative economy, championed by economist Richard Florida at the University of Toronto and others, is likely to remain, but machine learning may make it smaller and focused only on those tasks that require the sort of quirkiness that is particularly human.

Those creative jobs are safe from machines and they are probably safe from illness as well, at least if they don't require too much face-to-face interaction. Random, in-person meetings have long been a part of our creative processes, but genius survives, even if subdued, in a virtual world.

Nonroutine physical or embedded jobs include everything from cutting lawns to installing solar panels to preparing lattes. The first two occupations differ significantly from the last, however, because they generally do not involve significant face-to-face interaction. The noninteractive workers are hired for their physical skills, not their winning personalities. No one ever fired a competent and honest plumber for lacking charm. By contrast, good waiters and waitresses are highly social, and are employed partially as a source of genial interaction.

The outdoor nonroutine physical tasks, including construction, can be done reasonably safely, even during a pandemic, but they are not light work. Construction is the economy's most common nonroutine physical task. It can be backbreaking labor. Construction employment has remained relatively stable despite the economic chaos that has accompanied COVID-19. In July 2019, 7.75 million Americans worked in the building trades. A year later, the sector had 7.42 million workers, a drop of only 4.3 percent. Similarly, the number of workers in warehousing and storage has been rock steady, moving down only from 1.181 million to 1.178 million.

How many of these jobs will remain when robots get better and better? The rise of autonomous vehicles puts America's 1.5 million trucking-related jobs at risk, but we'd bet that plumbers and electricians will survive. A lot of buildings—even high-rises—can be built in a capital-intensive factory and then plopped in place quickly with a minimum amount of human sweat, so demand for construction labor may fall—though not dry up entirely.

A giant third group of jobs that seems safer from automation depends on the pleasure of personal contact. A good barista excels at the task of producing beautiful foam, perhaps in the shape of a heart, but that bit of artistry has far more value because one enjoys seeing it done live. The warm glow of knowing that another person put in effort for your pleasure is enough to justify the cost.

Great providers of in-person services are artists of human interaction who know how to make you feel valued and entertained. Harry's Bar in Florence—the more elegant cousin of the Venetian original—was tended for decades by the great Leo, who wore his reading glasses elegantly dangling from his cheekbones. To him, every prosperous middle-aged tourist was a contessa, every young would-be rake was Byron on a Grand Tour. It was all a mirage, of course, but he was a maestro of mixed drinks, not because his martinis were better, but because he made his customers feel special. Many found this was an experience well worth paying for.

On a smaller scale, such skills appear everywhere in the great urban service economy. All of us have our favorites, service providers who turn a task into an act of simulated—and maybe even real—friendship. Most of us are willing to pay extra for all manner of pleasant human engagement.

Over the past thirty years, the number of Americans working in restaurants has almost doubled, from 6.5 million in 1990 to 12.3 million in February 2020. The number of bartenders increased by almost 50 percent between 2010 and 2020, despite declining alcohol consumption. The numbers of people working as waiters and waitresses increased by 18 percent between 2010 and 2019. These are not well-paying, prestigious jobs, but they have offered reliable employment for millions of ordinary Americans, especially in cities where abundant numbers of educated urbanites are willing to spend on a pleasant personal interaction.

America's shift to service-sector jobs is not an unalloyed blessing. Critics emphasize the often degrading nature of having to please customers for a living. We are describing, not lauding, the pre-2020 status quo.

But our larger point is that the shift toward a predominantly service economy left the wealthy world, and especially the US, far more vulnerable to pandemic than in the past. The urban service industries were the epicenter of economic dislocation during the COVID-19 pandemic and urban service workers were disproportionately likely to suffer from the illness.

Employment and Illness during the COVID-19 Pandemic

As the pandemic raged, a flood of economic pain was unleashed on those urban service workers. America shut down and small businesses were shuttered. One of us (Glaeser) coauthored a series of papers based on a repeated survey of small business owners who were affiliated with Alignable, an online referral network for small businesses that has over five million members. We assured ourselves that the respondents were reasonably representative of small business owners across the US.

As of April 1, 2020, one half of all the retailers in our sample were closed. One half of all the jobs at those firms were gone. Fifty-four percent of restaurants were closed. Seventy-one percent of businesses specializing in the arts and entertainment had shuttered themselves or been shuttered by ordinance. The ordinary service jobs that employed Americans who don't have bachelor's degrees or higher vanished by the millions.

Many lower-income Americans faced a no-win situation. If their jobs were essential, they could keep on working and face the risk of getting the disease. If their jobs were nonessential, they could stay safe at home, but they would stop getting a paycheck. The link between occupation and illness is clear in the cities—such as New York, Philadelphia, and Chicago—that experienced the full brunt of the pandemic in March, April, and early May. In New York City zip codes where many workers were either in essential industries or in jobs that couldn't telecommute, mobility was much higher and COVID-19-related cases and deaths were more prevalent. We estimated that a 10 percent reduction in mobility led to a 20 percent reduction in the number of COVID-19 cases. Unsurprisingly, telecommuting was far more common in America's better-educated industries and wealthier zip codes.

In April, many small business owners had little confidence about their ability to recover. Forty-four percent of the retailers in our sample guessed that they would still be closed in December. Fifty-four percent of restaurateurs expected to stay dark for that long. The typical small business owner keeps only a small nest egg of cash to tide them over. In our sample, the average firm had about two weeks' worth of its regular expenses on hand. When their customers stayed home because they feared illness, the companies had little chance of survival without government assistance.

Public help materialized on a grand scale. The last time the economy faced such damage—the Great Recession of 2007–09—the federal government allocated $787 billion to economic stimulus, equivalent to $965 billion in 2020. The Obama administration deliberately brought the cost in under $800 billion to blunt public criticism of its apparent extravagance. Even with that sop, only sixty-one senators brought themselves to vote for the stimulus. In 2020, the Coronavirus Aid, Relief, and Economic Security (CARES) Act carried a cost of $2.2 trillion and sailed through the Senate 96–0. The CARES Act was easily the largest dollop of federal largesse in the history of America, and not a single senator argued against it.

Small businesses benefited most from the act's Paycheck Protection Program (PPP), which in 2020 lent $649 billion to firms with fewer than five hundred employees. The scale of this program is mind-boggling. The PPP cost $2,000 for each man, woman, and child in the country. Moreover, the loans are forgiven for firms that maintained their pre-COVID level of employment and used the money to pay wages and other core business expenses.

The cash came in two waves. The first wave ran woefully short, but by the end of the second wave, funds were available for everyone who was remotely eligible and managed to get through the paperwork. The first-wave loans were allocated by the banks, and in one of our surveys, we found that loans were more likely to go to businesses that reported little or no impact of the illness on their revenues. Banks tended to lend to firms that had more cash, not less, and to lend to longer-term borrowers that already had lines of credit. When hundreds of billions of dollars is given to the financial service industry, few strings attached, those firms direct the money first to their best customers.

We used a number of techniques to see what America had bought with $649 billion worth of credit. As of late April 2020, the companies that received the loans were somewhat more optimistic about their future. The firms that got loans were 14 percent more likely to be operational in July. Their self-assessed probability of survival increased by about fifteen percentage points. But there was little obvious impact on employment. The loans certainly helped many small businesses survive, but at an enormous cost.

Despite the federal aid, unemployment still soared, especially in the urban service sectors. As noted above, the overall unemployment rate rose from 3.5 percent in February to 14.7 percent in April. It settled down at 10.2 percent in July and remained at 6.7 percent through December. That overall figure hides dramatic differences between the old economy, which is as robust to pandemic as it was in 1918, and the new economy, which is not. The unemployment rate among leisure and hospitality workers was 25 percent in July 2020. The unemployment rate was only 5.7 percent among farmers and 8.6 percent among manufacturing workers.

Some thought that the economic decline was caused by a hysterical governmental response to the pandemic: the lockdown regulations that made it impossible for businesses to keep going. On April 29, 2020, Florida's governor, Ron DeSantis, began reopening his state, declaring that its biggest obstacle was "fear sparked by constant doom and gloom and hysteria that has permeated our culture for the last six weeks." Apparently, partiers had nothing to fear but fear itself. Florida reopened in a burst of optimism. The state had seemed almost immune to the pandemic, having until then experienced only 33,000 cases and 1,200 deaths across a total population of 21.5 million. But the economic consequences had been vast. Nearly a third of the state's employment in hospitality and leisure was laid off between February and April.

It was not obvious that people would start going back out again, even with the governor giving the OK. According to cell-phone data, people stopped moving around before most states put in lockdown orders, suggesting that fear, not government order, kept people inside. One striking piece of research compared the economic impact of COVID-19 in Denmark, which had stringent social-distancing laws, and nearby Sweden, which did not. Bank-account data revealed a 29 percent drop in spending in Denmark and a 25 percent drop in Sweden, which led the researchers to conclude that "most of the economic contraction is caused by the virus itself and occurs regardless of social distancing." In Brazil, there was also little link between government lockdown regulations and mobility, which seem driven by fear more than government directive.

But when DeSantis reopened, people started going out again. Perhaps Floridians were desperate for human contact, or perhaps they had confidence that their government wouldn't reopen unless it was safe. After all, the governor had assured them on April 28 at the White House that "Florida's done better" because "we had a tailored and measured approach, that not only helped our numbers be way below what anyone predicted, but also did less damage to our state going forward." That "tailored and measured approach" surely meant that if the state was reopening, then eating out wasn't risky.

If Florida had tested the asymptomatic, as Ardern and Bloomfield did in New Zealand, the state would have known if the illness was gone or merely gathering steam silently. Florida did not. It turned out that COVID-19 was still widespread.

The best data on dining out comes from the cell-phone records that the SafeGraph company assembled and made public during the COVID pandemic. Visits to sit-down restaurants were 68 percent below the pre-COVID norm in Florida by April 21. Visits to bars were almost 80 percent below what they had been pre-COVID. By June 22, restaurant and bar visits in Florida were back up to 87 and 74 percent respectively of their pre-COVID levels.

With the reopening came an increase in cases and deaths. Florida had 100,000 COVID-19 cases by June 22, and the state started to reregulate. Florida shut down its bars on June 26, but by July 11, Florida's case load had already grown to 250,000. The state's largest county, Miami-Dade, shut down all of its restaurants on July 6, and still by August 5 more than half a million Floridians had gotten sick. Two weeks after that date, Florida's death toll surpassed 10,000. By the end of 2020, the number of deaths in Florida had exceeded 20,000. More than one out of every thousand residents in the state perished. Florida could no longer boast of its "tailored and measured approach." The lesson of the Sunshine State is that if you put the economy ahead of health, you end up with neither. The government needs to measure the prevalence of disease, not act on the basis of wishful thinking.

Some services can be made safe for workers, but customers will still be at risk and demand will still be low. Bartenders can work at solo stations behind a clear wall, but a bar isn't fun if everyone is drinking in their own walled-off cubicle. You might as well drink in a closet at home. The whole point of a face-to-face service economy is to be close to other humans. That can't survive the threat of deadly contagion. Stopping the risk of illness is the first step toward creating the face-to-face jobs of the future.

The Pre-COVID Decline in American Entrepreneurship

Thousands of firms have permanently closed because of the pandemic. New enterprises will need to take their place. How easy will that be? The sad answer is that it will be quite difficult. Americans think of themselves as dynamic and full of entrepreneurial spirit, but the reality is that new firm formations have been declining in the US for decades.

Historically, entrepreneurship has been critical for urban reinvention. Writing in the late 1950s, the economist Benjamin Chinitz posited that New York was more resilient than Pittsburgh because of a culture of entrepreneurship that was inculcated at the breakfast table and on the street corner. In the 1950s, New York's garment industry had more workers than the steel industry in Pittsburgh or the automobile industry in Detroit. Even more importantly, the Garment District had vastly more entrepreneurs.

Anyone with a good idea and a sewing machine could start making and selling dresses—witness the scruffy operation run by Mrs. Maisel's father-in-law in her eponymous Amazon Prime series—but who was going to compete with U.S. Steel in Pittsburgh or the Big Three in Detroit? Pittsburgh and Detroit trained company men, not entrepreneurs.

Businessmen who got started in the garment industry went on to found companies that made many things other than clothing. Samuel Goldwyn (born Gelbfisz) got started sewing and then selling gloves before founding Goldwyn Pictures. A. E. Lefcourt moved from clothing to building Art

Deco skyscrapers. The children of dressmakers, like Sandy Weill of Citi-group, would end up being lions of Wall Street.

The comparison between Pittsburgh and New York City generalizes. Cities with access to coal and iron mines over a century ago ended up with larger companies, less competition, and eventually fewer new firms and less growth.

Unfortunately, the dynamism of the American economy is failing. Economists track job creation—the share of jobs from new or expanding establishments relative to overall employment. Job creation "averaged 18.9 percent in the late 1980s and decreased in what appears to be a roughly stepwise pattern following recessions to an average of 15.8 percent in the 2004–2006 period," which represents a 16 percent decline in the pace of job creation over twenty years. The share of employment at firms less than five years old "declined from an average of 18.9 percent in the late 1980s to an average of 13.4 percent at the peak before the Great Recession, a 29 percent decline over a 17-year period."

There is no scientific consensus on why America's start-up rate has fallen. Cross-country evidence finds that "regulations hamper the creation of new firms," but one study concludes that in the US, "rising federal regulation cannot explain secular trends in economic dynamism." The start-up rate has not fallen faster in those industries where federal regulations have risen the most.

Yet many of the biggest regulatory burdens facing new entrepreneurs are imposed by states and localities, not the federal government. One helpful, if somewhat outdated, checklist from the City of Boston contains eighteen regulatory steps, including the "weights and measures inspection," the storefront sign review process, and the dumpster placement permit. The prospective small business owner in New York City faces eight distinct regulatory bodies, all of which have different licensing and inspection processes.

Many regulations are unnecessary and serve only to protect insiders at the expense of outsiders. Occupational licensing for jobs with few safety implications, like florists or interior decorators, act primarily to protect incumbents from competition. Between the 1950s and today, the share of the population that works in a licensed occupation rose from 5 percent to over 20 percent. Occupational licensing does not generally seem to increase quality, but it does lead to higher prices. The insiders win, while the outsiders lose.

One of us (Cutler) studied restrictions on the activities of registered nurses relative to doctors. The country has a shortage of primary care providers, but many states prohibit nurses from using the full range of their skills. That policy entrenches the status of doctors and limits ordinary people's access to needed medical care.

An understandable frustration with regulation can lead to an overly simplistic opposition to all public rules, but there is a good case for regulating food and factory safety. An effective public sector imposes only rules that have benefits that exceed their costs, and then makes complying with those rules relatively easy. Unfortunately, urban leaders today typically embrace entrepreneurship in spirit, but then accept a web of local regulations that makes it difficult to start new businesses.

Policy can be improved first by making better decisions about what to regulate, and then by making the approval process easier and more transparent. One proposal is for the federal government to underwrite cost-benefit analysis of local rules by funding an independent evaluation team, along the lines of the federal Congressional Budget Office. That team would provide expert analysis of regulations, free of charge, to state and local governments. They would indicate which regulations are likely to have benefits that exceed the costs, and which do not. Localities would not have to follow the advice, but at least voters would get an independent evaluation. Both Democratic and Republican administrations, as well as expert bodies such as the National Academy of Medicine, have shamed excessive regulations, but there is little credible evaluation of local regulations.

Second, the process of permitting can be made more efficient through innovations like one-stop permitting. Consider an example in our home state, Massachusetts. In the wake of the 1996 closure of the Devens army base, which had been an influenza pandemic hot spot after World War I, the state of Massachusetts established the Devens Enterprise Commission. The commission aimed to encourage new business formation with a streamlined one-stop permitting process.

While there is no academic evaluation of the Devens experiment, the plan seems to have been moderately successful. A number of jobs were created and housing was built, though not as much as was hoped. The regional newspaper, the *Lowell Sun*, recently wrote that the "Devens Enterprise Zone already has shown that the ability to offer a variety of amenities along with a streamlined permitting process can serve as an economic-development magnet," and "that formula already has attracted more than 100 companies of all sizes to the self-contained community."

Permitting should be made just as transparent in inner city neighborhoods and low-density, disadvantaged locales. Indeed, we should particularly target permitting innovations toward areas with lower incomes and low employment rates because we regulate the entrepreneurship of the poor far more strictly than we regulate the entrepreneurship of the rich. It is easier to start a social network—now large enough to influence elections—in a Harvard college dorm than it is to start a small grocery store a few blocks away.

Permitting reform is particularly important because of the small-business Armageddon created by COVID-19. It will take years to work our way through all the bankruptcies that the pandemic will create. It would be impossible to save all the businesses affected, and frankly, one shouldn't try. We have an obligation to protect every person from hunger and deprivation, but not every business needs to be kept afloat. A full-scale business permitting overhaul is ideal but might take too long. In the short term, cities could create a one-stop permitting office that is directed to get new firms open as soon as possible. That office can then provide a model for permitting reform in the longer run.

Even beyond COVID-19, permitting reform was essential. In the pre-COVID era, jobs were plentiful in the growing coastal cities, but there were far fewer of them in the states of America's eastern heartland, like Ohio, West Virginia, and Mississippi, or in the old industrial regions of England, or in the growing cities of sub-Saharan Africa. These places need more entrepreneurship too.

Land use policy also matters. Many of the areas where jobs are plentiful are too expensive to live in. An out-of-work barber might move from Minnesota to San Francisco, but good luck finding affordable housing or commercial space. We shall turn to the cost of real estate in chapter 8.

In places where joblessness is high, policies can do more to encourage job creation, like providing employment tax credits and allowing disabled workers to earn more money before they lose access to their disability insurance payments.

The Future of the Service Sector

There is no going back to widespread manufacturing employment, either for the US or other rich countries. Nor will we return to dispersed agricultural jobs. The face-to-face service economy must continue providing employment possibilities for people without a computer science degree. Any job that relies on face-to-face interactions with strangers, like the personal trainers of today and unlike the domestic servants of 1918, is vulnerable to pandemic.

Before COVID-19 struck, there was a lively debate about the right policy response when the rise of robots leaves humanity with nothing to do. One line of reasoning, advanced by former presidential candidate Andrew Yang, is that as work disappears, we should provide everyone with an unconditional check from the government, called universal basic income. If vast numbers of Americans were paid for doing nothing, then the economy could indeed become pandemic-proof. The relatively small number of working Americans could oversee the robots and do highly intellectual, creative, and well-compensated tasks. The rest of the country could cash their checks (virtually, of course) and enjoy the delights of video-gaming.

America and Europe are not yet wealthy enough to afford such a generous welfare state, but they probably will be within the lifetimes of many of our students. The resources available to the nonworking will be limited, but they will have food, medical care, and abundant access to the internet. They also won't have to go out—essentially ever—and so they'll be safe from contagious illness.

At first thought, this scenario may seem attractive. The great economist John Maynard Keynes certainly thought so eighty years ago when he wrote his classic essay "Economic Possibilities of Our Grandchildren." But the data say otherwise. Joblessness, especially among prime-aged men, is associated with misery, suicide, and divorce. The problem is not so much material deprivation as social isolation and a sense of worthlessness. When purpose and social interaction vanish, humans often drift and can become dejected.

Gender norms make the situation somewhat different for women. Even officially "nonworking" women do plenty of work, taking care of children and family members and volunteering in the community. Jobless men watch an average of five hours of television every day. The issues around women and work are too deep and important for us to address satisfactorily here, but we think it is unlikely that the majority of nonworking men will ever manage to make their lives joyful and productive. At the end of the day, there is simply no viable alternative to a strong service sector. Thus, our efforts to combat pandemic are doubly important—to prevent death, and to keep the jobs that prevent misery.

But even if the service jobs remain, we need to worry about where they are located. Millions of those who live and work in cities are poor. Will the rich abandon them for leafy suburbs with the fastest possible Zoom connections? We turn to that possibility next.

Chapter 7

WHAT IS THE FUTURE

OF DOWNTOWN?

Forty years ago, the futurist Alvin Toffler predicted that the industrial "second wave" of smokestacks and assembly lines would be followed by an information- and technology-intensive "third wave," in which a "new production system could shift literally millions of jobs out of the factories and offices into which the Second Wave swept them and right back where they came from originally: the home."

Until 2020, offices seemed remarkably resilient, even in the technology sector. Google bought the Googleplex and tried to make it as welcoming as possible for the young and the fun. In 2013, Yahoo! CEO Marissa Mayer banned remote work, declaring, "We need to be one Yahoo!, and that starts with physically being together."

But with COVID-19, the dominance of office life disappeared. Google told its workers that they could stay remote until the summer of 2021. Facebook said the same. In one survey, which Glaeser helped analyze, more than 40 percent of employers predicted that 40 percent or more of their workers who switched to telecommuting during the pandemic would stay remote. Zoom became a ubiquitous noun, verb, and lifestyle.

Some workers become more productive if they don't have to commute. Natalia Emanuel and Emma Harrington, two former PhD students in the economics department at Harvard, analyzed data from a major online US retailer. In early 2018 the retailer allowed more remote work because it was running out of space in some of its call centers. Emanuel and Harrington compared the call volume for workers who were allowed to work at home before and after they switched to remote work. They found that "at the time of the transition to remote work, hourly calls rose by 7.5%," despite finding no change in the composition of calls. There was a reduction in unexcused absences, and little change in the ratings customers gave the workers for their calls. Similarly, when call-center workers were forced to go home because of COVID-19, productivity increased by 8 percent.

If people and businesses conclude that they are more productive from home, we could well see cities break apart. Rich people will live with other rich people in Zoom-friendly enclaves. Middle-class people will do the same, albeit in less luxurious surroundings. And poor people will inherit what is left of downtowns. Such a radical shift in the location of work would fundamentally transform the world's cities. Will it happen?

Cities will certainly change with COVID-19. But we suspect that there will be less of a transformation than many predict. While some cities are in danger, the downtown in most places is far from dying. A greater share of routine and easily evaluated work will be done at home, probably saving one or two commutes per week, but the most important moments on the job will still happen around coworkers. Commercial rents will certainly fall, and some commercial space will be converted to residences or allocated to scrappier start-ups. But the city itself will continue to be a home to rich and poor.

The office will not be vanquished, because in-person interaction is so much richer than working remotely. Jobs where work is relatively independent and output can be readily evaluated, like call-center work, can be done from home, but such jobs can also be outsourced to Asia or automated. Most workers produce output that is less easily quantified and less able to be done alone. Middle managers, executive assistants, and architectural draftspersons all benefit from the spark of in-person interaction. If work continues its evolution to more interactive and ephemeral tasks, as discussed in the previous chapter, then offices will become even more vital.

Fundamentally, people value cities because they value personal connection. Zoom-based jobs can quickly turn transactional; personal interaction allows for more inspiration and enjoyment. While some may leave cities because of pandemic fears, others will be there to take their place.

But this is still a moment of peril and opportunity for many city governments. COVID-19 has made large-scale corporate relocation vastly more plausible. Some telecommuters have moved to nicer and cheaper locales even while the pandemic still roars. That trickle could become a flood if companies decide that they too have no reason to remain in New York City or San Francisco. Relocation will become even more appealing if governments raise taxes. Cities that have long regarded their wealthier residents and businesses as permanent fixtures might see both leave. In the next few years, cities will have to fight even harder to attract nomadic talent. The need to retain the rich means that cities that want to do more for the poor will need to increase their competence rather than just redistribute income.

The Dance of Urbanizing and Dispersing Technologies

Cities are defined by the absence of physical distance. Cities exist to reduce the costs of connection, and consequently urban fortunes are determined by transportation technology. Changes in the ability to move people or goods or ideas over space all impact the demand for physical proximity in cities.

Almost thirty years ago, Nobel Prize–winning economist Paul Krugman formulated the basic tenets of economic geography. His papers focused on the balance between centripetal or urbanizing forces, which pull people toward cities, and centrifugal or dispersing factors, which lead people to move apart. Krugman's first spatial model balanced the desire to reduce the cost of moving manufactured goods between industrial firms and workers (the urbanizing or centripetal force) with the need to access agriculture (the dispersing or centrifugal force).

This framework matched the experience of nineteenth-century cities such as Chicago, which benefited both from industrial firms clustering near one another and from proximity to the rich farmland of Iowa. But the dance between centripetal and centrifugal is ever changing. Innovations that reduce the benefits of density, like cars and televisions, lead to deurbanization. Breakthroughs that make clustering more valuable pull people toward cities. The nineteenth century was strongly centripetal and dominated by urbanizing breakthroughs, including the streetcar, the steam train, the elevator, and the skyscraper. Sewers and aqueducts helped too.

The twentieth century was a centrifugal era, especially in the US, marked by the spread of innovations that enabled humans to disperse, including the internal combustion engine, the radio, and the television. The failures of urban government, including rising crime levels and problematic urban schools, also sent people to the suburbs. With the benefit of hindsight, we know whether an epoch was centrifugal or centripetal, but in the moment, it is often hard to spot which way the winds are blowing.

Observing the island of Manhattan from the window seat of an airplane provides a bird's-eye view of how nineteenth-century transportation technologies shaped the city. The elevator that enabled commuters to ride up and down gave the city its vertical height. The trains that speed noisily underground allowed the city to stretch from Battery Park to the Cloisters.

The midair observer of New York quickly notices the twin peaks of skyscrapers. There is a southern cluster perched at the bottom of the island and a central hulk of buildings anchored around Forty-Second Street. City guides sometimes perpetuate what economist Jason Barr of Rutgers University calls the Bedrock Myth, that "skyscrapers are constructed in Downtown and Midtown because bedrock is easily accessible there." But you don't need bedrock to build up. Chicago—the city that gave us the skyscraper—is built on mud.

Manhattan's architectural shape owes more to water than stone. The older Downtown cluster grew up around the ships that once docked at the south of the city. New York's stock exchange began with an agreement signed under a buttonwood tree on Wall Street, by men such as Ephraim Hart—sadly, they were all men—whose livelihoods were tied to the wharves. Hart listed his occupation in 1816 as a dock builder.

The Midtown cluster is anchored by the city's two major rail stations: Grand Central Terminal and Pennsylvania Station. Penn Station's location is linked to the Hudson River, which was far harder to cross than the modest waterways that separate Manhattan from Long Island and the Bronx. Large buildings, like those that A. E. Lefcourt erected in New York's once mighty Garment District, sprang up near these rail hubs to make it easier for commuters to come in and for finished goods to leave.

Those building heights required two urbanizing innovations of the nineteenth century: the safety elevator and the metal-framed skyscraper. The skyscraper has a long history. Joseph Paxton, an English gardener, architect, and member of Parliament, borrowed the metal framing of greenhouses for his design of the Crystal Palace that defined London's Great Exhibition of 1851. That building seems to have inspired the French architect Victor Baltard, who brought iron framing to Paris for the marketplace of Les Halles and the church of Saint-Augustin. The American architect William Le Baron Jenney studied in Paris and inserted a partial steel frame into Chicago's Home Insurance Building, which is sometimes credited as being the world's first skyscraper. Skyscrapers replace horizontal space with height.

There was little demand for many-storied buildings until elevators eliminated the need to tromp up all those flights. Elisha Otis produced the first safety elevator, which he demonstrated, coincidentally, at New York's 1853 Crystal Palace exhibition. He stood on an elevator deck and dramatically cut the only rope that was holding him aloft. The crowd watched as the Otis mechanism stopped the deck's downward trajectory and kept its inventor safe. It took Jenney thirty more years to build Home Insurance, but in 1853, New York had both the metal frame and the safe vertical-motion machine that would enable the climb to the sky.

The aerial view of Manhattan also reveals a long narrow stretch of buildings surging up the island. The northward march of the metropolis was its own saga of nineteenth- and twentieth-century city building. The structures first followed the paths of avenues, like Broadway, and then the course of trains that ran first above and then below ground. Abraham Brower pioneered public transportation in New York in 1827, when he sent a horse-drawn omnibus up Broadway from the Battery to Bleecker Street, roughly two miles.

John Stephenson, an Irish immigrant to New York, was the human link between the streetcar and the railroad. Stephenson began as one of Brower's apprentices, and then started his own business building coaches for Brower. He was approached by a banker who had received a charter in 1832 to build a street railroad reaching the eight miles from Prince Street to the Harlem River. The carriages would still be pulled by horses, but they would face far less friction traveling on rails. Stephenson's railroad design took twenty years to complete, but it eventually traveled the length of the island. The permission to build in the unpopulated north end of the city was uncontroversial, but the railroad's charter went through multiple amendments before it got the right to run through the city's densely packed south.

On the other side of the Atlantic, George Stephenson—no relation to John—was pioneering trains powered by steam rather than horses. Stephenson was an engineer from the north of England, a tinkerer without much formal education. His steam engines were seen as a nuisance in dense cities. In 1844, New York's city council refused to allow steam trains south of

Thirty-Second Street. Ten years later, they moved the no-steam zone ten blocks north, which determined the location of Grand Central Terminal, also known as Grand Central Station. Tall buildings would eventually cluster around that station, but it would take another eighty years before demand for space near that station was strong enough for rents to be high enough to cover the cost of skyscrapers.

The link between real estate and transportation was there from the beginning. Historian Harry Carman notes how Samuel Ruggles, the "owner of large tracts of real property between Third and Fourth Avenue, in the vicinity of Irving Place and Lexington Avenue, was untiring in his efforts to obtain public support and approval" for the railroad during the 1830s. He had strong financial incentives to do so, for "as well as being a large landholder, he was also a director and one of the largest stockholders of the New York and Harlem Railroad Company." Cornelius Vanderbilt was another director of the New York and Harlem. He pushed the construction of the Grand Central Depot that would eventually morph into Grand Central Station. As the railroad stretched north from Grand Central, the city expanded alongside the rails.

All cities are both nodes on the vast transportation network that spans the globe and hubs of their own local transportation system that allows travel across their metropolitan region. Global trade expanded enormously in the nineteenth century as first ships and then railroads traveled from one dense urban area to another. Both transportation technologies involved large vehicles and expensive local infrastructure. Both required large scale and so they were urbanizing, centripetal forces. It makes little sense to build a huge terminal where there aren't many people.

Railroads and streetcars enabled the spread of nineteenth-century cities by extending the reach of urban connection, but they still were best matched with densely packed offices and apartments. The subways may have traveled the whole length of Manhattan and beyond, but subway commuters still needed to stroll from the station to their final destinations. That walking ensured that buildings would be packed tightly enough to enable pedestrian mobility and that the city would remain a coherent whole.

The Centrifugal Twentieth Century

If the centripetal transportation technologies of the nineteenth century powered urban growth, the twentieth century's centrifugal marvels enabled an urban exodus. An air flight over Chicago, or almost any non-coastal American metropolis, makes it easy to see this transformation. A tall center stands at the middle of a web of large gray ribbons that shoot out radially. To the sides of those gray ribbons are houses—not the crowded tenements of nineteenth-century city dwellers or the glazed brick buildings built for middle-income urbanites after World War II—but single-family housing going on seemingly forever. These homes are arrayed along small roads that feed into the large gray ribbons that funnel commuters into the central city core.

In the northeastern part of the country, there is often copious greenery amid the ranch houses and colonials. In the Southwest, the homes are packed more efficiently together. Texans flying into Massachusetts for the first time are often amazed by the preponderance of trees. The difference between Boston and Houston reflects both climate and a massively regulated Massachusetts land market that makes it difficult to add the density that keeps Houston so much more affordable.

Suburban Chicago has less greenery and more closely packed homes. The abundant supply of suburban homes in the Midwest also helps prices remain moderate. The median-priced home in the Chicago metropolitan area sold for $270,000 in the first quarter of 2020. The comparable figure for Boston was $494,000, and it was $985,000 in San Francisco. Prices in the Bay Area reflect the collision of robust demand for technology jobs and pleasant Mediterranean weather with a set of local policies that drastically limit new supply.

Most American suburbs are affordable because the post–World War II highway system made the supply of land available for housing feel almost unlimited. In 1949, Americans allocated less than 1 percent of the country's land areas, 18 million out of 2.27 billion acres, for "urban" living. That official definition of urban includes pretty much every US suburb. America used less land for city living in 1949 than it did for rural roads. Sixty years later, the nation's "urban" land increased to 70 million acres, which is still less than 3 percent of the nation's total acreage, and less than the US uses growing soybeans.

The interstate highway system made living space within commuting distances of city centers abundant, and that land became even more attractive with other technological breakthroughs. Radio became ubiquitous in the 1930s; televisions blanketed America in the 1950s. Living on a farm in 1900 was practically synonymous with dreariness. Living in a suburban ranch home in 1960 meant an abundant array of television programming, classical music on the radio, and the joys of TV dinners. Perhaps it wasn't entirely Eden, but the long-distance transmission of entertainment allowed for connections to the wider world—a death of distance—that was at least as important for low-density living as the internet is today.

The national government supported suburbanization both by funding the highway system and by providing tax benefits for home owning. Nathaniel Baum-Snow of the University of Toronto estimated that each new highway that ran through a metropolitan area reduced the central city's population by 18 percent relative to the surrounding suburbs. The federal highway subsidy has actually increased over time, because the gas tax that funds the Highway Trust Fund has been fixed at 18.4 cents per gallon since 1993. As inflation has eroded that tax's real value, Washington has used general tax revenues to fund roads, which effectively subsidizes driving and energy use.

The home mortgage interest deduction was originally part of the tax code because all interest that households paid was deductible. The Tax Reform Act of 1986 eliminated the more general interest deduction, but the favoritism shown to homeowners remained. After World War II, the federal government expanded its support for home buying with Veterans Administration loans for returning soldiers. Between 1940 and 1960, the homeownership rate increased from 44 to 62 percent. There is a tight link between ownership type and structure type. Eighty-two percent of single-family homes are owner-occupied, but 87 percent of multifamily homes, such as apartment buildings, are rented. Thus, when the federal government subsidizes home owning, it also encourages Americans to leave urban apartments and move to suburban tract homes.

While the national government was implicitly subsidizing suburbanization, city governments were having a hard time keeping people within their boundaries. Millions of American parents took to the highways in the 1960s and 1970s because they thought that the suburbs would do a better job of educating their children. Some of those parents may have been motivated by racism, but as we will discuss in chapter 9, the work of our colleague Raj Chetty and his many coauthors finds that children who grew up outside of big city school districts became more successful as adults, even after controlling for the effect of their parents' incomes. Other suburbanizers, including both parents and companies, were motivated by rising urban crime levels and high taxes.

Chicago's greatest nineteenth-century industry, measured by value added, was meatpacking, and it clustered around the gigantic Union Stock Yards that were right next to the rail station. Moving cows, even when they were slaughtered, remained challenging and it made sense to keep distances from slaughterhouses to railroads short. All of America's older cities were anchored by close relationships between business and transportation.

But the centrifugal transportation innovations of the twentieth century enabled the flight of factories from the city. The view from the sky over Chicago reveals a vast number of sprawling businesses along with single-family houses. This was partly driven by technology. Early factories were dense and labor-intensive, which made them a good fit for central cities. Over the postwar decades, machines increasingly replaced human labor, and that meant that factories needed large amounts of space. The average manufacturing plant in 2006 used 892 square feet per worker, which is far more than a typical office or retail store. As factories used more square footage, they left city centers for cheaper land. By 2006, more than 68 percent of the jobs in the Chicago metropolitan area were more than ten miles from the city's center. As a result, the American Midwest is dotted with cities, like Wheeling, West Virginia, and Hamilton, Ohio, that are much smaller today than they were at their industrial height.

No industry moved itself more radically and quickly than New York City's garment sector, which we discussed in the previous chapter. In 1947, New York City had 140,000 workers making women's outerwear alone, which was 45 percent of all US employment in that industry. By 1982, the number of women's outerwear workers in New York had fallen to less than 70,000.

New York City had once been a fantastic place to make clothes, with a seaport and railyards that made both importing fabric and exporting dresses easy. An abundance of immigrant labor kept costs down. Garments were made by small sewing machines, not mechanical behemoths, so they could even be sewn in small tenement rooms. Visitors to New York are amazed at what was then the small size of the typical clothing "factory." The city's dense, stylish markets enabled designers to try out new ideas, which could then be marketed by the city's inventive advertising industry and lovingly depicted in the pages of the city's many magazines.

Ralph Lauren (born Lifshitz) may be the most successful example of the Garment District's ability to manufacture both clothes and creativity. His father painted houses, but Lauren liked clothes and his friends' parents produced garments. Lauren started selling ties, first at Brooks Brothers and then in the Beau Brummell tie company's Empire State Building shop. Beau Brummell gave him his own division, but Lauren rejected their offer to make ties in Ohio. He wanted producers nearby who could capture his vision in silk. He hit it big partnering with Bloomingdale's department store. Like generations of garment industry pioneers before him, Lauren proved his commercial viability by selling vast numbers of clothes to the fussy customers living on Manhattan's Upper East Side. And like generations of garment industry pioneers before him, Lauren proved the flexibility of entrepreneurial talent by moving beyond clothes to sell a vast number of different products.

Lauren's career has become legend, and New York City continues to produce important fashion designers, such as Donna Karan and Marc Jacobs. But the actual manufacturing of clothing left the five boroughs. There were cheaper factories in right-to-work states, where an absence of unions kept wages and benefits low. Labor costs were even lower in China and Bangladesh. Container shipping was so inexpensive that any labor-intensive activity was pushed toward places with the lowest wages. The shift was sufficiently sweeping that demand for the lower-cost workers of Asia reduced global inequality by raising wages in previously poor places. But the exodus of manufacturing jobs from New York left the city in crisis.

Other urban traumas accompanied the collapse of manufacturing. Cities were rocked by race riots in the 1960s. Crime rose steadily through the 1970s. City governments needed to increase spending to deal with urban inequities and disorder, but the city's tax base had become more mobile. In the 1970s, when cities like New York tried to tax companies and the rich, those taxpayers fled to lower tax locations. The downward spiral discussed in our introduction, where decline begets decline, seemed to foretell the future of cities. That is the backdrop for Alvin Toffler's 1980 prognostication about the rise of telecommuting.

Alvin Toffler and the
Triumph of Telecommuting

Alvin Toffler was a true scion of New York City. His father made furs, the products of the clothing industry that go back to the beaver pelts bought by the Dutch during the early seventeenth century. Toffler met his wife, Heidi, who deserves much of the credit for his writing, at New York University. The Tofflers left New York for Cleveland, were married by an inebriated justice of the peace, and built their careers writing about the economy.

In 1970, Toffler struck publishing gold with *Future Shock*, a two-word phrase defined as the "dizzying disorientation brought on by the premature arrival of the future," which Toffler argued "may well be the most important disease of tomorrow." Writing in the 1960s, Toffler perceived "a greatly accelerated rate of change in society," which he thought responsible for "malaise, mass neurosis, irrationality, and free-floating violence." Toffler coupled this diagnosis with a prescription that "the only remedy for the phenomenon of future shock" is to form a "clearer, better, stronger conception of what lies ahead." The world needed what Toffler himself became: a futurist.

Among the less accurate claims in *Future Shock* is an alleged "trend towards residential renting" that "underscores the tendency towards ever-briefer relationships with the physical environment." In fact, surging suburbanization meant the share of American households living in rental units was declining steadily from 56 percent in 1940 to 37 percent in 1970. Instead of "breeding a new race of nomads," as Toffler wrote, the geographic mobility of Americans is far lower today than it was in 1970.

The 1970s were a catastrophic decade for much of urban America. When Toffler followed *Future Shock* with *The Third Wave* in 1980, he expressed far less confidence that cities would survive. The main thesis of that later book was that humanity had experienced a first "wave" during the agricultural

revolution ten millennia ago and a second wave during the Industrial Revolution. The third wave was "the death of industrialism and the rise of a new
civilization" that could be only imperfectly labeled with the phrases "information age, electronic era, or global village."

Toffler was writing just as the easier shipment of goods was killing off
urban manufacturing. He naturally hypothesized that easier transmission of
knowledge would have a similar impact on information-intensive urban industries. But as we have noted, it can be hard to tell at the time whether a
moment is centripetal or centrifugal, and information technology did more
than just enable home offices.

The Third Wave made one big prediction that proved completely correct:
computerization did radically change the world. But the book's subsidiary
predictions, such as how the third wave "will topple bureaucracies, reduce
the role of the nation-state, and give rise to semi-autonomous economies in
a post-imperialist world," fared less well. Like many Silicon Valley tech barons over the past forty years, Toffler underestimated the resilience of old
political institutions, including bureaucracies and the nation-state. We particularly regret that we have seen little to support Toffler's prediction of future "governments that are simpler, more effective, yet more democratic than
any we know today."

Toffler also underestimated the sticking power of cities. He saw his third
wave as a giant centrifugal event: "The Third Wave alters our spatial experience by dispersing rather than concentrating population." He supported this
contention by citing "the new allure of small-city and rural life," perhaps
reflecting his own earlier decision to relocate from New York to Ohio. He
wrote that "city dwellers by the millions yearn for the countryside, and the
Urban Land Institute reports a significant population shift toward rural
areas." Yet even during the troubled 1970s, America's urban population had
grown more quickly than its rural population. During the twenty years after

The Third Wave, America's urbanization rate rose from 74 percent to 79 percent, as many cities, including New York, Boston, and San Francisco, experienced economic renaissances. Between 1970 and 2010, the population of urban American grew by almost 100 million, while the population of rural America grew by less than 6 million. In countries with less overall population growth, such as the United Kingdom, rural population actually fell over the same time period.

Toffler's turn against cities followed from his third-wave vision that the workplaces of the future would be "electronic cottages" built for telecommuting. *The Economist* magazine used that term in 1974 when it predicted that "as there is no logical reason why the cost of telecommunication should vary with distance, quite a lot of people by the late 1980s will telecommute daily to their London offices while living on a Pacific island." Toffler riffed off *The Economist*'s prediction for an entire chapter, arguing that the third wave would mean "a return to cottage industry on a new, high, electronic basis, and with it a new emphasis on the home as the center of society."

Toffler was right that an increasing number of jobs could be done from home, partially because of the declining "number of workers who actually have to manipulate physical goods." He understood that telecommuting would "reduce energy requirements" from driving, which would generate environmental benefits. He correctly anticipated that "'low-abstraction' office workers" who work "entering data, typing, retrieving, totaling columns of figures, preparing invoices" and similar jobs "could perhaps be most easily shifted into the electronic cottage." He seems to have underestimated, however, the extent to which the march of machines would cause those jobs to disappear entirely.

Toffler worried, "What happens to society when an increased amount of human interaction on the job is vicarious while face-to-face, emotion-to-emotion interaction intensifies in the home?" But he did not foresee the loneliness experienced by millions who lived alone and were unable to interact with their coworkers in 2020. Of course, he was imagining only telecommuting, not ubiquitous social distancing.

Toffler thought that "our biggest factories and office towers may, within our lifetimes, stand half empty, reduced to use as ghostly warehouses or converted into living space," even "if as few as 10 to 20 percent of the work force as presently defined were to make this historic transfer" to electronic cottages. Yet before COVID-19, more than one tenth of the workforce in the Netherlands and Finland worked from home, and these societies have certainly not been "altered almost beyond our recognition," as Toffler predicted. Among other issues, he forgot that office rents will fall to offset a drop in demand. We shall return to this equilibrating force later.

The pre-COVID share of Americans working from home is not entirely known, partially because many adopt a hybrid arrangement that involves working at home, the office, and even the occasional Starbucks. One 2018 census figure is that 5 percent of Americans reported their standard commute as within their own household, which means that 95 percent of workers left their home on the majority of weekdays. However, there was also remote work, most of which reflected people leaving the office with laptop in tow. The Bureau of Labor Statistics reports that one fifth of workers did some share of their work at home during a given day in 2019, and that 84 percent of workers left home to work every day. A 2016 Gallup poll found that 43 percent of American workers "spent at least some of their time working in a location different from that of their coworkers." Out of this group, 55 percent spent more than four tenths of their time "working remotely." Yet before COVID-19, many employers provided space for every mid-level worker who could possibly show up, which meant a lot of underused real estate in the offices of peripatetic professions, like management consulting.

Both the Bureau of Labor Statistics and the Gallup figures, but not the census figure, suggest that over one fifth of Americans worked from home pre-COVID, but that did not turn commercial skyscrapers into "ghostly warehouses" or alter "our entire economy, our cities, our ecology, our family structure, our values and even our politics beyond our recognition," as Toffler forecast.

Why didn't information technology do to urban knowledge workers what container ships did to urban seamstresses? And why did the telecommuting that did occur alter society so much less than Toffler predicted?

The answer to the second question is a failure to account for the continuing growth in the size of the labor force. Between 1980 and February 2020, the total number of employed Americans increased by 68 percent, from 90 million to 152 million. Toffler analyzed demand for urban space holding everything else constant (the Latin phrase that economists use is *ceteris paribus*)— especially the number of workers. If the labor force had been fixed and one fifth of workers had become telecommuters, then there would have been 18 million empty offices. But given the actual growth in the labor force, even with a 20 percent switch to telecommuting, America still needed to build an extra 30 million offices.

But Toffler was wrong for a deeper reason as well. He thought that computers would be like the telegraph and act mainly to allow more long-distance communication. Instead, technological change made our economy vastly more knowledge intensive, connection intensive, and unequal. Those forces turned the past forty years into a centripetal, urbanizing era. Toffler freely admitted that "we did get a few things wrong," but he would "always get a laugh from an audience" after admitting an error, by saying that "we futurists have a magic button; we follow every statement about a failed forecast with 'yet.'" Late in life, he stood by the prediction of electronic cottages, though he emphasized work from home more than work outside urban areas.

The Return of the City

By the 1990s, evidence was increasingly rejecting Toffler's hypothesis that technology was eliminating either face-to-face contact or the cities that facilitate that contact. Wall Street boomed in the 1980s with information-intensive finance firms leading the way. Margaret Thatcher awoke London's once sleepy financial services industry with her deregulatory "Big Bang" in 1986. London was soon fighting its way back to global preeminence. Between 1980 and 1990, nominal home values in Los Angeles County increased by 132 percent, or 35 percent after adjusting for inflation. Cities weren't turning into ghost towns.

But the most glaring fly in Toffler's intellectual ointment was Silicon Valley. By the early 1980s, Silicon Valley's set of geographically proximate, highly interactive companies had become the world's leading example of industrial clustering. Countries everywhere were trying to create their own Silicon Alleys, Fens, Glens, Roundabouts, and Wadis. AnnaLee Saxenian's *Regional Advantage* attributed Silicon Valley's dominance to "the region's dense social networks and open labor markets" that "encourage experimentation and entrepreneurship" through "informal communication and collaborative practices." That communication was occurring face-to-face both in offices and at watering holes like Walker's Wagon Wheel.

Here was an industry that, as Toffler wrote, "can be described, in the words of one researcher, as nothing but 'people huddled around a computer.'" Yet Silicon Valley belied his claim that "put the computer in people's homes, and they no longer need to huddle." Even with a server in every basement, there was still a great deal of huddling at work.

Toffler had given himself an out that perhaps explained the Silicon Valley conundrum: "'ultrahigh-abstraction' workers—researchers, for example, and economists, policy formulators, organizational designers—require both high-density contact with peers and colleagues and 'time to work alone.'"

Toffler clearly viewed such workers as the rare exception, but that was changing in the decades after 1980, when computers and globalization were radically increasing the returns to skill and innovation. Middle-skill, less abstract jobs had been replaced by machines, and workers had to become more innovative to thrive. Even seemingly solitary deep thinking may benefit from the presence of other humans; a recent study showed that chess players forced to play online by the COVID pandemic made worse moves than the same players did when they played in person.

The changing nature of work meant that vastly more people, especially those in Silicon Valley, did those difficult, collaborative tasks that benefit from face-to-face interaction. As problems became more complex, there were more nuances to lose in translation. The extra hints that come with live interaction became more valuable. Communicating complexity benefits from "all the subliminal and nonverbal communication that accompanies [face-to-face] contact," in Toffler's own words. Try teaching someone to prove the fundamental theorem of algebra over email. One study showed that the response time to emergency calls in Manchester, England, was shorter when the person who answered the phone and the person who dispatched the police were in the same room, and shorter still when their desks were closer together.

More complicated tasks often make output harder to measure, which makes proximity between manager and subordinate more valuable, both to watch for overlong coffee breaks and to create some team spirit. In New York's Garment District, workers were paid based on the number of dresses they sewed. Counting was easy enough, workers were motivated by piece wages, and the dresses could be made at home. That is true of the call center today. But Marissa Mayer needed abstract thinking and sophisticated coordination to reboot Yahoo!, and those things can't be paid by the piece.

Even within a job, the degree of interaction has changed. Take our own profession: academia. Economists typically wrote their papers by themselves during the 1960s. Over the thirty years leading up to 1995, coauthorship increased dramatically, partially because improvements in communications technology made coordination easier. Papers also became more complicated, which required a wider range of skills. Yet much of that coauthorship occurred within the same city or building and involved plenty of face-to-face contact. Even when we work together, our productivity depends on both live meetings and sharing data and drafts electronically. Evidence suggests that proximity matters for quality too. Coauthored articles are cited more when the coauthors have offices located closer together, even in the same building.

In the twenty-five years since then, economics has increasingly been done in labs, modeled after the biological sciences, that are even more interactive than the two-person teams of the 1990s. Those labs depend upon technology, especially computers, to crank the vast data sets that uncover new nuggets about human existence. Until the pandemic struck, the people in those labs almost always felt the need to congregate in person, to provide direction, share information, and deliver encouragement.

The idea that more effective electronic interactions will simply replace face-to-face meetings is a simple, static view that misses the impact of communications technology on overall human connectivity. Just as cheaper energy led people to use more energy-intensive means of production, cheaper communication leads to more overall communication, and in turn more need to meet. Email, Twitter, and Facebook may save some meetings with existing friends, but they may also lead to having more friends, many of whom will want to meet in person. Business travel soared in the 1980s, despite the supposed ability of calls and faxes to substitute for those long-distance trips. Business service providers, including Toffler's own consulting firm, took meetings with hundreds of clients annually, despite their access to the most up-to-date information technology. In the language of economics, electronic interactions don't just substitute for face-to-face meetings, they also complement those meetings. And being in a city makes in-person meetings easier.

There was plenty of evidence—even in 1980—that new media forms often complemented interacting face-to-face. Phone calls were more common between people who lived nearby and who were more likely to see one another. Today, Facebook friendships are more common among people who live close by.

The human ability to transmit knowledge over long distances has been improving for centuries. Until 2020, those communications advances never seemed to do cities much harm. The dissemination of Gutenberg's Bibles to far-flung farm communities might have first seemed like a blessing for low-density living in the early sixteenth century. Rural pastors certainly found it easier to accurately recite the Gospels or the latest Lutheran prayers. But many of the farmers' children started reading the Bible themselves, and an increasingly literate population sought its fortunes in cities like Frankfurt and Berlin. Nineteenth-century prognosticators thought that telephones would limit twentieth-century urban growth. They didn't. After 1980, computers ended up helping, rather than harming, the world's cities.

Inequality and the Telecommuting Boom of 2020

When the COVID pandemic struck, Toffler's speculative vision of a dispersed world came back to life. In May of 2020, 35 percent of American workers—49 million people—told the Bureau of Labor Statistics that they were teleworking because of the pandemic. This number does not include the Americans who were already working remotely before the onset of COVID-19, so the total number of employed Americans who worked remotely was over 40 percent, which is the figure reported by Stanford economist Nicholas Bloom.

May was particularly remarkable because 50 million Americans also reported that they lost their jobs because of the pandemic, which meant that
in two months almost 100 million Americans had stopped going in to work.
That staggering number was equally split between the lucky and the comfortable who were Zooming their way to a paycheck, and the less fortunate
who were hoping that the federal government would cover their lost wages.

But the numbers of those working at home slowly receded. By November, the share who were teleworking because of COVID-19 had already declined to 22 percent, which meant that 33 million Americans were still
dialing it in. The share declined because some unemployed went back to
work and some who were Zooming resumed their office commute. By November, the number of Americans who were unable to work because of
COVID had fallen to 15 million.

The almost identical numbers of Americans who were working remotely
and who were not working at all because of COVID-19 in May reminds us
of the very different economic experiences wrought by the pandemic. Many
of the luckier telecommuters were finding work less stressful; certainly, the
commute was easier. Few of the jobless were having such a pleasant experience. These two populations were both vast, and they came from different
parts of the education and income distribution.

In May 2020, 36 out of the 49 million who were working remotely came
from the cluster of jobs that the Bureau of Labor Statistics calls management, professional, and related occupations. That privileged stratum represented 42 percent of American workers in February 2020, and 73 percent of
the Americans who were working from home in May. Only 15 percent of
those in management and professional occupations had lost their jobs in
May because of COVID-19. Only 7 percent of finance and insurance sector
employees were jobless because of the disease in that month.

At the other end of the spectrum, only 1.5 million out of 22 million employed service workers were telecommuting in May. Thirty-two percent of

service sector workers were jobless because of the pandemic. Over 40 percent of leisure and hospitality workers had lost their jobs.

Those differences across occupations translated into differences across education. Two thirds of employed adults with advanced degrees were telecommuting in May, compared to only 5 percent of high school dropouts. Fifty-four percent of adults with college degrees but only 15 percent of high school graduates who had not been to college were working remotely. By November, the share that worked remotely had declined, but the education gaps still remained. Nearly half of workers with advanced degrees were remote in November, compared to less than 10 percent of adults without a college degree. Our own experience is perhaps representative: one of us (Cutler) entered his office building exactly once between early March 2020 and the dawn of 2021—a half-hour visit to collect the mail. The other (Glaeser) didn't go at all.

Nowhere in Toffler's vision did he mention the terribly unequal nature of the switch to remote work. Like almost every major technological innovation of the past forty years, the electronic interfaces that allow us to connect virtually have strongly favored the rich and educated. Working remotely was not some universal panacea. It protected those, like your authors, who were lucky enough to have secure jobs where some facsimile of our services could be provided via Zoom. It did much less for the 14 percent of Americans, and 21 percent of African Americans, who told the census in December that their household sometimes did not have enough to eat in the last week. Moreover, the teleworking of the educated rippled throughout the economy, because we were no longer buying our lunches from restaurants or food trucks, or our coffees from Starbucks. That meant even more unemployment among people without advanced degrees.

The joblessness among the less educated tells only one half of the story. Millions of less wealthy Americans work in essential industries, and they did not lose their jobs. They continued to operate grocery cash registers and clean up nursing homes. Those workers were also more likely to catch

COVID-19. If they were older or burdened by chronic disease, they were more likely to die.

In the Middle Ages, the ships that brought *Yersinia pestis* into European ports were mostly carrying luxury goods for the rich. Today again, the world's rich and well-educated global citizens have the greatest propensity to spread pandemic. COVID-19 came to America carried by well-paid business travelers returning from China and prosperous tourists who had been vacationing in Northern Italy. A single health technology conference in Boston managed to spread COVID-19 to hundreds of thousands. Yet once the pandemic had arrived, the rich protected themselves by telecommuting, while the less fortunate remained vulnerable. Not since Nero have the pleasures of the rich imposed such costs upon the poor.

Remote Productivity before
and during the Pandemic

How has productivity been affected by the COVID-19 pandemic? There is not a single story. We noted earlier the finding of Emanuel and Harrington that remote working was associated with improved productivity in call centers. That holds up in randomized trials as well. Stanford economists Nicholas Bloom and John Roberts, along with colleagues in China, analyzed data from a Chinese travel agency that conducted an experiment with working at home. Among workers who were interested in remote work, the firm randomized some to work at home and some to continue coming to the office. The workers who were allowed to work from home were 13 percent more productive than the workers who had to commute.

If call-center work is more productive at home, why did companies wait until COVID-19 to go remote? Emanuel and Harrington's data suggest one possible answer. When the company hired for purely remote jobs, it attracted less productive workers. They find that "remote workers answered 9–11% fewer calls than on-site workers prior to Covid-19," despite the fact that when workers switched to remote, they become more productive. The remote workers "spent 45–61 additional seconds on each call" and "much longer calls did not make for much more satisfied customers." In 2020, when "all workers were remote due to COVID-19," they found that "those who were hired into remote jobs were 12% less productive than those hired into on-site jobs." Thus, "remote work attracts unobservably less productive workers."

This "selection effect" is one obstacle limiting the widespread persistence of remote work post-COVID. If firms attract more engaged, ambitious people when they make them come into the office, then firms that value internal drive are going to keep their office space.

Moreover, many people don't have adequate workspaces at home. One quarter of Americans do not have residential broadband, and even when they do, it is often too slow for remote work. Working at home may also involve more interruptions from lonely children or other distractions. Christopher Stanton's research found that "prior to the pandemic, remote households' expenditure share on housing was over eight percent higher than similar non-remote households." They presumably needed the extra space to work effectively. In a city full of cramped apartments, like London, few workers are going to love the loss of their offices. Telecommuting doesn't eliminate the need for working space. It switches the burden of supplying that space from a company to its employees.

Finally, even seemingly routine work may involve complex tasks for which coordination is important. Even in the call centers studied by Emanuel and Harrington, more complex calls are given to more senior workers. Presumably, neophytes are more likely to learn how to handle these difficult situations if they sit near experienced coworkers who are talking an irate client through a complaint.

These factors shouldn't prevent more part-time working from home. Indeed, we are quite confident that many of the world's knowledge workers will do more Zooming in the future. However, unlike Toffler, we see such changes as more marginal than revolutionary, and unlikely either to solve our traffic problems or lead to empty office towers.

To examine the heterogeneous impact of remote working across industries, one of us (Glaeser) was part of a team that analyzed two surveys taken at the height of the pandemic. The first survey reached the small business leaders in the Alignable network, noted above. The second survey went to economists at larger businesses affiliated with the National Association for Business Economics (NABE). The Alignable CEOs were asked to give a numerical value capturing the change in productivity experienced by their workers who went remote. The NABE economists grouped outcomes in broad categories.

Most of the NABE economists did not think that working remotely generated a significant output loss. Twenty-eight percent of them thought that efficiency increased after telecommuting, which is in line with the findings of Bloom and Roberts, and Emanuel and Harrington. Twenty-nine percent of the Alignable CEOs also said that productivity rose with telecommuting, although many of them experienced significant disruption.

On average, the Alignable CEOs thought that productivity fell by 20 percent when their workers went remote. Those Alignable businesses in low-skill sectors found remote work particularly problematic. The productivity drop was also more severe in the larger Alignable companies, suggesting the difficulties of managing many workers over the internet.

We can understand even more about the future of remote work by looking at online job advertisements. One of our graduate students, José Ramón Morales-Arilla, and his coauthor, Carlos Daboin, looked at the time path of both employment and job postings aggregated by Burning Glass Technologies, which includes almost every online want ad. They split jobs into work that can be done remotely and work that must be done face-to-face. As we discussed earlier, employment dropped precipitously in the early days of the pandemic in those jobs that must be done in person, liking waiting on tables. Employment did not drop as much for jobs that could be done over the internet, like being an accountant. Job postings fell both for in-person jobs and potentially remote jobs early in the pandemic. Jobs that could be made remote were made remote, but new hiring stopped.

By September, employment had significantly recovered for the in-person jobs. Postings had also come back, and in many cases surged past pre-pandemic levels. There were 66 percent more postings for industrial truck and tractor operators in September 2020 than there had been in February 2020. There were 42 percent more postings for industrial food workers, specializing in mixing and blending ingredients.

But job postings did not come back for those occupations that had largely gone remote. In September of 2020, job postings for occupations that could go remote were down by over one third relative to February. While researchers at Microsoft found that "productivity, when measured using engineering system data, appears to be stable or slightly improved," overall want ads for software engineers collected by Burning Glass were down by 42 percent in September relative to February. There was a 40 percent drop in the postings for financial analysts over the same time period. Some of this decline may reflect a reduced need to replace workers (quit rates fell during the early months of the pandemic), and a contraction in the overall amount of work to be done. Yet the steady employment of old workers and the sharp decline in new hires also suggests that companies could coast on years of in-person social capital to keep the old workers going, but feared beginning new relationships over Zoom.

For over a century, economists largely agreed with the great English economist Alfred Marshall who wrote that in dense industrial clusters, "the mysteries of the trade become no mystery but are, as it were, in the air." We have all learned things from nearby colleagues and from unplanned inter-actions at the lunch table and the watercooler. When people move from a lower-wage city to a higher-wage city, their wage rises over time. But it is not all in one jump. Rather, the accrual occurs over months and years, presum-ably because of what people learn from their environment.

Emanuel and Harrington find that "on-site representatives are signifi-cantly more likely to be promoted to senior positions that let them make higher stakes decisions and handle higher volume clients," presumably be-cause they are learning by watching and listening. Bloom and Roberts's study of Chinese travel agents also found that remote workers were less likely to be promoted, holding productivity constant, which they associated with a failure to bond with the boss. Humans have an enormous capacity to soak up knowledge from people around us, even when we are unaware of that unconscious education. As information technology and globalization increase the returns to skill and innovation, face-to-face contact becomes even more valuable.

We have yet to learn if the in-person opportunities for learning can be duplicated virtually. We are doubtful that they all can. We are even more skeptical that the internet can ever replace the joy of working around real people or being in a real city.

When Social Animals Shelter in Place

Humans are social creatures, and we value live human company. Online interaction is better than no interaction, but a bevy of studies show that people are happier with in-person meetings than with exclusively online communication. Studies showing this have been conducted in many coun-tries, including the United States, Canada, and China. People prefer live meetings when groups are randomized into in-person or online interactions.

People prefer connecting in person in professional as well as personal settings. Even conflict resolution is easier in person than through written communication.

The additional emotional connection that comes with face-to-face contact suggests an even larger reason why fears of an entirely remote existence are wrong: meeting in person makes work as well as life more enjoyable. Most people want more social bonds, and even small, staged interactions with peers help. The pleasure of real live connection helps explain why technology company offices have games and couches and why many cities recovered after 1980. The urban television shows of the 1990s, like *Friends*, *Seinfeld*, and *Sex and the City*, mostly just celebrated the pleasures of hanging out in coffee shops and bars.

The employers of highly skilled, young technology workers—like Google, Apple, and Uber—all tried to make their offices into playgrounds. When work is fun, employees stay longer and gripe less. They put in more effort. When work is just programming alone—to borrow a phrase from our colleague Bob Putnam—then it is only a path to a paycheck. Without a sense of communal mission, people put in less effort, unless they do simple work or get paid with a piece rate. The quality of new hires falls as well. Paying for expensive urban office space enabled employers to hire younger workers who want to be part of a creative team.

There are perhaps life-stage differences in who is lured by physical connection. Middle-aged workers with life partners, children, and many community relationships are less likely to want to hang out at work until midnight. Consequently, the switch to remote work will have more appeal for the dull and middle-aged, such as your authors, than for the young and hip.

The fun side of face-to-face contact also helps explain some of the comeback of cities like New York, London, and San Francisco. Economists measure urban appeal using wages and prices. If a place has high pay relative to living costs, then something else must be wrong with the location, like the weather. Not surprisingly, wages are high in Alaska. If a place has prices higher than wages would justify, then people like something about the locale other than its labor market. Hawaii and the Cote d'Azur both fit this category. In cities where prices rise faster than income for many years, the odds are good that something is making that place nicer.

During the twenty-five years after 1980, price growth outpaced income growth in cities like New York, London, and San Francisco. People wanted to live in those urban playgrounds. In the 1970s, one needed to pay workers a high wage relative to the cost of living to get them to put up with New York City; think of it as combat pay. By 2005, workers were willing to take a pay cut to live in the place of pleasure depicted in *Sex and the City*.

Urban innovation includes leisure activities as well. The abundance of urban food entrepreneurs, who are often immigrants, produces great restaurants at every price point. The ability of large numbers of urbanites to share the fixed costs of paying for common infrastructure enables the pleasures of museums and concert halls. Most importantly, the massing of young single people in a single dense place has a tremendous appeal to other young single people.

About ten years ago, business journalists began to notice that some technology companies, like Zynga and Salesforce, were locating in the city of San Francisco itself rather than Silicon Valley. Other companies, like Google, ended up busing their workers from the city to their office's suburban locale. These companies and workers weren't in the city for access to its harbor or railyards. They were there because urban living was fun. Some tech companies have already announced their plans to expand their post-COVID-19 presence in New York. As we look past the pandemic, the ability of cities to enable the joys of human interactions and shared experiences may be their greatest protection against urban exodus.

The pleasures of face-to-face connections also occur in elementary and high schools, as we have seen with our children. When schools went remote in the spring, much of our children's coursework remained the same. As parents, we were grateful that our children still seemed to be learning. But the joy was gone. The fun of just running into friends and laughing had largely disappeared. As the world becomes wealthier, work will continue to become more about enjoyment and less about a paycheck. Already, the lucky knowledge workers who were capable of working remotely are rarely engaged in drudgery. Before COVID-19 struck, firms were competing to attract talent by building workplaces that were pleasant as well as productive. They will do so again, even if the technology exists to just dial it in.

Urban Futures in the Balance

The urban edge in enabling interaction seems to ensure the future of urban office space, but it provides no such guarantee for any individual city. The rise of remote work means that companies will find it far easier to relocate. Some older, wealthier individuals will assuredly find it more pleasant to do their work without commuting into the city at all. This extra dose of flexibility means that cities will have to work harder than they have since the 1970s to hold on to their tax bases. Urban success depends more than ever on delivering public services with intelligence and decency.

Our surveys of NABE economists and Alignable entrepreneurs suggested that 20 percent of the workers who went remote will stay remote. In the Alignable survey, about one fourth of jobs had switched to telecommuting. If those predictions hold true for the entire economy, then about seven million pre-COVID jobs will go remote—a little less than 5 percent of the American workforce. That doesn't mean acres of empty offices. The total number of jobs in the US grew by more than seven million workers between 2016 and 2020, which suggests that even a massive shift toward remote working will be reversed by normal job growth in five to ten years.

But that job growth need not happen in the same cities where workers go remote. New businesses can start anywhere. Many of them will be drawn to the low prices and low taxes of places like Austin, Texas. Vail and Boulder, Colorado, offer natural beauty. Kansas City emits an unbridled commitment to entrepreneurship. A renewed innovation economy will be looking across the world's landscape, knowing that its prospective business partners have become more comfortable than ever taking a meeting over Zoom.

How will this play out? In cities where more workers stay remote, demand for urban real estate will fall. The good news for cities is that rents are flexible. If the demand for office space in downtown Boston or Chicago drops because of a surge in working at home, commercial landlords will cut rents. They might also upgrade services, which amounts to the same thing—a reduction in price per quality-adjusted square foot. City space will become more affordable, and that's good for all those who are not trying to rent out an office building.

Can the demand for city space fall so much that office towers will become vacant, as Toffler envisioned forty years ago? As long as commercial rents remain comfortably above operating expenses, then buildings will still get leased, but there comes a point at which landlords walk away instead of covering the costs of utilities, maintenance, and taxes. In about one fourth of America's major office markets, commercial rents averaged less than twenty-four dollars per square foot per year in the third quarter of 2020. These areas, such as Cleveland, Ohio, and Grand Rapids, Michigan, face the greatest risk of long-term vacancies. In about one fifth of office markets, rents were above forty-two dollars per square foot, and they are above sixty dollars per square foot in New York City and greater San Francisco. For these places, the post-COVID reset will mean lower prices but not empty buildings.

Within localities, some buildings will face sharper drops in demand and greater risk of vacancy. The oldest office buildings—those with the fewest amenities and likely the worst hygiene profile—are likely to suffer most. Newer buildings with better ventilation systems should fare better.

As office space becomes more affordable, businesses that have been priced out of cities will start to rethink an urban location. Ten years ago, Boston's mayor Thomas Menino launched an innovation district on the waterfront. It was meant to catalyze Boston's entrepreneurial community with a cluster that was dedicated to creativity. The area's motto, "Work, Live, Play," was designed to appeal to 24-7 tech hipsters who wanted to have as much fun in their private lives as they had planning their start-ups.

The district was a roaring success. Boston is cramped and there was robust demand for sleek new urban space. But the district always faced the problem that start-ups aren't rich enough to outbid banks for the city's best space. Mayor Menino didn't want a new financial zone, but before 2020 that seemed like the future for the innovation district. The entrepreneurs relocated to cheaper, poorer parts of the city, which led to the fights over gentrification that are the topic of the next chapter.

But if the banks go remote or move to another city, then the space becomes available again. Jane Jacobs, author, journalist, and activist, was among the wisest observers of twentieth-century urban America. Her 1961 book, *The Death and Life of Great American Cities*, remains one of the true masterpieces of nonfiction writing. In that book, Jacobs wrote that cities needed "cheap and makeshift" space to permit the growth of new businesses. She was right about that, although she incorrectly thought that historic preservation would promote affordability. If remote working leads old jobs to relocate, then new jobs can emerge to take their place, assuming that the city makes it easy enough to start new businesses.

In some cities—regulation permitting—offices may be turned into apartments. Business owners may decide that they don't need as much space for face-to-face contact, but younger Americans have resoundingly shown that they are desperate to see each other again live and in person. The demand for an in-person social life explains the recovery of restaurant-going after Florida eased its lockdowns in May. That demand also explains that anger that many college students felt when their life on campus was replaced by online lectures watched from their childhood bedrooms. The problem wasn't so much the low quality of online classes—not every teacher became a TikTok superstar, but many put enormous effort into it—but rather the isolation from other students. Living at home provides nowhere near the social experience of living on campus.

If more of the middle-aged move out of cities and more of the young move in, the urban composition of cities will shift. That is not a bad thing, but it will require rethinking on the part of city governments. Before 2020, many of the most successful cities felt as if they were exclusively the preserve of the wealthy. Strict building codes meant that house prices had risen to a point where the young couldn't possibly buy, and many couldn't even rent. The young will care more about relaxing these restrictions than the old.

Cities will need to strike a tricky balance between helping less-advantaged outsiders and driving away the rich. America's polarization means that its cities, which have long tilted left, are more progressive than ever. As long as the federal government fails to take action on causes like climate change and income inequality, urbanites will look to their city governments to respond. There is much to admire in activism that fights for the future of the planet and the fates of the poorest Americans. But that activism must recognize the limits that cities face, especially when the tax base is untethered.

Urbanites over the age of fifty remember what happened when progressive mayors of cities like New York and Detroit ignored the exit option enjoyed by their wealthier residents. People left in droves. We could see the same again if cities treat the rich as a piggy bank to be cracked open or if the quality of public services declines.

Fortunately, urban progressives can do plenty of good without large increases in local tax rates. They can fight to make schools more effective for all children. They can agitate to reduce the barriers that prevent the construction of affordable housing and the entrepreneurship of the poor. They can create community organizations that promote the safety of their neighborhoods both from crime and police abuse.

The rise of Zoom will not endanger urban life as a whole, but it increases the risk facing any individual city. It creates the perilous possibility that long-simmering urban problems may lead to a cycle of decline. We visit these urban problems in the next sections: underperforming urban schools, police violence, and mass incarceration. We turn first to the battles over gentrification that reflect the larger crisis of urban affordability.

Chapter 8

THE BATTLE FOR BOYLE HEIGHTS AND THE CLOSING OF THE METROPOLITAN FRONTIER

A t 2:35 p.m. on the afternoon of September 11, 2001, New York mayor Rudy Giuliani told CNN that "I want the people of New York to be an example to the rest of the country and the rest of the world that terrorism can't stop us." The city had suffered a terrifying attack that seemed likely to usher in a new age of global terrorism. A great chunk of downtown real estate had been destroyed. The tourist revenues that sustained the city's economy were at risk. Every major world city—from Mumbai to London to Madrid—seemed likely to be targets for violent opponents of democracy. New York City appeared to face an almost existential threat at least as perilous as the COVID-19 pandemic.

Or did it? As we saw with the Plague of Justinian, the impact of an adverse shock depends on the preexisting strength of civil society. By 2001, New York had been on an upward trajectory since the nadir of the 1970s. The city had seen its crime rate plummet and its population increase during

the 1990s. The economic engine of financial services was sufficiently entrenched not to flee at the first sign of trouble, but voters still understood
that the city needed to deliver core services to keep its tax base. A political
consensus supported pragmatic city leadership, and that consensus became
stronger after terrorists destroyed the Twin Towers. New York survived, and
even thrived, in the aftermath of the terrorist attack.

But twenty years later, that consensus seems as foreign as the near-
universal acclaim that Mayor Giuliani enjoyed after the attack. Anger at the
status quo—much of it understandable—has replaced a shared belief in a
common purpose and destiny. Inequality has widened. Many have come to
see the police as oppressors rather than as the protectors who ran into the
burning Twin Towers and died trying to save their fellow citizens. Gentrification has engendered conflict, and acrimony has replaced hope in the
world's wealthiest cities.

That discord makes New York and other Western cities far weaker facing
the COVID-19 pandemic than they were on September 11, 2001. The work
of urban and environmental economist Matthew Kahn shows that the same
earthquake will kill far fewer people in a well-managed, well-educated society than in a country with a weak government and limited education. A
2010 earthquake in Chile, which has long prioritized education reform,
killed only 525 people; a smaller earthquake in Haiti during the same year
tragically killed over 100,000. The pandemic that struck Constantinople in
541 CE was catastrophic because it hit a Mediterranean world that was already on the edge of chaos. The cholera epidemics of the nineteenth century
did little to ruffle the rapidly industrializing cities of the West.

America's cities in 2020 are in better shape than Rome in 541 CE, but
they face fierce challenges: a limited supply of housing that generates high
prices and acrimonious battles over gentrification, a criminal justice apparatus that seems particularly cruel to African Americans, and increasing inequality that is not offset by upward mobility. Many see a broken system,

and their anger flared into street protests after the killing of George Floyd. The combination of profound challenges and political wildfire makes the post-COVID urban landscape far more treacherous.

This chapter focuses on gentrification and the economic forces that turned neighborhoods like Los Angeles's Boyle Heights into flashpoints. In the next chapter, we turn to race and policing and limited upward mobility. The common theme of these traumas, and the limits that local regulations place on the entrepreneurship of the poor, is that our cities—like our societies as a whole—do too much to protect insiders and too little to empower outsiders.

We make sure that wealthy apartment owners won't have their views spoiled by a new high-rise. We don't care about the young family that can't afford to live in the city. We accept brutal policing as the price of safer streets. We don't worry about the young men who waste years trapped in the prison system. We protect bad teachers from pay cuts or losing their jobs. We accept that the children of the poor pay the cost of lousy teaching. In every case, we privilege insiders over outsiders.

There is a simple narrative that frames our urban conflicts as battles that pit whites against African Americans or Latinos against Yanquis. That narrative is true to history—for centuries, whites enslaved Africans and slaughtered Native Americans—but false to the underlying economics and the fundamental nature of urbanism. The battle over gentrification can be portrayed as a battle between white gentrifiers and long-term ethnic residents—but in fact, both groups have the same, common interest in expanding the amount of urban space. Both groups have a common enemy in the anti-growth activists and the land-use bureaucrats who stop new construction. It may seem as if we are stuck in the old fight of race against race, but the real fight pits the status quo against change. The real fight is the city's need to expand against the enemies of urban growth.

At its heart, urbanism is about opportunity. Cities have made space and enabled economic miracles for white, Black, Mexican American, and

Chinese immigrants. The ground-level view of the gentrification battle sees only the fixed set of current resources, but cities are anything but a zero-sum game. We can make our metropolitan areas more equitable and humane, but only if we allow them to transform themselves. We can make space for all, but only if we understand that our real enemies are the artificial limits on growth, not our neighbors who happen to have a different skin color.

Background to Battle:
The Making of Boyle Heights

Racial and ethnic divisions loom so large in our cities both because urban density means that people with different heritages live cheek-by-jowl, and because urban history is replete with racial exclusion and discrimination. Boyle Heights is an epicenter of the gentrification battles because the neighborhood has a history of both discrimination and tolerance. Boyle Heights also illustrates the ability of urban density to empower the coordination that makes protests against discrimination more effective.

The Boyle Heights neighborhood of East Los Angeles was named for Andrew Boyle, a nineteenth-century Irish immigrant who ended up in the hills of Southern California. Boyle came west to sell shoes to prospectors during the Gold Rush. He later became the first Anglo settler on the eastern side of the Los Angeles River. Boyle's daughter, Maria, married a migrant from the Midwest, William Workman. Workman was a development dynamo who named, subdivided, and sold off the Boyle Heights neighborhood during the great Los Angeles property boom of the 1880s.

"Uncle Billy" Workman was one of those mighty builders of Los Angeles legend who combined real estate speculation with politics and a certain type of self-interested philanthropy. Workman was the city's mayor in 1888 at the height of its early real estate frenzy. He was the city's treasurer who oversaw the first bond issue for the aqueduct that would take water from the Owens River and bring it to the growing metropolis. He donated land to build "churches and public schools" and public spaces, including both MacArthur Park and Hollenbeck Park. Perhaps that was charity, but Workman's gifts also had the salubrious effect of making his real estate more valuable.

The film industry has turned the nefarious Los Angeles real estate developer into a stock villain in the mold of *Chinatown*'s Noah Cross. Certainly, city builders sometimes take ethical shortcuts. Yet even when a developer's actions are motivated by greed, the outcome can still be a city that provides homes to millions. Workman's subdevelopment turned Boyle's vineyard into a diverse and vibrant ethnic neighborhood. If the land had been protected by rigorous zoning rules like those that prevail in some counties outside of San Francisco today, it might have remained a weekend home for a wealthy, white Angeleno. Instead, it houses tens of thousands. The development of Boyle Heights helped Los Angeles become as important a gateway for Mexican Americans as Ellis Island had once been for Irish Americans.

Somewhat surprisingly, the nineteenth-century boosters of Boyle Heights saw a bit of diversity as a good thing. An 1899 pamphlet, titled *Beautiful Highlands of Los Angeles*, extols the virtues of the neighborhood, and of Workman himself, "who is the father and founder of Boyle Heights, is always foremost in all enterprises that will ennure [*sic*] to the benefit of this section of the city." But along with a picture of Workman's substantial home, the booklet also features an image of the somewhat more modest house belonging to Mr. Chan Kin Sing. The language about Sing is patronizing ("Mr. Sing, with his wife and pretty little oriental children, lives in a cozy little cottage") but positive ("there is one element of our population which never loses its interest, that is the Chinese"). Sing himself was a solidly middle-class civil servant: a court interpreter.

The house of Mr. J. A. Bernal is pictured on the same page. Bernal receives the same banal positive treatment as everyone else in the book ("a well-known surveyor"), but his Mexican heritage is not mentioned. The volume uses his initials rather than his full name of José Adolfo. Workman sold to Mexican Americans, but his promotional materials chose not to emphasize that fact to other potential buyers.

Nonetheless, the future of Boyle Heights would be diverse, and eventually Latino. In 1899, Boyle Heights was not in the center of Los Angeles, and its "healthfulness and pleasant location" appealed to grandees, like Workman and his friend John Hollenbeck, as well as to more modest people like Sing and Bernal. In the late nineteenth century, urban plagues still troubled high-density cities like New York, and living on the airier, hopefully healthier, heights above Los Angeles seemed like a distinct plus.

But over the next fifty years, cars enabled the grandees to move out, and poorer people moved into the area. This process occurred in most of America's cities from 1900 to 1970 as multiple forces turned areas near to the city center into neighborhoods for poorer urbanites. In a sense, the modern gentrification process is a reversal of the evolution from rich to poor that occurred in Boyle Heights a century ago.

Houses naturally move from richer to poorer owners because of a process of decay that urban economists call filtering. Poorer people often buy older cars that were previously owned by wealthier people. Like cars, houses break down over time unless they are maintained meticulously. Since most people don't fix every little problem, homes typically depreciate just like automobiles, and thus richer homeowners may move from one new house to another new house, leaving their old homes to someone willing to put up with something shabbier.

A flood of lower- and middle-income people wanted to come to cities like Los Angeles in the first half of the twentieth century. Many of them didn't have the resources to buy their own cars. They migrated to areas like Boyle Heights that were close to the city center and had abundant public transit. Los Angeles was a great hub of buses in those days. The city's streetcars—the large Red Cars and nimble Yellow Cars—regularly rolled through Boyle Heights, which meant that middle-income residents didn't need an automobile. Then, as now, one of the great advantages of urban living was the ability to share common resources, like public transportation.

Richer Angelenos had automobiles by the 1920s, and that made it easy for them to move just a little bit farther out. While Workman lived and died in Boyle Heights, the next generations of successful real estate developers lived at greater distances from the city center, first to the west of the city in Windsor Square, then in Blair Hills and Beverly Hills. They still built in Boyle Heights, though, which provided abundant space for thousands of newcomers to Los Angeles, many of them Jewish.

Even when migrants had financial resources, legal barriers such as restrictive covenants prevented them from moving into newer, more suburban developments. In 1917, the Supreme Court unanimously decided that local governments could not explicitly zone by race. But this did not stop segregation in private housing developments. Thus, private builders adopted restrictive covenants, which prevented selling to minorities and presumably could guarantee a homogeneous community to future home buyers. Many white buyers found racial homogeneity attractive, either because they were racists themselves or because they thought that future white buyers wouldn't want neighbors of color.

These covenants held sway until 1948, when the Supreme Court ruled that racial covenants could be written but not enforced by the police power of the state. While the government would do far more to fight racial segregation with the 1968 Fair Housing Act, the earlier ruling provides an example of libertarian progressivism in which the government does good for the disadvantaged by doing less. The appeal of restrictive covenants is illustrated by the fact that three Supreme Court justices recused themselves from the case because they themselves lived in properties covered by such covenants.

City governments also promoted segregation by restricting the construction of higher-density housing that might appeal to poorer residents. After
1921, Los Angeles banned multifamily building from the fanciest parts of
the city. Even today, areas of cities that allow multifamily dwellings are
significantly more diverse than neighboring communities that permit only
single-family homes. But by 1921, Boyle Heights was already mixed ethni-
cally, and was certainly not elite enough to be placed in the restrictive "A"
class of single-family neighborhoods.

When the US government began supporting loans through the Federal
Housing Administration and the Home Owners' Loan Corporation, Boyle
Heights was one of the urban communities that was redlined and made ineligible for federally supported lending. The federal administrators decided that
if a neighborhood wasn't sufficiently white, then it wasn't sufficiently reliable.

One Home Owners' Loan Corporation report on Boyle Heights describes the area's "class and occupation" as "Jewish professional & business
men, Mexican laborers, WPA [Works Progress Administration] workers,
etc." The report claimed that the neighborhood was "literally honeycombed
with diverse and subversive racial elements," and its writers doubted "whether
there is a single block in the area which does not contain detrimental racial
elements." The report was written in April 1939, a little more than two years
before America went to war against the racist regime of Nazi Germany.

While Boyle Heights wasn't going to get subsidized mortgages, the area
would receive other, less beneficial forms of attention from the federal government. The Home Owners' Loan Corporation report notes without edito-
rial comment that "the Federal Government, in conjunction with the city
government are undertaking a slum clearance project covering 41 acres in
the extreme northeast part of the area." As slums were cleared, public housing projects, like Ramona Gardens and Estrada Courts, were built. As Jane
Jacobs would warn twenty years later, replacing dense slums with new

projects often transformed functional, if gritty, urban spaces into crime-ridden no-man's-lands. These projects have had their share of fire bombings, but the magnificent murals that adorn their walls remind us that urban creativity can survive even postwar urban planning.

The federal government's largest investments in Boyle Heights were highways that sliced through the neighborhood and polluted its air. Constructing the interstate highway system was uncontroversial and relatively inexpensive in rural Iowa, but putting massive concrete edifices into already built-up urban spaces was more complex, just as the railroad had been in the southern portion of nineteenth-century Manhattan. Roads were typically designed to run through central neighborhoods with relatively poorer and less-empowered citizens. New York's master builder, Robert Moses, famously cut the middle-income Tremont neighborhood of the Bronx in two with the Cross-Bronx Expressway. Boston's road builders separated the poorer North End off from the rest of the city with an elevated highway.

Boyle Heights was vulnerable to such road building because it had a central location and little political clout. Between 1944 and 1965, federal infrastructure spending turned the neighborhood into one of the great highway interchanges of the world, covering 135 acres of land with road. The historian Gilbert Estrada writes that "to construct such a mammoth structure, engineers used thirty-two bridges, twenty walls, excavated 1,500,000 cubic yards of earth, laid 23,545 feet of concrete pipe, used 4,200,000 yards of structural steel and 13,200,000 pounds of reinforced steel."

Highways 5, 10, 60, and 101 course through the neighborhood and intersect with each other above its streets. One estimate is that 2.4 million cars drive through Boyle Heights every day. Hollenbeck Park, the once beautiful piece of nature donated by William Workman and Hollenbeck's widow, now abuts the mass of what is now Interstate 5. The excellent air quality that was so touted by Boyle Heights's early promoters became a nostalgic memory.

Some Boyle Heights residents tried to fight the freeways as early as 1953. Estrada writes that "groups like the Brooklyn Avenue Business Men's Association, the Eastside Citizen Committee Against the Freeway, and the Anti-Golden State Freeway Committee were the most structured groups unifying multicultural and working-class Eastside community members against freeway encroachment." The protesters were loud, and they kept yelling right up to the moment that they lost.

Many more decided to vote with their feet against the freeways and left the area. The old neighborhood, marked both by its diversity and its Jewishness, became an overwhelmingly Latino neighborhood. By 2000, 95 percent of the residents of Boyle Heights would identify themselves as Hispanic or Latino to the US census. Some have guessed that there were one million Mexicans and Mexican Americans living in East Los Angeles by 1960. Boyle Heights still offered proximity to Central Los Angeles, and it became even more inexpensive because the freeways filled the air with smog and noise.

The new residents of Boyle Heights weren't rich enough to have easy relocation options. For them to get a better political deal, they would need to speak up. Gradually Boyle Heights, and the rest of East Los Angeles, found its voice in anger over poor school conditions. Children who grew up in the neighborhood during the 1930s and 1940s became the leaders of a movement that flexed its muscles during the 1960s.

Sal Castro, Julian Nava, and the Making of the East LA Walkouts

All immigrants face the conflict between heritage and assimilation, but groups usually benefit from having some members who join the mainstream of American society and others who remain rooted in their ethnic community. Boyle Heights certainly gained from the remarkable partnership of Dr. Julian Nava, a Harvard-educated member of the Los Angeles School Board who would later serve as US ambassador to Mexico, and Sal Castro, the fiery high school teacher who led the East Los Angeles walkouts. Those walkouts were a turning point in the history of Latino political agency in urban America.

In the HBO film *Walkout*, Castro is portrayed by Michael Peña (who is probably best known as the lovable Luis in *Ant-Man*) and Nava is played by Edward James Olmos, who also directed the movie. *Walkout* tells the story of the thousands of Latino students and teachers who marched out of their Los Angeles public schools to demand bilingual education, better facilities, and protection against political reprisals.

The foot soldiers in this massive uprising were young, but the protest roared because it had older, savvier leaders, like Castro, and friends on the inside, like Nava. Castro and Nava were both born in Boyle Heights, in 1933 and 1927 respectively. Nava writes in his memoirs that "my memory starts when we lived in East Los Angeles in a neighborhood called Boyle Heights," which he describes as "like the United Nations because of all the immigrant children in school from different countries." Nava courageously signed up as a seventeen-year-old to fly in World War II, but he wasn't trained in time to fight. He wore his navy uniform to his graduation from Roosevelt High School. Nava's career provides a textbook example of how educational opportunities, created in his case by the GI Bill and California's early commitment to higher education, can enable talent to both succeed and serve the wider world.

Nava went first to East Los Angeles Junior College then to Pomona College and then to Harvard, where he received a fellowship to do graduate work. An old newspaperman who had spent time in the frigid East gave Nava his wool coat to take with him. Nava escaped the New England cold by spending time in Venezuela researching his dissertation on a nineteenth-century dictator. He received his PhD from Harvard in 1955 and began teaching at Cal State Northridge two years later. He would teach there for another forty-three years.

While Nava was entering the edges of the American establishment, his older brother, Henry, remained rooted in the barrio as head of the Boyle Heights–based Community Service Organization (CSO). Henry was an ally of Edward Roybal, who first represented Boyle Heights in the Los Angeles City Council and then in the US House of Representatives. The CSO was an urban training ground for community organizers. Cesar Chavez would learn his political skills in the East LA CSO and then use those skills to organize Latino farmworkers throughout the Southwest. Nava became so close to Chavez that he was a pallbearer at Chavez's funeral.

In 1967, Nava was persuaded to run for the Los Angeles Board of Education. Nava's broad support, among both the great and the ordinary, enabled him to become the first Mexican American to serve on that board. Nava remembered that "countless" graduates of Roosevelt High School "rallied to help just because I was a fellow 'Rough Rider.'" At the other end of the spectrum, movie star Gregory Peck and television pioneer Steve Allen cohosted a fundraiser in honor of both Nava and Chavez. Nava's election also benefited from the fact that the incumbent "said in public that Mexican-American children were poor academic students because they were just lazy."

Nava's position on the school board put him in the eye of the storm when thousands of Latino "students paraded down the streets protesting against inferior education and discrimination" in 1968. Nava may have been on the inside, but he saw Sal Castro, the teacher who was advising the student protesters, as a "hero" who was "teaching the students things you don't learn in books." Castro also grew up in Boyle Heights and used education to escape poverty. He had worked on Nava's school board campaign.

Like Nava, Castro served in the armed forces, but Castro didn't have a PhD from Harvard, and he taught in an inner-city high school, not a major university. Castro's father had been forcibly repatriated to Mexico when he was a child.

According to Nava, "the Los Angeles police and the school district police worked together and soon discovered that a high school teacher at Lincoln High School was advising the students." As a school board member, Nava knew about the investigation and he warned Castro, calling him on a public pay phone because he "feared" his own "phones were tapped." A friend in the school district's security team had whispered to Nava about the bugged phones, which led him to make "misleading remarks on the office phone" to misdirect the "recorders." Nava told Castro that "law enforcement was organizing to put down this student revolt." He also cautioned Castro about the wiretaps, but Castro laughingly replied that he had stopped using his own phone a long time ago.

Nava tried to protect Castro from being fired, but there was nothing he could do when Castro was arrested on fifteen counts of conspiracy to disturb the peace and the same number of counts of conspiracy to disrupt the schools. Castro spent five days in jail. While the charges were eventually dropped, the school district still kicked him out. Nava lobbied unsuccessfully for Castro's retention, but thousands of friends in the barrio ended up being worth more than one friend on the school board. For Castro's sake, they marched and they sat in. The students even staged a "sleep in" at the board of education auditorium. Castro got his job back.

The East LA walkouts did not overturn centuries of prejudice against Mexican Americans. They did not end injustice in the Los Angeles school district, but they did inspire hope. The *Los Angeles Times* reported that "the walkouts' greatest accomplishment was fostering in the Mexican American community a sense of possibility" and that "a year after the walkouts, UCLA's enrollment of Mexican Americans soared from 100 to 1,900." Nava thought that "the walkouts actually made it easier for me to get more things done, because now the board could see the alternative to educational reform." Castro's protests helped change the schools, partially because they were followed by years of earnest effort by empowered insiders, like Nava. Those who wish to reform schools and policing today through protest must recognize that they will also need their own Navas to turn their hopes into any kind of lasting change.

The walkouts galvanized a generation of Mexican American activists and spawned imitations throughout the Southwest. Sal Castro had been supported by a small group of young protesters who had called themselves the Brown Berets since 1967. Urban proximity often enables the random meeting of politically like-minded individuals and the organization of mass movements.

The Brown Berets emerged out of conversations that young Mexican Americans had during a student conference held in Los Angeles. Members of the Brown Berets had strongly supported Nava's election to the school board and they helped galvanize the walkouts. According to one of the organization's leaders, Carlos Montes, "the Brown Berets were the first to run into the high schools, yelling 'Walk out! Walk out!'" Like Castro, the Berets also benefited from the protection provided by Nava's insider information.

At one school board meeting, Nava received a tip that the Berets' headquarters were going to be raided by policemen looking for drugs. Nava called the Brown Beret Leader, David Sanchez, and then raced to the corner of Soto Street and Brooklyn Avenue to meet with him. Brooklyn Avenue now bears the name of Nava's friend Cesar Chavez. Nava warned Sanchez about the police bust, and Sanchez raced back. As Nava recounts it, "by the time the police arrived minutes later, the young people had turned their offices inside out and found a plastic bag with drugs inside the toilet water tank." The alliance between moderate insiders and radical outsiders protected the outsiders from arrest.

The Brown Berets also played an outsized role in organizing the Chicano Moratorium of 1970, in which tens of thousands of Latino marchers protested the Vietnam War. The demonstration's epicenter was Laguna Park, on the edge of Boyle Heights, which is now named after a reporter for the *Los Angeles Times*, Ruben Salazar. Salazar was killed by a canister of gas that the police dropped on the protesters during the march.

Yet memories of the walkouts and the political activity remain. Sal Castro is still a name to conjure with. Some young men who grow up in poverty in Boyle Heights still dream of leading a social revolution. Those memories are easily rekindled when white gentrifiers start occupying visible pieces of real estate in Boyle Heights.

Thanks partially to Nava and Castro, Boyle Heights became something of a Latino success story, at least measured in terms of upward mobility. The work of our colleagues Raj Chetty and Nathaniel Hendren as well as their coauthors measures the upward mobility of children born between 1978 and 1983 who lived in different neighborhoods. Their most standard measure is the average income achieved by those children when they reach young adulthood.

Many urban neighborhoods look terrible by this measure, especially for minorities, but Boyle Heights is an exception. On average, the data shows that a Hispanic child of poor parents growing up in greater Los Angeles earned $35,000 as an adult, and this is also true for Los Angeles County. In parts of Central Los Angeles, the average adult earnings for children of poorer Hispanics is under $30,000, but a poor Hispanic child growing up in Boyle Heights earned on average $39,000 as an adult. A poor white child growing up in Los Angeles took home $41,000 later in life. In other words, living in Boyle Heights closed two thirds of the opportunity gap between the average Hispanic and the average white child with low income parents.

Boyle Heights experienced many of the ravages of inner-city America, including terrible violence, but the community also displayed great strength. It gave birth to a protest movement. It has an artistic tradition that is displayed in extraordinary murals, such as those in the Estrada Courts housing project, and in the musicians of Mariachi Plaza. It has managed to produce

modest upward mobility, thanks partially to a tradition of community organization. No wonder that non-Hispanic Angelenos would see Boyle Heights
as an attractive place to relocate.

Gentrification Explodes

The original Anglo and Jewish exodus from Boyle Heights occurred during
a time in which highways and unfettered home building meant that the
southern California housing supply was expanding enormously. Between
1950 and 1970, the number of housing units in Los Angeles County increased by 76 percent, from 1.4 million to 2.5 million. An ocean of tract-
level housing was erected along the new freeways that surged through the
metropolitan area. That new construction meant that housing remained
affordable, despite the palm trees and movie stars.

The paradox of diamonds and water is that diamonds are far more expensive than water despite the fact that water is essential for existence and diamonds are not. The explanation for this paradox is that water is abundant but
diamonds are rare. If something is easy to get or to build, its price is likely to
remain low even if it is vital or beautiful. Los Angeles had cheap housing in
1970 because postwar California was a builders' paradise.

By 2010, coastal California had become a builders' hell. Local land-use
regulations mandated minimum lot sizes. The California Supreme Court
ruled that every major new project needed to go through an environmental
impact review. Those reviews added costs and blocked new projects—and
they were terribly one-sided.

Building in coastal California is intrinsically green because the region's
Mediterranean climate needs much less artificial cooling and heating than
the rest of the US. Building in California therefore lowers America's carbon
footprint, and should be ardently encouraged by environmentalists. However,

the court-mandated environmental review evaluates only the harm to the local environment, not the benefit created by building in a low-carbon part of the country. Local anti-growth activists don't get to stop all development in the US. They can make sure only that the development doesn't happen near them. When building is stopped near the intrinsically green region near San Francisco or Los Angeles, it gets displaced to the outer exurbs or to Houston or Las Vegas, where building does far more environmental harm.

Between 1990 and 2015, the number of housing units in LA County rose by only 11 percent or 340,000 housing units. That paltry supply of new homes couldn't possibly satisfy the robust demand driven by coastal California's climate and an economic boom. Central Los Angeles became more attractive for young urbanites who wanted sunshine, beaches, and a denser, hipper environment. After the city's metro opened the Gold Line in 2009, Boyle Heights gained a direct, traffic-free connection to the center of the city, and it became a gentrification magnet.

Urban economists often make the seemingly paradoxical point that investments in poor places can make the poor residents of those places worse off, especially if they are renters. A new subway stop may revitalize an area but still create nothing but headaches and higher living costs for long-term residents who don't want to take the train. Indeed, the coming of the Gold Line to Boyle Heights in 2009 is frequently cited as a starting point for the area's gentrification. The core area of Downtown Los Angeles has gradually been reborn as a more pedestrian-friendly, public transit–friendly place. Many hipper urbanites were eager to explore nearby neighborhoods, like Boyle Heights, that became accessible by rail.

Many of the first movers were more affluent Latinos, who liked the proximity, low prices, and cultural heritage of the area. Locals called that process "gentefication," which embeds the Spanish word *gente* or people. By 2016, the web was ablaze with headlines like IN BOYLE HEIGHTS, THE SIGNS OF GEN-TRIFICATION ARE EVERYWHERE. In 2017, the brilliant and funny Marvin

Lemus had produced a few digital episodes of *Gentefied*, which was turned into a full-fledged and generally acclaimed Netflix series in 2020.

The series uses Boyle Heights's gentrification to explore the conflict between financially rewarding integration and socially rewarding community loyalty. This is an old and central theme in many cities. The core conflict of the world's first talking movie—*The Jazz Singer*—is the hero's agonizing decision about whether to take his father's place singing the Kol Nidre at Yom Kippur or to perform his starring role in the premiere of a Broadway show. The jazz singer does sing the Kol Nidre, but luckily in Hollywood's version, his jazz career recovers. *Gentefied*'s Chris Morales is similarly torn between saving his grandfather's taco shop and attending Le Cordon Bleu in Paris.

But while there is internecine agonizing within the Latino community about "acting white," there is far less ambiguity—either in the show or real life—about non-Mexican gentrifiers in Boyle Heights. In the show, they are generally depicted as crass, rich, or foolish. In real life, gentrifiers are often seen as pure villains. Defend Boyle Heights, one anti-gentrification organization, declares that "gentrification is the true, highest form of hate crime," which is quite a claim given the twentieth century's history of genocide.

Weird Wave Coffee, which opened in 2017 near the spot where Julian Nava warned the Brown Berets about the forthcoming police raid, "almost immediately became ground zero for the very public discussion about gentrification." Weird Wave is an unlikely villain, with its homespun decor, octopus logo, and stated mission "to bring community together." Nonetheless, the protests and vandalism were ubiquitous. When the coffee shop's glass windows were smashed, Defend Boyle Heights did not claim credit for the action, but it did "cheer it on."

Still Weird Wave survives. Positive Yelp reviews urge prospective customers to "ignore the uninformed protestors," who don't know or care "that one of the owners is Salvadorean." Other gentrifiers faced rougher treatment and just gave up.

When a coffee shop opens in a gentrifying neighborhood, that shop is hoping to provide a morning beverage—and perhaps some home-baked muffins—to local residents as well as outside visitors. When an art gallery opens in a gentrifying neighborhood, it is looking for cheap space to show expensive merchandise to customers from somewhere else. Maybe some local businesses will benefit, but residents are more likely to lose out from a higher cost of living. When art galleries started opening in Boyle Heights in 2016, they were far easier to demonize than the hipsters who founded Weird Wave.

Just across the river from Boyle Heights, Los Angeles's Arts District has been gentrifying for decades. The downtown area was industrial. Artists moved into lofts. They started painting rarely authorized murals that now adorn public walls. Gallery owners bought the once inexpensive space. Since the area was filled with warehouses, not longtime residents, there was little resistance to change.

Hip eateries and cool clubs opened. Museums, like the Institute of Contemporary Art and the A+D (Architecture and Design Museum), located in the district. The Arts District seemed to offer a real urban experience amid all of Los Angeles's highways and Mediterranean-style homes, and so by 2015, the district was attracting technology entrepreneurs. Costs were soaring, with studio apartments renting for more than $2,000 per month and one-bedroom apartments costing $1 million or more.

The walk from the Institute of Contemporary Art to Weird Wave Coffee in Boyle Heights is only 2.5 miles, and gentrification oozes over space. Businesses and residents looking for cheaper quarters peek just over the horizon to the next, nearest neighborhood that hasn't yet seen its prices rise. Boyle Heights was much less expensive than the Arts District and so a wave of art galleries opened there, apparently oblivious to the neighborhood's long tradition of organized protest.

Paramilitary uniforms, like those once worn by the Brown Berets, reappeared on activists belonging to the Boyle Heights Alliance Against

Artwashing and Displacement (BHAAAD). BHAAAD's soldiers wear black jumpsuits and red ski masks. The organization is a highly vocal and effective coalition against the art galleries. The galleries were defaced with crude vandalism. More sophisticated protesters crossed the continent to disrupt one gallery owner's exhibition at the Whitney Museum in New York. The video of that protest shows a lot of blasé New Yorkers doing their best to ignore the interlopers from the other coast.

One gallery website was hacked so that it contained a fake formal apology from "hipster bro gentrifiers who have colonized Boyle Heights with our gallery." Some gallery owners even reported receiving death threats. By 2018, at least four of the galleries had had enough and decamped elsewhere. The first generation of Boyle Heights protesters had faced off against the LAPD and centuries of Anglo domination. Unsurprisingly, this new generation of protesters found it far easier to dispatch art gallery owners. Even those who didn't take the death threats seriously wanted to protect their reputations from the tinge of political incorrectness.

These gentrification battles rage so fiercely because Los Angeles's supply of affordable space is so limited. The median sales price of a Los Angeles condominium was over $470,000 in 2019, according to the National Association of Realtors, which is higher than any other metropolitan area in the United States, except for the even-pricier city of San Francisco. The median price for a Los Angeles home was over $600,000, over 60 percent more than the median price of a home in greater New York City.

Los Angeles has culture, climate, and a strong and diversified local economy. It is a natural entry point for Mexican immigrants. There is robust demand for the City of Angels. When that demand is met with insufficient supply, prices rise and there is conflict over space. Los Angeles doesn't have to be that expensive, and it wasn't particularly expensive before the 1970s, when there was still abundant new construction.

In 1970, the median home price in California was $23,100, which translates to $158,000 in 2020 dollars. This was 36 percent above the national average, but lower than median home prices in states like New Jersey and Connecticut. By 1990, California's median housing price had skyrocketed to $196,000 or $400,000 in 2020 dollars, 145 percent above the national average. In 1970, California was a normal state and Los Angeles was a normal city, at least in terms of its housing prices. By 1990, the Golden State and its great coastal cities had entered a real estate stratosphere that they have essentially never left.

California's climate did not change between 1970 and 1990. The state's economy was already strong in 1970. Arguably, that economy became even more successful relative to America's frostier states over the next twenty years, but the biggest change was the collapse in housing construction that we have already mentioned. The supply of new homes in Los Angeles County fell from over 50,000 per year between 1940 and 1970 to less than half that amount over the next thirty years.

The low level of construction in Los Angeles County does not reflect a lack of land. Los Angeles County contains an astounding three million acres. Currently, there are only 1.38 housing units per acre there, and that includes condominiums. Los Angeles is a great city, and great cities can easily house fifty people on an acre of land. But LA has chosen to pretend that it is still the land of orange groves and gentle hills that it was when Billy Workman first developed Boyle Heights.

Who Should the Protesters Be Protesting?

The protesters of Boyle Heights have a real point. Their rents are too damn high. Yet they blame the outsiders who are willing to pay higher rents—not the rules that ultimately cause their rents to rise. That is a mistake that ignores a fundamental problem with urban politics in the twenty-first century. Our laws and institutions have evolved to protect insiders, whether they are suburban homeowners or local activists, against change. By freezing our urban spaces, we ensure that cities can't grow enough to allow room for everybody. Land-use regulations create heightened competition for a limited resource. Instead of fighting the gentrifiers, who are also victims of Los Angeles's failure to build, the protesters should be joining them to battle the NIMBYists who restrict the amount of space available for everyone. They should both be fighting together with the small, but vigorous, movement of YIMBYists (which stands for Yes in My Back Yard) who want to allow more new construction and have been chronicled extensively by Conor Dougherty.

There is plenty of land in Los Angeles County on which to build art galleries and apartment buildings without bothering Boyle Heights. Too much of that space is off-limits because of fifty years of land-use restrictions and legal rulings that have protected the status quo. Those decisions worked out marvelously for people who bought homes in Los Angeles County in 1970, but not for newcomers and renters. Boyle Heights is the place where rules hatched to protect older and wealthier suburban homeowners engender conflict between less fortunate Angelenos of different races.

Proposition 13 provides a particularly egregious example of how the deck became stacked for insiders against outsiders. In most of America, homeowners pay for rising prices with rising property taxes, but in 1978, California voters gave their incumbent owners a safe harbor. Proposition 13, which passed in that year, mandates that "the maximum amount of any ad valorem tax on real property shall not exceed One percent (1%) of the full cash value of such property," and where the "full cash value" means the county assessor's valuation of real property as shown on the 1975–76 tax bill under "full cash value" or, thereafter, the appraised value of real property when purchased, newly constructed, or a change in ownership has occurred.

The insider bias comes not from the 1 percent tax cap, but from the definition of "full cash value," which remains at its mid-1970s assessed value for older homeowners, with a maximum annual increase for inflation of 2 percent, but resets with new construction or whenever the home is sold. The nominal price of homes in Los Angeles has increased nineteenfold between 1975 and 2020, which means that older Angelenos who haven't sold their homes since then might be paying one tenth of what a new buyer would face in property taxes. The proposition creates a massive disparity between insiders and outsiders, and a strong incentive for insiders not to sell their homes, which further freezes the Los Angeles property market.

If the city is frozen, then Boyle Heights will always be under threat. If building expands anyplace that prices are rising, then rents will moderate and there will be less pressure to cross the river into East LA. Many gallery owners would have been delighted to stay in the Arts District if that area made it easy to build new space. Many residents of Boyle Heights would be far more open to change if that change wasn't accompanied by soaring rents. The catalyst for the TV show *Gentefied*'s conflicts over identity is the grandfather's fight to save his taco shop, which is at risk because of rising rents. The struggle between Mexican roots and assimilation is inescapable, but it would be far less painful if living and working space were abundant and inexpensive. If protesters focused more on expanding the total amount of livable space in Los Angeles, then there could be plenty of room for both taco shops and art galleries.

Insiders, Outsiders, and the Closing of the Metropolitan Frontier

Cities often enable completely different peoples to peacefully coexist through a combination of urbane culture, law enforcement, and the desire to make a buck even by selling to people that you don't like. But close proximity always creates the potential for conflict, especially because there are so many instances when one person's action impacts his neighbor's well-being. No abutter will be disturbed by an overly loud radio played on an Iowa farm, but many neighbors will suffer from noise pollution in a dense urban area. Cities become hellish when people dump their waste into the street, congest the roads with traffic, and steal anything that is not locked down.

These negative effects of density are solved through collective actions, like investing in sewers, charging drivers a congestion fee, or hiring a night watchman. Yet the ability of cities to solve these problems is undermined by what the economist Mancur Olson called the free-rider problem. When the benefits of group activity go to everyone in the group, then each individual has a private incentive to coast along on the efforts of others. This free-rider problem bedevils any shared endeavor, from a high school science club to a great metropolis, and it becomes worse in larger groups.

Olson wrote in *The Rise and Decline of Nations* that "the incentive for group action diminishes as group size increases, so that large groups are less able to act in their common interest than small ones." Everyone has at some time found that it is easier to get something done with a band of three than a group of thirteen. With larger groups, it is harder to come to agreement and harder to ensure that everyone pulls their own weight. Olson argued that this fact implies that stable societies would eventually become dominated by small, narrowly focused, and well-organized interest groups. Olson also argued that the power of these groups would eventually cause economic stagnation and decline.

In Olson's view, groups of insiders fear change and competition. They put barriers in place to stymie the success of others, like bans on food trucks, or at least to stop any diminution of their own authority. He saw this process repeated over and over—in the fall of the Roman Republic, the stagnation of Tokugawa Japan, and Britain's travails during the 1970s. In each case, he argued, powerful insiders—the trade guilds of premodern Japan or English labor unions—enforced rules that limited innovation and harmed outsiders. Those insiders would maintain their invention-sucking hold on power, according to Olson, until there was a major shock to the system. He thought that Germany and Japan's post–World War II booms reflected the temporary elimination of insider power by military defeat.

For most of America's history, from 1800 to 1970, the country was changing too rapidly for insiders to control the future. If incumbents grabbed power in the Massachusetts State House, then outsiders would move west to the more fertile soil of the Ohio River Valley. If the cotton industry became dominated by a small number of great plantation owners and cotton traders, entrepreneurs could start steel factories in Birmingham, Alabama.

Moreover, some groups of insiders had strong financial incentives to cater to outsiders. In their influential and insightful book *Urban Fortunes*, Harvey Molotch and John Logan write about the urban "growth machines" that often dominated Sunbelt cities during their expansion spurts. "Uncle Billy" Workman, the Los Angeles mayor who once owned Boyle Heights, embodied the combination of financial and political muscle that sits at the top of these machines. These growth machines were small interest groups that catered to the city's richest bankers, employers, and real estate developers, but all of them wanted urban growth. That growth meant more lending for the bankers, more workers for the employers, and more building for the developers.

There was nothing altruistic about these characters and, as Molotch and Logan correctly note, they did plenty of unattractive and even immoral things, from stealing farmers' water to polluting the local waterways. They used the system to benefit themselves. Yet because their fundamental goal required the city to attract outsiders, the growth machines were focused both on making the city attractive to migrants and on producing new housing. Since each city's urban growth machine had to compete with every other city's growth machine, they had strong incentives to provide inexpensive homes for outsiders.

For several centuries, America's cities provided a metropolitan frontier that was far more important than the wilder frontier in the West. In 1893, Frederick Jackson Turner claimed "up to our own day American history has been in a large degree the history of the colonization of the Great West," and that "the existence of an area of free land, its continuous recession, and the advance of American settlement westward, explain American development." For decades, historians would debate Turner's essay on "The Significance of the Frontier in American History," but the fact is that in 1890, the ten states and territories that composed that frontier contained about the same population as the island of Manhattan.

The physical frontier may have loomed large in Turner's psyche, but America's growing cities were vastly more important for ordinary people. The population of urban America had increased from 6.2 million to 22 million in the thirty years before 1890, and that population would rise to 69 million in the thirty years after Turner's essay. Olson was right that small interest groups could sometimes dominate by solving their own free-rider problems. New York's Tammany Hall got its political foot soldiers to work with promises of public jobs and free turkeys. But before World War I, those interest groups typically wanted the wealth that would come with urban growth.

Gradually, however, a new anti-growth model was emerging in America's suburbs. In 1873, prosperous Brookline refused to be mixed into the city of Boston's melting pot. That town's wealthier citizens didn't want to be overruled by the city's bosses, and they didn't want to be overrun by Irish immigrants. Nineteenth-century Brookline stopped annexation, but they had limited legal resources to prevent new building. Those would emerge only in the early twentieth century. Zoning codes swept the nation in the 1920s after the Supreme Court's 1926 ruling that the regulations imposed by the town of Euclid, Ohio, were not an unwarranted "taking" of the property rights of Ambler Realty. Ambler argued that the new regulations illegally reduced the value of its real estate, but the Supreme Court held that physically separating homes from industrial pollution and harmful activities more generally was a legitimate use of public power. The Supreme Court had earlier reversed local attempts to explicitly zone by race. Many have thought that Euclidean zoning was popular because it implicitly segregated by race and income, for example by banning apartment buildings from wealthy suburbs.

These codes were allegedly motivated by health concerns, like keeping small children away from the masses of animals in Chicago's stockyards, but they came to exert wide-ranging control over the activities allowed in any locale. They also had unfortunate gender implications. Suburbs could be kept free not only from factories but also from office parks or chain stores, which were major employers of women after World War II. Caroline Criado Perez writes that because women "are most likely to have the primary caring responsibilities over children and elderly relatives, the legal separation of the home from formal workplaces can make life incredibly difficult."

The legal separation of the home from work also meant that suburbs were full of homeowners, who didn't want the crowding or the nuisances that came with new construction. They didn't want wages to fall for local employers and they didn't care much about new business for local bankers. Sometimes suburbs still had large real estate developers, and they would fight to allow the full development of their property. But once those developments were done, then no one was left to argue for the upside of new construction.

In a sense, the political structure of America's metropolitan areas made it easy for interest groups of insiders to take control of vast land areas. The older parts of America were settled in a pre-car and even pre-rail era, when ten miles was a long distance. Consequently, our oldest metropolitan areas have a proliferation of small local governments, which once corresponded to small local economies. Eventually, those tiny townships became part of one large metropolitan area, like New York or Boston or Philadelphia, and sometimes they also became part of one large city government. New York City consumed its outer boroughs in its 1898 consolidation.

Yet as the example of Brookline illustrates, wealthier suburbs learned how to say no. As Kenneth Jackson documents in his magisterial history of the American suburb, before 1900, suburbs usually said yes, but after that period they increasingly opposed annexation. So large metropolitan areas were honeycombed with small, independent polities with land that attracted those who were wealthy enough to own a car. Starting in the 1920s, a vast reorientation from city to suburb occurred throughout the US. The political impact of that migration was that wealthy homeowners managed to get control of their own local governments.

Those governments then served as homeowners' cooperatives. They were small towns tailor-made for takeover by the upper middle class, who used their power for good and ill. They often invested in good schools to save parents the cost of paying for private education. They provided policemen who protected private property. And they restricted new construction, especially smaller homes and apartments that would attract poorer residents, who would pay less in taxes than they cost in public services.

This process was well underway by the 1960s, but pockets of metropolitan America were still open to new construction. Sunbelt cities built in the car era are much larger than their eastern counterparts. Boston has 48 square miles of land; Phoenix has 517. Consequently, there was room to build within the central city, and those central cities had plenty of pro-growth voices, like the bankers, employers, and real estate developers that composed the urban growth machines. There was also room to build where the suburbs ended, where farmers wanted the windfalls that came if developers bought and built on their land. Moreover, there were some places, like unincorporated Las Vegas County, that remained a political free-for-all open to builders.

Yet since 1970, those remaining spaces on the metropolitan frontier have been increasingly captured by insiders as well. Within city limits, community activists, including the great Jane Jacobs, learned how to stop the mighty from bulldozing their neighborhoods. Jacobs brilliantly and intuitively understood the free-rider problems that Olson discussed. She helped lead Greenwich Village's opposition to the Lower Manhattan Expressway. This was an early example of the freeway revolts that would emerge in wealthier and better-organized communities to oppose highway construction.

Fighting a highway that might cut through your neighborhood is far more justifiable than fighting a medium-density housing project that might provide homes for some slightly poorer people. Yet the same organizing strategy that is used to fight a road can be used to fight a multistory building. When Jacobs's former neighborhood became the Greenwich Village Historic District in 1969, it was protected not only from Robert Moses's roads but from virtually all change whatsoever.

City after city made decision after decision that privileged current homeowners (and sometimes renters) against outsiders who might potentially benefit from inclusion. Along with these political changes, there was a change in mindset where we came to accept that people are entitled to the status quo. If you have always had a park out of your window, then no one is entitled to build in a way that blocks that view, even if they bought the land when there was no regulatory reason that they couldn't build. If there has never been an art gallery in your neighborhood, then you have a right to stop one from moving in.

As the metropolitan frontier closed, America became a less dynamic country. The economists Raven Malloy, Christopher Smith, and Abigail Wozniak, the first two at the Federal Reserve Board in Washington and the third at the Federal Reserve Bank of Minneapolis, document that between 1970 and 2010, the rate of interstate migration fell by half, and the rate of within-state migration fell by a third. People used to seek their fortunes elsewhere. Increasingly, they stay put, which helps explains why long-term joblessness has become a permanent part of America's economic landscape.

The jobless remain rooted in place partially to avoid paying the housing costs of moving to more economically dynamic and expensive locales. Many of the jobless live with their parents, and they would have to give up that free space to find opportunity somewhere else. Before 1980, less-educated Americans migrated to states with higher incomes, but the economists Peter Ganong and Daniel Shoag find that this "directed" migration has essentially disappeared, partially because high-wage places don't build enough.

The movement of poor people into productive places has been part of American history from its beginning. Farmers left rocky New England in the early nineteenth century for the rich soil of the Ohio River Valley. African Americans fled the Jim Crow South for higher wages and political freedom in northern cities. The Dust Bowl led thousands to flee Oklahoma for California. The limits on building in productive places makes that process far more difficult.

Historically, the migration of poor people into rich places helped smooth out income differences across space. As new workers came to high-wage areas, wages inevitably fell, just as they rose in low-wage areas after workers left. For 140 years, incomes rose more quickly in poorer parts of the country than in richer parts of the country. Since 1980, that process of regional convergence has stopped. Instead, we have a geographic stasis where places marked by high levels of long-term joblessness in 1980, like the Rust Belt, Appalachia, and the Mississippi Delta region, still had high rates of long-term joblessness in 2015.

America's most productive cities are failing the larger economy, partially because they don't provide enough space for ordinary people to live. The economists Chang-Tai Hsieh of the University of Chicago and Enrico Moretti of UC Berkeley estimate that the US economy would be substantially larger if people could move more easily to productive areas, like New York City and San Francisco. If workers are 30 percent more productive in Silicon Valley than in Detroit, then America automatically becomes more productive when migrants go west. Yet they do not, because the high costs of housing eat away the benefits of higher wages.

As housing prices soared in places like Los Angeles, America experienced a massive shift in wealth from the young to the old. In 1983, the median 35-to-44-year-old had $56,000 in housing wealth (in 2013 dollars). Thirty years later, the median 35-to-44-year-old had only $6,000 in housing wealth. By contrast, the median 65-to-74-year-old experienced a 20 percent increase in housing wealth over the same time period. The 95th percentile 65-to-74-year-old experienced a growth in housing wealth from $427,000 to $701,000 correcting for inflation. This redistribution is an example of insiders becoming richer and outsiders losing out.

New construction also reduces house price fluctuations, because the ability to supply new homes sates demand during boom periods. As housing supply has become more limited, price booms and busts have become more extreme. Bigger and more destructive housing bubbles are another side effect of the limits that insiders have placed on new housing construction.

Forty years ago, Olson's thesis seemed a poor fit for enduring American dynamism, but he seems more prescient today. American cities and states have increasingly protected and empowered insiders. A web of local regulation stymies entrepreneurship, and America's overall rate of business formation is far lower than it was in the 1980s. Younger Americans, who are more often outsiders, pay the price, just as they pay the price for the high housing costs that come from limitations on new growth.

In the next chapter, we turn to police tactics, long prison sentences, and underperforming urban schools, which can also be seen as protecting insiders and punishing outsiders. But there is a major difference between the underbuilding problem and either schools or policing. There is a simple, natural fix for underbuilding: allow cities to grow upward. There is no simple solution for urban crime and police brutality, for cities have an obligation to protect both their children against violence and their citizens against cops who kill. Fixing schools is even more difficult. This will take us into the complexities of institutional reform and designing government policy, where it is hard to get things exactly right.

Chapter 9

URBANIZATION
AND ITS DISCONTENTS

O
n May 25, 2020, George Floyd allegedly passed a counterfeit twenty-dollar bill at a convenience store in a gentrifying neighborhood of Minneapolis. The store called the police. The police arrived and asked Floyd to get out of his car. They were neither particularly polite nor brutal. Floyd was terrified and struggled but did not strike the police. He was an unarmed suspect accused of a crime that could have been innocently perpetrated by any of us.

Derek Chauvin, a nineteen-year veteran of the Minneapolis Police Department, arrived on the scene and was determined to impose order. Chauvin pinned Floyd and kept his knee on the back of Floyd's neck. Floyd cried for air. Bystanders started taking photographs and asked Chauvin to let Floyd free. Chauvin ignored their cries and crushed Floyd's windpipe for over eight minutes. Floyd died.

In 2018 alone, police killed 259 African Americans, twenty-eight of whom were, like Floyd, clearly unarmed, according to the Mapping Police Violence database. Yet most killings do not lead to a murder conviction, because there is ambiguity. Chauvin could never plausibly claim self-defense, because the bystanders' videos show that Floyd was helpless and Chauvin was surrounded by other officers. Those videos turned George Floyd from a data point into a cause. As of December 1, 2020, the five most-watched videos of Floyd's death had over fifty million YouTube views.

The horror of those videos powered the protests that followed. Despite the risk of COVID-19, the streets exploded. Societies are more vulnerable to pestilence or natural disaster when they are already riven by conflict. Anger over the slaying of George Floyd brought people out even in the face of an airborne pandemic.

We don't know if the protests spread COVID-19, but in 1918, patriotic rallies were thought to do "little to end the war and much to spread the deadly flu." One 2020 study found that "in the eight cities analyzed, all had positive abnormal growth in infection rate" after the George Floyd–related protests occurred. But another paper found "no evidence that urban protests reignited COVID-19 case or death growth after more than five weeks following the onset of protests," possibly because non-protesters became more careful. Mistrust of the police can hamper pandemic-fighting if it leads either to social gathering or to civil disobedience of public health rules, like not wearing masks in crowded areas.

Urban diversity can easily turn into distrust and then conflict, unless cities enable all of their residents to flourish. The enormous inequality of urban wealth is only tolerable when cities fulfill their historic role of transforming poorer children into richer adults. Yet the amazing data troves on upward mobility unearthed by our colleagues and friends Raj Chetty, John Friedman, Nathaniel Hendren, and their coauthors show that American cities do a worse job of empowering poor kids than we would like to believe. Children who grow up just outside the border of a big-city school district earn more and are less likely to be incarcerated as adults relative to those just inside the school district. Underperforming city schools and overly punitive law enforcement come together to perpetuate poverty across generations.

Urban schools and law enforcement both favor insiders over outsiders.

With law enforcement, the insiders are wealthy urbanites, who demand safety, and police unions, who protect abusive officers from punishment. The outsiders are the young men who are stopped, frisked, and sentenced for life. With schools, the insiders are suburban parents (like us) and the teachers' unions, who protect tenured teachers (again, like us) from being fired. The outsiders are the children of lower-income parents.

Anger and outrage alone cannot fix these problems. Like public health, schools and policing require a serious and sustained commitment to institutional reform. The politically simple shortcut is to embrace rules like "three strikes and you're out" or "defund the police." Governments are quick to do easy things, like imposing occupational licensing requirements or cutting checks to pay for Medicare, and slow to do hard things, like building a functional public health system or fixing urban schools.

Changing the rules that restrict building or business formation should be enough to provide new housing and jobs, because the private sector can deliver abundant homes and start a panoply of new firms. But on its own, the private sector will neither educate the poor nor protect them from harm. In this chapter, we focus on the shared public strength that is needed in both policing and schooling. In both cases, we contrast top-down legislation, which can never alone deliver what cities ultimately need, and the ground-level management that is both difficult and vital.

We start with the dramatic changes in law enforcement since the 1980s. Between 1988 and 2006, the share of Americans who were incarcerated more than doubled. Between 1993 and 2008, the share of female African Americans who were murdered between the ages of fourteen and seventeen—the age range reported by the Bureau of Justice Statistics, a part of the FBI—fell by almost two thirds, from 13.1 per 100,000 to 4.6 per 100,000. We now turn to the rise of aggressive policing and long sentences, and how to keep our cities' streets safe without locking up so many young men.

Three Strikes and You're Out

At 5:30 p.m. on September 26, 1988, a twenty-nine-year-old advertising executive, Diane Ballasiotes, left her job and headed for her car, which was parked near Seattle's Pioneer Square. Ballasiotes was a model of Reagan-era preppy professionalism, with "curly, shoulder-length auburn hair" and wearing a "navy skirt and tennis sweater." She never made it to her car. For a week, she was missing and posters were "nailed everywhere." Her body was finally discovered a week later, by a "Park Department employee," who was "looking for garbage being dumped in another part of town."

Gene Raymond Kane was convicted of the crime. Kane was "a convicted sex offender who had served thirteen years in prison and was, at the time of the murder, a resident of a work-release program in downtown Seattle," a block away from Pioneer Square and Ballasiotes's parking garage. Rachel Blacher wrote in the *Mercer Law Review* that "Kane had not received treatment as a sexual psychopath because he was considered too dangerous for treatment in the mental hospital where the treatment program was then located." Apparently, he was not deemed too dangerous for an essentially unsupervised release.

Ida Ballasiotes, Diane's mother, became the organizer of a grassroots social movement that was every bit as successful in its way as Jane Jacobs's fight to preserve Greenwich Village. According to the *Los Angeles Times*, Ida's "first thought, upon hearing the criminal history of the man who'd killed and raped her daughter," was "What was this guy doing out of jail?" Ida Ballasiotes successfully sued the state Department of Corrections for willful misconduct and won. More significantly, she spearheaded Washington's push for longer sentences. Eventually, she would file the State of Washington's Initiative 593, which required that "criminals who are convicted of 'most serious offenses' on three occasions" shall be "sentenced to life in prison without parole." It passed by an overwhelming three-to-one margin in 1993.

Diane Ballasiotes's murder had such impact because it did not occur in a political vacuum. Five days before Diane was killed, a Republican political action committee began showing an ad called "Weekend Passes" that blamed Democratic presidential candidate Michael Dukakis for giving convicted murderer Willie Horton a weekend furlough from a Massachusetts prison. Horton fled the state and committed rape and armed robbery. In his first term, Dukakis had vetoed a bill that "abolished furloughs for first-degree lifers" because he thought it would "cut the heart out of efforts at inmate rehabilitation."

The US homicide rate had risen only from 7.9 to 8.7 murders per 100,000 from 1984 to 1989. But since the time when Ida Ballasiotes turned twenty-one in 1957, the murder rate was up 118 percent. To many Americans of her generation, America seemed to have slipped from order to chaos. Those Americans were more concerned about the safety of their children than the rights of the accused. Dukakis hoped that even killers could be redeemed and rehabilitated, but voters were looking for vengeance and safety. In the days after Diane Ballasiotes's murder, the Willie Horton ad ran night after night, and as it ran, Ida Ballasiotes helped organize the Friends of Diane, which "began staging rallies and circulating petitions."

Each new crime helped their cause. In December 1988, a twenty-three-year-old Washington State woman was raped and "slashed," by Gary Minnix, "who'd been charged with four vicious knife-related rapes in 1986 and linked by Seattle police to 22 other such cases." He was on a weekend furlough from a mental hospital, because "he'd been found incompetent to stand trial" because of his low IQ.

On Saturday, May 20, 1989, "a 7-year-old boy riding his bike near his Tacoma home was dragged into the nearby woods, raped, choked nearly to death and sexually mutilated." The boy was able to identify his persecutor: a serial sex offender and killer named Earl Shriner, whose shoes were found to be "stained with mud and blood" and whose soles "appeared to match tread-marks at the scene." Shriner was charged with attempted first-degree mur-der and both rape and assault in the first degree. Over the next week, story after story "focused on the fact that so many officials had known of Shriner's history and had predicted he would commit acts of violence." His low IQ had saved him from criminal conviction. On Thursday, May 25, Ida Balla-siotes's fifty-third birthday, *The Seattle Times* "reported that the felony charges against Shriner in 1987 and 1988 were reduced to misdemeanors because the 'children who were the victims of his assault couldn't be made to testify against him in court.'"

As the video of George Floyd's death illustrates, a single graphic incident can be vastly more powerful than a mountain of statistics. The day after the *Seattle Times* article, "a group of protesters gathered on the steps of the Cap-itol Building in Olympia to demand that the Governor call a special session of the legislature to enact tougher penalties for sex offenders, including life imprisonment for repeat sex offenders." Diane Ballasiotes's brother was one of the group's organizers. The Democratic governor convened a task force led by a Republican district attorney who had sought to defeat him in the last election. Ida Ballasiotes was one of the two mothers of victims to join the task force, although she was also calling for immediate legislation.

The task force recommended tougher sentencing and registration of sex offenders. Prisoners who had served their time could still be committed if they were deemed to be a "sexually violent predator." The Washington state legislature put those recommendations into law unanimously in 1990, but Ballasiotes told the *Los Angeles Times* that this sexual predator law was "just a good first step."

Ballasiotes was elected to the Washington House of Representatives in

1992, and she would serve there until she was sixty-six years old. She teamed up with a right-wing radio and television commentator named John Carlson to lead the fight for tougher sentences. They gathered over 250,000 signatures for their three-strikes initiative and put it on the ballot.

Ballasiotes's law became a model followed by California and many other states. Congress passed and President Clinton enthusiastically signed into federal law the Violent Crime Control and Law Enforcement Act of 1994, which included a three-strikes provision. Clinton had watched the Willie Horton ads; he knew what happened when Democrats were seen as soft on crime. At the 1994 crime act's signing, Clinton intoned that "gangs and drugs have taken over our streets and undermined our schools" and the act took steps "toward bringing the laws of our land in line with the values of our people." He was pleased that the three-strikes provision would provide "the means by which we can say that punishment will be more certain." In 1995, a bevy of states decided to go even further and pass two-strikes laws that lowered the standard for life imprisonment.

In 2015, President Clinton would apologize for supporting the bill. At that point, he told the NAACP National Convention that "I signed a bill that made the problem worse and I want to admit it." But in 1994, he was a politician who was giving voters what they wanted: more punishment and less crime.

This history presents a warning to the would-be avengers of George Floyd today. The activists who imposed the draconian laws that imprisoned so many young men were also fueled by an understandable rage. To them, no policy could go too far if it protected a future Diane Ballasiotes. Today, some protesters seem to think no policy can go too far if it protects some future George Floyd. Both perspectives are comprehensible. Unfortunately, both are wrong. We must find the middle ground that protects our children from both private violence and police malfeasance.

Did Longer Sentences
Lead to Less Crime?

As if on cue, crime immediately started to fall after the three-strikes laws were passed. The national homicide rate dropped every year from 1993 to 2000, reaching 5.5 murders per 100,000 in the last year of Clinton's presidency. The number of murders in New York City fell from 2,245 in 1990 to 673 in 2000. Between 2016 and 2019, New York saw fewer than 350 murders per year, which is less than 4 murders per 100,000. Not only is New York much safer than it was, but it is now safer than the nation as a whole, at least as measured by homicides.

Were the three-strikes laws, and increased incarceration more generally, responsible for the increased safety of America's cities after 1993? Unfortunately, the answer is unclear. There are other suspects for the drop in crime, including increasing numbers of police (especially in New York City), changing police strategies, fewer drug-related gang conflicts, legalized abortion, and reduced exposure of children to lead. Some even argue that video games led to less crime.

Mass incarceration can impact crime through three distinct channels. First, prisons can deter crime, as longer sentences may make criminals warier of risking arrest. Second, prisons can incapacitate crime-prone individuals. Ida Ballasiotes certainly did not believe that Gene Kane and Earl Shriner could be scared straight, but she did believe that if they were locked up, they would do less harm. Third, exposure to other criminals while in prison may lead to more crime when a released convict finds it difficult to get a legal job.

One recent study by Eric Helland of Claremont McKenna College and Alex Tabarrok of George Mason University focuses specifically on the deterrent effect of three strikes. The study is ingenious. It compares two sets of criminals, all of whom have been charged for two serious offenses. Some of those criminals were convicted of two offenses and will be in prison ("out") for life on their next conviction. Others of those criminals were convicted on one serious and one lesser offense and will not be sentenced to life for their next conviction. By comparing these two groups, the authors estimate the deterrent effect of being at risk of going to jail forever.

Their estimate is that the three-strikes law reduced the crime rate for these two-crime offenders by about one fifth. However, the public cost of imprisoning a person is large, about $35,000 per person per year, and that's not including the more onerous burden borne by the prisoner. As a result, when they compare costs and benefits, they find that every crime avoided costs almost $150,000 in additional jail spending. Other estimates suggest a social benefit of $34,000 per crime avoided. A meta-analysis of prison sentencing studies (funded by Open Philanthropy, a foundation dedicated to prison reform) "calls even those mild estimates into question." The deterrence impact of longer sentences seems only moderately beneficial at best.

The case is stronger for the connection between incapacitation and crime. A classic study by economist Steven Levitt of the University of Chicago looked at the timing of American Civil Liberties Union (ACLU) lawsuits about prison overcrowding. These lawsuits led to the release of prisoners, and those releases were followed by increases in crime nearby. Analysts who have followed up Levitt's methodology estimate that a 10 percent increase in the number of prisoners released led to a 4.5 percent increase in the amount of violent crime and a 2.5 percent increase in the amount of property crime. Letting violent criminals out of jail appears to increase violence, which isn't all that surprising. That may have also happened after COVID-19-related prison releases in 2020.

But might longer sentences offset the incapacitation effect by increasing criminal activity after release? That effect would not have troubled Ida Ballasiotes, because she was campaigning to get people locked up for life. But for most minor crimes, there is life after prison, and long sentences may produce more habitual criminals. The evidence on this point is not entirely clear. A number of studies find that longer prison sentences raise the odds of rearrest. But if courts sentence prisoners who are more aggressive or crime-prone to more years in prison, then that can create the illusion that longer sentences are making prisoners more harmful to society. Those crime-prone or aggressive individuals would have been more likely to break the law in the future anyway. Other studies using more random sources of sentence length reach the opposite conclusion. Economist Ilyana Kuziemko of Princeton (a former student of ours) looks at how prison sentences are related to recidivism. By examining how somewhat random changes in eligibility for parole are related to length of time in prison, and in turn how that change in prison time relates to recidivism, she concludes that "prison time reduces recidivism risk."

The most critical step in social science is to recognize the limits of our knowledge. With so many different studies, the science is not clear about the effects of prison terms on post-prison behavior. But the fact that prisons reduce crime by keeping potential criminals off the street is supported both by rigorous statistical work and by common sense. Gene Kane would not have killed Diane Ballasiotes if he had been behind bars, and she might well be alive today.

That fact does not mean that three-strikes rules are good policy. Rather, it shows that there are trade-offs. Longer prison terms provide more safety for the outside world but impose costs on the imprisoned and on taxpayers. Clearly, we need some balance. Locking up thousands of young men for their entire lives is both brutal and inhumane. Yet there are some people, like Kane and Shriner, who do terrible things when they are left free.

In the past few decades, the pendulum has swung one way: toward longer sentences and more people in jail. It is appalling that more than 2 million Americans were incarcerated in 2018, and another 4.4 million were on probation and parole. Almost 500,000 of those Americans are imprisoned for drug crimes, and "nonviolent drug convictions remain a defining feature of the *federal* prison system." No other democratic nation has numbers that look anything like those. Among other harmful features, the crowding of jails and prisons makes them particularly vulnerable to infectious disease outbreaks. Reduced penalties for nonviolent drug crimes could shrink prison populations with limited risk to public safety.

The problem with mass incarceration is not that all incarceration is wrong. Gene Kane and Earl Shriner both should have been locked up. The problem is that we vastly increased incarceration with almost no focus on the long-term welfare of those who were sent to jail for life. We acted as if the safety of insiders was worth everything and the rights of outsiders were worth nothing. We follow the same lopsided approach when we encourage the police to stop and frisk any young minority male who happens to be walking down the street.

Ray Kelly: The Personification
of Policy Reform

Ida Ballasiotes's victory in the three-strikes law required political capacity, but it did not require sustained oversight of a public bureaucracy. Changing rules is relatively straightforward. As recent history has shown, we can readily move the needle back and forth between locking people up and letting them out. It is far harder to improve policing in a way that reduces both the number of crimes and the number of prisoners. That requires stronger public institutions with clearer accountability and improved management; these are not easy to build.

The good news is that police departments have repeatedly proven capable of reinventing themselves in the past, even if we don't like where they are today. In the 1970s and 1980s, police departments organized themselves around responding to 911 calls. In the 1990s and 2000s, departments became less reactive and more proactive in reducing crime. Partly as a result, the homicide rate in cities with more than a million inhabitants fell from over 35 per 100,000 in 1991 to under 12 per 100,000 in 2008. The police don't deserve all the credit for that change, but they deserve some.

Consider the career of Raymond Kelly. Kelly first became New York City police commissioner in 1992, when the police budget was $3.18 billion in 2020 dollars and 1,995 New Yorkers were murdered. Kelly's second term as commissioner ended in 2013, when the city spent $5.27 billion on policing and experienced only 333 murders. Kelly served two years under Mayor Dinkins, another twelve under Mayor Bloomberg. At the end of his tenure, Kelly had "the highest approval rating ever recorded for a New York City police commissioner."

Kelly's popularity is the executive branch counterpart to the overwhelming majority received by Ida Ballasiotes's three-strikes initiative. A frightened public cheered for tough policing, worrying little about its human costs. Yet unlike Ballasiotes, Kelly ran a public agency that employed over fifty thousand people, and was charged with protecting the safety of over eight million. He was applauded not just for being anti-crime, but also for being an "administrative magician" whose "management creed is to control everything he can control."

Kelly graduated with a degree in business administration from Manhattan College in 1963. He served as an officer in Vietnam and remained in the marine reserves for decades, rising to the rank of colonel. When he returned to New York in 1966, he "patrolled the Upper West Side for only seven months before getting promoted." Over the next quarter century, "he would command precincts in Brooklyn and Queens, obtain a master's degree from Harvard, and run the department's Office of Management Analysis and

Planning, which handled statistics" in the precomputer years. He was then "promoted over several superiors to the department's No. 2 post: first deputy." By the time Kelly became police chief in 1992, he had a lifetime of leadership experience from the Bronx to Southeast Asia.

Strong lieutenants make effective leaders. Kathy Ryan was Kelly's deputy chief in charge of the domestic violence unit. Under Ryan, the number of "police visits to homes with histories of domestic violence" rose from 33,400 in 2001 to 76,000 in 2007. Between 2001 and 2007, the number of women murdered in New York City fell by 38 percent, and *New York* magazine reported that "the big decline in domestic-violence murders occurred in households that police already knew were problem homes."

Police visits are intrusive. One of their objectives "is to give abusers a sense of being watched." These visits can also "give the weaker party in the home a sense of having allies," and "even catch an offender lording over a household that he's barred from by a court order." Ryan was also a pioneer in a "stern and futuristic" experiment with ankle bracelets, so that if a domestic violence offender "wanders too close to a home, school, or workplace covered by a protection order, a radio car will automatically be dispatched to the site and a call will be placed to the individual in danger." Ryan and Kelly used the power of policing to protect women from male violence. They innovated in the use of public strength to protect the vulnerable, instead of accepting the status quo.

Kelly also led an innovative fight against terrorism. On May 1, 2010, a car bomb was left to explode in crowded Times Square, but two street vendors "flagged down a mounted police officer after they noticed smoke coming from the Pathfinder, which had been parked haphazardly at the curb with its engine running." Jane Jacobs emphasized that crowds provide the "eyes on the street" that cry out when they see crime.

Kelly's high-tech bomb squad showed up with its "robot that looked like a moon rover." The bomb was defused. The case was cracked in fifty-three hours, just in time for the suspect to be removed from a plane headed for Dubai. Kelly took the failed terrorist attack as a justification "to spend $40 million to wire up midtown with more surveillance cameras."

Kelly's anti-terrorism efforts involved organizational, as well as technological, change. As the "city charter forbids cops on the NYPD payroll to work in other law-enforcement jurisdictions," Kelly used the private non-profit New York City Police Foundation to fund "the International Liaison Program, where NYPD detectives are sent to Tel Aviv, Amman, London," and other cities. Those global connections feed the NYPD tips about terrorist attacks from elsewhere on the planet.

The Rise and Fall of Stop and Frisk

The most controversial of Kelly's actions was the stop and frisk program. That tactic was tied to Operation Impact, which aimed "to reduce crime throughout the city by deploying more officers to high-crime hot spots, known as 'Impact Zones.'" In those areas, police would stop people who they thought might be criminals, ask them questions, and frisk them, searching for weapons or contraband. The police department claimed that Operation Impact was "integral" to their "unprecedented achievements." In practice, stop and frisk meant millions of body searches of unarmed African Americans and Latinos.

The scientific literature generally agrees that targeting police resources toward high-crime areas reduces crime. A recent meta-analysis concludes that "hot spots policing is an effective crime prevention strategy." A study conducted by John MacDonald of the University of Pennsylvania, Jeffrey Fagan of Columbia, and Amanda Geller of NYU finds that "impact zones were significantly associated with reductions in total reported crimes, assaults, burglaries, drug violations, misdemeanor crimes, felony property crimes, robberies, and felony violent crimes," as well as "increases in total reported arrests, arrests for burglary, arrests for weapons, arrests for misdemeanor crimes, and arrests for property felony crimes."

However, the literature has been less clear about the efficacy of using stop and frisk as part of a hot-spots strategy. The study with favorable results about impact zones also concluded that "the bulk of the investigative stops [stop and frisk] did not play an important role in the crime reductions." Another study, by Franklin Zimring of New York University, archly notes that the police believe that the "more than half a million stops in 2009 and two hundred thousand misdemeanor arrests" help "increase the effectiveness of preventive interventions, but there is no rigorous evidence on the value added in New York City."

The racial overtones of stop and frisk were particularly noticeable. A federal class-action lawsuit was filed in 2013 on behalf of minority civilians of New York City. Ray Kelly and Michael Bloomberg were both named defendants. The case was heard by Judge Shira Scheindlin. The judge noted that "between January 2004 and June 2012" the NYPD made 4.4 million stops and "over 80% of these 4.4 million stops were of blacks or Hispanics."

There is a *Saturday Night Live* skit from 1978 with a horribly apt parody. The experienced baggage inspector, played by Dan Aykroyd, tells his trainee to "always check black people!" They find an obviously innocent seed on the shirt of an African American man, played by Garrett Morris, that they claim is marijuana and submit him "to a personal search." They let the white John Belushi, who is positively overflowing with cocaine, pass by.

That sketch suggests the logic of a common social-science test of whether stop and frisk disproportionately searched minorities. If police target minorities too much given crime rates, then the minorities who are stopped will be less likely to have done anything wrong, like Garrett Morris's innocent traveler. Conversely, if targeting is race-blind, rates of arrests after the stops should be similar across racial groups. Studies have looked at this question, unfortunately with conflicting results. Decio Coviello of the Institute of Applied Economics in Canada and Nicola Persico of Northwestern find no evidence of bias: white pedestrians are "slightly less likely than African-American pedestrians to be arrested conditional on being stopped." However, research by Harvard PhD student John Tebes finds that African Americans who are stopped are more likely to be innocent. Of course, subsequent arrest by itself does not prove the policy was not biased. The decision to arrest given a stop may also be made on racial grounds.

In her ruling, Judge Scheindlin expressed no opinion on "the effectiveness of stop and frisk in deterring or combating crime." But the judge rebuked Kelly and Bloomberg by ruling that "the city acted with deliberate indifference towards the NYPD's practice of making unconstitutional stops and conducting unconstitutional frisks." She argued that "no one should live in fear of being stopped whenever he leaves his home to go about the activities of daily life," and ruled that "the police are not permitted to target people for stops based on their race."

The scale of stop and frisk was staggering. Judge Scheindlin noted that "in 98.5% of the 2.3 million frisks, no weapon was found," and that "between 2004 and 2009, the percentage of stops where the officer failed to state a specific crime rose from 1% to 36%," and that "88% of the 4.4 million stops resulted in no further law enforcement action." Additionally, she notes that "each stop is also a demeaning and humiliating experience." Since more than four fifths of the stops involved African Americans and Hispanics, minorities suffered more than 80 percent of the humiliation. Large racial disparities in police stops also exist in the UK, despite a legacy of limiting police aggression that goes back to prime minister Robert Peel.

When Mayor Bloomberg was replaced by Mayor de Blasio, all official opposition to Scheindlin's ruling ended, and so did the era of Ray Kelly. His legacy will always be tarnished by stop and frisk, but he was also an extraordinarily capable leader of the NYPD. Moreover, he was giving New York what it wanted. If the voters had made it clear that they found aggressive policing intolerable, then Kelly would have used different tactics, as his successor did after 2013. Looking forward, voters will need to give their police chiefs a clear dual mandate to both fight crime and respect the dignity of every citizen. But to impose the reforms that can reduce brutality on a recalcitrant police department, the voters will also need leaders who are just as effective as Kelly was at controlling his bureaucracy.

Police Insiders

The Police Officers Federation of Minneapolis declares that their "job is to improve working conditions for our members—police officers who work in Minneapolis—and to make certain their rights are protected." After George Floyd's murder, the president of the Minneapolis police union, Lieutenant Bob Kroll, made it clear that the union's labor attorneys were going to fight for the jobs of the four policemen involved because "they were terminated without due process." For good measure, he threw in the accusation that the media was covering up "the violent criminal history of George Floyd" and suggested that the protesters were a "terrorist movement." Kroll himself has been the subject of twenty-two internal affairs complaints.

The Wall Street Journal reports that "between 1995 and 2019, the Minneapolis contract between the police union and the city grew to 128 pages from 40," and "it now includes more protections such as a two-day waiting period before interviewing officers in investigations of misconduct and other matters; mandatory paid leave for officers involved in critical incidents; and erasing misconduct records when complaints don't lead to disciplinary action." One Reuters study found that a majority of police union "contracts call for departments to erase disciplinary records, some after just six months, making it difficult to fire officers with a history of abuse."

On October 20, 2014, Chicago police officer Jason Van Dyke fired sixteen shots at Laquan McDonald and killed him. CNN reported that "on at least 20 occasions in that police officer's 14-year career, citizens have filed complaints against Van Dyke." The ensuing report of Chicago's Police Accountability Task Force found that "the collective bargaining agreements between the police unions and the City have essentially turned the code of silence into official policy," and that "even after a misconduct complaint is sustained, the collective bargaining agreements provide a grievance procedure that can minimize the severity of the punishment or overturn it completely."

A study by Dhammika Dharmapala, Richard McAdams, and John Rappaport of the University of Chicago investigates the impact of union contracts by examining a 2003 judicial decision in which "county sheriffs' deputies won the right to organize for collective bargaining." Those sheriffs' deputies could be compared with municipal police departments that "had the right to bargain collectively both before and after that date." The authors' "estimates imply that collective bargaining rights led to a substantial increase in violent incidents of misconduct among sheriffs' offices, relative to police departments."

Police unions will always try to protect their members. But why do cities and counties sign contracts that allow the suppression of disciplinary records after six months? A simple story is that public sector workers can either be paid with obscure benefits, like arcane pension promises and protection from future discipline, or obvious wage increases. Local governments want to show voters that they are careful stewards of their cash, so their contracts provide protection for bad cops instead of pay raises. If voters are willing to pay more to get greater police accountability, then the many good police officers that do exist will take that deal.

The adoption of body cameras in Boston shows that unions will accept sensible reforms that benefit everyone. The Boston Police Patrolmen's Association initially filed suit to stop "a program requiring officers to wear body cameras." But police commissioner William Evans and the union both had the humility to learn. They compromised on a pilot program with just one hundred cameras randomly allocated among officers. When "complaints brought against officers were cleared by videos," the union started seeing the upsides of transparency. Moreover, a randomized control trial found that body cameras "generate small but meaningful benefits to the civility of police-citizen civilian encounters." The union accepted the cameras.

Should We Defund the Police?

Defunding the police may seem like a natural response to the lawless behavior displayed by Derek Chauvin. But an underfunded police department will not improve the safety of minority neighborhoods. If fewer police lead to more crime, then the poor will suffer disproportionately. Moreover, a more stressed police force could easily become a more brutal police force.

In 2018, the police killed 259 African Americans and 490 whites. That same year, 7,407 African Americans and 6,088 whites were victims of non-police homicide. Non-police homicides are both much more frequent than police homicides and more likely to target African Americans. Given the terrible toll that crime takes on disadvantaged and minority communities, it seems unwise to weaken the law enforcement mission.

The work of our colleague Roland Fryer and former student Tanaya Devi suggests that when investigations of bias lead the police to avoid minority neighborhoods, then minorities themselves can suffer. The Justice Department's Civil Rights Division has the power to investigate cases involving a "pattern or practice of conduct by law enforcement officers" that violates federal law. Fryer and Devi found that "for investigations that were preceded by a viral incident of deadly force—Baltimore, Chicago, Cincinnati, Riverside and Ferguson—there is a marked increase in both homicide and total crime" following the investigation. They explain that "the leading theory for why some investigations have led to an increase in crimes is a striking decrease in the quantity of police activity." After Chicago's investigation, they find an 89 percent reduction in "police-civilian interactions" and report that a reduction in police activity "is evident in all cities we were able to collect data." To test whether the crime surge primarily reflects anger at the police, they also investigate "cities that had viral shootings but no investigation," where they find "no significant level breaks for homicides or total crime," despite the widespread anger. Their back-of-the-envelope calculations imply that these cities will have experienced over 1,200 excess homicides by the time they return to their pre-investigation levels.

To stop murders, police need to solve murders. After falling from over 30 murders per 100,000 in the early 1990s to about 15 murders per 100,000 between 2005 and 2014, Chicago's homicide rate began to spike again, first to 17 per 100,000 in 2015 and then to 27 per 100,000 in 2016. Historically, the share of murders that lead to a criminal charge is more than 60 percent in the US, but in 2016, Chicago's murder clearance rate dropped to under 30 percent. Since 2017, Chicago has hired more detectives, the clearance rate has risen to about 50 percent, and the murder rate has come down.

Police reform needs to be about more than cutting spending or eliminating law enforcement. The key is recognizing that we care about more than just reducing crime. As Tracey Meares of Yale Law School writes, "security from government overreach and oppression is also a key element of public safety." That line would be greeted warmly by any right-wing, libertarian audience. In a coauthored article written after the George Floyd killing, Meares calls for "a relationship in which state and community co-produce public safety, with an emphasis on transitioning power from the police to community-led organizations." This co-production of public safety fits in well with community policing's objective of getting ordinary people to cooperate with the police.

Cooperation is particularly difficult when people fear reprisals. The murder spike of the late 1980s was associated with gangs like the Bloods, the Crips, and the Cobras who fought over the trade in crack cocaine. Effective gangs entrench themselves in the community through a combination of fear and favors. Consequently, police investigating gang crimes run into a wall of silence.

Community policing is designed to break through that wall by building trust between the police and the neighborhood. Often, police work in tandem with community organizations to do so. In Boston, for example, religious leaders came together into a TenPoint Coalition after a 1992 gang war targeted a church. That coalition helped the Boston Police Department shed its reputation for insularity and racism, and develop the skills needed for making friends with normal people.

Those skills are built by ordinary interactions with interested citizens, like the Coffee with a Cop program that began in Hawthorne, California, in 2011. There is now a Coffee with a Cop nonprofit that provides training for the interactive side of the events (presumably the cops know how to order coffee already). Local Starbucks and Dunkin's provide free java and receive some pleasant publicity. The program's website claims that "Coffee with a Cop events are now held in all 50 states" and that it is "one of the most successful community oriented policing programs across the country."

Some interpret "defunding the police" to mean moving funds from police to other government agencies that can potentially reduce violence. Rashawn Ray of the Brookings Institution notes that "9 out of 10 calls for police service are for nonviolent encounters," and that "police respond to everything from potholes in the street to cats stuck up a tree." According to Ray, "police officers are mostly trained in use-of-force tactics and worst-case scenarios to reduce potential threats," but "most of their interactions with civilians start with a conversation." Perhaps more of those interactions should occur with non-police public employees who don't carry firearms.

Tracey Meares, noted above, also supports funding nongovernmental entities, including LIFE Camp in New York, Upswell in Chicago, and Advance Peace in Richmond, California, that can co-produce safer streets.

Some cities are acting on this. For example, Baltimore plans to redirect police "funding to recreational centers, trauma centers, and forgivable loans for Black-owned businesses." One of the big payoffs from early childhood programs is that they can reduce crime levels for those children when they become adults, but it isn't clear that forgivable loans will either reduce crime or yield benefits that cover their costs.

Governments should fund more neighborhood amenities in high-poverty neighborhoods. The return to doing so is doubly high if they reduce crime. But the decision to spend more on non-police activities should be decoupled from the decision about how much to spend on policing itself. The size of the city budget for those two activities is not fixed, nor is the police department a piggy bank that can be emptied to provide extra funding for other goals.

Security and Freedom

Instead of thinking about police reform as a budgetary issue, we should start by thinking organizationally. Society has two goals: to keep crime as low as possible and to ensure that all citizens are treated with dignity and fairness. Rather than swing the pendulum one way or the other, we need to do both. That will require more spending, not less, and it will require us to start measuring dignity and fairness.

Crime drives voters and police behavior partially because it has such numerical clarity. The past thirty years of reform have strengthened the link between numerical crime data and the success of police superintendents and captains. If there is to be a dual mandate for low crime rates and good police behavior, then the measurement of police behavior must also be made more systematic. This observation reflects a basic principle of both bureaucracy and politics: things we measure get focused on, while things we do not measure get downplayed. If we want to balance safety and equal protection, we will need to comprehensively measure both.

Measuring how police interact with people must have several dimensions. An annual independent survey of neighborhood satisfaction with the police can measure the quality of community engagement. Such a survey should be large enough to shed light on every precinct, so it can be used to evaluate the performance of each captain as well as the police department overall. The survey, as well as other measures of community satisfaction, can be used to hold police chiefs accountable for their overall performance.

What should be the exact questions? Some experimentation is in order. The community could ask how often citizens have been stopped for minor transgressions. They could ask about overall satisfaction with the police, or trust of the police. They could focus on the number of unpleasant (or pleasant) experiences that citizens have with police officers.

Each city can decide on its own priorities, but the survey doesn't need to be designed anew each time. One model is that a few big cities, like New York and Los Angeles, could lead and other cities could adapt their surveys. Alternatively, the federal government could support the development and administration of a survey that could then be modified to meet local needs. The survey must not be administered by the police department or any entity associated with it so that the community has faith in its independence and integrity.

No survey will be perfect, but it will give a dual mandate for crime reduction and upholding citizens' dignity a chance. Once better measurement of community satisfaction is in hand, the mayor and police chief must decide how to make the dual mandate work. It must start at the top. Police chiefs must set benchmarks along both dimensions and agree to leave if they fail to meet those goals.

Since it makes sense to have both a belt and suspenders when it comes to community well-being, community watchdog organizations should supplement the survey. These organizations can both support the police in providing safety and also report on the police. The mayor should keep enough discretion to be able to punish his or her police chief if those organizations produce robust evidence of unacceptable behavior.

Beyond measuring the police force's performance and establishing community watchdogs, it makes sense to let chiefs design their own systems of operation and supervision. If the police chief likes an idea, then it will get implemented with or without external rules. If the police chief doesn't like an idea, then the chief can gut it internally through poor enforcement even if there is an outside mandate. Past disciplinary procedures have often failed to control police, because they have not had the support of the organization. That support must start at the top.

Good police chiefs can mold their departments through the standard tools of bureaucratic control: monitoring, incentives, training, hiring, and retention. Body cameras can ensure that every encounter is watched, especially involving police officers like Derek Chauvin who have a history of complaints. Police captains who fail to improve community satisfaction can be demoted. Sergeants can go through intensive training. Officers can be selected partially on the basis of their ability to work well with the community. A good police superintendent will figure out what works if they have the right goals. A dual mandate with the right measurement can give superintendents the incentive to make policing more humane.

One fear is that police are so entrenched in their current culture that even the most well-meaning police commissioner cannot change their ways. Here again, we need to accept that there is no free lunch. If we want the police to do more, we will need to pay them more. Unions will need to get higher wages if they are to agree that their members will be punished and fired more for misbehavior.

The Urban Opportunity Gap

A police department's DNA has roots in the regimented legions of ancient Rome, but a public school's antecedents lie in the chaotic Socratic dialogues in the agora of Athens. Top-down reform comes far more naturally to one than the other. No school district superintendent has ever enjoyed the power that Ray Kelly wielded over the New York City Police Department. Reforming education is difficult because different people want different things from our schools, and because measuring school performance is even harder than measuring the decency of police departments.

Since the 1960s, parents have used the interstate highway system to relocate to suburbs for access to supposedly better public schools. This process fed on itself. As middle-class parents left, those who stayed increasingly thought about exit as well. Their taxes went up, and the perceived quality of schools fell. Race added to this spiral, especially after a pair of Supreme Court decisions pretty much ensured that many white parents would leave the city.

The 1971 case of *Swann v. Charlotte-Mecklenburg Board of Education* ruled that school districts needed to eliminate racially segregated schools even if that meant busing children long distances. Three years later, in *Milliken v. Bradley*, the court ruled that while busing within districts was absolutely necessary, children could never be forced to bus across school districts. Parents who stayed in the city had to accept that their children could be bused to a racially mixed school. Parents who moved to a suburb could guarantee that their child was educated in an almost entirely white environment close to their home. The busing battles in our hometown of Boston were particularly notorious.

Urban high schools have long scored poorly on standardized tests, but is this because the schools are a problem or because urban children start with terrible disadvantages? The Opportunity Atlas, created by Raj Chetty, John Friedman, Nathaniel Hendren, and their collaborators, mentioned briefly in the previous chapter, helps answer this question. The Atlas is a monumental attempt to measure upward mobility in every American neighborhood.

Children born between 1978 and 1983 are followed throughout their lives. The Atlas focuses on the adult earnings of children born to parents who were at the 25th percentile of the income distribution in the year the children were born—they were richer than one quarter of families and poorer than three quarters. The data paints a dire picture of opportunity in urban America. If one ranked all 330 million Americans today in terms of income, a child of low-income parents born in a dense American metropolitan area in 1980 would today be 13 million Americans behind the same child born in a lower-density part of America. In the US, urban density appears to be good for productivity and bad for upward mobility.

A graduate student at Harvard, Brandon Tan, has worked together with one of us (Glaeser) to establish a number of facts about urban mobility using the Opportunity Atlas. Within the typical metropolitan area, a child growing up in the densest part of the city ends up about 15 million Americans behind a child growing up in the least dense part of the city. A child born at the city center ends up 20 million people behind a child growing up ten miles out.

While opportunity increases steadily with distance from the city center, there is a distinct jump just at the edge of the central city school district. Relocating right outside the city, in the closest suburb, moves the child at least 6 million Americans ahead in the income distribution as an adult. The share of children who are incarcerated as adults also drops when they move just outside the central city school district, from about 2.75 percent to 2.1 percent.

The Opportunity Atlas shows that neighborhood matters for upward mobility, even within a single school district. On average, a child of poor Hispanic parents who grew up in the Skid Row neighborhood of Central Los Angeles earned an average of $24,000 as an adult. Children who grew up just a few blocks north, near the Little Tokyo area, earned $30,000 annually when grown. If a child grew up just a little bit to the south of Skid Row along Olympic Boulevard, then they earned an average of $36,000 after they entered the labor market.

The importance of neighborhood is particularly large for African Americans, and especially for African American boys. Racial segregation compounds the downsides of urban school districts just as it does urban policing. Ellora Derenoncourt of UC Berkeley (and a former student of ours) has conducted research illustrating how the bright promise offered by northern cities to African Americans just after World War II turned into a nightmare for many. The segregation of northern cities created poor and isolated communities where crime ran unchecked. The deindustrialization of America's cities then particularly harmed those with less formal schooling.

The Great Migration of African Americans from the South to northern cities increased earnings for them dramatically, because there had been a big difference in incomes between city and non-city residents. David Autor of MIT found that in 1970, an urbanite with a high school diploma or less did substantially better than his nonurban equivalent, and that was roughly true everywhere, from Detroit to Dallas. By 2020, the urban wage premium was gone in less-educated cities, and since that was where less-educated workers typically lived, they earned no more than in rural America. The more-educated "superstar" cities, like New York, Boston, and Seattle, reinvented themselves as capitals of the information age—at least until the COVID-19 pandemic. Wages are higher there for everyone, even for low-income workers. Wages of rich and poor alike increase with the education of people around them, and that fact is particularly true in the developing world.

The trade-off, however, is that housing supply is limited in places with more years of schooling. Low-income people earn more in those educated cities, but the cost of housing and of all goods that require space, like supermarkets, are so much higher that they do not feel richer.

Cities have long seethed with inequality, as Plato noted in the *Republic*, because they attract both rich and poor. Urban inequality serves a larger purpose if poor urban children move up the income distribution. The problem, as we have discussed, is that they do not. If cities are going to succeed in recovering from COVID-19 and beyond, they will have to provide more opportunity for children born of poorer parents.

One policy approach to low urban mobility is to encourage low-income families to move to neighborhoods that appear to engender success. The Moving to Opportunity for Fair Housing experiment randomly allocated housing vouchers to poorer parents almost thirty years ago. The results were initially unpromising, because teenagers seemed to gain little from moving to better neighborhoods. However, when the parents of younger children received vouchers, those small children grew up to be far more successful as adults. Chetty and his partners have started a program in Seattle targeting housing vouchers to parents with small children and then helping those parents move to high-opportunity neighborhoods.

Race to the Top and Top-Down Educational Reform

Directing housing aid to parents with young children provides one means of supporting opportunity, but education remains our primary public tool for enhancing economic success. Poorer children born in Sweden or Germany have much higher levels of upward mobility than their American counterparts, partially because those countries educate their disadvantaged children so much better than America does.

Schooling represents the single largest failure of America's cities, and perhaps the largest failure of American society. Schools protect insiders, including poorly performing teachers with tenure, and fail outsiders, like the children of the poor. Just as with law enforcement, school reform has legislative components, such as the No Child Left Behind and Race to the Top initiatives, and institution building, which is the work of school principals and school district leaders. Legislation is easy to understand and suggests the possibility of national impact with a few strokes of a pen, but schools will not get better without the harder work of ground-up institutional reform.

We begin with legislation, just as we did with criminal justice. The 2008 Democratic platform wanted to "promote innovation within our public schools—because research shows that resources alone will not create the schools that we need to help our children succeed" and to "adapt curricula and the school calendar to the needs of the 21st century." Yet schooling, like land-use regulation, is a hyper-local affair in the United States. To change either schools or zoning, the federal government must first get the states on board, and then the states must force change on recalcitrant localities.

The Obama administration's Race to the Top program offered $4.35 billion to state governments in a contest where "states seeking funds will be pressed to implement four core, interconnected reforms." The program was sold as a "once-in-a-lifetime opportunity for the federal government to create incentives for far-reaching improvement in our nation's schools." States certainly fell into line eager for the recognition and the cash, which was especially welcome since the Great Recession had slashed state tax revenues.

The four "interconnected reforms" that were prioritized by Education Secretary Arne Duncan were "to reverse the pervasive dumbing down of academic standards and assessments," "to monitor growth in student learning—and identify effective instructional practices," "to identify effective teachers and principals," and "to turn around the lowest-performing schools." The program hoped that a dollop of federal cash could revolutionize entrenched institutions throughout the US: "states and districts must be ready to institute far-reaching reforms, replace school staff, and change the school culture."

The awards were based on a 500-point system, which gave 65 points for "Articulating State's education reform agenda and LEAs' [Local Education Agencies] participation in it," 58 points for "improving teacher and principal effectiveness based on performance," and 40 points for "developing and adopting common standards."

The short-run effects were astounding: "a total of 46 states and the District of Columbia put together comprehensive education reform plans to apply for Race to the Top in Phases 1 and 2." There were two winners in the first round and ten winners in the second round, including New York (which won $700 million) and Washington, DC ($75 million). The Department of Education claimed that because of the contest, "35 states and the District of Columbia have adopted rigorous common, college and career-ready standards in reading and math, and 34 states have changed laws or policies to improve education." At the time, this was an almost miraculous achievement, where the dreams of school reformers were becoming reality thanks to a little bit of funding and the magic of good tournament design.

Yet while the state governments got on board, localities pushed back. A system that looks great on paper can fail on the ground, perhaps because teachers and complicit principals fudge the test scores that are supposed to measure performance, or perhaps because common standards fit the local context poorly.

States received full points for the "common standards" component of the contest by participating in a consortium that "includes a significant number of States," who were "working toward jointly developing and adopting a common set of K-12 standards (as defined in this notice) that are supported by evidence that they are internationally benchmarked and build toward college and career readiness." The only multistate consortium that fit this definition in 2009 was the Common Core State Standards Initiative, which included 47 states and the District of Columbia. That initiative was, in principle, "state-led," convened by the National Governors Association (NGA)

Center for Best Practices and the Council of Chief State School Officers (CCSSO).

The CCSSO and NGA Center had been supported for years by organizations committed to education reform, especially the Gates Foundation. The Gates Foundation granted the NGA Center $19.6 million in 2005 "to provide states with grants and assistance to develop and implement comprehensive plans for high school redesign and increase college-ready high school graduation rates," and the CCSSO $9.97 million in 2009 "to increase the leadership capacity of chiefs by focusing on standards and assessments, data systems, educator development and determining a new system of supports for student learning." One of us (Glaeser) had a somewhat inside view on that process as a member of the Gates Foundation's US Program Advisory Panel.

Developing the standards took only thirteen months, from May 2009, when the development of the "core and college ready standards" began, to June 2010, when the NGA and CCSSO released "the final Common Core State Standards." The process was inclusive, involving "mountains of feedback" including "a feedback committee, a validation committee, and educator organizations brought in by CCSSO and NGA," as well as "something like 10,000 public comments from individuals and organizations." A 2012 paper on the Common Core State Standards for Mathematics (CCSSM) "found a very high degree of similarity between CCSSM and the standards of the highest-achieving nations," which is presumably what America should want, so that it can catch up with better-performing countries like South Korea and the Netherlands.

Any attempt to impose education standards in the US will always face three problems. First, high-performing districts will complain that their existing standards are more rigorous than any new Common Core and they do not want to "dumb down." Second, outside of the quantitative disciplines, standards will inevitably involve cultural aspects that will run into the buzz saw of America's social heterogeneity. Third, any standard requires good local implementation, and that means hard managerial and administrative work. A change in the rules does not automatically bring a change in the organization.

In Massachusetts, which had high standards before 2010, James Stergios of the Pioneer Institute led the charge against those who defended Race to the Top (including Glaeser), by arguing that "for Massachusetts and many other high-standard states," the Common Core will mean a dramatic "lowering" of "their standard of instruction and learning." Stergios's institute commissioned a white paper, titled "Lowering the Bar: How Common Core Math Fails to Prepare High School Students for STEM," which emphasized that even one of the Common Core authors had admitted that "the concept of college readiness is minimal and focuses on non-selective colleges." Those words evoked terror among the ambitious parents of Boston's education-intensive suburbs. As the Common Core was rolled out nationally before it was tested, Stergios could plausibly claim that "the feds are pushing stuff that is at best untested and in many cases has proven to be wrong-headed and harmful to improvements in student achievement."

A few states, including Massachusetts, could legitimately fear that common standards would involve dumbing down, but that wasn't true for much of America. Yet everywhere the Common Core could be opposed as an overreach of federal power. As it moved beyond the STEM fields, it would be accused of imposing the cultural values of coastal elites on the rest of America.

Conservative enemies of the Common Core called it a tool of "progressive educators" who are "well known for pushing to make changes in attitudes, values and beliefs through curriculum which often causes children to oppose their parents who have traditional views." In 2014, the former Fox News firebrand Glenn Beck published *Conform: Exposing the Truth about*

Common Core and Public Education, in which he argued that the Common Core's focus on "informational texts" is a "systematic approach to dumb down our kids and further remove parents from the process so that students will be easier to indoctrinate and control."

But the largest Race to the Top problem came in the translation from legislation to administration. New York State's 449-page Race to the Top application, dated June 1, 2010, promised that "all schools will implement the new Common Core Standards by the 2011–12 school year," and that "teachers and principals will be evaluated using student growth data beginning in the 2011–12 school year." In response to such a far-reaching commitment, New York was awarded $700 million, which was the largest single Race to the Top grant.

It turned out that changing a school system that employs thousands and educates millions is much harder than writing a law or a proposal. Writing in 2015, Governor Cuomo's task force reported that "in the press to implement the Common Core Standards in New York beginning in 2009 . . . educators were inundated with confusing information and new material without having first been brought into the process of developing how these new approaches were to be integrated into curricula and taught to students." Further, "due to these missteps, thousands of parents, educators, and other education stakeholders now associate the phrase Common Core with this rushed and failed attempt at implementation that caused undue disruption in our schools." While the state adopted the Common Core at the start of 2011, the state's department of education "did not post the majority of the entire Standards-aligned curriculum resources before the start of the 2012–2013 school year, leaving teachers unable to adapt or select curriculum, update their lesson plans and routine assessments of student learning, or rearrange classroom learning to be Standards-aligned."

One analysis of the New York Race to the Top highlights five distinct managerial failures. First, "local budgets were strained" because Race to the Top "took a relatively modest amount of federal money and leveraged local budgets to implement desired reform policies." Second, the rush to implement meant that the new "curriculum was not piloted, validated or field-tested" and "modules were still missing when the year began." Modules, especially in the math section, had errors. Third, the testing regime meant that "many districts felt compelled to rely heavily, if not exclusively," on modules that micromanaged teaching by providing "day-by-day highly scripted lesson plans for each grade level and subject." Fourth, the rush led to "inaccurate data," such as a state report that indicated that only 62 percent of the 2012 high school graduates of the South Orangetown district were still in college, while "the district calculated 89%." Fifth, there was enormous parental opposition to the time spent on standardized tests and union opposition to basing teacher pay on those tests.

Governor Cuomo, who was the head of the state government overseeing this debacle, washed his hands of it, declaring in a 2014 political debate that "I have nothing to do with common core." The task force that he convened suggested a slightly slower timetable. The system should wait "until the start of the 2019-2020 school year" before "results from assessments aligned to the current Common Core Standards" should "be used to evaluate the performance of specific teachers or students."

The Race to the Top experiment had its embarrassing moments, but it was not a terrible fiasco. It was also not "the equivalent of education reform's moon shot," as Secretary Duncan proclaimed in 2009. The Department of Education's National Assessment of Educational Progress (NAEP) tests assess fourth-, eighth-, and twelfth-grade students in several subjects and provide the "largest nationally representative assessment of what students across the United States know and can do." The average NAEP score for twelfth graders in mathematics was unchanged between 2009 and 2013, and the math score has fallen since then. The twelfth-grade reading score is similarly lower in 2019 than it was in 2009.

It is hard to think about how any low-cost, rule-based approach could fix the problems of city schools. Improving education requires serious management, and even the brightest stars can fail to survive the rough politics around schooling in the big city.

Michelle Rhee in Washington, DC

Michelle Rhee bestrides the cover of the December 8, 2008, issue of *Time* magazine like a colossus of educational management. The cover states "How To Fix America's Schools" and suggests that Rhee's "battle against bad teachers . . . could transform public education." At that point, Rhee was the chancellor of the Washington, DC, public school system and the superstar of school reform.

Rhee is the daughter of Korean immigrants who began as an educator in the elite Teach for America program. She then formed her own successful spinoff: The New Teacher Project. She was talented and charismatic, but she hadn't gone through decades of administrative (and real) warfare, like Ray Kelly had. Her administrative inexperience made her ill-prepared for the messy work of running a complex, highly politicized institution.

The leaders of America's big-city school districts are either selected by a popularly elected board, such as the one that Julian Nava served on in Los Angeles, or by the mayor, either directly or through a board the mayor appoints. In 2007, DC followed the lead of Chicago and New York and switched to mayoral appointment. The spirit behind mayoral control is that voters should be able to hold the mayor accountable for school quality, and thus the mayor should control who runs the schools.

One advantage of the 2007 act that switched DC schools to mayoral control is that it required a detailed evaluation of the Washington, DC, public schools, and a serious three-hundred-plus-page document duly appeared in 2015. The DC Council deserves credit for embedding this evaluation in the legislation and turning to an able and independent evaluator: the National Academy of Sciences (NAS). As Rhee and her successor had led the district since the switch to executive accountability, the NAS report can essentially be read as a verdict on their tenures.

The results are slightly positive. While test scores "increased between 2007 and 2014 across most student groups," it was also noted that "the increase is larger for math than it is for reading" and "indicators of proficiency in both subjects remain low." Moreover, "graduation rates have fluctuated from year to year, with no discernible pattern" and "they, too, remain disturbingly low." For example, the gap between DC and the nation on the eighth-grade mathematics component of the NAEP test shrank by 28 percent, from 32 points to 23 points. These results are not a failure, but they are not a transformation either.

The NAEP tests are administered independently, and consequently provide a legitimate measure of a school's progress, but most standardized testing is done by the schools themselves. An experienced administrator, or even one who had read about teacher cheating in *Freakonomics*, should have known that judging teachers with tests that they themselves administer is just asking for trouble. Yet that is exactly what Michelle Rhee did.

A *USA Today* investigation focused on Washington's Crosby S. Noyes Education Campus, now known as Noyes Elementary School. In 2006, only 10 percent of the students at the school "scored 'proficient' or 'advanced' in math on the standardized tests required by the federal No Child Left Behind law. Two years later, 58% achieved that level." The Department of Education named Noyes a National Blue Ribbon School. Rhee rewarded

Noyes's staff financially, and "in 2008 and again in 2010, each teacher won an $8,000 bonus, and the principal won $10,000." Much of the money came from philanthropy and was raised by Rhee.

USA Today found that "for the past three school years most of Noyes's classrooms had extraordinarily high numbers of erasures on standardized tests," where "the consistent pattern was that wrong answers were erased and changed to right ones." While high numbers of erasures do not prove cheating, they are a red flag. The newspaper reported Noyes's principal, Adell Cothorne, walking into a room with three staff members, one of whom was holding an eraser, with "over 200 test books spread out on desks." One of the staff said "in a light-hearted sort of way, 'Oh, Principal, I can't believe this kid drew a spider on the test and I have to erase it." Teachers had an incentive to cheat both because high test scores meant bonuses and because low tests scores could lose them their jobs. Rhee "let go dozens of principals and fired at least 600 teachers."

Firing bad teachers provides a potential path to better teacher quality. The education economist Eric Hanushek has long documented the disparities in teacher effectiveness. As Hanushek noted in one paper, the gap in quality between the worst teachers and average teachers is sufficiently large that "replacing the bottom 5–8 percent of teachers with average teachers could move the U.S. near the top of international math and science rankings." He calculated that the additional earnings that resulted from this would be worth roughly $100 trillion in present value.

Still, this path is fraught with difficulty. Typically, union contracts make such radical personnel changes impossible. However, in exchange for "a large, general salary increase for teachers," Rhee got the DC teachers' union members to agree to a contract that would fire teachers who were rated as "ineffective" on her IMPACT merit system. After the release of IMPACT scores in the summer of 2010, "Rhee was ready to announce that she planned to fire the 165 teachers who had received IMPACT ratings of 'ineffective' as well as 76 teachers who had not met qualifications based on their certification."

Even before that, administrative and political problems dogged Rhee's attempt to fire the new teachers who weren't protected by contract. "In February 2009, an independent arbitrator reversed her 2008 firing of 75 teachers, ruling that although Rhee had the right to fire teachers during their two-year probationary period, she could only do so if they had received negative feedback from school principals." The arbitrator said that "the 'glaring and fatal flaw' in Rhee's move was that the teachers were not offered reasons for their terminations, as required by their contract." Rhee made things worse by responding that "I got rid of teachers who had hit children, who had had sex with children, who had missed 78 days of school," which led people to ask why Rhee wasn't prosecuting teachers for criminal behavior instead of firing them. The union organized an anti-Rhee rally.

Two years after Rhee appeared on the cover of *Time*, the Democratic voters of Washington, DC, fired her boss, Mayor Adrian Fenty. *The Washington Post* wrote that his "School Chancellor Michelle A. Rhee's dismissal of hundreds of teachers and dozens of principals for what she said was poor performance" had managed to "alienate" these voters. One fundamental political problem facing public sector leaders is that public sector workers are also voters. Even non-teachers who worked for city government may have worried that the loss in job security for teachers would spill over to them and voted against Fenty. Rhee resigned the next month.

In the end, Rhee didn't become toxic among DC residents, but she wasn't exactly a hero. Rhee is exceptionally talented, and she proved that unions will accept accountability in exchange for higher pay. Yet the limits on her achievement point to the larger difficulties of reforming schools. Classrooms are complex. No teacher will inspire students if he or she is simply following a centrally planned script. Students are even more difficult to control, especially if they are just Zooming into class.

Teachers vs. Students
in a Time of COVID

The battle between insiders and outsiders in the classroom became particularly painful during the COVID-19 pandemic. In Florida and Georgia, teachers' unions sued to stop school reopening plans, claiming that these plans failed to protect teacher safety. Workplace safety is always an appropriate concern for unions, but online learning is a poor substitute for being in the classroom physically, especially for the very young. Preteen students and children who don't have great Wi-Fi—the real outsiders—suffer most when schools don't reopen. As understandable as the unions' concerns may be, they were still fighting for insiders against outsiders.

In both of these cases, appellate courts rejected the lawsuits. In Florida the court found no evidence "that any teacher was forced to return to the classroom, denied a requested accommodation from their employing school district, and then suffered harm." The schools did reopen, and they appear to have been pretty safe. As of December 8, 2020, the COVID-19 School Response Dashboard cocreated by Brown's Emily Oster showed that less than one fourth of one percent of elementary school teachers had tested positive for COVID-19. Less than one eighth of one percent of elementary school students had tested positive.

The challenge of getting school reform past teachers' unions is illustrated by the stance taken by the California Teachers Association (CTA) during the summer of 2020: "school districts lack the authority to force teachers to do live online instruction or to record lessons for later use." As Claudia Briggs of the CTA put it, "our position is that teachers will not be required to conduct live video over their objection."

The law in question is California Education Code Section 51512, a privacy rule written in 1976. The law specifies that "the Legislature finds that the use by any person, including a pupil, of any electronic listening or re-cording device in any classroom of the elementary and secondary schools without the prior consent of the teacher and the principal of the school given to promote an education purpose disrupts and impairs the teaching process and discipline in the elementary and secondary schools, and such use is pro-hibited." In normal circumstances, the rule gives teachers the right to veto any attempt to monitor their teaching via video. In times of a pandemic, the rule was interpreted by the CTA to mean that teachers didn't have to Zoom with their students either.

Luckily, the absurdity of this stance led to a legal fix. In September 2020, California passed legislation stating that "notwithstanding Section 51512 or any other law, the prior consent of the teacher or the principal of a school is not required for the adoption or implementation of the use of synchronous or asynchronous video for purposes of distance learning provided pursuant to this section." If teachers, for their own safety, were spared the need to come into class, at least they would be required to provide long distance in-struction.

The health concerns of teachers are real. Our own university shut down in-person classes for all of 2020–21 as a health measure. We have also tried to avoid exposure to the COVID-19 virus. Nor should the surreal nature of this debate distract us from the fact that the overwhelming majority of Cal-ifornia teachers were working harder than ever to teach over Zoom. Many of them were doing heroic things, trying to make up for the lack of face-to-face contact with even more hours of instruction. The teaching profession is mostly made up of good people. But the unions' inclination to protect its members at all costs still makes reform difficult.

Teacher compensation provides another example of the insider bias in union negotiations. In public sector union contracts, older retirees get a great deal relative to their private sector equivalents. Younger workers earn far less. The work of Maria Fitzpatrick at Cornell shows that younger teachers would much rather have smaller pensions and more pay up front. In one setting, Illinois teachers were given an opportunity to top up their pensions at a tiny fraction of the cost to the state of providing those pensions. Younger teachers said no. They wanted more money now—not more generous pensions in forty years. If public schools want to attract more young, idealistic teachers, then they will have to pay younger workers more.

Public school pay packages favor retirement and health benefits for the same reason police contracts erase evidence of misbehavior. Voters find it difficult to understand the cost of future pension promises. In fact, pension assumptions are far more optimistic than analysts think is reasonable, making the cost of pensions appear to be far lower than they are likely to be. Down the road, that will be a problem for taxpayers, but that will be someone else's problem.

If teachers were paid like private sector workers, with higher wages upfront and portable, defined payment pensions, then they would hop more often from district to district or from teaching to another career. In many ways, this would be a healthier situation, but it would mean a far weaker bond between each teacher and their union. Public sector pensions help explain why government workers quit their jobs so much less often than private sector workers.

There is a final reason to dislike the public sector pension system, especially in jobs that provide opportunities for overtime. The work of former Harvard students Natalia Emanuel—whose analysis of remote work we discussed earlier—and Valentin Bolotnyy showed that male transit workers in Boston earned much more than their female counterparts, even though the contract made no distinction between genders. The reason is that older male workers grabbed many more of the extra overtime gigs. In contrast, older women were weighed down by family responsibilities and found it harder to work on the weekends. That difference in overtime compensation then translates to a significant difference in lifetime pensions. Gender inequities become embedded in a system that rewards men who feel less obligation to care for their sick parents or children.

Vocational Training for Our Cities

We don't have a silver bullet for urban public schools that can thread the political barriers that have prevented change for the past thirty years. We do, however, have a more modest suggestion for improved vocational training that would allow the federal government to directly build its own institutional capacity to promote opportunity.

With predictable regularity, Americans rediscover the German apprenticeship system and learn that it seems to provide employable skills for kids who aren't academic superstars. Over half of German secondary school students enroll in apprenticeships, splitting time between classroom vocational work and on-the-job training. This leads to calls for following Germany and tracking children at age fourteen into highly practical learning that takes them off any possible college track. The smart thing about this enthusiasm for the apprenticeship system is that it recognizes the importance of providing skills with value in the labor market. However, it is silly to think that an institution that has evolved over centuries in Germany can just be grafted onto a setting in which it has no roots. The idea that one can tell whether a fourteen-year-old is fit for college is not reasonable in the US context.

A natural alternative is to provide wraparound vocational training that operates after school hours, on weekends, and during the summer. This can use the existing schools' physical infrastructure, but it should be funded and managed outside of the school system. To avoid any sense of limiting possibilities and thorny arguments with the teachers' unions, the vocational training will always be a supplement to current education, never a substitute that threatens the jobs of unionized teachers.

Like charter schools, extra vocational training can take advantage of the competitive energy that exists in any large metropolitan area. Large urban scale enables segregation, which is bad for schools and neighborhoods, and competition, which can be good. If the vocational training program is open to any provider—private or public, for-profit or nonprofit—then it can unleash entrepreneurial energy in the service of greater equity.

One of the downsides of for-profit schools is that they can focus more on bilking students out of money than on providing skills. The beauty of vocational training is that we can pay for performance, because the quality of the training should be clear immediately after the class or shortly thereafter. The programs do not get paid unless the students prove that they can do the work—whether as computer programmers or plumbers—using independent evaluations of ability.

Outsourced vocational education can also respond more readily to changing economic conditions. We don't know what skills will have the highest value in 2035; no one does. Providing training outside of the conventional teaching environment enables far easier adaption to changing conditions.

We are not advocating a new national education program. Rather, we are advocating experimentation and evaluation. A common theme of this book is that the great fights of the twenty-first century, whether against COVID-19 or urban inequality, must start from a place of humility. We don't know what will work, and what works today may not work in the future. We must innovate, test, and continually revise, using the best science.

Cities for Outsiders

Policing, schools, and business and housing regulation provide four different areas in which American cities, and our country as a whole, protect insiders at the expense of outsiders. Most of the wealthy world erects barriers to building and to forming new businesses. These protect the current urban incumbents.

The natural response of outsiders is to demand their fair share. If the rich have housing regulations, then the poor should get subsidized housing. If there are barriers to business formation, there should also be forgivable government loans targeted toward new business owners from underrepresented groups. If the old receive billions in Medicare, the young should be forgiven their student loans.

A tit-for-tat approach to government policy leads to a society in which everyone fights for their share of a fixed set of resources, instead of a society that expands the total resources available. To get to an urban world that is both equitable and dynamic, we need to be smarter: reduce regulations that limit home building and entrepreneurship and encourage more businesses. We must undertake the changes that will strengthen police departments and schools.

The COVID-19 pandemic revealed the weakness of our cities, our health-care system, and our public sphere. The failure is not just a lack of equity. It is a lack of capacity. If we are going to build back better from COVID-19, we must have policies that are both fairer and more effective. Most importantly, we need more capable public sectors if our societies are going to empower individuals to remake our world.

Chapter 10

A FUTURE WITH MORE
HOPE THAN FEAR

In the plague year of 2020, COVID-19 killed well over 300,000 Americans and perhaps as many as three million across the planet. Billions have experienced some form of social distancing, keeping themselves from friends, family, and the ordinary social connections that are the stuff of life. On January 14, 2021, *The Wall Street Journal* reported that there were "more than 821,000 additional deaths that aren't accounted for in governments' official COVID-19 death counts." Those extra deaths might be uncounted COVID deaths or suicides or deaths from illnesses that went untreated by people who suffered without adequate medical care. Like many people, we too have lost close friends over this year, without being able to say goodbye to them or be with their families.

Humanity is not meant to live alone. As isolated individuals, we are physically weak and psychologically vulnerable. The most important characteristics of our species, like our ability to communicate with language, enable us to survive collectively and achieve great things. There was no Zoom in the African habitats of our ancestors. We evolved to be together physically, not just in cyberspace.

After the vaccines roll out and we reemerge from our cocoons, we must begin by recognizing the importance of real, live human interactions. Every smile is a gift. Every handshake is a link. Every shared laugh is a celebration.

We have gone without those things for too long, and we must do whatever we can to minimize the chance that we have to go through this again. As we rebuild our world, we must ensure that we are far less vulnerable to the pandemics of the future. We must make investments both in health and education. We must reform our rules to make more space for outsiders. We need more entrepreneurs and fewer prisoners.

Humanity crafted itself an urban world because proximity is valuable. Face-to-face interaction enables the collaborative chains of creativity, which gave us the philosophy of classical Athens and the art of Amsterdam's golden age. Urban agglomerations enable commerce, entrepreneurship, and enjoyment. That urban world is unfortunately more open to the viruses and bacteria that also move through human contact. We cannot relish the good of cities without risking the bad. Our urban areas can thrive only if we do battle against the demons that come with density, which include crime, traffic congestion, high housing costs—and especially contagious disease.

COVID-19 teaches us that our globally connected world has made pandemic not only possible but probable. We have learned that even an illness with a relatively low death rate can have terrible economic and social consequences. Imagine if we face a new threat with the deadliness of *Yersinia pestis* or cholera morbus and the contagiousness of COVID-19. But we have also learned that our medical researchers can do miraculous things, like producing a phalanx of effective vaccines within a year. That knowledge gives us hope that the right combination of public and private effort can prevent the plagues of the future.

In this concluding chapter, we suggest paths forward for the world, for our nation, for cities, and for ordinary people like ourselves. Some of our suggestions focus on US institutions and problems, but others have more global relevance. We begin with policies directly linked to health and pandemic.

That must be the highest priority. We then turn to strengthening our social infrastructure. Thousands risked disease to protest policing during 2020. Future pandemics will be safer with a stronger sense of a shared destiny.

These recommendations all embed the three central themes of this book. The world needs public executive capability strong enough to protect us from future pandemics but accountable enough not to abuse its power—a shared strength that serves. That public power must ultimately empower rather than restrict individual autonomy—the freedom to flourish. We must recognize that we don't know all the answers and we must undertake an aggressive campaign to discover what works—the humility to learn, and to learn constantly.

We begin with our recommendations for a proposed global organization—a NATO for health—to monitor outbreaks and manage a global swap where rich countries provide aid for health-related infrastructure and poor countries agree to rules involving water, sewers, and separating humans from sources of new pandemics. We then turn to the US, though our recommendations would be similar for any large wealthy nation. The most important step is to preemptively invest in the public health tools to fight the next outbreak. That includes ventilators and personal protective equipment, along with a battery of vaccine production tools pretested for safety.

We must go beyond health, though. Every weak link puts society at risk. National governments need to reduce the number of weak links going forward. In the US, the level of vulnerability and lost opportunity is so enormous that we will need massive change. Fifty years ago, Americans went to the moon because of a Herculean effort of research and rocket building. We must put even more resources into empowering today's children to fight tomorrow's battles—learning what works and expanding it as rapidly as we can.

American states and cities cannot prevent a global plague, but they can help contain it, and they can strengthen civil society. States control community colleges, which can help provide a chance for students who have fewer resources or have lost their way in high school. States can rewrite local regulations to enhance new business formation and new housing construction. Cities must address the discontent that helped generate protests and riots. Policing must be made more accountable for community well-being without allowing increases in criminal victimization.

Private citizens can also act. Philanthropists can fund research, both in medicine and in education. Ordinary citizens can learn and teach and hold our leaders more accountable, by focusing more on the services we all need from our governments rather than on the issues that divide us.

Cities will survive this pandemic and many will thrive, but COVID-19 is the tip of an existential threat. The isolation and deaths due to the disease have been terrible, but it could have been much worse. We must never again allow our public sector to be so weak or our urban world to be so unprotected.

For the World: A NATO for Health

The essence of a pandemic is that a disease that starts in one location poses risks to all countries. Unless all countries close their borders completely and permanently—an unimaginable and awful possibility—then monitoring outbreaks in Azerbaijan will be as important as monitoring them in Atlanta. An effective global organization that can track and then swiftly contain illness is a first step toward a pandemic-proof future.

Reducing the risk of future pandemics is a global problem. Like preventing nuclear wars and addressing climate change, preventing pandemic disease is so big that one country cannot solve it on its own. In each of these areas, multilateral action is essential, because when it comes to nuclear fallout, carbon emissions, and COVID-19, all nations are intertwined. Indeed, preventing global pandemic inherently involves a more diverse group of countries than controlling nuclear technology or reducing greenhouse gases.

The poorest countries of the world neither spend on nuclear weapons nor emit much carbon, but they disproportionately contribute to the potential spread of new diseases.

At a technical level, we know what to do to reduce the risk of pandemic. The world must prevent risky interactions, detect outbreaks early, and contain those outbreaks before they become pandemics. Prevention includes avoiding close contact between animal species and humans where infections are likely to spread. Containment involves widespread testing for disease, contact tracing of positive cases, isolating infected people, and safely treating those who get sick. All of this is common scientific knowledge.

The issue for the world is not that we do not understand the science of reducing pandemic disease, although each contagion is subtly different. Rather, the issue is that our institutions have not taken appropriate actions. After the Ebola outbreak of 2014, the World Health Organization established a Global Preparedness Monitoring Board, headed by Gro Harlem Brundtland, the former WHO director-general and Norwegian prime minister, and Elhadj As Sy, the former secretary general of the International Federation of the Red Cross and Red Crescent Societies. In September 2019, on the eve of the COVID-19 outbreak, the board released a report, *A World at Risk*, noting that "for too long, we have allowed a cycle of panic and neglect when it comes to pandemics: we ramp up efforts when there is a serious threat, then quickly forget about them when the threat subsides. It is well past time to act."

Addressing pandemic preparedness will cost money. Estimates from the consulting firm McKinsey suggest that the cost might be $100 billion up front followed by annual spending of $20–40 billion. Vaccine development is a major part of that, as is expanding the health systems of low-income countries, where there are too few health-care workers and too little equipment.

Still, by any metric, this cost is a small share of the potential gains. COVID-19 by itself may cost the United States $16 trillion. A future disease that had a higher case fatality rate would cost even more. Even if the US financed the whole investment on its own, the increase in federal government spending would be a barely noticeable 0.1 percent, and the gains would be enormous.

Not money but leadership is lacking. There has been nothing to compel national governments to act. The World Health Organization's *A World at Risk* report concludes, "What we need is leadership and the willingness to act forcefully and effectively." Alas, the world failed to act, and we paid the costs of COVID-19.

As we go forward, we must not only spend but spend effectively. We cannot follow the Medicare model of just writing checks. We need to develop an effective institution to protect global health. The World Health Organization is not the right model. The WHO can discuss issues and make recommendations, but it cannot enforce. The WHO also contains an uncomfortable mix of science and politics. Science suggests both being skeptical of claims by governments with a history of understating infectious disease (like China) and calling out new outbreaks as soon as they are observed (as with Ebola). Politics pushes in the opposite direction. When politics trumps science, people die.

A stronger international organization is required, with a clear mission that is scientific, not political. The goal is to prevent pandemics, not to avoid offending member countries. Countries must be either in or out. If a country joins, then it receives aid, not only against future pandemics, but also support for medical training and sanitary infrastructure. But to stay in the system, countries must adhere to guidelines about reducing pandemic risk. They must limit exposure between humans and sources of cross-species infection, like bats. They must ensure that poor houses actually connect to sewers that are built with foreign aid. They must report all new outbreaks honestly.

Countries that stay out of the system forgo funding and may face other restrictions. Travelers to or from outside countries may have to undergo medical testing, which they pay for themselves. Shipping may have to undergo extra screening. The travel of people and goods to and from a country is inherently more dangerous if that country is not adopting rules to prevent the spread of illness.

Two global organizations emerged after World War II to ensure that Europe would not burn for a third time in the twentieth century. The United Nations was a broad coalition spanning the globe that had the right to bless defensive warfare and sanction combat but had little direct capacity for action. The North Atlantic Treaty Organization (NATO) was initially an alliance of twelve states that had come to realize that an amorphous parliament of nations was insufficient to counter Joseph Stalin and the Soviet threat. NATO played a major role in limiting armed conflict between the West and the Soviet Union during the Cold War, at least in Europe. Since the end of the Cold War, it has expanded into other areas that threaten member countries, including terrorism and cybersecurity. The European Union may have played the larger role in keeping the peace between the Western powers, but NATO had the military strength to balance the threat from the East.

NATO does not deserve sole credit for the fact that World War II was the last major war in Europe outside of the Balkans—the European Union was also critically important—but it surely deserves some credit. One measure of NATO's success is that more countries want to join. NATO's membership has grown from twelve countries in 1949 to thirty in 2020. President George W. Bush said that "NATO is the most successful alliance in the history of the world. . . . Because of NATO, Europe is whole and united and at peace." President Obama noted that "it is because of the strength of NATO and the Transatlantic partnership, this Transatlantic Alliance, that I'm confident that, despite these choppy waters, we will be able to continue to underscore and underwrite the peace and security and prosperity that has been the hallmark of the Transatlantic relationship for so many decades."

The NATO model would need to be modified for a health context. An organization with both rich and poor countries must naturally operate differently than one with only rich countries. Further, military matters are different from health. But the principles remain the same. Pandemic preparedness must have the same urgency as military defense. An effective anti-pandemic organization must impose requirements that can be enforced. Rich countries will foot the bill, but rich and poor together must agree to minimize the risk of contagion and prevent the spread of infectious disease as much as they can.

For the Nation, Part 1:
Preempting Pandemic

The US will also need to act domestically to bolster its pandemic preparedness. The most fundamental challenge in the health-care arena is to transform a system that is oriented around private health into one with a greater focus on public health, and to push a medical research budget that is targeted toward chronic illness to do more on contagious illness.

When COVID-19 first appeared in the West, a legitimate debate ensued about whether to lock down or let the disease proceed through the population. Most wealthy countries quickly decided that they couldn't tolerate the deaths that would pile up on the way to herd immunity, and so they shut themselves down. The hope was that either the disease would mutate into irrelevance or that a vaccine would appear.

If there is a much deadlier contagious disease than COVID-19 in the future, then there will be no debates about getting to herd immunity. Fewer will argue to keep the bars open if the disease kills half of those who get sick. In that case, we will have to hunker down and wait. The degree of suffering will be determined by the time it takes to distribute a safe and ef-fective vaccine.

The good news is that it took Moderna and the National Institutes of Health exactly two days to design a vaccine after Chinese scientists shared the genetic sequence to COVID on January 11, 2020. The bad news is that it took another eleven months for the vaccine to be tested and approved. Moderna took twenty-five days to produce the vaccine and forty-two days to begin the phase 1 trials. By the time COVID-19 cases were starting to add up in the US, the vaccine was already available. During the eight months of testing, about 240,000 Americans died. Distributing vaccines globally will take months if not years. The post-approval delivery of vaccines could have been much faster if more vaccines were manufactured during the testing period.

One key to reducing the risks from future pandemics is to shrink the time period between vaccine concept and vaccine distribution. One possibil-ity is to pay pharmaceutical companies to build up extra production capacity that they can use during emergencies—either with direct payment or tax credits. Another possibility is to pretest a battery of potential vaccines for safety on animals. Just as well-run industrial companies analyze every phase of the production process to search for waste and inefficiency, we must go over the FDA's trial and approval process to figure out how things can be sped up. Any investment that can be made ahead of time should be.

America also needs to reduce high-risk human-to-human and animal-to-human contact, set up better disease monitoring systems, and improve con-tainment when an outbreak is detected. Unlike many countries—especially those with significant experience in preventing HIV spread—the United States is not skilled in contact tracing. This will mean spending more, but relative to either the cost of the pandemic or America's normal health-care costs, the amount involved is trivial.

Current public health spending is only 2 percent of total medical spending and an even smaller share of total government spending. Governments across the US could increase the amount spent on public health many times over with relatively little impact on their overall budgets. Indeed, public health budgets rose considerably in the few years after the terrorist attacks of September 2001 before declining again.

Beyond increasing resources for public health, the US should improve other aspects of its health system. Because out-of-pocket medical costs are so high, people delay going to the doctor. In a world of potential pandemics, the last thing we want is for high co-payments to stop people from being properly diagnosed or treated. The US has an overabundance of specialists and an appalling lack of primary care physicians. Thus, when people need to access primary care in a pandemic, the system can rapidly become overburdened. Medical records are not generally shared across institutions, or between health-care organizations and other interested parties. Thus, if a person has been diagnosed with a communicable disease at a doctor's office, it is unlikely that clinicians at the local emergency department will be aware of that, should a person happen to twist an ankle on a Sunday. Nor are public health officials able to monitor infectious disease trends through medical records in real time.

The idea that medical care needs reform is not new. Indeed, one of us (Cutler) has written two books and many articles on the subject. COVID-19 certainly adds impetus to the need to address the health-care system. It also points out several areas that need to move up on the priority scale. Not being able to share medical information across organizations is an annoyance when it occurs for someone with a chronic disease but can be deadly when infectious disease is rampant. Retooling the medical care system for an era of potential pandemics will change where we focus our attention.

In addition, the United States needs to more seriously address the health behaviors responsible for so much illness. As good libertarians, we believe that people should generally be free to do what they choose, provided they know what they are doing and there are no harms to others from their choices. COVID-19 teaches us that these external harms are bigger than we thought. Obesity, tobacco use, unsafe sexual practices, and the use of illegal drugs have all helped to spread infectious disease. Had the US been better about reducing obesity over the years, the COVID-19 epidemic would have killed fewer people. Every tobacco company, food or beverage producer, or pharmaceutical company that promotes addiction to products associated with the spread of infectious disease is putting the health of all of us at risk. Unfortunately, our regulatory and punishment systems that are meant to protect public health are too weak. Education is a key component as well. People with more years of schooling have universally healthier behaviors, which is why schools are not just about economic and social mobility but also about protection from illness.

For the Nation, Part 2: An Apollo Program for Opportunity

In the previous two sections, we have focused on policy reforms that deal directly with health. We now move to nonmedical policies that will make us healthier and strengthen our cities.

The COVID-19 pandemic did the most damage where there were preexisting problems, such as urban schools where many students were only marginally committed to their classrooms before they were sent home. Over the years, America's test scores have fallen further behind. If one tenth or more of the children in Los Angeles and Boston dropped out of their virtual educations in 2020, as some reports suggest, then we risk another lost generation. These disruptions create a new urgency about improving the world's schooling.

We believe in investing in human capital from the egg to the grave, and in every form, from pre-K programs to graduate degrees in molecular biophysics. But the most important health-related educational investments should target the poorest parts of the population. Too many Americans—and Britons and Spaniards—are being left behind economically and socially. Since they are cut off, the world loses their skills and ideas. When an individual lacks the ability to be economically productive, all of society loses. We lose their earnings and their tax payments. We often must provide aid to help them survive. They become a burden on the health system and have a greater chance of being unhealthy themselves. They are even, potentially, a source of contagion.

Unlike in most wealthy countries, where education is a national commitment, schooling is seen as a local responsibility in the US. American parents like the control that comes from having their child in a locally run school district. But the unfortunate side effect of local schooling is that underperforming school districts often fail to help lower-income children escape poverty. Every educator knows that it is far more difficult to teach in a disadvantaged community, where parents may be absent and children may see little reason to study. As a result, the current system creates an intolerable level of vulnerability. Urban children need help.

Why should the nation make a commitment to help empower every child? First, only the national government has the ability to borrow large amounts for the needed investment in America's young. Second, an Apollo program for opportunity hinges on our ability to uncover new solutions, and that requires a national network of connected experiments. Third, localities can't be in charge of social justice policies, because if they take from the rich and give to the poor, the rich just leave. Investing in the skills of poor children is the most feasible way of producing a more just society without destroying economic dynamism. It will require a national effort.

The challenge is that we can't just write a big check, as we did with the

Marshall Plan and as we do with Medicare. A clear lesson from the school finance literature is that money by itself does not solve the problem. No Child Left Behind, the most significant federal intervention in education over the past twenty years, coupled a mild increase in spending with stronger incentives for good performance. The plan followed the standard economic reasoning that school districts would fix things on their own if given the right incentives and resources. A general summary of this effort is that the combination of modest cash infusion and modest incentives may have helped, but it did not eradicate American inequality.

The same is true about the Obama administration's Race to the Top initiative, which cleverly held out a cash reward for producing an innovative education plan. Race to the Top was a good way to get some bang for a limited amount of federal bucks. Its tournament structure provides a good model for rewarding innovations in education, but not for supporting long-term institutional reform.

In 2020, the United States loaned small businesses $649 billion through the Paycheck Protection Program, and we did little to make sure that much of it wasn't wasted. Surely, we can imagine spending another $100 billion per year to reduce the number of poorly trained adults. NASA's spending on the moon launch maxed out at almost $6 billion in 1966, which is $45 billion in 2020 dollars. At the time, it was almost 5 percent of the US government's budget. If we were to spend that share of the federal budget on an Apollo program for opportunity, the amount would be over $250 billion.

The beauty of investing in children is that in the long run it pays for itself, as documented by the work of our colleagues Nathaniel Hendren and Benjamin Sprung-Keyser. They show that education investments have covered their costs through higher tax revenue and lower outlays for social programs. There is no reason to expect anything different in the future. As a side benefit, investing in education will also reduce the risk of pandemic.

A $100 billion increase in federal spending on education would triple the budget of the Department of Education, which would be revolutionary in Washington but not in classrooms. States and localities spent $660 billion on schools in 2017. Increasing total school spending by 15 percent could be game-changing only if it were spent really effectively.

At the moment, neither economists nor educators know how to turn $100 billion into a vast improvement in American schools. Smaller class sizes have been shown to improve test scores in a landmark Tennessee experiment. But the estimated effects were small and the financial cost was large. Some charter schools have done a great job of raising test scores, especially in troubled urban neighborhoods, but their impact on long-run earnings is still being debated. Better teachers make a huge difference, and principals know how to identify those teachers even without fancy statistics. But none of this adds up to a complete plan. That's why we are calling for an Apollo program rather than a Marshall Plan. We didn't know how to send a person to the moon when we started the space program. Indeed, we didn't even know how to get a person safely into orbit. We had to learn first. With education, we must also begin with the humility to learn.

There are certainly places to start. Some charter schools have done well. One-on-one instruction is very effective relative to normal classroom lecturing. New teaching models can combine electronic workbooks with personalized instruction. In the previous chapter, we pushed for competitively sourced vocational training that wrapped around current education models.

These ideas are enough to start spending money on education experiments. Every child who needs it ideally should receive some form of extra education support, some in the school and some at home. The nature of that support could involve many experiments. We could then learn which new programs had the largest effects on tests scores and other outcomes.

Gradually, as we learn what is effective, we can scale up. At every point, we continue evaluating. When something ceases to succeed, then it gets scaled back. We start with experimentation and create an administrative machine for constant learning. We consistently adapt and figure out how to use our resources effectively. Once we learn how to spend wisely, we spend massively.

We have just described a model for a government effort that sounds like nothing the US government has done in decades. But it is how private industry works. New products are constantly tested. Tech companies in Silicon Valley imagine an experiment in the morning and implement it in the afternoon. The results are available the next day. Companies expand their markets and advertising when their products prove popular. The products get shut down when they fail. Huge numbers of people and machines are enlisted to develop, produce, and market something new, and those resources are then allocated somewhere else.

Governments can do this too. They have pursued campaigns like that in the past, most notably during World War II. The Allied effort involved vast resources and plenty of discretion for individual field commanders. There was a great deal of science, including the research that unlocked the power of the atom. There was a long period of training and preparation before the massive invasion hit the Normandy beaches on June 6, 1944. George Marshall was at the center of that as well as the later cash infusion sent into postwar Europe. Maybe we are talking about a Marshall Plan after all.

For States and Cities: Reducing Vulnerability and Promoting Opportunity

State and local governments don't need to wait on federal aid to increase opportunity and reduce vulnerability. A more decentralized opportunity agenda that improves skill acquisition, particularly for the most vulnerable, is a necessary complement to an Apollo program for human capital. States and cities can enable small business entrepreneurship by paring back barriers like business regulation and occupational licensing rules. State governments can reverse the overregulation of building and land use that makes it so hard for poor people to move to richer areas. States and local governments can create more freedom to flourish without spending a single dollar.

States and localities deliver education to American children. They operate schools and community colleges. If we are going to acquire the knowledge that we need to improve educational outcomes, then states and cities must take the lead. America's meta-error when fighting COVID-19 was to make policy without facts. New Zealand did so well because they devoted resources to measuring the path of the disease among the asymptomatic.

Every state should have a serious effort dedicated to educational innovation and measuring the impact of that innovation, with federal coordination and data transfer. Schools and teachers try new things every day, but unless those new ideas are evaluated, the larger world learns nothing. If we innovate without evaluating, then we lose the ability to learn, and that learning creates 99 percent of the benefit of innovation. The search for a COVID-19 vaccine was a serious effort that created success. The search for better cures for poverty must be just as serious.

Community colleges represent both a challenge and an opportunity. The community college system faces terrible funding shortfalls. Community college teachers try to teach millions of students who didn't learn basic skills in high school. There is no quick fix here, but there is more room to maneuver within community colleges than within high schools. Courses can be offered and dropped. More than one half of the students are taught by part-time, untenured faculty who can be promoted or fired. The political challenges with experimental forms of education are smaller with older students who choose to enroll.

Successful community colleges often work together with local businesses to produce students who will find jobs after graduation. For example, Siemens partners with Central Piedmont Community College in Charlotte, North Carolina, to provide apprenticeships to those who have taken the school's mechatronics program. Apprenticeships are easy for Siemens to use because the college's program is "aligned by competencies with 3rd party industry recognized certifications of Siemens Mechatronics Systems Certification Program."

Vocational training for younger workers can also integrate better with the local economy. Earlier in this book, we emphasized the value of experimental vocational training. A particularly attractive model is to work together with companies that need skilled workers to develop these programs. In some cases, the company may want to try teaching the skills itself. In other cases, it may make more sense to outsource instruction.

One model is to roll vocational training programs together with a larger push to empower local job creation. In the first half of the 2010s, one of us (Glaeser) cochaired a committee to design an entrepreneurship district in a poorer part of Boston, which would provide a more inclusive version of the glossy innovation district that had risen on Boston's waterfront. A designated coworking and innovation space was one part of the model, based on the waterfront area's extremely successful District Hall. The Roxbury Innovation Center was created to provide a similar experience in the heart of Boston.

The second part of the vision was to work with local institutions to ramp up vocational training opportunities. Madison Park Vocational Technical School is close to the Roxbury Innovation Center. Roxbury Community College is also nearby. Even Northeastern University is in walkable distance. Northeastern has enjoyed a spectacular transformation from former YMCA night school to educational powerhouse, partially because of its "apprenticeship and training program." Part of the challenge with children in poor urban households is that they can be isolated from the city as a whole.

Building connections to these institutions can integrate them into Boston's creative economy.

But there was also a third element in the entrepreneurship district: one-stop permitting. Just as a single enterprise commission eases the process of starting something new in Devens, Massachusetts, there can also be one-stop permitting in Liverpool and the South Side of Chicago and the favelas of Rio de Janeiro. When one agency is in charge of all business permitting, it is easier to hold that agency accountable for permitting delays.

Faster permitting is particularly vital as the American economy re-emerges from its COVID-19 shelter. Vast numbers of businesses have closed. New businesses will need to take their place. This process will require permits. We should not let a byzantine regulatory system stop the economy from rebooting. If we can start emergency fast tracks for new businesses in a few major cities, then these will provide models for fast-tracking programs everywhere in the future.

We also need to rethink our regulatory process for new housing. Homes are too expensive because we have restricted the supply of structures in the most desirable parts of the US, especially coastal areas like California. In some large cities, there is appetite for reform at the local level. Big-city mayors often like the jobs, taxes, and economic activity that come with large building projects. They sometimes even have the courage to push new projects through, despite community opposition. But suburban homeowners will never become pro-development on their own. To a homeowner, more affordability means a decline in the value of their most important asset.

To change these communities, states must act. In the US, the direct regulation of building is typically done by local governments, but the powers of America's local governments are determined by their state governments. Several times in past years, the California state legislature has come close to chipping away at the right of localities to block anything they want. Massachusetts has its statewide Chapter 40B, which provides builders with a means of bypassing local restrictions when building affordable housing. Creating more homes in high-wage areas empowers mobility by enabling more Americans to earn higher wages. State legislatures must step in to remove the burdens that local governments have placed on home builders.

For the States and Cities: More Effective and Balanced Criminal Justice

Criminal justice reform is a vital public good in its own right; it is also bound together with the pandemic, because packed prison populations spread viruses and because anti-police protests create the potential for more contagion. States must rethink laws that lock up too many people. Cities must reform police departments that fail to respect the lives and dignity of every citizen.

In both cases, these reforms must be calibrated so they do not take us back to the crime waves of the 1970s and 1980s. Policing is not a discretionary public service. Effective law enforcement is vital for our cities. When order breaks down, it is the poor and vulnerable who suffer must. In 1991, homicides killed 5.5 out of every 100,000 whites but 39.3 out of every 100,000 African Americans.

Policing reform will take years, effort, and expense, but sentence lengths can change whenever state governments choose to alter penalties for specific crimes. Smarter sentencing means evaluating when the benefits of longer jail time exceed the human costs of locking someone up. Prison sentences deter crime and incapacitate criminals. Yet there is little evidence that ultra-long jail times, like life sentences for drug dealers, achieve much extra deterrence. What nineteen-year-old cares if a crime carries a forty-five- or fifty-year sentence? Yet five extra years of jail time is an enormous expense for the system, as well as for the elderly prisoner. Moreover, people change. Few sixty-year-olds pose the same risks to society or themselves as they did at twenty.

The incapacitation value of ultra-long sentences makes sense only for really extreme cases, like the man who killed Diane Ballasiotes. We should be smart enough to target our penalties at the true threats and let others resume their lives. We should have a legal system that is able to distinguish between a repeat, highly violent sex offender and a repeat purveyor of marijuana.

Of course, we need punishment to deter misbehavior. For violent criminals, this will always mean prisons. For nonviolent crimes, cash fines that generate revenues are far more efficient than prison time. We should think harder about non-prison punishments of all forms, including community service.

Police reform is vital but more difficult. We have proposed a few simple tools: outside measurement of community experience with the police, judging police departments on both crime and assessments by ordinary citizens, and empowering police chiefs to make major changes. Our basic model is to hire an effective manager and provide reasonable benchmarks that will make success contingent on treating community members with respect and dignity.

Unfortunately, one can't give managers extra objectives without also providing them with extra resources. A more inclusive vision of public safety will require spending more, not less. And within this framework, it is reasonable for cities, or police chiefs themselves, to experiment with transferring some current police services to non-armed first responders. This might provide a better community experience or it might not. Only experience and experiment will tell.

There is also every reason to encourage stronger community organizations that can partner with the police to prevent crime. Cities should certainly experiment with funding effective community alliances, as long as they have a credible mechanism for evaluating that funding. Good communities protect themselves as much as they are protected by police.

For the Rest of Us: Learning and Teaching and Caring

The year of the pandemic was terrible. We all learned what it was like to lose companionship. We must not lose it again. Ordinary people can also help protect our planet from future pandemic risk, by learning and working together for this common goal.

Those who can, can help to improve the health, education, and government systems. Even those without money or technical expertise can become smarter voters or health or education activists. We can vote for politicians who focus on delivering better public services and help constrain disease.

Unfortunately, the US, along with many countries, has been riven by a political tribalism that drowns out the search for a more effective public sector. For forty years, Americans have been arguing about bigger or smaller government. This is a diversion; the real question is how to get *better* government. The governments of New Zealand, South Korea, and Germany were much more effective than the US in addressing the pandemic. These nations are not as wealthy as the US, although they are not starved for resources either. There is no reason the US could not have one of the strongest public sectors in the world. After World War II, we accomplished great things, in the military and space.

We have tried to deliberately avoid attacking individuals in this book, because blaming people obscures the fact that the system as a whole failed. Some leaders did perform terribly, but the world's safety requires more than just changing the names at the top. Further, the world needs to step back from anger and hate and recognize just how much we depend on the rest of humanity.

Months of isolation teach us that being alone is difficult and being connected is a treasure. We should redouble our commitment both to our friends and to the strangers around us. We should remember that we are all in a linked family. We have been through many months when every new person was a possible source of contagion. When that risk abates, let us remember that every new person is also a possible source of joy, and that every city should be a place of hope and shared human strength.

ACKNOWLEDGMENTS

This book was the work of eight months. It was also the work of thirty years. Consequently, it has benefited not only from the relatively small set of people who directly interacted with us on this volume but also the large number of friends, colleagues, and students who have helped us to better understand cities and health over many decades.

We begin our thanks with special appreciation for Scott Moyers, who has been a superb editor, full of wisdom about the big picture and care for the smallest detail. He pushed us to look beyond the pandemic and focus on the larger challenges facing urban life. He has been an unfailing source of careful queries and warm support. We are also grateful to Ann Godoff for overseeing this enterprise, and for her insight and good humor.

We are similarly thankful to our UK editor, Sarah Caro, who provided sage advice and keen notes and pushed us to make this book more international. By pressing us to better understand Joseph Bazalgette, she also helped us better understand the divergence between the localized US approach to public health and the more centralized approach in the UK. As we write these words, we are watching with envy the faster vaccine rollout in the UK.

Suzanne Gluck made all of this happen. She is our agent and our guide through the word of professional publishing. We are enormously grateful to her.

The book's production relied on four terrific research assistants: Madeline Kitch, Sravya Kuchibhotla, Jimmy Lin, and Jessica Wu. They prepared the footnotes and caught our errors. We are thankful that they gave us their winter break. Susan VanHecke was a superb copy editor and we are most grateful for her care.

We benefited enormously from the extensive comments we received from Giacomo Ponzetto, Tzachi Raz, Andrei Shleifer, and Larry Summers. Our discussion of the Black Death in particular benefited from Tzachi. Giacomo helped us with a more European perspective. Andrei, as he has for three decades, provided us with clarity about which themes and topics were most important. Larry pushed us to clarify our thoughts, which aided us immensely.

We have been blessed with many colleagues who have taught us a great deal over the decades. We are particularly grateful to Claudia Goldin and Larry Katz, whose intellectual imprint lies all over this book. We are also thankful for our colleagues in the applied microeconomics group at Harvard: Raj Chetty, Roland Fryer, Nathan Hendren, Jeffrey Miron, Amanda Pallais, and Stephanie Stantcheva. The work of Chetty and Hendren on intergenerational mobility helped to shape this book. Fryer's work on race and policing has been similarly influential. None of these colleagues are officially health-care experts or urban economists, but they are immensely talented and wonderful scholars.

The broad health policy community at Harvard is outstanding, and we are grateful to all of them. Particular thanks for so many conversations over the years go to fellow economists Amitabh Chandra, Leemore Dafny, Richard Frank, Rob Huckman, Tom McGuire, and Joe Newhouse. We are particularly grateful to Marcella Alsan, who has now rejoined this community.

We have benefited from our intellectual partners in study in the economic course of the pandemic, especially Alex Bartik, Zoe Cullen, Caitlin Gorback, Mike Luca, Stephen Redding, and Chris Stanton. Their work is also reflected in these pages. Joseph Gyourko provided thoughtful insights on commercial real estate, and years of keen economic insight and warm friendship. Marcella Alsan is something of a hero in this book, as she is in real life. We are grateful that she corrected a few of our errors.

This has been a season of great loss for our department, as well as our world. In the eighteen months between June 2019 and January 2021, we have lost six colleagues: Martin Feldstein, Martin Weitzman, Gary Chamberlain, Alberto Alesina, Emmanuel Farhi, and Richard Cooper. Marty Feldstein was the undergraduate thesis advisor to one of us (Cutler) and a mentor to both of us. Alberto Alesina wrote a book with one of us (Glaeser) and was a dear friend to us both. Gary Chamberlain was always a brilliant and kind presence at seminars. Marty Weitzman's lively curiosity and intellectual vibrancy were always wonderful to witness. Richard Cooper's enduring commitment to economics was inspiring. The loss of Emmanuel Farhi was particularly painful, because of his youth, brilliance, and charm. Edward Lazear also died in 2020. He was a thesis advisor to one of us (Glaeser) and a source of unfailing good spirits and perpetual insight to economists everywhere. We are also grateful for the many decades of advice and friendship given to us by Jim Poterba and Jose Scheinkman.

We would also like to thank the current and former students who contributed to this book. We have drawn heavily on the work of Valentin Bolotnyy, Natalia Emanuel, Emma Harrington, José Ramón Morales-Arilla, Gregor Schubert, Karen Shen, Brandon Tan, and John Tebes. Carlos Daboin was particularly helpful in providing data from Burning Glass. There are so many more; listing them all would require a volume of its own.

Finally, we would like to thank our families. Glaeser is grateful to his children—Theodore, Eliza, and Nicholas—who have patiently endured both the writing and the sacrifices required by the pandemic. They are a great source of strength and joy. Nancy Schwartz Glaeser is not only a loving spouse, but a major partner in this enterprise, who read every page again and again, correcting not only grammar but folly, bringing both her kindness and her keen intellect to every conversation. Cutler is grateful to his children—Kate and Allie—who continue to push for a better world. Thanks to Mary Beth Landrum, Cutler's spouse, for support during the writing process and for providing stability in a crazy world.

Without fear of contradiction, we accept responsibility for any errors that remain. The world is not perfect. Unfortunately, neither are we.

NOTES

CHAPTER 1: THE CITY BESIEGED

1 **Earthquake and invasion:** Mark, "Knossos."

1 **Data from cellular phones:** Glaeser et al., "Learning from Deregulation: The Asymmetric Impact of Lockdown and Reopening on Risky Behavior During COVID-19."

2 **32 million Americans:** US Bureau of Labor Statistics, "Table B-1. Employees on Nonfarm Payrolls by Industry Sector and Selected Industry Detail."

2 **UK employment in accommodation:** UK Office for National Statistics, "Employment by Industry."

2 **22 percent of those:** McKinsey, "COVID-19 in the UK."

2 **The semi-urban inhabitants:** Lieberman, *The Story of the Human Body: Evolution, Health, and Disease.*

2 **Cities long depended on net migration:** Davenport, "Urbanization and Mortality in Britain, c. 1800–50."

2 **But by 1940, vaccination:** Haines, "The Urban Mortality Transition in the United States, 1800–1940."

2 **By 2020, urbanites:** Singh and Siahpush, "Widening Rural-Urban Disparities in Life Expectancy, U.S., 1969–2009."

4 **Before 2020, our cities:** Chetty et al., "Where Is the Land of Opportunity? The Geography of Intergenerational Mobility in the United States."

4 **Almost 70 percent:** US Bureau of Labor Statistics, "Labor Force Statistics from the Current Population Survey: Supplemental Data Measuring the Effects of the Coronavirus (COVID-19) Pandemic on the Labor Market."

5 **only 5 percent of people:** US Bureau of Labor Statistics, "Labor Force Statistics."

5 **"any city, however small":** Plato, *The Republic*, 423.

6 **New York's Croton Aqueduct:** Ashraf, Glaeser, and Ponzetto, "Infrastructure, Incentives, and Institutions."

6 **In 2011, demonstrators seized:** Gabbatt, Townsend, and O'Carroll, "'Occupy' Anticapitalism Protests Spread around World."

6 **Two months after the COVID lockdowns:** Sullivan and Morrison, "George Floyd Fallout: Unrest Overshadows Peaceful Protests for Another Night."

6 **Seattle's "Capitol Hill Autonomous Zone":** Bush, "Welcome to the Capitol Hill Autonomous Zone, Where Seattle Protesters Gather without Police."

7 **The patricians who fled:** Borà, "Historical and Monumental Itineraries of Capri."

7 **In our own time, one of:** "Coronavirus in the U.S.: Latest Map and Case Count," *The New York Times.*

9 **long-term impairments:** del Rio, Collins, and Malani, "Long-Term Health Consequences of COVID-19."

10 **"there are no atheists in foxholes":** "Religion: Atheists & Foxholes," *Time.*

10 The pro- and anti-government divide: Siegler, "Biden's Win Shows Rural-Urban Divide Has Grown Since 2016."

11 $16 trillion by the time: Cutler and Summers, "The COVID-19 Pandemic and the $16 Trillion Virus."

11 Pfizer and Moderna: Thomas, "The Coronavirus Vaccines Will Probably Work. Making Them Fast Will Be the Hard Part."

11 building of sewers and aqueducts: Ashraf, Glaeser, and Ponzetto, "Infrastructure, Incentives, and Institutions."

11 US spends by far the most: Harvard Chan School of Public Health, "The Most Expensive Health Care System in the World."

12 the federal government became a great: Jennings and Nagel, *Federal Workforce Statistics Sources: OPM and OMB*.

12 almost two thirds of all: Jessie and Tarleton, *2012 Census of Governments: Employment Summary Report*.

12 Clear objectives have typically: Ferreira and Gyourko, "Do Political Parties Matter?"

12 "there is no Republican": "The Bloomberg Bus," *Observer*.

12 "politics stops at the water's edge": Lieber, "Politics Stops at the Water's Edge?"

14 "not wisely but too well": Shakespeare, *Othello*, 5.2.360.

14 "there ain't no such thing as a free lunch": Twin, "There Ain't No Such Thing as a Free Lunch (TANSTAAFL) Explained."

14 "among democratic nations": Tocqueville, *Democracy in America*, 597.

15 "Americans of all ages": Tocqueville, 596.

15 "can achieve almost nothing by themselves": Tocqueville, 597.

15 "stadtluft macht frei": Glaeser, "City Air Makes You Free."

16 Los Angeles sharply restricts: Glaeser, "Reforming Land Use Regulations."

18 The stellar performance of New Zealand: "Coronavirus: How New Zealand Relied on Science and Empathy," BBC News.

19 "there's no reason to be": "Fact Check: Outdated Video of Fauci Saying 'There's No Reason to Be Walking Around with a Mask,'" Reuters.

19 "although travel restrictions may intuitively": Turak, "UAE to Suspend All China Flights except for Beijing as Coronavirus Toll Mounts."

23 viral videos, like the one: "Man without Face Mask Refuses to Leave SEPTA Bus; Police Pull Him Off," NBC10 Philadelphia.

CHAPTER 2: WILL GLOBALIZATION LEAD TO PERMANENT PANDEMIC?

25 The first well-chronicled: Thucydides, *History of the Peloponnesian War*.

25 the epidemic began "in Ethiopia": Thucydides, book 2, 48.

25 "our city is open to the world": This quote was part of Pericles's Funeral Oration, which was written for Pericles by Thucydides. Thucydides, book 2, 39.

25 Athens was at war: Knowledge of the Athenian plague in this paragraph comes from Thucydides.

25 As many as one quarter of Athenians died: Robert J. Littman, "The Plague of Athens: Epidemiology and Paleopathology."

25 the case fatality rate perhaps twenty-five times that of COVID-19: Most of the population of Athens was infected with the plague, and up to 25 percent of the population died. At the time of publication, the case fatality rate of COVID-19 was estimated to be around 1 percent, as per Johns Hopkins Coronavirus Resource Center, "Mortality Analyses."

25 the city-state surrendered: "Peloponnesian War," History.com.

26 The first farming: Lieberman, *The Story of the Human Body: Evolution, Health, and Disease*.

26 many of those who died: Thucydides.

26 The oldest means: Tognotti, "Lessons from the History of Quarantine, from Plague to Influenza A."

26 The Athenians did not: Tognotti.

26 But the history of quarantines: Tognotti.

27 Herodotus, sometimes: Cicero called him the father of history. Mark, "Herodotus."

27 arrived in Athens around: Knowledge of Herodotus's life in this paragraph comes from

Herodotus, *The Landmark Herodotus: The Histories*.

27 Herodotus "flattered the Athenians": Plutarch, *Plutarch's Miscellanies and Essays: Comprising All His Works Collected Under the Title of "Morals,"* vol. 4, 346.

27 Pericles's own paramour: "Aspasia: Influential Concubine to Pericles," World History Encyclopedia.

27 Anaxagoras, like Herodotus: Knowledge of Anaxagoras comes from Curd, "Anaxagoras."

27 The mathematician Theodorus relocated: Bulmer-Thomas, "Theodorus of Cyrene."

27–28 Protagoras, a Thracian: Bonazzi, "Protagoras."

28 In the fifth century BCE: Mark, "Athens."

28 Herodotus answered Pericles's: Astour, "Ancient Greek Civilization in Southern Italy."

28 Protagoras would write: Bonazzi.

28 The great tragedian: Podlecki and Taplin, "Aeschylus."

28 Aristotle, who lived a century later: Aeschylus lived between 525 BC and 455 BC, according to Podlecki and Taplin. Aristotle lived between 384 BC and 322 BC, according to Shields, "Aristotle."

28 After coming to: Shields.

28 Athens relied on imported food: Garnsey, "Grain for Athens."

28 Demosthenes reported that: Demosthenes, *Against Leptines*, 32.

28 Athens exported olive oil: Cartwright, "Trade in Ancient Greece."

28 "allies who were originally": Thucydides, book 1, 97.

28 In 432, the Spartans: Cartwright, "Peloponnesian War."

29 "slavish to give in to them": Thucydides, book 1, 141.

29 "which are just as strong as anything they could build": Thucydides, book 1, 142.

29 "we have nothing to fear from their navy": Thucydides, book 1, 14.

29 "could harass the coastal": Kagan, *The Peloponnesian War*, 86.

29 Athens teemed with refugees: Knowledge of the Peloponnesian War in this paragraph comes from Kagan.

29 No one knows whether: Littman.

29 The refugees were "particularly affected": Thucydides, book 2, 52.

29 Just as in the case of COVID-19: Artiga et al., "COVID-19 Risks and Impacts among Health Care Workers by Race/Ethnicity—Issue Brief."

29 "dying like sheep": Thucydides, book 2, 51.

29 "carried away all alike": Thucydides, book 2, 5.

29 Unlike COVID-19: Johns Hopkins Coronavirus Resource Center, "Mortality Analyses."

29 "those with naturally strong . . . to resist the disease": Thucydides, book 2, 51.

29 "men, not knowing": Thucydides, book 2, 52.

30 "Athens owed to": Thucydides, book 2, 53.

30 "never affected the Peloponnese at all": Thucydides, book 2, 54.

30 Plato was born in the city: Knowledge of Plato in this section comes from Meinwald, "Plato." Plato lived between 428 BC and 348 BC.

30 "The disease inflicted a blow": McNeill, *Plagues and Peoples*, 121.

30 The scholarly investigators who: Cohen and Armelagos, *Paleopathology at the Origins of Agriculture*.

31 Some organisms, like lice: Polgar (1964) emphasizes the external organisms. Cockburn (1967) discusses the internal protozoa. Polgar, "The Evolution and Eradication of Infectious Diseases." Cockburn, *Infectious Diseases; Their Evolution and Eradication*.

31 Diseases like sleeping: Steverding, "The History of African Trypanosomiasis"; Neghina et al., "The Roots of Evil: The Amazing History of Trichinellosis and *Trichinella* Parasites."

31 The agricultural revolution: "Neolithic Revolution," History.com.

31 "products of domesticated animals": Armelagos et al., "Disease in Human Evolution: The Re-Emergence of Infectious Diseases in the Third Epidemiological Transition," 3.

31 Records of pre-Athenian plagues: Ehrenkranz and Sampson, "Origin of the Old Testament Plagues: Explications and Implications."

31 Some biblical scholars: Rendsburg, "The Date of the Exodus and the Conquest/Settlement: The Case for the 1100s."

31 The events of the *Iliad*: Apollo sends a plague upon the Greek Army in Book 1. Homer, *The Iliad*.

31 Sanskrit sources: Mouritz, *"The Flu": A Brief History of Influenza in U.S. America, Europe, Hawaii*.

31 These shreds of evidence: Norrie, "How Disease Affected the End of the Bronze Age."

32 Massive grain shipments: Rickman, "The Grain Trade under the Roman Empire."

32 Urban proximity linked: Dalzell, "Maecenas and the Poets."

32 "the Han histories record": The quotes in this section come from Raoul McLaughlin, *Rome and the Distant East: Trade Routes to the Ancient Lands of Arabia, India and China*, 59.

33 The Antonine Plague that came: McNeill.

33 the Chinese empire seems: Clements, *A Brief History of China: Dynasty, Revolution and Transformation: From the Middle Kingdom to the People's Republic*.

33 A second pandemic came: McNeill.

33 "one advantage that Christians had": The quotes in this section come from McNeill, 121–122.

33 The Antonine Plague struck: McNeill.

33 The second plague: McNeill.

33 Diocletian began: Cousin, "Diocletian."

33 Byzantium, would serve: Norwich, *Byzantium: The Early Centuries*.

33 In his Foundation trilogy: Asimov, *The Foundation Trilogy (Foundation, Foundation and Empire, Second Foundation); The Stars, Like Dust; The Naked Sun; I, Robot*.

33 Constantinople built: Nicol and Matthews, "Constantine I."

33 "built just in time": Norwich, 153.

33 Constantinople's Pandidakterion: "Pandidakterion," World Heritage Encyclopedia.

33 "the vacant throne": Gibbon, *The History of the Decline and Fall of the Roman Empire*, 93.

34 The moment for imperial renewal: Procopius, *History of the Wars, Volume II: Books 3–4 (Vandalic War)*.

34 "gold and carriages": Both quotes come from Procopius, *History of the Wars, Volume II: Books 3–4 (Vandalic War)*, IX [4-11], 281.

34 "during these times": Procopius, *History of the Wars, Volume I: Books 1–2 (Persian War)*, XXI [30-XXII.1], 451.

34 "it started from": Both quotes come from Procopius, *History of the Wars, Volume I: Books 1–2 (Persian War)*, XXII [1-7], 453.

34 The modern scientific: Morelli et al., "*Yersinia pestis* Genome Sequencing Identifies Patterns of Global Phylogenetic Diversity."

34 primarily because of DNA: Harbeck et al., "*Yersinia pestis* DNA from Skeletal Remains from the 6th Century AD Reveals Insights into Justinianic Plague."

35 Justinian's plague appears: Harbeck et al. Spyrou et al., "Analysis of 3800-Year-Old *Yersinia pestis* Genomes Suggests Bronze Age Origin for Bubonic Plague."

35 That serial slaughterer: Rasmussen et al., "Early Divergent Strains of *Yersinia pestis* in Eurasia 5,000 Years Ago."

35 The standard view is that: Morelli et al. *The New York Times* contains a helpful explanation in Wade, "Europe's Plagues Came from China, Study Finds."

35 *Yersinia pestis* was to haunt Europe: Rascovan et al., "Emergence and Spread of Basal Lineages of *Yersinia pestis* during the Neolithic Decline."

35 *Y. pestis* is a bacterium spread: "Plague (Yersinia Pestis)," *Harvard Health Publishing*.

35 Roughly half: DeWitte and Kowaleski, "Black Death Bodies."

35 "living conditions in these": Rascovan et al.

36 agrarian "mega-settlements": Rascovan et al.

36 Procopius's narrative of the plague: All quotes from this paragraph come from Procopius, *History of the Wars, Volume I: Books 1–2 (Persian War)*, XXII [30-XXIII.4], 463–465.

36 "confusion and disorder everywhere": Procopius, *History of the Wars, Volume I: Books 1–2 (Persian War)*, XXII [36-XXIII.4], 465.

36 "giving out the emperor's money": Procopius, *History of the Wars, Volume I: Books 1–2 (Persian War)*, XXIII [4–10], 467.

36 "those who in times": Procopius, *History of the Wars, Volume I: Books 1–2 (Persian War)*, XXIII [10–15], 469.

36 "supposing that they would die": Procopius, *History of the Wars, Volume I: Books 1–2 (Persian War)*, XXIII [15–19], 471.

36 In the spring of 2020, the streets: Wilson, "Coronavirus in N.Y.C.: Eerie Streetscapes Are Stripped of Commerce."

36 **"it seemed no easy thing":** Procopius, *History of the Wars, Volume I: Books 1–2 (Persian War),* XXIII [15–19], 471.

37 **He sent Belisarius back:** Knowledge in this paragraph comes from Procopius, *History of the Wars, Volume I: Books 1–2 (Persian War).*

37 **The plague came and went:** Horgan, "Justinian's Plague (541–542 CE)." At least one set of scholars has argued that Justinian's Plague was "an inconsequential pandemic" because of the absence of physical evidence, such as in Mordechai et al., "The Justinianic Plague: An Inconsequential Pandemic?"

37 **the Arab conquests:** Horgan.

37 **Antibiotics cure most cases:** US Centers for Disease Control and Prevention, "Plague FAQ."

37 **But Alexander Fleming only:** Gaynes, "The Discovery of Penicillin—New Insights after More Than 75 Years of Clinical Use."

37 **The same was true for COVID-19:** Pfizer and BioNTech first announced a vaccine candidate was over 90 percent effective in early November 2020. Pfizer, "Pfizer and Biontech Announce Vaccine Candidate Against COVID-19 Achieved Success in First Interim Analysis from Phase 3 Study."

38 **"all the days wherein the plague":** Lev. 13:46 (KJV).

38 **The Indian Lepers Act of 1898:** Buckingham, *Leprosy in Colonial South India.*

38 **The act was only:** Jyoti, "1898 Indian Lepers Act to Be repealed Finally."

38 **"on her pledge to give up her":** The quotes here come from Soper, "The Curious Career of Typhoid Mary," 708–709.

38 **symptomatic, as in the case of COVID-19:** COVID-19 spreads while people are asymptomatic. Johansson et al., "SARS-CoV-2 Transmission from People without COVID-19 Symptoms."

38 **"sitting in their houses" in Procopius's narrative:** Procopius, *History of the Wars, Volume I: Books 1–2 (Persian War),* XXIII [15–19], 471.

38 **Only 13 percent of:** US Bureau of Labor Statistics. "Supplemental Data Measuring the Effects of the Coronavirus (COVID-19) Pandemic on the Labor Market."

39 **cordon sanitaire:** *Cordon sanitaire* is French for "sanitary cordon," denoting a quarantine zone from which those inside are not allowed to leave. Hoffman and Hoffman, "Ethical Considerations in the Use of Cordons Sanitaires."

40 **The population of Rome:** Twine, "The City in Decline: Rome in Late Antiquity."

40 **trade reemerged both:** Hibbert, "Hanseatic League."

40 **Ties between European towns:** Cartwright, "Trade in Medieval Europe."

40 **Dubrovnik's picturesque red rooftops:** Dubrovnik is the main location in which King's Landing scenes from *Game of Thrones* were filmed. "King's Landing Dubrovnik: *Game of Thrones* Filming Locations in Dubrovnik, Croatia," *King's Landing Dubrovik.*

40 **It successfully linked the East:** Knowledge of Ragusan history in this section comes from Tomić and Blažina, *Expelling the Plague: The Health Office and the Implementation of Quarantine in Dubrovnik, 1377–1533.*

41 **In 1204, Venetians:** Cartwright, "1204: The Sack of Constantinople."

41 **In May 1363:** All quotes in this paragraph come from Tomić and Blažina, *Expelling the Plague,* 52.

41 **US banned travel from China:** "Proclamation on the Suspension of Entry as Immigrants and Non-Immigrants of Certain Additional Persons Who Pose a Risk of Transmitting Coronavirus Disease," White House.

42 **"Veniens de locis":** In 1377, Ragusa passed legislation to "prevent the spread of the pandemic." Vuković, "Dubrovnik: The Medieval City Designed around Quarantine."

42 **The rule established two:** Tomić and Blažina, *Expelling the Plague.*

42 **since the plague's incubation:** US Centers for Disease Control and Prevention, "Plague FAQ."

42 **England wouldn't have:** Tognotti, "Lessons from the History of Quarantine, from Plague to Influenza A."

42 **Ships from diseased ports:** Tognotti.

42 **America's own Ellis:** Ellis Island was in operation from 1890 to 1954. "Overview + History—Ellis Island," The Statue of Liberty—Ellis Island Foundation.

42 **The fictional Vito Corleone:** Coppola, Francis Ford, dir., *The Godfather Part II.*

42 **Before 1377:** Roos, "Social Distancing and Quarantine Were Used in Medieval Times to Fight the Black Death."

43 **many countries and even:** Schwartz, "I'm a U.S. Citizen. Where in the World Can I Go?" and "Thinking of Traveling in the U.S.? Check Which States Have Travel Restrictions."

43 **In 1390, the city appointed:** Tomić and Blažina, *Expelling the Plague.*

43 **"by the middle of the":** Cipolla, *Fighting the Plague in Seventeenth-Century Italy,* 4.

43 **Ragusa would eventually:** Tognotti.

43 **Jesus wandered:** Matt. 4:12 (NIV).

43 **Moses spent forty days:** Exod. 24:18 (NIV).

43 **Noah traveled forty days:** Gen. 8:6 (NIV).

43 **And the Israelites wandered:** Num. 14:33 (NIV).

43 **"entire districts within":** All quotations are from Crawshaw, *Plague Hospitals: Public Health for the City in Early Modern Venice,* 14–15.

44 **The beaked nose:** "The Plague Doctor Mask: The Most Unsettling of All Venetian Masks," Ca' Macana.

44 **"an information network":** Konstantinidou et al., "Venetian Rule and Control of Plague Epidemics on the Ionian Islands during 17th and 18th Centuries."

44 **Plenty of Americans:** Walker, "'If We Get It, We Chose to Be Here': Despite Virus, Thousands Converge on Sturgis for Huge Rally."

45 **Between 550 and 1450:** Knowledge of the history of Europe in this section comes from Salmon et al., "History of Europe."

46 **though some suggest:** Spyrou et al.

46 **"when the smallpox began":** The quotation is Motolinia, 1541, borrowed from Hopkins, *The Greatest Killer: Smallpox in History,* 206.

46 **"they fell down so generally":** "William Bradford on the Great Sickness among New England Indians (1633)," Westshore Community College.

46 **Some estimate that up to 90 percent:** Marr and Cathey, "New Hypothesis for Cause of Epidemic among Native Americans, New England, 1616–1619."

47 **Europeans turned to quarantine:** Tognotti.

47 **Syphilis seems to have been:** Nunn and Qian, "The Columbian Exchange: A History of Disease, Food, and Ideas." Harper et al., "The Origin and Antiquity of Syphilis Revisited: An Appraisal of Old World Pre-Columbian Evidence for Treponemal Infection."

47 **Since Africa became part:** Chippaux and Chippaux, "Yellow Fever in Africa and the Americas: A Historical and Epidemiological Perspective."

47 **Yellow fever is an arbovirus:** World Health Organization, "Yellow Fever."

47 **despite the existence:** Frierson, "The Yellow Fever Vaccine: A History,"

47 *Aedes aegypti* **mosquito to inhabit:** World Health Organization. "Yellow Fever."

47 **Yellow fever became endemic:** Blake, "Yellow Fever in Eighteenth Century America."

48 **The historian Billy Smith's:** The following description comes from the plot of Smith, *Ship of Death: A Voyage That Changed the Atlantic World.*

48 **Old Slaughter's Coffee House:** John Timbs, "Slaughter's Coffee House," 99–104.

48 **even that early intercontinental:** "Extracts from David Williams's Autobiography," *The American Historical Review,* 810.

48 **The plan was:** Knowledge in these two paragraphs from the plot of Smith, *Ship of Death.*

48 **The miasma theory emphasized:** Knowledge of both theories comes from Bell, *Plague in the Early Modern World: A Documentary History.*

49 **The celebrated Dr. Benjamin Rush:** "Diseases of the Mind: Highlights of American Psychiatry through 1900: Benjamin Rush, M.D. (1749–1813): 'The Father of American Psychiatry,'" US National Library of Medicine.

49 **Twenty thousand other Philadelphians:** Gum, "Philadelphia Under Siege: The Yellow Fever of 1793."

49 **yellow fever would kill one tenth:** Ruane, "Yellow Fever Led Half of Philadelphians to Flee the City. Ten Percent of the Residents Still Died."

49 **"in no one instance":** Both quotes in this paragraph come from Rush, *An Account of the Bilious Remitting Yellow Fever, as It Appeared in the City of Philadelphia, in the Year 1793,* 72.

49 **The African American community:** Gum.

49 **Rush's medical cure for yellow fever:** Gum.

50 **In 1804, he wrote that:** All quotes in this paragraph come from Butterfield, *Letters of Benjamin Rush: Volume II: 1793–1813*, 881.

50 **strictly human contact:** Yellow fever is transmitted by mosquitoes. World Health Organization, "Yellow Fever."

50 **Drawing on his Caribbean roots:** McKay, "Hamilton and Yellow Fever: The Library Where It Happens."

50 **Mosquitoes can travel:** US Centers for Disease Control and Prevention, *How to Prevent the Spread of the Mosquito That Causes Dengue.*

50 **quarantine in 1793:** Finger, "Yellow Fever."

51 **Both yellow fever:** There is natural vertical transmission of the yellow fever virus in *Aedes aegypti* mosquito (Fontenille et al., "First Evidence of Natural Vertical Transmission of Yellow Fever Virus in *Aedes aegypti*, Its Epidemic Vector"), as there also is with the Zika virus (Izquierdo-Suzán, "Natural Vertical Transmission of Zika Virus in Larval *Aedes aegypti* Populations, Morelos, Mexico"); mosquitoes infected in the fall could have transmitted the disease to their progeny that became active in the spring.

51 **Philadelphia would end up:** Gum.

51 **The true understanding of yellow fever:** Knowledge in this paragraph comes from Chastel, "Centenary of the Discovery of Yellow Fever Virus and Its Transmission by a Mosquito (Cuba 1900–1901)."

51 **Philadelphia was a pioneer:** Gum.

51 **Quarantines continued to be common:** Price, "Epidemics, Outsiders, and Local Protection: Federalism Theater in the Era of the Shotgun Quarantine."

52 **When the plague appeared:** Luttrell, *The Making of Christian Malta: From the Early Middle Ages to 1530.*

52 **The disease seems to have been kept:** Zwilling, "Poor Leadership during Times of Disease: Malta and the Plague of 1813."

53 **The village of Eyam in:** Wallis, "A Dreadful Heritage: Interpreting Epidemic Disease at Eyam, 1666-2000."

53 **As the deaths started:** Wallis, 2.

53 **"259 of a population of 330 died":** Wallis, 3.

53 **Roads and bridges leading:** Condie and Folwell, *History of the Pestilence, Commonly Called Yellow Fever, Which Almost Desolated Philadelphia, in the Months of August, September & October, 1798.*

53 **Empress Maria Theresa:** Boro, "Austrian Measures for Prevention and Control of the Plague Epidemic along the Border with the Ottoman Empire during the 18th Century."

53 **first used in 1821:** Nichols, *The European Pentarchy and the Congress of Verona, 1822.*

54 **variants across the globe:** US Centers for Disease Control and Prevention, "About Variants of the Virus That Causes COVID-19."

54 **China managed to stop the flow:** Feng and Cheng, "As China's Wuhan Ends Its Long Quarantine, Residents Feel a Mix of Joy and Fear."

54 **Similarly, Marshal Tito:** Flight, "Smallpox: Eradicating the Scourge."

55 **laws requiring that:** US Centers for Disease Control and Prevention, "Mandatory Reporting of Infectious Diseases by Clinicians."

55 **waiting until the end of January:** Chinazzi et al., "The Effect of Travel Restrictions on the Spread of the 2019 Novel Coronavirus (COVID-19) Outbreak."

55 **The international body most responsible:** Knowledge of the World Health Organization comes from "World Health Organization," *Encyclopædia Britannica Online.*

56 **the WHO tweeted that "preliminary investigations":** World Health Organization (@WHO), "Preliminary investigations conducted by the Chinese authorities have found no clear evidence of human-to-human transmission of the novel #coronavirus (2019-nCoV) identified in #Wuhan, #China."

56 **echoed official Chinese information:** The WHO reported on official Chinese government findings that "there is no clear evidence that the virus passes easily from person to person" on January 12, 2020. World Health Organization, "Novel Coronavirus—China."

56 **known by scientists in Wuhan:** Page and Khan, "How It All Started: China's Early Coronavirus Missteps."

56 **in Thailand:** World Health Organization. "Novel Coronavirus—Thailand (Ex-China)."

56 **vast numbers of people:** Page and Khan. Knowledge of China and the World Health Organization's missteps in this section also comes from Bollyky and Patrick, "Improving Pandemic Preparedness: Lessons From COVID-19."

56 **China is a major funder of the WHO:** At the end of 2019, China had contributed a total of $86 million to the WHO, $75.8 million in assessed contributions and $10.2 million in voluntary contributions. World Health Organization, "Programme Budget Web Portal."

56 **The WHO was also late:** Ebola was confirmed on March 22, 2014, but a public health emergency of international concern was not declared until August 8, 2014. Hoffman and Silverberg, "Delays in Global Disease Outbreak Responses: Lessons from H1N1, Ebola, and Zika." Knowledge of the World Health Organization's missteps also comes from Bollyky and Patrick.

57 **In January of 2021, China blocked:** Regand and Sidhu, "WHO Team Blocked from Entering China to Study Origins of Coronavirus."

57 **Membership in the WHO:** World Health Organization, "Countries Overview."

57 **"to guarantee the freedom":** North Atlantic Treaty Organization, "What Is NATO?"

57 **translated into strategic concepts:** North Atlantic Treaty Organization, "Strategic Concepts."

57 **The NATO secretary general:** North Atlantic Treaty Organization, "Principal Officials." North Atlantic Treaty Organization, "NATO Secretary General."

58 **$2.5 billion per year:** The WHO runs on a two-year budget cycle. According to the WHO website, its total budget for 2020–2021 is around $5.8 billion; its total budget in 2018–2019 was around $4.4 billion. World Health Organization, "Budget."

58 **money spent on pandemic:** World Health Organization, "Programme Budget 2020–2021."

58 **NATO's annual budget:** The total civil and military budget for NATO in 2021 is around €1.9 billion, or around $2.3 billion. NATO, "NATO Agrees 2021 Civil and Military Budgets."

58 **three times greater than the WHO's:** In the fiscal year 2018, funding for the CDC was $8.25 billion. US Centers for Disease Control and Prevention, "CDC's Funding."

58 **The Food and Drug Administration's budget:** In the fiscal year 2019, funding for the FDA was $5.9 billion. US Food and Drug Administration, "Fact Sheet: FDA at a Glance."

58 **The governing board:** World Health Organization, "Composition of the Board."

58 **Major operational decisions:** World Health Organization, "WHO and the WHA—an Explainer."

58 **Consensus bodies often:** Tansey, "Lowest Common Denominator Norm Institutionalization: The Anti-coup Norm at the United Nations."

58 **NATO also works by consensus:** North Atlantic Treaty Organization, "Consensus Decision-Making at NATO."

58 **an attack on all:** North Atlantic Treaty Organization, "Collective Defence—Article 5."

59 **After World War II, the West invented:** North Atlantic Treaty Organization, "Collective Defence—Article 5."

CHAPTER 3: CAN INDIAN SEWERS MAKE INDIANA HEALTHIER?

61 **the pandemic was far deadlier:** Adhikari et al., "Assessment of Community-Level Disparities in Coronavirus Disease 2019 (COVID-19) Infections and Deaths in Large US Metropolitan Areas."

62 **costing trillions:** Cutler and Summers, "The COVID-19 Pandemic and the $16 Trillion Virus."

62 **the number of people who die:** In 2016, 2420 deaths due to cholera were reported to WHO worldwide. World Health Organization, "Cholera."

62 **antibiotics and oral rehydration therapy:** World Health Organization, "Cholera." US Centers for Disease Control and Prevention, "Epidemic Typhus."

63 **Before 1815:** Napoleon Bonaparte was defeated at the Battle of Waterloo in 1815. Godechot, "Napoleon I."

64 **the military misadventures:** Willsher, "Story of Cities #12: Haussmann Rips Up Paris—and Divides France to This Day."

64 **great-grandfather had participated:** Collins, "Family Networks and Social Connections in the Survival of a Seventeenth-Century Library Collection."

64 **Rawdon grew up in:** National Park Service, "Francis Rawdon."

64 **personally executed Joseph Warren:** Russell, *Essays, and Sketches of Life and Character.*

64 **Rawdon went to India in 1813:** Rawdon-Hastings, *The Private Journal of the Marquess of Hastings.*

64 **"the dreadful epidemic disorder":** Rawdon-Hastings, 317.

64 **Rawdon is splendidly buried:** National Park Service, "Francis Rawdon."

65 **"to the memory":** Holmes and Co. (Calcutta), *The Bengal Obituary,* 161.

65 **Jameson died young:** "James Jameson (1786–1823)," Find A Grave Memorial.

65 **Jameson is known today:** Jameson, *Report on the Epidemick Cholera Morbus: As It Visited the Territories Subject to the Presidency of Bengal, in the Years 1817, 1818 and 1819.*

65 **"endemical in Bengal":** Jameson, 2–3.

65 **Portuguese traders reported:** Ryan, "Eyes on the Prize: Lessons from the Cholera Wars for Modern Scientists, Physicians, and Public Health Officials."

65 **"on the 28th of":** Jameson, 2–3.

66 **"the marked disposition":** Jameson, 102.

66 **"after the middle of September":** Jameson, 8.

66 **In one month:** The range of the speedy spread makes it possible that the disease had already traveled considerably before the outbreak in Jessore.

66 **"it at once raged":** Jameson, 9.

66 **"a new stream of":** Jameson, 11.

66 **"did no great mischief":** Jameson, 11.

66 **"the disease put forth":** Jameson, 12.

66 **the reverse of the movement:** Sagonowsky, "Biogen Superspreader Meeting Spawned 300,000-plus U.S. Coronavirus Cases: Study."

66 **"after creeping about":** All quotes from this paragraph come from Jameson, 12–13.

67 **"there is an opinion":** All quotes in this paragraph come from Rawdon-Hastings, 317–318.

67 **"were predisposed to receive":** Both quotes come from Rawdon-Hastings, 319.

67 **Like COVID-19, cholera:** Those with certain medical conditions are at "increased risk of severe illness" due to COVID-19. US Centers for Disease Control and Prevention, "People with Certain Medical Conditions."

67 **"debility from previous illness":** Rawdon-Hastings, 319.

67 **"broad and clear stream":** All quotes in this paragraph come from Rawdon-Hastings, 320–321.

68 **Cholera would occur and reoccur:** Chhabria, "Manufacturing Epidemics: Pathogens, Poverty, and Public Health Crises in India."

68 **epidemic that began in the 1890s:** Echenberg, "Pestis Redux: The Initial Years of the Third Bubonic Plague Pandemic, 1894-1901."

68 **The influenza pandemic of 1918–19 killed:** Chandra and Wray, "Mortality from the Influenza Pandemic of 1918–1919: The Case of India."

68 **The British elites:** Prashad, "The Technology of Sanitation in Colonial Delhi."

68 **"until 1928 excrement":** Mann, "Delhi's Belly: On the Management of Water, Sewage and Excreta in a Changing Urban Environment during the Nineteenth Century."

69 **Six great waves of cholera:** "Cholera," History.com.

69 **The second pandemic began:** Chan et al., "Historical Epidemiology of the Second Cholera Pandemic: Relevance to Present Day Disease Dynamics."

69 **across the mountains of Afghanistan:** Bosin, "Russia, Cholera Riots of 1830–1831."

69 **just as Chinese tourists:** Two tourists from China in Italy were confirmed to have COVID-19 on January 30, 2020. The US travel ban on China took effect on January 31, 2020. Apolone, "Unexpected Detection of SARS-CoV-2 Antibodies in the Prepandemic Period in Italy."

70 **By October 8, 1831:** Kell, *On the Appearance of Cholera at Sunderland in 1831: With Some Account of That Disease.*

70 **"no efficient measures"**: Kell, 19.

70 **More than 20,000 Britons**: Underwood, "The History of Cholera in Great Britain."

70 **On the fifteenth of March**: Moreau De Jonnes, "Statistical Remarks on the Effects of Cholera in France During the Epidemic of 1832."

70 **94,666 kills in France in 1832**: *The Lancet*, vol. 1, 690.

70 **means that the death rate**: As of January 18, 2021, there were 70,283 confirmed deaths due to COVID-19 in France ("France Coronavirus Map and Case Count," *The New York Times*). France's population in 2019 was 67,059,887 (World Bank, "Population, Total—France"), yielding a death rate of about 0.1 percent. There were about 32.6 million people in France in 1830 (Mitchell, *European Historical Statistics, 1750–1975*) and 94,666 deaths due to cholera in 1832, yielding a death rate of about 0.3 percent.

70 **One out of every fifty Parisians**: There were about 785,000 Parisians in 1831 (*A Handbook for Visitors to Paris; Containing a Description of the Most Remarkable Objects in Paris . . . With Map and Plans*, 40) and "almost twenty thousand" deaths in 1832 (Heine, "'A Riot of the Dead: A German Poet Reports from the Paris Cholera Outbreak of 1832"), yielding a death rate of around 2 percent.

70 **in two central districts**: In S'Jacques and Hotel de Ville, death rates were over five percent. Heine.

70 **"the cholera evidently"**: All three quotes come from Heine.

71 **had overthrown one monarch in 1830**: "July Revolution." *Encyclopædia Britannica Online*.

71 **enforce the rules**: Patterson, "The Cholera Epidemic of 1832 in York, Upper Canada."

71 **"merely separated those"**: Both quotes come from Patterson, 169.

71 **"the roads, in all directions"**: All three quotes come from Rosenberg, *The Cholera Years: The United States in 1832, 1849, and 1866*, 28.

71 **population of 220,000**: New York City's population in the 1830 US Census was 202,000 and the city's population in the 1840 US Census was 313,000. We assumed a constant growth rate over that date, and applied that

rate to produce an estimate of 220,000 for 1832.

71 **five times New York City's death rate**: As of January 18, 2021, New York's York County's death rate is about 209 per 100,000, or around 0.2 percent. "New York Coronavirus Map and Case Count," *The New York Times*.

72 **those city's slum dwellers**: Malani et al., "Seroprevalence of SARS-CoV-2 in Slums and Non-slums of Mumbai, India, during June 29–July 19, 2020."

72 **John Jacob Astor**: New York Public Library, "History of the New York Public Library."

72 **Theodore Roosevelt Sr., the president's father**: National Park Service, "Theodore Roosevelt, Sr.—Theodore Roosevelt Birthplace, National Historic Site, New York."

72 **Peter Cooper tried to**: The Cooper Union, "Peter Cooper's Vision."

72 **"spearheaded one"**: Gerber, "'Pure and Wholesome': Stephen Allen, Cholera, and the Nineteenth-Century New York City Water Supply," 1.

72 **Allen's father was a "superior and expert"**: Allen, *The Memoirs of Stephen Allen*, 4.

72 **Allen's mother "consented to permit"**: Allen, *The Memoirs of Stephen Allen*, 21.

72 **"was left with a family"**: Allen, *The Memoirs of Stephen Allen*, 54.

72 **Americans "constantly unite together"**: Tocqueville, *Democracy in America*, 363.

72 **At one point in his memoirs**: Allen, *The Memoirs of Stephen Allen*.

73 **The most important of Allen's**: Allen, *The Memoirs of Stephen Allen*.

73 **For 150 years, Tammany Hall's**: "Tammany Hall," *Encyclopædia Britannica Online*.

73 **Tweed Courthouse still stands**: City of New York, "A Brief History of Tweed Courthouse."

73 **"partly political and partly charitable"**: Allen, *The Memoirs of Stephen Allen*, 115.

73 **"any assistance I can give"**: Allen writes this in a letter addressed to Jesse Hoyt on November 28, 1832. Mackenzie, *The Lives and Opinions of Benj'n Franklin Butler, United States District Attorney for the Southern District of New-York; and Jesse Hoyt, Counsellor at Law*, 71.

73 **"a clear head and a sound heart"**: Allen, *The Memoirs of Stephen Allen*, p. 2 of Introduction.

73 "bringing in of good and wholesome": Hunt, *Lives of American Merchants, Volume 2*, 177.

73 "the route from the best source": Allen, *The Memoirs of Stephen Allen*, 145.

74 the Manhattan Company: JPMorgan Chase, "History of Our Firm."

74 While the Manhattan Company was busy: Allen, *The Memoirs of Stephen Allen*.

74 The aqueduct's advocates marshaled: Allen, *The Memoirs of Stephen Allen*.

74 In 1833, the governor of New York: Allen, *The Memoirs of Stephen Allen*.

75 "ripe scholar": Koeppel quotes Allen in his book, *Water for Gotham: A History*, 184.

75 In 1837, construction: Jervis, Lankton, and Clement. "Old Croton Aqueduct."

75 Croton cost nine million dollars: Croton took six years to construct. Thus, about $1.5 million per year. Lindert says income was $120 per capita in 1840 (Table 4). Population was 327,000. Thus, total income was $39 million per year. $1.5/$39 = 0.038. The cost of the Croton Aqueduct comes from "New York City Waterworks," Documentary History of American Water-works. The per capita income comes from Lindert and Williamson, "American Incomes 1774–1860," table 4.

75 "clean water was responsible": Cutler and Miller, "The Role of Public Health Improvements in Health Advances: The 20th Century United States."

75 23 to 1: Cutler and Miller.

76 the opposite is true: Alsan and Goldin, "Watersheds in Child Mortality: The Role of Effective Water and Sewerage Infrastructure, 1880 to 1920."

76 "one of the hottest": Ashton, *One Hot Summer: Dickens, Darwin, Disraeli, and the Great Stink of 1858*, 1.

76 London's sanitary master: "Sir Joseph William Bazalgette," *Encyclopædia Britannica Online*.

76 "That noble river": Disraeli, "First Reading—Metropolis Local Management Act Amendment Bill."

77 360 million pounds today: "Why a Pound Today Is Worth Only 0.8% of a Pound in 1858," CPI Inflation Calculator.

77 "constructed the system": Halliday, "Death and Miasma in Victorian London: An Obstinate Belief."

77 His sewers are still used today: Everett, "How London Got Its Victorian Sewers."

77 The speedier UK rollout: Hui, "UK Ramps Up Vaccine Rollout, Targets Every Adult by Autumn."

77 At the turn of the twentieth century: Glaeser, "Cities and Pandemics Have a Long History."

78 This spending was possible only: Cutler et al., "Evidence on Early-Life Income and Late-Life Health from America's Dust Bowl Era."

78 "sewer socialism": "Milwaukee Sewer Socialism," Wisconsin Historical Society.

78 systematically underserved: Troesken, *Water, Race, and Disease*.

79 "it doesn't matter if a cat": Simpson and Speake, "It Doesn't Matter If a Cat Is Black or White, as Long as It Catches Mice."

79 can cost over $1,000: Ashraf, Glaeser, and Ponzetto, "Infrastructure, Incentives, and Institutions."

79 less than $2,000 per year: World Bank, "GDP per Capita (Current US$)—Zambia."

80 second cholera epidemic: Rosenberg, "The Cholera Epidemic of 1832 in New York City."

80 A third cholera wave: "Asiatic Cholera Pandemic of 1846–63," Fielding School of Public Health, UCLA.

80 While the second epidemic: Summers, "Broad Street Pump Outbreak."

80 Dr. John Snow: Tuthill, "John Snow and the Broad Street Pandemic: On the Trail of an Epidemic."

80 5,000 New Yorkers: Wilford, "How Epidemics Helped Shape the Modern Metropolis."

80 2,300 free hydrants: Ashraf, Glaeser, and Ponzetto.

80 Death rates were higher: Glaeser, "The Health of the Cities."

81 pathogen-free milk: Ullmann, "Louis Pasteur."

81 Robert Koch: Stevenson, "Robert Koch."

81 Florence Nightingale carries: Selanders, "Florence Nightingale."

81 Excluded by Nightingale: "Mary Seacole," *Encyclopædia Britannica Online*.

81 **He was also the founder:** Rosen, "Tenements and Typhus in New York City, 1840–1875."

81 **"small farm in the highlands":** Rosen, 590.

81 **"upon examination":** Rosen, 590.

81 **"fever nest":** Rosen, 590.

81 **In New York at the time:** Knowledge of Smith's work comes from Rosen.

82 **landmark 1865 report:** Citizens' Association of New York, Council of Hygiene and Public Health, *Report of the Council of Hygiene and Public Health of the Citizens' Association of New York upon the Sanitary Condition of the City.*

82 **"contained not less than":** All quotes in this section come from Citizens' Association of New York, Council of Hygiene and Public Health.

82 **"emaciated to a skeleton":** Citizens' Association of New York, Council of Hygiene and Public Health, 49.

82 **That law required one indoor:** New York State Department of Health, *Tenement-house Acts, Chapter 908, Laws of 1867 (as Amended by Chapter 504, Laws of 1879, and Chapter 399, Section 1, Laws of 1880): An Act for the Regulation of Tenement and Lodging Houses in the Cities of New York and Brooklyn, Passed May 14, 1867.*

83 **The Metropolitan Health Bill:** Knowledge of the Metropolitan Health Bill comes from Brieger, "Sanitary Reform in New York City: Stephen Smith and the Passage of the Metropolitan Health Bill."

83 **In early 1879, Congress authorized:** Smillie, "The National Board of Health: 1879–1883."

83 **"Stephen Smith":** Smillie.

83 **"congress would lose interest":** Smillie.

84 **The secretary:** Smillie.

84 **"accepted the commissionership":** Waring, "The Cleaning of a Great City," originally published in *McClure's*, April 1897.

84 **"the practice of standing":** Waring.

84 **Mobs rioted when:** "TimesMachine: Sunday May 12, 1895," *The New York Times*.

84 **"within less than six":** Waring.

85 **"His power to dismiss me":** Waring.

85 **When Teddy Roosevelt:** Cooper, "Theodore Roosevelt."

85 **"splendid little war":** Burrows and Wallace, "Splendid Little War."

85 **A far more catastrophic:** Erkoreka, "Origins of the Spanish Influenza Pandemic (1918–1920) and Its Relation to the First World War."

86 **Jameson's narrative:** Jameson.

86 **The influenza pandemic of 1918–19:** Erkoreka.

86 **the Spanish flu did not originate:** Taubenberger, "The Origin and Virulence of the 1918 'Spanish' Influenza Virus."

86 **from human to human:** "Influenza Pandemic of 1918–19," *Encyclopædia Britannica Online.*

86 **extreme immune system response:** McAuley et al., "Host Immunological Factors Enhancing Mortality of Young Adults during the 1918 Influenza Pandemic."

86 **lack of exposure to similar diseases:** Shanks and Brundage, "Pathogenic Responses among Young Adults during the 1918 Influenza Pandemic."

87 **killing perhaps 50 million:** US Centers for Disease Control and Prevention, "1918 Pandemic (H1N1 Virus)."

87 **In 2020, the global:** The global population in 2020 was around 7.7 billion people. US Census Bureau, "U.S. and World Population Clock."

87 **over 90 percent fewer:** At the time of publication, the total number of confirmed deaths due to COVID-19 was around 2 million globally. "Coronavirus (COVID-19) Deaths—Statistics and Research," Our World in Data.

87 **most extreme in India:** Kant and Guleria, "Pandemic Flu, 1918: After Hundred Years, India Is as vulnerable."

87 **Large public gatherings:** Mihm, "Lessons From the Philadelphia Flu of 1918."

87 **objected to them vociferously:** Hauser, "The Mask Slackers of 1918."

87 **meticulously linked:** Barro, "Non-Pharmaceutical Interventions and Mortality in U.S. Cities during the Great Influenza Pandemic, 1918–1919."

87 **"although an increase in NPIs":** Barro, 1.

87 **"the most deadly single event":** Shanks and Brundage.

88 **Most pandemics are zoonotic:** Olival et al., "Host and Viral Traits Predict Zoonotic Spillover from Mammals."

88 **COVID-19 (bats):** Mallapaty, "Coronaviruses Closely Related to the Pandemic Virus Discovered in Japan and Cambodia."

88 **Ebola (bats):** World Health Organization, "Ebola Virus Disease."

88 **AIDS (chimpanzees):** Sharp and Hahn, "Origins of HIV and the AIDS Pandemic."

88 **Lyme disease (deer and mice):** US Centers for Disease Control and Prevention, "Lyme Disease."

88 **the Black Death (rodents, transmitted with the help of fleas):** US Centers for Disease Control and Prevention, "Plague FAQ."

88 **Mosquitoes are the source:** Moreno-Madriñán and Turell, "History of Mosquitoborne Diseases in the United States and Implications for New Pathogens."

88 **Birds are thought:** World Health Organization, "Influenza (Avian and Other Zoonotic)."

88 **Smallpox was circulating:** Spinney, "Smallpox and Other Viruses Plagued Humans Much Earlier Than Suspected."

88 **AIDS emerged in the Congo:** Sample, "HIV Pandemic Originated in Kinshasa in the 1920s, Say Scientists."

88 **COVID-19 had only:** Taylor, "The Coronavirus Pandemic: A Timeline."

89 **Domesticated animals are generally:** "Eastern Equine Encephalitis Virus (EEEV): The Role of Diagnostics," American Society for Microbiology.

89 **The Northeast of the US:** Levine et al., "Mice as Reservoirs of the Lyme Disease Spirochete." US Centers for Disease Control and Prevention, "Lyme Disease."

89 **Eastern equine encephalitis:** US Centers for Disease Control and Prevention, "Eastern Equine Encephalitis."

89 **since the H1N1:** Taubenberger.

89 **The ancient Romans:** "Cloaca Maxima," *Encyclopædia Britannica Online.*

89 **Dr. Benjamin Rush wanted:** Gum.

89 **Mussolini assembled:** Russell, "Agricultural Colonization in the Pontine Marshes and Libya."

89 **Mao exerted:** Fu, "The Secret Maoist Chinese Operation That Conquered Malaria—and Won a Nobel."

89 **his locust- and famine-inducing:** Steinfeld, "China's Deadly Science Lesson: How an Ill-Conceived Campaign against Sparrows Contributed to One of the Worst Famines in History."

90 **"boards of health were created":** Brinkley and Vitiello, "From Farm to Nuisance: Animal Agriculture and the Rise of Planning Regulation."

90 **a law in 1705:** Brinkley and Vitiello.

90 **"issued ordinances":** Brinkley and Vitiello.

90 **twenty-three thousand dairy cows:** Brinkley and Vitiello.

90 **New York City's 1916 law:** City of New York, Board of Estimate and Apportionment, "Building Zone Resolution (Adopted July 25, 1916)."

90 **dedicated urban farmers:** Black, "Urban Agriculture: Can It Feed Our Cities?"

90 **the free-ranging goats:** Saurine, "Slum Tour in Dharavi, Mumbai with Reality Tours and Travel."

91 **It is speculated that AIDS:** Sharp and Hahn.

91 **Middle East Respiratory Syndrome:** Baharoon and Memish, "MERS-CoV as an Emerging Respiratory Illness: A Review of Prevention Methods."

91 **Malayan pangolins:** Xiao et al., "Isolation of SARS-CoV-2-Related Coronavirus from Malayan Pangolins."

91 **"elevated metabolic":** Schountz, "Immunology of Bats and Their Viruses: Challenges and Opportunities."

91 **consumption of disease-ridden insects:** Gorman, "How Do Bats Live With So Many Viruses?" Calisher et al., "Bats: Important Reservoir Hosts of Emerging Viruses."

91 **"it is highly likely":** Fan et al., "Bat Coronaviruses in China."

91 **"suggest that global changes":** Gibb et al., "Zoonotic Host Diversity Increases in Human-Dominated Ecosystems."

91 **"conservation of protected":** Intergovernmental Science-Policy Platform on Biodiversity and Ecosystem Services (IPBES), *Workshop Report on Biodiversity and Pandemics of the Intergovernmental Platform on Biodiversity and Ecosystem Services (IPBES).*

92 **US foreign aid packages:** Franz, "The Legacy of Plan Colombia."

92 **US foreign aid seems:** Dreher et al., "Does US Aid Buy UN General Assembly Votes? A Disaggregated Analysis."

92 **America's current foreign aid:** Ingram, "What Every American Should Know about US Foreign Aid."

92 **The Marshall Plan was:** O'Hare, "The History of US Foreign Aid and Why It's as Important as Ever."

92 **"our political obligations":** O'Hare.

93 **For example, using satellites:** Marconcini et al., "Outlining Where Humans Live, the World Settlement Footprint 2015."

94 **Through her clinical work:** Kammili et al., "Plasmid-Mediated Antibiotic Resistance among Uropathogens in Primigravid Women—Hyderabad, India."

94 **Bacteria have a variety:** US Centers for Disease Control and Prevention, "How Antibiotic Resistance Happens."

94 **sometimes as a secondary therapy:** LaRocque and Harris, "Cholera: Clinical Features, Diagnosis, Treatment, and Prevention."

94 **412 prescriptions per 1,000 Indians:** Farooqui et al., "Outpatient Antibiotic Prescription Rate and Pattern in the Private Sector in India: Evidence from Medical Audit Data."

94 **Hyderabad itself is:** Donthi, "Hyderabad Pharma City: A Toxic Cluster in the Making."

94 **Dr. Alsan's work:** Kammili et al.

95 **One of us (Glaeser) studies water in Lusaka ... for days on end:** Ashraf et al., "Water, Health, and Wealth."

95 **There are two types:** Ashraf et al.

96 **young women then spend less:** Ashraf et al.

96 **Rather, we all:** Nair et al., "Spread of *Vibrio cholerae* 0139 Bengal in India."

CHAPTER 4: CAN OUR BODIES BE MORE PANDEMIC-PROOF?

97 **When COVID-19 first hit:** Pearce, "Obesity a Major Risk Factor for COVID-19 Hospitalization."

97 **In the US, African Americans:** US Centers for Disease Control and Prevention, "Risk for COVID-19 Infection, Hospitalization, and Death by Race/Ethnicity."

97 **Hispanics were at higher risk:** US Centers for Disease Control and Prevention, "Risk for COVID-19 Infection, Hospitalization, and Death by Race/Ethnicity."

97 **people of Asian and Caribbean heritage:** Platt and Warwick, Are Some Ethnic Groups More Vulnerable to COVID-19 Than Others?

97 **not all of which:** Sze et al., "Ethnicity and Clinical Outcomes in COVID-19: A Systematic Review and Meta-analysis."

97 **in Massachusetts in 2020:** Commonwealth of Massachusetts. "Weekly COVID-19 Public Health Report."

97 **Close living quarters:** "More Than One-Third of U.S. Coronavirus Deaths Are Linked to Nursing Homes," *The New York Times*.

97 **Health-related choices:** American Medical Association, *Issue Brief: Reports of Increases in Opioid- and Other Drug-related Overdose and Other Concerns during COVID Pandemic.*

98 **Cigarette smoking contributes:** World Health Organization, "Smoking and COVID-19."

98 **without a bachelor's degree:** US Centers for Disease Control and Prevention, "People with Certain Medical Conditions."

98 **who have completed college:** Scommegna, "Opioid Overdose Epidemic Hits Hardest for the Least Educated."

98 **as much as ten years on average:** New York City Department of Health and Mental Hygiene, "Suicides in New York City, 2000 to 2014."

99 **The magnitude of modern urban:** Mitcham, "The Statistics of the Disaster."

99 **didn't even give him that victory:** Grynbaum, "New York Plans to Ban Sale of Big Sizes of Sugary Drinks."

99 **absent from observant Mormon households:** Fuchs, *Who Shall Live?*

100 **schooling is the strongest predictor:** Cutler and Glaeser, "What Explains Differences in Smoking, Drinking, and Other Health Related Behaviors?"; Lawrence, "Why Do College Graduates Behave More Healthfully Than Those Who Are Less Educated?"

101 **life-expectancy areas—and then some:** Chetty et al., "The Association between Income and Life Expectancy in the United States."

101 **The bottom of the list:** McCann, "Most & Least Educated Cities in America."

101 **the Jim Crow South:** Smithsonian National Museum of American History, "Separate Is Not Equal: Brown v. Board of Education: Jim Crow Laws."

101 **Behaviors, healthy and unhealthy:** Allen et al., "Comparing the Influence of Parents and Peers on the Choice to Use Drugs: A Meta-analytic Summary of the Literature."

101 **Peers can influence:** Allen et al.

102 **San Jose, Boston:** Marcoux, "These Are the 25 Richest Cities in America."

102 **To paraphrase Tolstoy:** Tolstoy, *Anna Karenina*.

102 **A forty-year-old living:** Chetty et al., "The Association between Income and Life Expectancy."

103 **The smoking rate among:** Data from Chetty et al., "The Association between Income and Life Expectancy"; Buttar et al., "Prevention of Cardiovascular Diseases: Role of Exercise, Dietary Interventions, Obesity and Smoking Cessation."

103 **less heart disease, cancer:** Buttar et al.

103 **so poor in Glasgow?:** Cowley et al., "Unravelling the Glasgow Effect: The Relationship between Accumulative Bio-Psychosocial Stress, Stress Reactivity and Scotland's Health Problems."

103 **the "French paradox":** Ferrières, "The French Paradox: Lessons for Other Countries."

103 **Health insurance is universal:** Tikkanen et al., "England."

103 **In France, Paris has:** European Commission, "Eurostat: Database."

103 **In Spain, it is Madrid:** "People in Community of Madrid Live Longer, Compared to Other Europeans: European Regions with Highest Life Expectancies 2016," RList.

103 **In Canada:** Statistics Canada, "Health At a Glance, 2011"; Weigh2Healthy, "Top 5 Healthiest Cities in Canada," *Weigh2Healthy*.

103 **But all are rich:** McGillivray, "Ottawa."

103 **almost one year per mile:** Citizens' Committee for Children, "Life Expectancy."

103 **In the Camden borough:** "Life Expectancy by London Borough," Trust for London.

104 **Indeed, Brownsville:** New York City Department of Health and Hygiene, Community Health Profiles, "Brownsville"; Culliton, "This is The Deadliest Neighborhood in New York City."

104 **The smoking rate in Brownsville:** Chan, "Data Show Manhattan is Svelte and Bronx is Chubby, Chubby."

104 **The poorest quarter:** Wilson, "These Graphs Show How COVID-19 Is Ravaging New York City's Low-Income Neighborhoods."

104 **cell phones and subway turnstiles:** Glaeser, Gorback, and Redding, "JUE Insight: How Much Does COVID-19 Increase with Mobility? Evidence from New York and Four Other U.S. Cities."

104 **Almost 75,000:** Bowles and Shaviro, "Bearing the Brunt: Where NYC's Hard-Hit Sector Workers Live."

105 **median household income is $55,000:** "NYC-Queens Community District 3— Jackson Heights & North Corona PUMA, NY," Census Reporter.

105 **seeded the disease:** Bengali, Linthicum, and Kim, "How Coronavirus—a 'Rich Man's Disease'—Infected the Poor."

105 **With contagious disease:** Beachum, "New York's 'Patient Zero' Breaks His Silence after Surviving Covid-19."

105 **Like the game:** Smith, "Proof! Just Six Degrees of Separation between Us."

105 **One quarter of adults in:** US Centers for Disease Control and Prevention, "Hospitalization Rates and Characteristics of Patients Hospitalized with Laboratory-Confirmed Coronavirus Disease 2019—COVID-NET, 14 States, March 1–30, 2020"; Lighter et al., "Obesity in Patients Younger Than 60 Years Is a Risk Factor for COVID-19 Hospital Admission."

105 **The biology of:** Wadman et al., "Why COVID-19 Is More Deadly in People with Obesity—Even If They're Young."

106 **The Centers for Disease Control and Prevention suggests:** US Centers for Disease Control and Prevention, "Certain Medical Conditions and Risk for Severe COVID-19 Illness."

106 **antibodies by July 2020:** Malani et al., "Seroprevalence of SARS-CoV-2 in Slums and Non-Slums of Mumbai, India, during June 29-July 19, 2020."

106 **yet the death:** Raj and Ploriya, "Prevalence of Obesity among Rehabilitated Urban Slum Dwellers and Altered Body Image Perception in India (PRESUME)."

106 **rate in San Francisco:** "High Rate of Obese and Overweight Kids Poses Problems for SF," *San Francisco Examiner.*

106 **When people consume:** "Counting Calories: Get Back to Weight-Loss Basics," Mayo Clinic.

107 **In nineteenth-century Chicago:** Wilson, "Cyrus McCormick."

107 **During the twentieth century:** Cutler, Glaeser, and Shapiro, "Why Have Americans Become More Obese?"

107 **By the 1960s, we were almost:** Fryar et al., "Prevalence of Overweight, Obesity, and Severe Obesity among Adults Aged 20 and Over: United States, 1960–1962 through 2015–2016."

107 **The rise in American obesity:** Cutler, Glaeser, and Shapiro, "Why Have Americans Become More Obese?"

107 **The US government gets a picture:** A random group of people is given a food diary and asked to fill it out for a few days, including what was eaten and in what quantity. The results are then tabulated to determine caloric consumption.

108 **one fifth over thirty years:** Cutler, Glaeser, and Shapiro, "Why Have Americans Become More Obese?"

108 **Why has food:** Ritchie and Roser, "Obesity."

108 **One could watch:** "Julia Child," PBS.

108 **More than three quarters:** Poti et al., "Is the Degree of Food Processing and Convenience Linked with the Nutritional Quality of Foods Purchased by US Households?"

108 **Today, they are ubiquitous:** Poti et al.

108 **potato chips and a soda:** Buccholz, "Are Fast-Food Establishments Making Americans Fat?"

108 **Data from British food diaries:** Griffith, Lluberas, and Lührmann, *Gluttony in England? Long-Term Change in Diet: IFS Briefing Note BN142*; Harper and Hallsworth, "Counting Calories."

109 **competitors and its workforce:** Satterthwaite et al., "Urbanization and Its Implications for Food and Farming."

109 **the Loose-Wiles Biscuit Company:** "Loose-Wiles Biscuit Tins."

110 **The author E. B. White:** Martinelli, "The Factory That Oreos Built."

110 **The key to Nabisco's:** "Book Review: Packaging in Today's Society, 3rd Edition, Robert J. Kelsey, Technomic Publishing Co., Inc., Lancaster, PA (1989)," in *Journal of Plastic Film & Sheeting*; Warner, *Pandora's Lunchbox: How Processed Food Took Over the American Meal.*

110 **"Controlled atmosphere packaging":** Testin, "New Packaging Technologies."

110 **Since the 1970s, food irradiation:** US Food and Drug Administration, "Food Irradiation: What You Need to Know."

110 **A persistent problem in food:** Cutler, Glaeser, and Shapiro, "Why Have Americans Become More Obese?"

110 **In addition, the food industry:** Schlosser, *Fast Food Nation.*

111 **and alter the food's texture:** Kelsey, *Packaging in Today's Society.*

111 **is commonly called "freezer burn":** Library of Congress, "What Is 'Freezer Burn'?"

111 **By 1999, 83 percent did:** Energy Information Administration, "Households with Selected Appliances and Types of Maine Heating Fuel, Selected Years."

111 **Consider the ordinary loaf:** McCulloch, "Is It Safe to Eat Moldy Bread?"

111 **Today, sorbic acid is bought:** "Sorbic Acid," ScienceDirect Topics.

112 **Preservatives reduce the need:** "Food Preservative," ScienceDirect Topics.

112 **A whole literature:** Hilmers et al., "Neighborhood Disparities in Access to Healthy Foods and Their Effects on Environmental Justice"; Lewis et al., "African Americans' Access to Healthy Food Options in South Los Angeles Restaurants."

112 "predominantly black": Powell et al., "The Availability of Fast-Food and Full-Service Restaurants in the United States: Associations with Neighborhood Characteristics."

112 "neighborhood deprivation": Cummins et al., "McDonald's Restaurants and Neighborhood Deprivation in Scotland and England."

112 ate fast food daily: Fryar et al., *Fast Food Consumption among Adults in the United States, 2013–2016.*

113 between 1970 and 2000: "How Many Calories in McDonald's French Fries, Large," CalorieKing.

113 Jack (J.R.) Simplot: Davis and Stilwell, *Aristocrat in Burlap: A History of the Potato in Idaho*; Hadley, "Mr. Spud."

113 Like Nabisco, Simplot was: Martin, "J.R. Simplot, Farmer Who Developed First Frozen French Fries, Dies at 99."

113 woo pickier postwar consumers: "1940s: The Company's Beginnings," J.R. Simplot Company.

113 Simplot's star: Davis and Stilwell.

114 The resulting potato retained: Dunn, "J.R. Simplot."

114 The ability to make food: Nierenberg and Nink, "Here's Why Industrial Food Is Deceivingly Cheap."

114 between technological change: Lakdawalla and Philipson, "The Growth of Obesity and Technological Change."

114 Obesity has increased everywhere: Lakdawalla and Philipson.

114 The US, the UK, Canada, and Australia: Clower, "Why English Is 'the Language of Obesity'"; Cutler, Glaeser, and Shapiro, "Why Have Americans Become More Obese?"

114 the German Reinheitsgebot: Nicholson, "Germany's Beer Purity Law Is 500 Years Old. Is It Past Its Sell-By Date?"

115 their culinary traditions: Dessaux, "Chemical Expertise and Food Market Regulation in *Belle-Epoque* France."

115 The real cost: US Department of Labor and US Bureau of Labor Statistics, *100 Years of U.S. Consumer Spending: Data for the Nation, New York City, and Boston.*

115 easily accessible on demand: Drayer, "The Non-alcoholic's Guide to Drinking Less Alcohol."

116 instantaneous gratification: O'Donoghue and Rabin, "The Economics of Immediate Gratification."

116 twenty minutes less per day: Gershuny and Harms, "Housework Now Takes Much Less Time: 85 Years of US Rural Women's Time Use."

116 "stubbornly persistent plague": Koch, "Needed: Federal Anti-Drug Aid."

117 Those drugs, especially opioids: US Centers for Disease Control and Prevention, "Overdose Deaths Accelerating During COVID-19."

117 Heroin needles: Latkin et al., "Predictors of Sharing Injection Equipment by HIV-Seropositive Injection Drug Users."

117 250,000 drug overdose deaths: US Centers for Disease Control and Prevention, "Data Overview: The Drug Overdose Epidemic: Behind the Numbers."

117 "joy plant": Saunders, *The Poppy: A History of Conflict, Loss, Remembrance, and Redemption.*

117 The town of Belmont: "Cushing Estate, 'The Bellmont' (Now in Belmont, MA)," Digital Public Library of America.

117 Twenty percent of Chinese men: "Opium throughout History," PBS.

117 respiration and cardiac activity: Cleveland Clinic, "Opioids."

117 Heroin is a particularly deadly: Gable, "Comparison of Acute Lethal Toxicity of Commonly Abused Psychoactive Substances."

118 In 1676, the London physician: "Thomas Sydenham," *Encyclopædia Britannica Online.*

118 "inability or listlessness": Estes, "John Jones's Mysteries of Opium Reveal'd (1701): Key to Historical Opiates."

118 Friedrich Sertürner separated: Krishnamurthi and Rao, "The Isolation of Morphine by Serturner."

118 "free from the more": Musto, *Drugs in America: A Documentary History.*

118 Robiquet discovered: "Pierre-Jean Robiquet," *Encyclopædia Britannica Online.*

118 **"Heroin is completely devoid"**: "Felix Hoffmann," Science History Institute.

119 **"possesses many advantages"**: Daly, "A Clinical Study of Heroin."

119 **Heroin was marketed**: "From Cough Medicine to Deadly Addiction, a Century of Heroin and Drug-Abuse Policy," Yale School of Medicine.

119 **Bayer did better**: "Felix Hoffmann."

119 **For almost eighty years**: Sneader, "The Discovery of Aspirin: a Reappraisal."

119 **natural entry point for imported drugs**: US Drug Enforcement Administration, "2018 National Drug Threat Assessment (NDTA)."

119 **Dense urban markets**: Cerdá et al., "Revisiting the Role of the Urban Environment in Substance Use: The Case of Analgesic Overdose Fatalities."

119 **sharing needles helped spread**: Mandell et al., "Correlates of Needle Sharing among Injection Drug Users."

119 **After sharing roughly one hundred needles**: US Centers for Disease Control and Prevention, "HIV and Injection Drug Use"; Peters et al., "HIV Infection Linked to Injection Use of Oxymorphone in Indiana, 2014–2015."

119 **1 percent of the county**: Gonsalves and Crawford, "Dynamics of the HIV Outbreak and Response in Scott County, IN, USA, 2011–15: A Modelling Study."

120 **Mike Pence, approved**: Associated Press, "Pence's Handling of 2015 HIV Outbreak Gets New Scrutiny."

120 **Deaths from opioids are fewer**: Clay, "How Portugal Is Solving Its Opioid Problem."

120 **In 1995, Purdue Pharma**: Leslie, "The Contin Delivery System: Dosing Considerations."

120 **"Contin" system**: In 1984, Purdue Pharma tried this approach with MS Contin, which delivered morphine slowly into the body. Physicians' experiences with morphine led them to be fearful, from "Origins of the Opioid Epidemic: Purdue Pharma Knew of OxyContin Abuse in 1996 but Covered It Up," Democracy Now!

120 **revolutionized drug sales**: Podolsky et al., "Preying on Prescribers (and Their Patients)—Pharmaceutical Marketing, Iatrogenic Epidemics, and the Sackler Legacy."

121 **"consulting contract"**: Commonwealth of Massachusetts v. Purdue Pharma, First Amended Complaint and Jury Demand, January 31, 2019.

121 **"11,882 patients"**: Porter and Jick, "Addiction Rare in Patients Treated with Narcotics."

121 **opioids "should be used"**: "101 Words That Spelled Death," *Freedom*.

121 **Users started crushing**: National Drug Intelligence Center, "Abuse"; Zhang, "The One-Paragraph Letter from 1980 That Fueled the Opioid Crisis."

121 **The death rate from drug overdoses**: The early 1990s were also known as the period of "heroin chic," when popular musicians such as Kurt Cobain were known for their heroin use.

121 **"the Pike County"**: National Drug Intelligence Center.

121 **"the earliest reported cases"**: Tough, "The Alchemy of OxyContin."

122 **Policy makers started to crack down**: *Evaluating the Propriety and Adequacy of the Oxycontin Criminal Settlement: Hearing Before the Committee on the Judiciary, United States Senate*, 110th Cong., First Session, July 31, 2007.

122 **laws between 2006 and 2012**: Meara et al., "State Legal Restrictions and Prescription-Opioid Use among Disabled Adults."

122 **Lawsuits began**: Kornfield et al., "Purdue Pharma Agrees to Plead Guilty to Federal Criminal Charges in Settlement over Opioid Crisis."

122 **In August 2010**: Zhu et al., "Initial Opioid Prescriptions among U.S. Commercially Insured Patients, 2012–2017."

122 **fell by 27 percent**: Bonnie et al., *Pain Management and the Opioid Epidemic: Balancing Societal and Individual Benefits and Risks of Prescription Opioid Use*.

122 **One third of opioid users**: Cicero and Ellis, "Abuse-Deterrent Formulations and the Prescription Opioid Abuse Epidemic in the United States."

122 **more potent than heroin**: US Centers for Disease Control and Prevention, "Synthetic Opioid Overdose Data."

122 **Fentanyl is so concentrated**: Horwitz and Higham, "The Flow of Fentanyl: In the Mail, over the Border."

122 **cause of overdose deaths:** US Centers for Disease Control and Prevention, "Understanding the Epidemic"; Evans et al., "How the Reformulation of OxyContin Ignited the Heroin Epidemic."

123 **As opioids shifted from:** US Centers for Disease Control and Prevention, "Urban-Rural Differences in Drug Overdose Death Rates, by Sex, Age, and Type of Drugs Involved, 2017."

123 **three times higher:** Scommegna, "Opioid Overdose Epidemic Hits Hardest for The Least Educated."

123 **The less educated:** Cutler et al., "Socioeconomic Status and the Experience of Pain: An Example from Knees."

123 **create lasting pain:** Stevenson and Wolfers, "Subjective Well-Being and Income: Is There Any Evidence of Satiation?"

123 **"deaths of despair":** Zarroli, "'Deaths of Despair' Examines the Steady Erosion of U.S. Working-Class Life."

123 **"stresses related to the COVID-19":** Stephenson, "Drug Overdose Deaths Head toward Record Number in 2020, CDC Warns."

124 **crack cocaine epidemic:** Turner, "Crack Epidemic"; Grogger and Willis, "The Emergence of Crack Cocaine and the Rise in Urban Crime Rates."

124 **High crime rates caused people:** Cullen and Levitt, "Crime, Urban Flight, and the Consequences for Cities."

124 **The federal government:** Medicare, "Pain Management."

125 **Big tobacco:** Maloney and Chaudhuri, "Against All Odds, the U.S. Tobacco Industry Is Rolling in Money."

125 **In response to landmark studies:** Cummings et al., "Failed Promises of the Cigarette Industry and Its Effect on Consumer Misperceptions about the Health Risks of Smoking"; Hilts, "Tobacco Chiefs Say Cigarettes Aren't Addictive."

125 **the Sugar Research Foundation:** Kearns et al., "Sugar Industry and Coronary Heart Disease Research."

125 **Meat producers have used:** Gustin, "This Is How the Government Decides What You Eat."

125 **The makers of electronic cigarettes:** Sharpless, "How FDA Is Regulating E-Cigarettes."

125 **"it is not from the benevolence":** Smith, *The Wealth of Nations.*

126 **lasting damage may result:** Martuzzi, "The Precautionary Principle: In Action for Public Health."

126 **penalties for opioid malfeasance:** Spector, "In Emails, Sacklers Fret over Wealth, Opioid Business."

126 **related to secondhand smoke:** World Health Organization, "Worldwide Burden of Disease from Exposure to Second-Hand Smoke."

126 **One in four:** US Centers for Disease Control and Prevention, "Impaired Driving: Get the Facts"; US Department of Transportation, National Highway Traffic Safety Administration, *Traffic Safety Facts: Alcohol-Impaired Driving 2016 Data.*

126 **And excessive opioid use helps spread HIV:** US Centers for Disease Control and Prevention, "HIV and Substance Use."

127 **education is associated:** Hummer and Hernandez, "The Effect of Educational Attainment on Adult Mortality in the United States."

127 **Schooling also increases:** Wong et al., "Successful Schools and Risky Behaviors Among Low-Income Adolescents."

128 **There is virtually no one:** Novotney, "The Psychology of Scarcity."

128 **Years of schooling:** Organisation for Economic Co-operation and Development, *Equity and Quality in Education: Supporting Disadvantaged Students and Schools.*

128 **education has spillover effects:** Benos and Karagiannis, "Do Education Quality and Spillovers Matter? Evidence on Human Capital and Productivity in Greece."

128 **$5.85 per pack:** Whittaker, "Cigarette Tax Hike Proposed For New York State."

128 **In Indiana, the tax is $1:** Carden, "Indiana Lawmakers Eyeing Cigarette Tax Hike to Reduce Hoosier Smoking Rate."

128 **Restrictions on smoking:** US Centers for Disease Control and Prevention, "State Smoke-Free Laws for Worksites, Restaurants, and Bars—United States, 2000–2010."

128 **Peer effects:** Fletcher and Marksteiner, "Causal Spousal Health Spillover Effects and Implications for Program Evaluation."

129 **almost any plague:** The 1919 pandemic is the rare exception where a healthy immune system could actually make things worse.

129 **Half the people:** US Centers for Disease Control and Prevention, "Smoking Cessation: Fast Facts."

129 **Opioid addiction has declined in some areas:** US Department of Health and Human Services, "Opioid Crisis Statistics."

129 **cancers, and musculoskeletal pain:** Cutler et al., "A Satellite Account for Health in the United States"; Dieleman et al., "US Health Care Spending by Payer and Health Condition, 1996–2016."

CHAPTER 5: WHY DID SO MUCH HEALTH-CARE SPENDING PRODUCE SO LITTLE HEALTH?

131 **over \$3 trillion annually:** Johns Hopkins Coronavirus Resource Center, "Mortality Analyses"; Organisation for Economic Co-operation and Development, "Health Spending."

132 **city of Lubbock:** "City of Lubbock Reports 9 Additional COVID-19 Deaths, 312 New Cases," EverythingLubbock.

132 **Three aspects of health:** De Lew et al., "A Layman's Guide to the U.S. Health Care System."

132 **millions of Americans:** National Academies of Science, Engineering, and Medicine, *Communities in Action: Pathways to Health Equity.*

133 **All developed countries:** Scott, "9 Things Americans Need to Learn from the Rest of the World's Health Care Systems."

133 **two books:** Cutler, *The Quality Cure*; Cutler, *Your Money or Your Life.*

133 **a recent international survey:** Hero et al., "Understanding What Makes Americans Dissatisfied with Their Health Care System: An International Comparison."

133 **Far more Americans:** Tikkanen and Abrams, *U.S. Health Care from a Global Perspective, 2019: Higher Spending, Worse Outcomes?*

134 **The US spends:** "What Country Spends the Most on Healthcare?," Investopedia; Organisation for Economic Co-operation and Development, "Health Spending."

134 **"tapeworm on the economic system":** Lovelace, "Warren Buffett: Bezos, Dimon and I Aim for Something Bigger on Health Care Than Just Shaving Costs."

134 **were materially better than elsewhere:** Schoen and Doty, "Inequities in Access to Medical Care in Five Countries: Findings from the 2001 Commonwealth Fund International Health Policy Survey."

134 **Medicare pays about \$15,000:** Afana, Brinjikji, Cloft, et al., "Hospitalization Costs for Acute Myocardial Infarction Patients Treated with Percutaneous Coronary Intervention in the United States are Substantially Higher than Medicare Payments."

135 **more intensive care:** Yamada, "Verdugo Views: There Was a Time When a Hospital Stay Cost \$4 a Day."

135 **if they needed it:** "A Brief History of Private Insurance in the United States," Academic HealthPlans.

135 **During World War II:** Carroll, "The Real Reason the U.S. Has Employer-Sponsored Health Insurance."

136 **Insurers concentrated:** Marquis and Buntin, "How Much Risk Pooling Is There in the Individual Insurance Market?"

136 **By contrast, the US military:** Council on Foreign Relations, "Demographics of the U.S. Military"; Stockholm International Peace Research Institute, "SIPRI Military Expenditure Database."

137 **"a small number of men":** Wilson, *The New Freedom: A Call for the Emancipation of the Generous Energies of a People.*

137 **"the union of all":** "Progressive Party Platform of 1912," Teaching American History.

137 **"As long as we remain free":** "Address at the Jefferson Day Dinner," Harry S. Truman Library and Museum.

137 **"the Federal Government should":** "Special Message to the Congress Recommending a Comprehensive Health Program," Harry S. Truman Library and Museum.

138 **"ready access to all"**: "Special Message to the Congress Recommending Comprehensive Health Program," Healthcare Now!

138 **"the right to adequate"**: *Platforms of the Democratic Party and the Republican Party.*

138 **"there was probably"**: D. S. G., "Medical Care: Changes in the Political Terrain."

138 **"we reject any proposal"**: "1960 Democratic Platform," *Patriot Post.*

138 **In 1962, Congress**: "Medicare," *The Lancet*; Social Security Administration, "Social Security History: Chapter 4: The Fourth Round—1957 to 1965."

139 **"swung his present great popularity"**: "Medicare," *The Lancet.*

139 **"the most powerful man"**: Smith, "In 1974, a Stripper Known as the 'Tidal Basin Bombshell' Took Down the Most Powerful Man in Washington."

139 **"the concern for states' rights"**: Bertram, "Democratic Divisions in the 1960s and the Road to Welfare Reform."

139 **In March 1964**: Zelizer, *Taxing America: Wilbur D. Mills, Congress, and the State, 1945–1975.*

139 **the British National Health service**: Gorsky, "The British National Health Service 1948–2008: A Review of the Historiography."

140 **the Swedish system**: Shafrin, "The Development of Universal Health Care in Sweden."

140 **the Canadian system**: Canadian Health Coalition, "History of Canada's Public Health Care."

140 **Wilbur Mills put together**: Rose, *Financing Medicaid: Federalism and the Growth of America's Health Care Safety Net.*

140 **The bill sailed**: "50th Anniversary of Medicare and Medicaid," LBJ Presidential Library.

140 **"medically necessary or appropriate"**: Early Childhood Learning and Knowledge Center/Head Start, "Types of Grants."

140 **Unsurprisingly, medical spending**: Starr, *The Social Transformation of American Medicine.*

141 **about 4 percent**: Schieber, "Health Expenditures in Major Industrialized Countries, 1960–87."

141 **6 percent of GDP**: Kamal et al., "How Does Health Spending in the U.S. Compare to Other Countries?"

141 **One out of every**: Cutler and Ly, "The (Paper) Work of Medicine: Understanding International Medical Costs."

141 **less than half as large**: Cutler and Ly; Cutler, "Reducing Administrative Costs in U.S. Health Care."

142 **will not authorize additional scanners**: Martin et al., "Canada's Universal Health-Care System: Achieving Its Potential."

142 **Canada's rules can be**: Tikkanen et al., "Canada."

142 **"It's the Prices, Stupid"**: Anderson et al., "It's The Prices, Stupid: Why the United States Is So Different from Other Countries."

142 **Prescription drugs are the most notorious**: "Insulin Costs up to 10 Times More in US Compared with Other Nations," Kaiser Health News.

142 **Some Americans die**: Silverman, "One-Quarter of People with Diabetes in the U.S. Ration Their Insulin."

142 **Pharmaceutical companies charge**: "Ways and Means Committee Releases Report on International Drug Pricing," Ways and Means Committee.

142 **In the United Kingdom**: Gross et al., "International Pharmaceutical Spending Controls: France, Germany, Sweden, and the United Kingdom."

143 **Because highly educated people**: Cutler and Ly; Young, "The Economic Impact of Brain Drain."

143 **per capita than in other wealthy**: Kaiser Family Foundation, "The U.S. Has Fewer Physicians and Hospital Beds per Capita Than Italy and Other Countries Overwhelmed by COVID-19."

143 **physicians do in other countries**: US National Institutes of Health, "NIH-Funded Studies Show Stents and Surgery No Better than Medication, Lifestyle Changes at Reducing Cardiac Events."

144 **companies that wanted to earn**: Finkelstein, "The Aggregate Effects of Health Insurance: Evidence from the Introduction of Medicare."

144 **"signed deals"**: Gallagher, "Coronavirus Vaccine: UK Government Signs Deals for 90 Million Doses."

144 **deliverable in December**: "Pfizer and BioNTech Announce an Agreement with U.S.

Government for up to 600 Million Doses of mRNA-based Vaccine Candidate against SARS-CoV-2," *Business Wire*.

144 **In the face of:** Pérez-Peña, "How the Vaccine Rollout Will Compare in Britain, Canada and the U.S."

145 **was diagnosed on April 15:** World Health Organization, "Influenza-like Illness in the United States and Mexico."

145 **was approved in November:** US Centers for Disease Control and Prevention, "The 2009 H1N1 Pandemic: Summary Highlights, April 2009-April 2010."

145 **baked into the US:** Silverman, "Financing and Scaling Innovation for the COVID Fight: A Closer Look at Demand-Side Incentives for a Vaccine."

145 **In the late 1940s:** Cutler, *Your Money or Your Life*; Mampuya, "Cardiac Rehabilitation Past, Present and Future: An Overview."

145 **Coronary angiography:** Cutler, *Your Money or Your Life*; Aquilina et al., "Normal Adult Coronary Angiography."

145 **Fledgling efforts:** Cutler, *Your Money or Your Life*; Melly et al., "Fifty Years of Coronary Artery Bypass Grafting."

145 **In the early 1980s, physicians:** Cutler, *Your Money or Your Life*; Barton et al., "Balloon Angioplasty—The Legacy of Andreas Grüntzig, M.D. (1939–1985)."

145 **keep the artery open:** Cutler, *Your Money or Your Life*; Schmidt and Abbott, "Coronary Stents: History, Design, and Construction."

146 **The process of:** Starr, *The Social Transformation of American Medicine*.

146 **Today, there are forty:** "Physician Board Certification Is on the Rise: More Than 900,000 Are Certified in the US," American Board of Medical Specialties.

146 **Merritt Hawkins:** Merritt Hawkins, *2020 Review of Physician and Advanced Practitioner Recruiting Incentives and the Impact of COVID-19*.

146 **spending improved health outcomes:** Cutler, *Your Money or Life*.

146 **far less often than in the US:** Harding, "Heart Stents Used Twice as Often in U.S. vs. Canada"; Tu et al., "Use of Cardiac Procedures and Outcomes in Elderly Patients with Myocardial Infarction in the United States and Canada."

146 **telemedicine became ubiquitous:** Mehrotra et al., "The Impact of the COVID-19 Pandemic on Outpatient Visits: A Rebound Emerges."

147 **only some Medicaid patients:** Paradise, "Data Note: A Large Majority of Physicians Participate in Medicaid."

147 **needed to cut spending:** "Oil Crisis of the 1970s," Energy Education.

147 **"usual, customary":** HealthCare.gov, "UCR (Usual, Customary, and Reasonable)."

147 **in the private sector:** Chapin, "Why Insurance Companies Control Your Medical Care."

148 **In single-payer countries:** Haviland et al., "Consumer-Directed Plans Could Cut Health Costs Sharply, but Also Discourage Preventive Care."

148 **One quarter of privately insured:** Claxton et al., *Employer Health Benefits: KFF 2020 Annual Survey*.

148 **The hope is that people:** Manning et al., "Health Insurance and the Demand for Medical Care: Evidence from a Randomized Experiment."

148 **cholesterol (which are extremely cost effective):** Brot-Goldberg et al., "What Does a Deductible Do? The Impact of Cost-Sharing on Health Care Prices, Quantities, and Spending Dynamics."

149 **Another rationing:** Healthcare.gov, "Preauthorization."

150 **Travel to China:** "Partly False Claim: President Trump Signed Executive Order 13769, Temporarily Barring Foreigners from Entering the U.S. If They Had Been to China," Reuters.

150 **However, the Centers:** Willman, "Contamination at CDC Lab Delayed Rollout of Coronavirus Tests."

150 **Fixing this took weeks:** Lopez, "Why America's Coronavirus Testing Barely Improved in April."

150 **"The idea of anybody":** "Canada Shows How Easy Virus Testing Can Be," ResetEra.

150 **Treating people who:** Lagu et al., "Why Don't Hospitals Have Enough Masks? Because Coronavirus Broke the Market."

150 **cancellation of nonessential:** Chopra et al., "How Should U.S. Hospitals Prepare for Coronavirus Disease 2019 (COVID-19)?"

151 **The holdup was:** Ranney et al., "Critical Supply Shortages—The Need for Ventilators and Personal Protective Equipment during the Covid-19 Pandemic."

151 **The federal government neither procured:** Lopez, "Why America Ran out of Protective Masks—and What Can Be Done about It."

151 **how to obtain the necessary PPE:** Lagu et al. "Why Don't Hospitals Have Enough Masks? Because Coronavirus Broke the Market"; Lopez, "Why America Ran out of Protective Masks"; Ranney et al.

151 **situation played out with ventilators:** Kulish et al., "The U.S. Tried to Build a New Fleet of Ventilators. The Mission Failed."

151 **reagents needed to test people:** Pfeiffer et al., "Despite Early Warnings, U.S. Took Months to Expand Swab Production for COVID-19 Test"; Lopez, "Why America's Coronavirus Testing Barely Improved in April."

151 **"Trump would likely have":** Baccini et al., "The COVID-19 Pandemic and the 2020 U.S. Presidential Election."

151 **"Given the pre-existing conditions":** Leonard and Howitt, "Katrina as Prelude: Preparing for and Responding to Katrina-Class Disturbances in the United States—Testimony to U.S. Senate Committee, March 8, 2006."

152 **Joan of Arc:** "Joan of Arc (c. 1412–1431)," Biography.com.

152 **Herbert Hoover:** Kosar, "The Executive Branch's Response to the Flood of 1927."

152 **"First, agencies develop":** Leonard, "Command Under Attack: What We've Learned since 9/11 about Managing Crises."

152 **No one who:** Gates et al., "The Initial Response to the Boston Marathon Bombing: Lessons Learned to Prepare for the Next Disaster."

153 **The state of Massachusetts:** Commonwealth of Massachusetts, "Governor's FY2020 Budget Recommendation: Appropriation for Department of Public Health."

153 **budget of nearly $14 billion:** McCluskey, "Partners HealthCare Generates $14 Billion in Revenue."

153 **that works in Haiti and Lesotho:** Wallace-Wells, "Can Coronavirus Contact Tracing Survive Reopening?"

153 **While US medical spending:** Weber et al., "Hollowed-Out Public Health System Faces More Cuts amid Virus."

153 **outspends the US:** Source data from Chetty et al., "The Association between Income and Life Expectancy in the United States."

154 **come from public health:** "Ten Great Public Health Achievements—United States, 1900–1999," *JAMA.*

154 **including new vaccines:** "Impact of Vaccines Universally Recommended for Children—United States, 1900–1998," *JAMA.*

154 **advances in water:** Cutler and Miller, "The Role of Public Health Improvements in Health Advances: The 20th Century United States."

154 **and food safety:** US Centers for Disease Control and Prevention, "Safer and Healthier Foods."

154 **safer cars and roads:** US Centers for Disease Control and Prevention, "Motor-vehicle safety: a 20th century public health achievement."

154 **and reduced tobacco use:** US Centers for Disease Control and Prevention, "Motor-Vehicle Safety: A 20th Century Public Health Achievement."

154 **and spend less overall:** Cutler et al., "Explaining the Slowdown in Medical Spending Growth among the Elderly, 1999–2012."

154 **A good health system:** Daschle et al., *Critical: What We Can Do about the Health-Care Crisis.*

154 **fewer than four hundred geriatricians:** Petriceks et al., "Trends in Geriatrics Graduate Medical Education Programs and Positions, 2001 to 2018."

155 **Reed and Louis Pasteur:** "Louis Pasteur," *Encyclopædia Britannica Online.*

155 **exclusively on medical insurance:** Lubrano, "The World Has Suffered through Other Deadly Pandemics. But the Response to Coronavirus Is Unprecedented."

155 **mostly contained to Asia:** World Health Organization Global Influenza Program Surveillance Network, "Evolution of H5N1 Avian Influenza Viruses in Asia."

155 **The Obama administration got lucky:** McNeil, "U.S. Reaction to Swine Flu: Apt and Lucky."

156 **the MERS outbreak:** Oh et al., "Middle East Respiratory Syndrome: What We Learned from the 2015 Outbreak in the Republic of Korea."

156 **the Ebola outbreak:** US Centers for Disease Control and Prevention, "2014–2016 Ebola Outbreak in West Africa."

156 **Bill Gates of Microsoft fame:** Gates, "The Next Outbreak? We're Not Ready."

156 **Reflecting their experiences:** US Centers for Disease Control and Prevention, *National Strategy for Pandemic Influenza. Homeland Security Council*; Pandemic Prediction and Forecasting Science and Technology Working Group of the National Science and Technology Council, *Towards Epidemic Prediction: Federal Efforts and Opportunities in Outbreak Modeling*.

156 **a church service:** Sang-hun, "Shadowy Church Is at Center of Coronavirus Outbreak in South Korea."

156 **South Korea moved immediately:** Thompson, "What's Behind South Korea's COVID-19 Exceptionalism?

156 **the population of Daegu:** Martin and Yoon, "South Korea Widens Testing in Daegu as It Steps Up War on Coronavirus."

156 **Countries with notable success:** Bremmer, "The Best Global Responses to COVID-19 Pandemic."

156 **The East Asian countries:** LeDuc and Barry, "SARS, the First Pandemic of the 21st Century."

157 **Soldiers' Home:** Hamm, "Holyoke, Chelsea Soldiers' Homes Receive Coronavirus Vaccine."

157 **The home serves:** Commonwealth of Massachusetts, "Soldiers' Home in Holyoke."

157 **not adequately trained:** Jorgenson, "Holyoke Soldiers' Home, Site of Deadly Outbreak, Dealt with Systemic Issues for Years, Staffers and Union Say."

157 **Over the next week:** Associated Press, "2 Charged for Handling of Virus Outbreak at Veterans Home."

158 **"total pandemonium":** "Holyoke Soldiers' Home," *New England Journal of Medicine*.

158 **From late March:** Asiamah, "State: Deaths at Soldiers' Home in Holyoke Reaches 94, Covid-19 Retesting Shows Improvement."

158 **COVID-19, as did eighty-three employees:** Connors, "Management Change, Fewer Residents Eyed for Soldiers' Home."

158 **Retribution was swift:** Barry, "Independent Report on Holyoke Soldiers' Home COVID-19 Crisis Paints Early Decisions by Superintendent Bennett Walsh as 'a Catastrophe'."

158 **He had a distinguished:** Barry, "Former Holyoke Soldiers' Home Superintendent Bennett Walsh, Medical Director David Clinton Arraigned on Charges Linked to COVID-19 Outbreak."

158 **But the fault lies as:** "More Than One-Third of U.S. Coronavirus Deaths are in Nursing Homes," *The New York Times*.

158 **Running a nursing home:** Quadagno and Stahl, "Challenges in Nursing Home Care: A Research Agenda."

158–59 **about a third as much:** Sudo, "Long-Term Care Executive Salaries Rose 2.8% in 2019."

159 **attracting top-tier talent?:** Battenfeld, "Coronavirus Veteran Deaths in Holyoke Put Federal Heat on Charlie Baker."

159 **In Massachusetts, the share is . . . with high ratings:** Brown, "Nursing Homes Account for More Than Half of Total COVID-19 Deaths in Massachusetts."

159 **"49 percent":** Chen et al., "Nursing Home Staff Networks and COVID-19."

160 **"that also made pickups":** Tully et al., "70 Died at a Nursing Home as Body Bags Piled Up. This Is What Went Wrong."

160 **In cities with high rates:** Barnett et al., "Mortality, Admissions, and Patient Census at SNFs in 3 US Cities During the COVID-19 Pandemic."

160 **In Massachusetts, Medicaid payments:** "Nursing Home Costs and Ways to Pay," Care.com.

161 **Anyone with the virus:** Stack, "A Sudden Coronavirus Surge Brought Out Singapore's Dark Side."

161 **is where an outbreak occurred:** Stack.

161 **Foreign workers:** Beech, "Singapore Seemed to Have Coronavirus Under Control, until Cases Doubled."

163 **technical expertise and moral judgment:** "Why Pandemic Disease and War Are So Similar," *Business Insider*.

163 **By contrast, some:** "New Zealand," Worldometer.

163 **Containment is easier:** Roy, "'Can I Really Do This?' New Zealand's Ashley Bloomfield Reveals Self-Doubts at Height of Covid."

163 **first national leader to do so:** Meixler, "New Zealand's Jacinda Ardern Made History by Bringing Baby Neve to the U.N."

163 **Together they form:** World Health Organization, "New Zealand Takes Early and Hard Action to Tackle COVID-19."

163 **handwashing and social distancing:** Jefferies et al., "COVID-19 in New Zealand and the Impact of the National Response: A Descriptive Epidemiological Study."

164 **Between March 16:** Somerville, "New Zealand's Covid Response: Why Early Lockdown and Stringent Quarantine Kept Cases Down to Fewer Than 2,000."

164 **By March 25:** "New Zealand: Government Declares State of Emergency March 25 /Update 5," GardaWorld.

164 **New Zealand's Parliament:** New Zealand Government, "Managed Isolation and Quarantine"; "Focusing On Preservatives: How They Keep Food Fresh," ScienceDaily.

164 **The country did things:** "Coronavirus: How New Zealand Relied on Science and Empathy," BBC News.

164 **The number of new cases:** New Zealand Government, Ministry of Health, "COVID-19: Current Cases."

164 **By April 28:** New Zealand Parliament, "Daily Progress for Tuesday, 28 April 2020."

164 **During the first week:** New Zealand Government, "Alert Level 2."

165 **By the end of the year:** New Zealand Government, Ministry of Health.

165 **Moreover, the overall:** New Zealand Government, "About the Alert System."

165 **The final tribute:** "New Zealand Election: Jacinda Ardern's Labour Party Scores Landslide Win," BBC News.

165 **"we do consider":** "Jacinda Ardern: 'Tooth Fairy and Easter Bunny Are Essential Workers,'" BBC News.

165 **than most of her peers:** Burrows, "Ardern Responds to Fears Politicians Could Become COVID-19 'Super-Spreaders' during Election Campaign."

166 **had done poorly with SARS:** Overby et al., "The China Syndrome: The Impact of the SARS Epidemic in Southeast Asia."

166 **vice president of Taiwan:** Hernández and Horton, "Taiwan's Weapon against Coronavirus: An Epidemiologist as Vice President."

166 **Singapore also underperformed:** Sim, "From Sars to Covid-19, What Lessons Has Singapore Learned?"

166 **Germany and the Canadian province:** Ellyatt, "German Covid Cases are Rising Exponentially"; British Columbia Centre for Disease Control, "BC COVID-19 Cases."

166 **Neither Merkel nor:** "Why Germany's Low COVID-19 Death Rate Might Be a Mirage," CBC News.

166 **On March 22:** Posaner, "Germany's Merkel Bans Meetings of More Than 2 People to Slow Coronavirus."

167 **Germany had a testing system:** "Combating the Coronavirus Pandemic: Bosch Develops Rapid Test for COVID-19," Bosch Global.

167 **Robert Koch Institute:** Robert Koch Institute, "Navigation and Service."

167 **spending growth has slowed:** McWilliams et al., "Medicare Spending after 3 Years of the Medicare Shared Savings Program."

168 **The COVID pandemic created:** Goldstein, "Trump Administration Says It Will Pay Hospitals for Treating Uninsured Covid-19 Patients."

CHAPTER 6: DO ROBOTS SPREAD DISEASE?

169 **In February 2020:** US Bureau of Labor Statistics, "Databases, Tables & Calculators by Subject."

169 **American GDP shrank:** US Department of Commerce, Bureau of Economic Analysis, "Gross Domestic Product, Second Quarter

2020 (Advance Estimate) and Annual Update."

169 **In the UK:** UK Office for National Statistics, "GDP First Quarterly Estimate, UK."

169 **medieval serfs:** Routt, "The Economic Impact of the Black Death."

169 **Neither cholera nor yellow fever:** Davis, "An Annual Index of U. S. Industrial Production, 1790–1915."

169 **"substitute for the routine":** Autor, Katz, and Kearney, "The Polarization of the U.S. Labor Market."

171 **The Black Death wiped away:** Routt.

171 **"status quo":** Broadberry et al., *British Economic Growth, 1270–1870,* 207.

171 **"the economy":** Broadberry et al., 207.

171 **The price paid:** Data from Munro, "My Research Data Online: Spreadsheets, Tables, Publications."

172 **Individual barons:** Routt.

172 **"the landowners could not be united":** Domar, "The Causes of Slavery or Serfdom: A Hypothesis."

172 **"the Black Death set into motion":** Voigtländer and Voth, "How the West 'Invented' Fertility Restriction."

172 **The waves of war and conquest:** Meier, "The 'Justinianic Plague': The Economic Consequences of the Pandemic in the Eastern Roman Empire and Its Cultural and Religious Effects."

172 **increasing agricultural wealth:** Routt.

173 **Italy's cities were devastated:** Pamuk, "The Black Death and the Origins of the 'Great Divergence' across Europe, 1300–1600."

173 **"between 1500 and 1800":** Scott, *How the Old World Ended: The Anglo-Dutch-American Revolution 1500–1800.*

173 **The last major appearance:** Morrill, "Great Plague of London."

174 **"to the Old Exchange":** Pepys, "Friday 14 July 1665."

174 **"it is a wonder":** Pepys, "Sunday 3 September 1665."

174 **"durst not wear":** Pepys, "Sunday 3 September 1665."

174 **village of Eyam:** McKenna, "Eyam Plague: The Village of the Damned."

174 **cotton takes better:** Metcalfe, "The History of Woolsorters' Disease: A Yorkshire Beginning with an International Future?," 491–92.

174–75 **London's economic vulnerability:** Cummins, Kelly, and Ó Gráda, "Living Standards and Plague in London, 1560–1665."

175 **Pepys's own income:** Bryant, "Samuel Pepys: English Diarist and Naval Administrator."

175 **incomes had stagnated:** Crafts and Mills, "From Malthus to Solow: How Did the Malthusian Economy Really Evolve?"

176 **The first Robert Peel:** Leonard, "Sir Robert Peel—Arch Pragmatist or Tory Traitor?"

176 **one of an estimated ten:** "Who Wants to Be a Millionaire?," *The Guardian.*

177 **"no man in his senses":** Fitton, *The Arkwrights: Spinners of Fortune,* 152.

177 **The petitioners then turned:** Our understanding of these events is due entirely to a remarkably fine unpublished PhD dissertation by Carla Sue Patterson on the path to better health in British factories.

177 **"wide river of medical learning":** Guthrie, "The Influence of the Leyden School upon Scottish Medicine."

177 **Percival followed that flood:** Waterston, Shearer, and Royal Society of Edinburgh, *Former Fellows of the Royal Society of Edinburgh, 1783–2002,* 728.

177 **friends with Benjamin Franklin:** "Benjamin Franklin and the Manchester Lit & Phil," Manchester Literary and Philosophical Society.

177 **coined the term:** Waddington, "The Development of Medical Ethics—a Sociological Analysis," 36.

177 **He wrote scientific papers:** Waddington, 39.

177 **tested the water quality throughout:** Percival, "Experiments and Observations on the Waters of Buxton and Matlock, in Derbyshire, by Thomas Percival, of Manchester, M. D. and F. R. S."

177 **"great towns are":** Percival and Price, "V. Observations on the State of Population in Manchester, and Other Adjacent Places," 324.

177 **He also worked to improve:** Pickstone, "Thomas Percival and the Production of Medical Ethics."

177 **Percival studied:** Percival, *The Works, Literary, Moral, and Medical, of Thomas Percival, M.D.*, 297.

177 **"supported, diffused and aggravated":** Percival, *The Works.*

178 **In 1802, Peel:** Schregle, "Labor Law."

178 **ardent defense of the slave trade:** UK Parliament, "Petition from Manufacturers and Merchants of Manchester against the Foreign Slave Trade Abolition Bill."

178–79 **George Stigler . . . from outsiders:** Stigler, "The Theory of Economic Regulation."

179 **The US's Federal Employers' Liability Act:** Buford, "Assumption of Risk under the Federal Employers' Liability Act."

179 **"child workers received higher":** Fishback and Kantor, "'Square Deal' or Raw Deal? Market Compensation for Workplace Disamenities, 1884-1903."

179 **a poster recruiting young women:** National Park Service, "The Mill Girls of Lowell."

179 **The second Robert Peel's son:** Gash, "Robert Peel."

180 **The switch to cotton fabric:** Metcalfe, 491–92.

180 **Chicago's beef barons:** Specht, "The Price of Plenty: How Beef Changed America."

181 **The ergot fungus:** Schumann and Uppala, "Ergot of Rye."

181 **Nineteenth-century Americans:** Blum, "How Henry Heinz Used Ketchup to Improve Food Safety."

181 *Red River*: Hawks, dir., *Red River.*

181 *Sister Carrie*: Dreiser, *Sister Carrie.*

181 **Daniel Drew:** White, *The Book of Daniel Drew: A Glimpse of the Fisk-Gould-Tweed Régime from the Inside*, 44-54.

182 **Americans eat 50 . . . than salted beef:** Davis and Lin, *Factors Affecting U.S. Pork Consumption.*

182 **John Wayne's cinematic cattle drives:** Rydell, dir., *The Cowboys.*

182 **Gustavus Swift:** "Gustavus Swift." *Encyclopædia Britannica Online.*

182 **sophisticated urban societies:** "Gustavus Swift." *Encyclopædia Britannica Online.*

183 **French Academy of Sciences:** Farley and Geison, "Science, Politics and Spontaneous Generation in Nineteenth-Century France: The Pasteur-Pouchet Debate."

183 **Pasteur correctly grasped:** Ullmann, "Louis Pasteur."

184 **Nabisco's iconic bakery:** Grove, "Cookie Capital in the Universe of Cookie-Making, the Chicago Area Ranks as a Sweet, Hot, Big, Gooey Chocolate Chip."

184 **Upton Sinclair:** Lohnes, "The Jungle."

184 **"I aimed for the public's":** Beeston, "Book Club: The Jungle by Upton Sinclair."

184 **the Pure Food and Drug Act:** Lopez, "The War on Drugs, Explained."

184 **Yet even in 2008:** "Three More Hospitalised in Milk Scandal," *The Age.*

185 **the average textile mill:** Ronderos, *Stabilization of the U.S. Manufacturing Sector and Its Impact on Industrial Space*, 29.

185 **570 square feet:** Ronderos.

185 **675,000 people died:** Johnson and Mueller, "Updating the Accounts: Global Mortality of the 1918–1920 'Spanish' Influenza Pandemic," 111.

185 **It is estimated that one third:** Johnson and Mueller, 105.

185–86 **cloth masks became ubiquitous:** Strochlic and Champine, "How Some Cities 'Flattened the Curve' during the 1918 Flu Pandemic."

186 **François Velde:** Velde, "What Happened to the US Economy During the 1918 Influenza Pandemic? A View Through High-Frequency Data."

186 **In 1910, 31 percent:** Leon, "The Life of American Workers in 1915."

186 **In 2015, farmers:** Leon.

186 **44 percent:** Leon.

186 **12.5 percent by 2015:** Leon.

186 **9 percent:** US Bureau of Labor Statistics, "Table A-14. Unemployed Persons by Industry and Class of Worker, Not Seasonally Adjusted."

186 **sales by Woolworth:** Velde, 9.

187 **Spending on basic needs:** Karlamangla, "With Coronavirus Spreading in L.A. County Supermarkets, Here Are Some Tips for Shopping Safely."

187 **In 1910, only 14 percent:** Leon.

188 **Stanley Jevons:** Jevons, *The Coal Question: An Inquiry Concerning the Progress of the Nation, and the Probable Exhaustion of Our Coal-Mines.*

189 **an explosion of manufacturing:** *"Out-Producing the Enemy": American Production During WWII.*

189 **16.5 million:** Livingston, "Magnitude of Transition From War Production."

189 **America's manufacturing labor force:** Ghanbari and McCall, "Current Employment Statistics Survey: 100 Years of Employment, Hours, and Earnings."

189 **total nonfarm employment:** Data from US Bureau of Labor Statistics, "All Employees, Manufacturing/All Employees, Total Nonfarm."

190 **fewer than one:** Rhodes, "Manufacturing: Statistics and Policy," 3.

190 **below 12 percent:** "France Payroll Employment in Manufacturing," Trading Economics.

190 **The total number of Americans:** Data from US Bureau of Labor Statistics, "All Employees, Service-Providing."

190 **Between 1945 and 2004:** Data from US Bureau of Labor Statistics, "All Employees, Retail Trade."

190 **leisure and hospitality:** Data from US Bureau of Labor Statistics, "All Employees, Leisure and Hospitality."

190 **(12.3 million):** Data from US Bureau of Labor Statistics, "All Employees, Food Services and Drinking Places."

190 **(12.8 million):** Data from US Bureau of Labor Statistics, "All Employees, Manufacturing."

191 **21.5 million workers:** Data from US Bureau of Labor Statistics, "All Employees, Professional and Business Services."

191 **24.5 million workers:** Data from US Bureau of Labor Statistics, "All Employees, Education and Health Services."

191 **IBM's famed supercomputer:** Chen, "IBM's Watson Gave Unsafe Recommendations for Treating Cancer."

192 **creative economy:** Florida, *Rise of the Creative Class.*

192 **7.75 million Americans:** Data from US Bureau of Labor Statistics, "All Employees, Construction."

192 **1.181 million to 1.178 million:** Data from US Bureau of Labor Statistics, "All Employees, Warehousing and Storage."

192 **1.5 million trucking-related jobs:** Data from US Bureau of Labor Statistics, "All Employees, Truck Transportation."

193 **Harry's Bar in Florence:** "Harry's Bar, Florence, Italy," The Martini Hour.

193 **6.5 million in 1990 to 12.3 million:** Data from US Bureau of Labor Statistics, "All Employees, Food Services and Drinking Places."

193 **number of bartenders:** Data from US Bureau of Labor Statistics, "Employed Full Time: Wage and Salary Workers: Bartenders Occupations: 16 Years and Over."

193 **declining alcohol consumption:** Chaudhuri and Maloney, "As Americans Drink Less Alcohol, Booze Makers Look Beyond the Barrel."

193 **waiters and waitresses increased by 28 percent:** Data from US Bureau of Labor Statistics, "Employed Full Time: Wage and Salary Workers: Waiters and Waitresses Occupations: 16 Years and Over."

194 **As of April 1, 2020, one half:** Bartik et al., "How Are Small Businesses Adjusting to COVID-19?"

195 **We estimated that:** Glaeser, Gorback, and Redding, "JUE Insight: How Much Does COVID-19 Increase with Mobility? Evidence from New York and Four Other U.S. Cities."

195 **better-educated industries:** Glaeser, Gorback, and Redding, "JUE Insight: How Much Does COVID-19 Increase with Mobility? Evidence from New York and Four Other U.S. Cities."

195 **In April, many small business:** Bartik et al., "How Are Small Businesses Adjusting?"

195 allocated **$787 billion:** "Biden Says Some Waste Inevitable Part of Stimulus," Reuters.

195 **The Obama administration deliberately:** Grunwald, "Five Myths about Obama's Stimulus."

195 **only sixty-one senators:** Rogers, "Senate Passes $787 Billion Stimulus Bill."

195 **In 2020, the Coronavirus Aid, Relief:** Carney, "Obstacles Mount for Deal on next Coronavirus Bill."

195 **$649 billion to firms:** "The Paycheck Protection Program Is in Dire Need of Reform," *The Washington Post.*

196 **The first wave:** Bartik et al., "The Targeting and Impact of Paycheck Protection Program Loans to Small Businesses."

196 **Their self-assessed probability:** Bartik et al., "The Targeting and Impact."

196 **the overall unemployment:** US Bureau of Labor Statistics, "Unemployment Rate."

196 **The unemployment rate among:** US Bureau of Labor Statistics, "The Employment Situation—July 2020," 28.

197 **"fear sparked by":** "Donald Trump Ron DeSantis Press Conference Transcript."

197 **33,000 cases and 1,200 deaths:** Ross, "Florida Coronavirus Deaths Surpass 1,200, Cases Pass 33,000."

197 **Nearly a third of the state's:** US Bureau of Labor Statistics, "All Employees: Leisure and Hospitality in Florida."

197 **According to cell-phone data:** Glaeser et al., "Learning from Deregulation: The Asymmetric Impact of Lockdown and Reopening on Risky Behavior During COVID-19."

197 **One striking piece of research:** Sheridan et al., "Social Distancing Laws Cause Only Small Losses of Economic Activity during the COVID-19 Pandemic in Scandinavia."

197 **In Brazil, there was also little link:** Chauvin, Glaeser, and Kestelman, "Regulation and Mobility in Brazil."

197 **"Florida's done better":** "Donald Trump Ron DeSantis Press Conference Transcript," Rev.

198 **Ardern and Bloomfield did:** Cheng, "Covid 19 Coronavirus: Prime Minister Jacinda Ardern's D-Day Decision Already Made for Her."

198 **Visits to sit-down restaurants:** Glaeser et al., "Learning from Deregulation."

198 **100,000 COVID-19 cases by June 22:** "Florida Coronavirus Map and Case Count," *The New York Times*.

198 **on June 26:** Tisch et al., "Florida Suspends Drinking at Bars."

198 **grown to 250,000:** "Florida Coronavirus Map and Case Count."

198 **on July 6:** Selig and Vazquez, "Miami-Dade Closing Indoor Dining amid Coronavirus Spike; Gyms Can Now Stay Open."

198 **half a million Floridians:** "Florida Coronavirus Map and Case Count."

198 **Two weeks after that date:** "Florida Coronavirus Map and Case Count."

199 **the economist Benjamin Chinitz:** Chinitz, "Contrasts in Agglomeration: New York and Pittsburgh."

199 **In the 1950s, New York's:** Glaeser, *Triumph of the City*, 41.

199 **Mrs. Maisel's:** Sherman-Palladino, exec. prod. and dir., *The Marvelous Mrs. Maisel*.

199 **Samuel Goldwyn:** Amerman, "Sandy Weill 1933–."

200 **Cities with access to coal:** Glaeser, Kerr, and Kerr, "Entrepreneurship and Urban Growth: An Empirical Assessment with Historical Mines."

200 **"averaged 18.9 percent":** Decker et al., "The Role of Entrepreneurship in US Job Creation and Economic Dynamism."

200 **"declined from an average of 18.9 percent":** Decker et al. "The Secular Decline in Business Dynamism in the U.S."

200 **"regulations hamper the creation":** Klapper, Laeven, and Rajan, "Entry Regulation as a Barrier to Entrepreneurship."

200 **"rising federal regulation":** Goldschlag and Tabarrok, "Is Regulation to Blame for the Decline in American Entrepreneurship?"

200 **"weights and measures inspection":** City of Boston, *Licenses & Permits for Retail Shop Owners*.

200 **The prospective small business owner:** City of New York, "NYC Business: Get Help with Licenses and Permits."

201 **the share of the population:** US Department of the Treasury Office of Economic Policy, Council of Economic Advisers, and US Department of Labor, *Occupational Licensing: A Framework for Policymakers*; Kleiner and Krueger, "The Prevalence and Effects of Occupational Licensing."

201 **That policy entrenches:** Institute of Medicine, *The Future of Nursing: Leading Change, Advancing Health*.

201 **One proposal:** Glaeser and Sunstein, "Regulatory Review for the States."

201 **Both Democratic and Republican:** Cooper, *The War against Regulation: From Jimmy Carter to George W. Bush*; Institute of Medicine.

202 **Devens Enterprise Commission:** Bump, *Official Audit Report: Devens Enterprise Commission.*

202 **"Devens Enterprise Zone":** "Blockbuster Project Proof of Devons Lure." *The Sun* (Lowell).

204 **"Economic Possibilities of Our Grandchildren":** Keynes, "Economic Possibilities for Our Grandchildren (1930)."

204 **especially among prime-aged men:** Gulliford, "Research Indicates That Men Are More Likely to Suffer Adverse Health Consequences as a Result of Being Unemployed Than Women."

204 **five hours of television:** Krantz-Kent, "Television, Capturing America's Attention at Prime Time and Beyond."

CHAPTER 7: WHAT IS THE FUTURE OF DOWNTOWN?

207 **"new production system":** Toffler, *The Third Wave,* 210.

207 **"We need to be one Yahoo!":** Goudreau, "Back To the Stone Age?"

207 **Google told its workers:** Friedman, "Google Employees Will Work from Home until Summer 2021."

207 **In one survey:** Bartik et al., "What Jobs Are Being Done at Home During the Covid-19 Crisis?"

207 **Natalia Emanuel and Emma Harrington:** Harrington and Emanuel, "'Working' Remotely? Selection, Treatment, and Market Provision of Remote Work."

208 **"at the time of the transition":** Harrington and Emanuel.

209 **Paul Krugman formulated:** Krugman, "Increasing Returns and Economic Geography."

211 **"skyscrapers are constructed":** Barr, *Building the Skyline: The Birth and Growth of Manhattan's Skyscrapers.*

211 **built on mud:** Barr.

211 **New York's stock exchange:** "New York Stock Exchange," *Encyclopædia Britannica Online.*

211 **dock builder:** Hershkowitz, "Some Aspects of the New York Jewish Merchant and Community, 1654–1820."

211 **Joseph Paxton:** "Sir Joseph Paxton," *Encyclopædia Britannica Online.*

211 **Victor Baltard:** Ardagh, "Paris: The Halles."

211 **William Le Baron Jenney:** "William Le Baron Jenney," *Encyclopædia Britannica Online.*

211 **Elisha Otis:** "Elisha Otis." *Encyclopædia Britannica Online.*

212 **thirty more years:** "William Le Baron Jenney."

212 **Abraham Brower:** "New York City Transit—History and Chronology," World-Wide Business Centres.

212 **John Stephenson:** "Death of John Stephenson; the Builder of Street Cars Passes Away Suddenly," *The New York Times.*

212 **George Stephenson:** "George Stephenson," *Encyclopædia Britannica Online.*

213 **"owner of large tracts":** Carman, *The Street Surface Railway Franchises of New York City,* 23.

213 **"as well as being":** Carman, 23.

213 **Cornelius Vanderbilt:** "Cornelius Vanderbilt," *Encyclopædia Britannica Online.*

214 **sold for $270,000:** Rohde, "Why Investors Should Consider Chicago's Real Estate Market in 2021."

214 **Boston was $494,000:** Andreevska, "Where Should You Invest in the Boston Real Estate Market?"

214 **$985,000 in San Francisco:** National Association of Realtors, "Metro Home Prices Rise in 96% of Metro Areas in First Quarter of 2020."

215 **In 1949, Americans allocated:** Bigelow and Borchers, *Major Uses of Land in the United States, 2012.*

215 **Nathaniel Baum-Snow:** Baum-Snow, "Did Highways Cause Suburbanization?," 774.

215 **18.4 cents per gallon:** Peter G. Peterson Foundation, "The Highway Trust Fund Explained."

216 **increased from 44 to 62 percent:** "Homeownership—Past, Present, and Future," *U.S. Housing Market Conditions.*

216 **Eighty-two percent:** Hermann, "What Accounts for Recent Growth in Homeowner Households?"

216 **Raj Chetty:** Chetty et al., "Where Is the Land of Opportunity? The Geography of Intergenerational Mobility in the United States."

216 Chicago's greatest nineteenth-century industry: Wade, "Meatpacking."

217 more than 68 percent: Kneebone, "Job Sprawl
Revisited: The Changing Geography of Metropolitan Employment."

217 garment sector: Glaeser, *Triumph of the City*,
41.

217 140,000 workers making women's outerwear: Hum, "Mapping Global Production in
New York City's Garment Industry: The Role
of Sunset Park, Brooklyn's Immigrant Economy."

217 Ralph Lauren: "Ralph Lauren," Biography.

219 Alvin Toffler: Schneider, "Alvin Toffler, Author of 'Future Shock,' Dies at 87."

219 "dizzying disorientation": Toffler, *Future
Shock*, 11.

219 "the only remedy for the phenomenon of future shock": Toffler, "The Future as a Way of
Life."

219 "trend towards residential renting": Toffler,
Future Shock, 64.

219 56 percent in 1940 to 37 percent in 1970: Data
from www2.census.gov/programs-surveys/demo
/tables/geographic-mobility/time-series/historic
/tab-a-1.xls.

219 "breeding a new race of nomads": Toffler, *Future Shock*, 75.

220 "the death of industrialism": Toffler, *The Third
Wave*, 18.

220 "information age, electronic era, or global
village": Toffler, *The Third Wave*, 25.

220 "will topple bureaucracies": Toffler, *The Third
Wave*, 27.

220 "The Third Wave alters": Toffler, *The Third
Wave*, 312.

220 "the new allure of small-city and rural life":
Toffler, *The Third Wave*, 219.

220 "city dwellers by the millions": Toffler, *The
Third Wave*, 306.

221 rose from 74 percent to 79 percent: World
Bank, "Urban Population—United States";
World Bank, "Rural Population—United
States."

221 grew by almost 100 million: World Bank,
"Urban Population—United States"; World
Bank, "Rural Population—United States."

221 rural population actually fell: World Bank,
"Rural Population—United Kingdom."

221 "electronic cottages": Toffler, *The Third Wave*,
213.

221 "as there is no logical reason": Cox, "The Future of Work Looks like Staying Out of the
Office."

221 "a return to cottage industry": Toffler, *The
Third Wave*, 210.

221 "number of workers who actually": Toffler,
The Third Wave, 211.

221 "reduce energy requirements": Toffler, *The
Third Wave*, 221.

221 "'low-abstraction' office workers": Toffler,
The Third Wave, 213.

221 "What happens to society": Toffler, *The Third
Wave*, 222.

222 "our biggest factories": Toffler, *The Third
Wave*, 210.

222 "if as few as 10": Toffler, *The Third Wave*,
223.

222 more than one tenth: Indeed, Amsterdam
today would be quite recognizable not only to
a reader of Toffler from 1980 but also a reader
of Adam Smith from 1780. European Commission, "Eurostat: How Usual Is It to Work
from Home?"

222 "altered almost beyond our recognition": European Commission, "Eurostat: How Usual Is
It to Work from Home?"

222 One 2018 census: Data from https://data
.census.gov/cedsci/table?q=journey%20to
%20work&tid=ACSST1Y2018.S0801
&hidePreview=false.

222 one fifth of workers: US Bureau of Labor Sta-
tistics, "Table 7. Employed Persons Working
on Main Job at Home, Workplace, and Time
Spent Working at Each Location by Class of
Worker, Occupation, and Earnings, 2019
Annual Averages."

222 "spent at least some": Mann and Adkins,
"America's Coming Workplace."

223 "our entire economy": Toffler, *The Third Wave*,
223.

223 from 90 million to 152 million: Data from US
Bureau of Labor Statistics, "All Employees,
Total Nonfarm."

223 "we did get a few things wrong": Fisher,
"Alvin Toffler: The Thought Leader Interview."

223 Late in life: Fisher.

224 **back to global preeminence:** Z/Yen Group and China Development Institute, *The Global Financial Centres Index 20.*

224 **increased by 132 percent:** Data from US Federal Housing Finance Agency, "All-Transactions House Price Index for Los Angeles County, CA."

224 **AnnaLee Saxenian's** *Regional Advantage*: Saxenian, *Regional Advantage: Culture and Competition in Silicon Valley and Route 128, with a New Preface by the Author.*

224 **"can be described":** Toffler, *The Third Wave*, 215.

224 **"put the computer in people's homes":** Toffler, *The Third Wave.*

224 **"'ultrahigh-abstraction' workers":** Toffler, *The Third Wave*, 213.

225 **a recent study showed that chess players:** Künn, Seel, and Zegners, "Cognitive Performance in the Home Office—Evidence from Professional Chess."

225 **"all the subliminal":** Toffler, *The Third Wave*, 213.

225 **the response time:** Battiston, Blanes i Vidal, and Kirchmaier, "Is Distance Dead? Face-to-Face Communication and Productivity in Teams."

226 **Coauthored articles:** Lee et al., "Does Collocation Inform the Impact of Collaboration?"

227 **35 percent of American workers:** US Bureau of Labor Statistics, "One-Quarter of the Employed Teleworked in August 2020 Because of COVID-19 Pandemic."

227 **over 40 percent:** Bloom, "How Working from Home Works Out."

228 **50 million Americans:** Data from US Bureau of Labor Statistics, "Labor Force Statistics from the Current Population Survey: Supplemental Data Measuring the Effects of the Coronavirus (COVID-19) Pandemic on the Labor Market."

228 **In May 2020, 36 out of the 49:** US Bureau of Labor Statistics, "Labor Force Statistics from the Current Population Survey: Supplemental Data Measuring the Effects of the Coronavirus (COVID-19) Pandemic on the Labor Market."

229 **who told the census in December:** Center for Budget and Policy Priorities, "Tracking the

COVID-19 Recession's Effects on Food, Housing, and Employment Hardships."

230 **COVID-19 came to America:** Rabin, "First Patient with Wuhan Coronavirus Is Identified in the U.S."

230 **A single health technology conference:** Becker, "Biogen Conference in Boston Linked to More Than 300,000 COVID-19 Cases."

230 **Stanford economists:** Bloom et al., "Does Working from Home Work? Evidence from a Chinese Experiment."

231 **"remote workers answered":** Harrington and Emanuel.

231 **One quarter of Americans:** Pew Research Center, "Internet/Broadband Fact Sheet."

231 **"prior to the pandemic":** Stanton and Tiwari, "The Housing Consumption of Remote Workers."

232 **The first survey:** Bartik et al., "What Jobs Are Being Done at Home?"

232 **looked at the time path:** This work is ongoing and unpublished at the time of this writing.

233 **"productivity, when measured":** Ford et al., "A Tale of Two Cities: Software Developers Working from Home During the COVID-19 Pandemic."

233 **"the mysteries of the trade":** "In Praise of Boise," *The Economist.*

234 **"on-site representatives":** Harrington and Emanuel.

234 **including the United States:** Mallen, Day, and Green, "Online versus Face-to-Face Conversation: An Examination of Relational and Discourse Variables."

234 **Canada:** Helliwell and Huang, "Comparing the Happiness Effects of Real and On-Line Friends."

234 **China:** Lee et al., "Internet Communication versus Face-to-Face Interaction in Quality of Life."

234 **when groups are randomized:** Mallen, Day, and Green.

235 **People prefer connecting:** Harrington and Emanuel.

235 **Even conflict resolution:** Balliet, "Communication and Cooperation in Social Dilemmas: A Meta-analytic Review."

235 **Most people want more:** Anders and Pallais, "Why Can't We Be Friends?: Theory and Evidence on Friendship Formation."

236 **price growth outpaced income growth:** Himmelberg, *Mayer, and Sinai, Assessing High House Prices: Bubbles, Fundamentals, and Misperceptions.*

236 **Some technology companies:** Haag, "Manhattan Emptied Out During the Pandemic. But Big Tech Is Moving In."

237 **grew by more than seven million:** Data from US Bureau of Labor Statistics, "All Employees, Total Nonfarm."

238 **In about one fourth:** Ryan, "United States Office Outlook—Q3 2020."

239 **Thomas Menino launched:** ECPA Urban Planning, "Case Study: The Boston Waterfront Innovation District."

239 **"cheap and makeshift":** Jacobs, *The Death and Life of Great American Cities,* 397.

CHAPTER 8: THE BATTLE FOR BOYLE HEIGHTS AND THE CLOSING OF THE METROPOLITAN FRONTIER

243 **At 2:35 p.m.:** "New York's Governor and Mayor of New York City Address Concerns of the Damage."

243 **The city had seen its crime rate:** "New York Crime Rates 1960 to 2019," Disaster Center.

244 **Matthew Kahn:** Kahn, "The Death Toll from Natural Disasters: The Role of Income, Geography, and Institutions."

244 **A 2010 earthquake:** Bonnefoy and Lyons, "Why Chile's Latest Big Earthquake Has a Smaller Death Toll."

246 **The Boyle Heights neighborhood:** "Andrew A. Boyle, Namesake of Boyle Heights: An Immigrant's Story," *Boyle Heights History Blog.*

246 **Boyle's daughter:** "William Henry Workman: Founder of Boyle Heights," *Boyle Heights History Blog.*

247 **"churches and public schools":** Spitzzeri, "Sharing History with the Boyle Heights Historical Society."

247 **"who is the father":** *Beautiful Highlands of Los Angeles,* Comprising Boyle Heights, Brooklyn Heights, Euclid Heights, 6.

247 **"Mr. Sing, with his wife":** *Beautiful Highlands of Los Angeles,* 34.

248 **"a well-known surveyor":** *Beautiful Highlands of Los Angeles,* 28.

248 **The volume uses:** "José Adolfo Bernal: An 1899 Booster Pamphlet for Boyle Heights, Part 3," *Boyle Heights History Blog.*

248 **"healthfulness and pleasant location":** *Beautiful Highlands of Los Angeles,* 28.

249 **In 1917:** Ware, "Invisible Walls: An Examination of the Legal Strategy of the Restrictive Covenant Cases."

249 **These covenants held sway:** Silva, "Racial Restrictive Covenants History: Enforcing Neighborhood Segregation in Seattle."

249 **The appeal of restrictive:** Robson, "Public Interest Lawyering & Judicial Politics: Four Cases Worth a Second Look in Williams-Yulee v. The Florida Bar."

250 **After 1921:** Villianatos and Brozen, "Encouraging Diverse Missing-Middle Housing Near Transit."

250 **Even today, areas:** Resseger, "The Impact of Land Use Regulation on Racial Segregation: Evidence from Massachusetts Zoning Borders."

250 **ineligible for federally supported:** Reft, "Segregation in the City of Angels: A 1939 Map of Housing Inequality in L.A."

250 **"class and occupation":** Home Owners' Loan Corporation, "Security Map of Los Angeles County/Area Desription."

250 **"the Federal Government":** Home Owners' Loan Corporation.

250–51 **As Jane Jacobs . . . no-man's-lands:** Jacobs, *The Death and Life of Great American Cities.*

251 **Robert Moses:** Dunlap, "Why Robert Moses Keeps Rising from an Unquiet Grave."

251 **Between 1944 and 1965:** Estrada, "If You Build It, They Will Move: The Los Angeles Freeway System and the Displacement of Mexican East Los Angeles, 1944–1972."

251 **"to construct":** Estrada, 300.

251 **Highways 5, 10, 60, and 101:** Artsy, "Boyle Heights, the Land of Freeways."

252 **"groups like the":** Estrada, 299.

252 **By 2000:** Japanese American National Museum, "Exhibition Timeline: Boyle Heights Project."

252 **Some have guessed:** Avila, "East Side Stories: Freeways and Their Portraits in Chicano Los Angeles."

253 **the HBO film** *Walkout*: Olmos, dir., *Walkout.*

253 **"my memory starts":** Nava, *Julian Nava: My Mexican-American Journey,* 5.

254 **"countless":** Nava, 72.

254 **"said in public":** Nava, 72.

254 **Nava's position:** Nava, 82.

254 **"teaching the students":** Nava, 83.

255 **"the Los Angeles police":** Nava, 82.

255 **"phones were tapped":** Nava, 84.

255 **"sleep in":** Nava, 85.

255 **"the walkouts' greatest accomplishment":** Sahagún, "East L.A., 1968: 'Walkout!' The Day High School Students Helped Ignite the Chicano Power Movement."

255 **"the walkouts actually":** Nava, 85.

256 **"the Brown Berets":** San Francisco University High School, "The Brown Berets: Young Chicano Revolutionaries."

256 **"by the time":** Nava, 96.

257 **Their most standard measure:** Chetty et al., "Where Is the Land of Opportunity?"

257 **On average, the data shows:** Data from The Opportunity Atlas.

258 **Between 1950 and 1970:** US Census Bureau, *1990 Census of Population and Housing, Population and Housing Unit Counts, California.*

258 **The California Supreme Court:** California Department of Fish and Wildlife, "A Summary of the California Environmental Quality Act (CEQA)."

258 **Building in:** Glaeser and Kahn, "The Greenness of Cities: Carbon Dioxide Emissions and Urban Development."

259 **Between 1990 and 2015:** Glaeser, "The Nemeses of Cities."

259 **After the city's metro opened:** Becerra, "The Fast Track to Change."

259 **Locals called that process:** "From.Boyle Heights to Netflix . . . and Back to the Neighborhood," NPR.

259 IN BOYLE HEIGHTS: Brand, "In Boyle Heights, the Signs of Gentrification Are Everywhere."

259 **In 2017, the brilliant and funny:** "Marvin Lemus," IMDb.

260 **The core conflict:** Bahr, "'The Jazz Singer' Celebrates Yom Kippur."

260 **"gentrification is the true":** "Gentrification Is the True, Highest Form of Hate Crime!," *Defend Boyle Heights.*

260 **"almost immediately":** Elliott, "This New Boyle Heights Coffee Bar Has Become a Gentrification Battleground."

260 **"to bring community together":** "Meet Jackson Defa of Weird Wave Coffee in Boyle Heights," Voyage LA.

260 **"cheer it on":** Elliott, "Someone Smashed the Front Window of Divisive Boyle Heights Coffee Shop Again."

260 **"ignore the uninformed protestors":** "Wonderful coffee shop with free wifi. Ignore the uninformed protestors. They're usually not there. Owners work tirelessly inside. What these protestors don't realize is that one of the owners is Salvadorean," Yelp.

261 **Costs were soaring:** Khouri, "As New Apartments Flood Downtown L.A., Landlords Offer Sweet Deals."

262 **The video of that protest:** Velez, "Artwashing Fight Takes Twist with Gallery's Offer to 'Ceremonially' Close in Boyle Heights."

262 **"hipster bro":** Miranda, "The Art Gallery Exodus from Boyle Heights and Why More Anti-gentrification Battles Loom on the Horizon."

262 **By 2018:** Ahn, "More Galleries Are Leaving the Contested Los Angeles Neighborhood of Boyle Heights."

262 **The median sales:** National Association of Realtors, *Median Sales Price of Existing Apartment Condo-Coops Homes for Metropolitan Areas.*

262 **The median price for a Los Angeles:** National Association of Realtors, *Median Sales Price of Existing Single-Family Homes for Metropolitan Areas.*

262–63 **which translates to $158,000:** Derived from the US Census Bureau's "Historical Census of Housing Tables." Given that a 1970 dollar is worth 6.82 2020 dollars, we can calculate the adjusted value for California's median home price.

263 **The supply of new homes:** Data from Build-Zoom.

263 **there are only 1.38:** Los Angeles County contains 3,579,329 housing units. Dividing this by the area, 4,057.88 square miles converted to 2,579,043.2 acres, we get 1.378 units per acre. Data provided by US Census Bureau, "QuickFacts: Los Angeles City, California; Los Angeles County, California; California; United States."

264 **"the maximum amount":** "Tax Limitation, Article XIII A CONS § 1 (1978)," California Legislative Information, 1.

265 **The nominal price of homes:** Federal Housing Finance Agency, "Historical City-Level Housing Price Data."

266 **"the incentive for group":** Olson, *The Rise and Decline of Nations: Economic Growth, Stagflation, and Social Rigidities*, 31.

267 **Harvey Molotch and John Logan:** Logan and Molotch, *Urban Fortunes: The Political Economy of Place*, 218.

268 **"up to our own day":** Turner, *The Significance of the Frontier in American History*, 1.

268 **in 1890, the ten states:** Those states and territories housed 1.6 million inhabitants, or 2.5 percent of America's population. The US Census counted Manhattan's population at 1.5 million, but the New York City Police Census gave the island 1.7 million people.

268 **The population of urban America:** Data from the US Census.

268 **In 1873, prosperous:** "Annexation Spurned: Brookline's Rejection of Boston," Brighton Allston Historical Society.

268 **1926 ruling:** "Village of Euclid v. Ambler Realty Company," Oyez.

269 **"are most likely":** Perez, *Invisible Women: Data Bias in a World Designed for Men.*

270 **1898 consolidation:** Spellen, "Walkabout: 'The Great Mistake'—How Brooklyn Lost Its Independence, Part 2."

270 **As Kenneth Jackson documents:** Jackson, *Crabgrass Frontier: The Suburbanization of the United States.*

270 **48 square miles of land; Phoenix has 517:** As reported in the US Census Bureau, "QuickFacts."

271 **Manhattan Expressway:** Wainwright, "Street Fighter: How Jane Jacobs Saved New York from Bulldozer Bob."

272 **between 1970 and 2010:** Molloy, Smith, and Wozniak, "Internal Migration in the United States."

272 **Before 1980:** Ganong and Shoag, "Why Has Regional Income Convergence in the U.S. Declined?"

272 **For 140 years:** Austin, Glaeser, and Summers, "Jobs for the Heartland: Place-Based Policies in 21st Century America."

272–73 **The economists Chang-Tai Hsieh:** Hsieh and Moretti, "Housing Constraints and Spatial Misallocation."

273 **In 1983:** Glaeser and Gyourko, "The Economic Implications of Housing Supply."

CHAPTER 9: URBANIZATION AND ITS DISCONTENTS

275 **On May 25, 2020:** Hill et al., "How George Floyd Was Killed in Police Custody."

275 **Derek Chauvin:** Barker and Kovaleski, "Officer Who Pressed His Knee on George Floyd's Neck Drew Scrutiny Long Before."

275 **In 2018 alone:** Mapping Police Violence.

276 **As of December:** Taken from the YouTube website, December 1, 2020.

276 **"little to end the war":** "The Flu in Boston," PBS.

276 **"in the eight":** Valentine, Valentine, and Valentine, "Relationship of George Floyd Protests to Increases in COVID-19 Cases Using Event Study Methodology."

276 **"no evidence that urban":** Dave et al., "Black Lives Matter Protests and Risk Avoidance: The Case of Civil Unrest During a Pandemic."

276 **Mistrust of the police:** Murphy, "Police Forcibly Eject Man without Face Mask from SEPTA Bus."

276 **friends Raj Chetty:** Chetty et al., "Where Is the Land of Opportunity?"

276 **Children who grow:** Chetty et al., "The Opportunity Atlas: Mapping the Childhood Roots of Social Mobility."

277 **Between 1988 and 2006:** National Research Council, *The Growth of Incarceration in the United States: Exploring Causes and Consequences,* 35.

277 **Between 1993 and 2008:** Cooper and Smith, "Homicide Trends in the United States, 1980–2008."

278 **At 5:30 p.m. on September 26, 1988:** Siegel, "Locking Up 'Sexual Predators' : A Public Outcry in Washington State Targeted Repeat Violent Sex Criminals. A New Preventive Law Would Keep Them in Jail Indefinitely."

278 **"a convicted sex offender":** Boerner, "Confronting Violence: In the Act and in the Word."

278 **"Kane had not received":** Blacher, "Historical Perspective of the 'Sex Psychopath' Statute: From the Revolutionary Era to the Present Federal Crime Bill."

278 **"first thought":** Siegel.

278 **State of Washington's Initiative 593:** "Washington 'Three Strikes' Initiative 593 (1993)," Ballotpedia.

279 **"Weekend Passes":** Blakemore, "How the Willie Horton Ad Played on Racism and Fear."

279 **"abolished furloughs":** Thomas, "Easy Answer on Prison Furloughs Eludes Dukakis. Public Opinion Makes Bush's Job Easier."

279 **up 118 percent:** Fox and Zawitz, *Homicide Trends in the United States.*

279 **"began staging rallies":** Fox and Zawitz.

279 **In December:** Siegel.

279 **"a 7-year-old boy":** Siegel.

280 **The boy was able:** Boerner, 525.

280 **"focused on the fact":** Boerner, 529.

280 ***The Seattle Times:*** Boerner, 533.

280 **"a group of protesters":** Boerner, 534.

280 **"sexually violent predator":** Boerner, 540.

280 **"just a good first step":** Siegel.

281 **250,000 signatures:** Drosendahl, "Ida Ballasiotes Files Initiative That Will Become the Nation's First 'Three Strikes, You're Out' Law with Washington Secretary of State's Office on January 6, 1993."

281 **"gangs and drugs":** Clinton, "Remarks on Signing the Violent Crime Control and Law Enforcement Act of 1994," Public Papers of the Presidents of the United States: William J. Clinton (1994, Book II), 1539–1541.

281 **"I signed a bill":** "Bill Clinton Regrets 'Three Strikes' Bill," BBC News.

282 **The national homicide rate:** Levitt, "Understanding Why Crime Fell in the 1990s: Four Factors That Explain the Decline and Six That Do Not."

282 **The number of murders:** Pavia, "New York Streets Safest for 70 Years as Murders Plunge."

282 **Between 2016 and 2019:** Derived from New York City Police Department, "Historical New York City Crime Data."

282 **One recent study:** Helland and Tabarrok, "Does Three Strikes Deter?: A Nonparametric Estimation."

283 **Their estimate is:** Helland and Tabarrok.

283 **"calls even those mild":** Roodman, "The Impacts of Incarceration on Crime," 5.

283 **A classic study:** Levitt, "The Effect of Prison Population Size on Crime Rates: Evidence from Prison Overcrowding Litigation."

283 **4.5 percent increase:** Roodman, 5.

283 **COVID-19-related prison releases:** Rector, "Surge in South L.A. Bloodshed Tied to Gunfire from High-Capacity Firearms, Gang Feuds."

284 **raise the odds of rearrest:** Roodman.

284 **"prison time reduces recidivism risk":** Kuziemko, "How Should Inmates Be Released from Prison? An Assessment of Parole versus Fixed-Sentence Regimes," 1.

284 **more than 2 million:** Maruschak and Minton, *Correctional Populations in the United States, 2017–2018.*

285 **"nonviolent drug convictions":** Sawyer and Wagner, "Mass Incarceration: The Whole Pie 2020."

286 **35 per 100,000 in 1991 to under 12 per 100,000:** Fox and Zawitz.

286 **$3.18 billion in 2020 dollars:** Independent Budget Office of the City of New York, "Fiscal History: NYPD."

286 **1,995 New Yorkers were murdered:** Mitchell, "The Killing of Murder."

286 **"the highest approval":** Robbins, "Crime Is Up, and Ray Kelly Has Record High Approval Rating."

286 **Kelly ran a public agency:** Independent Budget Office of the City of New York.

286 "administrative magician": Gray, "Boss Kelly."
286 "patrolled the Upper West Side": Gray.
287 Under Ryan: Mitchell, "The Killing of Murder."
287 Between 2001 and 2007: New York City Department of Health and Mental Hygiene. "Female Homicide in New York City over 15 Years: Surveillance and Findings, 1995–2009."
287 "the big decline in": Mitchell, "The Killing of Murder."
287 "give the weaker party": Mitchell, "The Killing of Murder."
287 "flagged down": Grynbaum, Rashbaum, and Baker, "Police Seek Man Taped Near Times Sq. Bomb Scene."
287 "eyes on the street": Jacobs, The Death and Life of Great American Cities.
287 "robot that looked like": Fahim, "Bomb Squad Has Hard-Won Expertise."
288 "to spend $40 million": Gray.
288 "city charter forbids": Gray.
288 Operation Impact: New York City—Safety and Security, New York City Global Partners.
288 "integral" to their "unprecedented achievements": New York City—Safety and Security.
288 "hot spots policing": Braga, "The Crime Prevention Value of Hot Spots Policing."
288 "impact zones were": MacDonald, Fagan, and Geller, "The Effects of Local Police Surges on Crime and Arrests in New York City," 1.
289 "the bulk of the investigative": MacDonald, Fagan, and Geller, 1.
289 "more than half a million": Zimring, "The City That Became Safe: New York and the Future of Crime Control," 14.
289 "between January 2004": US District Court, Southern District Court of New York, Floyd v. The City of New York.
289 "always check": "SNL Transcripts: Chevy Chase: 02/18/78: Baggage Inspection Counter," SNL Transcripts Tonight.
290 "slightly less likely": Coviello and Persico, "An Economic Analysis of Black-White Disparities in NYPD's Stop and Frisk Program," 17.
290 African Americans who are . . . innocent: John Tebes, personal communication.

290 "the effectiveness of": US District Court, Southern District Court of New York, Floyd v. The City of New York, 2.
290 "the city acted": US District Court, Southern District Court of New York, Floyd v. The City of New York, 13
290 "no one should": US District Court, Southern District Court of New York, Floyd v. The City of New York, 3
290 "the police . . . race": US District Court, Southern District Court of New York, Floyd v. The City of New York, 14
290 Judge Scheindlin noted: US District Court, Southern District Court of New York, Floyd v. The City of New York, 6.
291 "job is to improve": "Police Officers Federation of Minneapolis," FindGlocal.
291 "they were terminated without": Matthews, "How Police Unions Became So Powerful—and How They Can Be Tamed."
291 "the violent criminal history": Sheehy, "George Floyd Had 'Violent Criminal History': Minneapolis Police Union Chief."
291 twenty-two internal affairs complaints: Belkin, Maher, and Paul, "Clout of Minneapolis Police Union Boss Reflects National Trend."
291 "between 1995 and 2019": Belkin, Maher, and Paul.
291 "contracts call for": Levinson, "Across the U.S., Police Contracts Shield Officers from Scrutiny and Discipline."
292 "on at least 20": McLaughlin, "Chicago Officer Had History of Complaints before Laquan McDonald Shooting."
292 "the collective bargaining agreements": Chicago Police Accountability Task Force, Recommendations for Reform: Restoring Trust between the Chicago Police and the Communities They Serve, 14, 85.
292 "county sheriffs'": Dharmapala, McAdams, and Rappaport, "Collective Bargaining Rights and Police Misconduct: Evidence from Florida," 2.
292 "estimates imply that": Dharmapala, McAdams, and Rappaport, 1.
292 "a program requiring officers": Associated Press, "Boston Police Union Goes to Court after Officers' Resistance to Wearing Body-Worn Cameras."

293 "complaints brought against officers": Miller, "Walsh Supportive of Body Cameras."

293 "generate small but meaningful": Braga, Barao, and Zimmerman, "The Impacts of Body Worn Cameras on Police-Citizen Encounters, Police Proactivity, and Police-Community Relations in Boston: A Randomized Control Trial."

293 In 2018, the police: Collins, "The Anger behind the Protests, Explained in 4 Charts."

293 That same year: Federal Bureau of Investigation, "Expanded Homicide Data Table 1: Murder Victims by Race, Ethnicity, and Sex, 2018."

293 The work of our colleague: Devi and Fryer, "Policing the Police: The Impact of 'Pattern-or-Practice' Investigations on Crime."

293 "pattern or practice": Devi and Fryer, 8.

293 "for investigations that were": Devi and Fryer, 4.

294 "the leading theory . . . to collect data": Devi and Fryer, 34.

294 back-of-the-envelope calculations: Devi and Fryer, 33.

294 After falling from: Fox and Zawitz.

294 the share of murders: Madhani, "Unsolved Murders: Chicago, Other Big Cities Struggle; Murder Rate a 'National Disaster.'"

294 Since 2017: Charles, "After 3 Years of Progress, Chicago's Murder Tally Skyrockets in 2020."

294 "security from government overreach": Meares, "Policing: A Public Good Gone Bad."

294 "a relationship in which": Meares, Goff, and Tyler, "Defund-the-Police Calls Aren't Going Away. But What Do They Mean Practically?"

295 In Boston, for example: "TenPoint Coalition Founder Departs," WBUR.

295 Coffee with a Cop: Coffee with a Cop, "About—Coffee with a Cop."

295 "defunding the police": Ray, "What Does 'Defund the Police' Mean and Does It Have Merit?"

296 Tracy Meares: Meares, Goff, and Tyler.

296 "funding to recreational centers": Ray.

296 early childhood programs: Heckman et al., "The Rate of Return to the High/Scope Perry Preschool Program."

299 The 1971 case: "Swann v. Charlotte-Mecklenburg Board of Education," Oyez.

299 Milliken v. Bradley: "Milliken v. Bradley, 418 U.S. 717 (1974)," Justia: US Supreme Court, 418.

299 The busing battles: "Violence Erupts in Boston over Desegregation Busing," History.com.

300 Children born between: Chetty et al., "The Opportunity Atlas."

300 If one ranked all 330 million: The Opportunity Atlas data provides outcomes in terms of percentiles in the income distribution. We have multiplied each percentile point by 1 percent of the total American population, or 3.28 million, and rounded.

300 A graduate student: Glaeser and Tan, "Why Do Cities Increase Productivity but Decrease Opportunity?"

300 Relocating right outside: Glaeser and Tan.

300 2.75 percent to 2.1 percent: Glaeser, "Urbanization and Its Discontents," 12.

300 The Opportunity Atlas shows: The Opportunity Atlas, "Explore Data."

301 Ellora Derenoncourt: Derenoncourt, "Can You Move to Opportunity?" Evidence from the Great Migration."

301 David Autor: Autor, "Work of the Past, Work of the Future."

301 Wages of rich and poor alike: Chauvin, Glaeser, Ma, and Tobio, "What Is Different about Urbanization in Rich and Poor Countries? Cities in Brazil, China, India and the United States."

301 do not feel richer: Glaeser, Triumph of the City.

301 As Plato noted: Plato, The Republic, 423.

302 The Moving to Opportunity: Chetty, Hendren, and Katz, "The Effects of Exposure to Better Neighborhoods on Children: New Evidence from the Moving to Opportunity Experiment."

303 "promote innovation within": "2008 Democratic Party Platform," The American Presidency Project.

303 "states seeking funds": US Department of Education, "The Race to the Top Begins—Remarks by Secretary Arne Duncan."

303 "interconnected reforms": US Department of Education, "The Race to the Top Begins."

304 **The awards were based:** US Department of Education, *Race to the Top Program: Executive Summary*, 3, 7, 9.

304 **"a total of 46 states":** US Department of Education, "Nine States and the District of Columbia Win Second Round Race to the Top Grants."

304 **"35 states and":** U.S. Department of Education, "Nine States and the District of Columbia Win."

304 **States received full points:** U.S. Department of Education, "Legislation, Regulations, and Guidance—Race to the Top Fund."

304 **The only multistate consortium:** National Governors Association, "Forty-Nine States and Territories Join Common Core Standards Initiative."

305 **"to provide states":** Bill and Melinda Gates Foundation, "How We Work: Grant: National Governors Association for Best Practices."

305 **"to increase the leadership":** Bill and Melinda Gates Foundation, "How We Work: Grant: Council of Chief State School Officers."

305 **Developing the standards:** Common Core State Standards Initiative, "Development Process."

305 **"mountains of feedback":** Zimba, "Straight Up Conversation: Common Core Guru Jason Zimba."

305 **"found a very high degree":** Schmidt and Houang, "Curricular Coherence and the Common Core State Standards for Mathematics," 1.

305 **South Korea and the Netherlands:** Organisation for Economic Co-operation and Development, *PISA 2012 Results in Focus: What 15-Year-Olds Know and What They Can Do with What They Know.*

306 **In Massachusetts, which had:** "Ed Glaeser Slips on a Banana Peel," Pioneer Institute.

306 **"for Massachusetts":** "Common Core Math Fails to Prepare Students for STEM | Common Core Math," Pioneer Institute.

306 **"the concept of college readiness":** Massachusetts Board of Elementary and Secondary Education, "March 2010 Meeting Agendas."

306 **"the feds are pushing":** "Ed Glaeser Slips on a Banana Peel."

306 **"progressive educators":** Murphy, "Common Core in Oklahoma."

306 *Conform: Exposing the Truth:* Beck and Olson, *Conform: Exposing the Truth about Common Core and Public Education*, 95.

307 **"all schools will implement":** New York State Education Department, "Race to the Top Application Phase 2, New York State," 9.

307 **"in the press to implement":** State of New York, *New York Common Core Task Force Final Report*, 1, 15.

307–8 **five distinct managerial failures:** Levy, "An Analysis of Race to the Top in New York State."

308 **"I have nothing to do":** Ujifusa, "Despite History, N.Y. Gov. Cuomo Says: 'I Have Nothing to Do with Common Core.'"

308 **"until the start":** State of New York, *New York Common Core Task Force Final Report*, 1.

308 **"the equivalent of education":** US Department of Education, "The Race to the Top Begins."

308 **"largest nationally representative":** "Focus on NAEP," The Nation's Report Card.

309 **twelfth-grade reading score:** *Results from the 2019 Mathematics and Reading Assessments at Grade 12*, The Nation's Report Card.

309 **"How To Fix":** "How to Fix America's Schools," *Time.*

310 **three-hundred-plus-page document:** National Research Council, *An Evaluation of the Public Schools of the District of Columbia: Reform in a Changing Landscape.*

310 **The results are:** National Research Council, *An Evaluation of the Public Schools*, 5.

310 **A *USA Today* investigation:** Gillum and Bello, "When Standardized Test Scores Soared in D.C., Were the Gains Real?"

311 **"over 200 test books":** Merrow, "Meet Adell Cothorne"; Breslow, "Education Department Finds No Evidence."

311 **"let go dozens":** Gillum and Bello.

311 **The education economist:** Hanushek, "The Economic Value of Higher Teacher Quality."

311 **"a large, general":** Winig, *Michelle Rhee and the Washington D.C. Public Schools.*

312 **problems dogged Rhee's attempt:** Winig.

312 **"School Chancellor Michelle A. Rhee's":** Stewart and Schwartzman, "Fenty Set Path, Oblivious to Terrain."

313 **In Florida:** Arkin, "Florida's Largest Teachers Union Sues State over Reopening Schools."

313 **Georgia, teachers' unions:** "Georgia Association of Educators Sue State, Paulding County over Early Reopening Plan for Schools," WSB-TV.

313 **"that any teacher":** Walsh, "Teachers' Rights Under COVID-19: Anxiety Meets Legality."

313 **As of December 8, 2020:** Data provided at COVID-19 School Response Dashboard.

313 **"school districts":** Fensterwald, "Some Teachers Unions, Districts at Odds over Live Distance Learning Instruction."

313 **"our position is":** Fensterwald.

313 **"the Legislature finds":** Taken from "State of California Education Section 51512," California Legislative Information.

314 **"notwithstanding Section 51512":** Travis, "Proposed Bill Seeks to Remove Limits on Classroom Recording."

315 **Illinois teachers were:** Firey, "A Better Solution to Maryland's Pension Problem?"

315 **Public sector pensions:** US Bureau of Labor Statistics, "Table 4. Quits Levels and Rates by Industry and Region, Seasonally Adjusted."

315 **Natalia Emanuel . . . and Valentin Bolotnyy:** Bolotnyy and Emanuel, "Why Do Women Earn Less Than Men? Evidence from Bus and Train Operators."

316 **This leads to calls:** Spees, "Could Germany's Vocational Education Training System Be a Model for the U.S.?"

CHAPTER 10: A FUTURE WITH MORE HOPE THAN FEAR

319 **In the plague year of 2020:** Overberg, Kamp, and Michaels, "The Covid-19 Death Toll Is Even Worse Than It Looks."

319 **"more than 821,000":** Overberg, Kamp, and Michaels.

323 **The poorest countries:** Oppenheim and Yamey, "Pandemics and the Poor."

323 **The world must:** World Health Organization, *Managing Epidemics: Key Facts about Major Deadly Diseases.*

323 **Prevention includes:** US Centers for Disease Control and Prevention, *Advancing the Global Health Security Agenda.*

323 **"for too long":** Global Preparedness Monitoring Board, *A World at Risk: Annual Report on Global Preparedness for Health Emergencies,* 6.

323 **Estimates from the consulting firm:** Craven, Sabow, Van der Veken, and Wilson, "Preventing Pandemics with Investments in Public Health."

323 **expanding the health systems:** National Academy of Medicine, *The Neglected Dimension of Global Security: A Framework to Counter Infectious Disease Crises.*

323 **may cost the United States $16 trillion:** Cutler and Summers, "The COVID-19 Pandemic and the $16 Trillion Virus."

324 **Even if the US financed:** As of October 2020, the IMF reports the US GDP at $20.81 trillion. Assuming an up-front cost of $15

billion, the federal government spending would be just .72 percent of GDP.

324 **"What we need":** Global Preparedness Monitoring Board, *A World at Risk,* 6.

325 **The North Atlantic Treaty Organization:** "NATO," History.com.

325 **expanded into other areas:** North Atlantic Treaty Organization, "Encyclopedia of NATO Topics."

325 **twelve countries in 1949 to thirty in 2020:** North Atlantic Treaty Organization, "Member Countries."

325 **"NATO is the most":** "President and Secretary General de Hoop Scheffer Discuss NATO Meeting," White House.

325 **"it is because":** "Remarks by the President and Secretary General Stoltenberg of NATO after Bilateral Meeting," White House.

327 **exactly two days:** Moderna, "Moderna's Work on Our COVID-19 Vaccine Candidate."

327 **During the eight months:** World Health Organization, "United States of America: WHO Coronavirus Disease (COVID-19) Dashboard."

327 **2 percent of total:** Himmelstein and Woolhandler, "Public Health's Falling Share of US Health Spending."

328 **rose considerably:** US Centers for Medicare & Medicaid Services, "National Health Expenditure Data."

328 **medical records in real time:** US Department of Health and Human Services, Office of the National Coordinator for Health Information Technology, 2016.

328 **two books and many articles:** Cutler, *Your Money or Your Life*; Cutler, *The Quality Cure*.

329 **Obesity, tobacco use:** Institute of Medicine (US) Committee on Health and Behavior: Research, Practice, and Policy, *Health and Behavior: The Interplay of Biological, Behavioral, and Societal Influences*.

329 **fallen further behind:** Brody and Koh, "WSJ News Exclusive | Student Test Scores Drop in Math Since Covid-19 Pandemic."

329 **If one tenth or more:** Korman, O'Keefe, and Repka, "Missing in the Margins: Estimating the Scale of the COVID-19 Attendance Crisis."

331 **No Child Left Behind:** Whitney and Candelaria, "The Effects of No Child Left Behind on Children's Socioemotional Outcomes."

331 **In 2020, the United States:** Campbell, Barcena, and David, "Hutchins Roundup: PPP Loans, Charter Schools and More."

331 **NASA's spending:** US Bureau of the Budget and US Office of Management and Budget, *The Budget of the United States Government for the Fiscal Year Ending June 30, 1967*.

331 **Nathaniel Hendren and Benjamin Sprung-Keyser:** Hendren and Sprung-Keyser, "A Unified Welfare Analysis of Government Policies."

331 **A $100 billion:** "Elementary and Secondary Education Expenditures," Urban Institute.

332 **Smaller class sizes:** Krueger and Whitmore, "The Effect of Attending a Small Class in the Early Grades on College-Test Taking and Middle School Test Results."

332 **Some charter schools:** Angrist et al., "Stand and Deliver: Effects of Boston's Charter High Schools on College Preparation, Entry, and Choice."

332 **Better teachers make a huge difference:** Kane and Staiger, "Estimating Teacher Impacts on Student Achievement: An Experimental Evaluation."

332 **principals know how to identify:** Jacob and Lefgren, "Principals as Agents: Subjective Performance Measurement in Education."

334 **New Zealand did so well:** Jefferies et al., "COVID-19 in New Zealand and the Impact of the National Response: A Descriptive Epidemiological Study."

334 **More than one half:** Center for Community College Student Engagement, *Contingent Commitments: Bringing Part-Time Faculty into Focus*.

335 **Siemens partners:** Davis, "Siemens AG."

335 **"aligned by competencies":** Central Piedmont Community College, "Mechatronics Engineering Technology."

335 **extremely successful District Hall:** Katz and Wagner, "The Rise of Innovation Districts."

335 **"apprenticeship and training program":** Northeastern University, "The Northeastern Joint Apprenticeship and Training Program (NEAT)."

336 **Chapter 40B:** Commonwealth of Massachusetts, "Chapter 40 B Planning and Information."

337 **In 1991, homicides:** Fox and Zawitz, *Homicide Trends in the United States*.

BIBLIOGRAPHY

Abrams, Hannah R., Lacey Loomer, Ashvin Gandhi, and David C. Grabowski. "Characteristics of U.S. Nursing Homes with COVID-19 Cases." *Journal of the American Geriatrics Society* 68, no. 8 (August 2020): 1653–56. https://doi:10.1111/jgs.16661.

"Address at the Jefferson Day Dinner." Harry S. Truman Library and Museum. www.trumanlibrary .gov/library/public-papers/68/address-jefferson-day-dinner.

Adhikari, Samrachana, Nicholas P. Pantaleo, and Justin M. Feldman. "Assessment of Community-Level Disparities in Coronavirus Disease 2019 (COVID-19) Infections and Deaths in Large US Metropolitan Areas." *JAMA Network Open*, July 28, 2020. https://doi.org/doi:10.1001 /jamanetworkopen.2020.16938.

Afana, Majed, Waleed Brinjikji, Harry Cloft, et al. "Hospitalization Costs for Acute Myocardial Infarction Patients Treated with Percutaneous Coronary Intervention in the United States are Substantially Higher than Medicare Payment." *Clinical Cardiology* 38, no. 1 (2015): 13–19. https://doi.org/10.1002/clc.22341.

Ahn, Abe. "More Galleries Are Leaving the Contested Los Angeles Neighborhood of Boyle Heights." *Hyperallergic*, May 4, 2018. https://hyperallergic.com/440967/mars-chimento-uta-artist-space -leaving-boyle-heights.

Ajuntament de Barcelona. "Safety Screens on Buses to Minimise the Risk of Infection." https:// ajuntament.barcelona.cat/bombers/en/noticia/safety-screens-on-buses-to-minimise-the -risk-of-infection_946277.

Alesina, Alberto, and Edward Glaeser. *Fighting Poverty in the US and Europe: A World of Difference.* Oxford, UK: Oxford University Press Oxford, 2004.

Allen, Mike, William A. Donohue, Amy Griffin, Dan Ryan, and Monique M. Mitchell Turner. "Comparing the Influence of Parents and Peers on the Choice to Use Drugs: A Meta-analytic Summary of the Literature." *Criminal Justice and Behavior* 30, no. 2 (April 2003): 163–86. https://doi:10.1177 /0093854802251002.

Allen, Stephen. *The Memoirs of Stephen Allen.* Typescript. Edited, with an introduction and notes by John C. Travis, 1927. Manuscripts and Archives Division, New York Public Library.

Alsan, Marcella, and Claudia Goldin. "Watersheds in Child Mortality: The Role of Effective Water and Sewerage Infrastructure, 1880 to 1920." *Journal of Political Economy* 127, no. 2 (April 2019): 586–638. https://doi.org/10.1086/700766.

Amazon Staff. "How We're Taking Care of Employees during COVID-19." About Amazon. March 24, 2020. www.aboutamazon.com/news/company-news/how-were-taking-care-of-employees-during -covid-19.

American Medical Association. *Issue Brief: Reports of Increases in Opioid- and Other Drug-related Overdose and Other Concerns during COVID Pandemic.* December 9, 2020, updated March 3, 2021. www.ama-assn.org/system/files/2020-12/issue-brief-increases-in-opioid-related-overdose.pdf.

Amerman, Don. "Sandy Weill 1933–." Reference for Business. Accessed January 9, 2021. www .referenceforbusiness.com/biography/S-Z/Weill-Sandy-1933.html.

"An Act Relative to Quarantine (1796)." Statutes and Stories. February 9, 2020. www.statutesandstories .com/blog_html/an-act-relative-to-quarantine.

Anders, Jenna, and Amanda Pallais. "Why Can't We Be Friends?: Theory and Evidence on Friendship Formation." *Harvard Mimeograph*, 2020.

Anderson, Gerard F., Uwe E. Reinhardt, Peter S. Hussey, and Varduhi Petrosyan. "It's the Prices, Stupid: Why the United States Is So Different from Other Countries." *Health Affairs* 22, no. 3 (May/June 2003): 89–105. https://doi.org/10.1377/hlthaff.22.3.89.

Andreevska, Daniela. "Where Should You Invest in the Boston Real Estate Market?" *Mashvisor*, November 16, 2017. www.mashvisor.com/blog/where-invest-boston-real-estate-market.

"Andrew A. Boyle, Namesake of Boyle Heights: An Immigrant's Story." *Boyle Heights History Blog*, August 26, 2009. http://boyleheightshistoryblog.blogspot.com/2009/08/andrew-boyle-namesake -of-boyle-heights.html.

"Angela Merkel." *Encyclopædia Britannica Online*. Accessed December 26, 2020. www.britannica.com /biography/Angela-Merkel.

"Angioplasty and Stent Placement—Heart." MedlinePlus. https://medlineplus.gov/ency/article /007473.htm.

Angrist, Joshua D., Sarah R. Cohodes, Susan M. Dynarski, Parag A. Pathak, and Christopher R. Walters. "Stand and Deliver: Effects of Boston's Charter High Schools on College Preparation, Entry, and Choice." *Journal of Labor Economics* 34, no. 2 (January 22, 2016): 275–318. https://doi .org/10.1086/683665.

"Annexation Spurned: Brookline's Rejection of Boston." Brighton Allston Historical Society. Accessed January 12, 2021. www.bahistory.org/HistoryAnnexBrookline.html.

Apolone, Giovanni, Emanuele Montomoli, Alessandro Manenti, Mattia Boeri, et al. "Unexpected Detection of SARS-CoV-2 Antibodies in the Prepandemic Period in Italy." *Tumori Journal*, November 11, 2020. https://doi.org/10.1177/0300891620974755.

Aquilina, O., V. Grech, H. Felice, J. Debono, and A. Fenech." Normal Adult Coronary Angiography." *Images in Paediatric Cardiology* 8, no. 2 (April–June 2006): 1–16. www.ncbi.nlm.nih.gov/pmc /articles/PMC3232562.

Ardagh, John Anthony Charles. "Paris: The Halles." *Encyclopædia Britannica Online*. www.britannica .com/place/Paris.

Arkin, Daniel. "Florida's Largest Teachers Union Sues State over Reopening Schools." NBC News, July 20, 2020. www.nbcnews.com/news/us-news/florida-s-largest-teachers-union-files-suit-against -state-over-n1234382.

Armelagos, George J., Kathleen C. Barnes, and James Lin. "Disease in Human Evolution: The Reemergence of Infectious Disease in the Third Epidemiological Transition." *AnthroNotes* 18, no. 3 (Fall 1996): 1–7. https://doi.org/10.5479/10088/22354.

Artiga, Samantha, Matthew Rae, Olivia Pham, Liz Hamel, and Cailey Muñana. "COVID-19 Risks and Impacts among Health Care Workers by Race/Ethnicity—Issue Brief." Kaiser Family Foundation. November 11, 2020. www.kff.org/report-section/covid-19-risks-and-impacts-among -health-care-workers-by-race-ethnicity-issue-brief.

Artsy, Avishay. "Boyle Heights, the Land of Freeways." KCRW, October 6, 2015. www.kcrw.com /culture/shows/design-and-architecture/boyle-heights-the-land-of-freeways.

Ashraf, Nava, Edward Glaeser, Abraham Holland, and Bryce Millett Steinberg. "Water, Health and Wealth." NBER Working Paper Series 23807, National Bureau of Economic Research, Cambridge, MA, September 2017. https://doi.org/10.3386/w23807.

Ashraf, Nava, Edward L. Glaeser, and Giacomo A. M. Ponzetto. "Infrastructure, Incentives, and Institutions." *American Economic Review* 106, no. 5 (May 2016): 77–82. https://doi.org/10.1257 /aer.p20161095.

Ashton, Rosemary. *One Hot Summer: Dickens, Darwin, Disraeli, and the Great Stink of 1858.* New Haven, CT, and London: Yale University Press, 2017.

Asiamah, Nancy. "State: Deaths at Soldiers' Home in Holyoke Reaches 94, Covid-19 Retesting Shows Improvement." WWLP, June 11, 2020. www.wwlp.com/news/local-news/hampden -county/state-deaths-at-soldiers-home-in-holyoke-reaches-94-covid-19-retesting-shows -improvement.

"Asiatic Cholera Pandemic of 1846–63," Fielding School of Public Health, UCLA. www.ph.ucla .edu/epi/Snow/pandemic1846-63.html.

Asimov, Isaac. *The Foundation Trilogy (Foundation, Foundation and Empire, Second Foundation); The Stars, Like Dust; The Naked Sun; I, Robot.* Book Sales, 1981.

"Aspasia: Influential Concubine to Pericles." World History Encyclopedia, January 18, 2012. www .ancient.eu/article/73/aspasia-influential-concubine-to-pericles.

Associated Press. "Boston Police Union Goes to Court after Officers' Resistance to Wearing Body-Worn Cameras." Police1. September 6, 2016. www.police1.com/police-products/body-cameras /articles/boston-police-union-goes-to-court-after-officers-resistance-to-wearing-body-worn -cameras-y8lF7jdjX4hCyNW2.

———. "Pence's Handling of 2015 HIV Outbreak Gets New Scrutiny." NBC News, February 28, 2020. www.nbcnews.com/politics/white-house/pence-s-handling-2015-hiv-outbreak-gets-new -scrutiny-n1144786.

———. "2 Charged for Handling of Virus Outbreak at Veterans Home." CNBC, September 25, 2020. www.cnbc.com/2020/09/25/2-charged-for-handling-of-virus-outbreak-at-veterans-home -.html.

Astour, Michael C. "Ancient Greek Civilization in Southern Italy." *Journal of Aesthetic Education* 19, no. 1 (Spring 1985): 23–37. https://doi.org/10.2307/3332556.

Austin, Benjamin A., Edward L. Glaeser, and Lawrence H. Summers. "Jobs for the Heartland: Place-Based Policies in 21st Century America." *Brookings Papers on Economic Activity* (Spring 2018): 151–232. https://doi.org/10.3386/w24548.

Autor, David H. "Work of the Past, Work of the Future." *American Economic Association Papers and Proceedings* 109 (May 2019): 1–32. https://doi.org/10.1257/pandp.20191110.

Autor, David H., Lawrence F. Katz, and Melissa S. Kearney. "The Polarization of the U.S. Labor Market." *American Economic Review* 96, no. 2 (May 2006): 189–94. https://doi.org/10.1257 /000282806777212620.

Avila, Eric. "East Side Stories: Freeways and Their Portraits in Chicano Los Angeles." *Landscape Journal* 26, no. 1 (January 2007): 83–97. https:// doi: 10.3368/lj.26.1.83.

Baccini, Leonardo, Abel Brodeur, and Stephen Weymouth. "The COVID-19 Pandemic and the 2020 U.S. Presidential Election." *Journal of Population Economics* 34, no. 2 (2021): 739–67. https://doi .org/10.1007/s00148-020-00820-3.

Baharoon, Salim, and Ziad A. Memish. "MERS-CoV as an Emerging Respiratory Illness: A Review of Prevention Methods." *Travel Medicine and Infectious Disease* 32 (November–December 2019): 101520. https://doi.org/10.1016/j.tmaid.2019.101520.

Bahr, Bob. "'The Jazz Singer' Celebrates Yom Kippur." *Atlanta Jewish Times*, September 24, 2020. https://atlantajewishtimes.timesofisrael.com/the-jazz-singer-celebrates-yom-kippur.

Balliet, Daniel. "Communication and Cooperation in Social Dilemmas: A Meta-analytic Review." *Journal of Conflict Resolution* 54, no. 1 (February 2010): 39–57. https://doi.org/10.1177 /0022002709352443.

Bank of England. "Inflation Calculator." Accessed January 25, 2021. www.bankofengland.co.uk /monetary-policy/inflation/inflation-calculator.

Barker, Kim, and Serge F. Kovaleski. "Officer Who Pressed His Knee on George Floyd's Neck Drew Scrutiny Long Before." *The New York Times*, July 18, 2020. www.nytimes.com/2020/07/18/us /derek-chauvin-george-floyd.html.

Barnett, Michael L., Lissy Hu, Thomas Martin, et al. "Mortality, Admissions, and Patient Census at SNFs in 3 US Cities During the COVID-19 Pandemic." *JAMA* 324, no. 5 (August 2020): 507–509. https://doi.org/10.1001/jama.2020.11642.

Barr, Jason M. *Building the Skyline: The Birth and Growth of Manhattan's Skyscrapers*. New York: Oxford University Press, 2016.

Barro, Robert J. "Non-Pharmaceutical Interventions and Mortality in U.S. Cities during the Great Influenza Pandemic, 1918–1919." NBER Working Paper Series 27049, National Bureau of Economic Research, Cambridge, MA, April 2020. https://doi.org/10.3386/w27049.

Barry, Stephanie. "Former Holyoke Soldiers' Home Superintendent Bennett Walsh, Medical Director David Clinton Arraigned on Charges Linked to COVID-19 Outbreak." MassLive, November 5, 2020. www.masslive.com/coronavirus/2020/11/former-holyoke-soldiers-home-superintendent -bennett-walsh-medical-director-david-clinton-arraigned-on-charges-linked-to-covid-19 -outbreak.html.

———. "Independent Report on Holyoke Soldiers' Home COVID-19 Crisis Paints Early Decisions by Superintendent Bennett Walsh as 'a Catastrophe.'" MassLive, June 24, 2020. masslive.com /boston/2020/06/independent-report-on-holyoke-soldiers-home-covid-19-crisis-paints-early -decisions-by-superintendent-bennett-walsh-as-a-catastrophe.html.

Bartik, Alexander W., Marianne Bertrand, Zoë B. Cullen, Edward L. Glaeser, Michael Luca, and Christopher T. Stanton. "How Are Small Businesses Adjusting to COVID-19? Early Evidence from a Survey." NBER Working Paper Series 26989, National Bureau of Economic Research, Cambridge, MA, April 2020. https://doi.org/10.3386/w26989.

Bartik, Alexander W., Zoe B. Cullen, Edward L. Glaeser, Michael Luca, and Christopher T. Stanton. "What Jobs Are Being Done at Home During the Covid-19 Crisis? Evidence from Firm-Level Surveys." NBER Working Paper Series 27422, National Bureau of Economic Research, Cambridge, MA, June 2020. https://doi.org/10.3386/w27422.

Bartik, Alexander W., Zoe B. Cullen, Edward L. Glaeser, Michael Luca, Christopher T. Stanton, and Adi Sunderam. "The Targeting and Impact of Paycheck Protection Program Loans to Small

Businesses." NBER Working Paper Series 27623, National Bureau of Economic Research, Cambridge, MA, July 2020. https://doi.org/10.3386/w27623.

Barton, Matthias, Johannes Grüntzig, Marc Husmann, and Josef Rösch. "Balloon Angioplasty—The Legacy of Andreas Grüntzig, M.D. (1939–1985)." *Frontiers in Cardiovascular Medicine* 1 (December 2014): 15. https://doi.org/10.3389/fcvm.2014.00015.

Battenfeld, Joe. "Coronavirus Veteran Deaths in Holyoke Put Federal Heat on Charlie Baker." *Boston Herald*, April 10, 2020. www.bostonherald.com/2020/04/10/coronavirus-veteran-deaths-in -holyoke-put-federal-heat-on-charlie-baker.

Battiston, Diego, Jordi Blanes i Vidal, and Tom Kirchmaier. "Is Distance Dead? Face-to-Face Communication and Productivity in Teams." *CEP Discussion Paper 1473*, Centre for Economic Performance, London, March 2017. https://ideas.repec.org/p/cep/cepdps/dp1473.html.

Baum-Snow, Nathaniel. "Did Highways Cause Suburbanization?" *Quarterly Journal of Economics* 122, no. 2 (May 2007): 775–805. https://doi.org/10.1162/qjec.122.2.775.

Beachum, Lateshia. "New York's 'Patient Zero' Breaks His Silence after Surviving Covid-19." *The Washington Post*, May 11, 2020. www.washingtonpost.com/nation/2020/05/11/patient-zero -new-york-coronavirus.

Beautiful Highlands of Los Angeles, Comprising Boyle Heights, Brooklyn Heights, Euclid Heights. Los Angeles, 1900. http://archive.org/details/beautifulhighlan00losa.

Becerra, Hector. "The Fast Track to Change." *Los Angeles Times*, November 30, 2008. www.latimes .com/archives/la-xpm-2008-nov-30-me-goldline30-story.html.

Beck, Glenn, and Kyle Olson. *Conform: Exposing the Truth about Common Core and Public Education.* New York: Threshold Editions, 2014.

Becker, Kaitlin McKinley. "Biogen Conference in Boston Linked to More Than 300,000 COVID-19 Cases." NBC Boston, December 11, 2020. www.nbcboston.com/news/coronavirus/biogen -conference-in-boston-now-tied-to-more-than-300000-coronavirus-cases/2254941.

Beech, Hannah. "Singapore Seemed to Have Coronavirus Under Control, until Cases Doubled." *The New York Times*, April 20, 2020. www.nytimes.com/2020/04/20/world/asia/coronavirus-singapore .html.

Beeston, Richard. "Book Club: The Jungle by Upton Sinclair." *The Times* (London), February 12, 2011. www.thetimes.co.uk/article/book-club-the-jungle-by-upton-sinclair-bcnlq6p7xkm.

Belkin, Douglas, Kris Maher, and Deanna Paul. "Clout of Minneapolis Police Union Boss Reflects National Trend." *The Wall Street Journal*, July 7, 2020. www.wsj.com/articles/robert-krolls-rise -from-barroom-brawler-to-minneapolis-police-union-boss-11594159577.

Bell, Dean Phillip. *Plague in the Early Modern World: A Documentary History.* New York: Routledge, 2019.

Bengali, Shashank, Kate Linthicum, and Victoria Kim. "How Coronavirus—a 'Rich Man's Disease'— Infected the Poor." *Los Angeles Times*, May 8, 2020. www.latimes.com/world-nation/story /2020-05-08/how-the-coronavirus-began-as-a-disease-of-the-rich.

"Benjamin Franklin and the Manchester Lit & Phil." Manchester Literary and Philosophical Society. Last modified July 13, 2016. www.manlitphil.ac.uk/news/benjamin-franklin-and-manchester -lit-phil.

Benos, Nikos, and Stelios Karagiannis. "Do Education Quality and Spillovers Matter? Evidence on Human Capital and Productivity in Greece." *Economic Modelling* 54 (April 2016): 563–73. https:// doi.org/10.1016/j.econmod.2016.01.015.

Bertram, Eva. "Democratic Divisions in the 1960s and the Road to Welfare Reform." *Political Science Quarterly* 126, no. 4 (Winter 2011): 579–610. https://doi.org/10.1002/j.1538-165X.2011.tb00713.x.

Biden, Joe. "Build Back Better: Joe Biden's Jobs and Economic Recovery Plan for Working Families." Joe Biden for President: Official Campaign Website. Accessed January 9, 2021. https://joebiden.com/build-back-better.

"Biden Says Some Waste Inevitable Part of Stimulus." Reuters, June 2, 2009. www.reuters.com/article/us-usa-biden-transparency-idUKTRE5516HE20090602.

Bigelow, Daniel P., and Allison Borchers. *Major Uses of Land in the United States, 2012.* US Department of Agriculture Economic Research Service, August 2017. www.ers.usda.gov/webdocs/publications/84880/eib-178.pdf?v=9775.2.

"Bill Clinton Regrets 'Three Strikes' Bill." BBC News. July 16, 2015. www.bbc.com/news/world-us-canada-33545971.

Bill and Melinda Gates Foundation. "How We Work: Grant: Council of Chief State School Officers." July 2009. www.gatesfoundation.org/How-We-Work/Quick-Links/Grants-Database/Grants/2009/07/OPP50935.

———. "How We Work: Grant: National Governors Association for Best Practices." March 2005. www.gatesfoundation.org/How-We-Work/Quick-Links/Grants-Database/Grants/2005/03/OPP38008.

Billings, Molly. "The 1918 Influenza Pandemic." Human Virology at Stanford, June 1997. https://virus.stanford.edu/uda.

Blacher, Rachel. "Historical Perspective of the 'Sex Psychopath' Statute: From the Revolutionary Era to the Present Federal Crime Bill." *Mercer Law Review* 46, no. 2 (March 1995): 889–920. https://digitalcommons.law.mercer.edu/jour_mlr/vol46/iss2/13.

Black, Jane. "Urban Agriculture: Can It Feed Our Cities?" *Food+City*. November 2017. https://foodandcity.org/urban-agriculture-can-feed-cities.

Blake, John B. "Yellow Fever in Eighteenth Century America." *Bulletin of the New York Academy of Medicine* 44, no. 6 (June 1968): 673–86.

Blakemore, Erin. "How the Willie Horton Ad Played on Racism and Fear." History. November 2, 2018. www.history.com/news/george-bush-willie-horton-racist-ad.

"Blockbuster Project Proof of Devons Lure." *The Sun* (Lowell), December 19, 2020. https://www.lowellsun.com/2020/12/19/blockbuster-project-proof-of-devens-lure.

Bloom, Nicholas. "How Working from Home Works Out." Stanford Institute for Economic Policy Research. June 2020. https://siepr.stanford.edu/research/publications/how-working-home-works-out.

Bloom, Nicholas, James Liang, John Roberts, and Zhichun Jenny Ying. "Does Working from Home Work? Evidence from a Chinese Experiment." *Quarterly Journal of Economics* 130, no. 1 (February 2015): 165–218. https://doi.org/10.1093/qje/qju032.

"The Bloomberg Bus." *Observer*, March 11, 2009. https://observer.com/2009/03/the-bloomberg-bus.

Blum, Deborah. "How Henry Heinz Used Ketchup to Improve Food Safety." *National Geographic*, January 15, 2019. www.nationalgeographic.com/magazine/2019/02/how-henry-heinz-used-ketchup-to-improve-food-safety.

Boerner, David. "Confronting Violence: In the Act and in the Word." *University of Puget Sound Law Review* 15, no. 3 (January 1992): 525–577. https://digitalcommons.law.seattleu.edu/cgi/viewcontent.cgi?article=1357&context=sulr.

Bollyky, Thomas J., and Stewart M. Patrick. "Improving Pandemic Preparedness: Lessons From COVID-19." Independent Task Force Report No. 78, Council on Foreign Relations, New York, October 2020. www.cfr.org/report/pandemic-preparedness-lessons-COVID-19/introduction.

Bolotnyy, Valentin, and Natalia Emanuel. "Why Do Women Earn Less Than Men? Evidence from Bus and Train Operators." Working Paper, Harvard University, November 28, 2018. https://scholar.harvard.edu/files/bolotnyy/files/be_gendergap.pdf.

Bonazzi, Mauro. "Protagoras," in *The Stanford Encyclopedia of Philosophy*. Edited by Edward N. Zalta. Stanford, CA: Metaphysics Research Lab, Stanford University, 2020. https://plato.stanford.edu/archives/fall2020/entries/protagoras.

Bonnefoy, Pascale, and Patrick J. Lyons. "Why Chile's Latest Big Earthquake Has a Smaller Death Toll." *The New York Times*, September 17, 2015. www.nytimes.com/2015/09/18/world/americas/chile-earthquake-tsunami-impact.html.

Bonnie, Richard J., Morgan A. Ford, and Jonathan K. Phillips. *Pain Management and the Opioid Epidemic: Balancing Societal and Individual Benefits and Risks of Prescription Opioid Use*. Washington, DC: National Academies Press, 2017.

"Book Reviews: *Packaging in Today's Society*, 3rd Edition, Robert J. Kelsey, Technomic Publishing Co., Inc., Lancaster, PA (1989)," in *Journal of Plastic Film & Sheeting* 5, no. 3 (1989): 176. https://doi.org/10.1177/875608798900500304.

Booth, Martin, *Opium: A History*. London: Simon and Schuster, 1996.

Borà, Salvatore. "Historical and Monumental Itineraries of Capri." CapriKronos. Accessed January 19, 2021. www.caprikronos.com/en/capri-island/#.YAaeXZNKgsk.

Boro, Bronza. "Austrian Measures for Prevention and Control of the Plague Epidemic along the Border with the Ottoman Empire during the 18th Century." *Scripta Medica* 50, no. 4 (January 2019): 177–84. https://doi.org/10.5937/scriptamed50-23457.

Bosin, Yury V. "Russia, Cholera Riots of 1830–1831," in *The International Encyclopedia of Revolution and Protest*. Edited by Immanuel Ness. Hoboken, NJ: Wiley-Blackwell, 2009. https://doi.org/10.1002/9781405198073.wbierp1282.

"Boston Police Union Goes to Court to Stop Mandatory Body Cams." CBS News, September 6, 2016. www.cbsnews.com/news/boston-police-union-goes-to-court-to-stop-mandatory-body-cams.

Bowles, Jonathan, and Charles Shaviro. "Bearing the Brunt: Where NYC's Hard-Hit Sector Workers Live." Center for an Urban Future. May 2020. https://nycfuture.org/research/where-hard-hit-sector-workers-live.

Braga, Anthony A. "The Crime Prevention Value of Hot Spots Policing." *Psicothema* 18, no. 3 (August 2006): 630–37.

Braga, Anthony A., Lisa M. Barao, and Gregory Zimmerman. "The Impacts of Body Worn Cameras on Police-Citizen Encounters, Police Proactivity, and Police-Community Relations in Boston: A Randomized Controlled Trial." Report to the Boston Police Department. School of Criminology and Criminal Justice, Northeastern University, July 27, 2018. https://news.northeastern.edu/wp-content/uploads/2018/08/BPD-BWC-RCT-Full-Report-07272018.pdf.

Braga, Anthony A., William H. Sousa, James R. Coldren Jr., and Denise Rodriguez. "The Effects of Body-Worn Cameras on Police Activity and Police-Citizen Encounters: A Randomized Controlled Trial." *Journal of Criminal Law and Criminology* 108, no. 3 (Summer 2018): 511–38. https://scholarlycommons.law.northwestern.edu/jclc/vol108/iss3/3.

Braga, Anthony A., Brandon S. Turchan, Andrew V. Papachristos, and David M. Hureau. "Hot Spots Policing and Crime Reduction: An Update of an Ongoing Systematic Review and

Meta-Analysis." *Journal of Experimental Criminology* 15, no. 3 (September 2019): 289–311. https://doi.org/10.1007/s11292-019-09372-3.

Brand, Madeleine. "In Boyle Heights, the Signs of Gentrification Are Everywhere." Union de Vecinos (blog), July 20, 2016. www.uniondevecinos.org/index.php/in-boyle-heights-the-signs-of-gentrification-are-everywhere.

Bremmer, Ian. "The Best Global Responses to COVID-19 Pandemic." *Time*, June 12, 2020. https://time.com/5851633/best-global-responses-covid-19.

Breslow, Jason M. "Education Department Finds No Evidence of Widespread Cheating on D.C. Exams." *Frontline*, January 8, 2013. www.pbs.org/wgbh/frontline/article/education-department -finds-no-evidence-of-widespread-cheating-on-d-c-exams.

"A Brief History of Private Insurance in the United States." Academic HealthPlans. Accessed January 30, 2020. www.ahpcare.com/a-brief-history-of-private-insurance-in-the-united-states.

Brieger, Gert H. "Sanitary Reform in New York City: Stephen Smith and the Passage of the Metropolitan Health Bill." *Bulletin of the History of Medicine* 40, no. 5 (1966): 407–29. http://www.jstor .org/stable/44450678.

Brinkley, Catherine, and Domenic Vitiello. "From Farm to Nuisance: Animal Agriculture and the Rise of Planning Regulation." *Journal of Planning History* 13, no. 2 (May 2014): 113–35. https:// doi.org/10.1177/1538513213507542.

British Columbia Centre for Disease Control. "BC Covid-19 Data." Accessed January 8, 2021. www .bccdc.ca/health-info/diseases-conditions/covid-19/data.

Broadberry, Stephen, Bruce M. S. Campbell, Alexander Klein, Mark Overton, and Bas van Leeuwen. *British Economic Growth, 1270–1870.* Cambridge, UK: Cambridge University Press, 2015.

Brody, Leslie, and Yoree Koh. "Student Test Scores Drop in Math Since Covid-19 Pandemic." *The Wall Street Journal*, November 21, 2020. www.wsj.com/articles/student-test-scores-drop-in-math -since-covid-19-pandemic-11605974400.

Brot-Goldberg, Zarek C., Amitabh Chandra, Benjamin R. Handel, and Jonathan T. Kolstad. "What Does a Deductible Do? The Impact of Cost-Sharing on Health Care Prices, Quantities, and Spending Dynamics." *The Quarterly Journal of Economics* 132, no. 3 (August 2017): 1261–1318. https://doi.org/10.1093/qje/qjx013.

Brown, Karen. "Nursing Homes Account for More Than Half of Total COVID-19 Deaths in Massachusetts." New England Public Media, May 29, 2020. www.nepm.org/post/nursing-homes -account-more-half-total-covid-19-deaths-massachusetts.

Bryant, Arthur. "Samuel Pepys: English Diarist and Naval Administrator." *Encyclopædia Britannica Online*. Last modified February 19, 2021. www.britannica.com/biography/Samuel-Pepys.

Buccholz, Todd G. "Are Fast-Food Establishments Making Americans Fat?" *Journal of Controversial Medical Claims* 10, no. 4 (November 2003): 1–10. www.ohio.k12.ky.us/userfiles/1153/Classes /34781/Are fast food making Amer fat.pdf.

Buckingham, Jane. *Leprosy in Colonial South India.* London: Palgrave Macmillan, 2002.

Buford, Edward P. "Assumption of Risk under the Federal Employers' Liability Act." *Harvard Law Review* 28, no. 2 (December 1914): 163–85. https://doi.org/10.2307/1325999.

Bulmer-Thomas, Ivor. "Theodorus of Cyrene." Encyclopedia.com. Accessed January 18, 2021. www .encyclopedia.com/science/dictionaries-thesauruses-pictures-and-press-releases/theodorus -cyrene.

Bump, Suzanne. *Official Audit Report: Devens Enterprise Commission.* Commonwealth of Massachusetts, Office of the State Auditor, May 6, 2015. https://archives.lib.state.ma.us/bitstream/handle /2452/265128/ocn910724896.pdf?sequence=1&isAllowed=y.

Burns, Joseph. "Prior Authorization Rules: Yet Another Way the Health Insurance System Frustrates Physicians and Patients." Association of Health Care Journalists (blog), August 9, 2018. https://healthjournalism.org/blog/2018/08/prior-authorization-rules-yet-another-way-the-health-insurance-system-frustrates-physicians-and-patients.

Burrows, Edwin G., and Mike Wallace. "Splendid Little War," in *Gotham: A History of New York City to 1898*. New York: Oxford University Press, 1998. https://erenow.net/modern/gotham-history-of-new-york-city-to-1898/69.php.

Burrows, Matt. "Ardern Responds to Fears Politicians Could Become COVID-19 'Super-Spreaders' during Election Campaign." MSN News, April 9, 2020. www.msn.com/en-nz/news/national/ardern-responds-to-fears-politicians-could-become-covid-19-super-spreaders-during-election-campaign/ar-BB18GWdA.

Bush, Evan. "Welcome to the Capitol Hill Autonomous Zone, Where Seattle Protesters Gather without Police." *Seattle Times*, June 10, 2020. www.seattletimes.com/seattle-news/welcome-to-the-capitol-hill-autonomous-zone-where-seattle-protesters-gather-without-police.

Buttar, Harpal S., Timao Li, and Nivedita Ravi. "Prevention of Cardiovascular Diseases: Role of Exercise, Dietary Interventions, Obesity and Smoking Cessation." *Experimental and Clinical Cardiology* 10, no. 4 (Winter 2005: 229–49. www.ncbi.nlm.nih.gov/pmc/articles/PMC2716237.

Butterfield, Lyman Henry. *Letters of Benjamin Rush: Volume II: 1793–1813*. Princeton, NJ: Princeton University Press, 2019.

California Code, Education Code, EDC § 51512. https://codes.findlaw.com/ca/education-code/edc-sect-51512.html.

California Department of Fish and Wildlife. "A Summary of the California Environmental Quality Act (CEQA)." Accessed January 13, 2021. https://wildlife.ca.gov/Conservation/CEQA/Purpose.

Calisher, Charles H., James E. Childs, Hume E. Field, Kathryn V. Holmes, and Tony Schountz. "Bats: Important Reservoir Hosts of Emerging Viruses." *Clinical Microbiology Reviews* 19, no. 3 (July 2006): 531–45. https://doi.org/10.1128/CMR.00017-06.

Campbell, Sophia, Lorena Hernandez Barcena, and Wessel David. "Hutchins Roundup: PPP Loans, Charter Schools and More." Brookings (blog), August 6, 2020. www.brookings.edu/blog/up-front/2020/08/06/hutchins-roundup-ppp-loans-charter-schools-and-more.

"Canada Shows How Easy Virus Testing Can Be." ResetEra. Accessed January 20, 2021. www.resetera.com/threads/canada-shows-how-easy-virus-testing-can-be.175157.

Canadian Health Coalition. "History of Canada's Public Health Care." Accessed January 20, 2021. www.healthcoalition.ca/tools-and-resources/history-of-canadas-public-health-care.

Carden, Dan. "Indiana Lawmakers Eyeing Cigarette Tax Hike to Reduce Hoosier Smoking Rate." *Times of Northwest Indiana*, December 17, 2020. www.nwitimes.com/news/local/govt-and-politics/indiana-lawmakers-eyeing-cigarette-tax-hike-to-reduce-hoosier-smoking-rate/article_a9cbb813-3f11-591c-81cb-8082c8377b25.html.

Carman, Harry James. *The Street Surface Railway Franchises of New York City*. New York: Columbia University, 1919.

Carney, Jordain. "Obstacles Mount for Deal on Next Coronavirus Bill." *The Hill*, May 3, 2020. thehill.com/homenews/senate/495760-obstacles-mount-for-deal-on-next-coronavirus-bill.

Carroll, Aaron E. "The Real Reason the U.S. Has Employer-Sponsored Health Insurance." *The New York Times*, September 5, 2017. www.nytimes.com/2017/09/05/upshot/the-real-reason-the-us-has-employer-sponsored-health-insurance.html.

Cartwright, Mark. "Peloponnesian War." World History Encyclopedia, May 2, 2018. www.ancient
.eu/Peloponnesian_War.

———. "Trade in Ancient Greece." World History Encyclopedia, May 22, 2018. www.ancient.eu
/article/115/trade-in-ancient-greece.

———. "Trade in Medieval Europe." World History Encyclopedia, January 8, 2019. www.ancient.eu
/article/1301/trade-in-medieval-europe.

———. "1204: The Sack of Constantinople." World History Encyclopedia, February 1, 2018. www
.ancient.eu/article/1188/1204-the-sack-of-constantinople.

Center for Budget and Policy Priorities. "Tracking the COVID-19 Recession's Effects on Food,
Housing, and Employment Hardships." Last modified March 5, 2021. www.cbpp.org/research
/poverty-and-inequality/tracking-the-covid-19-recessions-effects-on-food-housing-and.

Center for Community College Student Engagement. *Contingent Commitments: Bringing Part-Time
Faculty into Focus.* Austin: University of Texas at Austin, Program in Higher Education Leadership, 2014. www.ccsse.org/docs/PTF_Special_Report.pdf.

Central Piedmont Community College. "Mechatronics Engineering Technology." Accessed January
18, 2021. www.cpcc.edu/programs/mechatronics-engineering-technology.

Cerdá, Magdalena, Yusuf Ransome, Katherine M. Keyes, Karestan C. Koenen, Kenneth Tardiff,
David Vlahov, and Sandro Galea. "Revisiting the Role of the Urban Environment in Substance
Use: The Case of Analgesic Overdose Fatalities." *American Journal of Public Health* 103, no. 12
(December 2013): 2252–60. www.ncbi.nlm.nih.gov/pmc/articles/PMC3828967.

Chan, Christina H., Ashleigh R. Tuite, and David N. Fisman. "Historical Epidemiology of the Second
Cholera Pandemic: Relevance to Present Day Disease Dynamics." *PLoS ONE* 8, no. 8 (August
2013): e72498. https://doi.org/10.1371/journal.pone.0072498.

Chan, Sewell. "Data Show Manhattan is Svelte and Bronx is Chubby, Chubby." *The New York Times*,
July 21, 2009. www.nytimes.com/2009/07/22/nyregion/22fat.html.

Chandra, Siddharth, Goran Kuljanin, and Jennifer Wray. "Mortality from the Influenza Pandemic of
1918–1919: The Case of India." *Demography* 49, no. 3 (August 2012): 857–65. https://doi.org
/10.1007/s13524-012-0116-x.

Chapin, Christy Ford. "Why Insurance Companies Control Your Medical Care." The Conversation,
October 4, 2016. http://theconversation.com/why-insurance-companies-control-your-medical
-care-62540.

Charles, Sam. "After 3 Years of Progress, Chicago's Murder Tally Skyrockets in 2020." *Chicago Sun-
Times*, December 31, 2020. https://chicago.suntimes.com/crime/2020/12/31/22208002/chicago
-murders-2020-skyrocket-crime-violence-cpd-homicides.

Chastel, C. "Centenary of the Discovery of Yellow Fever Virus and Its Transmission by a Mosquito
(Cuba 1900–1901)." *Bulletin de la Société de Pathologie Exotique* 96, no. 3 (August 2003): 250–56.
https://www.researchgate.net/publication/9037638_Centenary_of_the_discovery_of_yellow
_fever_virus_and_its_transmission_by_a_mosquito_Cuba_1900-1901.

Chaudhuri, Saabira, and Jennifer Maloney. "As Americans Drink Less Alcohol, Booze Makers Look
Beyond the Barrel." *The Wall Street Journal*, January 17, 2019. www.wsj.com/articles/americans
-are-drinking-less-alcohol-11547733600.

Chauvin, J. P., Edward Glaeser, and Stephanie Kestelman. "Regulation and Mobility in Brazil."
Working Paper, 2021.

Chauvin, Juan Pablo, Edward Glaeser, Yueran Ma, and Kristina Tobio. "What Is Different about
Urbanization in Rich and Poor Countries? Cities in Brazil, China, India and the United States."
Journal of Urban Economics 98 (2017): 17–49. https://doi.org/10.1016/j.jue.2016.05.003.

Chen, Angela. "IBM's Watson Gave Unsafe Recommendations for Treating Cancer." *The Verge*, July 26, 2018. www.theverge.com/2018/7/26/17619382/ibms-watson-cancer-ai-healthcare-science.

Chen, M. Keith, Judith A. Chevalier, and Elisa F. Long. "Nursing Home Staff Networks and COVID-19." NBER Working Paper Series 27608, National Bureau of Economic Research, Cambridge, MA, July 2020. https://doi.org/10.3386/w27608.

Cheng, Derek. "Covid 19 Coronavirus: Prime Minister Jacinda Ardern's D-Day Decision Already Made for Her." *New Zealand Herald*, June 7, 2020. www.nzherald.co.nz/nz/covid-19-coronavirus-prime-minister-jacinda-arderns-d-day-decision-already-made-for-her/IY5QB46BKOXF44FKVFGRY2XRNY.

Chetty, Raj, John N. Friedman, Nathaniel Hendren, Maggie R. Jones, and Sonya R. Porter. "The Opportunity Atlas: Mapping the Childhood Roots of Social Mobility." NBER Working Paper Series 25147, National Bureau of Economic Research, Cambridge, MA, October 2018. https://doi.org/10.3386/w25147.

Chetty, Raj, Nathaniel Hendren, and Lawrence F. Katz. "The Effects of Exposure to Better Neighborhoods on Children: New Evidence from the Moving to Opportunity Experiment." *American Economic Review* 106, no. 4 (April 2016): 855–902. https://doi.org/10.1257/aer.20150572.

Chetty, Raj, Nathaniel Hendren, Patrick Kline, and Emmanuel Saez. "Where Is the Land of Opportunity? The Geography of Intergenerational Mobility in the United States." *The Quarterly Journal of Economics* 129, no. 4 (November 2014): 1553–1623. https://doi.org/10.1093/qje/qju022.

Chetty, Raj, et al. "The Association between Income and Life Expectancy in the United States." *JAMA* 315, no. 6 (April 2016): 1750–66. https://doi.org/10.1001/jama.2016.4226.

Chhabria, Sheetal. "Manufacturing Epidemics: Pathogens, Poverty, and Public Health Crises in India." *India Forum*, June 5, 2020. www.theindiaforum.in/article/manufacturing-epidemics.

Chicago Police Accountability Task Force. *Recommendations for Reform: Restoring Trust between the Chicago Police and the Communities They Serve.* April 2016. https://chicagopatf.org/wp-content/uploads/2016/04/PATF-Complete-Recommendations-.pdf.

Chinazzi, Matteo, Jessica T. Davis, Marco Ajelli, Corrado Gioannini, Maria Litvinova, Stefano Merler, Ana Pastore y Piontti, et al. "The Effect of Travel Restrictions on the Spread of the 2019 Novel Coronavirus (COVID-19) Outbreak." *Science* 368, no. 6489 (April 2020): 395–400. https://doi.org/10.1126/science.aba9757. https://doi.org/10.1177/0306422018800259.

Chinitz, Benjamin. "Contrasts in Agglomeration: New York and Pittsburgh." *American Economic Review* 51, no. 2 (1961): 279–89. https://www.sjsu.edu/faculty/watkins/chinitz01.htm.

Chippaux, Jean-Philippe, and Alain Chippaux. "Yellow Fever in Africa and the Americas: A Historical and Epidemiological Perspective." *Journal of Venomous Animals and Toxins Including Tropical Diseases* 24, no. 20 (August 2018). https://doi.org/10.1186/s40409-018-0162-y.

"Cholera." History.com. Last modified March 24, 2020. www.history.com/topics/inventions/history-of-cholera.

Chopra, Vineet, Eric Toner, Richard Waldhorn, and Laraine Washer. "How Should U.S. Hospitals Prepare for Coronavirus Disease 2019 (COVID-19)?" *Annals of Internal Medicine* 172, no. 9 (May 2020): 621–22. https://doi.org/10.7326/m20-0907.

Cicero, Theodore J., and Matthew S. Ellis. "Abuse-Deterrent Formulations and the Prescription Opioid Abuse Epidemic in the United States: Lessons Learned from OxyContin." *JAMA Psychiatry* 72, no. 5 (2015): 424. https://doi.org/10.1001/jamapsychiatry.2014.3043.

"Cincinnati, Ohio Population History 1840–2019." Biggest US Cities. Accessed November 18, 2020. www.biggestuscities.com/city/cincinnati-ohio.

Cipolla, Carlo M. *Fighting the Plague in Seventeenth-Century Italy.* Madison: University of Wisconsin Press, 1981.

Citizens' Association of New York, Council of Hygiene and Public Health. *Report of the Council of Hygiene and Public Health of the Citizens' Association of New York upon the Sanitary Condition of the City.* New York: D. Appleton and Company, 1865.

Citizens' Committee for Children. "Life Expectancy." Keeping Track Online. Accessed January 20, 2021. https://data.cccnewyork.org/data/map/1341/life-expectancy#1341/a/3/1573/25/a/a.

City of Boston. *Licenses & Permits for Retail Shop Owners.* www.cityofboston.gov/images_documents /AV%20Retail%20Printable%20updated_tcm3-27759.pdf.

"City of Lubbock Reports 9 Additional COVID-19 Deaths, 312 New Cases." EverythingLubbock, January 05, 2021. www.everythinglubbock.com/news/local-news/city-of-lubbock-reports-9-addi tional-covid-19-deaths-312-new-cases.

City of New York. "A Brief History of Tweed Courthouse." www.nyc.gov/html/om/html/tweed _courthouse.html.

———. "NYC Business: Get Help with Licenses and Permits." Accessed January 18, 2021. www1 .nyc.gov/nycbusiness/article/get-help-with-licenses-and-permits.

City of New York, Board of Estimate and Apportionment. "Building Zone Resolution (Adopted July 25, 1916)." www1.nyc.gov/assets/planning/download/pdf/about/city-planning-history/zr1916.pdf.

Claxton, Gary, Matthew Rae, Gregory Young, and Daniel McDermott. *Employer Health Benefits: KFF 2020 Annual Survey.* San Francisco: Kaiser Family Foundation, 2020. http://files.kff.org /attachment/Report-Employer-Health-Benefits-2020-Annual-Survey.pdf.

Clay, Rebecca A. "How Portugal Is Solving Its Opioid Problem." *Monitor on Psychology* 49, no. 9 (October 2018). www.apa.org/monitor/2018/10/portugal-opioid.

Clements, Jonathan. *A Brief History of China: Dynasty, Revolution and Transformation: From the Middle Kingdom to the People's Republic.* Clarendon, VT: Tuttle Publishing, 2019.

Cleveland Clinic. "Opioids." Accessed December 25, 2020. https://my.clevelandclinic.org/health /articles/21127-opioids.

Clinton, William J. "Remarks on Signing the Violent Crime Control and Law Enforcement Act of 1994." September 13, 1994. Public Papers of the Presidents of the United States: William J. Clin-ton (1994, Book II). US Government Publishing Office, 1994. www.govinfo.gov/content/pkg /PPP-1994-book2/html/PPP-1994-book2-doc-pg1539.htm.

"Cloaca Maxima." *Encyclopædia Britannica Online* May 22, 2009. www.britannica.com/topic/Cloaca -Maxima.

Clower, Will. "Why English Is 'the Language of Obesity.'" Mediterranean Wellness (blog), March 28, 2016. https://www.mymedwellness.com/Medwell_blog/2016/03/28/why-english-is-the-language -of-obesity.

Cockburn, Aidan. *Infectious Diseases; Their Evolution and Eradication.* Springfield, IL: Thomas, 1967.

Coffee with a Cop. "About—Coffee with a Cop." Accessed January 7, 2021. https://coffeewithacop .com/about.

Cohen, Mark Nathan, and George J. Armelagos. *Paleopathology at the Origins of Agriculture.* Gaines-ville: University Press of Florida, 2013.

Collins, Brenda. "Family Networks and Social Connections in the Survival of a Seventeenth-Century Library Collection." *Library & Information History* 33, no 2 (April 2017): 123–42. https://doi.org/10.1080/17583489.2017.1299427.

Collins, Sean. "The Anger behind the Protests, Explained in 4 Charts." *Vox*, May 31, 2020. www.vox.com/2020/5/31/21276004/anger-police-killing-george-floyd-protests.

"Combating the Coronavirus Pandemic: Bosch Develops Rapid Test for COVID-19." Bosch Global. Accessed December 25, 2020. www.bosch.com/stories/vivalytic-rapid-test-for-covid-19.

"Common Core Math Fails to Prepare Students for STEM." Pioneer Institute, October 1, 2013. https://pioneerinstitute.org/news/lowering-the-bar-how-common-core-math-fails-to-prepare-students-for-stem.

Common Core State Standards Initiative. "Development Process." Accessed January 24, 2021. www.corestandards.org/about-the-standards/development-process.

Commonwealth Fund. *2008 Commonwealth Fund International Health Policy Survey of Sicker Adults*. November 13, 2008. www.commonwealthfund.org/publications/surveys/2008/nov/2008-commonwealth-fund-international-health-policy-survey-sicker.

Commonwealth of Massachusetts. "Chapter 40 B Planning and Information." Accessed January 18, 2021. www.mass.gov/chapter-40-b-planning-and-information.

———. "Governor's FY2020 Budget Recommendation: Appropriation for Department of Public Health." Accessed January 20, 2021. https://budget.digital.mass.gov/govbudget/fy20/appropriations/health-and-human-services/public-health/?tab=historical-budget.

———. "Soldiers' Home in Holyoke." Accessed December 26, 2020. www.mass.gov/orgs/soldiers-home-in-holyoke.

———. "Weekly COVID-19 Public Health Report." December 10, 2020. www.mass.gov/doc/weekly-covid-19-public-health-report-december-10-2020/download.

Commonwealth of Massachusetts v. Purdue Pharma, First Amended Complaint and Jury Demand, January 31, 2019. www.reuters.com/investigates/special-report/assets/usa-courts-secrecy-judges/massachusetts-complaint-2.pdf.

Condie, Thomas, and Richard Folwell. *History of the Pestilence, Commonly Called Yellow Fever, Which Almost Desolated Philadelphia, in the Months of August, September & October, 1798.* Evans Early American Imprint Collection, Evans Text Creation Partnership, 2008. http://name.umdl.umich.edu/N26572.0001.001.

Connors, Michael. "Management Change, Fewer Residents Eyed for Soldiers' Home." *Daily Hampshire Gazette*, May 13, 2020. www.gazettenet.com/Soldiers-Home-Board-of-Trustees-give-update-at-meeting-34318222.

Cooper, Alexia D., and Erica L. Smith. "Homicide Trends in the United States, 1980–2008." Bureau of Justice Statistics, November 16, 2011. www.bjs.gov/index.cfm?iid=2221&ty=pbdetail.

Cooper, John Milton. "Theodore Roosevelt." *Encyclopædia Britannica Online*. www.britannica.com/biography/Theodore-Roosevelt.

Cooper, Phillip J. *The War against Regulation: From Jimmy Carter to George W. Bush.* Lawrence: University Press of Kansas, 2009.

The Cooper Union. "Peter Cooper's Vision." https://cooper.edu/about/history/peter-coopers-vision.

Cope, Zachary. "Dr. Thomas Percival And Jane Austen." *British Medical Journal* 1, no. 5635 (1969): 55–56.

Coppola, Francis Ford, dir. *The Godfather Part II*. Paramount Pictures/Coppola Company/American Zoetrope, 1974.

"Cornelius Vanderbilt." *Encyclopædia Britannica Online*. Accessed January 18, 2021. www.britannica .com/biography/Cornelius-Vanderbilt-1794-1877.

"Coronavirus (COVID-19) Deaths—Statistics and Research." Our World in Data. https:// ourworldindata.org/covid-deaths.

"Coronavirus: How New Zealand Relied on Science and Empathy." BBC News, April 20, 2020. www.bbc.com/news/world-asia-52344299.

"Coronavirus in the U.S.: Latest Map and Case Count." *The New York Times*. Accessed January 19, 2021. www.nytimes.com/interactive/2020/us/coronavirus-us-cases.html.

Council on Foreign Relations. "Demographics of the U.S. Military." Last modified July 13, 2020. www.cfr.org/backgrounder/demographics-us-military.

"Counting Calories: Get Back to Weight-Loss Basics." Mayo Clinic, December 8, 2020. www .mayoclinic.org/healthy-lifestyle/weight-loss/in-depth/calories/art-20048065.

Cousin, Jean. "Diocletian." *Encyclopædia Britannica Online*. www.britannica.com/biography/Diocletian.

"COVID-19 in the UK: Assessing Jobs at Risk and the Impact on People and Places." McKinsey, May 11, 2020. www.mckinsey.com/industries/public-and-social-sector/our-insights/covid-19-in-the -united-kingdom-assessing-jobs-at-risk-and-the-impact-on-people-and-places.

COVID-19 School Response Dashboard. Accessed December 8, 2020. https://covidschooldashboard .com.

Coviello, Decio, and Nicola Persico. "An Economic Analysis of Black-White Disparities in NYPD's Stop and Frisk Program." NBER Working Paper Series 18803, National Bureau of Economic Research, Cambridge, MA, February 2013. https://doi.org/10.3386/w18803.

Cowley, Joe, John Kiely, and Dave Collins. "Unravelling the Glasgow Effect: The Relationship between Accumulative Bio-Psychosocial Stress, Stress Reactivity and Scotland's Health Problems." *Preventive Medicine Reports* 4 (December 2016): 370–75. https://doi.org/10.1016/j.pmedr.2016 .08.004.

Cox, Kate. "The Future of Work Looks like Staying Out of the Office." Ars Technica, February 18, 2020. https://arstechnica.com/tech-policy/2020/02/employers-should-expand-not-cut-telework -into-the-future.

"Cracking the History of the Uncommon Common Cracker." New England Historical Society, January 24, 2014. www.newenglandhistoricalsociety.com/cracking-history-uncommon-common -cracker.

Crafts, Nicholas, and Terence C. Mills. "From Malthus to Solow: How Did the Malthusian Economy Really Evolve?" *Journal of Macroeconomics* 31, no. 1 (March 2009): 68–93. https://doi.org/10.1016 /j.jmacro.2007.08.007.

Craven, Matt, Adam Sabow, Lieven Van der Veken, and Matt Wilson. "Preventing Pandemics with Investments in Public Health." McKinsey, July 13, 2020. www.mckinsey.com/industries/public -and-social-sector/our-insights/not-the-last-pandemic-investing-now-to-reimagine-public -health-systems#.

Crawshaw, Jane L. Stevens. *Plague Hospitals: Public Health for the City in Early Modern Venice*. Surrey, UK: Ashgate, 2012.

"Cross Bronx Expressway: Historical Overview." NYCRoads.com. Accessed January 18, 2021. www .nycroads.com/roads/cross-bronx.

Cullen, Julie Berry, and Steven D. Levitt. "Crime, Urban Flight, and the Consequences for Cities." *Review of Economics and Statistics* 81, no. 2 (May 1999): 159–69. https://doi.org/10.1162/003465399558030.

Culliton, Kathleen. "This Is the Deadliest Neighborhood in New York City." Brownsville-East New York Patch, July 11, 2019. https://patch.com/new-york/brownsville/deadliest-neighborhood-new-york-city.

Cummings, K. M., C. P. Morley, and A. Hyland. "Failed Promises of the Cigarette Industry and Its Effect on Consumer Misperceptions about the Health Risks of Smoking." *Tobacco Control* 11 (2002): i110–17. https://doi.org/10.1136/tc.11.suppl_1.i110.

Cummins, Neil, Morgan Kelly, and Cormac Ó Gráda. "Living Standards and Plague in London, 1560–1665." *Economic History Review* 69, no. 1 (February 2016): 3–34. https://doi.org/10.1111/ehr.12098.

Cummins, Steven C.J., Laura McKay, and Sally MacIntyre. "McDonald's Restaurants and Neighborhood Deprivation in Scotland and England." *American Journal of Preventive Medicine* 29, no. 4 (November 2005): 308–10. https://doi.org/10.1016/j.amepre.2005.06.011.

Curd, Patricia. "Anaxagoras," in *The Stanford Encyclopedia of Philosophy*. Edited by Edward N. Zalta. Stanford, CA: Metaphysics Research Lab, Stanford University, 2019. https://plato.stanford.edu/archives/win2019/entries/anaxagoras.

"Cushing Estate, 'The Bellmont' (Now in Belmont, MA)." Digital Public Library of America. Accessed December 29, 2020. https://dp.la/item/a5659e02df76bfe779358456df64a91a.

Cutler, David M. "Nursing Our Way to Better Health." *JAMA* 322, no. 11 (2019): 1033–34. https://doi.org/10.1001/jama.2019.13834.

———. *The Quality Cure: How Focusing on Health Care Quality Can Save Your Life and Lower Spending Too.* 1st edition. Berkeley and Los Angeles: University of California Press, 2014.

———. "Reducing Administrative Costs in U.S. Health Care." The Hamilton Project, March 10, 2020. www.hamiltonproject.org/papers/reducing_administrative_costs_in_u.s_health_care.

———. *Your Money or Your Life: Strong Medicine for America's Health Care System.* Illustrated edition. New York: Oxford University Press, 2004.

Cutler, David M., Kaushik Ghosh, Kassandra Messer, Trivellore Raghunathan, Allison Rosen, and Susan Stewart. "A Satellite Account for Health in the United States." NBER Working Paper Series 27848, National Bureau of Economic Research, Cambridge, MA, September 2020. https://doi.org/10.3386/w27848.

Cutler, David M., Kaushik Ghosh, Kassandra L. Messer, Trivellore E. Raghunathan, Susan T. Stewart, and Allison B. Rosen. "Explaining The Slowdown in Medical Spending Growth among the Elderly, 1999–2012." *Health Affairs* 38, no. 2 (2019): 222–29. https://doi.org/10.1377/hlthaff.2018.05372.

Cutler, David M., and Edward Glaeser. "What Explains Differences in Smoking, Drinking, and Other Health Related Behaviors?" *American Economic Review* 95, no. 2 (May 2005): 238–42. https://doi.org/10.1257/000282805774670464.

Cutler, David M., Edward L. Glaeser, and Jesse M. Shapiro. "Why Have Americans Become More Obese?" *Journal of Economic Perspectives* 17, no. 3 (2003): 93–118. https://doi.org/10.1257/089533003769204371.

Cutler, David M., and Dan P. Ly. "The (Paper)Work of Medicine: Understanding International Medical Costs." *Journal of Economic Perspectives* 25, no. 2 (Spring 2011): 3–25. https://doi.org/10.1257/jep.25.2.3.

Cutler, David M., Ellen Meara, and Susan Stewart. "Socioeconomic Status and the Experience of Pain: An Example from Knees." NBER Working Paper Series 27974, National Bureau of Economic Research, Cambridge, MA, October 2020. https://doi.org/10.3386/w27974.

Cutler, David M., and Grant Miller. "The Role of Public Health Improvements in Health Advances: The 20th Century United States," *Demography* 42, no. 1 (2005): 1–22. https://doi.org/10.1353/dem.2005.0002.

Cutler, David M., Grant Miller, and Doug Norton. "Evidence on Early-Life Income and Late-Life Health from America's Dust Bowl Era." *Proceedings of the National Academy of Sciences* 104, no. 33 (August 2007): 13244–49. https://doi.org/10.1073/pnas.0700035104.

Cutler, David M., and Elizabeth Richardson. *Frontiers in Health Policy Research*. Vol. 2. Cambridge, MA: MIT Press, 1999.

Cutler, David M., and Lawrence H. Summers. "The COVID-19 Pandemic and the $16 Trillion Virus." *JAMA* 324, no. 15 (October 2020): 1495–96. https://doi.org/10.1001/jama.2020.19759.

Daly, James R. L. "A Clinical Study of Heroin." *Boston Medical and Surgical Journal* 142 (February 1900): 190–92. https://doi.org/10.1056/NEJM190002221420804.

Dalzell, A. "Maecenas and the Poets" *Phoenix* 10, no. 4 (Winter 1956): 151–62. https://doi.org/10.2307/1086017.

Daschle, Tom, Scott S. Greenberger, and Jeanne M. Lambrew. *Critical: What We Can Do about the Health-Care Crisis*. New York: St. Martins Griffin, 2009.

Dave, Dhaval M., Andrew I. Friedson, Kyutaro Matsuzawa, Joseph J. Sabia, and Samuel Safford. "Black Lives Matter Protests and Risk Avoidance: The Case of Civil Unrest During a Pandemic." NBER Working Paper Series 27408, National Bureau of Economic Research, Cambridge, MA, June 2020. Revised January 2021. https://doi.org/10.3386/w27408.

Davenport, Romola J. "Urbanization and Mortality in Britain, c. 1800–50." *Economic History Review* 73, no. 2 (May 2020): 455–85. https://doi.org/10.1111/ehr.12964.

Davis, Christopher G., and Biing-Hwan Lin. *Factors Affecting U.S. Pork Consumption*. United States Department of Agriculture, May 2005. www.ers.usda.gov/webdocs/outlooks/37377/15778_ldpm13001_1_.pdf.

Davis, James W., and Nikki Balch Stilwell. *Aristocrat in Burlap: A History of the Potato in Idaho*. Idaho Potato Commission. Accessed December 25, 2020. https://idahopotato.com/aristocrat-in-burlap/online/38.

Davis, Joseph H. "An Annual Index of U. S. Industrial Production, 1790–1915." *Quarterly Journal of Economics* 119, no. 4 (November 2004): 1177–1215. https://doi.org/10.1162/0033553042476143.

Davis, Lisa. "Siemens AG." Business Roundtable. Accessed January 18, 2021. www.businessroundtable.org/archive/skills-gap/siemens-ag.

"Death of John Stephenson; the Builder of Street Cars Passes Away Suddenly." *The New York Times*, August 1, 1893, www.nytimes.com/1893/08/01/archives/death-of-john-stephenson-the-builder-of-street-cars-passes-away.html.

Decker, Ryan, John Haltiwanger, Ron S. Jarmin, and Javier Miranda. "The Role of Entrepreneurship in US Job Creation and Economic Dynamism." *Journal of Economic Perspectives* 28, no. 3 (Summer 2014): 3–24.

———. "The Secular Decline in Business Dynamism in the U.S.," Working Paper, June 2014. http://citeseerx.ist.psu.edu/viewdoc/download?doi=10.1.1.391.3927&rep=rep1&type=pdf.

De Lew, Nancy, George Greenberg, and Kraig Kinchen. "A Layman's Guide to the U.S. Health Care System." *Health Care Financing Review* 14, no. 1 (1992): 151–69. www.ncbi.nlm.nih.gov/pmc /articles/PMC4193322.

Demosthenes. *Against Leptines*, section 32. Translated by C. A. Vince and J. H. Vince. Cambridge, MA: Harvard University Press; London: William Heinemann, 1926. www.perseus.tufts.edu /hopper/text?doc=Perseus%3Atext%3A1999.01.0072%3Aspeech%3D20%3Asection%3D32.

Derenoncourt, Ellora. "Can You Move to Opportunity? Evidence from the Great Migration." Working Paper, 2020. https://scholar.harvard.edu/elloraderenoncourt/publications/can-you-move-opportu nity-evidence-great-migration-job-market-paper.

DeSilver, Drew. "What's On Your Table? How America's Diet Has Changed over the Decades." Pew Research Center, December 13, 2016. www.pewresearch.org/fact-tank/2016/12/13/whats-on -your-table-how-americas-diet-has-changed-over-the-decades.

Dessaux, Pierre-Antoine. "Chemical Expertise and Food Market Regulation in *Belle-Epoque* France." *History and Technology* 23, no. 4 (September 2007): 351–68. https://doi.org/10.1080 /07341510701527427.

Devi, Tanaya, and Roland G. Fryer Jr. "Policing the Police: The Impact of 'Pattern-or-Practice' Inves tigations on Crime." NBER Working Paper Series 27324, National Bureau of Economic Re search, Cambridge, MA, June 2020. https://doi.org/10.3386/w27324.

Dewitte, Sharon N., and Maryanne Kowaleski. "Black Death Bodies." *Fragments: Interdisciplinary Approaches to the Study of Ancient and Medieval Pasts* 6 (2017): 1–37. http://hdl.handle.net/2027 /spo.9772151.0007.014.

Dharmapala, Dhammika, Richard H. McAdams, and John Rappaport. "Collective Bargaining Rights and Police Misconduct: Evidence from Florida." University of Chicago, Public Law Working Paper No. 655, August 1, 2019. https://doi.org/10.2139/ssrn.3095217.

Dickinson, Frank G. *Philanthropy and Public Policy*. New York: National Bureau of Economic Re search, 1962.

Dieleman, Joseph L., Jackie Cao, Abby Chapin, Carina Chen, Zhiyin Li, Angela Liu, et al. "US Health Care Spending by Payer and Health Condition, 1996–2016." *JAMA* 323, no. 9 (2020): 863. https://doi.org/10.1001/jama.2020.0734.

Dillon, Sam. "Eastern States Dominate in Winning School Grants." *The New York Times*, August 24, 2010. www.nytimes.com/2010/08/25/education/25schools.html.

"Diseases of the Mind: Highlights of American Psychiatry through 1900: Benjamin Rush, M.D. (1749–1813): 'The Father of American Psychiatry.'" US National Library of Medicine. Accessed January 13, 2021. www.nlm.nih.gov/hmd/diseases/benjamin.html.

Disraeli, Benjamin. "First Reading—Metropolis Local Management Act Amendment Bill." Decem ber 15, 1858, Hansard. UK Parliament. https://api.parliament.uk/historic-hansard/commons /1858/jul/15/first-reading.

"Dr. Deborah Birx on Efforts to Find COVID-19 Treatments, Vaccines and Push to Reopen Amer ica." Fox News, May 3, 2020. www.foxnews.com/transcript/dr-deborah-birx-on-efforts-to-find -covid-19-treatments-vaccines-and-push-to-reopen-america.

Domar, Evsey D. "The Causes of Slavery or Serfdom: A Hypothesis." *Journal of Economic History* 30, no. 1 (1970): 18–32. http://www.jstor.org/stable/2116721.

"Donald Trump Ron DeSantis Press Conference Transcript." Rev, April 28, 2020. https://www.rev .com/blog/transcripts/donald-trump-ron-desantis-press-conference-transcript.

Donev, J. M. K. C., et al. "Oil Crisis of the 1970s." Energy Education (2016). Accessed January 20, 2021. https://energyeducation.ca/encyclopedia/Oil_crisis_of_the_1970s.

Donthi, Narasimha Reddy. "Hyderabad Pharma City: A Toxic Cluster in the Making." *New Indian Express*, October 5, 2020. www.newindianexpress.com/states/telangana/2020/oct/05/hyderabad -pharma-city-a-toxic-cluster-in-the-making-2205942.html.

Douthat, Ross. "Prisons of Our Own Making." *The New York Times*, December 14, 2009. www .nytimes.com/2009/12/14/opinion/14douthat.html.

Drayer, Lisa. "The Non-alcoholic's Guide to Drinking Less Alcohol." CNN, November 3, 2017. www.cnn.com/2017/11/03/health/less-alcohol-food-drayer/index.html.

Dreher, Axel, Peter Nunnenkamp, and Rainer Thiele. "Does US Aid Buy UN General Assembly Votes? A Disaggregated Analysis." *Public Choice* 136, no. 1 (2008): 139–64.

Dreiser, Theodore. *Sister Carrie*. New York: Modern Library, 1999.

Drosendahl, Glenn. "Ida Ballasiotes Files Initiative That Will Become the Nation's First 'Three Strikes, You're Out' Law with Washington Secretary of State's Office on January 6, 1993." HistoryLink, November 19, 2015. www.historylink.org/File/11148.

D. S. G. "Medical Care: Changes in the Political Terrain." *Science* 135, no. 3498 (1962): 90–91. www .jstor.org/stable/1707551.

Dunlap, David W. "Why Robert Moses Keeps Rising from an Unquiet Grave." *The New York Times*, March 21, 2017. www.nytimes.com/2017/03/21/nyregion/robert-moses-andrew-cuomo-and-the -saga-of-a-bronx-expressway.html.

Dunn, Bill. "J.R. Simplot." Freedom from Religion Foundation. Accessed December 25, 2020. https://ffrf.org/news/day/dayitems/item/14774-j-r-simplot.

Early Childhood Learning and Knowledge Center/Head Start. "Types of Grants." December 3, 2018. https://eclkc.ohs.acf.hhs.gov/fiscal-management/article/types-grants.

"Eastern Equine Encephalitis Virus (EEEV): The Role of Diagnostics." American Society for Micro- biology, October 7, 2019. https://asm.org/Articles/2019/October/Eastern-Equine-Encephalitis -Virus-EEEV-the-Role-of.

Echenberg, Myron. "Pestis Redux: The Initial Years of the Third Bubonic Plague Pandemic, 1894– 1901." *Journal of World History* 13, no. 2 (Fall 2002): 429–49. https://doi.org/10.1353/jwh.2002 .0033.

ECPA Urban Planning. "Case Study: The Boston Waterfront Innovation District." Smart Cities Dive, 2017. www.smartcitiesdive.com/ex/sustainablecitiescollective/case-study-boston-waterfront -innovation-district/27649.

"Ed Glaeser Slips on a Banana Peel." Pioneer Institute, September 23, 2010. https://pioneerinstitute .org/news/ed-glaeser-slips-on-a-banana-peel.

Ehrenkranz, N. Joel, and Deborah A. Sampson. "Origin of the Old Testament Plagues: Explications and Implications." *Yale Journal of Biology and Medicine* 81, no. 1 (March 2008): 31–42. https:// www.ncbi.nlm.nih.gov/pmc/articles/PMC2442724.

"Elementary and Secondary Education Expenditures." Urban Institute, October 23, 2017. www .urban.org/policy-centers/cross-center-initiatives/state-and-local-finance-initiative/state-and -local-backgrounders/elementary-and-secondary-education-expenditures.

"Elisha Otis." *Encyclopædia Britannica Online*. Accessed January 18, 2021. www.britannica.com /biography/Elisha-Otis.

Elliott, Farley. "Someone Smashed the Front Window of Divisive Boyle Heights Coffee Shop Again." Eater Los Angeles, September 4, 2018. https://la.eater.com/2018/9/4/17819262/weird-wave -coffee-window-broken-smashed-news-update.

———. "This New Boyle Heights Coffee Bar Has Become a Gentrification Battleground." Eater Los Angeles, June 19, 2017. https://la.eater.com/2017/6/19/15818374/weird-wave-coffee-boyle-heights -protest-gentrification.

Ellyatt, Holly. "German Covid Cases Are Rising 'Exponentially'—And Its Vaccine Pause Could Make Things Worse," CNBC, March 17, 2021. www.cnbc.com/2021/03/17/german-covid-cases-rising -exponentially-amid-risky-vaccine-pause.html.

Energy Information Administration. 2003. "Households with Selected Appliances and Types of Main Heating Fuel, Selected Years," Available at http://www.eia.doe.gov/emeu/aer/txt/ptb0207 .html.

Erkoreka, Anton. "Origins of the Spanish Influenza Pandemic (1918–1920) and Its Relation to the First World War." *Journal of Molecular and Genetic Medicine* 3, no. 2 (December 2009): 190–94. https://www.ncbi.nlm.nih.gov/pmc/articles/PMC2805838.

Estes, J. W. "John Jones's Mysteries of Opium Reveal'd (1701): Key to Historical Opiates." *Journal of the History of Medicine and Allied Sciences* 34, no. 2 (April 1979): 200–9. https://pubmed.ncbi.nlm .nih.gov/381381.

Estrada, Gilbert. "If You Build It, They Will Move: The Los Angeles Freeway System and the Displacement of Mexican East Los Angeles, 1944-1972." *Southern California Quarterly* 87, no. 3 (October 2005): 287–315. https://doi.org/10.2307/41172272.

European Commission. "Eurostat: Database." https://ec.europa.eu/eurostat/web/main/data/database.

———. "Eurostat: How Usual Is It to Work from Home?" April 24, 2020. https://ec.europa.eu /eurostat/web/products-eurostat-news/-/DDN-20200424-1.

Evaluating the Propriety and Adequacy of the Oxycontin Criminal Settlement: Hearing Before the Committee on the Judiciary, United States Senate, 110th Cong., First Session, July 31, 2007. www.govinfo .gov/content/pkg/CHRG-110shrg40884/html/CHRG-110shrg40884.htm.

Evans, William N., Ethan M. J. Lieber, and Patrick Power, "How the Reformulation of OxyContin Ignited the Heroin Epidemic," *Review of Economics and Statistics* 101, no. 1 (March 2019): 1–15. www.mitpressjournals.org/doi/pdf/10.1162/rest_a_00755.

Everett, Bob. "How London Got Its Victorian Sewers," OpenLearn, August 30, 2019. www.open .edu/openlearn/science-maths-technology/engineering-technology/how-london-got-its -victorian-sewers.

"Explore Results for the 2019 NAEP Mathematics Assessment: Grade 12." The Nation's Report Card, 2019. www.nationsreportcard.gov/mathematics?grade=12.

"Extracts from David Williams's Autobiography," *The American Historical Review* 43, no. 4 (July 1938): 810–813. https://doi.org/10.1086/ahr/43.4.810.

"Fact Check: Outdated Video of Fauci Saying 'There's No Reason to Be Walking around with a Mask.'" Reuters, October 8, 2020. www.reuters.com/article/uk-factcheck-fauci-outdated-video -masks-idUSKBN26T2TR.

Fahim, Kareem. "Bomb Squad Has Hard-Won Expertise." *The New York Times*, May 3, 2010. www .nytimes.com/2010/05/03/nyregion/03squad.html.

Fan, Yi, Kai Zhao, Zheng-Li Shi, and Peng Zhou. "Bat Coronaviruses in China." *Viruses* 11, no. 3 (March 2019). https://doi.org/10.3390/v11030210.

Farley, John, and Gerald Geison. "Science, Politics and Spontaneous Generation in Nineteenth-Century France: The Pasteur-Pouchet Debate." *Bulletin of the History of Medicine* 48, no. 2 (1974): 161–98.

Farooqui, Habib Hasan, Aashna Mehta, and Sakthivel Selvaraj. "Outpatient Antibiotic Prescription Rate and Pattern in the Private Sector in India: Evidence from Medical Audit Data." *PLoS ONE* 14, no. 11 (November 2019). https://doi.org/10.1371/journal.pone.0224848.

Federal Bureau of Investigation. "Expanded Homicide Data Table 1: Murder Victims by Race, Ethnicity, and Sex, 2018." FBI Uniform Crime Reporting. https://ucr.fbi.gov/crime-in-the-u.s /2018/crime-in-the-u.s.-2018/tables/expanded-homicide-data-table-1.xls.

Federal Housing Finance Agency. "Historical City-Level Housing Price Data." January 19, 2021. www.fhfa.gov/DataTools/Downloads/Documents/HPI/HPI_AT_metro.txt.

"Felix Hoffmann." Science History Institute. Accessed January 20, 2021. www.sciencehistory.org /historical-profile/felix-hoffmann.

Feng, Emily, and Amy Cheng. "As China's Wuhan Ends Its Long Quarantine, Residents Feel a Mix of Joy and Fear." NPR, April 8, 2020. www.npr.org/2020/04/08/829574902/as-chinas-wuhan -ends-its-long-quarantine-residents-feel-a-mix-of-joy-and-fear.

Fensterwald, John. "Some Teachers Unions, Districts at Odds over Live Distance Learning Instruction." EdSource, July 2, 2020. https://edsource.org/2020/some-teachers-unions-districts-at-odds -over-live-distance-learning-instruction/635237.

Ferreira, Fernando, and Joseph Gyourko. "Do Political Parties Matter? Evidence from U.S. Cities." *Quarterly Journal of Economics* 124, no. 1 (February 2009): 399–422. https://doi.org/10.1162 /qjec.2009.124.1.399.

Ferrières, Jean. "The French Paradox: Lessons for Other Countries." *Heart* 90, no. 1 (January 2004): 107–11. ncbi.nlm.nih.gov/pmc/articles/PMC1768013.

"50th Anniversary of Medicare and Medicaid." LBJ Presidential Library. www.lbjlibrary.org/50th -anniversary-of-medicare-and-medicaid.

Finger, Simon. "Yellow Fever." *The Encyclopedia of Greater Philadelphia*. https://philadelphiaencyclo-pedia.org/archive/yellow-fever.

Finkelstein, Amy. "The Aggregate Effects of Health Insurance: Evidence from the Introduction of Medicare." *The Quarterly Journal of Economics* 122, no. 1 (February 2007): 1–37. https://doi .org/10.1162/qjec.122.1.1

Firey, Thomas A. "A Better Solution to Maryland's Pension Problem?" The Maryland Public Policy Institute, July 26, 2011. www.mdpolicy.org/research/detail/a-better-solution-to-marylands-pension -problem.

Fishback, Price V., and Shawn Everett Kantor. "'Square Deal' or Raw Deal? Market Compensation for Workplace Disamenities, 1884–1903." *Journal of Economic History* 52, no. 4 (December 1992): 826–48. https://www.jstor.org/stable/2123229.

Fisher, Lawrence M. "Alvin Toffler: The Thought Leader Interview." *Strategy+Business* 45 (Winter 2006). www.strategy-business.com/article/06408.

Fitton, Robert S. *The Arkwrights: Spinners of Fortune*. Manchester, UK, and New York: Manchester University Press, 1989.

Fletcher, Jason, and Ryne Marksteiner. "Causal Spousal Health Spillover Effects and Implications for Program Evaluation." *American Economic Journal. Economic Policy* 9, no. 4 (November 2017): 144–66. https://doi.org/10.1257/pol.20150573.

Flight, Colette. "Smallpox: Eradicating the Scourge." BBC. Last modified February 17, 2011. www
.bbc.co.uk/history/british/empire_seapower/smallpox_01.shtml.

"Florida Coronavirus Map and Case Count." *The New York Times*. Accessed January 18, 2021. www
.nytimes.com/interactive/2020/us/florida-coronavirus-cases.html.

Florida, Richard. *Rise of the Creative Class*. New York: Basic Books, 2019.

"The Flu in Boston." PBS. Accessed January 21, 2021. www.pbs.org/wgbh/americanexperience
/features/influenza-boston.

"Focus on NAEP." The Nation's Report Card. Accessed January 22, 2021. www.nationsreportcard
.gov/focus_on_naep.

"Focusing on Preservatives: How They Keep Food Fresh." ScienceDaily, November 13, 2002. www
.sciencedaily.com/releases/2002/11/021113070827.htm.

Fontenille, D., M. Diallo, M. Mondo, M. Ndiaye, and J. Thonnon. "First Evidence of Natural Vertical Transmission of Yellow Fever Virus in *Aedes aegypti*, Its Epidemic Vector." *Transactions of the
Royal Society of Tropical Medicine and Hygiene* 91, no. 5 (October 1997): 533–35. https://doi.org
/10.1016/s0035-9203(97)90013-4.

"Food Preservative." ScienceDirect Topics. Accessed December 25, 2020. www.sciencedirect.com
/topics/food-science/food-preservative.

Ford, Denae, Margaret-Anne Storey, Thomas Zimmermann, Christian Bird, Sonia Jaffe, Chandra
Maddila, Jenna L. Butler, Brian Houck, and Nachiappan Nagappan. "A Tale of Two Cities:
Software Developers Working from Home During the COVID-19 Pandemic." ArXiv:2008.11147
[cs.SE], August 25, 2020. http://arxiv.org/abs/2008.11147.

"Ford's Assembly Line Starts Rolling." History.com. Last modified November 30, 2020. www.history
.com/this-day-in-history/fords-assembly-line-starts-rolling.

Fox, James Alan, and Marianne W. Zawitz. *Homicide Trends in the United States*. Bureau of Justice
Statistics Crime Data Brief, January 1999. www.bjs.gov/content/pub/pdf/htiuscdb.pdf.

"France Coronavirus Map and Case Count." *The New York Times*. Accessed January 17, 2021. www
.nytimes.com/interactive/2020/world/europe/france-coronavirus-cases.html.

"France Payroll Employment in Manufacturing." Trading Economics. https://tradingeconomics
.com/france/manufacturing-payrolls.

Franz, Tobias. "The Legacy of Plan Colombia." Oxford Research Group, May 24, 2017. www
.oxfordresearchgroup.org.uk/blog/the-legacy-of-plan-colombia.

Friedman, Zack. "Google Employees Will Work from Home until Summer 2021." *Forbes*, July 27, 2020.
www.forbes.com/sites/zackfriedman/2020/07/27/google-amazon-facebook-microsoft-twitter.

Frierson, J. Gordon. "The Yellow Fever Vaccine: A History." *Yale Journal of Biology and Medicine* 83,
no. 2 (June 2010): 77–85. www.ncbi.nlm.nih.gov/pmc/articles/PMC2892770.

"From Boyle Heights to Netflix . . . and Back to the Neighborhood." NPR, March 20, 2020. www.npr
.org/2020/03/20/818806684/from-boyle-heights-to-netflix-and-back-to-the-neighborhood.

"From Cough Medicine to Deadly Addiction, a Century of Heroin and Drug-Abuse Policy." Yale
School of Medicine. Accessed December 25, 2020. https://medicine.yale.edu/news/yale
-medicine-magazine/from-cough-medicine-to-deadly-addiction-a-century.

Fryar, Cheryl D., Margaret D. Carroll, and Joseph Afful. "Prevalence of Overweight, Obesity, and
Severe Obesity among Adults Aged 20 and Over: United States, 1960–1962 through 2017–2018."
National Center for Health Statistics, Health E-Stats, 2020. www.cdc.gov/nchs/data/hestat
/obesity-adult-17-18/obesity-adult.htm#Citation.

Fryar, Cheryl D., Jeffrey P. Hughes, Kirsten A. Herrick, and Namanjeet Ahluwalia. *Fast Food Consumption among Adults in the United States, 2013–2016*. National Center for Health Statistics Data Brief 322, October 2018. www.cdc.gov/nchs/data/databriefs/db322-h.pdf.

Fu, Jia-Chen. "The Secret Maoist Chinese Operation That Conquered Malaria—and Won a Nobel." The Conversation, October 6, 2015. https://theconversation.com/the-secret-maoist-chinese -operation-that-conquered-malaria-and-won-a-nobel-48644.

Fuchs, Victor. "Who Shall Live?" in *Who Shall Live? Health, Economics, and Social Choice*. New York: Basic Books, 1974, 30–55.

Gabbatt, Adam, Mark Townsend, and Lisa O'Carroll. "'Occupy' Anti-capitalism Protests Spread around World." *The Guardian* (London), October 15, 2011. www.theguardian.com/world/2011 /oct/16/occupy-protests-europe-london-assange.

Gable, Robert S. "Comparison of Acute Lethal Toxicity of Commonly Abused Psychoactive Substances." *Addiction* 99, no. 6 (June 2004): 686–696. https://doi.org/10.1111/j.1360-0443.2004 .00744.x.

Gallagher, James. "Coronavirus Vaccine: UK Government Signs Deals for 90 Million Doses." BBC News, July 20, 2020. www.bbc.com/news/health-53469269.

Ganong, Peter, and Daniel W. Shoag. "Why Has Regional Income Convergence in the U.S. Declined?" NBER Working Paper Series 23609, National Bureau of Economic Research, Cambridge, MA, July 2017. https://doi.org/10.3386/w23609.

Garnsey, Peter. "Grain for Athens." *History of Political Thought* 6, no. 1/2 (1985): 62–75. https://www .jstor.org/stable/i26212456.

Garrett, Thomas A. Economic *Effects of the 1918 Influenza Pandemic: Implications for a Modern-Day Pandemic*. Federal Reserve Bank of St. Louis, November 2007. www.stlouisfed.org/~/media/files /pdfs/community-development/research-reports/pandemic_flu_report.pdf.

Gash, Norman. "Robert Peel." *Encyclopædia Britannica Online*. Last modified February 1, 2021. www .britannica.com/biography/Robert-Peel.

Gates, Bill. "The Next Outbreak? We're Not Ready." TED video, 8:24. March 2015. www.ted.com /talks/bill_gates_the_next_outbreak_we_re_not_ready/up-next?language=dz.

Gates, Jonathan D., Sandra Arabian, Paul Biddinger, Joe Blansfield, Peter Burke, Sarita Chung, Jonathan Fischer, et al. "The Initial Response to the Boston Marathon Bombing: Lessons Learned to Prepare for the Next Disaster." *Annals of Surgery* 260, no. 6 (December 2014): 960–66. https:// doi.org/10.1097/SLA.0000000000000914.

Gaynes, Robert. "The Discovery of Penicillin—New Insights after More Than 75 Years of Clinical Use." *Emerging Infectious Diseases* 23, no. 5 (May 2017): 849–53. https://doi.org/10.3201 /eid2305.161556.

"Gentrification Is the True, Highest Form of Hate Crime!" *Defend Boyle Heights*, November 3, 2016. http://defendboyleheights.blogspot.com/2016/11/gentrification-is-true-highest-form-of.html.

George, Justin, and Greg Jaffe. "Transit Workers Are Paying a Heavy Price during the Pandemic." *The Washington Post*, May 17, 2020. www.washingtonpost.com/local/trafficandcommuting/transit -workers-are-paying-heavy-price-in-the-coronavirus-pandemic/2020/05/17/d7251b18-8edc -11ea-a9c0-73b93422d691_story.html.

"George Stephenson." *Encyclopædia Britannica Online*. Accessed January 18, 2021. www.britannica .com/biography/George-Stephenson.

Georgia Association of Educators Sue State, Paulding County over Early Reopening Plan for Schools." WSB-TV, October 8, 2020. www.wsbtv.com/news/local/georgia-association-educators

-sue-state-paulding-county-over-early-reopening-plan-schools/6GQNCBRSYBHMXIUN-QLRTSGXWVE.

Georgina Gustin, "This Is How the Government Decides What You Eat." Food and Environment Reporting Network, April 18, 2016. https://thefern.org/2016/04/government-decides-eat.

Gerber, David E. "'Pure and Wholesome': Stephen Allen, Cholera, and the Nineteenth-Century New York City Water Supply." Pharos 76, no. 2 (Spring 2013): 18–27. https://alphaomegaalpha.org/pharos/PDFs/2013/1/Complete.pdf.

Gershuny, Jonathan, and Teresa Attracta Harms. "Housework Now Takes Much Less Time: 85 Years of US Rural Women's Time Use." Social Forces 95, no. 2 (December 2016): 503–24. https://doi.org/10.1093/sf/sow073.

Ghanbari, Lyda, and Michael D. McCall. "Current Employment Statistics Survey: 100 Years of Employment, Hours, and Earnings." Monthly Labor Review, US Bureau of Labor Statistics, August 2016. www.bls.gov/opub/mlr/2016/article/current-employment-statistics-survey-100-years-of-employment-hours-and-earnings.htm.

Gibb, Rory, David W. Redding, Kai Qing Chin, Christl A. Donnelly, Tim M. Blackburn, Tim Newbold, and Kate E. Jones. "Zoonotic Host Diversity Increases in Human-Dominated Ecosystems." Nature 584 (August 2020): 398–402. https://doi.org/10.1038/s41586-020-2562-8.

Gibbon, Edward. The History of the Decline and Fall of the Roman Empire. London: H. G. Bohn, 1854.

Gillum, Jack, and Marisol Bello. "When Standardized Test Scores Soared in D.C., Were the Gains Real?" USA Today, March 28, 2011. www.usatoday.com/news/education/2011-03-28-1Aschooltesting28_CV_N.htm.

Glaeser, Edward. "Cities and Pandemics Have a Long History." City Journal, Spring 2020. www.city-journal.org/cities-and-pandemics-have-long-history.

———. "City Air Makes You Free." NewBostonPost, March 26, 2016. https://newbostonpost.com/2016/03/26/city-air-makes-you-free.

———. "The Health of the Cities." Economix (blog), The New York Times, June 22, 2010. https://economix.blogs.nytimes.com/2010/06/22/the-health-of-the-cities.

———. "The Nemeses of Cities." City Journal, July 16, 2020. www.city-journal.org/perennial-threats-to-urban-life.

———. "Reforming Land Use Regulations." Brookings, April 24, 2017. www.brookings.edu/research/reforming-land-use-regulations.

———. Triumph of the City: How Our Greatest Invention Makes Us Richer, Smarter, Greener, Healthier, and Happier. New York: Penguin Press, 2011.

———. "Urbanization and Its Discontents." NBER Working Paper Series 26839, National Bureau of Economic Research, Cambridge, MA, March 2020. www.nber.org/system/files/working_papers/w26839/w26839.pdf.

Glaeser, Edward L., Caitlin Gorback, and Stephen J. Redding. "JUE Insight: How Much Does COVID-19 Increase with Mobility? Evidence from New York and Four Other U.S. Cities." Journal of Urban Economics, October 21, 2020. https://doi.org/10.1016/j.jue.2020.103292.

Glaeser, Edward, and Joseph Gyourko. "The Economic Implications of Housing Supply." Journal of Economic Perspectives 32, no. 1 (February 2018): 3–30. https://doi.org/10.1257/jep.32.1.3.

Glaeser, Edward L., and Matthew E. Kahn. "The Greenness of Cities: Carbon Dioxide Emissions and Urban Development." Journal of Urban Economics 67, no. 3 (May 2010): 404–18. https://doi.org/10.1016/j.jue.2009.11.006.

Glaeser, Edward L., Sari Pekkala Kerr, and William R. Kerr. "Entrepreneurship and Urban Growth: An Empirical Assessment with Historical Mines." *Review of Economics and Statistics* 97, no. 2 (May 2015): 498–520. https://doi.org/ doi:10.1162/REST_a_00456.

Glaeser, Edward, and Cass R. Sunstein. "Regulatory Review for the States." *National Affairs*, Summer 2014. www.nationalaffairs.com/publications/detail/regulatory-review-for-the-states.

Glaeser, Edward, and Brandon Tan. "Why Do Cities Increase Productivity but Decrease Opportunity?" Harvard University Working Paper, 2020.

Glaeser, Edward L., Ginger Zhe Jin, Benjamin T. Leyden, and Michael Luca. "Learning from Deregulation: The Asymmetric Impact of Lockdown and Reopening on Risky Behavior During COVID-19." NBER Working Paper Series 27650, National Bureau of Economic Research, Cambridge, MA, August 2020. https://doi.org/10.3386/w27650.

Global Preparedness Monitoring Board. *A World at Risk: Annual Report on Global Preparedness for Health Emergencies.* September 2019. www.preventionweb.net/publications/view/67706.

Green, Stephen, and Margot Hornblower. "Mills Admits Being Present during Tidal Basin Scuffle." *The Washington Post*, October 11, 1974. www.washingtonpost.com/wp-srv/local/longterm/tours /scandal/tidalbas.htm.

Griffith, Rachel, Rodrigo Lluberas, and Melanie Lührmann. *Gluttony in England? Long-Term Change in Diet: IFS Briefing Note BN142.* Institute for Fiscal Studies, November 2013. https://doi.org /10.1920/BN.IFS.2012.00142.

Godechot, Jacques. "Napoleon I." *Encyclopædia Britannica Online.* Accessed January 18, 2021. www .britannica.com/biography/Napoleon-I.

Goldschlag, Nathan, and Alex Tabarrok. "Is Regulation to Blame for the Decline in American Entrepreneurship?" *Economic Policy* 33, no. 93 (January 2018): 5–44. https://doi.org/10.1093/epolic /eix019.

Goldstein, Amy. "Trump Administration Says It Will Pay Hospitals for Treating Uninsured Covid-19 Patients." *The Washington Post.* April 23, 2020. www.washingtonpost.com/health/trump -administration-says-it-will-pay-hospitals-for-treating-uninsured-covid-19-patients/2020/04 /22/3df5fbb4-84b5-11ea-878a-86477a724bdb_story.html.

Goldstein, Dana, and Eliza Shapiro. "Teachers Are Wary of Returning to Class, and Online Instruction Too." *The New York Times*, July 29, 2020. www.nytimes.com/2020/07/29/us/teacher-union -school-reopening-coronavirus.html.

Gonsalves, Gregg S., and Forrest W. Crawford. "Dynamics of the HIV Outbreak and Response in Scott County, IN, USA, 2011–15: A Modelling Study." *The Lancet HIV* 5, no. 10 (October 2018): e569–77. https://doi.org/10.1016/s2352-3018(18)30176-0.

Gorman, James. "How Do Bats Live With So Many Viruses?" *The New York Times*, January 28, 2020. www.nytimes.com/2020/01/28/science/bats-coronavirus-Wuhan.html.

Gorsky, Martin. "The British National Health Service 1948–2008: A Review of the Historiography." *Social History of Medicine* 21, no. 3 (December 2008): 437–60. https://doi.org/10.1093/shm /hkn064.

Goudreau, Jenna. "Back To the Stone Age? New Yahoo CEO Marissa Mayer Bans Working from Home." *Forbes*, February 5, 2013. www.forbes.com/sites/jennagoudreau/2013/02/25/back-to-the -stone-age-new-yahoo-ceo-marissa-mayer-bans-working-from-home.

Gray, Geoffrey. "Boss Kelly." *New York*, May 14, 2010. https://nymag.com/news/crimelaw/66025.

Grogger, Jeff, and Michael Willis. "The Emergence of Crack Cocaine and the Rise in Urban Crime Rates." *Review of Economics and Statistics* 82, no. 4 (November 2000): 519–29. www.jstor.org /stable/2646648.

Gross, David J., Jonathan Ratner, James Perez, and Sarah L. Glavin. "International Pharmaceutical Spending Controls: France, Germany, Sweden, and the United Kingdom." *Health Care Financing Review* 15, no. 3 (Spring 1994): 127–40. www.ncbi.nlm.nih.gov/pmc/articles/PMC4193451.

Grove, Ben. "Cookie Capital in the Universe of Cookie-Making, the Chicago Area Ranks as a Sweet, Hot, Big, Gooey Chocolate Chip." *Chicago Tribune*, July 11, 1994.

Grunwald, Michael. "Five Myths about Obama's Stimulus." *The Washington Post*, August 10, 2012. www.washingtonpost.com/opinions/five-myths-about-obamas-stimulus/2012/08/10/7935341e -e176-11e1-ae7f-d2a13e249eb2_story.html.

Grynbaum, Michael. "New York Plans to Ban Sale of Big Sizes of Sugary Drinks." *The New York Times*, May 31, 2012. www.nytimes.com/2012/05/31/nyregion/bloomberg-plans-a-ban-on-large -sugared-drinks.html.

Grynbaum, Michael M., William K. Rashbaum, and Al Baker. "Police Seek Man Taped Near Times Sq. Bomb Scene." *The New York Times*, May 2, 2010. www.nytimes.com/2010/05/03/nyregion /03timessquare.html.

Gulliford, Jenny. "Research Indicates That Men Are More Likely to Suffer Adverse Health Consequences as a Result of Being Unemployed Than Women." London School of Economics and Political Science, June 16, 2014. https://blogs.lse.ac.uk/politicsandpolicy/men-are-more-likely-to -suffer-adverse-health-consequences-as-a-result-of-unemployment-than-women.

Gum, Samuel A. "Philadelphia Under Siege: The Yellow Fever of 1793." Pennsylvania Center for the Book. Accessed January 17, 2021. www.pabook.libraries.psu.edu/literary-cultural-heritage -map-pa/feature-articles/philadelphia-under-siege-yellow-fever-1793.

"Guns Germs & Steel: The Story Of . . . Smallpox—and Other Deadly Eurasian Germs," PBS. www .pbs.org/gunsgermssteel/variables/smallpox.html.

"Gustavus Swift." *Encyclopædia Britannica Online*. May 27, 1999. www.britannica.com/biography /Gustavus-Swift.

Guthrie, Douglas. "The Influence of the Leyden School upon Scottish Medicine." *Medical History* 3, no. 2 (1959): 108–22. https://doi:10.1017/S002572730002439X.

Haag, Matthew. "Manhattan Emptied Out During the Pandemic. But Big Tech Is Moving In." *The New York Times*, October 13, 2020. www.nytimes.com/2020/10/13/nyregion/big-tech-nyc -office-space.html.

Hadley, C. J. "Mr. Spud." *Range*, 1998. http://www.rangemagazine.com/archives/stories/summer98 /jr_simplot.htm.

Haines, Michael R. "The Urban Mortality Transition in the United States, 1800–1940." *Annales de démographie historique* 1, no. 1 (2001): 33–64. https://doi.org/10.3917/adh.101.0033.

Halliday, Stephen. "Death and Miasma in Victorian London: An Obstinate Belief." *BMJ* 323, no. 7327 (December 2001): 1469–71. https://doi.org/10.1136/bmj.323.7327.1469.

Hamm, Nia. "Holyoke, Chelsea Soldiers' Homes Receive Coronavirus Vaccine." NECN, December 29, 2020. www.necn.com/news/local/holyoke-chelsea-soldiers-homes-to-receive-coronavirus -vaccine/2378559.

A Handbook for Visitors to Paris; Containing a Description of the Most Remarkable Objects in Paris . . . With Map and Plans. London: John Murray, 1870.

Hanushek, Eric A. "The Economic Value of Higher Teacher Quality." *Economics of Education Review* 30, no. 3 (June 2011): 466–479. https://doi.org/10.1016/j.econedurev.2010.12.006.

Harbeck, Michaela, Lisa Seifert, Stephanie Hänsch, David M. Wagner, Dawn Birdsell, Katy L. Parise, Ingrid Wiechmann, et al. "*Yersinia pestis* DNA from Skeletal Remains from the 6th Century AD Reveals Insights into Justinianic Plague." *PLoS Pathogens* 9, no. 5 (May 2013). https://doi.org/10.1371/journal.ppat.1003349.

Harding, Anne. "Heart Stents Used Twice as Often in U.S. vs. Canada." Reuters, June 15, 2010. www.reuters.com/article/us-heart-stents-idUSTRE65E60220100615.

Harper, Hugo, and Michael Hallsworth. *Counting Calories: How Under-Reporting Can Explain the Apparent Fall in Calorie Intake.* London: Behavioural Insights Team, 2016.

Harper, Kristin N., Molly K. Zuckerman, Megan L. Harper, John D. Kingston, and George J. Armelagos. "The Origin and Antiquity of Syphilis Revisited: An Appraisal of Old World Pre-Columbian Evidence for Treponemal Infection." *American Journal of Physical Anthropology* 146, no. S53 (November 2011): 99–133. https://doi.org/10.1002/ajpa.21613.

Harrington, Emma, and Natalia Emanuel. "'Working' Remotely? Selection, Treatment, and Market Provision of Remote Work." Harvard University Working Paper, November 12, 2020.

Harris, Christopher J., and Robert E. Worden. "The Effect of Sanctions on Police Misconduct." *Crime & Delinquency* 60, no. 8 (December 2014): 1258–88. https://doi.org/10.1177/0011128712466933.

Harris, Jeffrey E. "The Subways Seeded the Massive Coronavirus Epidemic in New York City." NBER Working Paper Series 27021, National Bureau of Economic Research, Cambridge, MA, April 2020. https://doi.org/10.3386/w27021.

"Harry's Bar, Florence, Italy." The Martini Hour, June 3, 2011. https://martinicocktail.info/2011/06/03/harrys-bar-florence-italy.

Harvard Chan School of Public Health. "The Most Expensive Health Care System in the World." January 13, 2020. www.hsph.harvard.edu/news/hsph-in-the-news/the-most-expensive-health-care-system-in-the-world.

Hauser, Christine. "The Mask Slackers of 1918." *The New York Times*, August 3, 2020. www.nytimes.com/2020/08/03/us/mask-protests-1918.html.

Haviland, Amelia, Roland McDevitt, M. Susan Marquis, Neeraj Sood, and Melinda Beeuwkes Buntin. "Consumer-Directed Plans Could Cut Health Costs Sharply, but Also Discourage Preventive Care." RAND Corporation, June 28, 2012. www.rand.org/pubs/research_briefs/RB9672.html.

Hawks, Howard, dir. *Red River.* Monterey Productions, 1948.

He, Xi, Eric H. Y. Lau, Peng Wu, Xilong Deng, Jian Wang, Xinxin Hao, Yiu Chung Lau, et al. "Temporal Dynamics in Viral Shedding and Transmissibility of COVID-19." *Nature Medicine* 26, no. 5 (May 2020): 672–75. https://doi.org/10.1038/s41591-020-0869-5.

HealthCare.gov. "Preauthorization." Accessed December 26, 2020. www.healthcare.gov/glossary/preauthorization.

———. "UCR (Usual, Customary, and Reasonable)." Accessed January 20, 2021. www.healthcare.gov/glossary/ucr-usual-customary-and-reasonable.

Heckman, James J., Seong Hyeok Moon, Rodrigo Pinto, Peter A. Savelyev, and Adam Yavitz. "The Rate of Return to the High/Scope Perry Preschool Program." *Journal of Public Economics* 94, no. 1–2 (February 2010): 114–28. www.ncbi.nlm.nih.gov/pmc/articles/PMC3145373.

Heine, Heinrich. "'A Riot of the Dead: A German Poet Reports from the Paris Cholera Outbreak of 1832." *Lapham's Quarterly*, March 25, 2020. www.laphamsquarterly.org/roundtable/riot-dead.

Helland, Eric, and Alexander Tabarrok. "Does Three Strikes Deter?: A Nonparametric Estimation." *Journal of Human Resources* 42, no. 2 (Spring 2007): 309–30. https://doi.org/10.3368/jhr.XLII.2.309.

Helliwell, John F., and Haifang Huang. "Comparing the Happiness Effects of Real and On-Line Friends." *PLoS ONE* 8, no. 9 (September 2013). https://doi.org/10.1371/journal.pone.0072754.

Hendren, Nathaniel, and Ben Sprung-Keyser. "A Unified Welfare Analysis of Government Policies." *Quarterly Journal of Economics* 135, no. 3 (August 2020): 1209–1318. https://doi.org/10.1093/qje/qjaa006.

Hennessy-Fiske, Molly. "In Reversal, Texas and Florida Order Bars to Shut, Restaurants to Scale Back as Coronavirus Cases Surge." *Los Angeles Times*, June 26, 2020. www.latimes.com/world-nation/story/2020-06-26/texas-orders-bars-shut-restaurants-scale-back-coronavirus-spike.

Hermann, Alexander. "What Accounts for Recent Growth in Homeowner Households?" Joint Center for Housing Studies of Harvard University, November 26, 2018. www.jchs.harvard.edu/blog/what-accounts-for-recent-growth-in-homeowner-households.

Hernández, Javier C., and Chris Horton. "Taiwan's Weapon against Coronavirus: An Epidemiologist as Vice President." *The New York Times*, May 9, 2020. www.nytimes.com/2020/05/09/world/asia/taiwan-vice-president-coronavirus.html.

Hero, Joachim O., Robert J. Blendon, Alan M. Zaslavsky, and Andrea L. Campbell. "Understanding What Makes Americans Dissatisfied with Their Health Care System: An International Comparison." *Health Affairs* 35, no. 3 (March 2016): 502–09. https://doi.org/10.1377/hlthaff.2015.0978.

Herodotus. *The Landmark Herodotus: The Histories*. 1st ed. New York: Pantheon Books, 2007.

Hershkowitz, Leo. "Some Aspects of the New York Jewish Merchant and Community, 1654–1820." *American Jewish Historical Quarterly* 66, no. 1 (September 1976): 10–34. www.jstor.org/stable/i23880417.

Hibbert, Arthur Boyd. "Hanseatic League." *Encyclopædia Britannica Online*. Last modified October 21, 2019. www.britannica.com/topic/Hanseatic-League.

"High Rate of Obese and Overweight Kids Poses Problems for SF." *San Francisco Examiner*, December 13, 2013. www.sfexaminer.com/news/high-rate-of-obese-and-overweight-kids-poses-problems-for-sf.

Hill, Evan, Ainara Tiefenthäler, Christiaan Triebert, Drew Jordan, Haley Willis, and Robin Stein. "How George Floyd Was Killed in Police Custody." *The New York Times*, June 1, 2020. www.nytimes.com/2020/05/31/us/george-floyd-investigation.html.

Hilmers, Angela, David C. Hilmers, and Jayna Dave. "Neighborhood Disparities in Access to Healthy Foods and Their Effects on Environmental Justice." *American Journal of Public Health* 102, no. 9 (September 2012): 1644–54. https://doi.org/10.2105/ajph.2012.300865.

Hilts, Philip J. "Tobacco Chiefs Say Cigarettes Aren't Addictive." *The New York Times*, April 15, 1994. www.nytimes.com/1994/04/15/us/tobacco-chiefs-say-cigarettes-aren-t-addictive.html.

Himmelberg, Charles, Christopher Mayer, and Todd Sinai. *Assessing High House Prices: Bubbles, Fundamentals, and Misperceptions*. Federal Reserve Bank of New York, September 2005. https://www.newyorkfed.org/research/staff_reports/sr218.html.

Himmelstein, David U., and Steffie Woolhandler. "Public Health's Falling Share of US Health Spending." *American Journal of Public Health* 106, no. 1 (January 2016): 56–57. https://doi.org/10.2105/AJPH.2015.302908.

"History of Deadly Earthquakes." BBC News, August 19, 2018. www.bbc.com/news/world-1271 7980.

Hoffmann, Rachel Kaplan, and Keith Hoffmann. "Ethical Considerations in the Use of Cordons Sanitaires," *Clinical Correlations,* February 19, 2015. www.clinicalcorrelations.org/2015/02/19 /ethical-considerations-in-the-use-of-cordons-sanitaires.

Hoffman, Steven J., and Sarah L. Silverberg. "Delays in Global Disease Outbreak Responses: Lessons from H1N1, Ebola, and Zika." *American Journal of Public Health* 108, no. 3 (March 2018): 329–33. https://doi.org/10.2105/AJPH.2017.304245.

Holmes and Co. (Calcutta). *The Bengal Obituary, or, a Record to Perpetuate the Memory of Departed Worth: Being a Compilation of Tablets and Monumental Inscriptions from Various Parts of the Bengal and Agra Presidencies. To Which Is Added Biographical Sketches and Memoirs of Such as Have Preeminently Distinguished Themselves in History of British India, since the Formation of the European Settlement to the Present Time.* London: W. Thacker & Co., 1851.

"Holyoke Soldiers' Home." *New England Journal of Medicine* 250, no. 9 (1954): 398. https://doi.org /10.1056/nejm195403042500917.

Home Owners' Loan Corporation. "Security Map of Los Angeles County/Area Description." April 19, 1939. https://dsl.richmond.edu/panorama/redlining/#loc=17/34.046/-118.21&city=los-angeles -ca&area=D53&adimage=3/40/-155.724.

"Homeownership—Past, Present, and Future." *U.S. Housing Market Conditions.* US Department of Housing and Urban Development, Summer 1994. www.huduser.gov/periodicals/ushmc/summer94 /summer94.html.

Homer. *The Iliad.* Translated by Samuel Butler. Unabridged edition. Mineola, NY: Dover Publications, 2012.

Hopkins, Donald R. *The Greatest Killer: Smallpox in History.* Chicago: University of Chicago Press, 2002.

Horgan, John. "Justinian's Plague (541–542 CE)." World History Encyclopedia, December 26, 2014. www.ancient.eu/article/782/justinians-plague-541-542-ce.

Horwitz, Sari, and Scott Higham. "The Flow of Fentanyl: In the Mail, over the Border." *The Washington Post,* August 23, 2019. www.washingtonpost.com/investigations/2019/08/23/fentanyl-flowed -through-us-postal-service-vehicles-crossing-southern-border.

"Hospitals Are Paid Twice as Much (or More) by Private Insurers Than Medicare, Study Finds." Advisory Board, May 13, 2019. www.advisory.com/daily-briefing/2019/05/13/hospital-prices -rand.

"How to Fix America's Schools." *Time,* December 8, 2008. http://content.time.com/time/covers /0,16641,20081208,00.html.

"How Many Calories in McDonald's French Fries, Large." CalorieKing. Accessed December 29, 2020. www.calorieking.com/us/en/foods/f/calories-in-hot-fries-chips-french-fries-large /9OxHtBz6TT23cv9Osx5OnA.

Hsieh, Chang-Tai, and Enrico Moretti. "Housing Constraints and Spatial Misallocation." *American Economic Journal: Macroeconomics* 11, no. 2 (April 2019): 1–39. https://doi.org/10.1257/mac .20170388.

Hui, Sylvia. "UK Ramps Up Vaccine Rollout, Targets Every Adult by Autumn." Associated Press, January 10, 2021. https://apnews.com/article/international-news-england-coronavirus-pandemic -coronavirus-vaccine-ca01f408423b049a7625c6f431acdd8d.

Hum, Tarry. "Mapping Global Production in New York City's Garment Industry: The Role of Sunset Park, Brooklyn's Immigrant Economy." *Economic Development Quarterly* 17, no. 3 (August 2003): 294–309. https://doi.org/10.1177/0891242403255088.

Hummer, Robert A., and Elaine M. Hernandez. "The Effect of Educational Attainment on Adult Mortality in the United States." *Population Bulletin* 68, no. 1 (June 2013): 1–16. www.ncbi.nlm .nih.gov/pmc/articles/PMC4435622.

Hunt, Freeman. *Lives of American Merchants.* New York: Office of Hunt's Merchants' Magazine, 1858.

"Impact of Vaccines Universally Recommended for Children—United States, 1900–1998." *JAMA* 281, no. 16 (April 1999): 1482–83. https://doi.org/10.1001/jama.281.16.1482-JWR0428-2-1.

The Impacts of Body Worn Cameras on Police–Citizen Encounters, Police Proactivity, and Police–Community Relations in Boston: A Randomized Controlled Trial: Report to the Boston Police Department. Boston: School of Criminology and Criminal Justice, Northeastern University, July 27, 2018. https:// news.northeastern.edu/wp-content/uploads/2018/08/BPD-BWC-RCT-Full-Report -07272018.pdf.

"In Praise of Boise." *The Economist*, May 13, 2010. www.economist.com/united-states/2010/05/13 /in-praise-of-boise.

Independent Budget Office of the City of New York. "Fiscal History: NYPD." Accessed January 23, 2021. https://ibo.nyc.ny.us/RevenueSpending/nypd.html.

"Influenza Pandemic of 1918–19." *Encyclopædia Britannica Online.* July 7, 2020. www.britannica.com /event/influenza-pandemic-of-1918-1919.

Ingram, George. "What Every American Should Know about US Foreign Aid." Brookings, October 15, 2019. www.brookings.edu/policy2020/votervital/what-every-american-should-know-about -us-foreign-aid.

Institute of Medicine. *The Future of Nursing: Leading Change, Advancing Health.* Washington, DC: National Academies Press, 2011. https://doi.org/10.17226/12956.

Institute of Medicine (US) Committee on Health and Behavior: Research, Practice, and Policy. *Health and Behavior: The Interplay of Biological, Behavioral, and Societal Influences.* Washington, DC: National Academies Press, 2001. www.ncbi.nlm.nih.gov/books/NBK43733.

"Insulin Costs up to 10 Times More in US Compared with Other Nations." Kaiser Health News, October 7, 2020. https://khn.org/morning-breakout/insulin-costs-up-to-10-times-more-in-us -compared-with-other-nations.

Intergovernmental Science-Policy Platform on Biodiversity and Ecosystem Services (IPBES). *Workshop Report on Biodiversity and Pandemics of the Intergovernmental Platform on Biodiversity and Ecosystem Services (IPBES).* Bonn: IPBES Secretariat, October 29, 2020. https://doi.org/10.5281 /zenodo.4147317.

International Monetary Fund. "World Economic Outlook (October 2020)—GDP, Current Prices." Accessed January 17, 2021. www.imf.org/external/datamapper/NGDPD@WEO; Izquierdo-Suzán, Mónica, Selene Zárate, Jesús Torres-Flores, Fabián Correa-Morales, Cassandra González-Acosta, Edgar E. Sevilla-Reyes, et al. "Natural Vertical Transmission of Zika Virus in Larval *Aedes aegypti* Populations, Morelos, Mexico." *Emerging Infectious Diseases Journal* 25, no. 8 (August 2019): 1477–84. https://doi.org/10.3201/eid2508.181533.

"Jacinda Ardern: 'Tooth Fairy and Easter Bunny Are Essential Workers.'" BBC News, April 6, 2020. https://www.bbc.com/news/av/world-asia-52189013.

Jackson, Kenneth T. *Crabgrass Frontier: The Suburbanization of the United States.* 1st edition. New York: Oxford University Press, 1987.

Jacob, Brian A., and Lars Lefgren. "Principals as Agents: Subjective Performance Measurement in Education." *Journal of Labor Economics* 26, no. 1 (2008): 101–136. https://doi.org/10.1086 /522974.

Jacobs, Jane. *The Death and Life of Great American Cities.* New York: Vintage Books, 1992.

"James Jameson (1786–1823)." Find A Grave Memorial. www.findagrave.com/memorial/72990657 /james-jameson.

Jameson, James. *Report on the Epidemick Cholera Morbus: As It Visited the Territories Subject to the Presidency of Bengal, in the Years 1817, 1818 and 1819.* Calcutta: Balfour, 1820. http://resource.nlm.nih .gov/34720870R.

Japanese American National Museum. "Exhibition Timeline: Boyle Heights Project." Accessed January 11, 2021. https://www.janm.org/exhibits/boyle-heights.

Jefferies, Sarah, Nigel French, Charlotte Gilkison, Giles Graham, Virginia Hope, Jonathan Marshall, Caroline McElnay, et al. "COVID-19 in New Zealand and the Impact of the National Response: A Descriptive Epidemiological Study." *The Lancet Public Health* 5, no. 11 (November 2020): 612– 23. https://doi.org/10.1016/S2468-2667(20)30225-5

Jennings, Julie, and Jared C Nagel. *Federal Workforce Statistics Sources: OPM and OMB.* Congressional Research Service, October 23, 2020, 11.

Jervis, John B., Larry D. Lankton, and Daniel Clement. "Old Croton Aqueduct." Historic American Engineering Record NY-120. National Park Service, 1984. http://lcweb2.loc.gov/master/pnp /habshaer/ny/ny1100/ny1181/data/ny1181data.pdf.

Jessie, Lisa, and Mary Tarleton. *2012 Census of Governments: Employment Summary Report.* US Department of Commerce, March 6, 2014. https://www2.census.gov/govs/apes/2012_summary _report.pdf.

Jevons, William Stanley. *The Coal Question: An Inquiry Concerning the Progress of the Nation, and the Probable Exhaustion of Our Coal-Mines.* London: Macmillan, 1865.

"Joan of Arc (c. 1412–1431)" Biography.com. Updated March 4, 2020. www.biography.com/military -figure/joan-of-arc.

Johansson, Michael A., Talia M. Quandelacy, Sarah Kada, Pragati Venkata Prasad, Molly Steele, John T. Brooks, et al. "SARS-CoV-2 Transmission from People without COVID-19 Symptoms." *JAMA Network Open* 4, no. 1 (January 2021): e2035057. https://doi.org/10.1001/jamanet workopen.2020.35057.

Johns Hopkins Coronavirus Resource Center. "Mortality Analyses." Accessed January 18, 2021. https://coronavirus.jhu.edu/data/mortality.

Johnson, Niall P. A. S., and Juergen Mueller. "Updating the Accounts: Global Mortality of the 1918-1920 'Spanish' Influenza Pandemic." *Bulletin of the History of Medicine* 76, no. 1 (Spring 2002): 105–15. https://doi.org/10.1353/bhm.2002.0022.

Jonas, Michael. "Voc-Tech Woes Continue at Boston's Madison Park." *CommonWealth*, May 6, 2020. https://commonwealthmagazine.org/education/voc-tech-woes-continue-at-bostons-madison -park-2.

Jorgensen, Sarah. "Holyoke Soldiers' Home, Site of Deadly Outbreak, Dealt with Systemic Issues for Years, Staffers and Union Say." CNN, April 7, 2020. www.cnn.com/2020/04/06/us/holyoke -soldiers-home-coronavirus/index.html.

"José Adolfo Bernal: An 1899 Booster Pamphlet for Boyle Heights, Part 3." *Boyle Heights History Blog*, December 23, 2013. http://boyleheightshistoryblog.blogspot.com/2013/12/jose-adolfo-bernal -1899-booster.html.

JPMorgan Chase. "History of Our Firm." www.jpmorganchase.com/about/our-history.

"Julia Child." PBS. Accessed December 25, 2020. www.pbs.org/food/chefs/julia-child.

"July Revolution." *Encyclopædia Britannica Online*. July 20, 2020. www.britannica.com/event/July
-Revolution.

Jyoti, Archana. "1898 Indian Lepers Act to Be Repealed Finally." *The Pioneer*, June 13, 2016. www
.dailypioneer.com/2016/india/1898-indian-lepers-act-to-be-repealed-finally.html.

Kagan, Donald. *The Peloponnesian War*. London: Penguin Books, 2004.

Kahn, Matthew E. "The Death Toll from Natural Disasters: The Role of Income, Geography, and
Institutions." *Review of Economics and Statistics* 87, no. 2 (May 2005): 271–84. www.jstor.org
/stable/40042902.

Kaiser Family Foundation. "The U.S. Has Fewer Physicians and Hospital Beds per Capita Than Italy
and Other Countries Overwhelmed by COVID-19." March 27, 2020. www.kff.org/health-costs
/press-release/the-u-s-has-fewer-physicians-and-hospital-beds-per-capita-than-italy-and-other
-countries-overwhelmed-by-covid-19.

Kamal, Rabah, Giorlando Ramirez, and Cynthia Cox. "How Does Health Spending in the U.S.
Compare to Other Countries?" Peterson-KFF Health System Tracker, December 23, 2020.
www.healthsystemtracker.org/chart-collection/health-spending-u-s-compare-countries.

Kammili, Nagamani, Manisha Rani, Ashley Styczynski, Madhavi Latha, Panduranga Rao Pavuluri,
Vishnuvardhan Reddy, and Marcella Alsan. "Plasmid-Mediated Antibiotic Resistance among
Uropathogens in Primigravid Women—Hyderabad, India." *PloS One* 15, no. 5 (May 2020):
e0232710. https://doi.org/10.1371/journal.pone.0232710.

Kane, Thomas J., and Douglas O. Staiger. "Estimating Teacher Impacts on Student Achievement: An
Experimental Evaluation." NBER Working Paper Series 14607, National Bureau of Economic
Research, Cambridge, MA, December 2008. https://doi.org/10.3386/w14607.

Kant, Lalit, and Randeep Guleria. "Pandemic Flu, 1918: After Hundred Years, India Is as Vulnerable." *Indian Journal of Medical Research* 147, no. 3 (March 2018): 221–24. https://doi.org/10.4103
/ijmr.IJMR_407_18.

Karlamangla, Soumya. "With Coronavirus Spreading in L.A. County Supermarkets, Here Are Some
Tips for Shopping Safely." *Los Angeles Times*, December 20, 2020. www.latimes.com/california
/story/2020-12-20/covid-19-spreading-la-county-supermarkets-safety-tips-shopping.

Katz, Bruce, and Julie Wagner. "The Rise of Innovation Districts." Brookings, June 9, 2014. www
.brookings.edu/essay/rise-of-innovation-districts.

Kearns, Cristin E., Laura A. Schmidt, and Stanton A. Glantz. "Sugar Industry and Coronary Heart
Disease Research." *JAMA Internal Medicine* 176, no. 11 (November 2016): 1680–1685. https://
doi.org/10.1001/jamainternmed.2016.5394.

Kell, James Butler. *On the Appearance of Cholera at Sunderland in 1831: With Some Account of That
Disease*. Edinburgh: Adam and Charles Black, 1834. https://wellcomecollection.org/works
/usu29cpf.

Kelly, Jack. "Nearly 50 Million Americans Have Filed for Unemployment—Here's What's Really
Happening." *Forbes*, July 9, 2020. www.forbes.com/sites/jackkelly/2020/07/09/nearly-50-million
-americans-have-filed-for-unemployment-heres-whats-really-happening.

Kelsey, Robert J. *Packaging in Today's Society*. 3rd ed. Lancaster, PA: Technomic, 1989.

Keynes, John Maynard. "Economic Possibilities for Our Grandchildren (1930)," in *Essays in Persua-
sion*, 358–373. New York: Harcourt Brace, 1932.

Khouri, Andrew. "As New Apartments Flood Downtown L.A., Landlords Offer Sweet Deals." *Los Angeles Times*, August 4, 2016. www.latimes.com/business/la-fi-downtown-apartments-20160719-snap-story.html.

"King's Landing Dubrovnik: *Game of Thrones* Filming Locations in Dubrovnik, Croatia." Kings Landing Dubrovnik. www.kingslandingdubrovnik.com.

Klapper, Leora, Luc Laeven, and Raghuram Rajan. "Entry Regulation as a Barrier to Entrepreneurship." *Journal of Financial Economics* 82, no. 3 (December 2006): 591–629. https://doi.org/10.1016/j.jfineco.2005.09.006.

Klein, Alyson. "Race to the Top's Impact on Student Achievement, State Policy Unclear, Report Says." *EducationWeek*, October 26, 2016. www.edweek.org/policy-politics/race-to-the-tops-impact-on-student-achievement-state-policy-unclear-report-says/2016/10.

Kleiner, Morris M., and Alan B. Krueger. "The Prevalence and Effects of Occupational Licensing." *British Journal of Industrial Relations* 48, no. 4 (July 2010): 676–87. https://doi.org/10.1111/j.1467-8543.2010.00807.x.

Kneebone, Elizabeth. "Job Sprawl Revisited: The Changing Geography of Metropolitan Employment." Brookings, April 6, 2009. www.brookings.edu/research/job-sprawl-revisited-the-changing-geography-of-metropolitan-employment.

Koch, Edward I. "Needed: Federal Anti-Drug Aid." *The New York Times*, April 27, 1984. www.nytimes.com/1984/04/27/opinion/needed-federal-anti-drug-aid.html.

Koeppel, Gerard T. *Water for Gotham: A History*. Princeton, NJ: Princeton University Press, 2001.

Konstantinidou, Katerina, Elpis Mantadakis, Matthew E. Falagas, Thalia Sardi, and George Samonis. "Venetian Rule and Control of Plague Epidemics on the Ionian Islands during 17th and 18th Centuries." *Emerging Infectious Diseases* 15, no. 1 (January 2009): 39–43. https://doi.org/10.3201/eid1501.071545.

Korman, Hailly T.N., Bonnie O'Keefe, and Matt Repka. "Missing in the Margins: Estimating the Scale of the COVID-19 Attendance Crisis." Bellwether Education, October 21, 2020. https://bellwethereducation.org/publication/missing-margins-estimating-scale-covid-19-attendance-crisis.

Kornfield, Meryl, Christopher Rowland, Lenny Bernstein, and Devlin Barrett. "Purdue Pharma Agrees to Plead Guilty to Federal Criminal Charges in Settlement over Opioid Crisis." *The Washington Post*, October 22, 2020. www.washingtonpost.com/national-security/2020/10/21/purdue-pharma-charges.

Kosar, Kevin R. "The Executive Branch's Response to the Flood of 1927." History News Network. Accessed December 30, 2020. https://historynewsnetwork.org/article/17255.

Krantz-Kent, Rachel. "Television, Capturing America's Attention at Prime Time and Beyond." *Beyond the Numbers*, US Bureau of Labor Statistics, September 2018. www.bls.gov/opub/btn/volume-7/television-capturing-americas-attention.htm.

Krishnamurti, Chandrasekhar, and SSC Chakra Rao. "The Isolation of Morphine by Serturner." *Indian Journal of Anaesthesia* 60, no. 11 (November 2016): 861–62. www.ncbi.nlm.nih.gov/pmc/articles/PMC5125194.

Krueger, Alan B., and Diane M. Whitmore. "The Effect of Attending a Small Class in the Early Grades on College-Test Taking and Middle School Test Results: Evidence from Project STAR." *Economic Journal* 111, no. 468 (January 2001): 1–28. https://doi.org/10.1111/1468-0297.00586.

Krugman, Paul. "Increasing Returns and Economic Geography." *Journal of Political Economy* 99, no. 3 (June 1991): 483–99. https://doi.org/10.1086/261763.

Kulish, Nicholas, Sarah Kliff, and Jessica Silver-Greenberg. "The U.S. Tried to Build a New Fleet of Ventilators. The Mission Failed." *The New York Times*, March 29, 2020. www.nytimes.com/2020 /03/29/business/coronavirus-us-ventilator-shortage.html.

Künn, Steffen, Christian Seel, and Dainis Zegners. "Cognitive Performance in the Home Office— Evidence from Professional Chess." IZA Discussion Paper 13491, IZA Institute of Labor Economics, July 2020. https://covid-19.iza.org/publications/dp13491.

Kuziemko, Ilyana. "How Should Inmates Be Released from Prison? An Assessment of Parole versus Fixed-Sentence Regimes." *Quarterly Journal of Economics* 128, no. 1 (February 2013): 371–424. https://doi.org/10.1093/qje/qjs052.

Ladov, Mark. "Tenements." Encyclopedia.com, February 24, 2021. www.encyclopedia.com/literature -and-arts/art-and-architecture/architecture/tenements.

Lagu, Tara, Rachel Werner, and Andrew W. Artenstein. "Why Don't Hospitals Have Enough Masks? Because Coronavirus Broke the Market." *The Washington Post*, May 21, 2020. www .washingtonpost.com/outlook/2020/05/21/why-dont-hospitals-have-enough-masks-because -coronavirus-broke-market.

Lakdawalla, Darius, and Tomas Philipson. "The Growth of Obesity and Technological Change." *Economics and Human Biology* 7, no. 3 (December 2009): 283–93. https://doi.org/10.1016/j.ehb .2009.08.001.

The Lancet. Vol. 1. Edited by Thomas Wakley. London: Mills, Jowett, and Mills, 1833. https://books .google.com/books/about/The_Lancet.html?id=aLI1AQAAMAAJ&hl=en.

LaRocque, Regina, and Jason B. Harris. "Cholera: Clinical Features, Diagnosis, Treatment, and Prevention." UpToDate, December 2, 2020. www.uptodate.com/contents/cholera-clinical-features -diagnosis-treatment-and-prevention.

Latkin, Carl A., Amy S. Buchanan, Lisa R. Metsch, Kelly Knight, Mary H. Latka, Yuko Mizuno, and Amy R. Knowlton. "Predictors of Sharing Injection Equipment by HIV-Seropositive Injection Drug Users." *Journal of Acquired Immune Deficiency Syndrome* 49, no. 4, 447–50. https://doi .org/10.1097/QAI.0b013e31818a6546.

Lawrence, Elizabeth M. "Why Do College Graduates Behave More Healthfully Than Those Who Are Less Educated?" *Journal of Health and Social Behavior* 58, no. 3 (June 2017): 291–306. https:// doi.org/10.1177/0022146517715671.

LeDuc, James W., and M. Anita Barry. "SARS, the First Pandemic of the 21st Century." *Emerging Infectious Disease* 10, no. 11 (November 2004): e26. https://doi.org/10.3201/eid1011.040797_02.

Lee, Kyungjoon, John S. Brownstein, Richard G. Mills, and Isaac S. Kohane. "Does Collocation Inform the Impact of Collaboration?" *PLoS One* 5, no. 12 (December 2010): e14279. https://doi .org/10.1371/journal.pone.0014279.

Lee, Paul S. N., Louis Leung, Venhwei Lo, Chengyu Xiong, and Tingjun Wu. "Internet Communication versus Face-to-Face Interaction in Quality of Life." *Social Indicators Research* 100, no. 3 (February 2011): 375–89. https://doi.org/10.1007/s11205-010-9618-3.

Leon, Carol Boyd. "The Life of American Workers in 1915." *Monthly Labor Review*, US Bureau of Labor Statistics, February 2016. www.bls.gov/opub/mlr/2016/article/the-life-of-american-workers -in-1915.htm.

Leonard, Dick. "Sir Robert Peel—Arch Pragmatist or Tory Traitor?" in *Nineteenth-Century British Premiers: Pitt to Rosebery*. Edited by Dick Leonard, 180–99. London: Palgrave Macmillan, 2008.

Leonard, Herman B., and Arnold M. Howitt. "Katrina as Prelude: Preparing for and Responding to Katrina-Class Disturbances in the United States—Testimony to U.S. Senate Committee, March 8, 2006." *Journal of Homeland Security and Emergency Management* 3, no. 2 (2006). https://doi.org/10.2202/1547-7355.1246.

Leonard, Herman B., Arnold M. Howitt, Christine Cole, and Joseph W. Pfeifer. "Command Under Attack: What We've Learned since 9/11 about Managing Crises." The Conversation, September 9, 2016. https://theconversation.com/command-under-attack-what-weve-learned-since-9-11-about-managing-crises-64517.

Leslie, S. "The Contin Delivery System: Dosing Considerations." *The Journal of Allergy and Clinical Immunology* 78, no. 4, pt. 2 (October 1986): 768–73. https://doi.org/10.1016/0091-6749(86)90059-x.

Levine, J. F., M. L. Wilson, and A. Spielman. "Mice as Reservoirs of the Lyme Disease Spirochete." *American Journal of Tropical Medicine and Hygiene* 34, no. 2 (March 1985): 355–60. https://doi.org/10.4269/ajtmh.1985.34.355.

Levinson, Reade. "Across the U.S., Police Contracts Shield Officers from Scrutiny and Discipline." Reuters Investigates, January 13, 2017. www.reuters.com/investigates/special-report/usa-police-unions.

Levitt, Steven D. "The Effect of Prison Population Size on Crime Rates: Evidence from Prison Overcrowding Litigation." *The Quarterly Journal of Economics* 111, no. 2 (May 1996): 319–351. https://doi.org/10.2307/2946681.

———. "Understanding Why Crime Fell in the 1990s: Four Factors That Explain the Decline and Six That Do Not." *Journal of Economic Perspectives* 18, no. 1 (February 1, 2004): 163–90. https://doi.org/10.1257/089533004773563485.

Levy, Scott "An Analysis of Race to the Top in New York State." Unpublished report, December 2014.

Lewis, Lavonna Blair, David C. Sloane, Lori Miller Nascimento, Allison L. Diamant, Joyce Jones Guinyard, Antronette K. Yancey, and Gwendolyn Flynn. "African Americans' Access to Healthy Food Options in South Los Angeles Restaurants." *American Journal of Public Health* 95, no. 4 (April 2005): 668–73. https://doi:10.2105/ajph.2004.050260.

Li-xia, C., L. Ya-nan, L. Li, and T. Sheng. "Relationship Variables in Online versus Face-to-Face Counseling." *2010 IEEE 2nd Symposium on Web Society*, Beijing (2010): 77–82. https://doi.org/10.1109/SWS.2010.5607476.

Library of Congress. "What Is 'Freezer Burn'?" November 19, 2019. www.loc.gov/everyday-mysteries/food-and-nutrition/item/what-is-freezer-burn.

Lieber, Robert J. "Politics Stops at the Water's Edge? Not Recently." *The Washington Post*, February 10, 2014. www.washingtonpost.com/news/monkey-cage/wp/2014/02/10/politics-stops-at-the-waters-edge-not-recently.

Lieberman, Daniel. *The Story of the Human Body: Evolution, Health, and Disease*. Illustrated edition. New York: Vintage, 2014.

"Life Expectancy by London Borough." Trust for London. Accessed December 27, 2020. www.trustforlondon.org.uk/data/life-expectancy-borough.

Lighter, Jennifer, Michael Phillips, Sarah Hochman, Stephanie Sterling, Diane Johnson, Fritz Francois, and Anna Stachel. "Obesity in Patients Younger Than 60 Years Is a Risk Factor for COVID-19 Hospital Admission." *Clinical Infectious Diseases* 71, no. 15 (August 2020): 896–97. https://academic.oup.com/cid/article/71/15/896/5818333.

Lindert, Peter H., and Jeffrey G. Williamson. "American Incomes 1774–1860." *The Journal of Economic History* 73, no. 3 (September 2013): 725–765. https://doi.org/10.1017/S00220507130 00594.

Littman, Robert J. "The Plague of Athens: Epidemiology and Paleopathology." *Mount Sinai Journal of Medicine* 76, no. 5 (October 2009): 456–67. https://doi.org/10.1002/msj.20137.

Livingston, S. Morris. "Magnitude of Transition from War Production." *Survey of Current Business* 24, no. 8 (August 1944): 6–11. https://apps.bea.gov/scb/pdf/1944/0844cont.pdf.

Logan, John R., and Harvey Molotch. *Urban Fortunes: The Political Economy of Place*. 20th anniversary edition. Berkeley: University of California Press, 2007.

Lohnes, Kate. "The Jungle." *Encyclopædia Britannica Online*. Last modified December 19, 2019. www .britannica.com/topic/The-Jungle-novel-by-Sinclair.

"Loose-Wiles Biscuit Tins." Sussex-Lisbon Area Museum, March 24, 2017. https://slah.us/loose -wiles-biscuit-tins.

Lopez, German. "The War on Drugs, Explained." *Vox*, May 8, 2016. www.vox.com/2016/5/8 /18089368/war-on-drugs-marijuana-cocaine-heroin-meth.

———. "Why America Ran Out of Protective Masks—and What Can Be Done about It." *Vox*, March 27, 2020. www.vox.com/policy-and-politics/2020/3/27/21194402/coronavirus-masks-n95 -respirators-personal-protective-equipment-ppe.

———. "Why America's Coronavirus Testing Barely Improved in April." *Vox*, May 1, 2020. www .vox.com/2020/5/1/21242589/coronavirus-testing-swab-reagent-supply-shortage.

"Louis Pasteur." *Encyclopædia Britannica Online*. Accessed December 23, 2020. www.britannica.com /biography/Louis-Pasteur.

Lovelace, Berkeley, Jr. "Warren Buffett: Bezos, Dimon and I Aim for Something Bigger on Health Care Than Just Shaving Costs." CNBC, February 26, 2018. www.cnbc.com/2018/02/26/buffett -my-health-care-venture-with-bezos-and-dimon-is-going-for-something-bigger-than -shaving-a-few-percent-off-costs.html.

Lubrano, Alfred. "The World Has Suffered through Other Deadly Pandemics. But the Response to Coronavirus Is Unprecedented." *The Philadelphia Inquirer*, March 22, 2020. www.inquirer.com /health/coronavirus/coronavirus-philadelphia-spanish-flu-world-war-two-civil-war-pandemic -aids-20200322.html.

Luttrell, Anthony. *The Making of Christian Malta: From the Early Middle Ages to 1530*. 1st ed. London: Routledge, 2017.

MacDonald, John, Jeffrey Fagan, and Amanda Geller. "The Effects of Local Police Surges on Crime and Arrests in New York City." *PLoS One* 11, no. 6 (June 2016). https://doi.org/10.1371/journal .pone.0157223.

Mackenzie, William Lyon. *The Lives and Opinions of Benj'n Franklin Butler, United States District Attorney for the Southern District of New-York; and Jesse Hoyt, Counsellor at Law, Formerly Collector of Customs for the Port of New-York*. Boston: Cook & Company, 1845.

Madhani, Aamer. "Unsolved Murders: Chicago, Other Big Cities Struggle; Murder Rate a 'National Disaster.'" *USA Today*, August 10, 2018. www.usatoday.com/story/news/2018/08/10/u-s-homicide -clearance-rate-crisis/951681002.

"Madison Park High Rank." *U.S. News & World Report*, 2020. www.usnews.com/education/best -high-schools/massachusetts/districts/boston-public-schools/madison-park-high-9293.

Malani, Anup, Daksha Shah, Gagandeep Kang, Gayatri Nair Lobo, Jayanthi Shastri, Manoj Mohanan, Rajesh Jain, et al. "Seroprevalence of SARS-CoV-2 in Slums and Non-slums of Mumbai, India, during June 29–July 19, 2020." Preprint. *Epidemiology*, September 1, 2020. https://doi.org/10.1101/2020.08.27.20182741.

Mallapaty, Smriti. "Coronaviruses Closely Related to the Pandemic Virus Discovered in Japan and Cambodia." *Nature* 588, no. 7836 (November 2020): 15–16. https://doi.org/10.1038/d41586-020-03217-0.

Mallen, Michael J., Susan X. Day, and Melinda A. Green. "Online versus Face-to-Face Conversation: An Examination of Relational and Discourse Variables." *Psychotherapy: Theory, Research, Practice, Training* 40, no. 1–2 (2003): 155–63. https://doi.org/10.1037/0033-3204.40.1-2.155.

Maloney, Jennifer, and Saabira Chaudhuri. "Against All Odds, the U.S. Tobacco Industry Is Rolling in Money." *The Wall Street Journal*, April 23, 2017. www.wsj.com/articles/u-s-tobacco-industry-rebounds-from-its-near-death-experience-1492968698.

Mampuya, Warner M. "Cardiac Rehabilitation Past, Present and Future: An Overview." *Cardiovascular Diagnosis and Therapy* 2, no. 1 (March 2012): 38–49. https//doi.org/10.3978/j.issn.2223-3652.2012.01.02.

"Man without Face Mask Refuses to Leave SEPTA Bus; Police Pull Him Off." NBC10 Philadelphia, April 10, 2020. www.nbcphiladelphia.com/news/local/man-without-face-mask-refuses-to-leave-septa-bus-police-pull-him-off/2359607.

Mandell, W., D. Vlahov, C. Latkin, M. Oziemkowska, and S. Cohn. "Correlates of Needle Sharing among Injection Drug Users." *American Journal of Public Health* 84, no. 6 (June 1994): 920–23. https://doi.org/10.2105/ajph.84.6.920.

Mann, Annamarie, and Amy Adkins. "America's Coming Workplace: Home Alone." Gallup, March 15, 2017. https://news.gallup.com/businessjournal/206033/america-coming-workplace-home-alone.aspx.

Mann, Michael. "Delhi's Belly: On the Management of Water, Sewage and Excreta in a Changing Urban Environment during the Nineteenth Century." *Studies in History* 23, no. 1 (February 2007): 1–31. https://doi.org/10.1177/025764300602300101.

Manning, Willard G., Joseph P. Newhouse, Naihua Duan, Emmett B. Keeler, Arleen Leibowitz, and M. Susan Marquis. "Health Insurance and the Demand for Medical Care: Evidence from a Randomized Experiment." *American Economic Review* 77, no. 3 (June 1987): 251–77. www.jstor.org/stable/1804094.

Mapping Inequality: Redlining in New Deal America. Accessed January 10, 2021. https://dsl.richmond.edu/panorama/redlining.

Mapping Police Violence. Accessed January 5, 2021. https://mappingpoliceviolence.org.

Marconcini, Mattia, Annekatrin Metz-Marconcini, Soner Üreyen, Daniela Palacios-Lopez, Wiebke Hanke, Felix Bachofer, Julian Zeidler, et al. "Outlining Where Humans Live, the World Settlement Footprint 2015." *Scientific Data* 7, no. 1 (July 2020): 242. https://doi.org/10.1038/s41597-020-00580-5.

Marcoux, Steele. "These Are the 25 Richest Cities in America." *Veranda*, August 12, 2019. www.veranda.com/luxury-lifestyle/g28666999/richest-cities-usa.

Mark, Joshua J. "Athens." World History Encyclopedia, April 28, 2011. www.ancient.eu/Athens.

———. "Herodotus." World History Encyclopedia, March 27, 2018. www.ancient.eu/herodotus.

———. "Knossos." World History Encyclopedia, October 15, 2010. www.ancient.eu/knossos.

Markel, Howard. "69 Years Ago, a President Pitches His Idea for National Health Care." *PBS News Hour*, November 19, 2014. www.pbs.org/newshour/health/november-19-1945-harry-truman-calls -national-health-insurance-program.

Markey, Patrick, Charlotte Markey, and Juliana French. "Violent Video Games and Real-World Violence: Rhetoric versus Data." *Psychology of Popular Media* 4, no. 4 (January 2014): 277–95. https:// doi.org/10.1037/ppm0000030.

Marquis, M. Susan, and Melinda Beeuwkes Buntin. "How Much Risk Pooling Is There in the Individual Insurance Market?" *Health Services Research* 41, no. 5 (October 2006): 1782–1800. https:// doi.org/10.1111/j.1475-6773.2006.00577.x.

Marr, John S., and John T. Cathey. "New Hypothesis for Cause of Epidemic among Native Americans, New England, 1616–1619." *Emerging Infectious Diseases* 16, no. 2 (February 2010): 281–86. https://doi.org/10.3201/eid1602.090276.

Martin, Anne B., Micah Hartman, David Lassman, and Aaron Catlin. "National Health Care Spending In 2019: Steady Growth for the Fourth Consecutive Year." *Health Affairs* 40, no. 1 (January 2021): 14–24. https://doi.org/10.1377/hlthaff.2020.02022.

Martin, Danielle, Ashley P. Miller, Amélie Quesnel-Vallée, Nadine R. Caron, Bilkis Vissandjée, and Gregory P. Marchildon. "Canada's Universal Health-Care System: Achieving Its Potential." *The Lancet* 391, no. 10131 (2018): 1718–35. https://doi.org/10.1016/s0140-6736(18)30181-8.

Martin, Douglas. "J.R. Simplot, Farmer Who Developed First Frozen French Fries, Dies at 99." *The New York Times*, May 28, 2008. www.nytimes.com/2008/05/28/business/28simplot.html.

Martin, Timothy W., and Dasl Yoon. "South Korea Widens Testing in Daegu as It Steps Up War on Coronavirus." *The Wall Street Journal* March 4, 2020. www.wsj.com/articles/south-korea-widens -testing-in-daegu-as-it-steps-up-war-on-coronavirus-11583321995.

Martinelli, Katherine. "The Factory That Oreos Built." *Smithsonian*, May 21, 2018. www.smithson ianmag.com/history/factory-oreos-built-180969121.

Martuzzi, Marco. "The Precautionary Principle: In Action for Public Health." *Occupational and Environmental Medicine* 64, no. 9 (2007): 569–70. https://doi.org/10.1136/oem.2006.030601.

Maruschak, Laura, and Todd Minton. *Correctional Populations in the United States, 2017–2018*. US Department of Justice, Bureau of Justice Statistics, August 2020. www.bjs.gov/content/pub/pdf /cpus1718.pdf.

"Marvin Lemus." IMDb. Accessed January 11, 2021. www.imdb.com/name/nm3836245.

"Mary Seacole." *Encyclopædia Britannica Online*. January 1, 2021. www.britannica.com/biography /Mary-Seacole.

Massachusetts Board of Elementary and Secondary Education. "March 2010 Meeting Agendas." March 22, 2010. www.doe.mass.edu/bese/docs/fy2010/0310.

Matthews, Dylan. "How Police Unions Became So Powerful—and How They Can Be Tamed." *Vox*, June 24, 2020. www.vox.com/policy-and-politics/21290981/police-union-contracts-minneapolis -reform.

McAuley, Julie L., Katherine Kedzierska, Lorena E. Brown, and G. Dennis Shanks. "Host Immunological Factors Enhancing Mortality of Young Adults during the 1918 Influenza Pandemic." *Frontiers in Immunology* 6 (August 2015). https://doi.org/10.3389/fimmu.2015.00419.

McCann, Adam. "Most & Least Educated Cities in America." WalletHub, July 20, 2020. https:// wallethub.com/edu/e/most-and-least-educated-cities/6656.

McCluskey, Priyanka Dayal. "Partners HealthCare Generates $14 Billion in Revenue." *The Boston Globe*, December 6, 2019. www.bostonglobe.com/business/2019/12/06/partners-healthcare-generates -billion-revenues/bElEfqkxvxVMZ7sz6ROLNK/story.html.

McCulloch, Marsha. "Is It Safe to Eat Moldy Bread?" Healthline, February 22, 2019. www.healthline .com/nutrition/can-you-eat-bread-mold.

McGillivray, Brett. "Ottawa." *Encyclopædia Britannica Online.* Accessed December 27, 2020. www .britannica.com/place/Ottawa.

McKay, Katherine. "Hamilton and Yellow Fever: The Library Where It Happens." *NLM in Focus*, January 11, 2019. https://infocus.nlm.nih.gov/2019/01/11/hamilton-and-yellow-fever-the-library -where-it-happens.

McKenna, David. "Eyam Plague: The Village of the Damned." BBC News, November 5, 2016. www .bbc.com/news/uk-england-35064071.

McLaughlin, Eliott C. "Chicago Officer Had History of Complaints before Laquan McDonald Shooting." CNN, November 26, 2015. www.cnn.com/2015/11/25/us/jason-van-dyke-previous -complaints-lawsuits/index.html.

McLaughlin, Raoul. *Rome and the Distant East: Trade Routes to the Ancient Lands of Arabia, India and China.* London: Bloomsbury, 2010.

McNeil, Donald G., Jr. "U.S. Reaction to Swine Flu: Apt and Lucky." *The New York Times*, January 2, 2010. www.nytimes.com/2010/01/02/health/02flu.html.

McNeill, William. *Plagues and Peoples.* New York: Knopf Doubleday, 2010.

McWilliams, J. Michael, Laura A. Hatfield, Bruce E. Landon, Pasha Hamed, and Michael E. Chernew. "Medicare Spending after 3 Years of the Medicare Shared Savings Program." *New England Journal of Medicine* 379, no. 12 (2018): 1139–149. https://doi.org/10.1056/nejmsa1803388.

Meara, Ellen, Jill R. Horwitz, Wilson Powell, Lynn McClelland, Weiping Zhou, A. James O'Malley, and Nancy E. Morden. "State Legal Restrictions and Prescription-Opioid Use among Disabled Adults." *New England Journal of Medicine* 375, no. 1 (2016): 44–53. https://doi.org/10.1056 /nejmsa1514387.

Meares, Tracey L. "Policing: A Public Good Gone Bad." *Boston Review*, August 1, 2017. http:// bostonreview.net/law-justice/tracey-l-meares-policing-public-good-gone-bad.

Meares, Tracey, Phillip Atiba Goff, and Tom R. Tyler. "Defund-the-Police Calls Aren't Going Away. But What Do They Mean Practically?" NBC News, June 24, 2020. www.nbcnews.com/think /opinion/defund-police-calls-aren-t-going-away-what-do-they-ncna1231959.

"Medicare." *The Lancet* 279, no. 7241 (June 1962): 1231. https://doi.org/10.1016/S0140-6736(62)92271-7.

Medicare. "Pain Management." Accessed January 20, 2021. www.medicare.gov/coverage/pain -management.

"Medicare and Medicaid." LBJ Presidential Library. Accessed December 26, 2020. www.lbjlibrary .org/press/media-kit/medicare-and-medicaid.

"Meet Jackson Defa of Weird Wave Coffee in Boyle Heights." VoyageLA, September 8, 2020. http:// voyagela.com/interview/meet-jackson-defa-weird-wave-coffee-boyle-heights.

Mehrotra, Ateev, Michael Chernew, David Linetsky, Hilary Hatch, and David Cutler. "The Impact of the COVID-19 Pandemic on Outpatient Visits: A Rebound Emerges." Commonwealth Fund, May 19, 2020. www.commonwealthfund.org/publications/2020/apr/impact-covid-19-outpatient -visits.

Meier, Mischa. "The 'Justinianic Plague': The Economic Consequences of the Pandemic in the Eastern Roman Empire and Its Cultural and Religious Effects." *Early Medieval Europe* 24, no. 3 (July 2016): 267–92. https://doi.org/10.1111/emed.12152.

Meinwald, Constance C. "Plato." *Encyclopædia Britannica Online*. Last modified May 22, 2020. www.britannica.com/biography/Plato.

Meixler, Eli. "New Zealand's Jacinda Ardern Made History by Bringing Baby Neve to the U.N." *Time*, September 25, 2018. https://time.com/5405405/new-zealand-jacinda-ardern-baby-u-n.

Melly, Ludovic, Gianluca Torregrossa, Timothy Lee, Jean-Luc Jansens, and John D. Puskas. "Fifty Years of Coronary Artery Bypass Grafting." *Journal of Thoracic Disease* 10, no. 3 (March 2018): 1960–67. https://doi.org/10.21037/jtd.2018.02.43.

Merritt Hawkins. *2020 Review of Physician and Advanced Practitioner Recruiting Incentives and the Impact of COVID-19*. 2020. www.merritthawkins.com/uploadedFiles/MerrittHawkins_2020 _Incentive_Review.pdf.

Merrow, John. "Meet Adell Cothorne." *The Merrow Report*, January 9, 2013. https://themerrowreport .com/2013/01/09/meet-adell-cothorne.

Metcalfe, N. "The History of Woolsorters' Disease: A Yorkshire Beginning with an International Future?" *Occupational Medicine* 54, no. 7 (October 2004): 489–93. https://doi.org/10.1093 /occmed/kqh115.

"The Metropolitan Health Bill." *The New York Times*, March 24, 1862. www.nytimes.com/1862/03 /24/archives/the-metropolitan-health-bill.html.

Michaels, Matthew. "The 35 Most Expensive Reasons You Might Have to Visit a Hospital in the US—and How Much It Costs If You Do." *Business Insider*, March 1, 2018. www.businessinsider .com/most-expensive-health-conditions-hospital-costs-2018-2.

Mihm, Stephen. "Lessons from the Philadelphia Flu of 1918." Yahoo! Finance, March 30, 2020. https://finance.yahoo.com/news/lessons-philadelphia-flu-1918-153022624.html.

Miller, Julie. "The 1793 Yellow Fever Epidemic: The Washingtons, Hamilton and Jefferson." Library of Congress (blog), May 28, 2020. https://blogs.loc.gov/loc/2020/05/the-1793-yellow-fever -epidemic-the-washingtons-hamilton-and-jefferson.

Miller, Yawu. "Walsh Supportive of Body Cameras." *The Bay State Banner*, March 14, 2018. www .baystatebanner.com/2018/03/14/walsh-supportive-of-body-cameras.

"Milliken v. Bradley, 418 U.S. 717 (1974)." Justia: US Supreme Court. https://supreme.justia.com /cases/federal/us/418/717.

"Milwaukee Sewer Socialism." Wisconsin Historical Society, August 3, 2012. www.wisconsinhistory .org/Records/Article/CS428.

Miranda, Carolina A. "The Art Gallery Exodus from Boyle Heights and Why More Anti-gentrification Battles Loom on the Horizon." *Los Angeles Times*, August 8, 2018. www.latimes .com/entertainment/arts/miranda/la-et-cam-gentrification-protests-future-of-boyle-heights -20180808-story.html.

Mitcham, Lester. "The Statistics of the Disaster." Encyclopedia Titanica. Accessed January 03, 2021. www.encyclopedia-titanica.org/titanic-statistics.html.

Mitchell, Brian R. *European Historical Statistics, 1750–1975*. New York: Facts on File, 1980.

Mitchell, Chris. "The Killing of Murder." *New York Magazine*, January 4, 2008. https://nymag.com /news/features/crime/2008/42603.

Moderna. "Moderna's Work on Our COVID-19 Vaccine Candidate." Accessed January 18, 2021. www.modernatx.com/modernas-work-potential-vaccine-against-covid-19.

Molloy, Raven, Christopher L. Smith, and Abigail Wozniak. "Internal Migration in the United States." *Journal of Economic Perspectives* 25, no. 3 (September 2011): 173–96. https://doi.org /10.1257/jep.25.3.173.

Montes, Carlos. "The Brown Berets: Young Chicano Revolutionaries." *FightBack! News*, February 1, 2003. http://www.fightbacknews.org/2003winter/brownberets.htm.

Mordechai, Lee, Merle Eisenberg, Timothy P. Newfield, Adam Izdebski, Janet E. Kay, and Hendrik Poinar. "The Justinianic Plague: An Inconsequential Pandemic?" *Proceedings of the National Academy of Sciences* 116, no. 51 (December 2019): 25546–54. https://doi.org/10.1073/pnas.1903797116.

"More Than One-Third of U.S. Coronavirus Deaths Are Linked to Nursing Homes." *The New York Times*. Accessed January 22, 2021. www.nytimes.com/interactive/2020/us/coronavirus-nursing -homes.html.

Moreau De Jonnes, A. "Statistical Remarks on the Effects of Cholera in France During the Epidemic of 1832." *The Lancet*, 19, no. 495 (February 1833): 689–90. https://doi.org/10.1016/S0140 -6736(02)95229-3.

Morelli, Giovanna, Yajun Song, Camila J. Mazzoni, Mark Eppinger, Philippe Roumagnac, David M. Wagner, Mirjam Feldkamp, et al. "*Yersinia pestis* Genome Sequencing Identifies Patterns of Global Phylogenetic Diversity." *Nature Genetics* 42, no. 12 (October 2010): 1140–43. https://doi .org/10.1038/ng.705.

Moreno, Teresa, Rosa María Pintó, Albert Bosch, Natalia Moreno, Andrés Alastuey, María Cruz Minguillón, Eduard Anfruns-Estrada, et al. "Tracing Surface and Airborne SARS-CoV-2 RNA inside Public Buses and Subway Trains." *Environment International* 147 (February 2021): 106326. https://doi.org/10.1016/j.envint.2020.106326.

Moreno-Madriñán, Max J., and Michael Turell. "History of Mosquitoborne Diseases in the United States and Implications for New Pathogens." *Emerging Infectious Diseases* 24, no. 5 (May 2018): 821–26. https://doi.org/10.3201/eid2405.171609.

"More Than One-Third of U.S. Coronavirus Deaths Are Linked To Nursing Homes." *The New York Times*. Accessed January 12, 2021. www.nytimes.com/interactive/2020/us/coronavirus-nursing -homes.html.

Morrill, John S. "Great Plague of London." *Encyclopædia Britannica Online*. September 8, 2016. www .britannica.com/event/Great-Plague-of-London.

Mouritz, A. "*The Flu*": *A Brief History of Influenza in U.S. America, Europe, Hawaii*. Honolulu: Advertiser Publishing, 1921. http://www.gutenberg.org/ebooks/61607.

Munro, John. "My Research Data Online: Spreadsheets, Tables, Publications." December 31, 2012. www.economics.utoronto.ca/munro5/ResearchData.html.

Murphy, Darryl C. "Police Forcibly Eject Man without Face Mask from SEPTA Bus." WHYY, April 10, 2020. whyy.org/articles/viral-video-shows-police-forcibly-enforce-mask-mandate-on-septa -bus.

Murphy, Linda. "Common Core in Oklahoma." *Oklahoma Constitution*. Accessed January 22, 2021. www.oklahomaconstitution.com/ns.php?nid=459&pastissue=25.

Musto, David F. *Drugs in America: A Documentary History*. New York: New York University Press, 2002.

"The Mw 8.8 Chile Earthquake of February 27, 2010." *EERI Special Earthquake Report*, June 2010. www.eeri.org/site/images/eeri_newsletter/2010_pdf/Chile10_insert.pdf.

Nair, G. Balakrish, T. Ramamurthy, S. K. Bhattacharya, Asish K. Mukhopadhyay, Surabhi Garg, M. K. Bhattacharya, Tae Takeda, Toshio Shimada, Yoshifumi Takeda, and B. C. Deb. "Spread of *Vibrio cholerae* 0139 Bengal in India." *Journal of Infectious Diseases* 169, no. 5 (May 1994): 1029–34. https://doi.org/10.1093/infdis/169.5.1029.

National Academies of Sciences, Engineering, and Medicine; Health and Medicine Division; Board on Health Care Services; Committee on Ensuring Patient Access to Affordable Drug Therapies. *Making Medicines Affordable: A National Imperative, 3, Factors Influencing Affordability.* Edited by S. J. Nass, G. Madhavan, and N. R. Augustine. Washington, DC: National Academies Press, 2017.

National Academies of Sciences, Engineering, and Medicine; Health and Medicine Division; Board on Population Health and Public Health Practice; Committee on Community-Based Solutions to Promote Health Equity in the United States. *Communities in Action: Pathways to Health Equity.* Edited by Alina Baciu, Yamrot Negussie, Amy Geller, and James N. Weinstein. Washington, DC: National Academies Press, 2017.

National Academy of Medicine. *The Neglected Dimension of Global Security: A Framework to Counter Infectious Disease Crises.* Washington, DC: National Academies Press, 2016.

National Association of Realtors. *Median Sales Price of Existing Apartment Condo-Coops Homes for Metropolitan Areas.* Accessed January 11, 2021. https://cdn.nar.realtor/sites/default/files/documents/metro-home-prices-q3-2020-condo-co-op-2020-11-12.pdf.

———. *Median Sales Price of Existing Single-Family Homes for Metropolitan Areas.* https://cdn.nar.realtor/sites/default/files/documents/metro-home-prices-q3-2020-single-family-2020-11-12.pdf.

———. "Metro Home Prices Rise in 96% of Metro Areas in First Quarter of 2020." May 11, 2020. www.nar.realtor/newsroom/metro-home-prices-rise-in-96-of-metro-areas-in-first-quarter-of-2020.

National Drug Intelligence Center. "Abuse." In *OxyContin Diversion and Abuse.* January 2001. https://www.justice.gov/archive/ndic/pubs/651/abuse.htm.

———. *OxyContin Diversion and Abuse.* January 30, 2001. www.justice.gov/archive/ndic/pubs/651/index.htm.

National Governors Association. "Forty-Nine States and Territories Join Common Core Standards Initiative." June 1, 2009. https://web.archive.org/web/20131004230129/http://www.nga.org/cms/home/news-room/news-releases/page_2009/col2-content/main-content-list/title_forty-nine-states-and-territories-join-common-core-standards-initiative.html.

National Institute on Drug Abuse. "Drug Use and Viral Infections (HIV, Hepatitis) DrugFacts." Accessed January 20, 2021. www.drugabuse.gov/publications/drugfacts/drug-use-viral-infections-hiv-hepatitis.

National Park Service. "Francis Rawdon." Last modified July 2, 2020. www.nps.gov/people/francis-rawdon.htm.

———. "The Mill Girls of Lowell." November 15, 2018. www.nps.gov/lowe/learn/historyculture/the-mill-girls-of-lowell.htm.

———. "Theodore Roosevelt, Sr.—Theodore Roosevelt Birthplace, National Historic Site, New York." Accessed January 17, 2021. www.nps.gov/thrb/learn/historyculture/theodorerooseveltsr.htm.

National Research Council. *An Evaluation of the Public Schools of the District of Columbia: Reform in a Changing Landscape.* Washington, DC: National Academies Press, 2015. https://doi.org/10.17226/21743.

———. *The Growth of Incarceration in the United States: Exploring Causes and Consequences*. Washington, DC: National Academies Press, 2014. https://doi.org/10.17226/18613.

"National Trends." Mapping Police Violence. Accessed January 4, 2021. https://mappingpoliceviolence .org/nationaltrends.

"NATO." History.com. Last modified July 7, 2019. www.history.com/topics/cold-war/formation-of -nato-and-warsaw-pact.

Nava, Julian. *Julian Nava: My Mexican-American Journey*. Houston: Arte Público Press, 2002.

Neghina, Raul, Roxana Moldovan, Iosif Marincu, Crenguta L. Calma, and Adriana M. Neghina. "The Roots of Evil: The Amazing History of Trichinellosis and *Trichinella* Parasites." *Parasitology Research* 110 (2012): 503–8. https://doi.org/10.1007/s00436-011-2672-1.

"Neolithic Revolution." History.com. Accessed January 24, 2021. www.history.com/topics/pre-history /neolithic-revolution.

New York City Department of Health and Mental Hygiene. "Community Health Profiles 2018: Brownsville." https://www1.nyc.gov/assets/doh/downloads/pdf/data/2018chp-bk16.pdf.

———. "Female Homicide in New York City over 15 Years: Surveillance and Findings, 1995–2009." PowerPoint presentation, August 2011. https://www1.nyc.gov/assets/doh/downloads/pdf/ip/ip -femicide-stats-1995-2009.pdf.

———. "Suicides in New York City, 2000 to 2014." Epi Data Brief no. 75, September 2016. www1 .nyc.gov/assets/doh/downloads/pdf/epi/databrief75.pdf.

New York City Police Department. "Historical New York City Crime Data." Accessed January 7, 2021. www1.nyc.gov/site/nypd/stats/crime-statistics/historical.page.

New York City—Safety and Security. New York City Global Partners, July 2008. www.nyc.gov/html /unccp/gprb/downloads/pdf/NYC_Safety%20and%20Security_Operation%20Impact.pdf.

"New York City Transit—History and Chronology." World-Wide Business Centres, March 20, 2014. wwbcn.com/new-york-city-transit-history-chronology.

"New York City Waterworks." Documentary History of American Water-Works. http://waterworks history.us/NY/New_York_City.

"New York Coronavirus Map and Case Count." *The New York Times*. Accessed April 1, 2020. www .nytimes.com/interactive/2020/us/new-york-coronavirus-cases.html.

"New York Crime Rates 1960 to 2019." Disaster Center. www.disastercenter.com/crime/nycrime.htm.

New York Public Library. "History of the New York Public Library." www.nypl.org/help/about-nypl /history.

"New York's Governor and Mayor of New York City Address Concerns of the Damage." CNN transcript of broadcast aired 14:35 ET, September 11, 2001. http://transcripts.cnn.com/TRANSCRIPTS /0109/11/bn.42.html.

New York State Department of Health. *Tenement-house Acts, Chapter 908, Laws of 1867 (as Amended by Chapter 504, Laws of 1879, and Chapter 399, Section 1, Laws of 1880): An Act for the Regulation of Tenement and Lodging Houses in the Cities of New York and Brooklyn, Passed May 14, 1867*. 1880.

New York State Education Department. "Race to the Top Application Phase 2, New York State." June 1, 2010. http://usny.nysed.gov/rttt/application/criteriapriorities.pdf.

"New York Stock Exchange." *Encyclopædia Britannica Online*. Accessed January 18, 2021. www .britannica.com/topic/New-York-Stock-Exchange.

"New Zealand." Worldometer. Accessed December 26, 2020. www.worldometers.info/coronavirus /country/new-zealand.

"New Zealand Election: Jacinda Ardern's Labour Party Scores Landslide Win." BBC News, October 17, 2020. www.bbc.com/news/world-asia-54519628.

New Zealand Government. "About the Alert System." Accessed January 20, 2021. https://covid19.govt.nz/alert-system/about-the-alert-system.

———. "Alert Level 2." Unite Against COVID-19. Accessed December 30, 2020. https://covid19.govt.nz/alert-system/alert-level-2.

———. "Managed Isolation and Quarantine." Accessed December 30, 2020. https://covid19.govt.nz/travel-and-the-border/travel-to-new-zealand/managed-isolation-and-quarantine.

"New Zealand: Government Declares State of Emergency March 25 /Update 5." GardaWorld. Accessed December 26, 2020. www.garda.com/crisis24/news-alerts/326196/new-zealand-government-declares-state-of-emergency-march-25-update-5.

New Zealand Government, Ministry of Health. "COVID-19: Current Cases." Accessed January 20, 2021. www.health.govt.nz/our-work/diseases-and-conditions/covid-19-novel-coronavirus/covid-19-data-and-statistics/covid-19-current-cases.

New Zealand Parliament. "Daily Progress for Tuesday, 28 April 2020." Accessed January 20, 2021. www.parliament.nz/en/pb/daily-progress-in-the-house/daily-progress-for-tuesday-28-april-2020.

Nichols, I. C. *The European Pentarchy and the Congress of Verona, 1822.* The Hague: Springer Netherlands, 2012.

Nicholson, Esme. "Germany's Beer Purity Law Is 500 Years Old. Is It Past Its Sell-By Date?" NPR, April 29, 2016. www.npr.org/sections/thesalt/2016/04/29/475138367/germanys-beer-purity-law-is-500-years-old-is-it-past-its-sell-by-date.

Nicol, Donald MacGillivray, and J. F. Matthews. "Constantine I." *Encyclopædia Britannica Online.* Last modified December 28, 2020. www.britannica.com/biography/Constantine-I-Roman-emperor.

Nierenberg, Danielle, and Emily Nink. "Here's Why Industrial Food Is Deceivingly Cheap." *The Christian Science Monitor*, September 8, 2015. www.csmonitor.com/Business/The-Bite/2015/0908/Here-s-why-industrial-food-is-deceivingly-cheap.

"1940s: The Company's Beginnings." J.R. Simplot Company. Accessed December 25, 2020. www.simplot.com/sustainability/story_detail/1940s_the_companys_beginnings1.

"1960 Democratic Platform." *Patriot Post.* https://patriotpost.us/documents/484.

Norrie, Philip. "How Disease Affected the End of the Bronze Age." In *A History of Disease in Ancient Times: More Lethal Than War*, 61–101. London: Pargrave Macmillan, 2016.

North Atlantic Treaty Organization. "Collective Defence—Article 5." Last modified February 8, 2021. www.nato.int/cps/en/natohq/topics_110496.htm.

———. "Consensus Decision-Making at NATO." Last modified October 2, 2020. www.nato.int/cps/en/natohq/topics_49178.htm.

———. "Encyclopedia of NATO Topics." Accessed January 21, 2021. www.nato.int/cps/en/natohq/topics.htm.

———. "Member Countries." September 24, 2020. www.nato.int/cps/en/natohq/topics_52044.htm.

North Atlantic Treaty Organization. "NATO Agrees 2021 Civil and Military Budgets." December 17, 2020. www.nato.int/cps/en/natohq/news_180185.htm.

———. "NATO Secretary General." April 13, 2016. www.nato.int/cps/en/natohq/topics_50094.htm.

———. "North Atlantic Treaty." August 22, 2012. www.nato.int/cps/en/natohq/topics_89597.htm.

———. "Principal Officials." www.nato.int/cps/en/natohq/who_is_who_51639.htm.

———. "Strategic Concepts." Last modified September 24, 2020. www.nato.int/cps/en/natohq /topics_56626.htm.

———. "What Is NATO?" www.nato.int/nato-welcome/index.html.

Northeastern University. "The Northeastern Joint Apprenticeship and Training Program (NEAT)." Accessed January 18, 2021. https://www.neat1968.org/about-neat.

Norwich, John Julius. *Byzantium: The Early Centuries.* New York: Knopf, 1989.

Novotney, Amy. "The Psychology of Scarcity." *Monitor on Psychology* 45, no. 2 (February 2014): 28. www.apa.org/monitor/2014/02/scarcity.

Nunn, Nathan, and Nancy Qian. "The Columbian Exchange: A History of Disease, Food, and Ideas." *Journal of Economic Perspectives* 24, no. 2 (June 2010): 163–88. https://doi.org/10.1257/jep .24.2.163.

"Nursing Home Costs and Ways to Pay." Caring.com. Accessed December 26, 2020. www.caring .com/senior-living/nursing-homes/how-to-pay.

"NYC-Queens Community District 3—Jackson Heights & North Corona PUMA, NY." Census Reporter. Accessed December 25, 2020. https://censusreporter.org/profiles/79500US3604102 -nyc-queens-community-district-3-jackson-heights-north-corona-puma-ny.

O'Donoghue, Ted, and Matthew Rabin. "The Economics of Immediate Gratification." *Journal of Behavioral Decision Making* 13 (March 2000): 233–50. https://doi.org/10.1002/(SICI)1099 -0771(200004/06)13:2<233::AID-BDM325>3.0.CO;2-U.

Oh, Myoung-don, Wan Beom Park, Sang-Won Park, Pyoeng Gyun Choe, Ji Hwan Bang, Kyoung-Ho Song, Eu Suk Kim, Hong Bin Kim, and Nam Joong Kim. "Middle East Respiratory Syndrome: What We Learned from the 2015 Outbreak in the Republic of Korea." *Korean Journal of Internal Medicine* 33, no. 2 (March 2018): 233–46. https://doi.org/10.3904/kjim.2018.031.

O'Hare, James. "The History of US Foreign Aid and Why It's as Important as Ever." Global Citizen, June 13, 2017.

Olival, Kevin J., Parviez R. Hosseini, Carlos Zambrana-Torrelio, Noam Ross, Tiffany L. Bogich, and Peter Daszak. "Host and Viral Traits Predict Zoonotic Spillover from Mammals," *Nature* 546 (June 2017): 646–50. https://doi.org/10.1038/nature22975.

Olmos, Edward James, dir. *Walkout.* HBO, 2006.

Olson, Mancur. *The Rise and Decline of Nations: Economic Growth, Stagflation, and Social Rigidities.* New Haven, CT: Yale University Press, 1982.

"101 Words That Spelled Death." *Freedom*, September 28, 2018. www.freedommag.org/magazine /201809-almost-heaven/101-words-that-spelled-death.html.

"Opium throughout History." PBS. Accessed December 29, 2020. www.pbs.org/wgbh/pages/frontline /shows/heroin/etc/history.html.

Oppenheim, Ben, and Gavin Yamey. "Pandemics and the Poor." Brookings, June 19, 2017. www .brookings.edu/blog/future-development/2017/06/19/pandemics-and-the-poor.

The Opportunity Atlas. Accessed January 18, 2021. https://opportunityatlas.org.

Organisation for Economic Co-operation and Development. *Equity and Quality in Education: Supporting Disadvantaged Students and Schools.* Paris: OECD Publishing, 2012.

———. "Health Spending." Accessed January 18 and 22, 2021. https://data.oecd.org/healthres /health-spending.htm.

———. "Obesity Update." Accessed January 18, 2021. www.oecd.org/health/obesity-update.htm.

———. *PISA 2012 Results in Focus: What 15-Year-Olds Know and What They Can Do with What They Know.* 2014. http://www.oecd.org/pisa/keyfindings/pisa-2012-results-overview.pdf.

"Origins of the Opioid Epidemic: Purdue Pharma Knew of OxyContin Abuse in 1996 but Covered It Up." Democracy Now!, June 1, 2018. www.democracynow.org/2018/6/1/origins_of_the_opioid _epidemic_purdue.

"Out-Producing the Enemy": American Production During WWII. New Orleans: The National WWII Museum. www.nationalww2museum.org/sites/default/files/2017-07/mv-education-package.pdf.

Overberg, Paul, Jon Kamp, and Daniel Michaels. "The Covid-19 Death Toll Is Even Worse Than It Looks." *The Wall Street Journal*, January 14, 2021. www.wsj.com/articles/the-covid-19-death -toll-is-even-worse-than-it-looks-11610636840.

Overby, John, Mike Rayburn, Kevin Hammond, and David C. Wyld. "The China Syndrome: The Impact of the SARS Epidemic in Southeast Asia." *Asia Pacific Journal of Marketing and Logistics* 16, no. 1 (March 2004): 69–94. https://doi.org/10.1108/13555850410765131.

"Overview + History—Ellis Island." The Statue of Liberty—Ellis Island Foundation. Accessed March 4, 2020. www.statueofliberty.org/ellis-island/overview-history.

Page, Jeremy, Wenxin Fan, and Natasha Khan. "How It All Started: China's Early Coronavirus Missteps." *The Wall Street Journal*, March 6, 2020. www.wsj.com/articles/how-it-all-started-chinas -early-coronavirus-missteps-11583508932.

Pamuk, Sevket. "The Black Death and the Origins of the 'Great Divergence' across Europe, 1300– 1600." *European Review of Economic History* 11, no. 3 (December 2007): 289–317. www.jstor.org /stable/41378468

Pandemic Prediction and Forecasting Science and Technology Working Group of the National Science and Technology Council. *Towards Epidemic Prediction: Federal Efforts and Opportunities in Outbreak Modeling.* December 2016. https://obamawhitehouse.archives.gov/sites/default/files /microsites/ostp/NSTC/towards_epidemic_prediction-federal_efforts_and_opportunities.pdf.

"Pandidakterion." World Heritage Encyclopedia. www.self.gutenberg.org/articles/pandidakterion.

Paradise, Julia. "Data Note: A Large Majority of Physicians Participate in Medicaid." Kaiser Family Foundation, May 10, 2017. www.kff.org/medicaid/issue-brief/data-note-a-large-majority-of -physicians-participate-in-medicaid.

"Partly False Claim: President Trump Signed Executive Order 13769, Temporarily Barring Foreigners from Entering the U.S. If They Had Been to China." Reuters, March 20, 2020. www.reuters .com/article/uk-factcheck-trump-executive-order-idUSKBN21739V.

"Pasteurization." *Encyclopædia Britannica Online.* July 20, 1998. www.britannica.com/technology /pasteurization.

Patterson, Marian A. "The Cholera Epidemic of 1832 in York, Upper Canada." *Bulletin of the Medical Library Association* 46, no. 2 (April 1958): 165–84.

Pavia, Will. "New York Streets Safest for 70 Years as Murders Plunge." *The Times* (London), December 29, 2017. www.thetimes.co.uk/article/new-york-streets-safest-for-70-years-as-murders-plunge -sgrt9r8c8.

"The Paycheck Protection Program Is in Dire Need of Reform." *The Washington Post*, May 22, 2020. www.washingtonpost.com/opinions/the-paycheck-protection-program-is-in-dire-need -of-reform/2020/05/22/f5f3f01a-9b6f-11ea-a2b3-5c3f2d1586df_story.html.

Pearce, Katie. "Obesity a Major Risk Factor for COVID-19 Hospitalization." Hub, June 1, 2020. https://hub.jhu.edu/2020/06/01/david-kass-obesity-covid-19.

"Peloponnesian War." History.com. Last modified August 29, 2019. www.history.com/topics/ancient
    -history/peloponnesian-war.

"People in Community of Madrid Live Longer, Compared to Other Europeans: European Regions
    with Highest Life Expectancies 2016." RList. Accessed December 27, 2020. https://rlist.io/l
    /madrid-of-spain-tops-average-life-expectancy-in-eu.

Pepys, Samuel. "Friday 14 July 1665." The Diary of Samuel Pepys. www.pepysdiary.com/diary/1665
    /07/14.

———. "Sunday 3 September 1665." The Diary of Samuel Pepys. www.pepysdiary.com/diary/1665
    /09/03.

Percival, Thomas, and Dr. Price. "Observations on the State of Population in Manchester, and Other
    Adjacent Places, Concluded. By Thomas Percival, M. D. F. R. S. and S. A. Communicated by the
    Rev. Dr. Price, F. R. S." Philosophical Transactions of the Royal Society of London 65 (1775): 322–35.

Percival, Thomas. "Experiments and Observations on the Waters of Buxton and Matlock, in Der-
    byshire, by Thomas Percival, of Manchester, M. D. and F. R. S." Philosophical Transactions of the
    Royal Society of London 62 (1772): 455–64.

———. The Works, Literary, Moral, and Medical, of Thomas Percival, M.D. Cambridge, UK: Cambridge
    University Press, 2013.

Percival, Thomas, and Richard Price. "V. Observations on the State of Population in Manchester, and
    Other Adjacent Places." Philosophical Transactions of the Royal Society of London 64 (January 1,
    1774): 54–66. https://doi.org/10.1098/rstl.1774.0005.

Perez, Caroline Criado. Invisible Women: Data Bias in a World Designed for Men. New York: Harry N.
    Abrams, 2019.

Pérez-Peña, Richard. "How the Vaccine Rollout Will Compare in Britain, Canada and the U.S."
    The New York Times, December 12, 2020. www.nytimes.com/2020/12/12/world/americas/covid
    -vaccine-us-uk-canada.html.

Perper, Rosie. "China Is Injecting Millions into WHO as the US Cuts Funds. Experts Say Beijing Is
    Trying to Boost Its Influence over the Agency and Its 'Deeply Compromised' Chief." Business
    Insider, April 24, 2020. www.businessinsider.com/china-who-multimillion-dollar-contribution
    -political-power-move-2020-4.

Pessar, Patricia R. "Engendering Migration Studies: The Case of New Immigrants in the United
    States." American Behavioral Scientist 42, no. 4 (January 1999): 577–600. https://doi.org/10.1177
    /00027649921954372.

Peter G. Peterson Foundation. "The Highway Trust Fund Explained." August 14, 2020. www.pgpf
    .org/budget-basics/budget-explainer-highway-trust-fund.

Peters, Frank M. Cracker or biscuit machine. US Patent 724609A, filed November 16, 1901, and
    issued April 7, 1903. https://patents.google.com/patent/US724609A/en.

Peters, Philip J., et al. "HIV Infection Linked to Injection Use of Oxymorphone in Indiana,
    2014–2015." New England Journal of Medicine 375 (July 2016): 229–39. https://doi.org/10.1056
    /NEJMoa1515195.

Petriceks, Aldis H., John C. Olivas, and Sakti Srivastava. "Trends in Geriatrics Graduate Medical
    Education Programs and Positions, 2001 to 2018." Gerontology and Geriatric Medicine 4 (May
    2018): 233372141877765. https://doi.org/10.1177/2333721418777659.

Pew Research Center. "Internet/Broadband Fact Sheet." June 12, 2019. www.pewresearch.org/internet
    /fact-sheet/internet-broadband.

Pfeiffer, Sacha, Meg Anderson, and Barbara Van Woerkom. "Despite Early Warnings, U.S. Took Months to Expand Swab Production for COVID-19 Test." NPR, May 12, 2020. www.npr.org /2020/05/12/853930147/despite-early-warnings-u-s-took-months-to-expand-swab-production -for-covid-19-te.

"Pfizer and BioNTech Announce an Agreement with U.S. Government for up to 600 Million Doses of mRNA-based Vaccine Candidate against SARS-CoV-2." *Business Wire*, July 22, 2020. www .businesswire.com/news/home/20200722005438/en/Pfizer-BioNTech-Announce -Agreement-U.S.-Government-600.

Pfizer. "Pfizer and BioNTech Announce Vaccine Candidate against COVID-19 Achieved Success in First Interim Analysis from Phase 3 Study." November 9, 2020. www.pfizer.com/news/press -release/press-release-detail/pfizer-and-biontech-announce-vaccine-candidate-against.

"Physician Board Certification Is on the Rise: More Than 900,000 Are Certified in the US." American Board of Medical Specialties, November 19, 2020. www.abms.org/news-events/abms-releases -2018-2019-board-certification-report.

Pickstone, John V. "Thomas Percival and the Production of Medical Ethics," in *The Codification of Medical Morality*. Edited by Robert Baker, Dorothy Porter, and Roy Porter, 161–78. Dordrecht: Springer Netherlands, 1993. https://doi.org/10.1007/978-94-015-8228-5_8.

"Pierre-Jean Robiquet." *Encyclopædia Britannica Online*. Accessed December 25, 2020. www.britannica .com/biography/Pierre-Jean-Robiquet.

"Plague (Yersinia Pestis)." Harvard Health Publishing, December 2018. www.health.harvard.edu /a_to_z/plague-yersinia-pestis-a-to-z.

"The Plague Doctor Mask: The Most Unsettling of All Venetian Masks." Ca' Macana. www.camacana .com/en-UK/plague-doctor-mask-history.php.

Platforms of the Democratic Party and the Republican Party. Washington: U.S. Government Printing Office, 1940.

Plato. *The Republic*. Edited by G. R. F. Ferrari. Translated by Tom Griffith. Cambridge, UK: Cambridge University Press, 2000.

Platt, Lucinda, and Ross Warwick. *Are Some Ethnic Groups More Vulnerable to COVID-19 Than Others?* Institute for Fiscal Studies, May 2020. www.ifs.org.uk/inequality/wp-content/uploads/2020/04 /Are-some-ethnic-groups-more-vulnerable-to-COVID-19-than-others-V2-IFS-Briefing -Note.pdf.

Plutarch. *Plutarch's Miscellanies and Essays: Comprising All His Works Collected Under the Title of "Morals."* Corrected and revised by William W. Goodwin. Boston: Little, Brown, 1898.

Podlecki, Anthony, and Oliver Taplin. "Aeschylus." *Encyclopaedia Britannica Online*. www.britannica .com/biography/Aeschylus-Greek-dramatist.

Podolsky, Scott H., David Herzberg, and Jeremy A. Greene. "Preying on Prescribers (and Their Patients)—Pharmaceutical Marketing, Iatrogenic Epidemics, and the Sackler Legacy." *New England Journal of Medicine* 380, no. 19 (May 2019): 1785–87. https://doi.org/10.1056/nejmp1902811.

Polgar, Steven. "The Evolution and Eradication of Infectious Diseases." *American Anthropologist* 66, no. 6 (1964): 1457–58. https://doi.org/10.1525/aa.1964.66.6.02a00670.

"Police in 2020 Killed People at Similar Rates as Past Years," December 30, 2020. https:// mappingpoliceviolence.org/nationaltrends.

"Police Officers Federation of Minneapolis." FindGlocal, 2021. www.findglocal.com/US/Minneapolis /200372523486100/Police-Officers-Federation-of-Minneapolis.

"Population of the Major European Countries in the 19th Century." Table from website of History 203, Modern Europe, taught by Dr. David Morgan, Professor of History Emeritus and Tutor Emeritus, College of Social Studies, Wesleyan University, Middletown, CT. http://dmorgan .web.wesleyan.edu/materials/population.htm.

Porter, Jane, and Hershel Jick. "Addiction Rare in Patients Treated with Narcotics. *New England Journal of Medicine* 302 (January 1980): 123. https://doi.org/10.1056/NEJM198001103020221.

Posaner, Joshua. "Germany's Merkel Bans Meetings of More Than 2 People to Slow Coronavirus." *Politico*, March 22, 2020. www.politico.com/news/2020/03/22/germany-merkel-bans-meetings -two-people-142283.

Poti, Jennifer M., Michelle A. Mendez, Shu Wen Ng, and Barry M. Popkin. "Is the Degree of Food Processing and Convenience Linked with the Nutritional Quality of Foods Purchased by US Households?" *American Journal of Clinical Nutrition* 101, no. 6 (2015): 1251–262. https://doi.org /10.3945/ajcn.114.100925.

Powell, Lisa M., Frank J. Chaloupka, and Yanjun Bao. "The Availability of Fast-Food and Full-Service Restaurants in the United States: Associations with Neighborhood Characteristics." *American Journal of Preventive Medicine* 33, no. 4 (October 2007): S240–45. https://doi.org /10.1016/j.amepre.2007.07.005.

Prashad, Vijay. "The Technology of Sanitation in Colonial Delhi." *Modern Asian Studies* 35, no. 1 (2001): 113–55. https://www.jstor.org/stable/313090.

"President and Secretary General de Hoop Scheffer Discuss NATO Meeting." White House. News release, February 22, 2005. https://georgewbush-whitehouse.archives.gov/news/releases/2005 /02/20050222-3.html.

Price, Polly J. "Epidemics, Outsiders, and Local Protection: Federalism Theater in the Era of the Shotgun Quarantine." *University of Pennsylvania Journal of Constitutional Law*, December 2016; Emory Legal Studies Research Paper No. 15-352, August 5, 2015. https://doi.org/10.2139 /ssrn.2640182.

"Proclamation on the Suspension of Entry as Immigrants and Non-Immigrants of Certain Additional Persons Who Pose a Risk of Transmitting Coronavirus Disease." White House, January 25, 2021. https://www.federalregister.gov/documents/2020/02/05/2020-02424/suspension-of-entry -as-immigrants-and-nonimmigrants-of-persons-who-pose-a-risk-of-transmitting-2019.

Procopius. *History of the Wars, Volume I: Books 1–2 (Persian War)*. Translated by H. B. Dewing. London: W. Heinemann, 1914.

———. *History of the Wars, Volume II: Books 3–4 (Vandalic War)*. Translated by H. B. Dewing. Loeb Classical Library 81. Cambridge, MA: Harvard University Press, 1916.

———. *History of the Wars, Volume IV: Books 6.16–7.35 (Gothic War)*. Translated by H. B. Dewing. Loeb Classical Library 173. Cambridge, MA: Harvard University Press, 1924.

Procopius of Caesarea. *The Complete Works of Procopius of Caesarea*. East Sussex, UK: Delphi Classics, 2016.

"Progressive Party Platform of 1912." Teaching American History. Accessed January 18, 2021. https://teachingamericanhistory.org/library/document/progressive-platform-of-1912.

Quadagno, Jill, and Sidney M. Stahl. "Challenges in Nursing Home Care: A Research Agenda." *The Gerontologist* 43, no. suppl_2 (April 2003): 4–6. https://doi.org/10.1093/geront/43.suppl_2.4.

Rabin, Roni Caryn. "First Patient with Wuhan Coronavirus Is Identified in the U.S." *The New York Times*, January 21, 2020. www.nytimes.com/2020/01/21/health/cdc-coronavirus.html.

Raj, Jeffrey Pradeep, and Shervin Ploriya. "Prevalence of Obesity among Rehabilitated Urban Slum Dwellers and Altered Body Image Perception in India (PRESUME)." *Indian Journal of Endocrinology and Metabolism* 22, no. 1 (2018): 23–29. https://doi.org/10.4103/ijem.ijem _363_17.

"Ralph Lauren," Biography. September 13, 2019. www.biography.com/fashion-designer/ralph-lauren.

Ranney, Megan L., Valerie Griffeth, and Ashish K. Jha. "Critical Supply Shortages—the Need for Ventilators and Personal Protective Equipment during the Covid-19 Pandemic." *New England Journal of Medicine* 382, no. 18 (April 2020): e41. https://doi.org/10.1056/NEJMp2006141.

Rascovan, Nicolás, Karl-Göran Sjögren, Kristian Kristiansen, Rasmus Nielsen, Eske Willerslev, Christelle Desnues, and Simon Rasmussen. "Emergence and Spread of Basal Lineages of *Yersinia pestis* during the Neolithic Decline." *Cell* 176, no. 1 (January 2019): 295–305.e10. https://doi.org /10.1016/j.cell.2018.11.005.

Rashbaum, William K., and Al Baker. "Smoking Car to an Arrest in 53 Hours." *The New York Times*, May 4, 2010. www.nytimes.com/2010/05/05/nyregion/05tictoc.html.

Rasmussen, Simon, Morten Erik Allentoft, Kasper Nielsen, Ludovic Orlando, Martin Sikora, Karl-Göran Sjögren, Anders Gorm Pedersen, et al. "Early Divergent Strains of *Yersinia pestis* in Eurasia 5,000 Years Ago." *Cell* 163, no. 3 (October 2015): 571–82. https://doi.org/10.1016/j.cell.2015 .10.009.

Rawdon-Hastings, Francis, Marquess of Hastings. *The Private Journal of the Marquess of Hastings*. Allahabad: Panini Office, 1907.

Ray, Rashawn. "What Does 'Defund the Police' Mean and Does It Have Merit?" Brookings, June 19, 2020. www.brookings.edu/blog/fixgov/2020/06/19/what-does-defund-the-police-mean-and -does-it-have-merit.

"Reactions to Plague in the Ancient & Medieval World." World History Encyclopedia, March 31, 2020. www.ancient.eu/article/1534/reactions-to-plague-in-the-ancient—medieval-world.

Rector, Kevin. "Surge in South L.A. Bloodshed Tied to Gunfire from High-Capacity Firearms, Gang Feuds." *Los Angeles Times*, December 15, 2020. www.latimes.com/california/story/2020 -12-15/lapd-officials-lament-ongoing-surge-in-violence-in-south-and-central-los-angeles.

Reft, Ryan. "Segregation in the City of Angels: A 1939 Map of Housing Inequality in L.A." KCET, November 14, 2017. www.kcet.org/shows/lost-la/segregation-in-the-city-of-angels-a-1939-map -of-housing-inequality-in-la.

Regan, Helen, and Sandi Sidhu. "WHO Team Blocked from Entering China to Study Origins of Coronavirus." CNN, January 6, 2021. www.cnn.com/2021/01/05/china/china-blocks-who-team -coronavirus-intl-hnk/index.html.

Reinhart, Eric, and Daniel L. Chen. "Incarceration and Its Disseminations: COVID-19 Pandemic Lessons from Chicago's Cook County Jail." *Health Affairs* 39, no. 8 (August 2020): 1412–18. https://doi.org/10.1377/hlthaff.2020.00652.

"Religion: Atheists & Foxholes." *Time*, June 18, 1945. http://content.time.com/time/subscriber/article /0,33009,775935,00.html.

"Remarks by the President and Secretary General Stoltenberg of NATO after Bilateral Meeting." White House, April 4, 2016. https://obamawhitehouse.archives.gov/the-press-office/2016/04 /04/remarks-president-and-secretary-general-stoltenberg-nato-after-bilateral.

Rendsburg, Gary A. "The Date of the Exodus and the Conquest/Settlement: The Case for the 1100S." *Vetus Testamentum* 42, no. 4 (October 1992): 510–27. https://doi.org/10.2307/1518961.

Resseger, Matthew. "The Impact of Land Use Regulation on Racial Segregation: Evidence from Massachusetts Zoning Borders." Harvard University, November 26, 2013. https://scholar.harvard.edu/files/resseger/files/resseger_jmp_11_25.pdf.

Results from the 2019 Mathematics and Reading Assessments at Grade 12. The Nation's Report Card, 2019. www.nationsreportcard.gov/mathematics/supportive_files/2019_infographic_G12_math_reading.pdf.

Rhodes, Chris. "Manufacturing: Statistics and Policy." UK Parliament, House of Commons Library, January 10, 2020. https://commonslibrary.parliament.uk/research-briefings/sn01942.

Rickman, G. E. "The Grain Trade under the Roman Empire." *Memoirs of the American Academy in Rome* 36 (1980): 261–75. https://doi.org/10.2307/4238709.

Rio, Carlos del, Lauren F. Collins, and Preeti Malani. "Long-Term Health Consequences of COVID-19." *JAMA* 324, no. 17 (November 2020): 1723–24. https://doi.org/10.1001/jama.2020.19719.

Ritchie, Hannah, and Max Roser. "Obesity." Our World in Data, August 11, 2017. https://ourworldindata.org/obesity.

Robbins, Christopher. "Crime Is Up, and Ray Kelly Has Record High Approval Rating." *Gothamist*, January 17, 2013. https://gothamist.com/news/crime-is-up-and-ray-kelly-has-record-high-approval-rating.

Robert Koch Institute. "Navigation and Service." Accessed December 30, 2020. www.rki.de/EN/Home/homepage.html.

Robson, Ruthann. "Public Interest Lawyering & Judicial Politics: Four Cases Worth a Second Look in Williams-Yulee v. The Florida Bar." CUNY Academic Works, January 1, 2015. https://academicworks.cuny.edu/cl_pubs/40.

Rogers, David. "Senate Passes $787 Billion Stimulus Bill." *Politico*, February 13, 2019. www.politico.com/story/2009/02/senate-passes-787-billion-stimulus-bill-018837.

Rohde, Jeff. "Why Investors Should Consider Chicago's Real Estate Market in 2021." Roofstock, January 6, 2021. https://learn.roofstock.com/blog/chicago-real-estate-market.

Ronderos, L. Nicolas. *Stabilization of the U.S. Manufacturing Sector and Its Impact on Industrial Space.* NAIOP Research Foundation. Herndon, VA: 2013. www.naiop.org/-/media/Research/Research/Research-Reports/Stabilization-of-the-US-Manufacturing-and-Its-Impact-on-Industrial-Space/NAIOP_Ronderos_FINAL_web-version.ashx.

Roodman, David. "The Impacts of Incarceration on Crime." Open Philanthropy Project, September 2007. http://arxiv.org/abs/2007.10268.

Roos, Dave. "Social Distancing and Quarantine Were Used in Medieval Times to Fight the Black Death." History.com, March 27, 2020. www.history.com/news/quarantine-black-death-medieval.

Rose, Shanna. *Financing Medicaid: Federalism and the Growth of America's Health Care Safety Net.* Ann Arbor: University of Michigan Press, 2013.

Rosen, G. "Tenements and Typhus in New York City, 1840–1875." *American Journal of Public Health* 62, no. 4 (April 1972): 590–93. https://doi.org/10.2105/AJPH.62.4.590.

Rosenberg, Charles E. *The Cholera Years: The United States in 1832, 1849, and 1866.* Chicago: University of Chicago Press, 2009.

———. "The Cholera Epidemic of 1832 in New York City," *Bulletin of the History of Medicine* 33, no. 1 (January–February 1959): 37–49. www.jstor.org/stable/i40187015.

Ross, Allison. "Florida Coronavirus Deaths Surpass 1,200, Cases Pass 33,000." *Tampa Bay Times*, April 29, 2020. www.tampabay.com/news/health/2020/04/29/florida-coronavirus-deaths-surpass-1200-cases-pass-33000.

Routt, David. "The Economic Impact of the Black Death." EH.Net Encyclopedia. Edited by Robert Whaples, July 20, 2008. https://eh.net/encyclopedia/the-economic-impact-of-the-black-death.

Roy, Eleanor Ainge. "'Can I Really Do This?' New Zealand's Ashley Bloomfield Reveals Self-Doubts at Height of Covid." *The Guardian* (London), September 23, 2020. www.theguardian.com/world/2020/sep/24/can-i-really-do-this-new-zealands-ashley-bloomfield-reveals-self-doubts-at-height-of-covid.

Ruane, Michael E. "Yellow Fever Led Half of Philadelphians to Flee the City. Ten Percent of the Residents Still Died." *The Washington Post*, April 4, 2020. www.washingtonpost.com/history/2020/04/04/yellow-fever-led-half-philadelphians-flee-city-ten-percent-residents-still-died.

Rush, Benjamin. *An Account of the Bilious Remitting Yellow Fever, as It Appeared in the City of Philadelphia, in the Year 1793*. Edinburgh: John Moir, 1796.

Russell, E. J. "Agricultural Colonization in the Pontine Marshes and Libya." *The Geographical Journal* 94, no. 4 (October 1939): 273–89. https://doi.org/10.2307/1788096.

Russell, John. *Essays, and Sketches of Life and Character*. London: Forgotten Books, 2019.

Ryan, Edward T. "Eyes on the Prize: Lessons from the Cholera Wars for Modern Scientists, Physicians, and Public Health Officials." *The American Journal of Tropical Medicine and Hygiene* 89, no. 4 (October 2013): 610–14. https://doi.org/10.4269/ajtmh.13-0173.

Ryan, Phil. "United States Office Outlook—Q3 2020." Jones Lang LaSalle, October 14, 2020. www.us.jll.com/en/trends-and-insights/research/office-market-statistics-trends.

Ryan, Thomas J. "The Coronary Angiogram and Its Seminal Contributions to Cardiovascular Medicine over Five Decades." *Circulation* 106, no. 6 (August 2002): 752–56. https://doi.org/10.1161/01.CIR.0000024109.12658.D4.

Rydell, Mark, dir. *The Cowboys*. Warner Bros., 1972.

Sagonowsky, Eric. "Biogen Superspreader Meeting Spawned 300,000-plus U.S. Coronavirus Cases: Study." FiercePharma, December 15, 2020. www.fiercepharma.com/pharma/biogen-superspreader-meeting-associated-300-000-u-s-coronavirus-cases-study.

Sahagún, Louis. "East L.A., 1968: 'Walkout!' The Day High School Students Helped Ignite the Chicano Power Movement." *Los Angeles Times*, March 1, 2018. www.latimes.com/nation/la-na-1968-east-la-walkouts-20180301-htmlstory.html.

Salmon, John Hearsey McMillan, et al. "History of Europe." *Encyclopædia Britannica Online*. Accessed January 17, 2021. www.britannica.com/topic/history-of-Europe.

Sample, Ian. "HIV Pandemic Originated in Kinshasa in the 1920s, Say Scientists." *The Guardian* (London), October 2, 2014. www.theguardian.com/science/2014/oct/02/hiv-aids-pandemic-kinshasa-africa.

"Samuel Pepys and the Navy." Royal Museums Greenwich. www.rmg.co.uk/explore/samuel-pepys-and-navy.

San Francisco University High School. "The Brown Berets: Young Chicano Revolutionaries." Accessed January 11, 2021. http://inside.sfuhs.org/dept/history/US_History_reader/Chapter14/brownberets.htm.

Sang-hun, Choe. "Shadowy Church Is at Center of Coronavirus Outbreak in South Korea." *The New York Times*, February 21, 2020. www.nytimes.com/2020/02/21/world/asia/south-korea-coronavirus-shincheonji.html.

Satterthwaite, David, Gordon McGranahan, and Cecilia Tacoli. "Urbanization and Its Implications for Food and Farming." *Philosophical Transactions of the Royal Society B: Biological Sciences* 365, no. 1554 (2010): 2809–20. https://doi.org/10.1098/rstb.2010.0136.

Saunders, Nicholas J., *The Poppy: A History of Conflict, Loss, Remembrance, and Redemption.* London: Oneworld, 2014.

Saurine, Angela. "Slum Tour in Dharavi, Mumbai with Reality Tours and Travel." News.com.au, July 29, 2013. www.news.com.au/travel/world-travel/slum-tour-in-dharavi-mumbai-with-reality -tours-and-travel/news-story/7167502cc923fa1a0aa6bf983bfaed6f.

Sawyer, Wendy, and Peter Wagner. "Mass Incarceration: The Whole Pie 2020." Prison Policy Initiative, March 24, 2020. www.prisonpolicy.org/reports/pie2020.html.

Saxenian, AnnaLee. *Regional Advantage: Culture and Competition in Silicon Valley and Route 128, with a New Preface by the Author.* Cambridge, MA: Harvard University Press, 1996.

Schieber, G. J. "Health Expenditures in Major Industrialized Countries, 1960–87." *Health Care Financing Review* 11, no. 4 (Summer 1990): 159–67. www.ncbi.nlm.nih.gov/pmc/articles /PMC4193120.

Schlosser, Eric. *Fast Food Nation.* Barcelona: Debolsillo, 2007.

Schmidt, Torrey, and J. Dawn Abbott. "Coronary Stents: History, Design, and Construction." *Journal of Clinical Medicine* 7, no. 6 (May 2018): 126. https://doi.org/10.3390/jcm7060126.

Schmidt, William H., and Richard T. Houang. "Curricular Coherence and the Common Core State Standards for Mathematics." *Educational Researcher* 41, no. 8 (November 2012): 294–308. https:// doi.org/10.3102/0013189X12464517.

Schneider, Keith. "Alvin Toffler, Author of 'Future Shock,' Dies at 87." *The New York Times*, June 29, 2016. www.nytimes.com/2016/06/30/books/alvin-toffler-author-of-future-shock-dies-at-87.html.

Schoen, Cathy, and Michelle M. Doty. "Inequities in Access to Medical Care in Five Countries: Findings from the 2001 Commonwealth Fund International Health Policy Survey." *Health Policy* 67, no. 3 (March 2004): 309–22. https://doi.org/10.1016/j.healthpol.2003.09.006. PMID: 15036818.

Schountz, Tony. "Immunology of Bats and Their Viruses: Challenges and Opportunities." *Viruses* 6, no. 12 (December 2014): 4880–901. https://doi.org/10.3390/v6124880.

Schregle, Johannes. "Labor Law." *Encyclopædia Britannica Online.* Last modified September 25, 2019. www.britannica.com/topic/labour-law.

Schumann, G. L., and S. Uppala. "Ergot of Rye." The Plant Health Instructor, 2000. www.apsnet .org/edcenter/disandpath/fungalasco/pdlessons/Pages/Ergot.aspx.

Schwartz, Karen. "I'm a U.S. Citizen. Where in the World Can I Go?" *The New York Times*, March 15, 2021. www.nytimes.com/article/coronavirus-travel-restrictions.html.

———. "Thinking of Traveling in the U.S.? Check Which States Have Travel Restrictions." *The New York Times*, July 10, 2020. www.nytimes.com/2020/07/10/travel/state-travel-restrictions.html.

Scommegna, Paola. "Opioid Overdose Epidemic Hits Hardest for the Least Educated." Population Reference Bureau, January 10, 2018.

Scott, Dylan. "9 Things Americans Need to Learn from the Rest of the World's Health Care Systems." *Vox*, January 29, 2020. www.vox.com/health-care/2020/1/29/21075388/medicare-for-all -what-countries-have-universal-health-care.

Scott, Jonathan. *How the Old World Ended: The Anglo-Dutch-American Revolution 1500–1800.* New Haven, CT: Yale University Press, 2020.

"Second Round of PPP Loans Approved by Congress in New COVID-19 Stimulus Bill." StatesAttorney, January 2, 2021. www.statesattorney.org/2021/01/02/second-round-of-ppp-loans-approved-by-congress-in-new-covid-19-stimulus-bill.

Selanders, Louise. "Florence Nightingale." *Encyclopædia Britannica Online*. Last modified January 13, 2021. www.britannica.com/biography/Florence-Nightingale.

Selig, David, and Christina Vazquez. "Miami-Dade Closing Indoor Dining amid Coronavirus Spike; Gyms Can Now Stay Open." Local 10 News, July 6, 2020. www.local10.com/news/local/2020/07/06/miami-dade-closing-restaurants-amid-coronavirus-spike.

Shafrin, Jason. "The Development of Universal Health Care in Sweden." *Healthcare Economist*, December 6, 2011. www.healthcare-economist.com/2011/12/06/the-development-of-universal-health-care-in-sweden.

Shakespeare, William. *Othello*, Act V, Scene 2, 1605. Available from Folger Library. https://shakespeare.folger.edu/downloads/pdf/othello_PDF_FolgerShakespeare.pdf.

Shanks, G. Dennis, and John F. Brundage. "Pathogenic Responses among Young Adults during the 1918 Influenza Pandemic." *Emerging Infectious Diseases* 18, no. 2 (February 2012): 201–7. https://doi.org/10.3201/eid1802.102042.

Sharp, Paul M., and Beatrice H. Hahn. "Origins of HIV and the AIDS Pandemic." *Cold Spring Harbor Perspectives in Medicine* 1, no. 1 (September 2011). https://doi.org/10.1101/cshperspect.a006841.

Sharpless, Ned. "How FDA Is Regulating E-Cigarettes." US Food and Drug Administration. Last modified September 10, 2019. www.fda.gov/news-events/fda-voices/how-fda-regulating-e-cigarettes.

Sheehy, Kate. "George Floyd Had 'Violent Criminal History': Minneapolis Police Union Chief." *New York Post*, June 2, 2020. https://nypost.com/2020/06/02/george-floyd-had-violent-criminal-history-minneapolis-union-chief.

Sheridan, Adam, Asger Lau Andersen, Emil Toft Hansen, and Niels Johannesen. "Social Distancing Laws Cause Only Small Losses of Economic Activity during the COVID-19 Pandemic in Scandinavia." *Proceedings of the National Academy of Sciences* 117, no. 34 (August 2020): 20468–73. https://doi.org/10.1073/pnas.2010068117.

Sherman-Palladino, Amy, ex. prod. and dir. *The Marvelous Mrs. Maisel*. Prime Video, 2017–2019.

Shields, Christopher. "Aristotle," in *The Stanford Encyclopedia of Philosophy*. Edited by Edward N. Zalta. Stanford, CA: Metaphysics Research Lab, Stanford University, 2020.

Siegel, Barry. "Locking Up 'Sexual Predators': A Public Outcry in Washington State Targeted Repeat Violent Sex Criminals. A New Preventive Law Would Keep Them in Jail Indefinitely." *Los Angeles Times*, May 10, 1990. www.latimes.com/archives/la-xpm-1990-05-10-mn-1433-story.html.

Siegler, Kirk. "Biden's Win Shows Rural-Urban Divide Has Grown Since 2016." NPR, November 18, 2020. www.npr.org/2020/11/18/934631994/bidens-win-shows-rural-urban-divide-has-grown-since-2016.

Silva, Catherine. "Racial Restrictive Covenants History: Enforcing Neighborhood Segregation in Seattle." Seattle Civil Rights and Labor History Project, 2008. https://depts.washington.edu/civilr/covenants_report.htm.

Silverman, Ed. "One-Quarter of People with Diabetes in the U.S. Ration Their Insulin." *Stat*, October 20, 2019. www.statnews.com/pharmalot/2019/06/18/one-quarter-of-people-with-diabetes-in-the-u-s-are-rationing-their-insulin.

Silverman, Rachel, et al. "Financing and Scaling Innovation for the COVID Fight: A Closer Look at Demand-Side Incentives for a Vaccine." Center For Global Development, March 31, 2020. www .cgdev.org/publication/financing-and-scaling-innovation-covid-fight-closer-look-demand-side -incentives-vaccine.

Sim, Dewey. "From Sars to Covid-19, What Lessons Has Singapore Learned?" *South China Morning Post*, February 25, 2020. www.scmp.com/week-asia/health-environment/article/3052120/sars -covid-19-what-lessons-has-singapore-learned.

Simpson, John, and Jennifer Speake. "It Doesn't Matter If a Cat Is Black or White, as Long as It Catches Mice," in *The Oxford Dictionary of Proverbs*. Edited by John Simpson and Jennifer Speake. Oxford, UK: Oxford University Press, 2008. www.oxfordreference.com/view/10.1093/acref/978 0199539536.001.0001/acref-9780199539536-e-312.

Singh, Gopal K., and Mohammad Siahpush. "Widening Rural-Urban Disparities in Life Expectancy, U.S., 1969–2009." *American Journal of Preventive Medicine* 46, no. 2 (February 2014): e19–29. https://doi.org/10.1016/j.amepre.2013.10.017.

"Sir Joseph Paxton." *Encyclopædia Britannica Online*. Accessed January 18, 2021. www.britannica.com /biography/Joseph-Paxton.

"Sir Joseph William Bazalgette." *Encyclopædia Britannica Online*. March 24, 2020. www.britannica .com/biography/Joseph-William-Bazalgette.

Smillie, W. G. "The National Board of Health, 1879–1883." *American Journal of Public Health and the Nation's Health* 33, no. 8 (August 1943): 925–30. https://doi.org/10.2105/AJPH.33.8.925.

Smith, Adam. *The Wealth of Nations*. New York: Random House, 2020.

Smith, Billy. *Ship of Death: A Voyage That Changed the Atlantic World*. New Haven, CT: Yale University Press, 2013.

Smith, David. "Proof! Just Six Degrees of Separation between Us." *The Guardian* (London), August 2, 2008. www.theguardian.com/technology/2008/aug/03/internet.email.

Smith, Laura. "In 1974, a Stripper Known as the 'Tidal Basin Bombshell' Took Down the Most Powerful Man in Washington." *Medium*, September 18, 2017. https://timeline.com/wilbur-mills -tidal-basin-3c29a8b47ad1.

Smith, Wilbur S. "Interactions between Transportation and High-Rise, High-Density Living." *Ekistics* 53, no. 320/321 (1986): 336–44.

Smithsonian National Museum of American History. "Separate Is Not Equal: Brown v. Board of Education: Jim Crow Laws." Accessed December 27, 2020. https://americanhistory.si.edu/brown /history/1-segregated/detail/jim-crow-laws.html.

Sneader, Walter. "The Discovery of Aspirin: A Reappraisal." *British Medical Journal* 321 (December 2000): 1591–4. https://doi.org/10.1136/bmj.321.7276.1591.

"SNL Transcripts: Chevy Chase: 02/18/78: Baggage Inspection Counter." SNL Transcripts Tonight. https://snltranscripts.jt.org/77/77kcustoms.phtml.

Social Security Administration. "Social Security History: Chapter 4: The Fourth Round—1957 to 1965." Accessed December 26, 2020. www.ssa.gov/history/corningchap4.html.

Somerville, Ewan. "New Zealand's Covid Response: Why Early Lockdown and Stringent Quarantine Kept Cases Down to Fewer Than 2,000." iNews, October 28, 2020. https://inews.co.uk /news/world/new-zealand-covid-how-beat-coronavirus-free-lockdown-quarantine-coronavirus -cases-739493.

Soper, George A. "The Curious Career of Typhoid Mary." *Bulletin of the New York Academy of Medicine* 15, no. 10 (October 1939): 698–712. https://europepmc.org/backend/ptpmcrender.fcgi?accid =PMC1911442&blobtype=pdf.

"Sorbic Acid." ScienceDirect Topics. Accessed December 25, 2020. www.sciencedirect.com/topics /immunology-and-microbiology/sorbic-acid.

Specht, Joshua. "The Price of Plenty: How Beef Changed America." *The Guardian* (London), May 7, 2019. www.theguardian.com/environment/2019/may/07/the-price-of-plenty-how-beef-changed -america.

"Special Message to the Congress Recommending a Comprehensive Health Program." Harry S. Truman Library and Museum. Accessed January 20, 2021. www.trumanlibrary.gov/library/public -papers/192/special-message-congress-recommending-comprehensive-health-program.

Spector, Mike. "In Emails, Sacklers Fret over Wealth, Opioid Business." Reuters, October 21, 2020. www.reuters.com/article/purdue-pharma-opioids-investigations-ema-idUSKBN277070.

Spees, Ann-Cathrin. "Could Germany's Vocational Education Training System Be a Model for the U.S.?" World Education News and Reviews, June 12, 2018. https://wenr.wes.org/2018/06/could -germanys-vocational-education-and-training-system-be-a-model-for-the-u-s.

Spellen, Suzanne. "Walkabout: 'The Great Mistake'—How Brooklyn Lost Its Independence, Part 2." Brownstoner, September 3, 2015. www.brownstoner.com/history/brooklyn-history-consolidation -of-new-york-great-mistake.

Spinney, Laura. "Smallpox and Other Viruses Plagued Humans Much Earlier Than Suspected." *Nature* 584, no. 7819 (July 2020): 30–32. https://doi.org/10.1038/d41586-020-02083-0.

Spitzzeri, Paul R. "Sharing History with the Boyle Heights Historical Society." *The Homestead Blog*, May 7, 2019. homesteadmuseum.blog/2019/05/07/sharing-history-with-the-boyle-heights -historical-society.

Spyrou, Maria A., Rezeda I. Tukhbatova, Chuan-Chao Wang, Aida Andrades Valtueña, Aditya K. Lankapalli, Vitaly V. Kondrashin, Victor A. Tsybin, et al. "Analysis of 3800-Year-Old *Yersinia pestis* Genomes Suggests Bronze Age Origin for Bubonic Plague." *Nature Communications* 9, no. 1 (June 2018): 2234. https://doi.org/10.1038/s41467-018-04550-9.

Stack, Megan K. "A Sudden Coronavirus Surge Brought Out Singapore's Dark Side." *The New York Times*, May 20, 2020. www.nytimes.com/2020/05/20/magazine/singapore-coronavirus.html.

Stanton, Christopher, and Pratyush Tiwari. "The Housing Consumption of Remote Workers." *Harvard Mimeograph*, 2020.

Starr, Paul. *The Social Transformation of American Medicine*. New York: Basic Books, 2017.

"State of California Education Section 43503." California Legislative Information. Accessed January 8, 2021. http://leginfo.legislature.ca.gov/faces/codes_displaySection.xhtml?lawCode=EDC &sectionNum=43503.

"State of California Education Section 51512." California Legislative Information. Accessed January 8, 2021. http://leginfo.legislature.ca.gov/faces/codes_displaySection.xhtml?lawCode=EDC &sectionNum=51512.

State of New York. *New York Common Core Task Force Final Report*. 2015. https://www.governor.ny.gov /sites/governor.ny.gov/files/atoms/files/NewYorkCommonCoreTaskForceFinalReport2015.pdf.

Statistics Canada. "Health At a Glance, 2011, Appendix 1: Life Expectancy by Health Region, 2005– 2007." Accessed December 8, 2020. https://www150.statcan.gc.ca/n1/pub/82-624-x/2011001 /article/11427-01-app-eng.htm.

Steinfeld, Jemimah. "China's Deadly Science Lesson: How an Ill-Conceived Campaign against Sparrows Contributed to One of the Worst Famines in History." *Index on Censorship* 47, no. 3 (September 2018): 49. Stevenson, Betsey, and Justin Wolfers. "Subjective Well-Being and Income: Is There Any Evidence of Satiation?" *American Economic Review* 103, no. 3 (May 2013): 598–604. https://doi.org/10.1257/aer.103.3.598.

Stephenson, Joan. "Drug Overdose Deaths Head toward Record Number in 2020, CDC Warns." *JAMA Health Forum*, October 20, 2020. https://jamanetwork.com/channels/health-forum/fullarticle/2772241.

Stevenson, Lloyd Grenfell. "Robert Koch." *Encyclopædia Britannica Online*. Last modified December 7, 2020. www.britannica.com/biography/Robert-Koch.

Steverding, Dietmar. "The History of African Trypanosomiasis." *Parasites & Vectors* 1 (February 2008): 3. https://doi.org/10.1186/1756-3305-1-3.

Stewart, Nikita, and Paul Schwartzman. "How Adrian Fenty Lost His Reelection Bid for D.C. Mayor," *The Washington Post*. September 16, 2010.

Stigler, George J. "The Theory of Economic Regulation." *The Bell Journal of Economics and Management Science* 2, no. 1 (Spring 1971): 3–21. https://doi.org/10.2307/3003160.

Stockholm International Peace Research Institute. "SIPRI Military Expenditure Database." Accessed January 18, 2021. www.sipri.org/databases/milex.

Strochlic, Nina, and Riley Champine. "How Some Cities 'Flattened the Curve' during the 1918 Flu Pandemic." *National Geographic*, March 27, 2020. www.nationalgeographic.com/history/2020/03/how-cities-flattened-curve-1918-spanish-flu-pandemic-coronavirus.

Sudo, Chuck. "Long-Term Care Executive Salaries Rose 2.8% in 2019." *Senior Housing News*, February 14, 2020. https://seniorhousingnews.com/2020/02/14/long-term-care-executive-salaries-rose-2-8-in-2019.

Sullivan, Tim, and Aaron Morrison. "George Floyd Fallout: Unrest Overshadows Peaceful Protests for Another Night; No Apparent Injuries after Semitruck Drives into Minneapolis Demonstrators." *Chicago Tribune*, May 31, 2020. www.chicagotribune.com/nation-world/ct-nw-george-floyd-protests-minneapolis-nation-20200531-7qcojsy535bs7a56cxk3cnmrgq-story.html.

Summers, Judith. "Broad Street Pump Outbreak." UCLA Fielding School of Public Health Department of Epidemiology. Accessed January 17, 2021. www.ph.ucla.edu/epi/snow/broadstreetpump.html.

"Swann v. Charlotte-Mecklenburg Board of Education." Oyez. www.oyez.org/cases/1970/281.

Sze, Shirley, Daniel Pan, Clareece R. Nevill, Laura J. Gray, et al. "Ethnicity and Clinical Outcomes in COVID-19: A Systematic Review and Meta-analysis." *EClinicalMedicine* 29, no. 100630 (December 2020). https://doi.org/10.1016/j.eclinm.2020.100630.

"Tammany Hall." *Encyclopædia Britannica Online*. January 24, 2020. www.britannica.com/topic/Tammany-Hall.

Tansey, Oisín. "Lowest Common Denominator Norm Institutionalization: The Anti-Coup Norm at the United Nations." *Global Governance: A Review of Multilateralism and International Organizations* 24, no. 2 (August 2018): 287–306. https://doi.org/10.1163/19426720-02402008.

Taubenberger, Jeffery K. "The Origin and Virulence of the 1918 'Spanish' Influenza Virus." *Proceedings of the American Philosophical Society* 150, no. 1 (March 2006): 86–112. https://pubmed.ncbi.nlm.nih.gov/17526158.

"Tax Limitation, Article XIII A CONS § 1 (1978)." California Legislative Information. https://leginfo.legislature.ca.gov/faces/codes_displaySection.xhtml?lawCode=CONS&sectionNum=SECTION%201.&article=XIII%20A.

Taylor, Derrick Bryson. "The Coronavirus Pandemic: A Timeline." *The New York Times*, January 10, 2021. www.nytimes.com/article/coronavirus-timeline.html.

"Ten Great Public Health Achievements—United States, 1900–1999." *JAMA* 281, no. 16 (1999): 1481. https://doi.org/10.1001/jama.281.16.1481.

"TenPoint Coalition Founder Departs." WBUR, January 30, 2013. www.wbur.org/radioboston /2013/01/30/tenpoint.

Testin, Robert F. "New Packaging Technologies." *Food and Drug Law Journal* 1995, 50, no. 4: 399–413.

Thomas, Katie. "The Coronavirus Vaccines Will Likely Work. Making Them Fast Will Be the Hard Part." *The New York Times*, November 17, 2020. www.nytimes.com/2020/11/17/health /coronavirus-vaccine-operation-warp-speed.html.

Thomas, Owen. "Easy Answer on Prison Furloughs Eludes Dukakis. Public Opinion Makes Bush's Job Easier." *The Christian Science Monitor*, September 8, 1988. www.csmonitor.com/1988/0908 /afur.html.

"Thomas Sydenham." *Encyclopædia Britannica Online*. Last modified January 1, 2021. www.britannica .com/biography/Thomas-Sydenham.

Thompson, Derek. "What's Behind South Korea's COVID-19 Exceptionalism?" *The Atlantic*, May 6, 2020. www.theatlantic.com/ideas/archive/2020/05/whats-south-koreas-secret/611215.

"Three More Hospitalised in Milk Scandal." *The Age*, September 24, 2008. www.theage.com.au /world/three-more-hospitalised-in-milk-scandal-20080924-4mp8.html.

Thucydides. *History of the Peloponnesian War*. Edited by M. I. Finley. Translated by Rex Warner: London: Penguin Books, 1974.

Tikkanen, Roosa, and Melinda K. Abrams. *U.S. Health Care from a Global Perspective, 2019: Higher Spending, Worse Outcomes?* New York: Commonwealth Fund, 2020.

Tikkanen, Roosa, Robin Osborn, Elias Mossialos, Ana Djordjevic, and George A. Wharton. "Canada." Commonwealth Fund, June 5, 2020. www.commonwealthfund.org/international-health -policy-center/countries/canada.

Tikkanen, Roosa, Robin Osborn, Elias Mossialos, et al. "England." Commonwealth Fund, June 5, 2020. https://www.commonwealthfund.org/international-health-policy-center/countries/england.

Timbs, John. "Slaughter's Coffee House," in *Club Life of London with Anecdotes of the Clubs, Coffee-Houses and Taverns of the Metropolis During the 17th, 18th, and 19th Centuries*, Vol. 2. London: Richard Bentley, 1866. www.gutenberg.org/files/41516/41516-h/41516-h.htm#Page_99.

"TimesMachine: Sunday May 12, 1895." *The New York Times*, May 12, 1895. http://timesmachine .nytimes.com/timesmachine/1895/05/12/issue.html.

Tisch, Chris, Peter Talbot, Helen Freund, and Lawrence Mower. "Florida Suspends Drinking at Bars." *Tampa Bay Times*, June 26, 2020. www.tampabay.com/news/health/2020/06/26/drinking -alcohol-at-florida-bars-suspended.

Tocqueville, Alexis de. *Democracy in America*. Translated by Harvey C. Mansfield and Delba Winthrop. 1st edition. Chicago. University of Chicago Press, 2012.

———. *Democracy in America and Two Essays on America*. London: Penguin, 2003.

Toffler, Alvin. *Future Shock*. New York: Random House, 1970.

———. *The Third Wave*. New York: Morrow, 1980.

———. "The Future as a Way of Life." *Horizon* 7, no. 3 (Summer 1965): 108. Unidentified reprint at www.benlandau.com/wp-content/uploads/2015/06/Toffler-1965-The-future-as-a-way-of-life.pdf.

Tognotti, Eugenia. "Lessons from the History of Quarantine, from Plague to Influenza A." *Emerging Infectious Diseases* 19, no. 2 (February 2013): 254–59. https://doi.org/10.3201/eid1902.120312.

Tolstoy, Leo. *Anna Karenina*. London: Penguin Reader, 2001.

Tomić, Zlata Blažina, and Vesna Blažina. *Expelling the Plague: The Health Office and the Implementation of Quarantine in Dubrovnik, 1377–1533*. Montreal: McGill-Queen's University Press, 2015. www.jstor.org/stable/j.ctt14jxt9r.

"Top 5 Healthiest Cities in Canada." *Weigh2Healthy*, March 23, 2010. https://weigh2healthy.wordpress.com/2010/03/23/top-5-healthiest-cities-in-canada.

Tough, Paul. "The Alchemy of OxyContin." *The New York Times*, July 29, 2001. www.nytimes.com/2001/07/29/magazine/the-alchemy-of-oxycontin.html.

Travis, Michael T. "Proposed Bill Seeks to Remove Limits on Classroom Recording." Parker & Covert LLP (blog), September 2, 2020. www.parkercovert.com/2020/09/proposed-bill-seeks-to-remove-limits-on-classroom-recording.

Troesken, Werner. *Water, Race, and Disease*. Cambridge, MA: MIT Press, 2004.

Tu, Jack V., Chris L. Pashos, C. David Naylor, Erluo Chen, Sharon-Lise Normand, Joseph P. Newhouse, and Barbara J. McNeil. "Use of Cardiac Procedures and Outcomes in Elderly Patients with Myocardial Infarction in the United States and Canada." *New England Journal of Medicine* 336, no. 21 (May 1997): 1500–1505. https://doi.org/10.1056/NEJM199705223362106.

Tully, Tracey, Brian M. Rosenthal, Matthew Goldstein, and Robert Gebeloff. "70 Died at a Nursing Home as Body Bags Piled Up. This Is What Went Wrong." *The New York Times*, April 19, 2020. www.nytimes.com/2020/04/19/nyregion/coronavirus-nj-andover-nursing-home-deaths.html.

Turak, Natasha. "UAE to Suspend All China Flights except for Beijing as Coronavirus Toll Mounts." CNBC, February 3, 2020. www.cnbc.com/2020/02/03/coronavirus-uae-to-suspend-all-china-flights-except-for-beijing.html.

Turner, Deonna S. "Crack Epidemic." *Encyclopædia Britannica Online*. Accessed December 29, 2020. www.britannica.com/topic/crack-epidemic.

Turner, Frederick Jackson. *The Significance of the Frontier in American History*. London: Penguin, 2008.

Tuthill, Kathleen. "John Snow and the Broad Street Pump: On the Trail of an Epidemic." UCLA Fielding School of Public Health Department of Epidemiology. Accessed January 13, 2021. www.ph.ucla.edu/epi/snow/snowcricketarticle.html.

Tuttle, Carolyn. "Child Labor during the British Industrial Revolution." EH.Net Encyclopedia. Edited by Robert Whaples. August 14, 2001. https://eh.net/encyclopedia/child-labor-during-the-british-industrial-revolution.

Twede, Diana. "Uneeda Biscuit: The First Consumer Package?" *Journal of Macromarketing* 17, no. 2 (December 1997): 82–88. https://doi.org/10.1177/027614679701700208.

Twin, Alexandra. "There Ain't No Such Thing as a Free Lunch (TANSTAAFL) Explained." Investopedia, August 25, 2020. www.investopedia.com/terms/t/tanstaafl.asp.

Twine, Kevin. "The City in Decline: Rome in Late Antiquity." Department of Environmental, Urban & Geographic Studies, Montclair State College, n.d., 5.

"2008 Democratic Party Platform." The American Presidency Project. August 25, 2008. www.presidency.ucsb.edu/documents/2008-democratic-party-platform.

Ujifusa, Andrew. "Despite History, N.Y. Gov. Cuomo Says: 'I Have Nothing to Do with Common Core.'" *EducationWeek*, October 23, 2014. www.edweek.org/policy-politics/despite-history-n-y-gov-cuomo-says-i-have-nothing-to-do-with-common-core/2014/10.

Ullmann, Agnes. "Louis Pasteur." *Encyclopædia Britannica Online*. July 20, 1998. www.britannica .com/biography/Louis-Pasteur.

Underwood, E. Ashworth. "The History of Cholera in Great Britain." *Proceedings of the Royal Society of Medicine* 41, no. 3 (March 1948): 165–73. https://doi.org/10.1177/003591574804100309.

UK Ministry of Justice. *Statistics on Race and the Criminal Justice System 2008/09*. London: Ministry of Justice, June 2010. https://assets.publishing.service.gov.uk/government/uploads/system/uploads /attachment_data/file/217822/stats-race-and-the-criminal-justice-system-2008-09c1.pdf.

UK Office for National Statistics. "Employment by Industry." Accessed November 10, 2020. www.ons .gov.uk/employmentandlabourmarket/peopleinwork/employmentandemployeetypes/datasets /employmentbyindustryemp13.

———. "GDP First Quarterly Estimate, UK." August 12, 2020. www.ons.gov.uk/economy /grossdomesticproductgdp/bulletins/gdpfirstquarterlyestimateuk/apriltojune2020.

UK Parliament. "Petition from Manufacturers and Merchants of Manchester against the Foreign Slave Trade Abolition Bill." Accessed January 12, 2021. www.parliament.uk/about/living-heritage /transformingsociety/tradeindustry/slavetrade/from-the-parliamentary-collections/the -british-slave-trade/petition-against-the-foreign-slave-trade-abolition-bill-page-1.

US Bureau of the Budget and US Office of Management and Budget. *The Budget of the United States Government for the Fiscal Year Ending June 30, 1967*. Washington, DC: US Government Printing Office, 1966. https://fraser.stlouisfed.org/title/budget-united-states-government-54/fiscal-year -ending-june-30-1967-19020.

US Bureau of Labor Statistics. "All Employees, Construction." FRED, Federal Reserve Bank of St. Louis. https://fred.stlouisfed.org/series/USCONS.

———. "All Employees, Education and Health Services." Federal Reserve Bank of St. Louis. https:// fred.stlouisfed.org/series/USEHS.

———. "All Employees, Food Services and Drinking Places." FRED, Federal Reserve Bank of St. Louis. https://fred.stlouisfed.org/series/CES7072200001.

———. "All Employees, Leisure and Hospitality." Federal Reserve Bank of St. Louis. https://fred .stlouisfed.org/series/USLAH.

———. "All Employees, Manufacturing." FRED. https://fred.stlouisfed.org/series/MANEMP.

———. "All Employees, Manufacturing/All Employees, Total Nonfarm." FRED, Federal Reserve Bank of St. Louis. Accessed January 12, 2021. https://fred.stlouisfed.org/graph/?g=cAYh.

———. "All Employees, Professional and Business Services." FRED, Federal Reserve Bank of St. Louis. https://fred.stlouisfed.org/series/USPBS.

———. "All Employees, Retail Trade." FRED, Federal Reserve Bank of St. Louis. https://fred .stlouisfed.org/series/USTRADE.

———. "All Employees, Service-Providing." FRED, Federal Reserve Bank of St. Louis. https://fred .stlouisfed.org/series/SRVPRD.

———. "All Employees, Total Nonfarm." FRED, Federal Reserve Bank of St. Louis. https://fred .stlouisfed.org/series/PAYEMS.

———. "All Employees, Truck Transportation." FRED, Federal Reserve Bank of St. Louis. https:// fred.stlouisfed.org/series/CEU4348400001.

———. "All Employees, Warehousing and Storage." FRED, Federal Reserve Bank of St. Louis. https://fred.stlouisfed.org/series/CES4349300001.

———. "All Employees: Leisure and Hospitality in Florida." Federal Reserve Bank of St. Louis. https://fred.stlouisfed.org/series/FLLEIH.

———. "Databases, Tables & Calculators by Subject." Accessed December 29, 2020. https://www.bls.gov/data.

———. "Supplemental Data Measuring the Effects of the Coronavirus (COVID-19) Pandemic on the Labor Market." Accessed January 18, 2021. www.bls.gov/cps/effects-of-the-coronavirus-covid-19-pandemic.htm.

———. "Employed Full Time: Wage and Salary Workers: Bartenders Occupations: 16 Years and Over." FRED, Federal Reserve Bank of St. Louis. https://fred.stlouisfed.org/series/LEU0254493100A.

———. "Employed Full Time: Wage and Salary Workers: Waiters and Waitresses Occupations: 16 Years and Over." FRED, Federal Reserve Bank of St. Louis. https://fred.stlouisfed.org/series/LEU0254493400A.

———. "Employment by Major Industry Sector." Accessed December 29, 2020. www.bls.gov/emp/tables/employment-by-major-industry-sector.htm.

———. "Historical Census of Housing Tables: Home Values." Accessed January 14, 2021. www.census.gov/data/tables/time-series/dec/coh-values.html.

———. "Labor Force Statistics from the Current Population Survey: Supplemental Data Measuring the Effects of the Coronavirus (COVID-19) Pandemic on the Labor Market." Last modified February 23, 2021. www.bls.gov/cps/effects-of-the-coronavirus-covid-19-pandemic.htm#data.

———. "One-Quarter of the Employed Teleworked in August 2020 Because of COVID-19 Pandemic: The Economics Daily." Accessed September 15, 2020. www.bls.gov/opub/ted/2020/one-quarter-of-the-employed-teleworked-in-august-2020-because-of-covid-19-pandemic.htm.

———. "Table 4. Quits Levels and Rates by Industry and Region, Seasonally Adjusted." Accessed January 12, 2021. www.bls.gov/news.release/jolts.t04.htm.

———. "Table 7. Employed Persons Working on Main Job at Home, Workplace, and Time Spent Working at Each Location by Class of Worker, Occupation, and Earnings, 2019 Annual Averages." Accessed January 25, 2020. www.bls.gov/news.release/atus.t07.htm.

———. "Table A-14. Unemployed Persons by Industry and Class of Worker, Not Seasonally Adjusted." Accessed January 8, 2021. www.bls.gov/news.release/empsit.t14.htm.

———. "Table B-1. Employees on Nonfarm Payrolls by Industry Sector and Selected Industry Detail." Accessed January 8, 2021. www.bls.gov/news.release/empsit.t17.htm.

———. "The Employment Situation—July 2020." August 7, 2020. www.bls.gov/news.release/archives/empsit_08072020.pdf.

———. "Unemployment Rate." FRED, Federal Reserve Bank of St. Louis. Accessed January 18, 2021. https://fred.stlouisfed.org/series/UNRATE.

US Census Bureau. *1990 Census of Population and Housing, Population and Housing Unit Counts, California*. Washington, DC: US Government Printing Office, 1992.

———. "QuickFacts." Accessed January 12, 2021. www.census.gov/quickfacts/fact/table/US/PST045219.

———. "QuickFacts: Los Angeles City, California; Los Angeles County, California; California; United States." Accessed January 12, 2021. www.census.gov/quickfacts/fact/table/losangelescitycalifornia,losangelescountycalifornia,CA,US/PST045219.

———. *2010 Census of Population and Housing, Population and Housing Unit Counts, CPH-2-1, United States Summary.* Washington, DC: US Government Printing Office, 2012.

———. "U.S. and World Population Clock." Accessed January 17, 2021. www.census.gov/popclock.

US Centers for Disease Control and Prevention. "About Variants of the Virus That Causes COVID-19." Last modified February 12, 2021. www.cdc.gov/coronavirus/2019-ncov/transmission/variant .html.

———. *Advancing the Global Health Security Agenda: CDC Achievements and Impact—2018.* Washington, DC: Centers for Disease Control and Prevention, 2018.

———. "CDC's Funding." October 11, 2018. www.cdc.gov/about/report/cdc-funding.html.

———. "Data Overview: The Drug Overdose Epidemic: Behind the Numbers." December 7, 2020. www.cdc.gov/drugoverdose/data/index.html.

———. "Eastern Equine Encephalitis." October 21, 2020. www.cdc.gov/easternequineencephalitis /index.html.

———. "Epidemic Typhus." November 13, 2020. www.cdc.gov/typhus/epidemic/index.html.

———. "History of Quarantine." July 20, 2020. www.cdc.gov/quarantine/historyquarantine.html.

———. "HIV and Injection Drug Use." Accessed January 18, 2021. www.cdc.gov/hiv/basics/hiv -transmission/injection-drug-use.html.

———. "HIV and Substance Use." Last modified November 3, 2020. www.cdc.gov/hiv/basics/hiv -transmission/substance-use.html.

———. "Hospitalization Rates and Characteristics of Patients Hospitalized with Laboratory -Confirmed Coronavirus Disease 2019—COVID-NET, 14 States, March 1–30, 2020." April 17, 2020. www.cdc.gov/mmwr/volumes/69/wr/mm6915e3.htm.

———. "How Antibiotic Resistance Happens." Last modified February 10, 2020. www.cdc.gov /drugresistance/about/how-resistance-happens.html.

———. *How to Prevent the Spread of the Mosquito That Causes Dengue.* www.cdc.gov/dengue/resources /vectorcontrolsheetdengue.pdf.

———. "Impaired Driving: Get the Facts." August 24, 2020. www.cdc.gov/transportationsafety /impaired_driving/impaired-drv_factsheet.html.

———. "Lyme Disease." Accessed November 5, 2020. www.cdc.gov/lyme/index.html.

———. "Mandatory Reporting of Infectious Diseases by Clinicians." *Morbidity and Mortality Weekly Report* 39, no. 9 (June 22, 1990): 1–11, 16–17. www.cdc.gov/mmwr/preview/mmwrhtml /00001665.htm.

———. "Motor-Vehicle Safety: A 20th Century Public Health Achievement." *Morbidity and Mortality Weekly Report* 48, no. 18 (May 14, 1999): 369–374. https://www.cdc.gov/mmwr/PDF/wk /mm4818.pdf. Published correction appears in *Morbidity and Mortality Weekly Report* 48, no. 22 (June 11, 1999): 473. https://www.cdc.gov/mmwr/PDF/wk/mm4822.pdf.

———. *National Strategy for Pandemic Influenza. Homeland Security Council*, November 1, 2005. www .cdc.gov/flu/pandemic-resources/pdf/pandemic-influenza-strategy-2005.pdf.

———. "1918 Pandemic (H1N1 Virus)." March 20, 2019. www.cdc.gov/flu/pandemic-resources /1918-pandemic-h1n1.html.

———. "Overdose Deaths Accelerating During COVID-19." December 18, 2020. www.cdc.gov /media/releases/2020/p1218-overdose-deaths-covid-19.html.

———. "People with Certain Medical Conditions." Last modified February 22, 2021. www.cdc.gov /coronavirus/2019-ncov/need-extra-precautions/people-with-medical-conditions.html.

———. "Plague FAQ." November 26, 2019. www.cdc.gov/plague/faq/index.html.

———. "Preventing, Detecting, and Responding to Epidemics: CDC's Achievements." September 23, 2019. www.cdc.gov/globalhealth/security/ghsareport/2018/prevent-detect-respond.html.

———. "Risk for COVID-19 Infection, Hospitalization, and Death by Race/Ethnicity." Last modified February 18, 2021. www.cdc.gov/coronavirus/2019-ncov/covid-data/investigations -discovery/hospitalization-death-by-race-ethnicity.html.

———. "Safer and Healthier Foods." *Morbidity and Mortality Weekly Report* 48, no. 40 (October 1999): 905–13. https://pubmed.ncbi.nlm.nih.gov/12432905.

———. "Smoking Cessation: Fast Facts." Last modified May 21, 2020. www.cdc.gov/tobacco/data _statistics/fact_sheets/cessation/smoking-cessation-fast-facts/index.html.

———. "State Smoke-Free Laws for Worksites, Restaurants, and Bars—United States, 2000–2010." Accessed December 26, 2020. www.cdc.gov/mmwr/preview/mmwrhtml/mm6015a2.htm.

———. "Synthetic Opioid Overdose Data." March 19, 2020. www.cdc.gov/drugoverdose/data /fentanyl.html.

———. "Tobacco Use—United States, 1900–1999." *Morbidity and Mortality Weekly Report* 48, no. 43 (November 5, 1999): 986–93. https://www.cdc.gov/mmwr/PDF/wk/mm4843.pdf.

———. "2014–2016 Ebola Outbreak in West Africa." Last reviewed March 8, 2019. www.cdc.gov /vhf/ebola/history/2014-2016-outbreak/index.html.

———. "The 2009 H1N1 Pandemic: Summary Highlights, April 2009–April 2010." Last modified June 16, 2010. www.cdc.gov/h1n1flu/cdcresponse.htm.

———. "Understanding the Epidemic." Last modified February 12, 2021. www.cdc.gov/drugoverdose /epidemic/index.html.

———. "Urban-Rural Differences in Drug Overdose Death Rates, by Sex, Age, and Type of Drugs Involved, 2017." NCHS Data Brief, no. 345, August 2019. https://www.cdc.gov/nchs/products /databriefs/db345.htm.

US Centers for Medicare & Medicaid Services. "National Health Expenditure Data." Accessed January 18, 2021. www.cms.gov/research-statistics-data-and-systems/statistics-trends-and-reports /nationalhealthexpenddata.

"U.S. Crime and Imprisonment Statistics Total and by State 1960–2013." Disaster Center. Accessed January 18, 2021. http://disastercenter.com/crime.

US Department of Agriculture, Economic Research Service. "Nutrients." www.ers.usda.gov /webdocs/DataFiles/50472/nutrients.xls.

US Department of Commerce. *1992 Census of Population and Housing: Population and Housing Unit Counts.* Washington, DC: US Government Printing Office, 1992. https://www.census.gov/prod /cen1990/cph2/cph-2-6.pdf.

———. *2000 Census of Population and Housing: Population and Housing Unit Counts.* Washington, DC: US Government Printing Office, 2003. www.census.gov/library/publications/2003/dec /phc-3.html.

———. *2010 Census of Population and Housing: Population and Housing Unit Counts.* Washington, DC: US Government Printing Office, 2012. www.census.gov/prod/cen2010/cph-2-1.pdf.

US Department of Commerce, Bureau of Economic Analysis. "Gross Domestic Product, Second Quarter 2020 (Advance Estimate) and Annual Update." News release BEA 20-37, July 30, 2020. www.bea.gov/sites/default/files/2020-07/gdp2q20_adv_0.pdf.

US Department of Education. "Legislation, Regulations, and Guidance—Race to the Top Fund." Last modified May 17, 2016. www2.ed.gov/programs/racetothetop/legislation.html.

———. "Nine States and the District of Columbia Win Second Round Race to the Top Grants." August 24, 2010. www.ed.gov/news/press-releases/nine-states-and-district-columbia-win-second-round-race-top-grants.

———. "The Race to the Top Begins—Remarks by Secretary Arne Duncan." July 24, 2009. www2.ed.gov/news/speeches/2009/07/07242009.html.

———. *Race to the Top Program: Executive Summary*. November 2009. https://files.eric.ed.gov/fulltext/ED557422.pdf.

US Department of Health and Human Services. "Opioid Crisis Statistics." Accessed December 8, 2020. www.hhs.gov/opioids/about-the-epidemic/opioid-crisis-statistics/index.html.

US Department of Health and Human Services, Office of the National Coordinator for Health Information Technology, "2016 Report to Congress on Health IT Progress." www.healthit.gov/sites/default/files/2016_report_to_congress_on_healthit_progress.pdf.

US Department of Justice, Bureau of Justice Statistics. "New Report: U.S. Homicide Rate Falls to Lowest Rate in Four Decades." November 18, 2011. www.justice.gov/archives/opa/blog/new-report-us-homicide-rate-falls-lowest-rate-four-decades.

US Department of Labor and US Bureau of Labor Statistics. *100 Years of U.S. Consumer Spending: Data for the Nation, New York City, and Boston*. May 2006. www.bls.gov/opub/100-years-of-u-s-consumer-spending.pdf.

US Department of Transportation, National Highway Traffic Safety Administration. *Traffic Safety Facts: Alcohol-Impaired Driving 2016 Data*. October 2017. https://crashstats.nhtsa.dot.gov/Api/Public/ViewPublication/812450.

US Department of the Treasury Office of Economic Policy, Council of Economic Advisers, and US Department of Labor. *Occupational Licensing: A Framework for Policymakers*. July 2015. https://obamawhitehouse.archives.gov/sites/default/files/docs/licensing_report_final_nonembargo.pdf.

US District Court, Southern District of New York, "Floyd v. The City of New York," Opinion and Order, 08 Civ. 1034 (SAS), August 12, 2013. https://www.clearinghouse.net/chDocs/public/PN-NY-0009-0010.pdf.

US Drug Enforcement Administration. "2018 National Drug Threat Assessment (NDTA)." October 2, 2018. www.dea.gov/documents/2018/10/02/2018-national-drug-threat-assessment-ndta.

US Energy Information Administration. *Annual Energy Review*, 1978–2001. Available at www.eia.doe.gov/emeu/aer/txt/ptb0207.html.

US Federal Housing Finance Agency. "All-Transactions House Price Index for Los Angeles County, CA." FRED, Federal Reserve Bank of St. Louis. https://fred.stlouisfed.org/series/ATNHPIUS06037A.

US Food and Drug Administration. "Fact Sheet: FDA at a Glance." November 18, 2020. www.fda.gov/about-fda/fda-basics/fact-sheet-fda-glance.

———. "Food Irradiation: What You Need to Know." January 4, 2018. www.fda.gov/food/buy-store-serve-safe-food/food-irradiation-what-you-need-know.

US National Institutes of Health. "NIH-Funded Studies Show Stents and Surgery No Better than Medication, Lifestyle Changes at Reducing Cardiac Events." March 30, 2020. www.nih.gov/news-events/news-releases/nih-funded-studies-show-stents-surgery-no-better-medication-lifestyle-changes-reducing-cardiac-events.

Valentine, Randall, Dawn Valentine, and Jimmie L Valentine. "Relationship of George Floyd Protests to Increases in COVID-19 Cases Using Event Study Methodology." *Journal of Public Health* 42, no. 4 (November 2020): 696–97. https://doi.org/10.1093/pubmed/fdaa127.

Vandiver, John. "Kick Turkey Out of NATO? It Wouldn't Be Easy." *Stars and Stripes*, October 11, 2019. www.stripes.com/news/europe/kick-turkey-out-of-nato-it-wouldn-t-be-easy-1.602661.

Vaznis, James. "Timeline of Madison Park High School." *The Boston Globe*, October 12, 2014. www.bostonglobe.com/metro/2014/10/12/voctechtimeline/bvJAxOiTaxHghEmwHUwgkK/story.html.

Velde, François R. "What Happened to the US Economy During the 1918 Influenza Pandemic? A View Through High-Frequency Data." Federal Reserve Bank of Chicago, Working Paper WP 2020-11, July 7, 2020. https://doi.org/10.21033/wp-2020-11.

Velez, Jennifer. "Artwashing Fight Takes Twist with Gallery's Offer to 'Ceremonially' Close in Boyle Heights." *L.A. Taco*, April 24, 2018. www.lataco.com/artwashing-fight-takes-twist-with-gallerys-offer-to-ceremonially-close-in-boyle-heights.

"Village of Euclid v. Ambler Realty Company." Oyez. www.oyez.org/cases/1900-1940/272us365.

Villianatos, Mark, and Madeline Brozen. "Encouraging Diverse Missing-Middle Housing Near Transit." UCLA Lewis Center for Regional Policy Studies Policy Briefs, May 1, 2019. www.lewis.ucla.edu/research/encouraging-diverse-missing-middle-housing-near-transit.

"Violence Erupts in Boston over Desegregation Busing." History.com, September 12, 1974. www.history.com/this-day-in-history/violence-in-boston-over-racial-busing.

Voigtländer, Nico, and Hans-Joachim Voth. "How the West 'Invented' Fertility Restriction." *American Economic Review* 103, no. 6 (October 2013): 2227–64. https://doi.org/10.1257/aer.103.6.2227.

Vuković, Kristin. "Dubrovnik: The Medieval City Designed around Quarantine." BBC, April 22, 2020. www.bbc.com/travel/story/20200421-dubrovnik-the-medieval-city-designed-around-quarantine.

Waddington, I. "The Development of Medical Ethics—a Sociological Analysis." *Medical History* 19, no. 1 (January 1975): 36–51. https://doi.org/10.1017/S002572730001992X.

Wade, Louise Carroll. "Meatpacking." *Encyclopedia of Chicago*, 2004. www.encyclopedia.chicagohistory.org/pages/804.html.

Wade, Nicholas. "Europe's Plagues Came from China, Study Finds." *The New York Times*, October 31, 2010. www.nytimes.com/2010/11/01/health/01plague.html.

Wadman, Meredith. "Why COVID-19 Is More Deadly in People with Obesity—Even If They're Young." *Science*, September 8, 2020. www.sciencemag.org/news/2020/09/why-covid-19-more-deadly-people-obesity-even-if-theyre-young.

Wainwright, Oliver. "Street Fighter: How Jane Jacobs Saved New York from Bulldozer Bob." *The Guardian* (London), April 30, 2017. www.theguardian.com/artanddesign/2017/apr/30/citizen-jane-jacobs-the-woman-who-saved-manhattan-from-the-bulldozer-documentary.

Walker, Mark. "'If We Get It, We Chose to Be Here': Despite Virus, Thousands Converge on Sturgis for Huge Rally," *The New York Times*, August 11, 2020. www.nytimes.com/2020/08/07/us/sturgis-motorcyle-rally.html.

Wallace-Wells, Benjamin. "Can Coronavirus Contact Tracing Survive Reopening?" *The New Yorker*, June 12, 2020. www.newyorker.com/news/us-journal/can-coronavirus-contact-tracing-survive-reopening.

Wallis, Patrick. "A Dreadful Heritage: Interpreting Epidemic Disease at Eyam, 1666–2000." *History Workshop Journal* 61, no. 1 (Spring 2006): 31–56. https://doi.org/10.1093/hwj/dbi060.

Walsh, Mark. "Teachers' Rights under COVID-19: Anxiety Meets Legality." *EducationWeek*, November 19, 2020. www.edweek.org/teaching-learning/teachers-rights-under-covid-19-anxiety-meets -legality/2020/11.

Waltenburg, Michelle A., et al. "Update: COVID-19 among Workers in Meat and Poultry Processing Facilities—United States, April–May 2020." *Morbidity and Mortality Weekly Report* 69, no. 27 (July 2020): 887–92. www.cdc.gov/mmwr/volumes/69/wr/mm6927e2.htm?s_cid=mm6927e2_w.

Ware, Leland. "Invisible Walls: An Examination of the Legal Strategy of the Restrictive Covenant Cases." *Washington University Law Review* 67, no. 3 (1989): 737–72. https://openscholarship .wustl.edu/cgi/viewcontent.cgi?article=2010&context=law_lawreview.

Waring, George E. "The Cleaning of a Great City (*McClure's*, April 1897)." *The Brooklyn Rail*, March 2012. https://brooklynrail.org/2012/03/local/the-cleaning-of-a-great-city.

Warner, Melanie. *Pandora's Lunchbox: How Processed Food Took Over the American Meal*. New York: Scribner, 2014.

"Washington 'Three Strikes,' Initiative 593 (1993)." Ballotpedia. Accessed January 7, 2021. https:// ballotpedia.org/Washington_%22Three_Strikes%22,_Initiative_593_(1993).

Waterston, C. D., A. Macmillan Shearer, and Royal Society of Edinburgh. *Former Fellows of the Royal Society of Edinburgh, 1783–2002: Biographical Index*. Edinburgh: The Royal Society of Edinburgh, 2006.

Wayman, Erin. "Chile's Quake Larger but Less Destructive than Haiti's." *Earth*, March 1, 2010. www.earthmagazine.org/article/chiles-quake-larger-less-destructive-haitis.

"Ways and Means Committee Releases Report on International Drug Pricing." Ways and Means Committee, US House of Representatives, September 23, 2019. https://waysandmeans.house .gov/media-center/press-releases/ways-and-means-committee-releases-report-international -drug-pricing.

"What Country Spends the Most on Healthcare?" Investopedia, September 28, 2020. www .investopedia.com/ask/answers/020915/what-country-spends-most-healthcare.asp.

Weber, Lauren, Laura Ungar, Michelle R. Smith, et al. "Hollowed-Out Public Health System Faces More Cuts amid Virus." Kaiser Health News. Last modified August 24, 2020. https://khn.org /news/us-public-health-system-underfunded-under-threat-faces-more-cuts-amid-covid -pandemic.

White, Bouck. *The Book of Daniel Drew: A Glimpse of the Fisk-Gould-Tweed Régime from the Inside*. New York: Doubleday, Page & Company, 1910. http://archive.org/details/bookofdanieldrew00whit.

Whitney, Camille R., and Christopher A. Candelaria. "The Effects of No Child Left Behind on Children's Socioemotional Outcomes." *AERA Open* 3, no. 3 (July 2017). https://doi.org/10.1177 /2332858417726324.

Whittaker, John. "Cigarette Tax Hike Proposed for New York State." *Post-Journal* (Jamestown, NY), May 14, 2020. www.post-journal.com/news/page-one/2020/05/cigarette-tax-hike-proposed-for -new-york-state.

"Who Wants to Be a Millionaire?" *The Guardian* (London), September 28, 1999. www.theguardian .com/theguardian/1999/sep/29/features11.g2.

"William Henry Workman: Founder of Boyle Heights." *Boyle Heights History Blog*, September 23, 2009. http://boyleheightshistoryblog.blogspot.com/2009/09/william-henry-workman-founder-of -boyle.html.

"William Le Baron Jenney." *Encyclopædia Britannica Online*. Accessed January 18, 2021. www .britannica.com/biography/William-Le-Baron-Jenney.

Willsher, Kim. "Story of Cities #12: Haussmann Rips Up Paris—and Divides France to This Day," *The Guardian* (London), March 31, 2016. www.theguardian.com/cities/2016/mar/31/story-cities -12-paris-baron-haussmann-france-urban-planner-napoleon.

Wilson, Woodrow. *The New Freedom: A Call for the Emancipation of the Generous Energies of a People.* New York: Doubleday, Page & Company, 1913. www.gutenberg.org/files/14811/14811-h/14811-h.htm.

"Wonderful coffee shop with free wifi. Ignore the uninformed protestors. They're usually not there. Owners work tirelessly inside. What these protestors don't realize is that one of the owners is Salvadorean." Yelp, July 22, 2019. www.yelp.com/biz/weird-wave-coffee-brewers-los-angeles.

World Health Organization. "WHO and the WHA—an Explainer." Last modified November 9, 2020. www.who.int/about/governance/world-health-assembly/seventy-third-world-health-assembly /the-who-and-the-wha-an-explainer.

"Why a Pound Today Is Worth Only 0.8% of a Pound in 1858." CPI Inflation Calculator, January 13, 2020. www.in2013dollars.com/uk/inflation/1858.

"Why Germany's Low COVID-19 Death Rate Might Be a Mirage." CBC News, March 31, 2020. www.cbc.ca/news/world/germany-coronavirus-death-rate-reasons-1.5513816.

"Why Pandemic Disease and War Are So Similar." *Business Insider*, March 28, 2015. www .businessinsider.com/why-pandemic-disease-and-war-are-so-similar-2015-3.

Wilford, John Noble. "How Epidemics Helped Shape the Modern Metropolis." *The New York Times*, April 15, 2008. www.nytimes.com/2008/04/15/science/15chol.html.

"William Bradford on the Great Sickness among New England Indians (1633)." Westshore Community College. www.westshore.edu/personal/mwnagle/US1/NativeAmerDocs/Bradford -sickness.htm.

Willman, David. "Contamination at CDC Lab Delayed Rollout of Coronavirus Tests." *The Washington Post*, April 18, 2020. www.washingtonpost.com/investigations/contamination-at-cdc-lab -delayed-rollout-of-coronavirus-tests/2020/04/18/fd7d3824-7139-11ea-aa80-c2470c6b2034 _story.html.

Wilson, Chris. "These Graphs Show How COVID-19 Is Ravaging New York City's Low-Income Neighborhoods." *Time*, April 15, 2020. https://time.com/5821212/coronavirus-low-income -communities.

Wilson, Michael. "Coronavirus in N.Y.C.: Eerie Streetscapes Are Stripped of Commerce." *The New York Times*, March 21, 2020. www.nytimes.com/2020/03/21/nyregion/coronavirus-empty-nyc .html.

Wilson, Mitchell. "Cyrus McCormick." *Encyclopædia Britannica Online.* Last modified February 12, 2021. www.britannica.com/biography/Cyrus-McCormick.

Winig, Laura. *Michelle Rhee and the Washington D.C. Public Schools.* Harvard Kennedy School Case Program, April 5, 2012. https://case.hks.harvard.edu/michelle-rhee-and-the-washington-d-c -public-schools.

Wong, M. D., K. M. Coller, R. N. Dudovitz, D. P. Kennedy, R. Buddin, M. F. Shapiro, S. H. Kataoka, et al. "Successful Schools and Risky Behaviors among Low-Income Adolescents." *Pediatrics* 134, no. 2 (August 2014): e389–96. https://doi.org/10.1542/peds.2013-3573.

World Bank. "GDP per Capita (Current US$)—Zambia." Accessed January 17, 2021. https://data .worldbank.org/indicator/NY.GDP.PCAP.CD?locations=ZM.

———. "Population, Total—France." Accessed January 17, 2021. https://data.worldbank.org/indicator /SP.POP.TOTL?locations=FR.

———. "Rural Population—United Kingdom," 2018 revision. Accessed April 9, 2021. https://data
.worldbank.org/indicator/SP.RUR.TOTL?locations=GB.

———. "Rural Population—United States," 2018 revision. Accessed April 9, 2021. https://data
.worldbank.org/indicator/SP.RUR.TOTL?locations=US.

———. "Urban Population—United States," 2018 revision. Accessed April 9, 2021. https://data
.worldbank.org/indicator/SP.URB.TOTL?locations=US.

"World Health Organization." *Encyclopædia Britannica Online.* July 8, 2020. www.britannica.com
/topic/World-Health-Organization.

World Health Organization. "Budget." www.who.int/about/accountability/budget.

———. "Cholera." www.who.int/health-topics/cholera#tab=tab_1.

World Health Organization. "Composition of the Board." https://apps.who.int/gb/gov/en/composition
-of-the-board_en.html.

———. "Countries Overview." www.who.int/countries.

———. "Ebola Virus Disease." Last modified February 23, 2021. www.who.int/news-room/fact
-sheets/detail/ebola-virus-disease.

———. "Influenza (Avian and Other Zoonotic)." November 13, 2018. www.who.int/news-room
/fact-sheets/detail/influenza-(avian-and-other-zoonotic).

———. "Influenza-like Illness in the United States and Mexico." April 24, 2009. www.who.int/csr
/don/2009_04_24/en.

———. *Managing Epidemics: Key Facts about Major Deadly Diseases.* May 2018. www.who.int
/emergencies/diseases/managing-epidemics/en.

———. "New Zealand Takes Early and Hard Action to Tackle COVID-19." Accessed December 26,
2020. www.who.int/westernpacific/news/feature-stories/detail/new-zealand-takes-early-and-hard
-action-to-tackle-covid-19.

———. "Novel Coronavirus—China." January 12, 2020. www.who.int/csr/don/12-january-2020
-novel-coronavirus-china/en.

———. "Novel Coronavirus—Thailand (Ex-China)." Accessed January 17, 2021. www.who.int/csr
/don/14-january-2020-novel-coronavirus-thailand-ex-china/en.

——— (@WHO). "Preliminary investigations conducted by the Chinese authorities have found no
clear evidence of human-to-human transmission of the novel #coronavirus (2019-nCoV) identified in #Wuhan, #China." Twitter, January 14, 2020, 6:18 a.m. https://twitter.com/WHO
/status/1217043229427761152.

———. "Programme Budget 2020–2021." www.who.int/publications-detail-redirect/programme
-budget-2020-2021.

———. "Programme Budget Web Portal." https://open.who.int/2018-19/contributors/contributor.

———. "Smoking and COVID-19." Accessed January 20, 2021. www.who.int/news-room
/commentaries/detail/smoking-and-covid-19.

———. "United States of America: WHO Coronavirus Disease (COVID-19) Dashboard." Accessed
January 18, 2021. https://covid19.who.int.

———. "Worldwide Burden of Disease from Exposure to Second-Hand Smoke." February 9, 2011.
www.who.int/quantifying_ehimpacts/publications/shsarticle2010/en.

———. "Yellow Fever." May 7, 2019. www.who.int/news-room/fact-sheets/detail/yellow-fever.

World Health Organization Global Influenza Program Surveillance Network. "Evolution of H5N1 Avian Influenza Viruses in Asia." *Emerging Infectious Diseases* 11, no. 10 (October 2005): 1515–21. https://doi.org/10.3201/eid1110.050644.

Xiao, Kangpeng, Junqiong Zhai, Yaoyu Feng, Niu Zhou, Xu Zhang, Jie-Jian Zou, Na Li, et al. "Isolation of SARS-CoV-2-Related Coronavirus from Malayan Pangolins." *Nature* 583, no. 7815 (July 2020): 286–89. https://doi.org/10.1038/s41586-020-2313-x.

Yamada, Katherine. "Verdugo Views: There Was a Time When a Hospital Stay Cost $4 a Day." *Los Angeles Times*, November 17, 2012. www.latimes.com/socal/glendale-news-press/community/tn-gnp-1117-verdugo-views-there-was-a-time-when-a-hospital-stay-cost-4-a-day-story.html.

Young, Julie. "The Economic Impact of Brain Drain." Investopedia, September 29, 2020. www.investopedia.com/terms/b/brain_drain.asp.

Zarroli, Jim. "'Deaths of Despair' Examines the Steady Erosion of U.S. Working-Class Life." NPR, March 18, 2020. www.npr.org/2020/03/18/817687042/deaths-of-despair-examines-the-steady-erosion-of-u-s-working-class-life.

Zelizer, Julian E. *Taxing America: Wilbur D. Mills, Congress, and the State, 1945–1975.* Cambridge, UK: Cambridge University Press, 2000.

Zhang, Sarah. "The One-Paragraph Letter from 1980 That Fueled the Opioid Crisis." *The Atlantic*, June 2, 2017. www.theatlantic.com/health/archive/2017/06/nejm-letter-opioids/528840.

Zhu, Wenjia, Michael E. Chernew, Tisamarie B. Sherry, and Nicole Maestas. "Initial Opioid Prescriptions among U.S. Commercially Insured Patients, 2012–2017." *New England Journal of Medicine* 380, no. 11 (2019): 1043–52. https://doi.org/10.1056/nejmsa1807069.

Zimba, Jason. "Straight Up Conversation: Common Core Guru Jason Zimba." *Education Next*, February 28, 2013. http://www.educationnext.org/straight-up-conversation-common-core-guru-jason-zimba.

Zimring, Franklin E. "The City That Became Safe: New York and the Future of Crime Control." Straus Working Paper 09/11, Straus Institute, NYU School of Law, New York, NY, September 2011. www.law.nyu.edu/sites/default/files/siwp/WP9Zimring.pdf.

Zwilling, Andrew. "Poor Leadership during Times of Disease: Malta and the Plague of 1813." War on the Rocks, March 27, 2020. https://warontherocks.com/2020/03/poor-leadership-during-times-of-disease-malta-and-the-plague-of-1813.

Z/Yen Group and China Development Institute. *The Global Financial Centres Index 20.* September 2016. https://www.longfinance.net/media/documents/GFCI20_26Sep2016.pdf.

INDEX

New York City
anti-terrorism efforts in, 287–88
appeal of, 236
architecture of, 210–11
Bloomberg's health initiatives in, 99
board of health established in, 83
cholera outbreaks in, 71, 73, 74, 80
cigarette tax rate in, 128
COVID-19 pandemic in, 104, 195
and Cross-Bronx Highway, 251
disease-infested tenements of, 81–83
domestic violence in, 287
draining of swamps in, 84, 89
garment industry of, 199–203, 211,
217–18, 225
Gary, Indiana compared to, 102–3
health of poor in, 161–62
infrastructure investments in, 6
last-mile problem in, 80, 83
life-expectancy disparities in, 102, 103
livestock in, 90
obesity rates in, 105
police department of, 285–91, 297, 299
sanitation enforcement in, 82–86
and September 11, 2001, terrorist attacks,
6, 243
Smith's advocacy in, 81–83, 84
"stop and frisk" policies, 288–91
strength of civil society in, 243–44
violent crime in, 282, 286
water supply of, 72–75, 77, 79–80
New York State, 307–8
New Zealand, 18–19, 156, 163–65, 198,
334, 339
No Child Left Behind, 303, 310
non-pharmaceutical interventions (NPIs), 87
Noyes Elementary School, 310–11
nursing homes, 97, 157–60

Obama, Barack, 303–4, 325, 331
Obama administration, 155–56, 195, 331
obesity
and city life, 106
and COVID-19, 105–6
education differences in rates of, 98, 127–28
and fast foods, 112–15
and mass-produced foods, 109–12

place-based differences in, 103, 104
rise in rates of, 107
and sedentary lifestyles, 107
and trends in food consumption, 107–9,
115–16
occupational licensing, 200–201, 277, 334
Occupy movement of 2011, 4, 6
offices and office buildings
converted into housing, 17–18, 208, 239
future of, 237–39
and growth of labor force, 223
pre-pandemic resilience of, 207
Toffler's perspective on, 222–23
value of in-person interaction in, 208–9
Olson, Mancur, 266–67, 268, 271, 273
opioid epidemic
costs to public, 99–100
deaths associated with, 97–98, 117, 120, 121,
122–24, 129
and fentanyl, 122, 123, 129
and heroin use, 118–20, 122
history of opioid use, 117–19
and HIV transmission, 117, 118–20, 126
overdoses of, 117
and OxyContin, 120–22, 123, 124, 126
and penalizing deceitful practices, 124–26
and Purdue Pharma's marketing practices,
120–22, 125
Opportunity Atlas, 299–301
Oster, Emily, 313
Overton, Mark, 171
OxyContin, 120–22, 123, 124, 126. See also
opioid epidemic

pangolins, 91
Paris, 6, 70–71
pasteurization, 183
Paycheck Protection Program (PPP),
195–96, 331
Peels of Manchester, 176–80, 188, 189
peer effects, 128
Pence, Mike, 120
pension systems, 315–16
Pepys, Samuel, 174–75
Percival, Thomas, 177–78
Perez, Caroline Criado, 269
Pericles, 25, 27, 28, 29